D1033994

Humanitarian Intervention

University of Pennsylvania Press
Procedural Aspects of International Law Series

Burns H. Weston, Series Editor (1994–   )
Robert Kogod Goldman, Editor (1977–1994)
Richard B. Lillich, Editor (1964–1977)

A complete list of the books in this series
appears at the back of this volume.

Humanitarian Intervention

The United Nations
in an Evolving World Order

Sean D. Murphy

Volume 21, Procedural Aspects of International Law Series

PENN

University of Pennsylvania Press

Philadelphia

Printed in the United States of America on acid-free paper
10 9 8 7 6 5 4 3 2 1

Published by
University of Pennsylvania Press
Philadelphia, Pennsylvania 19104-6097

Library of Congress Cataloging-in-Publication Data

Murphy, Sean D.
   Humanitarian Intervention : the United Nations in an evolving
world order / Sean D. Murphy.
      p.   cm.—(Procedural aspects of international law series ;
v. 21)
   Based on the author's thesis (S.J.D.)—University of Virginia.
   Includes bibliographical references and index.
   ISBN 0-8122-3382-4 (alk. paper)
   1. Intervention (International law)   2. United Nations—Armed
Forces. I. Title. II. Series.
JX4481.M86   1996
341.5'84—dc20

96-32578
CIP

Contents

Editor's Foreword

Humanitarian Intervention: The United Nations in an Evolving World Order
is the twenty-first book in the Procedural Aspects of International Law
Series, the third to be published by the University of Pennsylvania Press.
It also is extremely timely. As it goes to press, governmental and nongovernmental officials probing the killing fields of Bosnia-Herzegovina
and Rwanda are resurrecting memories that, in the last three to four
years, have shocked the global conscience as has nothing since the Holocaust: tens and hundreds of thousands of desperate men, women, and
children fleeing their homes and across borders to escape "ethnic
cleansing" and other premeditated abuse; huddled refugees and
déplacés crammed into squalor and further victimized by starvation and
malnutrition, not unusually owing to deliberate policy; emaciated young
men, some old, clutching barbed wire prison fences, eyeballs sunken,
ribs protruding, the victims often of torture and comparable atrocity;
gaunt, terror-struck women haunted by systematic rapes and assaults, co-
erced pornography, and their forced witness to the sadistic murders of
their children, families, and friends; bloodied and dismembered bodies,
some the consequence of indiscriminate warfare, others of savage massacres, scattered on city streets and country hillsides, or heaped one
upon the other in open charnel pits swarming with flies; and more. The
enormity of the horror is only partially revealed by the claimed statistics:
in Bosnia-Herzegovina, as of the signing of the Dayton accord, more
than 200,000 killed and an estimated 2.5 million driven from their
homes since the outbreak of hostilities in 1990, the vast majority of them
of Muslim faith; in Rwanda, between 500,000 and one million Tutsis ex-
terminated during three months of fighting and up to 3.5 million external refugees and internally displaced persons since fighting began in
1994, an astounding three-fourths of the country's total population. In
towns and villages with unfamiliar names, nearly every building damaged
or destroyed, little or no running water, little or no electricity, little or no

government infrastructure. And as I write, Burundi threatens to do much the same, again.

These and other icons of late twentieth-century carnage and devastation, together with the post-Cold War revival of the United Nations Security Council, have prompted a clamor for forceful "humanitarian intervention," both unilateral and multilateral, that is perhaps unparalleled since the birth of the State system. Unparalleled but not surprising. With the spread of market forces and new communications technologies making it each day more difficult to ignore happenings in other parts of the world, it is not unreasonable that there should be an increasing worldwide desire to safeguard against the severe and widespread deprivations of human rights that arise from civil wars and from persecutions by autocratic governments. A central challenge for the next century will be, of course, how to reconcile existing constraints on the use of force with this increasing desire.

Sean D. Murphy, the author of this book, has anticipated this challenge with breadth, depth, acumen, and clarity. Formerly in the Office of the Legal Adviser of the U.S. Department of State and presently Counselor for Legal Affairs at the U.S. Embassy in The Hague, he has done so also with objectivity and sensitivity, capitalizing on his own governmental experience, but sparing from criticism no government, not even his own, when criticism is due.

Murphy writes, however, not to pronounce humanitarian intervention legal or illegal, moral or immoral, prudent or imprudent. Rather, viewing the values of justice and order as constituting a "fundamental dialectic" that requires accommodation constantly in everyday life, he explores the theory and practice of humanitarian intervention—"the threat or use of force by a state, group of states, or international organization primarily for the purpose of protecting the nationals of the target state from widespread deprivations of internationally recognized human rights" (pp. 11–12)—principally to assess the post-Cold War strengths and weaknesses of the United Nations and its Charter in this realm. He begins by placing the doctrine of humanitarian intervention in acutely nuanced theoretical and policy-oriented perspective. Next he considers the traditions, pre- and post-Charter, from which the contemporary international law on the use of force relative to human rights has emerged, and thereafter he examines the actual practice of states relative to humanitarian intervention up to the dissolution of the Soviet Union. Then, faithful to an enlightened methodological design, he considers, in a major chapter, six post-Cold War "incidents" of claimed humanitarian intervention: Liberia (1990), Iraq (1991–92), Bosnia-Herzegovina (1992), Somalia (1992), Rwanda (1994), and Haiti (1993–94). Separately and together, these case studies, rich in detail, provide a means for considering the desirability and utility of both the United Nations and regional organizations with respect to humanitarian intervention, which consideration he does give in the next two chapters. Finally, in a concluding chapter, the author explores the issue of unilateral humanitarian intervention, that is, intervention not formally authorized by the United Nations. In a world where multilateral approaches, particularly through the United Nations and cognate regional organizations, are seen increasingly to present more viable options for assessing and validating, possibly even exercising, the use of force, the issue is of course not without controversy.

This monograph, then, a prodigious effort by a meticulous scholar, which in an earlier incarnation served as the author's S.J.D. thesis at the University of Virginia, constitutes a systematic legal analysis of the doctrine of humanitarian intervention, accounting not only for the history and practice of states relative to humanitarian intervention before and after the adoption of the UN Charter, but also for insights of relevance to the future operations of the United Nations, regional organizations, and states acting on their own in this field. As such, befitting the work of an international lawyer who studied under Richard Gardner, Louis Henkin, and Oscar Schachter at the Columbia Law School, who received his LL.M. degree in international legal studies under Philip Allot, Derek Bowett, and Elihu Lauterpacht at Cambridge University, and who earned his S.J.D. in international law under Richard Lillich and John Norton Moore at the University of Virginia, it adds significantly to the literature. So far the only known integrated study of humanitarian intervention relative to the United Nations since the end of the Cold War, it firmly establishes itself as the leading work on this critical subject for years to come.

Thus it is with pride that I launch my tenure as Series Editor of the Procedural Aspects of International Law Series. I do so, moreover, with pleasure. Dr. Murphy is as gracious an author as he is meticulous a scholar, and I thank him for his courtesy and care. Also, I thank my former research assistant, Jason L. Letcher, now a graduate of The University of Iowa College of Law, for his truly generous help in proofing and cite-checking the author's many footnotes.

Burns H. Weston

Preface

When the Government of Iraq invaded Kuwait in August 1990, I was an attorney-adviser with the Office of the Legal Adviser of the United States Department of State in the section that handles politico-military affairs. For the most part, the international law issues that arose during that war could be addressed without great difficulty. Over the centuries, societies have developed normative constraints on the use of armed force in the conduct of foreign relations, and in the mid-twentieth century general consensus was reached among states that the use of military force for territorial aggrandizement was unacceptable. Consequently, the norms of international law posed no hindrance in rallying the international community to deploy a coalition of forces under the authorization of the United Nations to assist Kuwait in defending itself.

In the aftermath of that war, however, the Government of Iraq undertook ruthless and indiscriminate attacks against Iraqi Kurds in northern Iraq and against Iraqi Shiites in southern Iraq in an effort to quell rebel elements that challenged the Sunni-dominated regime of President Saddam Hussein. Here the international legal issues became more difficult, for the international community had to decide whether it should deploy forces into Iraq to assist Iraqi nationals in defending themselves against their own government. Shortly thereafter, other largely internal conflicts also cried out for intervention by the international community. In April 1994, for instance, Hutu militia in Rwanda systematically slaughtered at least a half million Rwandan Tutsis. In one incident in Nyarubuye, at a Catholic missionary compound, Tutsis were hacked to death while cowering midst the pews of the church and its adjacent classrooms; when the militia grew tired, they immobilized those still alive by slicing the tendons of their arms and legs, thereby allowing the militia time to rest before finishing the slaughter.

A central challenge for the next century rests in reconciling existing constraints on the use of armed force with the increasing desire to protect civilians and combatants from widespread and severe deprivations of human rights that arise from internal conflicts due to civil war or to the persecution of groups by autocratic governments. Should states be allowed to intervene in the affairs of other states to prevent deprivations of human rights, an action commonly referred to as "humanitarian intervention?" If so, under what conditions should such intervention occur? Finally, how best can the international community organize itself so as to ensure that such interventions are timely and effective?

In a 1995 supplement to his Agenda for Peace, United Nations Secretary-General Boutros Boutros-Ghali correctly observed:

> [S]o many of today's conflicts are within States rather than between States. The end of the cold war removed constraints that had inhibited conflict in the former Soviet Union and elsewhere. As a result there has been a rash of wars within newly independent States, often of a religious or ethnic character and often involving unusual violence and cruelty. The end of the cold war seems also to have contributed to an outbreak of such wars in Africa. In addition, many of the proxy wars fuelled by the cold war within States remain unresolved. Inter-state wars, by contrast, have become infrequent.[1]

The collapse of bipolar confrontation not only unleashed internal conflicts that heretofore were suppressed or at least controlled by that confrontation, but also unleashed in a fashion the collective security apparatus of the United Nations. Suddenly, in various situations, the members of the Security Council authorized the deployment of military forces under United Nations command, or more often under national command with United Nations backing, in an attempt to resolve forcibly what were largely internal, not transnational conflicts. Yet these deployments encountered tremendous difficulties, raising doubts about the true willingness of member states to provide the necessary military and financial support to the United Nations and about the ability of the United Nations to serve this function. Indeed, the Secretary-General's supplemental report may be read as a lament that after just a few years of trying to address conflicts "within states," the United Nations and its member states were confused, ambivalent, and battered by their efforts to build a "new world order" and uncertain how to proceed.

The outcome of the Iraq crisis, and of others that followed, prompted me to pursue an integrated legal study of the doctrine of "humanitarian intervention," with particular emphasis on the role of the United Nations in authorizing or itself conducting such intervention. My purpose is to explore the roots of contemporary norms on the use of force and on the protection of human rights, and then to relate them to con-

---

1. *Supplement to an Agenda for Peace: Position Paper of the Secretary-General on the Fiftieth Anniversary of the United Nations*, U.N. GAOR, 50th Sess., U.N. Doc. A/50/60 (1995).

temporary problems and possibilities that have arisen midst the aftershocks of the end of the Cold War. My observations and conclusions in this study are no doubt influenced and informed by my position as an attorney at the U.S. State Department; throughout, I have sought to draw upon my personal experience of observing how law affects the behavior of governments and international organizations. Moreover, in developing my own views, I have consciously sought the views of several of my colleagues in the Department. At the same time, I have sought to immerse myself in nongovernmental communities during formative stages of this project and to appraise the actions of the Government of the United States as critically as that of any other government. Indeed, all the views expressed herein are my own and do not necessarily reflect the views of any other persons or institutions, or of the United States Government. They reflect, simply, the views of one person who has sought to be as analytically objective as it is possible for any independent observer to be.

Acknowledgments

In writing this book, I have received support from various quarters; a written acknowledgment is an essential (but all too insufficient) means of expressing my gratitude for that support.

In 1993, the Office of the Legal Adviser of the United States Department of State permitted me to take a one-year leave of absence, during which I collected and consumed most of the materials used for this book, conducted interviews, and completed an initial draft. Various colleagues in the Legal Adviser's Office and other parts of the Department read all or portions of this book and provided very helpful comments and corrections.

During my leave of absence, I was in residence at the University of Virginia School of Law. Funding during that period was generously provided by the University of Virginia School of Law, the Ford Foundation, and the Council on Foreign Relations, including funding for conducting research in Washington, D.C., New York, and Europe. In June 1993 I presented the views expressed in chapter 6 at a seminar organized in New York by the Council on Foreign Relations, which provided an opportunity for several of the Council's fellows and members to point me in the right direction at an early stage in the development of this book.

After my return to the Department, I was considerably aided by the vast library holdings of the Department of State and of the Library of Congress, which respectively lay claim to being the oldest and the largest libraries in Washington, D.C. Both the United Nations Information Center in Washington, D.C. and the Peace Palace Library in The Hague were invaluable resources for tracking down both mainstream and off-beat United Nations materials. The staffs at each of these institutions proved first rate.

My observations and conclusions in this book have benefited from those in the academic community with whom I have had the great fortune to study: Richard Gardner, Louis Henkin, and Oscar Schachter of the Columbia Law School; Philip Allott, Derek Bowett, Christopher

Greenwood, and Elihu Lauterpacht of Cambridge University; and Richard Lillich, David Martin, and John Norton Moore of the University of Virginia School of Law. Special thanks are owed to Professor Lillich who read and commented on this entire study, correcting errors, suggesting improvements to arguments even when they contradicted his own well-crafted views in this area, and providing the encouragement necessary to bring this project to print.

Burns Weston thoroughly edited this book, correcting a range of substantive and syntactical lapses, thereby making this a stronger effort. Professor Weston's ability to challenge without discouraging an author reflects a well-honed skill, if not an art. My thanks also to Jason Letcher, a 1996 graduate of the University of Iowa College of Law, who provided extensive cite-checking support.

Finally, my wife Julie—to whom this book is dedicated—has contributed an enormous amount of patience, encouragement, and general good humor in allowing me to complete this project, notwithstanding two other small projects for which we share responsibility, Jack and Lisa. Without Julie, none of this would have been possible.

To go to war for an idea, if the war is aggressive, not defensive, is as criminal as to go to war for territory or revenue; for it is as little justifiable to force our ideas on other people, as to compel them to submit to our will in any other respect. But there assuredly are cases in which it is allowable to go to war, without having been ourselves attacked, or threatened with attack; and it is very important that nations should make up their minds in time, as to what these cases are.

—John Stuart Mill, "A Few Words on Non-Intervention" (1859)

Introduction

The collapse of the Soviet Union and the regimes of its allied states in the late 1980s was a seminal event in world relations. For more than forty years, the promise of "world order" heralded by the birth of the United Nations in 1945 lay unfulfilled, caught in a web of competing East-West ideologies. Powerful states, capable of projecting military force abroad, spoke in terms of political or economic justice but acted almost always with reference to maintaining the order of a bipolar balance of power—a game of cat and mouse in which rival factions battled worldwide, from the Korean peninsula to the Horn of Africa and beyond.

With the demise of the bipolar world, hopes reemerged for a "new world order," a world where the dictates of ideological competition would give way to greater political, social, and economic cooperation, built on the pillars of international law and international institutions. A resurgent United Nations, a dramatic reduction in nuclear and conventional weapons, and a flowering of democracies evidenced new opportunities for enhancing such cooperation. In early 1991, a carefully built coalition of nations, operating under the formal authorization of the United Nations, successfully checked and repelled Iraqi aggression in Kuwait, raising hopes that finally the prohibition on the use of war as an instrument of national policy had moved from ideal to reality.

Unfortunately, a genuinely cooperative world order seems, at present, as elusive as ever. With the thawing of the bipolar Cold War world have come new threats among peoples of long-suppressed ethnic, religious, and cultural differences. As Yugoslavia disintegrated during the early 1990s and Serbs, Croats, and Muslims took to slaughtering each other, the international community watched and wondered whether this anarchy was the first of a series of events that would play out in Central Europe, the former Soviet Union, and elsewhere. At the same time, other civil wars raged, disease flourished, and children starved in various African countries, for example Somalia, the Sudan, Liberia, and Angola.

Most striking about these post-Cold War crises has been the wanton disregard for basic human rights—the casual slaughter of innocents, the use of rape as an instrument of warfare, the indiscriminate shelling of civilians in their homes and on their streets. As the world moves into the twenty-first century, a critical question is whether, and if so how, the international community should forcibly intervene in the affairs of a nation whose citizens are subject to widespread human rights deprivations, an action commonly referred to as "humanitarian intervention."

The United Nations Charter and the practice of states under the Charter recognize the right of a nation to use military force in self-defense and, as well, the right of the United Nations to use military force to address threats to international peace and security. The Charter, however, does not expressly recognize the right to use military force to protect the people of a state against their own governing authorities or from an overall breakdown in governmental authority, even when they face genocide, widespread violence, starvation, or disease. In the context of projecting military force, the Charter is oriented to the preservation of order, not the protection of human rights.

Yet when cases of widespread human rights deprivations occur, this Charter orientation raises a fundamental and serious question: can any order be durable if it is not just? As seen in the emergence of international human rights law since the enactment of the Charter, the international community increasingly is interested in promoting justice in international relations and international law—a natural outgrowth of philosophical and legal traditions that date back centuries.

The purpose of this study is to assess the controversy over humanitarian intervention as a dialectic of international law, a competition between the values of order and justice. The post-Cold War world is undergoing a process of change, a process the rudimentary object of which should be to reconcile a traditional norm disfavoring transnational projections of force with emerging norms favoring human rights and respect for the dignity of persons. The object of this study, therefore, is not to declare humanitarian intervention legal or illegal, moral or immoral, prudent or imprudent, but to explore issues of legality, morality, and prudence in humanitarian intervention from the standpoint of competing values of world order and with particular attention to the potentially greater use of the United Nations after the Cold War. Though the United Nations is not a world government and though its powers and ability to generate and enforce its commands are constrained by political pressures and reliance on ad hoc economic and military actions, it nevertheless provides new opportunities for enhancing a just world order through the use of humanitarian intervention in appropriate situations. First, at our present stage in history, the United Nations provides the most realistic opportunity for developing reasonable rules in this area, grounded in the common experience of states and created with the participation of those states. Second, it provides the best opportunity for achieving an authoritative decision-making process for assessing whether a particular instance of humanitarian intervention is in fact just and is in accordance with those rules. Third, it provides opportunities for humanitarian intervention to be conducted under the direct command of the United Nations or in close cooperation with the United Nations.

Unfortunately, there are considerable weaknesses in the United Nations as currently structured for conducting humanitarian intervention. The Security Council is expected to be the vehicle for authorizing such intervention. As an institution, however, the Security Council has no infrastructure for, and little experience with, the management of such crises. It is reliant on a few major powers for the economic and military support that is needed to accomplish large-scale interventions to address humanitarian crises. The domination of those powers raises serious questions about the legitimacy of the process by which the Security Council authorizes humanitarian intervention. And while it may be willing to authorize the use of force to conduct humanitarian intervention, it does so without clear guidelines or even general principles as to how the intervention should be conducted and what ultimate objectives should be sought. This is due partly to the lack of a textual or even philosophical basis within the UN Charter for the authorization of such interventions, partly to a tendency to draw upon principles that operate in traditional peacekeeping operations undertaken with the consent of a host government but which are not suited to humanitarian intervention, and partly to a desire by member states to conduct each intervention on an ad hoc basis with as little control by the United Nations as possible. Moreover, there is a disturbing tendency in recent interventions for one or more member states to rush into humanitarian intervention under the authority of the United Nations, only to withdraw their forces hastily a few months later, insisting that the United Nations assume responsibility for the intervention.

This study argues that these weaknesses must be addressed if efforts in this area are to succeed and makes recommendations to this end.

Chapter 1 focuses on what is meant by "humanitarian intervention," a term fraught with ambiguity and subject to endless debate. The approach taken is to recognize that the concept of intervention encompasses a continuum of potential political, economic, and military actions by one state against another, but that a working definition of "humanitarian intervention" is best limited to the threat or use of force by a state, group of states, or international organization primarily for the purpose of protecting the nationals of the target state from widespread deprivations of internationally recognized human rights, whether or not the intervention is authorized by the target state or the international community. As such, the rescue by states of their own nationals is not recommended to be included within the scope of "humanitarian intervention." Neither is transboundary action by non-governmental organizations included within this scope. The focus here is upon state action.

Chapter 1 also addresses the relevance and efficacy of international law in this area and the role of morality and political theory. A full appreciation of the problem of humanitarian intervention, however, is not possible without reference to the philosophical, theological, and legal traditions from which contemporary international law has emerged. Thus, chapter 2 reviews the development of constraints on the use of force from ancient legal traditions through the enactment of the UN Charter as well as certain early developments in international human rights law. It also considers the dialectic of order and justice in law that underlies contemporary legal thought.

Chapter 3 briefly discusses the structure and content of the UN Charter regarding the use of force and the protection of human rights. Providing for a Security Council charged with the maintenance of international peace and security and taking into account regional organizations for assistance in this regard, the UN Charter is centrally focused on the preservation of international peace. Though its original design for the provision of troops by member states to the Security Council on an as-needed basis never has been implemented and though it leaves ambiguous the role of regional organizations within the UN scheme (and thereby fails to provide for systematic relationships), the UN Charter prohibits the use of force by a state against the territorial integrity or political independence of another nation except in self-defense or when authorized by the UN Security Council. Human rights are propounded and referenced in the UN Charter, but the nature and scope of those rights, and their relationship to the maintenance of international peace, are not addressed, leaving human rights something of a poor second cousin in the UN Charter scheme.

The Charter, however, is not a static document. Under any theory of international law, state practice is pivotal in assessing international law as it exists or as it is developing. Accordingly, chapter 4 analyzes incidents of intervention during the Charter era through the dissolution of the Soviet Union in the late 1980s that at times have been argued as humanitarian in nature. Assessing state practice requires assessing the ways in which power and authority have been used by various political actors and the conditions that accounted for them, including reviewing public statements by representatives of relevant states and international organizations and the legal theories upon which they are based. As will be seen, practice in this area is sporadic and, in most instances, the stated objective of the intervening state does not appear consistent with a candid assessment of the circumstances. At the same time, assessing the objective of an intervening state is a highly subjective task and suffers from a tendency to view state action as emanating from a single, conscious viewpoint. This chapter, therefore, discusses debates and actions by the UN General Assembly and its subsidiary organs, decisions of the International Court of Justice, and the development of significant human rights instruments since the entry into force of the UN Charter that are of relevance to this assessment. It also describes the debate during the Cold War era among legal scholars on the interpretation of the legality of humanitarian intervention under the UN Charter, observing that the debate among these scholars reflects differing, perhaps irreconcilable, epistemological views regarding international law.

Chapter 5 focuses on six cases of forcible intervention in the aftermath of the Cold War. Nations have forcibly intervened in Liberia, Iraq, Somalia, Rwanda, and Haiti to address differing levels of internal human rights deprivations. In Bosnia-Herzegovina, the international community forcibly intervened on a limited basis; although most of the atrocities were committed among Bosnians, this crisis is not a true example of humanitarian intervention since the conflict was in fact international in character. Greater attention is given to these case studies than to those that occurred during the Cold War for two reasons. First, they occurred in an environment in which the United Nations was available to serve, and in fact often did serve, as a meaningful participant. Second, they have not received as much attention from scholars assessing the doctrine of humanitarian intervention.

Having considered the context in which the United Nations was created and incidents of intervention during the Charter era, this study next explores, in chapter 6, various key issues regarding the role of the United Nations in relation to humanitarian intervention. One issue concerns the basis under Chapter VII of the UN Charter for the United Nations to engage in humanitarian intervention; the progressive expansion of the concept of "threat to the peace" and its implications for world order are assessed. Next considered is the claim that the United Nations not only is permitted to engage in humanitarian intervention but is bound to do so under the Charter. Further analyzed is the more subtle issue of the "legitimacy" of Security Council intervention of this type and whether there is a need for other UN organs, including the International Court of Justice, to play a significant role in sanctioning Security Council action. Consideration is given to the means by which the Security Council may conduct or authorize such interventions and the limits, if any, that may be derived from state practice. Recent incidents show that the United Nations is no more immune to the difficulties of conducting such interventions than are states, particularly to the difficulty of stabilizing the situation to allow withdrawal of the intervening forces. Finally, this chapter addresses next steps that might prove useful for directing the work of the United Nations in this area.

The UN Charter also envisions a role for regional organizations in the maintenance of international peace and security, a role that for the most part, as already intimated, has been underutilized. Chapter 7 considers the largely unexploited role of regional organizations in humanitarian intervention and considers the difficulties posed both within the UN Charter for independent decisionmaking by those organizations and within the charters of those bodies themselves for taking action to address deprivations of human rights within one of their member states. Still, certain incidents both during the Cold War era and in recent years indicate that regional organizations can perform significant functions in fostering or conducting humanitarian intervention and that greater use of these organizations for humanitarian intervention could yield significant benefits not achieved through use of the United Nations alone. If nothing else, regional organizations can perform important functions in conditioning the behavior of the United Nations. This study urges a more symbiotic relationship between the Security Council and relevant regional organizations to draw on their respective strengths and to confront their respective weaknesses.

Chapter 8 addresses unilateral action by a state or group of states, action outside the auspices of the United Nations or a regional security organization. It considers the legality and prudence of unilateral humanitarian intervention under various approaches: a rules-oriented approach that emphasizes the language of the UN Charter and state practice; a policy-oriented approach that favors resolving indeterminate rules through the advancement of certain values such as the dignity of persons or systemic stability; and a moral philosophy-oriented approach that favors application of a particular theory about the relationship of states to persons. Particular attention is given to the relevance for unilateral humanitarian intervention of a reinvigorated Security Council that can act as an authoritative decisionmaker regarding the appropriateness of an intervention. Finally, efforts to develop acceptable criteria for when states should be able to act unilaterally are considered and criticized.

Chapter 1
Humanitarian Intervention: Preliminary Considerations

International law as a discipline presents special problems for scholar and practitioner alike. In operation, it is significantly different from law as understood in national legal systems. With no centralized legislature, the rules and norms of international law—particularly in their adaptation over time—are less apparent and less precise than those found in national laws. With no generally competent judiciary, opaque terms used to express legal concepts (e.g. "sovereignty," "self-defense," "intervention") are primarily self-judged by states (at least initially), and disputes over the meaning of rules and norms are addressed in ad hoc fashion, if at all. The lack of authoritative, centralized institutions for generating, appraising, and enforcing the legality of state action magnifies inherent jurisprudential difficulties present in national law systems, such as what constitutes "law" and how, and in what way, it binds public and private actors. Moreover, traditional international law and theory is heavily oriented toward the nation-state as the relevant actor and has had difficulty taking account of nongovernmental organizations and individuals as competent actors in the transnational legal system. As a result, non-lawyers and non-international lawyers often are skeptical—even cynical—about the role of law in world affairs.

Nowhere is this skepticism more apparent than in relation to the international rules relating to the use of force. With national security interests normally at stake, skeptics presume that states will act pursuant to their short-term interests and that those interests, with some regularity, will conflict with the long-term interests and expectations of the international community. Efforts to identify and refine international rules regarding intervention to prevent widespread deprivations of internationally recognized human rights are considered noble but futile; such interventions are destined to occur on an ad hoc basis, so it is argued, uninfluenced by even rudimentary norms regarding the use of force.

To address some of these concerns as they relate to the issue of humanitarian intervention, this chapter first provides a working definition of humanitarian intervention. Though the term can have different meanings for different observers, a working definition assists in identifying the essential problem at stake in this area of international law and provides a basis for exploring the relevance of law, morality, and political science to humanitarian intervention. As will be seen, international law in its broadest sense should be regarded not merely as a system of rules but, rather, as a comprehensive process by which states and other international actors make authoritative and more or less controlling decisions, driven in part by past decisions and in part by contemporary community expectations. The chapter concludes with a discussion and explanation of the methodology used in the remaining chapters for assessing the status of international law as it relates to humanitarian intervention.

A. Humanitarian Intervention Defined

The term "humanitarian intervention" has gained great currency in recent years, yet a common definition is neither easily nor succinctly achieved. The adjective "humanitarian" is very broad and in common parlance is used to describe a wide range of activities by governmental and nongovernmental actors that seek to improve the status and well-being of individuals. Even if narrowed to a concept of protecting "human rights," that term potentially encompasses a broad array of political, social, and economic rights. The international community is not fully in agreement on the normative content of many human rights, let alone in agreement on whether there is a hierarchy of values to be ascribed to those rights. For example, in Vienna in 1993, the UN World Conference on Human Rights, attended by 171 states, declared that the "universal nature" of all human rights and fundamental freedoms embodied in the UN Charter, other instruments of human rights, and international law was "beyond question."[1] Yet the Vienna Conference itself revealed deep divisions among states as to whether, and if so which, rights are universally binding. The issue of cultural relativism was a centerpiece of the conference, pitting the Western, industrialized nations advocating the universality of human rights against many of the less-industrialized nations demanding varying standards. This tension is reflected in the declaration issued by the conference, which in one paragraph on the

1. Vienna Declaration and Programme of Action, Report of the World Conference on Human Rights, ch. I, para. 1, U.N. Doc. A/CONF.157/24 (Part I) (1993), *reprinted in* 32 I.L.M. 1661 (1993), 3 INTERNATIONAL LAW & WORLD ORDER III.u.2 (B. Weston ed., 1994) [hereinafter WESTON].

universality of human rights says that it is the duty of states "regardless of their political, economic, and cultural systems" to promote and protect all human rights, while at the same time asserting that "the significance of national and regional particularities" as well as historical, cultural, and religious factors had to be "borne in mind."[2] As discussed in Chapters 4 and 6, however, the practice of states and international organizations reveals that there is an implied hierarchy of human rights and that gross violations by states of certain internationally recognized human rights are accorded greater weight by the international community.

Assuming certain core human rights upon which there is more or less universal agreement, there is nevertheless an inherent subjectivity in assessing whether, for any given situation, those rights are threatened and must be protected. This subjectivity in turn raises important questions about who is competent to make the assessment. Is it important that the international community regard an intervention as "humanitarian," or is it sufficient that the state or group of states conducting the intervention consider it humanitarian? Is it important that the persons on whose behalf the intervention is being taken believe it to be "humanitarian," and if so how is this belief to be assessed, particularly when the crisis arises from competing factions within a state? If the view of the state or states conducting the intervention is relevant, must the intervention be exclusively "humanitarian" or is it acceptable that other motivations be present as well? If so, must the humanitarian motivation be dominant or merely present? If the view of the international community is relevant, what do we mean by "international community"—the United Nations, regional organizations, the general views expressed by governments, the views of only "disinterested" governments, or the views of such nongovernmental actors as human rights organizations or scholars?

The noun "intervention" is, likewise, quite broad and has been the subject of extensive debate in the United Nations[3] and of scholarly treatises on international law.[4] When a state, group of states, or international organization takes action against a state—publicly condemns the state, ceases diplomatic relations or expels the state from membership, provides funding to opposition groups in the other state, imposes economic sanctions, or withholds economic benefits—the state, group of states, or

---

2. *Id.*, para. 5.

3. Key resolutions of the U.N. General Assembly are discussed *infra* chapter 4.

4. *See, e.g.*, INTERVENTION IN WORLD POLITICS (H. Bull ed., 1984); LAW AND CIVIL WAR IN THE MODERN WORLD (J. Moore ed., 1974); E. STOWELL, INTERVENTION IN INTERNATIONAL LAW (1921); A. THOMAS & A. THOMAS, JR., NON-INTERVENTION: THE LAW AND ITS IMPORT IN THE AMERICAS (1956); R. VINCENT, NONINTERVENTION AND INTERNATIONAL ORDER (1974).

international organization "intervenes" in the affairs of that state in the lay sense of the term, even if no military coercion is brought to bear. Indeed, all of international law and international relations consists of varying levels of states interacting and thereby "intervening" in each other's affairs.[5] While recognizing that there is a continuum of actions that can constitute intervention, most writers on the topic of intervention narrow the concept to some form of objectionable or "dictatorial" interference in the affairs of a state.[6] Further, as a practical matter, writers on humanitarian intervention usually narrow the term even further to intervention by the threat or use of armed force.[7] This approach comports with the practice of states and the United Nations in the field of human rights generally; merely considering, debating, and making recommendations regarding a state's human rights record is not generally considered "intervention" in that state's internal affairs so long as there is no implication of enforcement action.[8] Thus, while a general declaration was issued by the 1993 Vienna Conference calling on all states to do better in upholding human rights, many of the Asian, Arab, and non-democratic countries turned back efforts to establish new human rights enforcement mechanisms because of opposition to such "intervention" in their "internal affairs."[9]

Even this narrower concept of intervention, however, has ambiguities and obscurities. For example, does a low-level, temporary deployment of military forces in which there is no intent to change political structures or territorial boundaries of the "target state"[10] (e.g. the airdropping of

5. *See* J. BRIERLY, THE LAW OF NATIONS 402 (H. Waldock ed., 6th ed. 1963) (*"Intervention* is a word which is often used quite generally to denote almost any act of interference by one state in the affairs of another"); W. Friedmann, *Intervention and International Law I, in* INTERVENTION IN INTERNATIONAL POLITICS 40, 42 (L. Jaquet ed., 1971) ("Every recall of a diplomat, every trade negotiation, every promise or withdrawal of economic assistance or commercial credit constitutes, in the relations of any two states, a form of intervention.").

6. *See, e.g.*, 1 OPPENHEIM'S INTERNATIONAL LAW (PEACE) 415–16 (H. Lauterpacht ed., 8th ed. 1955).

7. *See, e.g.*, T. Franck & N. Rodley, *After Bangladesh: The Law of Humanitarian Intervention by Military Force*, 67 AM. J. INT'L L. 275, 277 n.12 (1973).

8. *See* BRIERLY, *supra* note 5, at 294–95. *Contra* G. Gottlieb, *International Assistance to Civilians in Armed Conflicts*, 4 N.Y.U.J. INT'L L. & POL. 403, 410 (1971) (citing as humanitarian intervention General Assembly resolutions concerning South African human rights violations).

9. D. Ottaway, *Human Rights Post Suggested for U.N.*, WASH. POST, June 26, 1993, at A18; *Human Rights: Never Heard of Them*, ECONOMIST, June 12, 1993, at 48.

10. The term "target state" is unfortunate in the context of humanitarian intervention since the objective in the intervention purportedly is not to attack or subjugate the will of a state but, rather, to assist its nationals. Nevertheless, the term "target state" is useful in distinguishing the state against which the intervention is being taken from those states undertaking the intervention (the "intervening state(s)"), and in that spirit is used in this study.

food from military cargo planes) qualify as "intervention?" Such diffi-culties have led some to conclude that there is little use in trying to de-fine a doctrine of humanitarian intervention.[11] Nevertheless, at least a working definition of humanitarian intervention is useful as a basis for discussion.

Several writers have crafted their definition to describe a *right of states*, inserting conditions into the definition that render an intervention legal (at least in the eyes of the writer) when undertaken consistent with that definition.[12] A better approach, because it avoids normative ambiguity, is to craft a working definition that describes a *range of actions by states*, the permissibility or legality of which may then be assessed along with de-sirable restrictions or conditions. In so doing, lines must be drawn—some justifiable, others arbitrary—to provide general contours. This study proceeds with the following working definition of humanitarian intervention:

- Humanitarian intervention is the threat or use of force by a state, group of states, or international organization primarily for the pur-

11. *See, e.g.*, M. Bazyler, *Reexamining the Doctrine of Humanitarian Intervention in Light of the Atrocities in Kampuchea and Ethiopia*, 23 Stan. J. Int'l L. 547, 547 n.1 (1987).

12. For instance, Antoine Rougier, writing in the early part of this century on the theory of humanitarian intervention, asserted: "The theory of humanitarian intervention is that which recognizes *the right* of one state to exercise international control over the acts of another in regard to its internal sovereignty when contrary to the laws of humanity." A. Rougier, *La Théorie de l'Intervention d'Humanité*, 17 Rev. Gén. D. Int'l Pub. 468, 472 (1910) (author's translation; emphasis added). This formulation is picked up by some writers in the post-Charter era. *See, e.g.*, Thomas & Thomas, Jr., *supra* note 4, at 372 ("Humanitarian intervention can be defined as the right of one state to exercise international control over the acts of another in regard to its internal sovereignty when such acts are contrary to the laws of humanity.").

Also writing in the pre-Charter era, Ellery Stowell defined humanitarian intervention as "the reliance upon force for the *justifiable* purpose of protecting the inhabitants of another state from treatment which is so arbitrary and persistently abusive as to exceed the limits of that authority within which the sovereign is presumed to act with reason and justice." Stowell, *supra* note 4, at 53 (emphasis added); *see also* E. Stowell, *Humanitarian Intervention*, 33 Am. J. Int'l L. 733 (1939).

More recently, Professor Fernando Tesón, who approaches the issue from a neo-Kantian perspective on international law which sees sovereign rights as derived from the people, defines humanitarian intervention as "the *proportionate* transboundary help, including forc-ible help, provided by governments to individuals in another state who are being denied basic human rights *and who themselves would be rationally willing to revolt against their oppressive government*." F. Tesón, Humanitarian Intervention: An Inquiry into Law and Mo-rality 5 (1988) (emphasis added).

Conversely, at least one scholar regards intervention legally authorized by the United Nations as falling outside the scope of humanitarian intervention. *See* W. Verwey, *Humani-tarian Intervention Under International Law*, 32 Neth. Int'l L. Rev. 357, 375 (1985).

pose of protecting the nationals of the target state from widespread deprivations of internationally recognized human rights.

Each component of this working definition merits brief discussion.

1. "Threat or use of force"

As stated above, intervention may be defined to embrace situations where a state, group of states, or international organization undertakes actions that do not involve a threat or a use of force. This study, however, focuses on intervention primarily with reference to the threat or use of military force, although attention will also be paid to the increasing use of comprehensive economic sanctions as a means of coercing state behavior. While such a focus artificially limits the scope of intervention to be discussed, it also permits for a more detailed discussion of the most extreme form of international coercion. Furthermore, the essential feature of humanitarian intervention—and the reason for its controversial nature among governments and scholars—is the tension it engenders vis-à-vis the constraints developed by the international community on the use of force among states. With respect to state action, the centerpiece of contemporary restraints on the use of force (which will be discussed further in chapter 3) is Article 2(4) of the UN Charter, which prohibits states from "the threat or use of force" against other states in certain situations. Thus, humanitarian intervention that takes the form of a threat or use of force presents a direct conflict with a key norm of the UN Charter; the question then becomes whether, among the other norms of the Charter, one can find authority that renders the action lawful.

In most instances, humanitarian intervention as considered in this study involves the *actual* use of *armed* force through the *transboundary* projection of military units into a target state. These units usually have the task of suppressing local activities that endanger human rights, of reestablishing order, and of fostering conditions for relief operations, the return of refugees, and the avoidance of further deprivations. Nevertheless, it is important to recognize the possibility of humanitarian intervention where force is not projected into the territory of the target state, where the force is not armed force, and where force in the sense of Article 2(4) is not even used. Interventions come in all shapes and sizes, even among the ones discussed in this study, and therefore any working definition of humanitarian intervention should not be so rigid that it cannot take account of those differences.

First, humanitarian intervention may not involve the actual transboundary projection of military or police units into the target state. Military forces stationed outside the territory of the target state for purposes of impeding vessels and aircraft entering or departing the target state should be considered a use of force that, in appropriate circumstances, may qualify as intervention; it is usually recognized by the target state as an attack on its national security.[13]

Second, where there is only the "threat" of force, then obviously force itself is not actually being used. Instead, the intervening state, states, or international organization indicates that, unless the relevant authorities within the target state conform their behavior, the intervenors are prepared to use force. The threat of force falls within the ambit of restraints on the use of force since the international community recognizes that threats can be just as coercive as the actual use of force; indeed, states may be more tempted to use threats because they entail lower costs to the threat-issuing state than actually taking forcible action. In the case of humanitarian intervention, the threat of using force may be a preferred method of intervention if the intervenor seeks to protect persons prior to the deprivation of their human rights, since once deprivations occur their effects may be irreversible. As will be discussed in chapter 5, the 1994 intervention by the United States in Haiti involved a threat of forcible intervention, which led to the acceptance by the de facto authorities of the deployment of U.S. and other military forces to Haiti.

Third, where comprehensive economic sanctions are imposed on a target state with the effect of seriously impeding the ability of the state to provide goods and services to its people, then the type of coercion employed is not, by definition, armed force. The imposition of economic sanctions generally has not been regarded by states or scholars as a use of force within the scope of Article 2(4), but has been regarded as relevant to the principle of nonintervention.[14] Indeed, whenever coercion by a state, group of states, or international organization increases to a point where it deprives the target state of critical resources or otherwise fundamentally affects the ability of a target state to conduct its day-to-day affairs, then the coercion may well provoke the target state to react in a manner that threatens international peace and security. As such, this

13. *See, e.g.*, North Atlantic Treaty, Apr. 4, 1949, art. 6, 63 Stat. 2241, 2244, 34 U.N.T.S. 243, 246–48, *reprinted in* 2 WESTON, *supra* note 1, at II.D.9 ("For the purpose of Article 5 an armed attack on one or more of the Parties is deemed to include an armed attack . . . on the vessels or aircraft . . . of the Parties.").

14. *See, e.g.*, D. Bowett, *Economic Coercion and Reprisals by States*, 13 VA. J. INT'L L. 1, 1–2 (1972). Regarding the ability of the Security Council to undertake economic coercion in the exercise of its Chapter VII powers, see M. McDougal & W. Reisman, *Rhodesia and the United Nations: The Lawfulness of International Concern*, 62 AM. J. INT'L. L. 1 (1968).

higher level of coercion should properly be considered a form of intervention and, if done for humanitarian purposes, a form of humanitarian intervention.

2. "State, group of states, or international organization"

Humanitarian intervention may occur as a result of action by a single state, by a cluster of states acting together on an ad hoc basis or as part of a regional organization, or by a broad coalition of states representative of the various regions of the world. The state or states may be acting under the express authority of the UN Security Council pursuant to Chapter VII of the UN Charter, which in this study shall be referred to as "UN-authorized humanitarian intervention." As will be seen in chapter 5, some interventions that do not have the express authority of the UN Security Council may nevertheless be considered over time within the scope of authority granted by the United Nations. Alternatively, such intervention could be undertaken by a state or states acting without any UN authority but, rather, under the authority of a regional organization, which shall be referred to as "regional humanitarian intervention." Finally, humanitarian intervention could be undertaken by a state or states acting without the authority of either the United Nations or a regional organization, which for convenience shall be referred to as "unilateral humanitarian intervention," a somewhat misleading term since the intervention may be conducted by several states.

Reference to "state, group of states, or international organization" consciously excludes action by non-state entities designed to prevent widespread deprivations of internationally recognized human rights. Without question, nongovernmental organizations such as the International Committee of the Red Cross and Médecins sans Frontières (Doctors Without Frontiers) play a key role in addressing humanitarian crises as they unfold. Nevertheless, even when such organizations act without the consent of the local governing authorities, their intervention is qualitatively different from intervention by states, both in the likelihood of creating or aggravating a threat to international peace and security and in the legal norms of the UN Charter and state responsibility that are engaged.

3. "Primarily"

As will be seen in the discussion of incidents of intervention in chapters 2, 4 and 5, it is difficult to identify an intervention where the prevention of widespread deprivations of internationally recognized human rights is the sole reason for the intervention; often there are other issues at stake, such as the protection of persons who are not nationals of the target state or a claim in favor of vindicating treaty rights. Where those issues are peripheral to an overall purpose of the intervention to protect local nationals (e.g., in the course of protecting thousands of local nationals, the intervenor also protects a few nationals of its own or of a third country), the intervention is properly considered humanitarian intervention.

This is not to say that an intervenor motivated by a desire to prevent widespread deprivations of human rights is necessarily correct in asserting that such deprivations exist, nor that it is for the intervenor alone to self-judge the intervention, nor that intervention is the best means for preventing or ending human rights deprivations. Indeed, the violent nature of interventions, and the often vacillating means by which states and international organizations conduct them, typically leads to the deaths of some of those nationals the intervenor seeks to protect. Nevertheless, it is submitted that the crucial reference point for bringing an intervention within a working definition of humanitarian intervention is whether the intervention is undertaken primarily because of a perceived sense of altruism rather than for some other reason, such as advancing a state's own national interest.

To determine the primary purpose of an intervention, the statements of officials of the intervening state, states, or international organization are relevant. Governments, however, are notorious for providing public statements that are at odds with the actual internal events that inspire state action, and therefore statements of various kinds by various actors may be relevant. Of course, in speaking of a single "purpose," one risks assigning to states and international organizations anthropomorphic features they do not possess; there may be a range of motivating factors operating among the relevant regime elites of a state or international organization. Nevertheless, this approach provides a benchmark for inquiring into the nature of interventions as humanitarian interventions.

4. "Nationals of a target state"

In theory, the doctrine of "humanitarian intervention" could include intervention to protect or "rescue" one's own nationals (perhaps along with the nationals of a third state). The Israeli commando operation at Entebbe, Uganda in 1976 is the prototype rescue operation and was clearly an intervention motivated by humanitarian concerns. Including the protection of one's nationals as a component of humanitarian intervention is the approach that some commentators have taken, perhaps in the belief that forcible intervention either on behalf of one's own or a third state's nationals or on behalf of nationals of the target state is equally likely to endanger international peace and security or to violate international constraints on the use of force.

It is preferable, however, to restrict one's definition of humanitarian intervention to actions seeking to prevent human rights deprivations inflicted on the nationals of the target state. Government officials and scholars for the most part do not regard a state's intervention to protect one's own nationals as comparable to intervention to protect the nationals of the target state; the former has gained greater acceptance as a lawful act within the international community even in the post-Charter years.[15] This greater acceptance is not surprising. There is a juridical relationship between an intervening state and its nationals that is lacking with respect to the nationals of the target state. Further, as a practical matter, the pure rescue of nationals should be of a "get in and get out" nature; the objective can be achieved without altering significantly the activities of the local government authorities. As such, a pure rescue operation should have less implications for the territorial integrity and political independence of the target state. This study will consider only the issue of protection by a state of its own or a third state's nationals when considering the more general point of whether norms arising from the UN Charter can change over time in light of state practice.

Of course, operations to rescue nationals have the potential of expanding in scope beyond the original objective. Intervention by Belgian forces in the Congo in 1964 and U.S. forces in the Dominican Republic in 1965, in Grenada in 1983, and in Panama in 1989 were criticized as unlawful on this basis, and will be discussed further in chapter 4. Under the "primary purpose" test set forth above, in the event an intervention goes beyond what is necessary to rescue one's nationals, then it may be that the primary reason of the intervenor is to protect the nationals of the target state, in which case the intervention would be properly characterized as a humanitarian intervention.

5. "Widespread deprivations of internationally recognized human rights"

Most commentators that accept the legality of humanitarian intervention limit it to the prevention of widespread violations of certain fundamental human rights. This is because the most compelling arguments

---

15. 1 OPPENHEIM'S INTERNATIONAL LAW (PEACE) 440–42 (R. Jennings & A. Watts eds., 9th ed. 1992). For further discussion of the right of a state under international law to intervene for the protection of its own nationals, *see infra* chapter 8. This study also sets aside the issue of rescue of third-country nationals in the process of rescuing one's own nationals. Those rescues also fall within the scope of the more accepted doctrine of rescue or protection of nationals of the intervening states.

for the legality, morality, and prudence of such interventions arise from the rudimentary values at stake when human rights violations occur on a large scale, when they are persistent, and when, in some fashion, they "shock the conscience of humanity. Most state practice arguably within the realm of humanitarian intervention indicates that these are the conditions for which states may be willing expressly or implicitly to intervene for humanitarian reasons.

What is meant by a widespread violation of fundamental human rights, however, is not altogether clear.[16] As will be discussed in chapter 4, the phrase "gross violations" has gained some currency in the development of human rights law by the United Nations and serves as a basis for distinguishing between fundamental human rights and other human rights. Certain actions by states may be regarded as inherently gross violations of internationally recognized human rights (e.g., genocide, slavery, and torture), whereas other actions may be regarded as gross violations when they occur as part of a consistent pattern. A broader reading of fundamental human rights might include the right to be free of tyranny or to participate in free elections, in which case intervention for the purpose of overthrowing a nondemocratic regime would be considered "humanitarian intervention."[17]

The international law of human rights is viewed generally as law dealing with the protection of persons against violations *by their governments* of their internationally guaranteed rights.[18] Nevertheless, the loss of human rights need not necessarily be inflicted by the de jure government of a state; it might arise from the actions of rebel forces or of feuding factions within a state which are in de facto control of part of the country. Complicated circumstances may arise in which governmental or rebel forces are not directly inflicting violence on persons but, rather, are preventing the delivery of humanitarian relief to persons who are sick or

16. A review of various human rights instruments and associated commentary reveals a range of terms used to describe the more egregious forms of human rights violations. *See* Verwey, *supra* note 12, at 368–69 ("References are found to 'gross', 'massive', 'large-scale' or 'persistent' violations, of 'elementary' or 'fundamental' human rights, in such a way that 'atrocities', 'barbaric acts' or 'repulsive practices' are committed, which constitute 'crimes against (the laws of) humanity' or 'genocide', and are considered to 'shock the conscience of mankind' or 'flagrantly violate standards of morality and civilization', single or in combination, in most definitions of humanitarian intervention.") (citations omitted).

17. *See* A. D'Amato, *The Invasion of Panama Was a Lawful Response to Tyranny*, 84 AM. J. INT'L L. 516, 519 (1990); W. Reisman, *Coercion and Self-Determination: Construing Charter Article 2(4)*, 78 AM. J. INT'L L. 642 (1984); *contra* O. Schachter, *The Legality of Pro-Democratic Invasion*, 78 AM. J. INT'L L. 645 (1984).

18. *See* B. Weston, *Human Rights*, in HUMAN RIGHTS IN THE WORLD COMMUNITY: ISSUES AND ACTION 17 (R. Claude & B. Weston eds., 2d ed. 1992) ("At bottom, human rights limit state power.").

starving due to the outbreak of civil warfare. In these cases, the loss of certain fundamental human rights is more in the nature of a "deprivation" by the local authorities than direct "violation" of those rights. Consequently, for the purposes of this study, the broader formulation of "widespread deprivation of internationally recognized human rights" is used to capture the myriad of conditions that might arise where human rights on a large scale are in jeopardy.

6. The Issue of Consent by Local Authorities

It might be argued that when one speaks of a "threat or use of force against a state" there must be a lack of authorization or consent by authorities of that state; otherwise the threat is not really a threat and "the use of force" is better characterized as military cooperation. Under this reasoning, a definition of "humanitarian intervention" should be limited to situations where the local governing authorities of the target state have not authorized or consented to the interference in its affairs. If such an approach is taken, it invariably leads to arguments about whether highly coercive action taken by states or an international organization against another state is "humanitarian intervention" due to differences of view as to whether consent was provided or, if so, whether it was provided by the relevant authorities. As such, it introduces undesirable ambiguities about what constitutes "humanitarian intervention," confusing the descriptive with the prescriptive enterprise.

The approach taken in this study is to regard the issue of authorization by the target state as not central to whether certain actions should be categorized as "humanitarian intervention." The issue of authorization by the target state becomes important, rather, in assessing whether the humanitarian intervention should be regarded as permissible or lawful. As noted above, this definition of "humanitarian intervention" seeks to describe a range of actions that are in fact undertaken by states; the permissibility or legality of those actions may then be assessed along with desirable restrictions or conditions.

The means by which humanitarian intervention may be authorized will be explored more fully in subsequent chapters. However, some preliminary observations are appropriate since this study proceeds with its primary focus on humanitarian interventions where the target state has not directly authorized the intervention because such interventions pose the most acute difficulties in formulating principles for a just world order precisely because they have not been previously authorized. Where direct authorization from the target state is lacking, it is necessary to identify some other authority for the intervention to sustain its permissibility or legality. Indirect authorization by the target state may exist based on its acceptance, at the time it became a member of the United Nations, of the Security Council's authority under Chapter VII of the Charter. Alternatively, this study will consider whether authority might be derived from some other international instrument, such as the charter of a regional organization, or from customary rules of international law. If no authority for the intervention may be found, then presumably it is impermissible or unlawful.

Construing whether there is direct authorization for the intervention from the target state poses some difficulties; in crisis situations, the power structures within the target state are rarely monolithic. The local governing authorities may consist of a government that is de jure sovereign in the target state and is wholly or mostly in control of its territory, a government that is de facto sovereign in the target state (with the de jure government only partially in control of territory or in exile), or various factions de facto controlling different portions of the territory of the target state. This study focuses primarily on situations where direct authorization for intervention has not been obtained from all such entities that de jure or de facto control the target state's territory.[19]

In some cases, governmental order in a target state may have collapsed such that no authorities exist capable of authorizing an intervention, as arguably was the case in Somalia prior to the enforcement actions taken in December 1992. Nevertheless, the issue of authorization is still rele-

---

19. This approach comports with the classical rule in international law that, once an internal faction gains a certain amount of control in a state, it achieves a belligerent status that precludes foreign states from aiding the de jure government, and any such assistance to either side constitutes unlawful intervention. For a discussion of this traditional rule, see E. Borchard, *"Neutrality" and Civil Wars*, 31 AM. J. INT'L L. 304 (1937). Whether this traditional rule survived the Spanish Civil War is unclear. *See* L. HENKIN, HOW NATIONS BEHAVE: LAW AND FOREIGN POLICY 153–62 (2d ed. 1979); J. MOORE, LAW AND THE INDO-CHINA WAR 161–63 (1972).

Indeed, the question of external military assistance to factions fighting in a civil war is complicated and appears far from settled under contemporary international law. Such assistance would appear to violate the traditional norm under customary international law of nonintervention. The UN Charter, however, does not address the question. On the one hand, it may be argued that such assistance in favor of just one faction is a use of force against the territorial integrity and political independence of the target state; the civil war should be allowed to run its course before assistance may be given to the prevailing faction. On the other hand, since there is no government definitively in control of the state, it may be argued that assistance at the request of one of the factions is neither "against" the state's political independence nor a violation of its territorial integrity. L. Henkin, *International Law: Politics, Values and Functions*, 216 R.C.A.D.I. 9, 166 (1989-IV).

The legality of counterintervention by state C (alone or in conjunction with others) in state A to offset or neutralize substantial military participation by state B in favor of one of the factions in state A is also unsettled. If such counterintervention were forbidden, it would be difficult to deter interventions and would likely lead to results unacceptable to states. *Id.* at 168.

vant in such cases; it cannot somehow be assumed that authorization would be forthcoming if a recognized governmental authority or authorities existed. In most instances some type of controlling faction capable of granting authorization does exist for each of the different regions of the country, even if it is difficult to identify that faction.

B. Law, Morality, and Political Theory

Because this study seeks to explore issues of the legality, morality, and prudence of humanitarian intervention, a preliminary question arises as to why and in what way law, morality, and political theory are relevant to humanitarian intervention. Humanitarian intervention typically involves the decision by a state, group of states, or international organization to undertake violent action against a state that is threatening, engaging in, or tolerating violent action. As such, the issues of law and morality that arise are per se outside any one national legal system and often outside any one community bound together through a cultural, religious, or philosophical value system. Moreover, the violence inherent in both humanitarian intervention and the action justifying the intervention, reflecting respectively a disruption of transnational and national order, appears to defy the application of legal or moral norms. To address these concerns, the following subsections explore the relevance of law, morality, and political theory to humanitarian intervention.

1. International Law

The Rules-Oriented Approach

There is a tendency to regard international law as a system of rules that bind states. To divine these rules, one may look to the express obligations undertaken by states in international conventions and treaties, which can be ascertained through the "ordinary meaning" of the language of the agreement, supplemented by interpretive techniques similar to those applied for the interpretation of national statutes. One may look also to the customary practices of states that are undertaken in the belief they are legally compelled, which can be ascertained by observing what governments do and how they explain what they do. Other traditional sources of international law include "general principles" of law common to all states, decisions of international courts and tribunals, and the writings of "highly qualified publicists" or scholars. At its positivist extreme, this classical approach to international law regards rules as being "out there," needing simply to be found and applied to state actions to determine their legality.

Statesmen,[20] journalists,[21] and even lawyers themselves[22] have expressed skepticism, however, about the concept of legal rules "governing" international behavior, especially rules that relate to the use of armed force. Perhaps most telling has been the disdain of prominent international political theorists, sometimes referred to as "realists," who could have helped advance understanding about the nature and role of law in international affairs.[23] There are common themes to the criticisms.

First, it is said, the international system surrounding these "rules" compares poorly to national legal systems. There are no well-functioning international bodies capable of consistently enacting and amending these rules or adjudicating disputes over their interpretation. With an inordinate emphasis placed on the role of the International Court of Justice, which reviews and decides only a few cases each year, it is argued that the rules cannot be developed, refined, or amended over time to take account of new circumstances and experiences and do not deserve the name "law." Moreover, it is noted (in the spirit of John Austin[24]) there is no well-functioning body capable of enforcing sanctions against states found in violation of the rules.

Second, since there is no ability to police this system of rules, it is contended, deviations by states from "international law" are frequent, particularly by powerful states, which are capable of setting the agenda and determining outcomes regardless of the "rules." Indeed, it is said, states are bound only to their own sense of self-interest, by which they may or may not adhere to customary practices as they choose; the repeated willingness of states not to comply with these "rules" is evidence that the

20. *See, e.g.*, G. KENNAN, AMERICAN DIPLOMACY 1900–1950 95 (1951).

21. *See, e.g.*, C. Krauthammer, *The Curse of Legalism*, NEW REPUBLIC, Nov. 6, 1989, at 44; G. Will, *The Perils of "Legality"*, NEWSWEEK, Sept. 10, 1990, at 66.

22. *See, e.g.*, R. Bork, *The Limits of "International Law"*, NAT'L INTEREST, Winter 1989/90, at 3. More sophisticated, international law scholars, some associated with the critical legal studies movement, have challenged what they consider to be the incoherence of the fundamental theories upon which international law is based. *See, e.g.*, A. CARTY, THE DECAY OF INTERNATIONAL LAW? A REAPPRAISAL OF THE LIMITS OF LEGAL IMAGINATION IN INTERNATIONAL AFFAIRS (1986); D. KENNEDY, INTERNATIONAL LEGAL STRUCTURES (1987); M. KOSKENNIEMI, FROM APOLOGY TO UTOPIA: THE STRUCTURE OF INTERNATIONAL LEGAL ARGUMENT (1989).

23. H. MORGENTHAU, POLITICS AMONG NATIONS: THE STRUGGLE FOR POWER AND PEACE 4–5 (4th ed. 1967); K. WALTZ, THEORY OF INTERNATIONAL POLITICS 82–101 (1979). The view that nations are in an anarchical state of nature, driven inescapably by motives of self-preservation, derives from Hobbes. T. HOBBES, LEVIATHAN, OR THE MATTER, FORME AND POWER OF A COMMONWEALTH, ECCLESIASTICALL AND CIVIL (M. Oakeshott ed., New York, Macmillan 1962) (1651).

24. J. AUSTIN, THE PROVINCE OF JURISPRUDENCE DETERMINED, Lecture 1 (H. Hart ed., Weidenfeld & Nicolson 1954) (1832). Austin's concept of law is that of a sovereign command made effective by the application of sanction.

rules do not exist. States exhibiting greater fidelity to "international law," it is argued, are at a severe disadvantage vis-à-vis states that habitually ignore such rules with impunity. If such rules are reconceptualized as simply a reflection of how states behave in practice rather than as an independent structure to which states are bound, then, it is argued, these rules are not "legal rules" but, rather, a device for describing political behavior. They are an "apology" or justification for, rather than a restraint upon, action.

Third, it is noted, the rules of "international law," particularly those relating to the use of force, consist of fairly minimalist, indeterminate principles contained primarily in the UN Charter and other treaties. The reason the principles are minimalist or indeterminate is that, in lieu of an international legislature, the system relies upon the creation of rules only through the consensus of all states. Since states operate on the global plane under different legal, moral, and cultural traditions, these rules are forced to the lowest common denominator among all states. Further, many of these rules travel in complementary pairs, such that, for any given state action, a rule may be found supporting the action and another condemning it. Critics therefore argue that, at best, these so-called rules are but general, malleable principles, devoid of moral content.

Such skepticism is by no means unfounded, but it is usually overstated and often proceeds from a narrow view about the nature of law and its role in conditioning behavior. As is discussed in the next subsection, "law" is more than a set of rules governing social behavior. Yet, even if one focuses on law as a system of rules, it is appropriate to accept that law arises when one's conduct is in some sense made nonoptional or obligatory.[25] As such, law can arise either when one is obliged to act due to a threatened, effective sanction *or* when one is obliged to act due to social rules for which conformity is generally demanded and from which deviations are therefore met with social pressures large and small. These social rules operate as a guide to one's conduct even in the absence of a centrally organized system of inducement and punishment.

International law consists of some rules that are enforced by effective sanction and others that are adhered to because of complex relationships of interdependency operating among states. These rules are not some kind of black-letter restatement of scientifically derived principles isolated from "reality." They reflect, rather, underlying policy choices made by states (and in some cases nongovernmental organizations) over time and in the context of interactive processes inextricably related to the actors upon which the rules operate. One may observe states as hav-

25. H. Hart, The Concept of Law 77–96, 208–31 (1961).

ing the strongest allegiance to rules that are perceived as legitimate or have been rendered by legitimate rule-making institutions,[26] and where deviations from them are met with international approbation, entailing political and at times economic costs for the offending state (e.g., the U.S. embargo on sales of grain to the Soviet Union following Moscow's 1979 intervention in Afghanistan).

It is out of concern for these potential costs that states pay attention to international rules on the use of force and seek to conduct themselves and justify their actions in a manner consistent with those rules. Like individuals in domestic legal systems, there are times when states will act contrary to the rules to advance their own short-term self-interests and will successfully escape effective censure. Yet the self-interest of states is more often seen as reinforcing allegiance to these rules out of an appreciation for the benefits of an orderly system. International rules on the use of force were not created out of thin air nor did they spring forth from an academic mind. They are the culmination of centuries of experience with the carnage of war.

Despite the lack of detail associated with the international rules on the use of force, there is, in short, a core meaning to these rules that is understood and accepted by all states, even if their application to particular situations inevitably raises interpretive issues.[27] As discussed in detail in chapter 3, these rules make clear that states may not use armed force for aggrandizement but may use force for certain limited reasons, most notably necessary and proportionate self-defense. While there is no compulsory adjudication of these rules, resort by a state (or the United Nations) to the use of force is publicly and vociferously appraised by states, international organizations, nongovernmental organizations, and individuals, and that appraisal has a conditioning influence on the way states behave. Further, while the international community, including the United Nations, is deemed prohibited from intervening in matters that are considered wholly within the domestic jurisdiction of states (the principle of sovereignty), actions by a state against its nationals are not considered solely a matter of domestic jurisdiction.

There is particular hope for the efficacy of international rules relating to humanitarian intervention. In situations of unilateral humanitarian intervention, the primary reason for the intervention is not a state's own national interest or national security but, rather, its humanitarian concern for the nationals of another state or states. Since the benefits that accrue to the intervening state ordinarily are indirect or minimal, it will

26. *See generally* T. Franck, The Power of Legitimacy Among Nations (1990).

27. O. Schachter, *In Defense of International Rules on the Use of Force*, 53 U. Chi. L. Rev. 113, 119–21 (1986).

not wish to incur significant costs, political or economic, that may arise from the approbation of the world community. Consequently, the intervening state is less likely to disregard international rules governing humanitarian intervention and more likely to act consistent with those rules. Further, to extract its forces from the target state and to defray the financial costs of the intervention, the intervening state typically will have strong incentives to make use of any available opportunities for engaging the international community in the intervention, such as through the United Nations or regional organizations. Indeed, a central problem is the failure of states to act at all (whether through the United Nations, regional organizations, or otherwise) when faced with widespread violations of internationally recognized human rights, which is largely attributable to a perception that their own interests are not at stake.

The Policy-Oriented Approach

International law consists only partly of a set of rules governing international behavior; it consists of a variety of specialized social processes by which international society moves beyond rules developed in the past to address new problems as they arise in the present. Perhaps the best-developed theory of international law in this sense is the "policy-oriented" approach advanced by Myres McDougal, Harold Lasswell, and their associates.[28] McDougal and Lasswell argue that international law consists of more than just technical rules; it consists of processes for authoritative and controlling decisionmaking within wider contexts of morality and politics. Since technical rules commonly travel in pairs of complementary opposites, they are capable of reflecting a range of community demands and expectations. For McDougal, "In the process of decision-making in the world arena, the technical rules that constitute the *lex lata* are continually being defined and redefined in the application of policy to ever-changing facts in ever-changing contexts."[29] In determining the presence of international law, one must ascertain whether decisions by states are in conformity with community values and expectations and not based on naked power ("authoritative") and whether they are supported by enough power to be effective to a consequential degree ("controlling"). Further, technical rules often are ambiguous as

---

28. For an introduction to this "New Haven school," see M. McDougal, *International Law, Power and Policy: A Contemporary Conception*, 82 R.C.A.D.I. 137 (1953-I). For its elaboration, in two volumes, *see* H. LASSWELL & M. MCDOUGAL, JURISPRUDENCE FOR A FREE SOCIETY: STUDIES IN LAW, SCIENCE, AND POLICY (1992). For works by others in the "New Haven School," *see* TOWARD WORLD ORDER AND HUMAN DIGNITY: ESSAYS IN HONOR OF MYRES S. MCDOUGAL (W. Reisman & B. Weston eds., 1976).

29. McDougal, *supra* note 28, at 156.

to whether they are describing past events, describing how future events will likely be appraised, or describing how future events should be appraised. If one asserts that "the use of force to protect human rights is lawful under the UN Charter," for instance, it is unclear whether one is saying that in the past such action has been considered lawful, in the future it will continue to be considered lawful, or that as a normative aspiration it should be considered lawful. Based on this approach, McDougal, Lasswell, and their associates over the last half-century have produced studies that appraise different areas of international law, including that of the use of force.[30]

While much of this jurisprudential approach has been assimilated into international legal scholarship, other aspects of it have proved more contentious. McDougal and Lasswell believe that, because of the decentralized nature of the international system, the function of international law is less to constrain state behavior than to support the realization of community values. For them, the dominant challenge for international lawyers is to establish a public order in which the basic values of human dignity are sought, to wit, the greatest possible shaping and sharing of power, enlightenment, wealth, well-being, skill, affection, respect, and rectitude. McDougal and Lasswell claim that, by following certain analytical steps, one may reach a scientifically grounded answer to any given policy problem that is likely to promote a world order based on principles of human dignity.

Many scholars contend, however, that this approach creates too great an opportunity for the use of law as an instrument for powerful states to dictate their political interests. The essential problem is that two policymakers seeking to apply the "scientific" approach advocated by the McDougal/Lasswell jurisprudence can reach completely opposite policy conclusions.[31] This difficulty was particularly apparent during the turbulent years of the Cold War, when McDougal and some of his students insisted upon policy outcomes that advanced values derived from the experience of the nonsocialist West. At the same time, other students of the McDougal/Lasswell jurisprudence, such as Richard Falk, asserted that the jurisprudence was being used improperly simply to support consistently the policy position of the U.S. Government.

Falk regarded the value commitments of both the socialist and nonsocialist systems as flawed and believed that the threat of another world war called for policy approaches that fostered a world order based on

---

30. *E.g.*, M. McDougal & F. Feliciano, Law and Minimum World Public Order: The Legal Regulation of International Coercion (1961).

31. R. Falk, *Casting the Spell: The New Haven School of International Law*, 104 Yale L.J. 1991, 2000–1 (1995).

systemic stability. Rather than allow policymakers to use the law to advance their own particular agenda, Falk wrote:

The task of legal analysis is to find a middle ground, conjoining law to politics without collapsing the one into the other and attaining a realism that neither expects law to guarantee a peaceful world nor concludes that law is irrelevant to international peace.[32]

With the end of the Cold War, Falk now regards, in hindsight, the "ideological partisanship of McDougal and Lasswell as far preferable to my posture of nonpartisan criticism and emphasis on war avoidance," but he continues to maintain that the jurisprudence advocated by McDougal and Lasswell cannot provide "objective knowledge generative of 'correct' policy choices."[33] Further, Falk regards the McDougal/Lasswell jurisprudence as seriously deficient in failing to take account of critical perspectives of excluded constituencies, such as women, non-Westerners, and the poor.[34]

One of the fundamental challenges of legal scholarship today is to find the "middle ground," to develop a coherent theory that conjoins law to politics. To date, no single integrated theory has gained widespread adherence, largely because of the difficulty in applying subjective values (such as "human dignity" or "systemic stability") to concrete situations. In the case of humanitarian intervention, this difficulty is readily apparent. When "authorized persons or organs" in international society seek to decide whether a particular humanitarian intervention should be undertaken, there may be significant values of human dignity and justice advanced by the intervention but there will also be competing values favoring orderly and nonforcible resolution of such conflicts. This dilemma can lead to a conclusion that law in this area is contradictory and essentially indeterminate at its core.

While acknowledging this criticism, this study proceeds on the basis that the dilemma is but a manifestation of a core dialectic within law itself. In all of law, there is a fundamental conflict between subjective values of justice or equity and more objective norms established in favor of order. These competing values are the very "stuff" of law; the tension between them and the difficulty in reconciling them in international law are not indicative of incoherence but, rather, of the challenge faced by the international community in reconciling them in an era when numerous states are experiencing internal violence. The process is a legal one so long as "decisions are made by those authorized to do so, with impor-

32. R. Falk, The Status of Law in International Society 51 (1970).
33. Falk, *supra* note 31, at 2003.
34. *Id*. at 1999, 2002, & 2007–8.

tant guiding reliance on past decisions, and with available choices being made on the basis of community interests and for the promotion of common values."[35] As discussed in chapters 6 and 8, a striking development since the end of the Cold War is the emergence of the UN Security Council as an organ capable and more or less willing to engage in authoritative decisionmaking. Much of this study is dedicated to describing and analyzing how the Security Council has proceeded in weighing the values of order and justice when authorizing, or itself conducting, humanitarian intervention, and its strengths and shortcomings in doing so.

2. Moral Philosophy

This study is primarily about international law. It does not seek to provide a comprehensive discussion of moral philosophy as it relates to humanitarian intervention. Nevertheless, law does not operate in a vacuum. As discussed in the previous subsection, subjective values are of necessity a part of the law.

To appreciate fully the strengths and weaknesses of law with respect to humanitarian intervention, it thus is necessary to consider the role of morality; and while one might argue that international rules on the use of force are devoid of morality, there is in fact a moral element to existing rules on the use of force, self-defense, the peaceful settlement of disputes, and the treatment of individuals by states (human rights). For instance, the obligation for a society first to seek the peaceful settlement of a dispute, thereby providing full opportunity for avoidance of bloodshed, expresses a moral value whose lineage is traced to antiquity. Of newer vintage, but of considerable relevance to humanitarian intervention, is the concept of "crimes against humanity," which is based on what can only be considered civilized standards of morality. Morality as a system concerns itself with explaining right or wrong conduct; one segment of morality is the concept of justice.

If one accepts the relevance of moral values for international law, there are two ways to approach those values. One approach is to view international law as a common framework of rules that allows states with different values, concepts, and beliefs to coexist with one another. For instance, one could accept that international law should operate as a restraint on the pursuit of certain actions that threaten basic international order (e.g., territorial aggression) but not accept that it should attempt to establish shared values among states (e.g., improve the general welfare of individuals or foster democratic regimes). Under this

35. R. Higgins, Problems and Process: International Law and How We Use It 9 (1994).

approach, any rule permitting humanitarian intervention must "be reconciled with those that are fundamental to the idea of international society as a rule-governed association of states, one in which a multiplicity of diverse and independent political communities can accommodate themselves to each other's continued existence." [36]

Alternatively, one might argue that because international rules are incomplete in their meaning, they must be interpreted in light of a specific substantive moral philosophy. To do so, one must believe that there are certain universal principles of morality or justice that are discoverable and that can be applied by human reason. One such substantive moral philosophy underlies the principle of state sovereignty that has characterized most of history since the rise of the nation state and runs counter to the doctrine of humanitarian intervention. Under this philosophy, one argues that a state, as a member of international society, possesses moral rights similar to those of individuals in domestic society. The government of the state, regardless of whether its internal foundations are considered legitimate by other states, is competent to exercise this moral right of self-preservation so long as it is in effective control of the state's territory and population. Other states must respect this moral right and cannot use armed force against it lest international society degenerate into a state of armed conflict, a morally unacceptable situation. If the government of that state is withholding from its people certain fundamental rights, such as liberty or freedom, it is for those people to rise up and reconstitute their government. [37]

An alternative moral philosophy gives primacy to human rights over state rights, thereby justifying humanitarian intervention. [38] An essential element of this approach is the belief that the operative principle of morality is a principle of justice essentially derived from the "equality between human beings as moral persons." [39] Individuals have a moral right to self-preservation; the state's right of self-preservation is subordinate to this right. [40] This approach has its origins in the social contract theory of Locke, Rousseau, and Kant, to which Western democratic traditions can

36. T. Nardin, Law, Morality, and the Relations of States 239–240 (1983).

37. J. Mill, *A Few Words on Non-Intervention* (1859) *reprinted in* Essays on Politics and Culture 368, 382 (G. Himmelfarb ed., New York, Doubleday 1962) ("It can seldom, therefore—I will not go so far as to say never—be either judicious or right, in a country which has a free government, to assist, otherwise than by the moral support of its opinion, the endeavours of another to extort the same blessing from its native rulers."). Mill maintained some important exceptions to this general rule of nonintervention, however, which are discussed *infra* chapter 2.

38. *See generally* Tesón, *supra* note 12.

39. J. Rawls, A Theory of Justice 19 (1971).

40. C. Beitz, Political Theory and International Relations 51–53 (1979).

be traced. Its burden is to show that global moral harmony on this principle of justice exists despite competing philosophical traditions and
conflicting codes of values.

Law and morality can be, but are not always, congruent. A moral or
just act can be illegal; a legal act can be immoral or unjust. Scholars of
jurisprudence robustly debate whether a legal rule that fails to conform
to fundamental requirements of morality or justice should be considered
law.[41] Arguably, an international legal rule that prohibits humanitarian
intervention has no validity or is properly overlooked from the moral
standpoint.

Those who reject that a legal system must exhibit some specific conformity with morality or justice nevertheless normally will accept that morality has profoundly influenced the development of law.[42] In the context
of humanitarian intervention, the stature of rules prohibiting such intervention is tarnished if those rules are deemed inconsistent with moral
values, and even more so if the rules are periodically honored in the
breach. For these reasons, the role of morality and its relationship to
legal rules on the use of force will be considered in subsequent chapters.

3. Political Theory

While the disregard by political realists of the role of international law in
conditioning state behavior may properly be seen as deficient, there is,
similarly, a long-recognized tendency of international lawyers to neglect
the role of politics and political theory in the formation and implementation of international law.[43] Scholarship in international relations has
now moved well beyond the view that international politics is governed
by power and power alone. Increasingly sophisticated methods of mod-
elling state behavior based on the social sciences, such as economics and
"regime" theories, have been developed to further our understanding
of why states behave as they do. Yet, to its detriment, international legal
scholarship has been slow to look beyond its own disciplinary methods.[44]

41. *Compare* H. Hart, *Positivism and the Separation of Law and Morals*, 71 Harv. L. Rev. 593
(1958) *with* L. Fuller, *Positivism and Fidelity to Law—A Reply to Professor Hart*, 71 Harv. L.
Rev. 630 (1958).

42. Hart, *supra* note 25, at 181.

43. *See* Henkin, *supra* note 19, at 3–4; D. Forsythe, The Politics of International
Law: U.S. Foreign Policy Reconsidered 8 (1990).

44. For discussions of how international political theories might apply to international
legal scholarship, see F. Boyle, World Politics and International Law (1985); K. Ab-
bott, *Modern International Relations Theory: A Prospectus for International Lawyers*, 14 Yale J.
Int'l L. 335 (1989); A. Burley, *International Law and International Relations Theory: A Dual
Agenda*, 87 Am. J. Int'l L. 205 (1993).

This study draws upon political theory as appropriate, and upon contemporary political theorists who are actively considering various issues directly relating to humanitarian intervention, to provide insights into how international law currently operates and how it ought to operate in relation to humanitarian intervention. Humanitarian intervention by the United Nations, by regional organizations, or by individual states obviously entails significant choices about the means and ends of the intervention as well as about the rules and practices that ought to be followed. One key function of political theory is to formulate and analyze alternative possibilities for such means, ends, rules, and practices and to explain why some are more persuasive than others.

C. Methodology

Most treatises and casebooks on international law agree on the standard "sources" of international law (treaties, state practice, general principles, judicial decisions, views of scholars), but otherwise divergences exist regarding the means for assessing the process of lawmaking and law development. The traditional approach places primary emphasis on the "black-letter" rules contained in international agreements and judicial decisions, especially the judgments of the International Court of Justice. State practice also may generate international rules, but only if there is a consistent and widespread practice by states reflecting a belief that such practice is compelled by law. Much attention has been paid, also, to the potential creation of international law by international institutions, for example through resolutions of the UN General Assembly.

The traditional approach to lawmaking and law development notes the realities of international politics in the way that states behave but has not sought to assimilate political theory to its approach. The "policy-oriented" approach of McDougal and Lasswell, on the other hand, advances a broader approach to the study of international law. It urges that for any given issue, for example, the issue of humanitarian intervention, one must conduct a systematic and disciplined study that performs four intellectual tasks: (1) the clarification of the policy goals at stake; (2) the description of past trends in decisions related to the issue; (3) the projection of future trends to help predict future decisions; and (4) the appraisal of the compatibility of past and predicted decisions with the policy goals clarified and the invention of policy alternatives for better achieving those goals.

A common method of studying the process of international lawmaking and law development is to focus in depth on specific cases, incidents, or crises to see how, if at all, the law has affected the actions of states.[45] While these studies often conclude that law does affect the way states operate, they do not ordinarily extrapolate from this conclusion to comment on the content and state of international law generally that results as a consequence. In 1984, Michael Reisman called for a "new genre in the study of international law" through the study of particular "incidents" as law-shaping events,[46] seeking to establish the "incident" as a basis for "systematic observation and generalized observation of the law."[47] Some scholars, such as Richard Falk, have heralded this approach as providing a foundation for the realistic assessment of international law;[48] others, such as Derek Bowett, have doubted that the approach is novel and regard it as, at best, an adjunct to traditional methods of study.[49]

Thus there is not yet a unified methodology or theory of methodology for studying international law. The approach taken in this study draws upon various aspects of the approaches discussed above. Borrowing from traditional international law scholarship, the "black-letter" rules embodied in the UN Charter, Security Council and General Assembly resolutions, International Court of Justice decisions, treaties, and regional instruments will be analyzed and discussed in the context of their initial development. However, the appraisal of those rules must also be done in the context of their background, the world in which they operate at present, and the world in which they most likely will operate in the future. Borrowing from McDougal and Lasswell, efforts are made to appraise not just past trends but likely future trends and the policies that might

45. *See, e.g.*, G. ABI-SAAB, THE UNITED NATIONS OPERATION IN THE CONGO 1960–1964 (1978); R. BOWIE, SUEZ 1956 (1974); A. CHAYES, THE CUBAN MISSILE CRISIS (1974); T. EHRLICH, CYPRUS 1958–1967 (1974); R. FISHER, POINTS OF CHOICE (1978).

46. W. Reisman, *International Incidents: Introduction to a New Genre in the Study of International Law*, 10 YALE J. INT'L 1 (1984). Professor Reisman's approach was further developed and put into practice in collaboration with several of his law students. INTERNATIONAL INCIDENTS: THE LAW THAT COUNTS IN WORLD POLITICS (W. Reisman & A. Willard eds., 1988).

47. Reisman defines an incident as: (1) an overt conflict between two or more actors in the international system; (2) perceived as such by other key actors; (3) resolved in some non-judicial fashion; (4) such that the attitudes of "functional elites" as to whether the resolution was acceptable behavior may be assessed. Reisman, *supra* note 46, at 12.

48. R. Falk, *The Validity of the Incidents Genre*, 12 YALE J. INT'L L. 376, 379 (1987) (the genre of international incidents "provides the best available means of comprehending the legislative potential of facts in relation to different topics and different geopolitical configurations on a local, regional, or global scale").

49. D. Bowett, *International Incidents: New Genre or New Delusion?*, 12 YALE J. INT'L L. 386 (1987). Bowett sees the approach as useful in relation to major instances of the use of force since for those "incidents" it would be possible to assess the reactions of "functional elites." *Id.* at 388.

be pursued to reach the overall goals outlined in the Introduction. Where possible, the way in which law affects the steps taken by decision-makers will be indicated. Borrowing from the "incidents" genre, which is particularly well suited to the rare occurrences of humanitarian intervention, the reactions of key decisionmakers to particular incidents of humanitarian intervention will be emphasized. What is hoped to be achieved is a general understanding of the process and limits of international law in conditioning state behavior regarding humanitarian intervention.

Chapter 2
Humanitarian Intervention Prior to the UN Charter

Most contemporary lawyers writing about humanitarian intervention focus on the status of international law under the UN Charter with occasional reference to the status of customary international law prior to the Charter's enactment.[1] The UN Charter's prohibition on the resort to force (with certain stated exceptions) deserves a central focus in any study of this issue; therefore, it will be addressed in the next chapter. Nevertheless, a full understanding of humanitarian intervention under contemporary international law cannot be achieved without reference to the history and tradition from which that law developed. The relevance of this history and tradition may be noted in several ways.

First, international law as it relates to the use of force arose from two main jurisprudential approaches. The divine and secular natural law schools, which emerged from ancient traditions and dominated early writings on the nature and content of international law, stressed universal principles emanating from "right reason" as guides for the behavior of rulers and, later, states; rulers and states acting in accordance with principles of justice were justified in resorting to armed force. The positivist law school, which rose to prominence in the nineteenth century, took as self-evident that international legal rules relating to the use of force had their rudiments only in the self-interest of states, as expressed in international agreements and state practice, and not in independent principles derived from nature or divinity. As the law on the use of force

---

1. There are exceptions. For useful discussions of European Concert interventions in the pre-Charter era, see M. GANJI, INTERNATIONAL PROTECTION OF HUMAN RIGHTS 17–38 (1962); J. Fonteyne, *The Customary International Law Doctrine of Humanitarian Intervention: Its Current Validity Under the U.N. Charter*, 4 CAL. W. INT'L L.J. 203 (1974); T. Franck & N. Rodley, *After Bangladesh: The Law of Humanitarian Intervention by Military Force*, 67 AM. J. INT'L L. 275, 277–95 (1973); I. Pogany, *Humanitarian Intervention in International Law: The French Intervention in Syria Re-Examined*, 35 INT'L & COMP. L.Q. 182 (1986).

became more developed and systematic in the twentieth century, the influence of positivism became ascendant, thereby resulting in considerable emphasis on international agreements (such as the UN Charter) and state practice. Yet history shows that in situations where positive law is considered inadequate or unsatisfactory, it is common for jurists, scholars, and politicians to appeal to the older concepts of law embodied in the natural law traditions. Thus a complete picture of the law on the use of force, including that of humanitarian intervention, cannot ignore the continuing relevance of natural law.

Second, while the term "humanitarian intervention" is a product of legal writings during only the past century, the idea of resorting to war to support individuals suffering from unjust rule is older. It is clearly present in the writings of influential "fathers" of international law such as Grotius and Vattel, can be surmised in the philosophy of political theorists such as Mill and Kant, and is unevenly present in the practice of states during the nineteenth century. In assessing the justification for, or limitations on, humanitarian intervention today, consideration is due to the constructs by which this concept emerged.

Third, because, as is often said, society is condemned to repeat history unless it learns from it, it is important to appreciate that the inspiration for the United Nations (an ambitious attempt to ensure international peace and security through collective measures) lies in earlier efforts at multilateral diplomacy, the Concert of Europe and the League of Nations. Likewise, the conflicting views of scholars during the years preceding the Covenant of the League of Nations on the legality of unilateral humanitarian intervention under customary international law presaged the debates among international lawyers in the UN Charter era regarding the legality of unilateral humanitarian intervention under the Charter.

Fourth, it is useful to dispel certain common misperceptions regarding the status of international law prior to this century. The first is that, under customary international law, resort to the use of force was completely unregulated and therefore any actions that might be characterized as humanitarian intervention were simply a subset of an overall right to attack one's neighbor for whatever reason. To the contrary, there were doctrines regarding the waging of war, intervention, and self-defense under customary international law to which states paid heed.[2] A second

---

2. Scholarly efforts to describe international law from the early treatises, such as Grotius, ON THE LAW OF WAR AND PEACE, discussed *infra* at notes 42–51 and accompanying text, through treatises in the early part of this century, such as J. WESTLAKE, INTERNATIONAL LAW (2 vols. 1910), focused in substantial part on classifying the conditions under which states were justified in resorting to war and how they were to conduct themselves. Probably still

misconception is that the principle of state sovereignty reigned supreme in a state's conduct of its internal affairs. While the law of human rights as known today was not a significant feature of international law prior to this century, the internal conduct of a sovereign was for many jurists and philosophers in earlier times considered a matter of relevance to other sovereigns.[3]

A word of caution, however. The fact that older doctrines regarding the use of force may have included notions properly associated with humanitarian intervention, and that state practice may be shown to support such intervention, does not mean that a right of humanitarian intervention survived into this century, particularly after the entry into force of the UN Charter. Further, the collective action possible today through the operation of Chapter VII of the UN Charter is quite unlike state practice prior to this century, including that of the Concert of Europe.

A. Ancient Legal Traditions

The conduct of warfare in ancient times—whether by the Babylonian, Chinese, Egyptian, Greek, Persian, Roman, or other empires—exhibited considerable inhumanity and barbarity. Even so, most ancient civilizations developed some internal code or philosophy regulating the use of force, usually derived from purportedly universal (often religious) principles.[4] Typically, the code or philosophy referred to the preliminary ex-

---

the best survey of the pre-Charter doctrines on the use of force as they relate to the Charter is I. Brownlie, International Law and the Use of Force by States (1963). On the development of customary norms regarding the conduct of hostilities once commenced, which have been codified over the past century primarily in a series of conventions concluded in The Hague and in Geneva, see G. Best, Humanity in Warfare: The Modern History of the International Law of Armed Conflict (1983).

3. See, e.g., the discussion of the writings of Grotius and Vattel infra notes 42–53 and accompanying text.

4. For Africa before the advent of the Europeans, see African International Legal History 19–24, 111–15 (A. Mensah-Brown ed., 1975); for ancient China, see W. Tieya, International Law in China: Historical and Contemporary Perspectives, 221 R.C.A.D.I. 195, 209 (1990-II) (and sources cited therein); for ancient Greece and Rome, see II C. Phillipson, The International Law and Custom of Ancient Greece and Rome 166–348 (1911); for ancient India, see H. Bhatia, International Law and Practice in Ancient India 81–92 (1977); N. Singh, India and International Law 70–72 (1969). On the development of international law generally in antiquity, see A. Nussbaum, A Concise History of the Law of Nations 1–16 (rev. ed. 1954) (and sources cited therein).

For example, Coleman Phillipson, in his study of international law in ancient Greece and Rome, writes:

Now it was not at all considered by the ancient peoples that war was their normal condition. It was admittedly their frequent condition; but, at least amongst the Greeks and the

haustion of means of reconciliation, the need for a valid ground for commencing war, the requirement in some circumstances for a declaration of war prior to its commencement, rules on the conduct of the fighting, and rules on truces and cessation of the conflict. Of course, the ameliorating nature of these codes or philosophies should not be overemphasized; in many instances ancient warfare resulted in brutal massacres and abuses of men, women, and children and the widespread destruction or theft of property.

In the writings of the historians and philosophers of those early civilizations, the concept of "humanitarian intervention" does not appear as a valid cause for resorting to war per se. Nevertheless, the idea of justifying the use of force on the basis of a divine or just cause is readily apparent, as are self-imposed restrictions on how such action should be undertaken. This section focuses on such developments in ancient Israel, Greece, and Rome that are significant in understanding the development of European Christian doctrines, which in turn underlie the development of contemporary international law.

Max Weber described the God of the early Yahwist confederacy of Hebrew tribes as "first and foremost a god of war. . . . He thirsts for blood, for the blood of the enemies, the disobedient, the victims."[5] From the sources available to us it appears that this early confederation had no political organization on a national scale and that the wars it conducted were fundamentally defensive.[6] Over time, however, increasing threats from foreign powers forced Israel to abandon its approach of conducting defensive wars using largely improvised organization.[7] A permanent kingship emerged along with a professional army, and eventually, as seen in Deuteronomy, war became conceived as a means of attacking and destroying other tribes, not because Israel needed to expand its territorial dominion but rather because these other tribes adhered to gods other than Yahweh.[8] This more aggressive posture based on a divinely inspired cause, however, was concomitant with the development in Deuteronomy of canons of warfare, which contained detailed rules for the conduct of

---

Romans, certain clearly defined causes were recognized as occasioning legitimate war, that is, war in the regular, political acceptation of the term. And in the absence of these causes, to engage in warfare was conceived to be irregular, and forbidden by law and religion alike, and punishable by the gods; so that in these circumstances both the divine sanction and the positive exerted a deterrent influence.

PHILLIPSON, *id.*, at 167.

5. M. WEBER, ANCIENT JUDAISM 127 (H. Gerth & D. Martindale trans. & eds., 1952).
6. E. VOEGELIN, 1 ORDER AND HISTORY: ISRAEL AND REVELATION 204–05, 209 (1957).
7. *Id.* at 210.
8. *Id.* at 211, 376; *see* Deuteronomy 11:23, 19:1, 20:15.

officers and men in camp and for their conduct in battle, including the seige of cities.[9] This duality is worthy of note: at the same time that the notion of holy war emerged in Judaism (later picked up by Islam[10] and, during the Crusades, by Christianity) there emerged what are probably the oldest canons on the conduct of warfare.[11]

Ancient Greek attitudes regarding the use of force also reflect a striving for principles regarding the use of force in intercommunity relations. After the Greek city-states emerged, internal economic pressures forced each to undertake colonial expansion throughout the Mediterranean.[12] When this expansion stopped during the sixth century B.C., internal economic pressures for each city-state reemerged and were addressed by developing local production for external consumption, thereby forcing the city-states out of their parochialism and into greater economic interdependence among themselves.[13] Institutions emerged that moderated aggression among the city-states, such as religious festivals and leagues, athletic festivals, and treaties of alliance. Theorists such as Aristotle (384–322 B.C.) reflected this moderation by positing that war was a means to defend "the good life" and to help others "to share in the good life," but that resort to war was not "the good life" itself. In his *Politics*, Aristotle notes the reality that most rulers do seek domination over others, but states:

> Yet surely, if we are prepared to examine the point carefully, we shall see how completely unreasonable it would be if the work of a statesman were to be reduced to an ability to work out how to rule and be master over neighbouring peoples, with or without consent. How could that be a part of statecraft or lawgiving, when it is not even lawful in itself? To rule at all costs, not only justly but unjustly, is unlawful, and merely to have the upper hand is not necessarily to have a just title to it. . . . Certainly most people seem to think that mastery is statesmanship, and they have no compunction about inflicting upon others what in their own community they regard as neither just nor beneficial if applied to them-

9. Deuteronomy, 20:1–21, 21:10–14, 23:10–14.

10. The Islamic doctrine that emerged centuries later from Old and New Testament traditions was fundamentally oriented toward conquest in conducting warfare against non-Muslim countries. Under the Qur'an, a latent state of war exists against non-Muslim countries; it then rises to an actual state of war in the jihad. *See generally* M. KHADDURI, WAR AND PEACE IN THE LAW OF ISLAM bk. II (1955). Unbelievers must be either converted, subjugated, or killed, excepting women, children, and slaves. J. SCHACHT, AN INTRODUCTION TO ISLAMIC LAW 130 (1964). Even so, as early as the seventh century, Islamic doctrine too contained restrictions on the conduct of such warfare, which were in some respects superior to Christian doctrine of the same period. *See* NUSSBAUM, *supra* note 4, at 51–53.

11. NUSSBAUM, *supra* note 4, at 3; 1 VOEGELIN, *supra* note 6, at 375–76.

12. A. TOYNBEE, CIVILIZATION ON TRIAL 56 (1948).

13. *Id.* at 57–59.

selves. They themselves ask for just government among themselves; but in the treatment of others they do not worry at all about what measures are just.[14]

Aristotle then opines that since a state existing in complete isolation, without any need to resort to war, could be perfectly happy, then it leads to a simple conclusion.

The conclusion is obvious, we regard every provision made for war as admirable, not as a supreme end but only as serving the needs of that end. It is the task of a sound legislator to survey the state, the clan, and every other association and to see how they can be brought to share in the good life and in whatever degree of happiness is possible for them. There will of course be different rules laid down in different places; if there are neighbouring peoples, it will be part of the legislative function to decide what sort of attitude is to be adopted to this sort and that sort, and how to employ towards each the proper rules for dealing with each.[15]

Similar statements calling for states to exercise justice in relations with other states may be found in Thucydides, Plutarch, Plato, and Euripides.[16] This striving for justice in intercommunity relations, of course, did not necessarily match reality, as Aristotle himself recognized. Further, constraints on the use of force normally were applied only in relations among Greek city-states; for the most part, non-Greeks were simply considered barbarians destined to serve as Greek slaves.[17] Thus only in wars among Greek states does Plato argue that rulers should observe special rules which prohibit all cruelties, destruction of cities, enslavement, or wholesale killings.[18] Similarly, for Aristotle, the just cause for resorting to war was easily met with respect to non-Greeks; he considered as "just" any war against non-Greeks that refused to submit to servitude.[19]

Perhaps the most significant Greek influence on subsequent developments in Europe and elsewhere regarding law on the use of force

14. *Aristotle, The Politics* bk. 7, ch. 2, at 396–97 (T. Sinclair trans., T. Saunders ed., Penguin, London, rev. ed. 1992).

15. *Id.* at 397–98.

16. 1 R. PHILLIMORE, COMMENTARIES UPON INTERNATIONAL LAW 16–17 (3d ed. 1879).

17. NUSSBAUM, *supra* note 4, at 5.

18. THE REPUBLIC OF PLATO 469b–471c (F. Cornford ed., Oxford U. Press, Fair Lawn, NJ 1945).

19. In his *Politics*, Aristotle wrote:

If then nature makes nothing without some end in view, nothing to no purpose, it must be that nature has made all of them for the sake of man. This means that it is according to nature that even the art of war, since hunting is a part of it, should in a sense be a way of acquiring property; and that it must be used both against wild beasts and against such men as are by nature intended to be ruled over but refuse; for that is the kind of warfare which is by nature just.

ARISTOTLE, *supra* note 14, bk. 1, ch. 8, at 79.

derives from the development of natural law in Greek tradition. When the Greek city-states began to decline after the fourth century B.C., it was necessary to develop a philosophy capable of providing explanations that transcended principles originating with the city-state.[20] The Stoic philosophy of the third century B.C. promoted universally applicable principles arising from natural law or "right reason" of Man, not from positive law or divine revelation. Moreover, Stoic philosophy sought to achieve harmony among states through a system of universal values based on principles of equality (which, of course, was "equality" in a limited sense, given the attitudes at that time toward slaves, women, and others). Such egalitarianism was of particular appeal to minority groups within the Hellenic orbit, such as the Syrians and Phoenicians.[21] This Greek tradition, in turn, heavily influenced the development of Roman law, which recognized natural law principles in establishing rules of law which were directly applicable to relations with or between foreigners (*jus gentium*). These natural law principles derived from "right reason" and were considered fundamentally valid and just, universally applicable, and everlasting.[22]

Early Roman law also developed an elaborate internal proceeding for determining the existence of a just and pious cause for resorting to war (*bellum justum et pium*), premised on the fiction of an offense by non-Romans against the Roman people.[23] Over time, the use of this formal proceeding disappeared but the concept of a just war remained, albeit as a malleable one, with Roman scholars debating its true meaning. For Cicero (106–43 B.C.), the moral statesman should seek to avert war if possible; the justness of resorting to war then turned on whether it was a means of obtaining a lasting peace.[24]

Thus even in ancient civilizations rudimentary constraints on the use

---

20. F. Parkinson, The Philosophy of International Relations: A Study in the History of Thought 10 (1977).

21. *Id.* at 11, 13.

22. *Id.* at 12.

23. The proceeding involved a special group of priests meeting together (*collegium fetalium*) to advise on the resort by the state to war. *See* Nussbaum, *supra* note 4, at 10–11; 1 Phillimore, *supra* note 16, at 17–18. Interestingly, in Islam as well as in ancient Rome, not only was war to be just, it was to be pious, meaning in accordance with the sanction of religion and the implied commands of the gods. *See* J. Von Elbe, *The Evolution of the Concept of the Just War in International Law*, 33 Am. J. Int'l L. 665–88 (1939).

24. M. Cicero, *On Moral Duties* bk. 1, *reprinted in* The Basic Works of Cicero 32 (M. Hadas ed., Random House, New York 1951) ("Accordingly in settling a dispute the skill of the diplomatist is to be preferred to the valor of the soldier, but we should adopt this principle not through fear of war but on the ground of public expediency, and should only take up arms when it is evident that peace is the one object we pursue"). It must be noted, however, that Cicero is somewhat notorious in trying to promote the status and honors accorded to nonmilitary leaders, such as himself.

of force were present, at least in their internal philosophies and laws. At the same time, these constraints were not limited to the self-defense or self-preservation of a body politic; they embodied a notion of using force against a foreign people due to the failure of such people to conduct themselves in accordance with purportedly universal principles. Although not viewed as "international law" as we know it today, such concepts foreshadowed the emergence of the just war doctrine in the Middle Ages, which in turn heavily influenced the development of modern international law.

B. Christian Legal Traditions

Early Christian thinking opposed or, at best, was ambivalent regarding the participation of Christians in war and military service,[25] but once Christianity was adopted as the state religion of the Roman Empire in the fourth century A.D., and once that Empire began to disintegrate from the onslaught of "barbarian" tribes, a new approach was necessary.[26] Through the teachings of Augustine (354–430 A.D.), the Church adopted the position that, while waging war by temporal rulers for power or revenge was not justified, it was justified when it was either of a defensive character or waged on divine command (*bellum justissimum*).[27] Under this just war doctrine, wars in aid of Christian peace and against Christian evil were justified through a fusion of universal, natural law principles of justice and the divine authority of God.

Thomas Aquinas (1225?-1274) developed this construct by stating three conditions upon which the just war may be waged.[28] First, the resort to war must be based on right authority; a prince, who derives his authority from God, is capable of exercising the requisite right authority as a secular "minister of God." Second, the prince must have a just cause (*justa causa*), which exists when the target entity deserves to be fought for having acquired some form of guilt (*propter aliquam culpam*). This

25. Nussbaum, *supra* note 4, at 35.

26. Parkinson, *supra* note 20, at 15 ("Though neither the Empire in its state of depravity nor the de facto kingdoms which had arisen out of chaos, and which [St. Augustine] considered the products of robbery on a large scale, were worth defending in his eyes, the Church certainly was. St. Augustine was therefore faced with turning Christianity from an emphatically pacific into a fighting faith.").

27. Augustine of Hippo, De Civitate Dei (The City of God) bk. 19, at 7 (Doubleday, New York 1958) ("Those wars are customarily called just which have for their end the revenging of injuries, when it is necessary by war to constrain a city or a nation which has not wished to punish an evil action committed by its citizens, or to restore that which has been taken unjustly.").

28. T. Aquinas, Summa Theologica ch. II–II, quae. 40, art. 1, *reprinted in* St. Thomas Aquinas On Politics and Ethics 64–65 (P. Sigmund ed. & trans., W.W. Norton & Co., New York 1988); *see generally* F. Russell, The Just War in the Middle Ages (1975).

guilt did not arise solely from aggressive behavior, but also from other acts, such as heresy or the failure to pay a just debt. Finally, the prince must have a correct intention (*recta intentio*), by which was meant an intention to promote good and avoid evil. Thus, while Christendom gave up its early resistance to any resort to war, it retained certain conditions that sought to limit resort to war.

Initially, the just war doctrine was ambiguous as to whether it could justify resorting to war simply to attack or convert non-Christian people, even if they were peaceful. This ambiguity resulted in repeated debates among Church and temporal rulers, particularly with respect to the Crusades to the Holy Land after the eleventh century.[29] When unified Christendom broke down after the Protestant Reformation, the classic just war doctrine experienced a gradual decline and in its place arose two contending versions of just war doctrine: the doctrine of the holy war and a just war doctrine (discussed in the next section) embodied in a secularized law of nature.

The holy war version of the just war doctrine essentially set aside the limitations that had existed under the classic Christian just war doctrine.[30] Instead, it expressly advocated the justice of resorting to war to advance one's own religious purposes, especially the protection of persecuted religious minorities.[31] The emergence of this thinking fueled the vicious religious warfare among Europeans seen in the period of 1560–1660: the German civil wars between Catholic and Protestant leagues, the French wars of religion, the Puritan revolution in England, and the Thirty Years War. This thinking carried over as well to the European conquest of the indigenous peoples of the Western Hemisphere. In this expansive view of just war, a critical defect emerged—the egalitarianism of early Christianity, inherited from Stoic philosophy, was in conflict with a just war doctrine permitting attacks on others due to their religious beliefs.

Strictly speaking, the transitioning just war doctrine of this time was one of moral theology, not of jurisprudence or international law; it integrated natural law into Christian theology, with nature conceived as a manifestation of God. Further, the context of its development was not solely wars among nations ("public wars"), but also feuds within an empire among princes ("private wars"), a critical concern of the Church during the Middle Ages. Nevertheless, the impact of this thinking profoundly influenced later developments on international law relating to the use of force. The excesses that occurred from relying on religious

29. PARKINSON, *supra* note 20, at 17–20.
30. *See* J. JOHNSON, IDEOLOGY, REASON, AND THE LIMITATION OF WAR: RELIGIOUS AND SECULAR CONCEPTS 1200–1740, at 81–133 (1975).
31. 1 PHILLIMORE, *supra* note 16, at 621–22.

ideology in constructing rules on the use of force made Europeans reconstruct the just war doctrine using a secularized natural law base, the forerunner to modern international law doctrine.

C. The Rise of the Nation-State: Grotius and Vattel

With the Peace of Westphalia in 1648 the religious wars of Europe came to an end, and this date is typically cited as the turning point for the emergence of the state system,[32] when nation-states ruled by independent monarchies rose to dominance in Europe. Yet even before the Peace of Westphalia, some political theorists, reacting to the failure of feudal structures to provide guidance in the conduct of affairs of state, argued that a virtuous ruler is an effective one who sets aside Christian ethics and morality in favor of advancing the interests of the state by whatever practical means available.[33] It is at this stage that the principle of sovereignty was first enunciated, proclaiming that sovereign rulers alone were responsible for administering their internal affairs as they see fit to advance the interests of the state. Thus Niccolo Machiavelli's *The Prince* (1513) heralded the need for a ruler who would advance the interests of his realm through the most ruthless of means and with complete disregard for political morality.[34] Jean Bodin's *The Six Bookes of a Commonweale* (1576) argued in favor of an absolute theory of sovereignty, in which a monarch wielded absolute power over his people.[35]

This principle of sovereignty did not mean a prince was incapable of interfering in the affairs of another prince. On the contrary, princes were well within their rights to wage war on behalf of their state. Yet one effect of the greater emphasis on secular, princely power was a reinterpretation of the type of proper authority necessary to wage war. "Proper authority" came to mean the authority of the secular sovereign prince, whose rights derived not from God but from the community he represented.[36] As such, the prince was justified in resorting to war in self-defense or to punish those persons he believed had committed an injustice to him or his people. In theory, wars still could be waged for religious reasons against the enemies of the Church, but the rise of secular sovereigns led to a greater emphasis on waging wars for secular reasons.[37]

It was at this time, too, that international law proper began to receive

---

32. *See, e.g.*, H. MORGENTHAU, POLITICS AMONG NATIONS: THE STRUGGLE FOR POWER AND PEACE 264 (4th ed. 1967).

33. PARKINSON, *supra* note 20, at 30–32 (discussing Machiavelli).

34. N. MACHIAVELLI, THE PRINCE (W. Marriot trans., E.P. Dutton 1948) (1513).

35. J. BODIN, THE SIX BOOKES OF A COMMONWEALE (K. McRae trans., 1962) (1576).

36. JOHNSON, *supra* note 30, at 76.

37. *Id.* at 76–78.

widespread and systematic treatment, including the law that related to the use of force.[38] Early European writers on international law understood that anarchical religious wars arose from associating justice with religious principles, and consequently they constructed a system of international law on the basis of a secularized law of nature. Whether approaching the problem as theologians (Francisco Vitoria 1492–1546, Francisco Suarez 1548–1617) or as secular jurists (Alberico Gentili 1552–1608), they rejected the idea that war could be waged for religious reasons on the basis of revelation.[39] At the same time, however, they had some difficulty in determining the just causes of war that might arise from a natural law-based system. For instance, some theologians argued that a war may be simultaneously just on both sides of a conflict, which opened the door to greater application of the *jus in bello*, but which also confused the moral dimension of resorting to the use of force.[40]

This approach of maintaining the just war doctrine couched in secular-legal terminology dominated legal writings on the use of force up to the nineteenth century, including the writings of Hugo Grotius (1583–1645) and Emmerich de Vattel (1714–1767), both of whom were exceedingly influential in the development of modern international law.[41] In their writings, attention is explicitly given to the issue of armed intervention to assist persons suffering under an unjust sovereign. While both seem to have favored this type of intervention in certain circumstances, even at this early stage the tension between obtaining justice for such persons and simultaneously maintaining international peace was readily apparent.

In *On the Law of War and Peace*, Grotius maintained that resort to war was lawful, under natural law and the law of nations, when doing so was based on a just cause, such as defense against an injury, recovery of what is legally due, and the infliction of punishment on a wrongdoing state for excessive crimes.[42] Grotius did not address the issue of "humani-

---

38. *See* NUSSBAUM, *supra* note 4, 61–185; PARKINSON, *supra* note 20, 31–41; F. RUDDY, INTERNATIONAL LAW IN THE ENLIGHTENMENT 12–32 (1975).

39. *See* NUSSBAUM, *supra* note 4, at 61–101. For theologians such as Vitoria, the value base associated with just war is naturalist, albeit one that ultimately draws its sanction from God.

40. *Id*. at 97 (discussing Alberico Gentili's LAW OF WAR).

41. The rise of secular natural law thinking also resulted in arguments that international law, including law relating to the use of force, simply did not exist. Thomas Hobbes (1588–1679) believed there was no law among nations but, rather, the same savage conditions that man experienced before the creation of the state. T. HOBBES, LEVIATHAN, OR THE MATTER, FORME AND POWER OF A COMMONWEALTH, ECCLESIASTICALL AND CIVIL, bk. 1, ch. 13, at 101 (M. Oakeshott ed., Macmillan, New York 1962) (1651).

42. 2 H. GROTIUS, DE JURE BELLI AC PACIS LIBRI TRES (ON THE LAW OF WAR AND PEACE), bk. 2, ch. 1, para. 2.2 (Carnegie Classics of Int'l Law 1925) (F. Kelsey, trans.) (1646).

tarian intervention" in those terms; however, some count him as a "non-interventionist" because he granted considerable deference to sovereign authority and placed heavy emphasis on the obedience of an individual to one's sovereign.[43] Further, Grotius rejected the view that sovereign power is in some fashion vested in the sovereign's people such that they have a right to restrain and punish the sovereign for an abuse of his power.[44]

For others, however, such as Sir Hersch Lauterpacht, Grotius's treatise represented an early authoritative statement of the principle of humanitarian intervention.[45] As stated above, one of the justifiable reasons for a state going to war against another state is the punishment of excessive crimes (*punitio*); Grotius argued that sovereigns have the right to punish other sovereigns not only for injuries to themselves or their own subjects but also for gross violations of the laws of nature and of nations done to others. He wrote:

> The fact must also be recognized that kings, and those who possess rights equal to those kings, have the right of demanding punishments not only on account of injuries committed against themselves or their subjects, but also on account of injuries which do not directly affect them but excessively violate the law of nature or of nations in regard to any persons whatsoever. For liberty to serve the interests of human society through punishments, which originally, as we have said, rested with individuals, now after the organization of states and courts of law is in the hands of the highest authorities, not, properly speaking, in so far as they rule over others, but in so far as they are themselves subject to no one. For subjection has taken this right away from others.[46]

Further, in a chapter on "The Causes of Undertaking War for Others," Grotius asks whether there may be a just cause for undertaking war on

43. R. Vincent, *Grotius, Human Rights, and Intervention*, in HUGO GROTIUS AND INTERNATIONAL RELATIONS 241, 246–47 (H. Bull, B. Kingsbury & A. Roberts eds., 1992). On resistance to sovereign authority, Grotius wrote:

> By nature all men have the right of resisting in order to ward off injury, as we have said above. But as civil society was instituted in order to maintain public tranquillity, the state forthwith acquires over us and our possessions a greater right, to the extent necessary to accomplish this end. The state, therefore, in the interest of public peace and order, can limit that common right of resistence. That such was the purpose of the state we cannot doubt, since it could not in any other way achieve its end.

2 GROTIUS, *supra* note 42, bk. 1, ch. 4, para. 2.1.

44. 2 GROTIUS, *supra* note 42, bk. 1, ch. 3, para. 8.11.

45. H. Lauterpacht, *The Grotian Tradition in International Law*, 23 BR. YRBK. INT'L L. 1 (1946).

46. 2 GROTIUS, *supra* note 42, bk. 2, ch. 20, para. 40. In making this statement, Grotius notes that many of his contemporaries (such as Vitoria) hold a different view, whereby puni;hment may only be inflicted for injury to the intervening state or its subjects.

behalf of the subjects of another ruler who is treating them wrongly, and answers that if a ruler "should inflict upon his subjects such treatment as no one is warranted in inflicting," other rulers may exercise a "right vested in human society" to undertake war on behalf of those subjects.[47]

Thus, while Grotius was unwilling to accept that the subjects of a sovereign may rise up to redress grievances against their sovereign, he was willing to allow other sovereigns to do so when those grievances were of a certain magnitude. Grotius presciently warned, however, that interventions of this type "may often be used as the cover of ambitious designs."[48] Also, in the context of his times, he did not regard certain treatment of one's subjects that would today be regarded as horrendous (e.g., slavery) as per se a sufficient basis for intervention.[49]

It has been argued that Grotius' conception of international law contains a central assumption regarding the solidarity, or potential solidarity, of the states which make up international society that goes beyond matters to which those states have consented.[50] This solidarity led Grotius to accept that a ruler has a responsibility not just for the safety and welfare of the ruler's subjects, but also for the safety and welfare of other subjects. Beginning in the eighteenth century (the Age of Enlightenment), however, political and legal theorists became more skeptical about the advantages of absolutist rulers and tended to regard the relationship of states in more competitive terms.[51] The conclusions theorists drew from this tendency differed.

Vattel, writing 130 years after Grotius, asserted that a nation is under an obligation to "preserve" all its members; this duty flows from the very act of association as a nation.[52] Like Grotius, he generally supported the principle of sovereignty of nations even where the sovereign acts unjustly (e.g., by imposing excessive taxes or otherwise acting severely against the sovereign's subjects). Yet, he wrote:

But if a prince, by violating the fundamental laws, gives his subjects a lawful cause for resisting him; if, by his insupportable tyranny, he brings on a national revolt

47. 2 Grotius, *id.* bk. 2, ch. 25, para. 8.

48. 2 GROTIUS, *id.* bk. 3, ch. 15, para. 8.

49. 2 GROTIUS, *id.* bk. 2, ch. 22, para. 11.

50. H. Bull, *The Grotian Conception of International Society*, in DIPLOMATIC INVESTIGATIONS: ESSAYS IN THE THEORY OF INTERNATIONAL POLITICS 51 (H. Butterfield & M. Wight eds., 1966).

51. PARKINSON, *supra* note 20, at 62 (the thinkers of the Enlightenment "attacked the idea that interdynastic solidarity was the cornerstone of world peace, thereby questioning the underlying rationality of the international absolutist system").

52. 3 E. VATTEL, THE LAW OF NATIONS OR THE PRINCIPLES OF NATURAL LAW APPLIED TO THE CONDUCT AND TO THE AFFAIRS OF NATIONS AND OF SOVEREIGNS bk. 1, ch. 2, sec. 17 (C. Fenwick trans., Carnegie 1916) (1758).

against him, any foreign power may rightfully give assistance to an oppressed people who ask for its aid.[53]

Thus, although for Vattel the presumption of the solidarity of states is not as strong, Vattel followed Grotius in drawing a line beyond which a sovereign cannot go without foreign intervention being justified. This outlook found favor with democratic revolutionaries, such as the American colonists, who called upon natural law to justify resistance to unjust rule and welcomed foreign assistance in support of that cause.

At the same time, however, self-determination of a state meant that it was to be free from intervention by meddling foreign powers, particularly absolutist powers. For this latter reason, theorists such as Immanuel Kant (1724–1804) broadly condemned intervention. In his essay *Perpetual Peace*, Kant stated that "No state shall by force interfere with either the constitution or government of another state."[54] Yet Kant's emphasis on the need for republican forms of government to achieve lasting peace seems to have favored intervention to bring about the downfall of non-republican governments, a view some scholars propound today to justify unilateral humanitarian intervention.[55]

John Stuart Mill (1806–1873) also advocated nonintervention as a principle out of a desire not to disturb the balance of forces on which the permanent maintenance of national freedom depends.[56] Mill did not advocate intervention to assist citizens of a state in throwing off the tyrannical yoke of a government, absent some form of foreign support for that government.[57] In his view, if the local citizens did not have a sufficient love of liberty to take the matter into their own hands, then foreign intervention to assist them would not be sustainable in the long run.[58] While Mill does not explicitly address the general issue of a state

53. 3 id. at bk. 2, ch. 4, secs. 55–56.

54. I. KANT, PERPETUAL PEACE (Columbia U. Press, New York 1939) (1795).

55. *See, e.g.*, F. Tesón, *The Kantian Theory of International Law*, 92 COLUM. L. REV. 53, 96 (1992).

56. J. Mill, *A Few Words on Non-Intervention* (1859), *reprinted in* ESSAYS ON POLITICS AND CULTURE 368 (G. Himmelfarb ed., 1962).

57. Mill believed the principle of nonintervention did not apply among "civilized" nations in certain situations: (1) when the intervenor acts as a part of self-defense; (2) when the intervenor acts to assist people struggling against *foreign* tyranny; and (3) when the intervenor acts to assist people struggling against native tyranny upheld by *foreign* arms. *Id.* at 381–83. Further, Mill maintained an exception that should be discarded as unacceptable in contemporary international society; Mill believed "civilized" nations could intervene in "barbarous" nations since the latter "have not got beyond the period during which it is likely to be for their benefit that they should be conquered and held in subjection." *Id.* at 377.

58. *Id.* at 381–82.

committing severe and widespread human rights atrocities against its people, he does go so far as to say:

A case requiring consideration is that of a protracted civil war, in which the contending parties are so equally balanced that there is no probability of a speedy issue; or if there is, the victorious side cannot hope to keep down the vanquished but by severities repugnant to humanity, and injurious to the permanent welfare of the country. In this exceptional case it seems now to be an admitted doctrine, that the neighbouring nations, or one powerful neighbour with the acquiescence of the rest, are warranted in demanding that the contest shall cease, and a reconciliation take place on equitable terms of compromise. Intervention of this description has been repeatedly practised during the present generation, with such general approval, that its legitimacy may be considered to have passed into a maxim of what is called international law.[59]

The interventions to which Mill refers were those committed by European states in the first part of the nineteenth century (interventions throughout that century are considered in the next section). Of note is Mill's reference to "neighbouring nations" as the appropriate type of intervenor and the ability of several nations essentially to deputize a powerful neighbor to conduct the intervention. Mill's statement, however, is limited to a situation of a protracted civil war in which there are equally balanced contending parties. Nevertheless, some scholars today argue that Mill's stated exception to the nonintervention principle can be regarded as allowing intervention to uphold "communal autonomy" and on this basis advocate humanitarian intervention broadly as a legitimate exception to Mill's position.[60]

D. The Growth of Positive Law

As the Western world moved into the nineteenth century, a transition in international legal reasoning occurred. Natural law theory gave way to more positivist thinking; the rights and duties of the state under international law were to be derived less from "right reason" and more from the express will or consent of states, as evidenced in treaty relationships and state practice. As such, reliance on a just war doctrine as derived from divine or secular natural law dissipated. In its place arose somewhat uneven doctrines of *jus ad bellum* derived from the practice of states. On the one hand, states were considered free to resort to a formal state of war and to judge for themselves whether doing so was justified. On the other hand, measures short of declaring war were to be justified only by

59. *Id.* at 380.
60. *See* M. WALZER, JUST AND UNJUST WARS: A MORAL ARGUMENT WITH HISTORICAL ILLUSTRATIONS 90 (2d ed. 1992).

reference to certain concepts loosely grouped under the headings of self-defense or self-preservation, reprisal, intervention by virtue of treaty rights, and collective intervention.[61]

The concept of humanitarian intervention is explicitly present during this period also, although its exact nature is unclear and has been the subject of some debate. The lack of clarity arises from a differing, often imprecise, use of terminology among writers and from a lack of discipline in asserting what law *is* as opposed to what it *ought to be*. Some writers dogmatically rejected the legality of humanitarian intervention, while other writers did not.[62] The debate is interesting because it is similar to the one that continues today among international law scholars regarding the legality of unilateral humanitarian intervention in light of the UN Charter. Proponents of humanitarian intervention in the 1800s, lacking extensive, supportive state practice, appealed to notions of humanity and justice. Opponents of humanitarian intervention did not resist the moral imperatives, but absent state practice had difficulty finding the crystallization of a substantive rule of law on the issue. As the pre-World War I era drew to its close, one scholar observed that "As regards an intervention undertaken in the *cause of humanity* there seems to be a divergence of opinion among the most prominent writers. . . . "[63]

Nevertheless, the concept of humanitarian intervention did exist and presumably influenced the conduct of states during this period. One of the best and most influential articles on the doctrine of humanitarian intervention that emerged from this prewar period was written in 1910 by a French professor of law, Antoine Rougier.[64] For Rougier, humanitarian intervention was lawful, under certain appropriate conditions, when the public authorities of a target state violate fundamental human rights.[65] An essential condition was that the intervention—to be lawful—had to be "disinterested" in character, meaning that it was not undertaken for political or economic reasons.[66] Rougier expressed skep-

---

61. H. Wheaton, Elements of International Law sec. 290 (G. Wilson ed., Carnegie 1936) (1836); Brownlie, *supra* note 2, at 26–49.

62. For a review of various writers of this period on the issue of humanitarian intervention, *see* Fonteyne, *supra* note 1, at 215–224.

63. H. Hodges, The Doctrine of Intervention 87 (1915).

64. A. Rougier, *La théorie de l'intervention d'humanité*, 17 Rev. Gén. D. Int'l Pub. 468 (1910). Rougier was the first to deal exhaustively with the topic of humanitarian intervention, and his views are reflected in various subsequent authorities. *See, e.g.,* E. Borchard, The Diplomatic Protection of Civilians Abroad 14 (1915) (reprinted 1970); E. Stowell, Intervention in International Law 53 (1921); A. Thomas & A. Thomas, Jr., Non-intervention: The Law and Its Import in the Americas 372 (1956) (using Rougier's exact definition of humanitarian intervention without citation).

65. Rougier, *supra* note 64, at 512.

66. *Id.* at 502 ("Le désintéressement est une condition essentielle chez l'intervenant

ticism about humanitarian intervention by individual states, because such interventions are typically undertaken with a view to advancing that state's own exclusive interests. Looking back on the experience of the Concert of Europe, Rougier saw significant advantages to a system of collective intervention, in which powerful states with personal interests could be checked by more objective "third party" powers, and which would allow for a collective, unbiased decision on the legality of a particular intervention.[67] Rougier also warned that a concert of powers could not address all violations of human rights or play the role of "redresseur universal des torts." Rather, collective action should occur only when exceptionally serious violations take place that shatter ("bouleversent") the life of a nation.[68]

The shift in international law to an emphasis on positive law, as contained in international agreements and in state practice, encouraged states and scholars to look more closely at treaty rights and customary practice when pursuing interventions. For this reason, interventions by the Concert of Europe to protect Christians living under Ottoman Empire rule received close attention by nineteenth-century and early twentieth-century commentators on international law (e.g., Rougier). This practice also received considerable attention by twentieth-century scholars after entry into force of the UN Charter, due to an argument that a customary rule of humanitarian intervention survives the Charter and remains a part of international law today.[69] In view of the increased opportunities for the deployment of armed forces under UN auspices after the Cold War, the interventions of the Concert of Europe to protect Christians merit brief revisiting, for they reveal some of the inherent strengths and weaknesses in collective intervention.

E. The Era of the Concert of Europe

In 1806, Franz II, the last emperor of the Holy Roman Empire, abdicated, marking the Empire's formal dissolution. Shortly thereafter, the defeat of Napoleon led to the Congress of Vienna of 1815,[70] which adopted ambitious proposals for the institutionalized management of

---

dont l'action tend à faire respecter une règle de droit générale et non à poursuivre la réalisation d'un advantage individuel.").

67. *Id*. at 500.

68. *Id*. at 524.

69. Whether such a rule in fact survived the passage of the U.N. Charter is discussed in chapter 3 *infra*.

70. The final act of the Congress of Vienna was signed on June 9, 1815 by Austria, France, England, Portugal, Prussia, Russia, and Sweden. The dominant powers at that time were Austria, England, Prussia, and Russia, to be joined by France in 1818.

Europe by the major European powers. Differences in the policies and objectives of the great powers prevented such management from materializing but nevertheless ushered in an era of "diplomacy by conference," a practice commonly referred to as the Concert of Europe.[71]

In the early stages of the Concert of Europe, three of the major powers—Austria, Prussia, and Russia—united in a "Holy Alliance," the purpose of which was quite contrary to the concept of humanitarian intervention in that it sought through intervention to maintain absolutist regimes and suppress democratic movements.[72] On authorization from the Holy Alliance in 1823, Bourbon France militarily intervened in Spain to crush the Spanish revolution and to restore King Ferdinand VII fully to power;[73] and it was concern with the extension of this approach to Spanish colonies in the New World that prompted President James Monroe to announce, in 1823, that any such intervention by a European power in the affairs of emerging American states would be considered "unfriendly."[74] The Holy Alliance collapsed in the mid-1820s, but the ability of the European powers to act in concert remained for decades thereafter, as did the sentiment for suppressing revolutionary movements.

The Concert of Europe has been appropriately described as "an exclusive club for great powers, whose members were self-appointed guardians of the European community and executive directors of its affairs."[75] As such, the "club" periodically met in conference to discuss European political concerns, to establish standards of conduct by states, and, above all, to maintain peaceful conditions. The Concert was a system of joint consultation that led to collective diplomatic action for the peaceful

71. For histories of this period, *see* R. ALBRECHT-CARRIÉ, A DIPLOMATIC HISTORY OF EUROPE SINCE THE CONGRESS OF VIENNA (rev. ed. 1973); C. HOLBRAAD, THE CONCERT OF EUROPE: A STUDY IN GERMAN AND BRITISH INTERNATIONAL THEORY 1815–1914 (1970); H. KISSINGER, DIPLOMACY (1994); W. MEDLICOTT, BISMARCK, GLADSTONE, AND THE CONCERT OF EUROPE (1956).

72. WHEATON, *supra* note 61, sec. 64.

73. ALBRECHT-CARRIÉ, *supra* note 71, at 28.

74. In his seventh annual message to the Congress, President Monroe stated: "The political system of the allied powers is essentially different in this respect from that of America. . . . We owe it, therefore, to candor and to the amicable relations existing between the United States and those powers to declare that we should consider any attempt on their part to extend their system to any portion of this hemisphere as dangerous to our peace and safety." *Reprinted in* 1 DOCUMENTS OF AMERICAN HISTORY 235, 236 (H. Commager & M. Cantor eds., 10th ed. 1988). For interpretations and pronouncements by the U.S. Government regarding the doctrine, see 5 DIGEST OF INTERNATIONAL LAW 435 (G. Hackworth ed., 1943).

75. I. CLAUDE, JR., SWORDS INTO PLOWSHARES: THE PROBLEMS AND PROGRESS OF INTERNATIONAL ORGANIZATION 25 (4th ed. 1971).

resolution of disputes. Where peaceful resolution was not possible, the Concert would authorize military actions by one or more powers, at times imposing constraints on those actions.

Several interventions of the Concert might be characterized as humanitarian in character, their primary focus being to protect from persecution Christians located within, and therefore subjects of, the Ottoman Empire. Intervention based upon religious affinity among Christians might be dismissed as not reflective of a European view of the legality of humanitarian intervention but, rather, of a hatred of the non-Christian Turks and a belief that Turkey was outside the scope of European international law. While there is some merit to this view, particularly as it applies to the early part of the nineteenth century, the objection is not entirely convincing. Throughout this period, full diplomatic relations existed between the Ottoman Empire and the European states, numerous international treaties were concluded among them, and non-Christian Turkey was granted full status in the European system in 1856. Moreover, the fact that the interventions were motivated in part by religious affinity does not mean they were conducted for other than humanitarian reasons, the conservative views of the Holy Alliance having given way over time to more progressive thinking within the Concert. Progressive writers (e.g., John Stuart Mill) and statesmen (e.g., William Gladstone), deeply disturbed by the suffering of oppressed peoples, advocated intervention in certain situations as a means of either reforming the oppressor or liberating the oppressed.[76]

There are, however, other reasons why these interventions should be approached with caution. This period is one in which the Ottoman Empire was entering its final stages of political decay; as it crumbled, so did its ability to maintain order in many of its provinces, leading inexorably to greater autonomy and ultimately to independence for most of those provinces. At the same time, the increasingly dominant, industrializing, and economically robust European powers sought to extend their influence worldwide, including to areas under Ottoman rule. As part of this process, the Ottoman Empire was forced, throughout the nineteenth century, to grant various concessions to the European powers regarding the treatment of Christians within its empire. The concessions, which appear in treaties such as the General Treaty of Paris of 1856[77] and the

76. HOLBRAAD, *supra* note 71, at 162–76 (discussing the humanitarian ideas that animated the Concert).

77. General Treaty for the Re-establishment of Peace, March 30, 1856, 46 BRITISH AND FOREIGN STATE PAPERS 8, 12 (1855–56) (*see especially* Article 9, which makes reference to a prior Turkish edict guaranteeing certain fundamental political and civil rights to non-Moslem subjects).

Treaty of Berlin of 1878,[78] were viewed by the European powers as obligating Turkey to treat its subjects on the basis of religious and racial nondiscrimination. While a careful review of these concessions does not reveal an explicit legal right for European powers to intervene militarily in the event of mistreatment of Christians,[79] the European powers typically argued that their interventions were undertaken on the basis of a right of intervention to secure compliance with treaty rights and not on the basis of a general rule of international law regarding humanitarian intervention. This practice of relying on treaty-based justifications rather than a general right of humanitarian intervention foreshadowed interventions during the Cold War era under the UN Charter (explored in chapter 4), in which states did not assert a general right of humanitarian intervention but relied on the right of self-defense explicitly preserved in the UN Charter. Consider, thus, the most important instances of intervention during this Concert of Europe period.

1. Great Britain, France, and Russia in Greece (1827–30)

Beginning in the early 1800s, Ottoman control of Greece saw constant unrest by the local Greek population and concomitant friction with local Turkish authorities. Several massacres of Greek Christians during the 1820s prompted Great Britain, France, and Russia to conclude a treaty by which they agreed that bloodshed should be put to an end through limited autonomy for Greece within the Ottoman Empire. The three powers stated in the treaty that action was called for "no less by sentiments of humanity, than by interests for the tranquility of Europe."[80] Turkey rejected the proposal, arguing that the matter was an internal affair.[81] Thereafter, the three powers intervened in Greece with military forces primarily provided by Russia. Too weak to resist, Turkey acceded to the demands of the European powers[82] and ultimately to the independence of Greece in 1830.[83]

78. Treaty for the Settlement of Affairs in the East, July 13, 1878, 69 BRITISH AND FOREIGN STATE PAPERS 749, 753 (1877–78) [hereinafter Treaty of Berlin] (*see especially* arts. 5, 61, 62).

79. Fonteyne, *supra* note 1, at 207–08.

80. Treaty for the Pacification of Greece, July 6, 1827, Gr. Brit.-Fr.-Rus., 14 BRITISH AND FOREIGN STATE PAPERS 632, 633 (1826–27). For a discussion of the treaty, see WHEATON, *supra* note 61, sec. 70.

81. Manifesto of the Sublime Porte, Declining the Pacification with the Greeks, Proposed by the Mediating Powers (June 9, 1927), *in* 14 BRITISH AND FOREIGN STATE PAPERS 1042, 1044–46 (1826–27).

82. *See* Treaty of Adrinople, Sept. 14, 1829, 16 BRITISH AND FOREIGN STATE PAPERS 647 (1828–29).

83. Protocol (3.) de la Conférence tenue au Foreign Office, Feb. 3, 1830, 17 BRITISH AND FOREIGN STATE PAPERS 202–03 (1829–30).

On its face, this intervention has the character of a humanitarian intervention and was, in effect, considered as such by many writers of the pre-World War I era.[84] More recent writers, however, have pointed out that the desire to eliminate impediments to European commerce wrought by the unrest was one of the motivations of the intervening states[85] and that the intervention could be considered a lawful exercise of treaty concessions previously obtained from Turkey by Russia.[86] Neither position is wholly convincing; the action of the intervening states evidences a belief that widespread killing of persons is a matter of concern to other states and can serve as a basis for their intervention. Yet the intervention cannot be regarded as one conducted by states operating under the purest of motives, and the justification stated does not reflect explicit reliance on a right of humanitarian intervention under international law.

2. France in Syria (1860–61)

Massacres of Christians in Syria, carried out with the complicity of Turkish authorities, provoked deployment of European forces to Syria in 1860. This incident is particularly interesting because it involved intervention by a single nation pursuant to authorization by several nations. As early as 1842, the European powers complained to Turkey about the treatment of Christian minorities in Syria,[87] prompting Turkey to pursue special protections for the Christians from the local Muslim population. These protections, however, failed to prevent further massacres of the Christians in 1860; during a four-week period alone, an estimated 11,000 Christians were killed and another 100,000 made homeless.[88] Austria, France, Great Britain, Prussia, Russia, *and Turkey*, meeting in Paris, signed two protocols.[89] In the first, the parties agreed that a body of up

---

84. *See, e.g.*, 1 L. OPPENHEIM, INTERNATIONAL LAW, A TREATISE 194 (2d ed. 1912); 1 WESTLAKE, *supra* note 2, at 318–20.

85. Franck & Rodley, *supra* note 1, at 280 (citing to Wheaton).

86. M. GANJI, *supra* note 1, 23–24; A. Mandelstam, *La Protection des Minorités*, 1 R.C.A.D.I. 367, 374 (1923). Ganji argues that the 1774 Treaty of Kutchuk-Kainardji between Russia and the Ottoman Empire obligated the Sultan to provide certain protections for Christians.

87. "Syria" at this time consisted of present-day Lebanon, Jordan, Israel, Syria, the West Bank, and the Gaza Strip. The massacres and intervention occurred in an area now a part of Lebanon.

88. POGANY, *supra* note 1, at 184.

89. The two protocols in the original French appear at 51 BRITISH AND FOREIGN STATE PAPERS 278–79 (1860–61). The protocol authorizing the deployment of forces was incorporated in a Convention of September 5, 1860. For extracts in English of this convention, *see* L. SOHN & T. BUERGENTHAL, INTERNATIONAL PROTECTION OF HUMAN RIGHTS 156–58 (1973).

to 12,000 European forces would be sent to Syria to reestablish "tranquility," that France would furnish half these forces, and that the deployment would be limited to six months.[90] In the second protocol, presumably to establish the "disinterested" character of the intervention, the European powers declared they did not seek "any territorial advantages, any exclusive influence, or any commercial concession for their subjects which might not be granted to the subjects of all the other nations."[91] An international commission was established to set rules for regulating the intervening forces. The commission promulgated a new constitution for the region, which called for the appointment of a Christian governor responsible directly to the Ottoman Empire's Sublime Porte.[92] French forces were deployed to Syria in mid-August, only to find that the disturbances had basically subsided, and withdrew in 1861 after conducting various relief activities.

Some writers of both the pre-Charter and post-Charter era have characterized this incident as one of humanitarian intervention;[93] others have been skeptical regarding the innocence of the Christian population.[94] While the motivation of the European powers appears humanitarian in nature, the Turkish consent in this case (however reluctant) argues against regarding this incident as evidencing the legality of nonconsensual humanitarian intervention. Rather, the incident reflects a decaying Ottoman Empire, progressively incapable of maintaining consistent control over certain of its regions and grudgingly conceding the growing influence of the European powers. Of striking relevance today, however, is the effort to multilateralize the action and to impose constraints on the conduct of the intervening multilateral forces. By doing so, Britain (which otherwise might have protested) obtained a degree of comfort in allowing France to proceed.

3. Russia in Bosnia, Herzegovina, and Bulgaria (1877–78)

In actions that would be echoed some 115 years later, Serbia and Montenegro in 1876 declared war on Ottoman rule in Bosnia, Herzegovina, and Bulgaria, seeking to aid the Christians in those regions.[95] In re-

90. The duration of the intervention was subsequently extended. STOWELL, *supra* note 64, at 65–66.

91. 51 BRITISH AND FOREIGN STATE PAPERS 279 (1860–61).

92. Protocol Relative to the Administration of Lebanon, June 9, 1861, Annex, 51 BRITISH AND FOREIGN STATE PAPERS 287, 288–92 (1860–61).

93. *See, e.g.*, BROWNLIE, *supra* note 2, at 340; Rougier, *supra* note 64, at 474.

94. Franck & Rodley, *supra* note 1, at 282.

95. Proclamation of the Prince of Servia (June 18/30, 1876), *in* 67 BRITISH AND FOREIGN STATE PAPERS 1238 (1875–76).

sponse, the Sultan proposed certain reforms. He balked, however, at a demand by the European powers for an international commission to oversee their implementation. In the London Protocol of March 31, 1877, Austria-Hungary, France, Germany, Great Britain, Italy, and Russia affirmed their concern for the Christians and indicated they would take all necessary measures in the event the reforms were insufficient.[96] When Turkey rejected the protocol, Russia declared war on Turkey[97] and the other European powers declared their neutrality. The fighting lasted for less than a year, resulting in limited local autonomy for Bulgaria and the occupation of Bosnia and Herzegovina by Austria-Hungary.[98]

The general difficulty of assessing the reasons for an intervention is apparent in this case. Prior to declaring war, Russia asserted that it sought the provision of humane treatment proscribed by Turkey's treaty obligations to the European powers.[99] Britain, which did not support Russia's intervention, regarded it as a "power grab" with the ultimate objective to control the Bosporus Straits and even Constantinople.[100] Serbia may have had genuine humanitarian concerns but it also had strong historical interests in reasserting its own hegemony in the region. Also significant is that the prior demands of the Concert of Europe, rejected by Turkey, provided a certain level of Concert-"legitimization" to the intervention, even though the Concert as such neither authorized the intervention nor sent multinational forces. As will be seen in chapter 5, interventions pursued today under the aegis of the United Nations also have the potential for occurring without express Security Council authorization but, rather, on the basis of Security Council decisions that identify human rights abuses and demand action on the part of the target state.

4. The United States in Cuba (1898)

Harsh Spanish rule in Cuba at the end of the 1800s spawned an insurgency by Cuban guerrillas seeking greater autonomy.[101] In response,

---

96. London Protocol, Mar. 31, 1877, 68 BRITISH & FOREIGN STATE PAPERS 823 (1876–77).

97. Russian Note Declaring War Against Turkey (Apr. 12/24, 1877), *in* 68 BRITISH AND FOREIGN STATE PAPERS 844 (1876–77).

98. *See* Treaty of Berlin, *supra* note 78.

99. Russian Note (Nov. 7, 1876), *in* 67 BRITISH AND FOREIGN STATE PAPERS 328, 331 (1875–76).

100. Franck & Rodley, *supra* note 1, at 283.

101. For discussions of this incident, see G. O'TOOLE, THE SPANISH WAR: AN AMERICAN EPIC 1898 (1984); D. TRASK, THE WAR WITH SPAIN IN 1898 (1981); T. Behuniak, *The Law of Unilateral Humanitarian Intervention by Armed Force: A Legal Survey*, 79 MIL. L. REV. 157 (1978); D. Bogen, *The Law of Humanitarian Intervention: United States Policy in Cuba (1898) and in the Dominican Republic (1965)*, 7 HARV. INT'L L. CLUB J. 296 (1966).

Spain sought to hamper the guerrillas by herding the rural population into the cities, an approach that exacerbated matters drastically by increasing starvation and disease. Some estimates indicated that about 100,000 Cubans (approximately one-sixteenth of the population) died as a result of these "reconcentrations."[102] Public outcry in the United States, undoubtedly fueled by the "yellow," sensationalist journalism common at the time,[103] led the United States to issue protests to Spain and ultimately to intervene militarily in Cuba after the battleship *USS Maine* blew up in Havana Harbor (thus demonstrating that not all interventions in this late nineteenth century period were conducted by European powers).

When intervening, the United States claimed to be a disinterested state.[104] Certainly the outcry on the part of the U.S. public was largely motivated by what could fairly be described as humanitarian concerns. However, public cries for "Free Cuba" were accompanied by cries of "Remember the Maine," and President William McKinley's stated motivation for the intervention spoke of various factors, among them concerns for U.S. citizens, U.S. property, U.S. commerce, and U.S. national security.[105] The last factor was by no means the least; by challenging Spanish power, the United States reduced the overall Spanish influence in the Western Hemisphere. The subsequent Spanish-American War became a referendum on Spanish control of various colonies in Washington's claimed sphere of influence. Ultimately, the United States succeeded in obtaining control or dominance not just of Cuba but also of Puerto Rico, Hawaii, and the Philippines.

5. Greece, Bulgaria, and Serbia in Macedonia (1913)

For centuries, Macedonia was a region coveted by various powers, particularly Austria-Hungary and Russia. The broad mix of ethnic and religious minorities in Macedonia made for an unstable society, and as the Ottoman Empire weakened, in the early years of the twentieth century, unrest broke out there. Austria-Hungary and Russia, acting as mandatories of the European powers, demanded that Turkey implement cer-

102. TRASK, *supra* note 101, at 9.

103. One of the celebrated stories of this time is an exchange of telegrams between the New York Journal's William Randolph Hearst and Frederic Remington, who was sent to Cuba by Hearst to capture through drawings the events unfolding there. Remington, wishing to return to the United States, supposedly cabled to Hearst that everything was quiet and that there would be no war. Hearst is said to have replied: "Please remain. You furnish the pictures and I'll furnish the war." O'TOOLE, *supra* note 101, at 82.

104. STOWELL, *supra* note 64, at 121 n.53.

105. Address of President McKinley to Congress, *in* PAPERS RELATING TO THE FOREIGN RELATIONS OF THE UNITED STATES, 1878, at 750, 757 (1901).

tain reforms in Macedonia.[106] Turkey agreed,[107] but brutal efforts were nevertheless ultimately pursued by local Turkish leaders to "Turkify" the Christian Macedonian population. In 1912, to assist their Christian "brethren,"[108] Bulgaria, Greece, and Serbia declared war on Turkey,[109] and fighting raged in Macedonia for several months. It concluded with Turkey ceding most of Macedonia (as well as the island of Crete) to the Balkan states for partition.[110]

This intervention has the same characteristics as the earlier interventions—a collapsing Ottoman Empire and treaty rights purportedly owed to European powers. In addition, it reflects an actual territorial gain by several of the states that pursued the intervention, which suggests that the motivation for the intervention probably went beyond humanitarian concerns. Finally, it should be noted that, like the earlier intervention in Bosnia and Herzegovina, this intervention was not by the Concert of Europe as such but intervening states that cloaked themselves in the authority of the Concert based on the failure to provide protections for Christians previously demanded by the Concert.

F. The Covenant of the League of Nations and the Kellogg-Briand Pact

Europe soon fell into a brutal "world war" that lasted five years, redrawing political and geographical lines in Europe and spawning the first true attempt to institutionalize collective security under international law. In the aftermath of the war, President Woodrow Wilson sought the creation of an institution that would prevent future wars *and* address certain human rights concerns. For Wilson, the new institution needed to resolve the issue of decolonization in a manner other than simply turning over former German colonies to the victors. It also needed to address standards of social justice necessary to prevent renewal of the revolutionary fervor that led to war in the first place. Finally, the institution needed to address the fair treatment of labor, the protection of nationalities and of religious minorities, and the elimination of racial and gender discrimination.[111]

---

106. This program of reforms was referred to as the Mürzsteg Punctation. *See* British Note (Nov. 19, 1903), *in* 1 BRITISH DOCUMENTS ON THE ORIGINS OF THE WAR, 1898–1914 303–305 (G. Goach & H. Temperley eds., 1927).

107. *Id.* at 305.

108. Note Verbale of the Greek Government to the British Government (Oct. 4(17), 1912), *in* 106 BRITISH AND FOREIGN STATE PAPERS 1059, 1059 (1913).

109. *See* 106 BRITISH AND FOREIGN STATE PAPERS 1058–60 (1913).

110. A treaty resolving the status of Macedonia was concluded in London on May 30, 1913.

111. A. HECKSCHER, WOODROW WILSON 531 (1991).

The Covenant of the League of Nations addressed some but not all of these issues. The Covenant sought peace, inter alia, "by the acceptance of obligations not to resort to war" and "by the maintenance of justice . . . in the dealings of organized peoples with one another."[112] It did not, however, prohibit the use of force. Instead, it made the use of force a matter of concern to the institutions of the League and required League members to submit their disputes first to arbitral or judicial settlement, or to settlement by the League's Council.[113] So long as these steps were taken prior to the resort to the use of force, force could then be used. Resort to force without adhering to these steps constituted an act of war on all other members of the League and, in theory, would result in automatic sanctions against the transgressing member.

With respect to human rights issues, the Covenant required that states acting as mandatories on behalf of the League (administering areas previously under colonial rule) guarantee to the people within each mandate freedom of conscience and religion, and that they also prohibit abuses such as the slave trade.[114] All members were obligated to secure and maintain fair and humane labor conditions in accordance with the international conventions that were just beginning to be developed, including those under the auspices of the International Labor Organization.[115] Yet, neither the phrase "human rights" nor economic and social rights generally appears in the Covenant; most issues that arise in contemporary human rights law were considered solely within the domestic jurisdiction of states. Efforts by the United States to include protections for racial and national minorities failed, as did an effort by Japan to include a provision on the just treatment of nationals.[116] On the other hand, although not incorporated in the Covenant, an elaborate system for protecting the rights of minorities was developed under the League pursuant to which the League guaranteed certain linguistic and religious rights accorded under a series of treaties primarily relating to Eastern and Central Europe.[117]

112. League of Nations Covenant pmbl.

113. *Id.* arts. 12, 13, 15.

114. *Id.* art. 22.

115. *Id.* art. 23.

116. The U.S. proposal foundered when the Peace Conference decided that protection of minorities would be addressed in separate treaties and declarations, while Japan's proposal foundered because it frightened those states which restricted Asian immigration. R. Lillich, International Human Rights: Problems of Law, Policy, and Practice 2 (2d ed. 1991).

117. Under this system, minorities could submit petitions to the League charging violations of their rights. A committee of the League would then review the petition and any views submitted by the states concerned. When appropriate, the Permanent Court of Justice

The limited initial success of the League and its ultimate inability to prevent the outbreak of a Second World War are well known. With respect to the concept of humanitarian intervention in international law at that time, however, three points are worth noting.

First, nothing in the language of the Covenant prohibited humanitarian intervention. Indeed, other than requiring that a state undertake certain procedural steps to resolve a dispute before resorting to war, the Covenant did nothing to outline when the use of force is or is not permissible (e.g., self-defense). Consequently, in theory, a state that objected to human rights violations in another state could characterize its objection as a dispute, the dispute could be resolved in its favor, and the target state would be required in good faith to carry out any arbitral award, judicial decision, or unanimous report of the Council of the League regarding its treatment of its nationals. Failure to do so could result in sanctions against the target state, including the possibility of armed intervention.

Second, under the procedures established by the Covenant, a state engaged in human rights violations stood a good chance of avoiding censure by the League. Even if the state failed to accept an arbitral or judicial settlement and was taken before the Council, the Council was precluded from dealing with any matter which, under international law, was solely within the jurisdiction of the member state.[118] While certain human rights issues (e.g., slavery) were considered within the scope of international law at this time,[119] most were not. Consequently, unless a dispute brought before the Council arose out of a limited number of treaties addressing human rights issues, the Council likely would have dismissed the matter without recommendation.

Third, nothing in the practice of states during the inter-war period reveals a belief that the doctrine of humanitarian intervention was embodied in, or permitted by, the Covenant. If anything, this period reflected an increasing sense that war was wrong and that it could and should be avoided entirely, for whatever reason. Although the League sought to defuse armed conflict in several instances, the Council and Assembly of the League never dealt with human rights issues as such or any charges of violations of human rights.[120] Indeed, during this era the

---

was asked to render advisory opinions interpreting the rights of these minorities. *See, e.g.*, Advisory Opinion on Access to German Minority Schools in Upper Silesia, 1931 P.C.I.J. (ser. A/B) No. 40 (May 15).

118. LEAGUE OF NATIONS COVENANT art. 15, para. 8.

119. For instance, several international conventions abolished or limited the slave trade.

120. R. ASHER ET AL., THE UNITED NATIONS AND PROMOTION OF THE GENERAL WELFARE 648–49 (photo reprint 1980) (1957).

brutal suppression of human rights in the Soviet Union, Italy, and Nazi Germany were unaddressed by the League and not considered a basis for intervention by other states.

Wilsonian idealism captured a sense that war was not a necessary or inevitable state of affairs but one that could be avoided through appeals to reason and appropriate institutional machinery. The United States never joined the League of Nations, but it was instrumental in developing a pact calling on all nations to renounce war as an instrument of national policy in their relations with one another. The Kellogg-Briand Pact of August 27, 1928,[121] was a seminal event in world affairs; it codified within international law the idea that resort to the use of force to achieve foreign policy objectives was no longer permissible. Humanitarian intervention is not explicitly authorized or rejected by the Kellogg-Briand Pact, yet its tenor is to preclude the initiation of war by any nation when an international controversy arises; and while it failed to prevent the outbreak of the Second World War, its condemnation of the use of force became the centerpiece of postwar efforts to maintain international peace and security.

The pre-Charter, post-Kellogg-Briand Pact period nevertheless reveals some potential precedents for a state articulating a right of humanitarian intervention. Unfortunately, they relate to actions by Japan, Italy, and Germany, which reveal how a doctrine of humanitarian intervention may be severely abused.

1. Japan in Manchuria

When Japan invaded Manchuria in September 1931, it initially characterized the intervention as necessary to protect Japanese nationals and businesses from acts of violence by Chinese military forces.[122] As time passed and Japanese troops remained in Manchuria, the rationale shifted to an emphasis on a duty to protect the inhabitants of the region generally. Japan argued that:

It was Japan's clear duty to render her steps of self-defense as little disturbing as possible to the peaceable inhabitants of the region. It would have been a breach

---

121. General Treaty for the Renunciation of War, Aug. 27, 1928, 46 Stat. 2343, 94 L.N.T.S. 57, *reprinted in* 2 INTERNATIONAL LAW & WORLD ORDER: BASIC DOCUMENTS II.A.1 (B. Weston ed., 1994). Article 1 of the Treaty provides: "The High Contracting Parties solemnly declare in the names of their respective peoples that they condemn recourse to war for the solution of international controversies, and renounce it as an instrument of national policy in their relations with one another."

122. *See* Japanese Statement Issued After Extraordinary Cabinet Meeting (Sept. 24, 1931), *in* 1 PAPERS RELATING TO THE FOREIGN RELATIONS OF THE UNITED STATES: JAPAN: 1931–1941, at 11 (1943) [hereinafter JAPAN PAPERS]; Memorandum from the Japanese Embassy to the Department of State to be Presented to the Chinese Government on October 9, 1931 (Oct. 8, 1931), *in* 1 JAPAN PAPERS, *supra* at 15.

of that duty to have left the population a prey to anarchy—deprived of all the apparatus of civilized life. Therefore, the Japanese military have, at considerable sacrifice, expended much time and energy in securing the safety of persons and property in the districts where the native authorities had become ineffective. This is a responsibility which was thrust upon them by events, and one which they had as little desire to assume as to evade.[123]

The invasion of Manchuria, however, generally is regarded as an example of blatant aggression. Japan declared a new state of Manchukuo in 1932, occupied Shanghai later that same year, and embarked on full-scale war with China in 1937. It remained in Manchuria until the end of the Second World War.

2. Italy in Ethiopia

In October 1935 Italian forces invaded Ethiopia from their neighboring colony, Somaliland. The League of Nations condemned the invasion and imposed sanctions on the basis that Italy had violated its obligations under Article 12 of the Covenant of the League of Nations. Italy argued to the League that:

The Italian Government has abolished slavery in the occupied territories, giving to 16,000 slaves that liberty from which they would have awaited in vain from the Government of Addis Ababa, despite the clauses of the Covenant and the undertakings assumed at the moment of its admission as a member of the League of Nations. The liberated populations see in Italy, not the aggressor state, but the power which has the right and the capacity of extending that high protection which the very Covenant of the League of Nations, in its Article 22, recognizes as the civilizing mission incumbent upon the more advanced nations.[124]

The members of the League, however, rejected Italy's position, regarding it as an unlawful use of force. Unfortunately, the League's inability to agree upon forcible measures as a response to Italy's actions served to undermine its international standing. Italian forces remained in Ethiopia until 1941.

3. Germany in Czechoslovakia

On March 15, 1939 German military forces occupied the regions of Bohemia and Moravia in Czechoslovakia, declared them a protectorate of the Third Reich, and sent military officials to assume the functions of

123. Statement by the Japanese Government (Dec. 27, 1931), 1 JAPAN PAPERS, *supra* note 122, at 72, para. 1.

124. Note from the Italian Government Addressed to All Governments Which Voted for Sanctions Against Italy (Nov. 11, 1935), *in* 1 FOREIGN RELATIONS OF THE UNITED STATES, DIPLOMATIC PAPERS: 1935, at 684–87 (1953).

government.[125] Adolph Hitler's decree of March 16 on the establishment of the Protectorate of Bohemia and Moravia asserted that the Czechoslovak state and its rulers had not succeeded in organizing the different national groups present in Bohemia and Moravia, which in turn had led to "continuous disturbances in those regions," which were of "decisive importance" to Germany's own peace and security "and to the general welfare and the general peace."[126] The preamble to the decree ended with the following:

Filled with earnest desire to serve the true interests of the peoples dwelling in this area, to safeguard the national individuality of the German and Czech peoples, and to further the peace and social welfare of all, I therefore order the following, in the name of the German Reich, as the basis for the future common life of the inhabitants of these regions.[127]

Once again, the humanitarian concern for the welfare of the inhabitants of these regions does not bear up under scrutiny. As is well known, Hitler's invasion of Czechoslovakia was but the first in a series of acts of aggression that ultimately led to the Second World War.

G. Summary

The idea of one state (or group of peoples) using force against another for reasons other than self-defense or territorial aggrandizement can be traced to the earliest developments of law and philosophy, as can efforts to place restrictions on the practice of war. As may be seen in ancient Jewish, Greek, and Roman traditions, universally applicable principles derived from divine law, natural law, or the "right reason" of Man served as the basis for societies' perception of themselves and the justness of using force against others. The Christian just war doctrine emerged from these natural law principles and lay the foundation for both the Crusades of the late Middle Ages and the vicious religious wars that plagued Europe until the Peace of Westphalia.

The earliest writers on international law, most notably Hugo Grotius, observed how states reacted to the anarchy of associating justice with religious principles and proceeded by building a system of international law that sought to achieve greater stability and order through a more

125. Of the remaining portions of Czechoslovakia, the Slovakian President asked Adolph Hitler to declare Slovakia a protectorate, and Hungarian forces occupied the region of Ruthenia.

126. Decree of the Government of the Reich on the Protectorate of Bohemia and Moravia (Mar. 16, 1939), *in* 1 FOREIGN RELATIONS OF THE UNITED STATES, DIPLOMATIC PAPERS: 1939, at 45–47, 51–52 (1956).

127. *Id.*

secularized law of nature. In doing so, the necessity of obedience of persons to their sovereign was firmly stated, but so was the right of a sovereign to intervene to protect the subjects of another sovereign from harsh treatment. As was the case under Christian doctrine, however, delimiting the exact circumstances when such intervention was acceptable proved difficult. As positivist thinking rose to preeminence in the nineteenth century, close attention was paid to the practice of states in an effort to discern whether humanitarian intervention constituted a lawful basis for resort to force.

Various interventions during the nineteenth century, primarily by the European powers, indicate some level of acceptance, as a matter of international law, of the right to intervene for the protection of human rights. Of particular note, these interventions exhibit a belief that greater order in international relations could be achieved by authorizing these interventions through a multilateral decisionmaking process. In some cases the authorization was explicit and with express limitations, while in others the intervening state argued that authorization was implicit. At the same time, these interventions reveal the inherent difficulties in assessing the motivations of the intervening state(s), the tendency of states to seek other (or at least multiple) justifications for their conduct, and the difficulty in extrapolating general principles of law from fact-specific situations. The best that may be said of this practice is that a concept of humanitarian intervention was present in nineteenth century state practice, but its application was sporadic and uneven.

After the outbreak of World War I, there came a recognition that international law and international institutions should be used to try to avoid armed conflict and promote dispute resolution. Consequently, with the establishment of the League of Nations, the global community sought to create a collective security organization that did not prohibit, but did seek to rationalize, the resort to force. Although steps were taken to improve labor conditions and to protect the rights of minorities and populations within the mandate system, the protection of human rights generally was not a central feature of the League of Nations. Examples of intervention, purportedly for the protection of human rights during the League era, reflect the darker side of this doctrine; Japan, Italy, and Germany all appealed to this notion when intervening for what indubitably was territorial aggrandizement. If there was a general trend during the League era regarding the attitudes of states toward the use of force, it was one in favor of tightly restricting the use of force, as may be seen in the Kellogg-Briand Pact's general prohibition on resort to war as a means of foreign policy. It was, in short, a trend in favor of establishing international order even at the cost of neglecting certain values of justice. While the vitality of the doctrine of humanitarian intervention at the outbreak of the war cannot be conclusively denied, it would appear doubtful that the trend away from the availability of force as an instrument of national policy allowed for a continuing doctrine of humanitarian intervention. This trend did not forestall the outbreak of World War II. It did, however, carry over to efforts in the postwar era to succeed where the League failed. The next chapter examines those efforts.

Chapter 3
The UN Charter: Origins and Text

The atrocities committed by Germany against German nationals, particularly German Jews, during the Second World War constitute one the worst periods of human rights violations of any era. Nevertheless, the war that was fought against Germany and the other Axis Powers was not a war for human rights;[1] it was a war of self-defense. Of the major Allied Powers, Britain and France declared war on Germany after belatedly realizing that Hitler's fascism was a direct threat to their national interests. The United States expressed concern regarding Axis human rights abuses,[2] but entered the war only after a direct attack by Japan on U.S. territory; the United States then declared war on Germany in response to Germany's declaration of war against the United States.[3] The Soviet Union actively cooperated with Germany under the infamous Ribbentrop-Molotov Pact until the Soviets, too, were attacked by Germany in 1942. Consequently, while the atrocious human rights abuses committed by Germany provide in retrospect added moral justification for the Allied actions, it cannot be said that the Allied Powers initiated and maintained armed force against the Axis Powers largely out of a concern for human rights in Germany. In the aftermath of World War II, as is discussed in this chapter, human rights were expressly recognized as an im-

---

1. *Contra* F. TESÓN, HUMANITARIAN INTERVENTION: AN INQUIRY INTO LAW AND MORALITY 158 (1988).

2. The most cited example is President Franklin D. Roosevelt's "Four Freedoms" message to the Congress on January 6, 1941, *in* THE PUBLIC PAPERS AND ADDRESSES OF FRANKLIN D. ROOSEVELT, 1940, at 663 (S. Rosenman ed., 1941).

3. The war aims of the Allies gave a nod to human rights in the Axis territories as an ancillary matter. *See, e.g.*, Declaration by United Nations, Jan. 1, 1942, 55 Stat. 1600, 1600, *in* 4 DOCUMENTS ON AMERICAN FOREIGN RELATIONS: 1941–1942, at 203, 208 (L. Goodrich, ed. 1942) ("Being convinced that complete victory over their enemies is essential to defend life, liberty, independence and religious freedom, and to preserve human rights and justice in their own lands as well as in other lands, and that they are now engaged in a common struggle against savage and brutal forces seeking to subjugate the world").

portant element of the UN Charter, but the right of armed intervention to prevent human rights abuses was not.

A. Dumbarton Oaks

The seeds of the UN Charter were sown by the Declaration of Four Nations on General Security in 1943, which committed the major powers (the United States, Great Britain, the Soviet Union, and China) to the creation of an international organization "for the maintenance of international peace and security."[4] To this end, these powers met at Dumbarton Oaks, Washington, D.C., in the autumn of 1944 and drafted proposals for the establishment of the international organization.

The "Dumbarton Oaks proposals"[5] provided the basic framework for the UN Charter. In them, the major powers agreed on a comprehensive prohibition on the threat or use of force by states against other states.[6] They also agreed that a Security Council consisting of permanent and non-permanent members would be given primary responsibility for maintaining international peace and security, and that it could pursue forcible measures to restore peace and security once it determined there existed a "threat to the peace, breach of the peace or act of aggression." These provisions, with some modifications, survived the subsequent 1945 meeting in San Francisco and are present in the UN Charter.

Under the Dumbarton Oaks proposals, however, the "purposes" of the new organization did *not* include the protection of human rights, although they did speak of "international cooperation" in the solution of "humanitarian problems." The "principles" of the organization were oriented, rather, toward international security, stating that all members would settle their disputes by peaceful means and that "All members of the Organization shall refrain in their international relations from the threat or use of force in any manner inconsistent with the purposes of the Organization." The only significant provision relating to human rights appeared toward the end of the Dumbarton Oaks proposals; it called on the General Assembly, through an Economic and Social Council (ECOSOC), to "facilitate solutions of international economic, social and other humanitarian problems and promote respect for human

---

4. Declaration of Four Nations on General Security, Oct. 30, 1943, *in* 6 DOCUMENTS ON AMERICAN FOREIGN RELATIONS, 1943–1944, at 229, 229 (L. Goodrich & M. Carroll eds. 1945).

5. Proposals for the Establishment of a General International Organization, Oct. 7, 1944, 11 DEP'T ST. BULL. 368 (1944) [hereinafter Dumbarton Oaks Proposals].

6. *Id.* ch. 2, para. 4.

rights and fundamental freedoms."[7] The origin of this last provision is of interest.

The initial proposals of the United States and Great Britain at Dumbarton Oaks called for a provision on economic and social cooperation, including matters relating to cultural and educational affairs. The Soviet Union, however, believed that fostering such cooperation should be left to some other organization entirely, allowing the new organization to focus its attention exclusively on international security.[8] The compromise reached was to retain economic and social cooperation as a function of the new organization but to relegate it to a subsidiary body of the General Assembly. Pursuant to a Soviet proposal, the phrase "other humanitarian concerns" was inserted to replace "educational and cultural problems."[9]

The United States then proposed, somewhat belatedly, that the General Assembly be able to make recommendations "for the promotion of the observance of basic human rights." This proposal, however, met with resistance by Great Britain and the Soviet Union on the grounds that UN involvement in such issues would be a violation of a state's national sovereignty.[10] The United States, while accepting that the issue of human rights was an internal one, nevertheless wished to have some reference to human rights in the Charter. Consequently, it proposed that a provision be added making clear that the international organization should refrain from intervention in the internal affairs of any state since it was the "responsibility of each state 'to respect the human rights and fundamental freedoms' of its own people and to govern 'in accordance with the principles of humanity and justice.' "[11] Even this tame formulation was resisted by the other powers; the British expressed concern that it might still invite criticism by the organization regarding British rule in its colonies, while the Soviets saw the issue as wholly outside the scope of a security organization.[12] Ultimately, a compromise was reached in which the phrase "and promote respect for human rights and fundamental freedoms" was added to the ECOSOC provision.

Thus, the Dumbarton Oaks proposals transmitted to the intergovernmental negotiating conference in San Francisco in September 1945 were

7. *Id.* ch. 9, sec. A, para. 1.
8. R. HILDERBRAND, DUMBARTON OAKS: THE ORIGINS OF THE UNITED NATIONS AND THE SEARCH FOR POSTWAR SECURITY 86–87 (1990).
9. *Id.* at 90–91.
10. 1 E. LUARD, A HISTORY OF THE UNITED NATIONS: THE YEARS OF WESTERN DOMINATION, 1945–1955, at 31–32 (1982).
11. HILDERBRAND, *supra* note 8, at 91.
12. *Id.* at 91–92.

fundamentally oriented toward traditional concepts of threats to the peace. The major powers emphasized the need both to preserve international peace and security and to engage collective machinery to that end (and only that end) when necessary. The proposals contained but one reference to the need to promote respect for human rights, which was relegated to a minor position wholly outside the provisions relating to UN deployment or authorization of military force.

B. The Provisions of the UN Charter

The basic structure of the UN Charter as it emerged from the 1945 San Francisco Conference is well known. The Charter provides that the principal organs of the United Nations are the Security Council, the General Assembly, ECOSOC, the International Court of Justice, and the Secretariat, headed by the Secretary-General.[13]

The Security Council is the primary organ for addressing matters relating to the maintenance of international peace and security, pursuant to powers granted by Chapter VII of the UN Charter. The General Assembly may discuss any issues within the scope of the Charter, including matters relating to international peace and security,[14] and it also may make recommendations on matters of international peace and security. But it cannot bind states to adhere to those recommendations. If the Security Council is "exercising" the functions assigned to it relating to the maintenance of international peace and security, the General Assembly cannot issue recommendations.[15]

Matters relating to the protection of human rights and freedoms were assigned to the General Assembly, ECOSOC, and ECOSOC's Commission on Human Rights. There is, however, no express linkage in the Charter between the maintenence of international peace and security and the protection of human rights. Indeed, the human rights provisions of the Charter are separate from the provisions relating to the maintenance of peace and security and represent a grafting onto the Dumbarton Oaks proposals of concerns regarding human rights largely held by nongovernmental representatives and by states other than the major powers. To provide proper background to the issue of humanitarian intervention under the UN Charter, however, it is essential that they be reviewed along with the provisions relating to the use of force and collective security.

13. U.N. CHARTER art. 7. Article 7 also provided for a Trusteeship Council, but with the complete transition of trusteeships into sovereign states or freely associated states, the Trusteeship Council is no longer central to the activities of the United Nations.

14. U.N. CHARTER art. 11.

15. U.N. CHARTER art. 12.

1. Human Rights Provisions

At the San Francisco Conference, numerous states and nongovernmental organizations successfully insisted that more human rights provisions should be included in the UN Charter than had appeared in the Dumbarton Oaks proposals.[16] Thus the Preamble of the Charter reaffirms "faith in fundamental human rights, in the dignity and worth of the human person, in the equal rights of men and women and of nations large and small."[17] Among the purposes of the organization are the development of "friendly relations among nations based on respect for the principle of equal rights and self-determination of peoples" and the achievement of international cooperation in "promoting and encouraging respect for human rights and for fundamental freedoms for all without distinction as to race, sex, language, or religion."[18] Under Chapter IV, the General Assembly "shall initiate studies and make recommendations for the purpose of . . . (b) . . . assisting in the realization of human rights and fundamental freedoms for all without distinction as to race, sex, language, or religion."[19] Under Chapter IX on international economic and social cooperation, the United Nations is charged with promoting "universal respect for, and observance of, human rights and fundamental freedoms," and all members pledge to take joint and separate action with the United Nations to this end.[20] Under Chapter X, ECOSOC is empowered to make recommendations in this realm and is called upon to establish a commission for the promotion of human rights.[21] And in Chapter XII, echoing the Covenant of the League of Nations, the UN trusteeship system is instructed to encourage such rights and freedoms.[22]

There are certain issues, however, that the UN Charter did not address. Except in forbidding discrimination based on race, sex, language, or religion, it did not define what was meant by "human rights" and

16. For a discussion of the role of nongovernmental organizations and individuals in the creation of human rights norms in the U.N. Charter, see J. ROBINSON, HUMAN RIGHTS AND FUNDAMENTAL FREEDOMS IN THE CHARTER OF THE UNITED NATIONS: A COMMENTARY (1946). Some representatives argued at San Francisco that, unlike the League of Nations Covenant, the U.N. Charter should not be simply a legal document that seeks to prevent war but also a declaration regarding the fundamental rights of persons. See, e.g., LA CHARTE DES NATIONS UNIES: COMMENTAIRE ARTICLE PAR ARTICLE 2–4, 13–14 (J. Cot & A. Pellet eds., 2d ed. 1991) (discussing the role of South Africa's Prime Minister Jan Smuts).

17. U.N. CHARTER pmbl.
18. U.N. CHARTER art. 1, paras. 2–3.
19. U.N. CHARTER art. 13, para. 1.
20. U.N. CHARTER arts. 55–56.
21. U.N. CHARTER arts. 62, 68.
22. U.N. CHARTER art. 76.

"fundamental freedoms." Various proposals made by delegations to flesh out these concepts were postponed to a later time.[23] Further, the operative gerunds in these human rights provisions ("promoting," "encouraging," and "assisting in the realization of") are tepid and give little sense of the concrete powers and functions of the United Nations in promoting and protecting these rights and freedoms. In particular, there is no explicit provision authorizing the use of force either by states or by the United Nations for the purpose of enforcing these provisions. Tom J. Farer notes:

> Anyone who considers with some measure of objectivity the Charter's normative logic, its allocation of coercive jurisdiction, its omissions, as well as the preferences manifested by most participants in the drafting process and their immediately subsequent behavior, cannot help concluding that the promotion of human rights ranked far below the protection of national sovereignty and the maintenance of peace as organizational goals.[24]

The protection of national sovereignty and the maintenance of peace were indeed the central features of the UN Charter, and thus the provisions associated with those features merit attention.

2. Provisions on the Use of Force by States

The provisions of the UN Charter in its final form weigh heavily against the use of armed force solely to protect human rights in a target state. With respect to actions by member states, Article 2(4) of the Charter provides:

> All Members shall refrain in their international relations from the threat or use of force against the territorial integrity or political independence of any state, or in any other manner inconsistent with the Purposes of the United Nations.[25]

The broad term "use of force"—as opposed to the term "war," as used in the Kellogg-Briand Pact—reflected a desire to prohibit armed conflicts generally, not just conflicts arising from a formal state of war. As such, an initial reading of Article 2(4) suggests that the various doctrines of forcible self-help, reprisal, protection of nationals, and humanitarian intervention that had developed in the pre-Charter era[26] were now un-

---

23. *See* R. ASHER E AL., THE UNITED NATIONS AND PROMOTION OF THE GENERAL WELFARE 656–67 (photo. reprint 1980) (1957).

24. T. Farer, *An Inquiry into the Legitimacy of Humanitarian Intervention, in* LAW AND FORCE IN THE NEW INTERNATIONAL ORDER 185, 190 (L. Damrosch & D. Scheffer eds., 1991).

25. U.N. CHARTER art. 2, para. 4.

26. *Supra* ch. 2, n.61.

lawful. A closer reading of Article 2(4), however, affords two arguments for why these earlier doctrines survived Article 2(4).

The first argument is that the phrase "against the territorial integrity or political independence of any state" should be read to limit the prohibition to uses of force that are above a threshold where the territorial integrity or political independence of a state is impugned.[27] Actions by a state that annex territory or seek to depose a foreign government are prohibited because such actions are against a state's "territorial integrity or political independence." Other actions, however, may involve military action of a different type. For instance, perhaps a state may employ force to vindicate its legal rights as a response to unlawful (albeit nonforcible) behavior of another state; such a use of force does not impinge on the other state's "territorial integrity or political independence" because such integrity and independence are contingent on the other state's compliance with its legal obligations.[28] Similarly, the argument goes, humanitarian intervention falls below the threshold set in Article 2(4) since the intervenors (if the intervention is truly humanitarian) do not seek to deprive the state of its territorial or political attributes but, rather, to enhance them.[29]

The counter to this argument is that, according to the negotiating history of the Charter, the phrase "territorial integrity or political independence" reflected an effort to clarify, not curtail, the comprehensive nature of the prohibition.[30] This phrase was not considered necessary for inclusion by the major powers meeting at Dumbarton Oaks, but was inserted at San Francisco out of a belief among weaker states that it strengthened the concept that forcible actions against a state were impermissible. Indeed, arguing that the phrase was meant to expand the

27. This approach is heavily influenced by the work of Julius Stone. J. STONE, AGGRESSION AND WORLD ORDER: A CRITIQUE OF UNITED NATIONS THEORIES OF AGGRESSION (1958); *see also* D. BOWETT, SELF-DEFENCE IN INTERNATIONAL LAW (1958).

28. *See* W. REISMAN, NULLITY AND REVISION 844–51 (1971).

29. W. Reisman, *Humanitarian Intervention to Protect the Ibos, in* HUMANITARIAN INTERVENTION AND THE UNITED NATIONS 167, 177 (R. Lillich ed., 1973).

30. For the negotiating history of this phrase in Article 2(4), *see* I. BROWNLIE, INTERNATIONAL LAW AND THE USE OF FORCE BY STATES 265–68 (1963) ("The conclusion warranted by the *travaux préparatoires* is that the phrase under discussion was not intended to be restrictive but, on the contrary, to give more specific guarantees to small states and that it cannot be interpreted as having a qualifying effect."). *See also* LA CHARTE DES NATIONS UNIES: COMMENTAIRE ARTICLE PAR ARTICLE, *supra* note 16, at 125; THE CHARTER OF THE UNITED NATIONS: A COMMENTARY 117–18 (B. Simma ed., 1994); L. GOODRICH ET AL., CHARTER OF THE UNITED NATIONS: COMMENTARY AND DOCUMENTS 44–45 (3rd ed. 1969); 2 OPPENHEIM'S INTERNATIONAL LAW 153–54 (H. Lauterpacht ed., 7th ed. 1952); C. Waldock, *The Regulation of the Use of Force by Individual States in International Law,* 81 R.C.A.D.I. 451, 493 (1952-II).

ability of more powerful states to intervene in weaker states (even for altruistic purposes) is inconsistent with the overall noninterventionist tenor of the San Francisco debates. Further, the Article 2(4) phrase derives from similar language in the Covenant,[31] which had no reason to make these kinds of threshold distinctions between differing levels of force in fostering resort to peaceful settlement of disputes. Most scholars who have closely analyzed the negotiating history of the Charter accept that this formulation in Article 2(4) was not intentionally drafted so as to provide an opening for forcible conduct.[32]

A further counterargument is that humanitarian intervention, even if the phrase is regarded as prohibiting only uses of force over some threshold level of force, is demonstratively above that level. Humanitarian intervention *is* a violation of a state's territorial integrity (even if borders are not altered) as well as a violation of the political independence of a state; it typically involves the deployment of military personnel and equipment across a border, sometimes for an extended period of time and for the purpose of suppressing the political will of the de facto authorities in the target state. In some instances, the ruling government is toppled and a new one installed. Whether or not this action occurs in support of self-determination by the people of the state, the use of force is one against the "political independence" of the state in that it has the effect of altering political structures through external means.[33] Even if the intervention is only for a short term and is for a good purpose, it runs afoul of Article 2(4).[34]

The second argument for why certain pre-Charter doctrines survived the passage of Article 2(4) is the presence of the phrase "or in any other manner inconsistent with the purposes of the United Nations." This phrase, it is argued, allows for the use of force to protect certain essential rights set forth in the UN Charter (e.g., Article 1) in situations where there is no other means to protect them.[35] As noted above, those purposes include promoting respect for human rights and fundamental freedoms; thus humanitarian intervention would be an action consistent with the purposes of the Charter.

31. LEAGUE OF NATIONS COVENANT art. 10 ("The Members of the League undertake to respect and preserve as against external aggression *the territorial integrity and existing political independence* of all Members of the League.") (emphasis added).

32. *See, e.g.,* REISMAN, *supra* note 28, at 850–51.

33. O. Schachter, *The Legality of Pro-Democratic Invasion*, 78 AM. J. INT'L L. 645, 649 (1984) ("The idea that wars waged in a good cause such as democracy and human rights would not involve a violation of territorial integrity or political independence demands an Orwellian construction of those terms").

34. O. SCHACHTER, INTERNATIONAL LAW IN THEORY AND PRACTICE 112–13 (1991).

35. STONE, *supra* note 27, at 43, 95–96.

The counterargument observes that the "or" indicates that this phrase supplements, not qualifies, the initial text. In other words, states are always prohibited from threatening or using force against the territorial integrity or political independence of any state and are further prohibited from threatening or using force in any other manner inconsistent with the purposes of the United Nations. As before, the negotiating history supports the view that this phrase was not intended to have a restrictive effect on the Article 2(4) prohibition, although Ian Brownlie notes that it may have been intended to permit action by states when sanctioned by the UN Security Council.[36]

The primary exceptions to the prohibition on the use of force contained in Article 2(4) are the ability of a state to use force in self-defense (Article 51) or the authority of the UN Security Council to do so under Chapter VII.[37] Leaving the latter for consideration in the following section, it has been argued that nothing in the language of the Charter, including Article 2(4), has deprived states of their right under customary international law to engage in self-defense. Consequently, it is asserted that the Charter implicitly accepts that a state may defend its political independence, territorial integrity, the lives and property of its nationals, and even its economic independence.[38] There is some attraction to this view, inasmuch as the general understanding of the drafters of the Charter seems to have been that they had no intention of (and, indeed, no capacity for) precluding states from exercising their fundamental right of self-defense. The difficulty with this view, however, is that, in the context of assuring regional organizations that their right of *collective* self-defense was not impaired by the Charter, the drafters reached agreement in the Charter on an article that seems to announce the sole basis upon which self-defense is recognized, be it collective or individual.[39] Article 51 of the UN Charter provides:

Nothing in the present Charter shall impair the inherent right of individual or collective self-defense if an armed attack occurs against a Member of the United Nations, until the Security Council has taken measures necessary to maintain in-

36. BROWNLIE, *supra* note 30, at 208.

37. U.N. Charter Article 107 also provides an exception to the prohibition on the use of force contained in Article 2(4) for actions by states against World War II "enemy states." Presumably, circumstances have changed sufficiently since the time of the adoption of the Charter that this exception has no continuing effect. *See* THE CHARTER OF THE UNITED NATIONS: A COMMENTARY, *supra* note 30, at 119.

38. BOWETT, *supra* note 27, at 185–86.

39. *See* BROWNLIE, *supra* note 30, at 273 ("where the Charter has a specific provision relating to a particular legal category, to assert that this does not restrict the wider ambit of the customary law relating to that category or problem is to go beyond the bounds of logic").

ternational peace and security. Measures taken by Members in the exercise of this right of self-defence shall be immediately reported to the Security Council and shall not in any way affect the authority and responsibility of the Security Council under the present Charter to take at any time such action as it deems necessary in order to maintain or restore international peace and security.

The approach in Article 51 of not impairing "the inherent right"[40] of self-defense suggests that the UN Charter itself does not grant a right of self-defense but, rather, preserves a right that predated the UN Charter under customary international law. Most international law scholars agree upon this interpretation,[41] as does the International Court of Justice.[42] From here, however, there is a divergence of views. If rights are being preserved from the pre-Charter era, how broadly may one read the "right of self-defense?"

One indicia of the scope of "self-defense" contemplated by Article 51 is the reference to "armed attack," which may indicate that any use of armed force other than in response to an armed attack does not trigger a right of "self-defense."[43] If this restrictive view is correct, then Article 51 provides no basis for resort to humanitarian intervention. Under a more "expansive view" of the right of self-defense, however, use of force might be permitted in situations other than an armed attack on the territory of a state; it might be permitted in cases of anticipatory self-defense[44] or to protect one's nationals abroad.[45] This view would argue that the reference to "armed attack" was meant to be exemplary, not restrictive. If this view is correct, then one might ask whether an expansive view of the right of self-defense preserved by Article 51 includes the

40. In the French text, the phrase appears as "droit naturel."

41. *See, e.g.,* BOWETT, *supra* note 27, at 186; J. BRIERLY, THE LAW OF NATIONS 416–20 (H. Waldock ed., 6th ed. 1963).

42. In Military and Paramilitary Activities (Nicar. v. U.S.), 1986 I.C.J. 14, para. 176 (June 27), the Court construed Article 51 as a reference to customary international law.

43. *Id.*, paras. 194–95, 210–11 (the Court left open the issue of whether force may be used in anticipation of an armed attack); BROWNLIE, *supra* note 30, at 273–76; THE CHARTER OF THE UNITED NATIONS: A COMMENTARY, *supra* note 30, at 678; H. KELSEN, THE LAW OF THE UNITED NATIONS 269, 797–98 (1950); L. Henkin, *International Law: Politics, Values and Functions,* 216 R.C.A.D.I. 9, 156 (1989-IV); Q. Wright, *The Legality of Intervention Under the United Nations Charter,* 51 AM. SOC'Y INT'L L. PROC. 79, 88 (1957).

44. BOWETT, *supra* note 27, at 187–93; R. HIGGINS, THE DEVELOPMENT OF INTERNATIONAL LAW THROUGH THE POLITICAL ORGANS OF THE UNITED NATIONS 201 (1963); M. MCDOUGAL & F. FELICIANO, LAW AND MINIMUM WORLD PUBLIC ORDER: THE LEGAL REGULATION OF INTERNATIONAL COERCION 233–41 (1961); A. THOMAS & A. THOMAS, JR., NONINTERVENTION, THE LAW AND ITS IMPORT IN THE AMERICAS 123–25 (1956); J. Fawcett, *Intervention in International Law,* 103 R.C.A.D.I. 343, 360–62 (1961-II). *Contra* L. HENKIN, HOW NATIONS BEHAVE: LAW AND FOREIGN POLICY 141 (2d ed. 1979); O. Schachter, *The Right of States to Use Armed Force,* 82 MICH. L. REV. 1620, 1633–34 (1984).

45. *See infra* ch. 8.

right to undertake humanitarian intervention. Perhaps the concept of self-defense includes humanitarian intervention on a theory that the destruction of human rights values, at least on a large scale, threatens the stability and expectations of the global community. Such an expansive view of self-defense, however, might then be used to justify a wide range of coercive behaviors by states and ultimately eviscerate virtually all normative restraints on the use of force.

Considerations of this type relative to both Article 2(4) and Article 51 will be pursued further in later chapters. At present, it is sufficient to note that, notwithstanding the foregoing arguments in favor of humanitarian intervention, there is nothing explicit in either the text of the UN Charter or its negotiating history to support a right of unilateral humanitarian intervention by states.

3. Provisions on the Use of Force by the United Nations

Provisions of the Charter governing the actions of the United Nations itself (as opposed to the actions of the individual member states) also weigh against the use of armed force solely to protect against human rights abuses in the target state. Article 2(7) provides:

Nothing contained in the present Charter shall authorize the United Nations to intervene in matters which are essentially within the domestic jurisdiction of any state or shall require the Members to submit such matters to settlement under the present Charter; but this principle shall not prejudice the application of enforcement measures under Chapter VII.

This "intervention" prohibition is broader than the prohibition on the "threat or use of force" that applies to actions of individual states. Certainly the projection of armed force into the territory of another state, for whatever reason, would constitute intervention; and the records of the San Francisco Conference suggest that Article 2(7) was meant to extend beyond uses of armed force to include other types of interference in the domestic affairs of states, such as interference related to economic and social matters.[46] On the other hand, the provision is formulated not as a prohibition but as a statement that the "present Charter" does not authorize such action, leaving open the possibility that authorization might emanate from some other source, such as the inherent rights of states or subsequent state practice.

The provision echoes the Covenant of the League of Nations, with one important difference. Under the Covenant, the comparable provision

---

46. ASHER ET AL., *supra* note 23, at 661–62; *see also* THE CHARTER OF THE UNITED NATIONS: A COMMENTARY, *supra* note 30, at 142–43.

applied a standard of international law for determining whether a matter was within the domestic jurisdiction of a state and empowered the Council of the League to make such determinations.[47] Article 2(7) is considerably weaker; regardless what the international community may decide, any particular state may argue that it considers certain actions to be within its "domestic jurisdiction" and hence not subject to UN action.

Article 2(7) contains an important exception. The United Nations may intervene in the domestic affairs of a state when pursuing enforcement measures under Chapter VII of the Charter. Chapter VII[48] is the heart of the collective security machinery of the United Nations, and it is pursuant to this chapter that the UN Security Council may pursue economic or military measures against a state to maintain or restore international peace and security.[49] Unlike the approach taken in the League's Covenant, neither the Security Council nor member states are *required* by Chapter VII to take measures against an offending state. The Security Council, however, is *empowered* to take decisions binding on member states involving not just economic but also military measures; the Covenant's Council could recommend only military action.

A key feature of Chapter VII is that the Security Council must first determine that a "threat to the peace, breach of the peace, or act of aggression" exists before it may pursue measures under Chapter VII.[50] Chapter VII begins:

> The Security Council *shall* determine the existence of any threat to the peace, breach of the peace, or act of aggression and shall make recommendations, or decide what measures shall be taken in accordance with Articles 41 and 42, to maintain or restore international peace and security.[51]

The records of both the Dumbarton Oaks and San Francisco conferences confirm that this preliminary requirement was intended to prevent United Nations interference in matters unrelated to international security. The phrase "threat to peace" arose at the Dumbarton Oaks

47. The LEAGUE OF NATIONS COVENANT art. 15, para. 8. provided: "If the dispute between the parties is claimed by one of them, and is found by the Council, to arise out of a matter which by international law is solely within the domestic jurisdiction of that party, the Council shall so report, and shall make no recommendation as to its settlement."

48. U.N. CHARTER arts. 39–51.

49. Chapter VII also provides for nonenforcement measures by the Security Council, such as recommendations. U.N. CHARTER art. 39. It is unclear whether provisional measures under Article 40 should be considered "enforcement measures"; the language used in Article 40 ("may . . . call upon the parties concerned") is stronger than that of Article 39 ("make recommendations"), but weaker than that of Article 41 ("decide what measures") or Article 42 ("take . . . action").

50. THE CHARTER OF THE UNITED NATIONS: A COMMENTARY, *supra* note 30, at 610.

51. U.N. CHARTER art. 39 (emphasis added).

Conference in the context of how to handle "disputes" among states that could not be resolved peacefully. The Four Powers first established a procedure for the peaceful settlement of disputes, which became the basis for Chapter VI of the Charter. If a dispute could not be resolved peacefully, but the dispute was not itself a threat to the peace, the Security Council would be limited to *recommending* "appropriate procedures or methods of adjustment." The Four Powers denied the Security Council the power to impose the terms for dispute settlement after Great Britain pointed to the disastrous 1938 Munich settlement and to the unlikelihood that the less powerful states would favor such a power.[52] However, where the inability to resolve a dispute constituted a "threat" to the maintenance of international peace and security, then the Security Council could undertake enforcement measures.[53] As a separate matter, the Four Powers agreed that "in general" the Security Council should determine the existence of any "threat to the peace, breach of the peace or act of aggression," and make recommendations or decide upon measures "to maintain or restore peace and security."[54] At San Francisco, these two components—threats to the peace arising from the failure to resolve a dispute and threats arising more generally—were collapsed into one paragraph pursuant to a motion by China.[55] That paragraph ultimately became Article 39 of the Charter.

Chapter VII contains no definition as to what constitutes a "threat to the peace, breach of the peace, or act of aggression." Efforts to clarify this matter at San Francisco failed.[56] From the text and the negotiating history it is clear that a threshold was being set that would permit action by the Security Council, but among the varying levels of potential conflict it is unclear where that threshold lies. To allow the Security Council sufficient flexibility to discharge its duties, the conference committee charged with drafting the provision opted to leave it to the Security Council to decide what constitutes "a threat to peace, a breach of the peace, or an act of aggression."[57] Chapter VI of the Charter, which addresses the role of the United Nations (particularly the Security Council) in the pacific settlement of disputes, permits UN involvement in disputes the continuance of which is "likely to endanger the maintenance of international peace and security."[58] The phrase "likely to endanger" in

---

52. HILDERBRAND, *supra* note 8, at 136.
53. Dumbarton Oaks Proposals, *supra* note 5, ch. 8, sec. B, para. 1.
54. *Id.*, ch. 8, sec. B, para. 2.
55. Doc. 628, III/3/33, 12 U.N.C.I.O. Docs. 379, 379 (1945).
56. LA CHARTE DES NATIONS UNIES: COMMENTAIRE ARTICLE PAR ARTICLE, *supra* note 16, at 647–48; THE CHARTER OF THE UNITED NATIONS: A COMMENTARY, *supra* note 30, at 608.
57. Doc. 881, III/3/46, 12 U.N.C.I.O. Docs. 502, 505 (1945).
58. U.N. CHARTER arts. 34, 37, para. 2.

Chapter VI appears to set a lower threshold than the actual existence of a "threat to the peace," but the difference in practice between the two is not at all clear.

It should be noted that, unlike Chapter VI, Chapter VII does not speak of *international* peace, but simply of a threat or breach of *the* peace. A mere textual analysis of this omission might suggest that Chapter VII can be triggered by internal violence and unrest without any transnational nexus. If so, it would help explain why the exception in Article 2(7) is necessary; the United Nations cannot intervene in matters within the domestic jurisdiction of a state except where this is done under Chapter VII to address internal violence and unrest that threatens peace within that state.[59] The absence of "international" in Chapter VII, however, has not been accorded much significance, although in the early years of the Charter it led to some confusion. For instance, when hostilities broke out in Palestine in 1947 between Palestinian and Israeli forces, the General Assembly adopted a resolution partitioning Palestine and requesting the Security Council to consider whether the situation constituted "a threat to the peace" such that the Security Council could take measures under Chapter VII to empower the UN Palestine Commission to enforce its mandate.[60] The Security Council discussed at length the issue of what constituted a threat to the peace, with Great Britain stressing that it must be a threat to *international* peace, while the United States asserted that internal disorders and incursions by armed bands could constitute such a threat.[61]

On the assumption that some transnational nexus is necessary, common sense indicates that the armed attack by one state against another state would constitute a "threat to the peace," "breach of the peace," and "act of aggression," whereas a diplomatic protest would not (although one might conjecture extraordinary circumstances where it might constitute a threat to the peace). A low level of violence or unrest internal to a country for a short period of time (e.g., a riot in a city) probably would not constitute a threat to the peace, but as the violence increased in intensity, scope, and duration presumably the threshold would at some point be crossed. At the same time, a threat to the peace might arise if neighboring states provided financial or military assistance to dissident factions of a state, or if dissident forces were staged from

59. *But see* THE CHARTER OF THE UNITED NATIONS: A COMMENTARY, *supra* note 30, at 609, arguing that in light of Article 2(7), Article 39 must be viewed as referring only to international peace.

60. G.A. Res. 181 (II) A, U.N. Doc. A/519, at 131 (1948), *reprinted in* 3 INTERNATIONAL LAW AND WORLD ORDER III.Q.1 (B. Weston ed., 1994).

61. GOODRICH ET AL., *supra* note 30, at 296.

neighboring states, with or without the consent of the neighboring states. In such circumstances, the likelihood of conflict between two states is readily apparent and can be considered a threat to the peace.

But how far can one go in postulating events that might agitate other states into taking action, thus creating a "threat to the peace?" What if the internal violence results in the flow of refugees into neighboring states? Is this a "threat to the peace" and, if so, in what circumstances (large flows? continuous flows? flows of persons ethnically or culturally affiliated with, or antagonistic to, groups located in the neighboring states?). What if there are no flows or minimal flows of refugees but the internal violence is extraordinarily high? Does such violence constitute a "threat to the peace" only if large numbers of persons are injured or killed? Is it only a "threat to the peace" if television images and newspaper accounts report the carnage to neighboring or other states? Does it matter if the deaths or injuries are sustained by combatants as opposed to noncombatants? Does it matter if the deaths are the result of a civil war in which the opposing sides are evenly matched, as opposed to the infliction of violence by a government or rebel force that is vastly superior in strength to its opposition? Does the cause for which one or more of the factions involved is fighting (e.g., for democracy) make any difference in whether the internal violence is a "threat to the peace?" What if widespread deaths are occurring not from government or rebel actions but, rather, from starvation due to government neglect or incapacity? If one can identify international agreements (e.g., human rights instruments) which are being violated by a government's pursuit of such violence, does that make the matter a "threat to the peace?" What if there is no violence, but instead the widespread deprivation of certain political rights, such as the rights to speech, assembly, and free elections?

The Charter itself does not answer these questions; they will be explored in subsequent chapters in light of UN and state practice. Nevertheless, assuming that a "threat to the peace, breach of the peace, or act of aggression" can be determined to exist, Chapter VII sets forth steps that may be taken by the Security Council.[62]

Under Article 39, the Security Council can make recommendations, presumably to the parties to the conflict, other states, other UN enti-

---

62. Before making any recommendations or taking any measures, the Security Council can call upon the parties to a conflict or potential conflict to take provisional measures, which would be designed to prevent the conflict from escalating or occurring. U.N. CHARTER art. 40. The general view is that the Security Council must find a "threat to the peace, breach of the peace, or act of aggression" prior to calling upon the parties concerned to comply with provisional measures. *See* THE CHARTER OF THE UNITED NATIONS: A COMMENTARY, *supra* note 30, at 618; GOODRICH ET AL., *supra* note 30, at 303–05.

ties, or other international organizations. Under Article 41, the Security Council can decide upon measures not involving the use of armed force that are necessary to maintain or restore international peace and security. Article 41 states:

> The Security Council may decide what measures not involving the use of armed force are to be employed to give effect to its decisions, and it may call upon the Members of the United Nations to apply such measures. These may include complete or partial interruption of economic relations and of rail, sea, air, postal, telegraphic, radio, and other means of communication, and the severance of diplomatic relations.

Once decided upon by the Security Council, states are obligated to implement the measures called for. If these Article 41 measures do not or cannot work, the Security Council can decide upon measures involving military force pursuant to Article 42, which provides:

> Should the Security Council consider that measures provided for in Article 41 would be inadequate or have proved to be inadequate, it may take such action by air, sea, or land forces as may be necessary to maintain or restore international peace and security. Such action may include demonstrations, blockade, and other operations by air, sea, or land forces of the Members of the Security Council.

In light of the reference to Article 41, it appears that some form of non-military measures must first be considered before pursuit of military measures, although there is support in the Charter's negotiating history for the view that the Security Council may act immediately at least in the case of "flagrant aggression." [63] The ability of the Security Council to take military actions against a state was a radical advance over the collective security regime of the Covenant, which only provided for recommendations of such action by the unanimous vote of the League Council. While a "plain and natural meaning" reading of the Charter suggests that all military actions by the Security Council would arise under Article 42, in fact, since early in the Charter years, most UN military actions have occurred under Article 39 [64] or as "peacekeeping operations" conducted with the consent of the host state. [65]

The Charter envisioned states making available to the Security Council armed forces, assistance, and facilities that could be called upon as necessary to maintain international peace and security. [66] The Charter did not call for the creation of some sort of "standing army"; indeed, pro-

63. GOODRICH ET AL., *supra* note 30, at 314.

64. This was the basis for the U.N. action to assist South Korea against aggression from North Korea. *See generally* U.N. SCOR, 5th Sess., 473d-474th mtgs. (1950).

65. To date more than thirty peacekeeping operations have taken place, based variously on Chapter VI and Chapter VII.

66. U.N. CHARTER art. 43.

posals of this kind were rejected at both Dumbarton Oaks and San Francisco. The provision of this "on-call" support was to occur through special agreements between states and the Security Council (referred to as "Article 43 agreements"), but to date no such agreements have been concluded. Although it might be argued that "enforcement action" under Chapter VII (for purposes of Article 2(7)) must occur pursuant to such agreements, or at least under the direct control of the Security Council, current practice suggests that any forcible action taken as authorized by the Security Council under Chapter VII constitutes enforcement action. Indeed, the Charter contemplated joint action among states on behalf of the United Nations to maintain international peace and security even without the entry into force of such agreements (while such action was authorized only during a transition period to allow for the conclusion of Article 43 agreements, that transition period has not yet ended).[67] A Military Staff Committee, consisting of the Chiefs of Staff of the permanent members of the Security Council, was established to "advise and assist" the Security Council on an array of military issues, including "the Security Council's military requirements for the maintenance of international peace and security" and "the employment and command of forces placed at its disposal."[68]

The UN Charter also recognized the importance of regional arrangements or agencies for maintaining international peace and security.[69] The Charter states that such arrangements and agencies are appropriate so long as they operate consistently with the purposes and principles of the UN Charter. Regional arrangements and agencies may pursue pacific settlement of local disputes and may be used by the Security Council for enforcement action under Security Council authority, although the Charter prohibits enforcement action under such arrangements or agencies absent authorization of the Security Council.[70]

In summary, the UN Charter is built around a fundamental belief that the use of force by states against other states must be prohibited unless that force is in self-defense or is under the authority of the Security Council when responding to a threat to, or breach of, the peace or to an act of aggression. What constitutes a "threat to the peace" is not defined in the Charter; the drafters purposefully left out such definitions for fear of inhibiting the ability of the Security Council to act. Human rights were addressed in the UN Charter, but, as noted earlier, were attached to the Dumbarton Oaks proposals in a manner that accords them secondary

67. U.N. CHARTER art. 106; *see* THE CHARTER OF THE UNITED NATIONS: A COMMENTARY, *supra* note 30, at 1150.

68. U.N. CHARTER art. 47, para. 1.

69. *See* U.N. CHARTER arts. 52–54.

70. U.N. CHARTER art. 53, para. 1.

status to the provisions addressing peace and security. The provisions providing authority to UN organs to address human rights issues are at tension with other provisions calling upon states and the United Nations not to interfere in the internal affairs of states. Lines were not drawn in the Charter indicating how far the United Nations or states may go in reviewing, assessing, and acting upon human rights deprivations occurring in states. Mere discussion of human rights violations by organs of the United Nations was clearly permissible, but clarifying what steps might be taken beyond discussion was left to be developed by the United Nations and states. The next chapter assesses these developments during the Cold War.

Chapter 4
Intervention During the Cold War (1945–89)

Chapter 3 indicated that the language and intent behind the UN Charter does not provide an express legal basis for the conduct of humanitarian intervention by states or by regional organizations, and that it is at best ambiguous as to whether humanitarian intervention may be conducted by the United Nations itself. Drafted in the aftermath of a global war triggered by the transnational aggression of a few militant states, the Charter's core provisions reflect a clear moral and political decision in favor of strict prohibitions on the transnational use of force and a preference for collective action over unilateral action. Yet the UN Charter—as both a treaty and the constitution of an organization—cannot be viewed as a static document. Changes may occur in the meaning of the UN Charter, either through a difficult amendment process[1] or through a process of interpretation and application by the UN organs or the member states to situations as they arise.[2]

While the meaning of the UN Charter may change over time, there is no single, authoritative means for its interpretation. At San Francisco, it was decided that each of the organs of the United Nations should itself interpret those parts of the UN Charter that applied to its particular functions. A statement issued at San Francisco on this point asserted that:

1. Amendments to the U.N. Charter require a vote of two-thirds of the General Assembly and ratification by two thirds of the U.N. members, including all of the permanent members of the Security Council. U.N. CHARTER art. 108. Alternatively, a General Conference of U.N. members may be called by the General Assembly to recommend alterations to the Charter, which then take effect when ratified by two-thirds of the U.N. members, including all the permanent members of the Security Council. U.N. CHARTER art. 109. While a few amendments to the Charter have occurred pursuant to the first procedure, the procedure for amendment by Conference has never been invoked.

2. O. SCHACHTER, INTERNATIONAL LAW IN THEORY AND PRACTICE 118–19 (1991) ("The Charter is, as often stated, a living instrument. It is, like every constitutional instrument, continuously interpreted, molded and adapted to meet the interests of the parties.").

two organs may conceivably hold and may express or even act upon different views. Under unitary forms of national government the final determination of such a question may be vested in the highest court or in some other national authority. However, the nature of the Organization and of its operation would not seem to be such as to invite the inclusion in the Charter of any provision of this nature. If two Member States are at variance concerning the correct interpretation of the Charter, they are of course free to submit the dispute to the International Court of Justice as in the case of any other treaty. Similarly, it would always be open to the General Assembly or to the Security Council, in appropriate circumstances, to ask the International Court of Justice for an advisory opinion concerning the meaning of a provision of the Charter.[3]

This approach to the interpretation of the UN Charter resulted in a wide array of means for interpreting the Charter. Organs of the United Nations are capable of making interpretations of functions relating to them, but for political reasons it may not be possible to make such interpretations, and (when made) these interpretations may not be acceptable to other organs. The Security Council and the General Assembly are by their nature political, not judicial, organs, and therefore their interpretations are more apt to be dictated by political rather than juridical reasoning.

For these reasons, anyone interested in ascertaining the current state of international law under the Charter must consider the practice of UN organs and UN member states in interpreting the Charter over time. In the field of human rights generally, the Cold War era saw an impressive amount of lawmaking through the United Nations. As a part of that lawmaking, various UN-sponsored conventions as well as UN resolutions and declarations undertook the difficult task of balancing the desire to protect human rights with concern against intervention in the internal affairs of states. Yet that same era saw no incidents of humanitarian intervention by or under the authority of the United Nations. Ideological divergences virtually prevented the Security Council from acting in cases of outright aggression, let alone in cases involving widespread deprivations of internationally recognized human rights. Consequently, it was left to states to address those crises in their individual or regional capacities, and to justify their actions under the UN Charter.

This chapter first assesses incidents of intervention by states during the Cold War (1945–89) that in some fashion implicated humanitarian concerns. As will be seen, these interventions were episodic; they do not represent a pattern of consistent state practice. Furthermore, states rarely justified such interventions by crafting a careful, coherent position articulated in the context of international law; when they did, in no instance did a state assert that its intervention was justified solely on the basis of a right of humanitarian intervention. This is not to say that states

3. Doc. 933, IV/2/42(2), 13 U.N.C.I.O. Docs. 703, 709 (1945).

did not at times invoke human rights arguments, but these arguments never were central to the asserted justification.

The chapter then proceeds to assess relevant activities of the organs of the United Nations during this period, including the development of UN-sponsored human rights conventions and the development of regional organizations. The chapter concludes with a brief review of the opinions of scholars on the issue of humanitarian intervention during the Cold War.

A. Incidents of Intervention

As indicated, interventions during the Cold War that might be considered humanitarian interventions were limited and episodic. Nevertheless, there were several incidents where the intervention had the effect of ending a severe and widespread deprivation of human rights. Virtually all of them were cases of unilateral intervention, by which is meant intervention by a state or states without the authorization of the United Nations or a regional organization.

In assessing these incidents, the initial line of inquiry is whether the intervening state's primary reason for intervening was to prevent the severe and widespread deprivation of human rights. If this cannot be said, then the intervention is not evidence of a belief by the intervening state that a right of unilateral humanitarian intervention exists under the UN Charter. In most of the cases discussed below, government officials of the intervening state (rightly or wrongly) based the legality of that state's action on one or more other reasons. In some cases, the intervening state justified its action primarily on the basis of self-defense, such as the interventions by Tanzania in Uganda in 1979 and Vietnam in Cambodia in 1978. In other cases, the intervening state asserted that it had been invited to intervene by the target state or by a local insurgency that had toppled the target state's regime, such as was claimed by France (at least initially) when intervening in Central Africa in 1979. In still other cases, complicated mixtures of rights based on consent, rescue of nationals, regional organization authorization, and rights under international agreements were put forth, such as the intervention by Western states in the Congo in 1964 and the interventions by the United States in Latin and Central America in 1965, 1984, and 1989.

Of course, the justifications stated by intervening states may have differed from what some or all of the relevant actors in the intervening state in fact believed. Consequently, to the extent possible, the inquiry must look beyond public justifications to see if other reasons for the intervention may be discerned. Such an inquiry is admittedly subjective but must be guided by as objective an assessment of the facts as possible.

A secondary line of inquiry is whether the international community appraised the intervention as lawful or unlawful. If the reason for the intervention was humanitarian and criticism by the international community was muted or nonexistent, the incident may stand as an example of acceptance or tolerance by the international community of unilateral humanitarian intervention under the UN Charter. If the international community was highly critical of the intervention, then even if the intervening state's primary reason for intervening was to protect human rights, it cannot be said that the incident supports the legality of unilateral humanitarian intervention under the UN Charter. As will be seen, the action of the intervening state in many of these cases was censured by third states and the United Nations.

To appraise these interventions, a modified form of the "incidents" method of study advocated by Michael Reisman is used.[4] First, the facts of the incident are stated. Second, the claims made by the intervening state and those of the target state are reviewed. Third, the reactions of the global community (through the representatives of governments or "regime elites") are assessed, usually in the form of the debates and voting practices at the United Nations. Finally, an appraisal is provided of how, in light of these factors, the incident advances our understanding of the state of international law.

In the context of this study, not all of the interventions that took place during the Cold War can be assessed. Those interventions selected for assessment here purportedly have some humanitarian characteristic on the basis of either the reasons stated by the intervening state or the facts of the intervention itself. It should be noted that this chapter does not focus on the myriad Cold War situations when states could have intervened on humanitarian grounds and yet failed to do so. Such an inquiry is certainly relevant in the event one considers states as *obligated* to undertake humanitarian intervention, but it is less probative of whether states are permitted to undertake humanitarian intervention should they wish to do so.[5]

1. The Soviet Union in Eastern Europe

Inquiries into the conduct of humanitarian intervention usually do not refer to interventions by the Soviet Union in Eastern Europe. Nevertheless, these interventions are a useful reminder of the grave abuse that

4. *See supra* chapter 1 nn.46–47 and accompanying text.

5. This point is particularly stressed by Thomas Franck and Nigel Rodley in rejecting the legality of a unilateral right of humanitarian intervention. T. Franck & N. Rodley, *After Bangladesh: The Law of Humanitarian Intervention by Military Force*, 67 AM. J. INT'L L. 275, 290–98 (1973).

may be made of a doctrine of humanitarian intervention. As will be seen, these incidents cannot be characterized as humanitarian intervention; they do, however, demonstrate how a powerful state intent on protecting its own national interests will distort international legal norms to justify its intervention and how the involvement of a multilateral organization is no guarantee to an altruistic intervention.

Hungary (1956)

Hungary was an ally to the Axis powers during World War II. After the defeat of the Axis, a new Hungarian republic was proclaimed, and a 1947 Treaty of Peace established Hungary's borders and imposed conditions for reparations and disarmament.[6] The initial coalition government was replaced in May 1949 by a communist government whose Moscow-directed collectivization and industrialization program led to sporadic social unrest. On October 23, 1956, this unrest resulted in violent disturbances in Budapest when Hungarian police fired into a crowd of students and workers seeking better wages and greater liberty. Unrest began spreading throughout the country, and the next morning certain members of the Hungarian government, later identified by Radio Budapest as Prime Minister Andras Hegedus and the First Secretary of the Hungarian Workers Party, requested assistance from Soviet military forces already stationed in Hungary.

Due to public pressure, however, the Presidential Council of Ministers met on October 24 and duly elected, in a manner consistent with the Hungarian Constitution of August 20, 1949, a new Prime Minister, former Prime Minister Imre Nagy. Nagy declined responsibility for inviting assistance from Soviet forces and sought, instead, a negotiated withdrawal of Soviet forces stationed in Budapest. He also proposed several reforms, such as free elections, the abolition of the one-party system, and the end of forced collectivization.

On October 30, the Soviet Union announced a willingness to enter into negotiations regarding the presence of its troops in Hungary and, as well, its willingness to withdraw the forces when deemed necessary by the Hungarian government. On November 1, Imre Nagy demanded that Soviet forces be withdrawn from Hungary, gave notice of Hungary's intent to terminate adherence to the Warsaw Pact, and declared Hungary's neutrality.

---

6. This subsection is based largely on the following discussions of the intervention and the primary sources to which they refer: INTERNATIONAL COMMISSION OF JURISTS, THE HUNGARIAN SITUATION AND THE RULE OF LAW (1957); J. SZIKSZOY, THE LEGAL ASPECTS OF THE HUNGARIAN QUESTION (1963); Q. Wright, *Intervention, 1956*, 51 AM. J. INT'L L. 257 (1957).

The Soviet Union's October 30 statement, however, had also expressed confidence that the "peoples of the socialist countries will not permit foreign and international reactionary forces to undermine the basis of the people's democratic regimes . . ."[7] On November 4, Soviet forces attacked and occupied Budapest and deposed the Nagy regime. Radio Budapest and Radio Moscow announced the formation of a Revolutionary Worker-Peasant Party headed by Janos Kadar, which requested aid from Soviet troops to restore order. Hungarian regular and irregular forces resisted, but were unable to withstand the more powerful Soviet Army. By the time hostilities ended in mid-November, some 20,000 Hungarians and 3,000 Soviets were dead and some 170,000 refugees had fled Hungary, mostly to Austria. The Kadar government successfully consolidated its power. Nagy and several of his supporters were subsequently tried and executed.

The legal basis asserted by the Soviet Union for its actions was the invitation by the pre-Nagy Government of Hungary, using military forces lawfully present in Hungary pursuant to its Warsaw Pact obligations.[8] Since the Warsaw Pact envisaged use of force only against attacks by other states and not to suppress internal uprisings, however, Soviet lawyers characterized the intervention as a defensive response to the foreign funding of subversive activities and armed bands within Hungary for purposes of overthrowing the democratically elected government.[9]

The reaction of the international community was to condemn the Soviet intervention as suppressing, not advancing, human rights. Although distracted by the pending Suez crisis, the United States proposed a Security Council resolution calling on the Soviet Union to desist from its intervention. When the resolution was vetoed by the Soviet Union on November 4, a similar resolution was approved by the General Assembly pursuant to which the General Assembly considered the social unrest in Hungary as manifesting "clearly the desire of the Hungarian people to exercise and to enjoy fully their fundamental rights, freedom and independence" and condemned the Soviet actions to suppress these efforts.[10] Hungary and the Soviet Union rejected efforts by the United Nations to

7. Text of Soviet Statement (Oct. 30, 1956), *in* 35 Dep't St. Bull. 745, 746 (1956).

8. *See* U.N. GAOR, 2d Emergency Special Sess., 564th mtg., paras. 100–113, U.N. Doc. A/PV. 564 (1956).

9. *See* Broadcast Interview of G.P. Zadorozhny, Doctor of Law (Nov. 18, 1956) and Broadcast Interview of Eugenyi A. Korovin, Professor of Law and Corresponding Member, U.S.S.R. Academy of Sciences (Nov. 26, 1956), *in* International Commission of Jurists, *supra* note 6, apps. B(a), B(b).

10. G.A. Res. 1004, U.N. GAOR, 2d Emergency Special Sess., Supp. No. 1, at 2, U.N. Doc. A/3355 (1956). In the resolution, the General Assembly said it was "[c]onvinced that recent events in Hungary manifest clearly the desire of the Hungarian people to exercise and to enjoy fully their fundamental rights, freedom and independence" and that it was

send UN observers to Hungary. However, a special committee of the General Assembly issued a report, stating:

It is incontrovertible that the Nagy Government, whose legality under the Hungarian Constitution, until it was deposed, cannot be contested, protested against the entry and the use of Soviet forces on Hungarian territory, and not only asked that these forces should not intervene in Hungarian affairs, but negotiated and pressed for their ultimate withdrawal. The actions of the Nagy Government give proof of the firm desire of the Hungarians, as long as they could publicly express their aspirations, to achieve a genuinely independent international status for their country.[11]

The reason for the intervention asserted by the Soviet Union was thus certainly not convincing. Even if an invitation by the Hungarian government existed on October 24 for Soviet assistance, that consent was gone by November 1. The Soviet military actions on November 4 were not authorized by the Nagy government. The ex post facto request for assistance by the Kadar government cannot provide a sufficient basis for the deposition of the Nagy government. Nor does permission arise from the Soviet Union's rights and obligations under the Warsaw Pact; Articles 4 and 5 of the Warsaw Pact speak of consultation and assistance upon request in the event of an "armed attack" by another state or group of states, an event clearly lacking in this situation.

If the Soviet Union's asserted basis for its intervention is unconvincing, can a justification nevertheless be found in the Soviet Union's claimed desire to protect the human rights of Hungarian nationals? The Soviet statements do refer to the presence in Hungary of "reaction and counter-revolution, which are trying to take advantage of the discontent of part of the working people to undermine the foundations of the people's democratic order in Hungary and to restore the old landlord and capitalist order."[12] Such statements reflect standard Leninist-Stalinist theory that the dictatorship of the proletariat must suppress counterrevolutionary actions by capitalist and fascist forces. As such, the statements are infused with notions familiar to the realm of human rights, that of pre-

---

"condemning the use of Soviet military forces to suppress the efforts of the Hungarian people to reassert their rights." The vote passed 50–8 with 15 abstentions.

Subsequent resolutions also emphasized that the Soviet action deprived the Hungarian people of the exercise of their fundamental rights. G.A. Res. 1005, U.N. GAOR, 2d Emergency Special Sess., Supp. No. 1, at 2, U.N. Doc. A/3355 (1956); G.A. Res. 1127, U.N. GAOR, 11th Sess., Supp. No. 17, at 63, U.N. Doc. A/3572 (1956); G.A. Res. 1130, U.N. GAOR, 11th Sess., Supp. No. 17, at 63, U.N. Doc. A/3572 (1956); G.A. Res. 1131, U.N. GAOR, 11th Sess, Supp. No. 17, at 64, U.N. Doc. A/3572 (1956).

11. *Report of the Special Committee on the Problem of Hungary*, U.N. GAOR, 11th Sess., Supp. No. 18, para. 366, U.N. Doc. A/3592 (1957).

12. Text of Soviet Statement (Oct. 30, 1956), *supra* note 7, at 746.

serving and protecting economic and social rights. Nevertheless, at their heart, the actions of the Soviet Union were designed not to foster the basic human rights of the Hungarian people but, rather, to maintain a Hungarian government allied closely with the Soviet Union, one willing to retain Soviet forces on Hungarian soil. As such, the intervention arose less from a Soviet concern with the human rights of the Hungarian people than from a concern that Soviet geo-political interests in Hungary, and perhaps in the rest of Eastern Europe, were seriously threatened.

Czechoslovakia (1968)

Social unrest in Eastern Europe was not unique to Hungary. For several years leading up to 1968, leading intellectuals and officials in Prague challenged the Czechoslovakian Communist Party's domestic and foreign policy, including the policies that had led to economic stagnation.[13] By 1968, Antonin Novotny, the conservative Czech President and Communist Party First Secretary, had lost considerable support from moderate and progressive forces in Czechoslovakia. Consequently, on January 5, he resigned his position as First Secretary and Alexander Dubček, considered a loyal communist by Moscow, was then named Communist Party First Secretary. In response to increasing public and media demands, however, Dubček pushed for greater political and social reforms. His actions, including leadership changes within the government and Party, all suggested that Czechoslovakia was on the verge of pursuing a much more liberal, progressive policy, oriented away from the Soviet bloc and toward Western Europe.

After Czech public opinion forced the resignation of Novotny from the Czech presidency in March 1968 without Soviet consent, the Soviet Union convened meetings of Soviet bloc countries to consider the potential reforms in Czechoslovakia and then began massing troops along the Czech border. On August 20 and 21, an estimated 600,000 military forces from the Soviet Union, Poland, the German Democratic Republic, Bulgaria, and Hungary crossed the border into Czechoslovakia. They met no armed resistance from the Czech government and were completely successful in occupying Czechoslovakia. The Czech government, however, followed a policy of active, nonviolent resistance, with all the major

---

13. This subsection is based largely on the following discussions of the intervention and the primary sources to which they refer: P. BERGMANN, SELF-DETERMINATION: THE CASE OF CZECHOSLOVAKIA 1968–1969 (1972); K. DAWISHA, THE KREMLIN AND THE PRAGUE SPRING (1984); G. GOLAN, THE CZECHOSLOVAK REFORM MOVEMENT: COMMUNISM IN CRISIS 1962–1968 (1971); H. SKILLING, CZECHOSLOVAKIA'S INTERRUPTED REVOLUTION (1976); J. VALENTA, SOVIET INTERVENTION IN CZECHOSLOVAKIA, 1968: ANATOMY OF A DECISION (1979).

organs of the government protesting the occupation and demanding withdrawal of the foreign forces. A one-week stalemate was broken when Soviet and Czech representatives, meeting in Moscow, compromised their positions. Certain Czech policies pursued in the spring were allowed to remain, as was the existing Czech government, albeit with certain personnel changes; the Soviet Union promised not to interfere further in Czech internal affairs; and Czechoslovakia accepted the temporary stationing of foreign troops in the country pending a withdrawal and promised to carry out "effective measures serving Socialist powers."

While the Soviet Union initially claimed that Czech party and government leaders had requested assistance in repulsing reactionary forces, [14] the Soviet Union eventually justified its actions by arguing that the world Socialist community had the right to intervene whenever socialism was under attack in a fraternal socialist country. In an article in *Pravda*, it argued:

The anti-Socialist elements in Czechoslovakia actually covered up the demand for so-called neutrality and Czechoslovakia's withdrawal from the Socialist community with talk about the right of nations to self-determination. . . . Such self-determination, as a result of which NATO troops would have been able to come up to the Soviet border, while the community of European Socialist countries would have been split, in effect encroaches upon the vital interests of the peoples of these countries and conflicts, as the very root of it, with the right of these people to Socialist self-determination. Discharging their internationalist duty toward the fraternal peoples of Czechoslovkia and defending their own Socialist gains, the USSR and the other Socialist states had to act decisively, and they did act against the anti-Socialist forces in Czechoslavkia. [15]

Outside the Soviet bloc, the international community once again criticized the intervention. The Security Council considered the situation at five meetings held between August 21 and August 24, 1968. A draft Security Council resolution condemning the intervention and calling for the withdrawal of foreign forces [16] obtained ten votes but failed to pass due to a negative vote by a permanent member, the Soviet Union. After Soviet and Czech representatives reached agreement in Moscow on nor-

---

14. On the day of the intervention, Moscow's explanation to President Lyndon Johnson, passed through Soviet Ambassador to the United States Anatoly Dobrynin, was that there had been "a conspiracy of internal and external reaction against the social system" in Czechoslovakia and that the Warsaw Pact nations had intervened in response to a request for help from the Czech government. A. Dobrynin, In Confidence: Moscow's Ambassador to America's Six Cold War Presidents 180 (1995).

15. The article, written by Pravda's specialist in ideological matters, appeared on September, 26, 1968. Facts on File 1968: World News Digest with Index 417–18 (1968). For a translation, *see Text of Pravda Article Justifying Invasion of Czechoslovakia*, N.Y. Times, Sept. 27, 1968, at 3, *reprinted in* 7 I.L.M. 1323.

16. U.N. SCOR, 23rd Sess., 1442d mtg. at 3, U.N. Doc. S/8761 and Add.1 (1968).

malization of relations, the matter was withdrawn from the Security Council's agenda and was not voted on in the General Assembly.

As in the case of Hungary, this intervention spoke rhetorically of protecting economic and social rights while in fact it thwarted the aspirations of the Czech people who, operating through their existing constitutional and political structures, sought greater political and economic freedom. Once again, the Soviet Union and its satellite states feared not just the defection of Czechoslovakia from Soviet bloc control but also the implications for similar changes in other Soviet bloc states, all of which were experiencing varying levels of social unrest. An interesting element of the intervention is that, unlike the intervention in Hungary, it was conducted under the auspices of a multinational force. This approach presumably lent greater credence to the Soviet theory that Socialist states must together ensure the preservation of working class rights and that, to that end, political sovereignty of any particular state must give way to a higher political and moral authority exercised pursuant to the collective interests of Socialist states. Although this theory of limited sovereignty has antecedents in earlier events, such as the intervention in Hungary, the theory is commonly known as "the Brezhnev doctrine." The Brezhnev doctrine expresses an ideological view to justify states collectively intervening in the affairs of another state; the doctrine itself, however, may have withered away even during the Cold War when the Soviet Union signed the 1975 Helsinki Accords.[17]

2. Belgium and the United States in the Congo (1964)

On July 30, 1960, Belgium granted the Democratic Republic of the Congo its independence.[18] The ensuing political instability and violence resulted in the deployment of UN peacekeeping forces to the Congo, which remained until June 30, 1964. After the UN forces departed, Prime Minister Moise Tshombe was sworn in as the leader of a government of reconciliation. But civil war raged in the Congo, with rebel forces in control of most of the countryside. On August 5, 1964, rebel forces took Stanleyville. One month later the rebels proclaimed a new

17. Final Act of the Conference on Security and Cooperation in Europe, Aug. 1, 1975, Dep't St. Pub. No. 8826, Gen. Foreign Pol'y Series 298, *reprinted in* 14 I.L.M. 1292, 1 International Law & World Order: Basic Documents I.D.9 (B. Weston ed., 1994) [hereinafter Weston] (principle eight provides that all people have the right to determine their internal status without external interference).

18. This subsection is based largely on the following discussions of the intervention and the primary sources to which they refer: H. Epstein, Revolt in the Congo (1965); Franck & Rodley, *supra* note 5, at 287–89; H. Weisberg, *The Congo Crisis 1964: A Case Study in Humanitarian Intervention*, 12 Va. J. Int'l L. 261 (1972).

"Popular Revolutionary Government," headed by Christophe Gbenye. In late September, Gbenye announced that some 1,300 foreigners in Stanleyville (mostly Belgians, Britons, Canadians, Greeks, and Italians) would not be allowed to leave. By November there were reports that several of the foreigners had been slain and that more deaths were likely. On November 21, Tshombe authorized the Belgian government to send a military force to rescue the foreigners, with the United States furnishing transportation. The mission commenced on November 24 with the airdropping of Belgian paratroopers and lasted about one week. Some 2,000 people were evacuated to safe territory, virtually all of them foreigners.

Belgium and the United States characterized their intervention as a humanitarian rescue mission carried out with the authority of the legitimate government of the Congo.[19] In their statements, the primary concern for their own nationals is apparent, but also apparent is a concern for the well-being of "civilians in general in the region of Stanleyville" and the lives of "innocent Congolese." Thus, while the statements suggest that the intervention by Belgium and the United States was undertaken primarily to rescue their own nationals, a conscious decision was made by them to include in the evacuation any other civilians considered threatened.

During the debates in the Security Council, there was vociferous reaction to the intervention by much of the international community. Some states asserted that the intervention represented white racism (whites shooting blacks to save whites). Others charged that the intervention was a pretext for assisting the pro-Western Tshombe government in the Congo and the product of a colonialist mentality. Interestingly, a few African states expressly stated that force could not be used to protect human rights.[20] The debate resulted in a Security Council resolution that deplored the events in the Congo but did not condemn the intervention.[21]

There is no reason to believe that the motive for the intervention was primarily to protect the human rights of Congolese nationals. The apparent threat to foreigners and the limited nature of the operation (regardless of the incidental evacuation of some Congolese as well) essentially confirm the primary justification asserted by the intervening

19. For Belgium, *see* Statement by the Belgian Government (Nov. 20, 1964), *in* 51 Dep't St. Bull. 840 (1964). For the United States, see Department of State Press Release 499 (Nov. 24, 1964), *in* 51 Dep't St. Bull. 841 (1964); U.S. Letter to the Security Council (Nov. 21, 1964), *in* 51 Dep't St. Bull. 840 (1964).

20. For a discussion of these debates, *see* Weisberg, *supra* note 18, at 266–74.

21. S.C. Res. 199, U.N. SCOR, 19th Sess., 1189th mtg. at 18, U.N. Doc. S/INF/19/Rev.1 (1966).

states. Further, the express consent to the intervention by the widely recognized government of the Congo weighs against regarding the intervention as evidencing a right of unilateral humanitarian intervention, although the minimal territorial control of the Tshombe government may call into question whether its consent alone was sufficient.

3. The United States in the Dominican Republic (1965)

For thirty years (1930–61), General Rafael Trujillo served as the authoritarian ruler of the Dominican Republic, a reign characterized by terror and violence.[22] Ultimately, diplomatic and economic sanctions imposed by other Organization of American States (OAS) members encouraged internal efforts to depose Trujillo, who was assassinated on May 30, 1961. A violent and protracted leadership crisis ensued. In 1963, the democratically elected Juan Bosch was ousted in a military coup. A three-man civilian junta led by President Reid Cabral assumed power. Cabral proved an unpopular leader, and on April 24, 1965 a revolt broke out within the military, with the rebels calling for reinstatement of the constitutionally elected Bosch. These "constitutionalists," who arguably included communist supporters, were opposed by other elements of the military (the "loyalists"). After several days of fighting, the constitutionalists had gained the upper hand, but the situation had deteriorated to the extent that the United States asserted that the safety of its nationals in Santo Domingo was threatened.

On April 28 the United States intervened with several hundred troops, which grew over several days to nearly 23,000. The U.S. deployment was designed in part to protect and evacuate its nationals, but also to prevent further fighting and to create a security zone around the U.S. and foreign embassies. Due to criticisms by other states, the United States sought to multilateralize the intervention by securing the involvement of the OAS. On the night of April 29–30, the Council of the OAS called upon the Dominican Republic factions to cease fighting and to allow the establishment of an "international neutral zone of refuge, encompassing

---

22. This subsection is based largely on the following discussions of the intervention and the primary sources to which they refer: J. Cabranes, *Human Rights and Non-Intervention in the Inter-American System*, 65 MICH. L. REV. 1147, 1171–75 (1967); C. Fenwick, *The Dominican Republic: Intervention or Collective Self-Defense?*, 60 AM. J. INT'L L. 64 (1966); D. KURZMAN, SANTO DOMINGO: REVOLT OF THE DAMNED (1965); A. LOWENTHAL, THE DOMINICAN INTERVENTION (1972); V. Nanda, *The United States' Action in the 1965 Dominican Crisis: Impact on World Order* (pt. 1), 43 Denv. L.J. 439 (1966), (pt. 2), 44 DENVER L.J. 225 (1967); J. SLATER, INTERVENTION AND NEGOTIATION: THE UNITED STATES AND THE DOMINICAN REVOLUTION (1970); T. SZULC, DOMINICAN DIARY (1965); A. Thomas, Jr. & A. Thomas, *The Dominican Republic Crisis 1965: Legal Aspects, in* THE DOMINICAN REPUBLIC CRISIS 1965, at 1 (J. Carey ed., 1967).

the geographic area of the city of Santo Domingo immediately surrounding the embassies of foreign governments, the inviolability of which will be respected by all opposing forces and within which nationals of all countries will be given safe haven."[23] On May 1, an OAS meeting of Ministers of Foreign Affairs established a five-member commission to investigate and seek a diplomatic solution to the crisis.[24] The same group, on May 6, by a very narrow vote, requested the OAS states to make forces available to form an inter-American force for use in the Dominican Republic under OAS authority to maintain, among other things, "the security of [Dominican Republic] inhabitants and the inviolability of human rights."[25] The force was formed and placed under the command of a general of the Brazilian Army on May 31. U.S. forces under U.S. command were then largely withdrawn, but U.S. troops formed the core of the multinational force. Efforts by various entities to mediate a resolution of the crisis were initially unsuccessful, but a three-man Ad Hoc Committee authorized by the OAS[26] eventually produced a political solution. General elections were held in June 1966 and all foreign forces were withdrawn by September of that year.

The United States initially asserted that its intervention was necessary to protect U.S. nationals and to escort them and nationals of other countries to the United States.[27] Moreover, the United States asserted that its presence was requested by "military authorities in the Dominican Republic," by which was meant the loyalists.[28] Although the United States clung to this justification in the first two days of the intervention, thereby provoking criticism that the extensive deployment went beyond this objective, ultimately it claimed that the additional deployment of forces was to preserve the Dominican people's right to a free choice of government

23. Council Resolution of April 29–30, 1965, OEA/Ser.G/III/C-sa-569(4), *reprinted in* O.A.S. ANN. REP. SECRETARY GEN. FISCAL YEAR 1964–1965, OEA/Ser.D/III.16 at 19; 52 DEP'T ST. BULL. 741 (1965).

24. *Special Committee to Seek the Re-establishment of Peace and Normal Conditions in the Dominican Republic*, May 1, 1965, *reprinted in* O.A.S ANN. REP. SECRETARY GEN. FISCAL YEAR 1964–1965, OEA/Ser.D/III.16 at 4; 52 DEP'T ST. BULL. 741 (1965). The member states of this committee were Argentina, Brazil, Colombia, Guatemala, and Panama.

25. *Urgent Appeal for Aid to the Dominican Republic*, May 6, 1965, *reprinted in* O.A.S. ANN. REP. SECRETARY GEN. FISCAL YEAR 1964–1965, OEA/Ser.D/III.16 at 4–5; 52 DEP'T ST. BULL. 862–63 (1965) (para. 2).

26. *Ad Hoc Committee for the Restoration of Democratic Order in the Dominican Republic*, June 2, 1965, *reprinted in* O.A.S. ANN. REP. SECRETARY GEN. FISCAL YEAR 1964–1965, OEA/Ser.D/III.16 at 6; 52 DEP'T ST. BULL. 1018 (1965).

27. *See, e.g.,* U.N. SCOR, 20th Sess., 1200th mtg. at 5–6, U.N. Doc. S/PV.1200 (1965) (statement of U.S. representative to the Security Council).

28. Statement by President Lyndon Johnson (Apr. 28, 1965), *in* 52 DEP'T ST. BULL. 738, 738 (1965); U.S. Letter to the Security Council (Apr. 29, 1965), *in* 52 DEPT. ST. BULL. 739 (1965).

and to prevent the forcible seizure of power by Communists.[29] Amidst these statements are references to avoiding a "bloodbath," creating a safe area for "humanitarian reasons," and avoiding physical danger to Dominican Republic nationals.[30] The United States asserted that it had the evidence to prove the threat of a Communist takeover, but that it could not release the evidence for security reasons.[31] After the OAS Council passed its April 30 resolution, the United States justified its efforts to create a security zone on that basis.[32]

Although several countries supported the intervention (Britain, France, The Netherlands, and Taiwan), many states were openly critical during the Security Council debate on this matter. They accepted the right to protect one's own nationals, but criticized the United States for exceeding this step by maintaining its forces in the Dominican Republic. Some expressly charged that the United States had intervened to prevent the "leftist" constitutionalists from prevailing, while others viewed the action as symptomatic of U.S. "imperial" hegemony and "gunboat diplomacy." The United States sought to argue that it was for the OAS in the first instance to address the crisis; the Soviet Union and Cuba responded that even such action by the OAS was enforcement action and, under Chapter VIII of the Charter, could not proceed without Security Council authorization.[33] The U.S. effort to engage the OAS in the resolution of the crisis undoubtedly assisted in deflecting criticism that might otherwise have existed.[34] Ultimately the Security Council did not condemn the action (it would have faced a certain veto from the United States). In-

29. *See, e.g.*, T. Mann, The Dominican Crisis: Correcting Some Misconceptions, Address Before the Inter-American Press Association (Oct. 12, 1965), *in* 53 DEP'T ST. BULL. 730, 736 (1965) (Under Secretary of State) ("All those in our Government who had full access to official information were convinced that the landing of additional troops was necessary in view of the clear and present danger of the forcible seizure of power by the Communists."). For other citations, *see* Nanda (pt. 2), *supra* note 22, at 226–230.

30. *See, e.g.*, Statement by President Johnson (Apr. 30, 1965), *in* 52 DEP'T ST. BULL. 742, 742 (1965) ("There is a great danger to the life [sic] of foreign nationals and of thousands of Dominican citizens, our fellow citizens of this hemisphere.").

31. *See* Nanda (pt. 2), *supra* note 22, at 228–29.

32. Statement by President Johnson (May 1, 1965), *in* 52 DEP'T ST. BULL. 743 (1965).

33. U.N. SCOR, 20th Sess., 1196th mtg. at 44, U.N. Doc. S/PV.1176 (1965); U.N. SCOR, 20th Sess., 1198th mtg. at 16,29, U.N. Doc. S/PV.1198 (1965); U.N. SCOR, 20th Sess., 1200th mtg. at 19–20, U.N. Doc. S/PV.1200 (1965).

34. *See, e.g.*, the statement of the representative of The Netherlands to the Security Council, which concluded:

For all of these reasons which I have mentioned—tradition, the text of the Charter of the United Nations, and practical considerations—my delegation believes that the Security Council should, in compliance with Article 52, paragraph 3 . . . encourage, in the

stead, it passed a resolution calling for a ceasefire and for the Secretary-General to send an observer to the Dominican Republic.[35]

There undoubtedly were some concerns by the United States for the well-being of U.S. and foreign nationals in the Dominican Republic. The scope of the intervention, however, makes clear that this was not the primary reason for the intervention. The U.S. government position that there existed a threat of imminent Communist takeover is difficult to accept without any convincing evidence; indeed, the evidence made publicly available suggests that the perception of such a threat was not wellfounded.[36] In the end, however, such a perception, well-founded or not, appears to have existed within the U.S. government and among many members of the Congress, and this perception, along with the desire to protect American lives, served as the basis for convincing the American public that the intervention was necessary. As such, the primary reason for the U.S. intervention appears to lie more with a concern with the national security of the United States than with the human rights of the people of the Dominican Republic. Much of the U.S. rhetoric was infused with notions familiar to the realm of human rights, that of preserving and protecting political rights and freedoms and of preventing bloodshed. Still, the actions of the United States arose less from a concern with the human rights of the people of the Dominican Republic—rights that had been largely ignored by the United States for decades—than from a concern (valid or not) that its geo-political interests in the Caribbean were threatened.

4. India in East Pakistan (1971)

When Pakistan gained its independence from Great Britain, it was a divided country perched on the northwest and northeast flanks of also

---

words of the Charter, the settlement of this local dispute through regional arrangements, which means in this case through the Organization of American States.

U.N. SCOR, 20th Sess., 1202 mtg. at 4, U.N. Doc. S/PV.1202 (1965).

35. S.C. Res. 203, U.N. SCOR, 20th Sess., 1208th mtg. at 10, U.N. Doc. S/INF/20/Rev.1 (1967).

36. T. Draper, *The Dominican Crisis: A Case Study in American Policy*, COMMENTARY, Dec. 1965, at 33. Draper conducts an extensive study of the day-by-day events surrounding the intervention. Based on that study, he concurs with Senator William Fulbright's assessment, 111 CONG. REC. 23001 (Sept. 15, 1965), that, right from the start, the U.S. intervention was for the purpose of preventing the victory of a revolutionary force that was judged to be Communist dominated. *Id.* at 50. At the same time, Draper concludes that this judgment was based largely on the views of two men—U.S. Ambassador W. Tapley Bennett Jr. and special presidential envoy John Bartlow Martin—who had no basis for those views. *Id.* at 52–62.

newly independent India.[37] Both halves of Pakistan shared a Muslim faith, but otherwise were quite different ethnically and linguistically. Although East Pakistan had the greater population, West Pakistan was economically and militarily dominant and controlled the dictatorial Pakistani government.

West Pakistani denial of political rights to East Pakistan led to widespread social and political unrest. Although national elections were held in 1970 to appease this unrest, the government refused to summon the National Assembly when East Pakistan's autonomy-oriented political party (the Awami League) won a majority of the seats in the National Assembly. At the same time, the Pakistani army engaged in certain hostile acts against India, including the bombing of Indian villages along the India-Pakistan border.

In March 1971, after the leader of the Awami League issued a "Declaration of Emancipation," the West Pakistani army began indiscriminately to destroy property and to murder, torture, and rape unarmed East Pakistani civilians, with deaths estimated as high as one million. Some 10 million East Pakistani refugees fled, mostly into India. On November 21, 1971 India intervened in East Pakistan and engaged the Pakistani army. After one month the latter surrendered. East Pakistan was proclaimed a new state—Bangladesh—which was subsequently recognized by the international community and admitted to the United Nations.

The crisis was discussed by the UN Security Council on December 4 and the UN General Assembly on December 7. India stated to both organs that it had intervened militarily in response to aggression committed by Pakistan, consisting of the bombing of Indian villages and the creation of conditions for a massive migration of refugees into India. At the same time, India made note of the human rights atrocities committed by the Pakistani army and contended that "civilized behavior" called upon India to protect the East Pakistanis.

---

37. This subsection is based largely on the following discussions of the intervention and the primary sources to which they refer: M. Akehurst, *Humanitarian Intervention, in* INTERVENTION IN WORLD POLITICS 95 (H. Bull ed., 1984); *Documents: Civil War in Pakistan*, 4 N.Y.U. J. INT'L L. & POL. 524 (1971); Franck & Rodley, *supra* note 5; V. Nanda, *Self-Determination in International Law: The Tragic Tale of Two Cities—Islamabad (West Pakistan) and Dacca (East Pakistan)*, 66 AM. J. INT'L L. 321 (1972); V. Nanda, *A Critique of the United Nations Inaction in the Bangladesh Crisis*, 49 DENV. L.J. 53 (1972); M. Nawaz, *Bangla Desh and International Law*, 11 INDIAN J. INT'L L. 251 (1971); J. Salzberg, *U.N. Prevention of Human Rights Violations: The Bangladesh Case*, 27 INT'L ORG. 115 (1973); F. TESÓN, HUMANITARIAN INTERVENTION: AN INQUIRY INTO LAW AND MORALITY 179–188 (1988); N. RONZITTI, RESCUING NATIONALS ABROAD THROUGH MILITARY COERCION AND INTERVENTION ON GROUNDS OF HUMANITY 95–97 (1985).

India's assertion that it was acting in response to aggression does not seem credible given the relatively minor bombing incidents along the border. Such skirmishes had been a feature of Indian-Pakistani relations ever since their independence, and in any event the skirmishes were wildly disproportionate to full-scale intervention by India in East Pakistan. Whether the massive flow of refugees can also be considered an "act of aggression" is likewise doubtful; a better case is made that they were a threat to international peace and security in the region.

Although India's statements emphasized self-defense as the primary justification for its intervention, it seems more likely that India had other reasons. First, in light of the enmity between India and Pakistan, India likely believed that its geo-political interests were advanced by a partitioning of Pakistan.[38] Second, India undoubtedly had a general concern for maintaining peace and security in the region, which was threatened by continued unrest in East Pakistan. Third, due perhaps to its ethnic links, India likely intervened due to three humanitarian concerns: the widespread abuses by the Pakistani army in East Pakistan, the massive suffering caused by the movement of refugees out of East Pakistan, and the efforts by the East Pakistanis to gain their autonomy.

With the exception of a few states (Bulgaria, Czechoslovakia, Hungary, Poland, the Soviet Union), the international community did not condone India's intervention. The debates in both the Security Council and the General Assembly indicate that, notwithstanding the human rights situation in East Pakistan, India's intervention was viewed as itself a threat to international peace. During the fighting, due to the negative vote of the Soviet Union, the Security Council was deadlocked and referred the matter to the General Assembly.[39] The General Assembly declared that the hostilities between India and Pakistan were a threat to international peace and security and called upon both parties to withdraw their forces, which in effect was directed at Indian forces in Pakistan since there were no Pakistani forces in India. At the same time, the General Assembly urged that "efforts be intensified," in accordance with the principles and purposes of the Charter, to bring about the restoration of "conditions necessary for the voluntary return of . . . refugees,"

---

38. *See* S. Talbot, *The Subcontinent: Ménage à Trois*, 50 FOREIGN AFF. 698, 698 (1971–72); S. Schanberg, *Pakistan Divided*, 50 FOREIGN AFF. 125, 126 (1971).

39. S.C. Res. 303, U.N. SCOR, 26th Sess., 1608th mtg. at 10, U.N. Doc. S/INF/27 (1972), *reprinted in* 11 I.L.M. 123. The vote was 11–0, with four abstentions. After the fall of Dacca, the Security Council passed a resolution calling for a ceasefire and withdrawal of all armed forces to their respective territories. S.C. Res. 307, U.N. SCOR, 26th Sess., 1621st mtg. at 11, U.N. Doc. S/INF/27 (1972), *reprinted in* 11 I.L.M. 125. The vote was 13–0, with two abstentions.

which in effect was directed at the human rights atrocities of the Pakistani army.[40] The overall tenor of the resolutions, confirmed by the debates, is that the issue of human rights in East Pakistan, while of concern to the international community, did not justify India's resort to armed intervention.

Ultimately, the intervention in East Pakistan stands as a good example of how an intervention that yields significant human rights benefits may nevertheless raise considerable concerns about its effect on the maintenance of international peace. It is also a good example of how the weighing of those two concerns will not necessarily favor the protection of human rights.

5. Syria in Lebanon (1976)

Always a crossroads of the Middle East, Lebanon in the post-World War II era comprised a patchwork of ethnic and religious communities.[41] Muslim Sunni, Shia, and Druze communities coexisted with Christian Maronite, Greek Orthodox, and Greek Catholic communities under a constitution that sought to take account of all of these factions, and in so doing left a relatively weak central government.

After 1948, Palestine refugees flowed into Lebanon and, by the 1970s, some 400,000 were living in rudimentary camps, including armed militants seeking recovery of their lands from Israel.[42] The Lebanese Maronite Christians—the richest group in Lebanon—perceived a threat to the stability of Lebanon from the presence of the Palestinians, and in April 1975 violence broke out between the communities which could not be controlled by the weak Lebanese government. This led to full-scale civil war, with the possibility that the Palestinians—in alliance with Druze Muslims—could take control of the country.

While such an outcome might have seemed welcome to Lebanon's Muslim neighbor Syria, in fact Syria's President Hafiz Assad feared it would inevitably lead to a military confrontation between Syria and Israel for which Syria was not prepared. From April to December 1975, Syria sought through noncoercive, diplomatic means to bring an end to the fighting. When these efforts failed, Syria, in the first half of 1976, sup-

---

40. G.A. Res. 2793, U.N. GAOR, 26th Sess., Supp. No. 29, at 3, para. 2, U.N. Doc. A/8429 (1972). The vote was 104–11, with ten abstentions.

41. This subsection is based largely on the following discussions of the intervention and the primary sources to which they refer: A. DAWISHA, SYRIA AND THE LEBANESE CRISIS (1980); D. HIRO, LEBANON FIRE AND EMBERS: A HISTORY OF THE LEBANESE CIVIL WAR 31–51 (1993); S. MACKEY, LEBANON: DEATH OF A NATION 165–68 (1989); N. WEINBERGER, SYRIAN INTERVENTION IN LEBANON: THE 1975–76 CIVIL WAR (1986).

42. *See* P. CALVOCORESSI, WORLD POLITICS SINCE 1945, at 248 (5th ed. 1987).

ported the Palestinian/Druze forces as a means of ending the fighting, but this merely exacerbated the problem. On June 1, 1976, about 4,000 Syrian troops and 250 tanks moved into Lebanon, engaged the Palestinian/Druze forces, and actively supported the Christians in regaining military dominance.[43]

By the end of September, Syrian forces had inflicted a total defeat on the Palestinian/Druze forces, forcing them to accept a ceasefire. Facing political realities, a mini-summit of Arab leaders in Riyadh on October 16 and a full Arab summit in Cairo on October 25 endorsed Syria's action. While the Cairo summit called for the establishment of a 30,000-strong multinational Arab peacekeeping force to implement the ceasefire and a final settlement, only token numbers of forces could be provided by the other Arab states; Syrian forces remained the backbone of the peacekeeping operation. Ultimately, a multifactional Lebanese government was established under a Maronite Christian President.

The intensity of geo-politics in the Middle East make this intervention difficult to assess. President Assad asserted two years later, on August 9, 1978, that the intervention was "in response to requests and pleas for assistance, which came to us from hundreds of families, from thousands of Lebanese citizens, and from many [different] sides; and [we entered] with the approval of the legitimate authorities in Lebanon."[44] While it appears that some Lebanese citizens did request assistance from Syria, the de jure Lebanese authorities, including the President of Lebanon, apparently were not aware of Syria's plans to intervene.[45] Certainly Syria eventually succeeded in reducing the widespread fighting that was causing the deaths of thousands of persons (including innocent civilians) and in preventing the creation of a Muslim government that might have shown little care for Lebanese Christians. Yet Syria did so by conducting a major military operation that crushed Palestinian and Druze forces. Syria's primary motivation appears not to have been the well-being of the Christian communities but, rather, its own national security interests, which were closely tied to Palestinian activities in Lebanon and their propensity for provoking war with Israel. One careful analysis of the intervention makes the case that the Syrian decisionmakers perceived the domestic conflict in Lebanon as a clear and ominous threat to fundamental Syrian values that had to be defended at all times, even at the risk of military involvement.[46] Syria's concerns appear borne out by the facts; Syria was primarily successful in disarming Palestinians in the north of

43. Dawisha, *supra* note 41, at 135–38.

44. Syrian Institute Interview with Syrian President Hafiz Assad (Aug. 9, 1978), *quoted in* Weinberger, *supra* note 41, at 140.

45. Weinberger, *supra* note 41, at 210–11.

46. *See generally* Dawisha, *supra* note 41.

Lebanon, but the continued fighting between Palestinians and Christians in the south of Lebanon ultimately led to the establishment by Israeli forces in southern Lebanon of a semi-independent Christian state as a "security zone." [47]

The intervention was not well received by the international community. Syria was reviled by most of the Arab world for supporting the Lebanese Christian community: the Saudis expressed their disapproval, Egypt withdrew its diplomatic mission from Damascus, and Iraq cut off oil exports to Syria. Syria's superpower sponsor, the Soviet Union, called for an end to the intervention. [48] The United States, however, was not critical; Assad assured the United States that Syria's objective was solely to end the fighting in Lebanon and that it would pose no threat to Israel's security. [49] The matter was not raised in either the Security Council or the General Assembly, where Middle East questions were dominated by the conflict between Israel and its Arab neighbors.

Thus, there were humanitarian benefits to the Syrian intervention. Syria's primary motivation and the conduct of the intervention indicate, however, that it does not stand as an example of humanitarian intervention.

6. Vietnam in Cambodia (1978)

For centuries, the declining empire of Kampuchea (or Cambodia) struggled to preserve its territorial integrity from encroachments by its neighbors to the east (Vietnam) and to the West (Laos). [50] Over time, it lost areas historically under its control, which then became inhabited by demographic mixtures ethnically and culturally associated with both Cambodia and its neighbors. Prince Norodom Sihanouk ruled Cambodia from 1941 until 1970, when he was overthrown by an internal coup. Whereas Sihanouk ostensibly pursued a policy of neutrality with respect to the war that raged in Vietnam during the 1960s, his successor, General

47. This security zone covers approximately one-tenth of Lebanon's total area. In 1982, Israel also invaded deep into Lebanese territory in an effort to destroy Palestinian military capability.

48. *See generally* DAWISHA, *supra* note 41, at 135–38.

49. HIRO, *supra* note 41, at 39.

50. This subsection is based largely on the following discussions of the intervention and the primary sources to which they refer: M. Bazyler, *Reexamining the Doctrine of Humanitarian Intervention in Light of the Atrocities in Kampuchea and Ethiopia*, 23 STAN. J. INT'L L. 547 (1987); W. BURCHETT, THE CHINA-CAMBODIA-VIETNAM TRIANGLE (1981); CAMBODIA 1975–1978: RENDEZVOUS WITH DEATH (K. Jackson ed., 1989); N. CHANDA, BROTHER ENEMY: THE WAR AFTER THE WAR (1986); G. KLINTWORTH, VIETNAM'S INTERVENTION IN CAMBODIA IN INTERNATIONAL LAW (1989).

Lon Nol, openly sided with the South Vietnamese forces and the United States. This open association prompted North Vietnamese and Chinese support for a Cambodian communist insurgency, the Khmer Rouge, which plunged Cambodia into civil war. The civil war, along with heavy U.S. bombing in Cambodia of North Vietnamese and Viet Cong forces, resulted in massive population displacement and serious losses in food production in Cambodia. Lon Nol was himself overthrown in April 1975 by the Khmer Rouge, just as the North Vietnamese were consolidating their power in Vietnam.

Within a year of assuming power, the Khmer Rouge (led by Pol Pot) began a campaign of remaking Cambodian society by emptying the cities and destroying everybody and everything associated with the prior regime or with Western countries. The widespread killings, torture, and persecution by the Khmer Rouge from 1975 through 1979 have been amply documented; it is estimated that more than one million Cambodians (perhaps up to one-quarter of the population of 7.3 million) perished. At the same time, and despite the initial support the Khmer Rouge received from North Vietnam, the Khmer Rouge pursued an anti-Vietnamese posture. They not only killed Vietnamese civilians living in Cambodia, but also, by April and May 1977, began destroying Vietnamese villages and killing Vietnamese civilians in a series of raids along the Cambodia-Vietnam border, in some instances penetrating as much as four miles inside Vietnam.[51] These incursions were more than skirmishes; they were multidivisional attacks backed up by the massing of some 100,000 troops along the border.[52]

On December 25, 1978, Vietnamese forces crossed into Cambodia, accompanied by forces of a newly formed "United Front for the National Salvation of Kampuchea" led by a former Khmer Rouge military commander, Heng Samrin. Within two weeks, these forces sent Khmer Rouge forces fleeing into rural areas and seized the capital, Phnom Penh. On January 8, 1979, a new People's Republic of Kampuchea was established, headed by Heng Samrin. Domestic communist and noncommunist resistance to the regime, however, compelled Vietnam to keep its forces stationed in Cambodia throughout the 1980s. On October 23, 1991, a set of accords aimed at bringing national reconciliation to Cambodia was signed in Paris, leading to 1993 elections supervised by the United Nations and the restoration of King Norodom Sihanouk as a constitutional monarch.

Vietnam's primary justification for its intervention was self-defense.

51. KLINTWORTH, *supra* note 50, at 19.
52. *Id.* at 22.

The Vietnamese Foreign Ministry claimed that the Khmer Rouge had waged a "large-scale aggressive war" against Vietnam to which it was entitled to respond.[53] Vietnam also stated that Pol Pot had been deposed by the United Front, which Vietnam had assisted at its request.[54] Only in passing did Vietnamese statements refer to the human rights abuses committed by the Khmer Rouge.

Despite what appeared to be a significant gain for humanity in the overthrow of Pol Pot, the international community, with the exception of the Soviet bloc, condemned the intervention. After a proposed Security Council resolution calling for the withdrawal of Vietnamese forces was vetoed by the Soviet Union, the General Assembly censured the intervention.[55] Few countries engaged in diplomatic or commercial relations with the Heng Samrin regime, and the UN General Assembly consistently voted to reject its credentials. The explanation for this condemnation undoubtedly lies in the global isolation of communist Vietnam after the withdrawal of U.S. forces from that country and the fall of Saigon, in the concern of states with Vietnam's own human rights record, and in the concern that Vietnam's reasons for intervening might be a precursor to greater regional ambitions. Although not advanced by Vietnam as a primary reason for its intervention, it should be noted that, in the General Assembly debates, several states argued that Vietnam could not justify its use of force in order to protect human rights in Cambodia.[56]

The evidence of Cambodian aggression against Vietnam is sufficient to support a proportionate response in self-defense by Vietnam to neutralize the military forces along its border. Whether this response justifiably included seizure of the capital, installation of a puppet regime, and maintenance of Vietnamese forces in Cambodia for a decade is less clear. An argument can be made that, notwithstanding its superior forces, Vietnam believed that the only way of eliminating the threat from Cambodia was to depose the Pol Pot regime. In any event, whether Vietnam intervened also out of concern for the human rights of Cambodians is even less clear; at best it would appear a secondary consideration. The traditional antipathy between Cambodians and Vietnamese suggests that, absent a threat to Vietnamese security or a perceived strategic gain for

53. Foreign Ministry Statement (Jan. 6, 1979), *in* F.B.I.S., ASIA/PAC. DAILY REP., Jan. 8, 1979, at K6, K6.

54. U.N. SCOR, 34th Sess., 2108th mtg. at 13, U.N. Doc. S/PV.2108 (1979).

55. G.A. Res. 34/22, U.N. GAOR, 34th Sess., Supp. No. 46, at 16, U.N. Doc. A/34/46 (1980), called for the "immediate withdrawal of all foreign forces from Kampuchea." The vote was 91–21, with 29 abstentions.

56. For citations, *see* D. Wolf, *Humanitarian Intervention*, 9 MICH. Y.B. INT'L LEGAL STUD. 333, 352 n.94 (1988).

Vietnam, it is unlikely that Vietnam would have intervened solely or even largely to prevent human rights abuses against Cambodians.

7. Tanzania in Uganda (1979)

Idi Amin came to power in Uganda in 1971, and during his dictatorial regime extensive atrocities were committed against the Ugandan people, including some 300,000 deaths.[57] Tanzania's President Julius Nyerere considered Amin a murderer and refused to sit with him on the Authority of the East African Community. In October 1978, Amin ordered his troops to cross Uganda's border with Tanzania and to occupy an area in Tanzania known as the Kagera Salient, ostensibly as a matter of Ugandan self-defense against support funnelled through that area to Ugandan dissidents. On November 1, 1978, Amin purported to annex the Kagera Salient to Uganda. President Nyerere declared the annexation an act of war and, lacking international support, Amin offered to withdraw his forces if Tanzania agreed to cease its support for Ugandan dissidents. Tanzania refused, arguing that a state of war existed due to the death, suffering, and destruction wrought by Ugandan troops in Tanzania. Amin began to withdraw his troops voluntarily, but on November 15 Tanzania attacked the Ugandan forces and Nyerere asserted his intention to depose Amin. By January 1979, some 20,000 Tanzanian forces were in Uganda, supporting a group of Ugandan rebels called the Ugandan National Liberation Front (UNLF). Amin threatened to punish Ugandans who supported the invading forces, but his forces continued to be pushed back. By late April, Tanzanian forces occupied the Ugandan capital of Kampala, Amin fled Uganda, and a new government was formed.

Initially, President Nyerere justified the intervention as a reaction to Uganda's armed attack on Tanzania, which in some instances was characterized as punitive in nature and at other times as self-defense. Also, as the intervention proceeded and Ugandan rebel forces became a factor in the intervention, Nyerere made statements stressing that the overthrow of Amin was the responsibility of the Ugandan people. Tanzania

---

57. This subsection is based largely on the following discussions of the intervention and the primary sources to which they refer: S. Chatterjee, *Some Legal Problems of Support Role in International Law: Tanzania and Uganda*, 30 INT'L & COMP. L.Q. 755 (1981); F. Hassan, *Realpolitik in International Law: After Tanzanian-Ugandan Conflict "Humanitarian Intervention" Reexamined*, 17 WILLAMETTE L. REV. 859 (1981); RONZITTI, *supra* note 37, at 102–106; TESÓN, *supra* note 37, at 159–175; C. Rousseau, *Chronique des Faits Internationaux*, 83 REV. GÉN. D. INT'L PUB. 998, 1058–59 (1979); U. Umozurike, *Tanzania's Intervention in Uganda*, 20 ARCHIV DES VÖLKERRECHTS 301 (1982); I. Wani, *Humanitarian Intervention and the Tanzania-Uganda War*, 3/2 HORN OF AFRICA 18 (1980).

continued to support the UNLF, which professed its belief in restoring democracy and human rights in Uganda. After occupying Kampala, Nyerere said that Tanzania had to "act the policeman" because Amin had said repeatedly that he would invade the Kagera Salient again.[58]

Except for a few countries (Kenya, Libya, Nigeria, Sudan), the intervention was tolerated by the international community. It was not debated in either the Security Council or the General Assembly. The Secretary-General was involved only in the latter stages of the intervention in an effort to mediate a ceasefire. The Organization for African Unity (OAU) sought to mediate at an earlier stage, but never condemned the intervention, despite nonintervention principles in the OAU Charter similar to provisions in the UN Charter, and the new government of Uganda was quickly recognized by other states. It cannot be said definitively that the international community accepted as the sole justification for the intervention either self-defense or the protection of human rights; most governments in some fashion noted both circumstances as elements of the intervention. The reaction of international scholars to the legality of the intervention was mixed. On the theory that once the Ugandan forces were removed from Tanzania there was no further right to enter Uganda and depose Amin from power, some writers have rejected the claim that Tanzania was acting in self-defense.[59]

While it is not possible in this study to assess thoroughly the nature and scope of the right of self-defense in international law, it is not self-evident that a state's right of self-defense dissipates once invading forces are expelled from that state. Indeed, a review of prior incidents of self-defense involving invading and occupying forces—from those that occurred during the Second World War up to the 1990–91 Iraq-Kuwait crisis—indicates a widespread acceptance that the defending state(s) may not only expel the occupying forces but may pursue them into their

---

58. 16 Africa Research Bulletin (Political, Social and Cultural Series) 5224 (1979), *cited in* Ronzitti, *supra* note 37, at 104.

59. Ronzitti, *supra* note 37, at 102; Tesón, *supra* note 37, at 167. Although Ronzitti asserts that the intervention in Uganda cannot be characterized as one of self-defense, he also asserts that it is not one of humanitarian intervention. Ronzitti notes that during the course of the military action, Nyerere argued that there existed "two wars," one limited to the border area fought by Tanzanian forces, which was justified on the basis of Tanzanian self-defense, and one fought by Ugandan insurgents to topple Idi Amin, which presumably does not need to be justified under international law since it was an internal conflict. However, once both rebel and Tanzanian forces succeeded in occupying the capital, Ronzitti argues that Tanzania switched its justification for intervening from self-defense to the promotion of "freedom, justice and human dignity," purely because its limited self-defense justification no longer held water. Ronzitti concludes that the humanitarian justification was not the real reason but, rather, that Nyerere wished to punish Amin for invading Tanzania. *Id.* at 103–4.

own territory and, in some instances, depose their government if necessary to prevent recurrence of the initial attack. Consequently, Tanzania's claim that it was acting in self-defense is not clearly erroneous, unless it is shown that Tanzania's security would not have been further threatened if Idi Amin remained in power. At the same time, it is evident that President Nyerere was genuinely concerned about Amin's human rights violations, considered Amin a murderer, and most likely wanted to avoid a bloodbath in Uganda from a failure to remove Amin from power. For several years, Nyerere had not considered Amin's human rights abuses as sufficient justification for invading Uganda, but once the justification of self-defense existed for intervening in Uganda the desire to prevent further human rights atrocities surely was a factor in assessing how far to carry the intervention. As such, the reason for Tanzania's intervention is best characterized as one involving mixed reasons of self-defense and protection of human rights.

8. France in Central Africa (1979)

For the first half of the twentieth century, Central Africa was a French colony.[60] The French Constitution of 1958, creating the Fifth French Republic, provided for the free association of autonomous republics within the French community. Central Africa became one of these autonomous republics and achieved full independence in 1960 under President David Dacko. Dacko's rule was characterized by severe political and economic difficulties, and in January 1966 Dacko's military Chief of Staff, Jean-Bedel Bokassa, engineered a coup d'état. Initially there was hope that Bokassa would pursue needed reforms as well as elections, so France provided Bokassa with economic and political support (the currency of the Central African Republic was tied to the French franc thereby providing significant economic stability). Bokassa, however, proved to be a ruthless and eccentric ruler, going so far as to proclaim himself emperor in December 1976. For the next two years, political opposition grew and, in response, Bokassa's forces undertook brutal atrocities. In April 1979, Bokassa's forces rounded up students and other young people suspected of opposing Bokassa and beat at least 100 to death in the presence of, and probably with the participation of, Bokassa himself.[61] That massacre prompted the Sixth Franco-African Congress meeting in Kigali in May

---

60. This subsection is based largely on the following discussion of the intervention and the primary sources to which they refer: T. O'TOOLE, THE CENTRAL AFRICAN REPUBLIC: THE CONTINENT'S HIDDEN HEART (1986); TESÓN, *supra* note 37, at 175–79; Y. ZOCTIZOUM, HISTOIRE DE LA CENTRAFRIQUE: VIOLENCE DU DÉVELOPPEMENT, DOMINATION ET INÉGALITÉS (1983).

61. O'TOOLE, *supra* note 60, at 54.

1979 to convene a Commission of Inquiry composed of judges from five African states[62] to look into the affair. The Commission's report found that Bokassa had personally participated in the massacre. In September 1979, while Bokassa was in Libya, some 1,800 French commandos were flown to Central Africa along with David Dacko. A bloodless coup occurred, and Dacko was restored to power.

Initially, the French government issued statements suggesting that first an internal coup deposed Bokassa and then the new Central African regime invited in French troops. Within a short time, however, it was quite clear that the sequence was the other way around; the French intervention had led to the coup. Once that became clear, the French government indicated that the intervention was based on humanitarian concerns.[63]

There is no reason to regard France's stated humanitarian reason as disingenuous; France had previously expressed grave concerns about the human rights situation in Central Africa. Unlike the interventions with respect to East Pakistan, Cambodia, and Uganda, there was absolutely no self-defense justification for the French intervention, either expressed by France or objectively discernible from the facts. France itself achieved no territorial gains, although for decades it had a close political and economic relationship with the Central African Republic, and the intervention solidified that relationship. Except for a few countries (Benin, Libya, Chad), the intervention was accepted by the international community. There were no resolutions issued by the Security Council or the General Assembly criticizing the intervention. An interesting feature of the intervention is that it occurred immediately after a multinational entity, the Commission of Inquiry, had determined that Bokassa had personally engaged in an incident of human rights atrocities. Overall, this incident is probably the best example of humanitarian intervention during the Cold War that was accepted as lawful by the international community.

9. The United States in Grenada (1983)

In 1974 the Caribbean Island of Grenada received its independence from Great Britain.[64] After a few years of parliamentary rule, a bloodless coup brought Maurice Bishop to power.

62. The judges were from the Ivory Coast, Liberia, Rwanda, Senegal, and Togo.
63. *See* TESÓN, *supra* note 37, at 177.
64. This subsection is based largely on the following discussion of the intervention and the primary sources to which they refer: O. Audéoud, *L'Intervention Américano-Caraibe à la Grenade*, 29 ANNUAIRE FR. D. INT'L 217 (1983); F. Boyle et al., *International Lawlessness in Grenada*, 78 AM. J. INT'L L. 172 (1984); I. Dore, *The U.S. Invasion of Grenada: Resurrection of*

The Bishop regime defined itself as Marxist-Leninist in ideological orientation and in alliance with Cuba and the Soviet Union. As such, it ended freedom of the press and other political freedoms. In mid-October 1983, disagreements within the Bishop regime led to another coup by Bishop's deputy, Bernard Coard, deposing Bishop. When Bishop's supporters marched on an army barracks where Bishop and some of his cabinet ministers were held, Coard's army fired on them, killing several. Bishop and several of his ministers were also killed, possibly by summary execution. A new "Revolutionary Military Council" declared a 96-hour shoot-on-sight curfew and the Grenadan schools and airport were closed.

The United States expressed concern about some 100 U.S. students attending medical school in Grenada, but requests to evacuate them by air and sea were denied. On October 25, 1,900 U.S. troops and 300 security personnel from neighboring islands landed in Grenada and within three days gained control of the island. An interim government was established, which ultimately led to multi-party elections in late 1984. Foreign military forces withdrew from Grenada by December 15, 1983.

The United States justified its intervention based on an invitation from the Grenadan Governor General to restore order to the island, a request from the Organization of East Caribbean States for collective security action in Grenada, and the need to protect U.S. nationals in Grenada. The United States did not advance a general right of humanitarian intervention.[65]

The legitimacy of the U.S. justifications was widely debated at the time and will not be repeated here. From a legal standpoint, the first two justifications raise some questions, but cannot be dismissed as clearly un-

---

the *"Johnson Doctrine?"* 20 STAN. J. INT'L L. 175 (1984); L. Doswald-Beck, *The Legality of the United States Intervention in Grenada*, 31 NETH. INT'L L. REV. 355 (1984); H. Fraser, *Grenada—The Sovereignty of a People*, 7 W. INDIAN L.J. 205 (1983); W. GILMORE, THE GRENADA INTERVENTION: ANALYSIS AND DOCUMENTATION (1984); E. Gordon et al., *International Law and the United States Action in Grenada: A Report*, 18 INT'L LAW. 331 (1984); C. Joyner, *The United States Action in Grenada: Reflections on the Lawfulness of Invasion*, 78 AM. J. INT'L L. 131 (1984); M. Levitin, *The Law of Force and the Force of Law: Grenada, the Falklands, and Humanitarian Intervention*, 27 HARV. INT'L L.J. 621 (1986); J. Moore, LAW AND THE GRENADA MISSION (1984); J. Moore, *Grenada and the International Double Standard*, 78 AM. J. INT'L L. 145 (1984); V. Nanda, *The United States Armed Intervention in Grenada—Impact on World Order*, 14 CAL. W. INT'L L.J. 395 (1984); TESÓN, *supra* note 37, at 188–200; D. Vagts, *International Law Under Time Pressure: Grading the Grenada Take-Home Examination*, 78 AM. J. INT'L L. 169 (1984); L. Wheeler, Note, *The Grenada Invasion: Expanding the Scope of Humanitarian Intervention*, 8 B.C. INT'L & COMP. L. REV. 413 (1985).

65. Statement of Deputy Secretary of State Kenneth Dam (Nov. 4, 1983), *in* DEP'T ST. BULL., Dec. 1983, at 79; Letter of State Department Legal Adviser Davis R. Robinson (Feb. 10, 1984), *in* 18 INT'L LAW. 381, 386 (1984).

sound. The third supports the actions designed to rescue U.S. nationals, but cannot justify the more extensive nature of the intervention. Looking beyond these justifications to see if some other underlying reason existed, some have argued that the intervention was human-rights based, in light of concerns expressed by the United States regarding human rights and the need to restore democracy in Grenada.[66] Yet an overall assessment of the intervention leads to the conclusion that the primary reason for the intervention was a desire by the U.S. Reagan Administration to reclaim Grenada from the Soviet/Cuban orbit. This was part of its overall policy to "roll-back" communism in Central America,[67] a theme that was playing out in Nicaragua and El Salvador at the same time. While in the abstract this ideological approach subsumed concerns for human rights violations by communist regimes, the dominant feature is less "pro-human rights" and more "anti-communism"; if the governing regime had committed the same abuses but had not been Marxist-Leninist oriented, it seems unlikely the United States would have intervened.

To the extent that this intervention nevertheless advanced the rights of Grenadan nationals, those rights were qualitatively different from the widespread atrocities and violence seen in the incidents discussed above. The situation in Grenada was certainly confused and even chaotic in late October 1983, but the likelihood of widespread atrocities and violence appears to have been minimal. In fact, it appears that many more persons died during the intervention (which included the inadvertent bombing of a Grenadan hospital) than died during violence following the mid-October coup. Rather, the intervention would be characterized as a new breed of humanitarian intervention, such as "intervention to restore democracy" or "pro-democratic invasion."[68]

The U.S. position, supported by leaders of the Organization of Eastern Caribbean States, generally was not accepted by the international com-

---

66. Tesón, *supra* note 37, at 192–200; A. D'Amato, International Law: Process and Prospect 354 (2d ed. 1995).

67. In his memoirs as U.S. Secretary of State, George Schultz characterizes the decision to intervene in Grenada as follows: "President Reagan's reaction was decisive. What kind of country would we be, he asked, if we refused to help small but steadfast democratic countries in our neighborhood to defend themselves against the threat of this kind of tyranny and lawlessness? Furthermore, Americans were in serious danger of being killed or taken hostage." G. Schultz, Turmoil and Triumph: My Years as Secretary of State 329 (1993).

68. For a spirited exchange in the wake of the Greneda intervention on whether international law admits a right of a state to use armed force to overthrow a despotic government, *see* W. Reisman, *Coercion and Self-Determination: Construing Charter Article 2(4)*, 78 Am. J. Int'l L. 642 (1984); O. Schachter, *The Legality of Pro-Democratic Invasion*, 78 Am. J. Int'l L. 645 (1984).

munity. A draft resolution placed before the UN Security Council condemning the intervention could not pass due to U.S. opposition. The General Assembly, however, condemned the intervention as a violation of international law;[69] the debate in the General Assembly focused primarily on the intervention as a violation of Article 2(4) of the Charter, paying little attention to the issue of human rights. No OAS member even introduced a resolution on the intervention before the OAS.[70]

Characterizing this intervention as a case of humanitarian intervention is inconsistent with the stated justifications of the main intervenor. Looking beyond the stated justifications, this intervention might be considered an example of humanitarian intervention if the denial of free elections is encompassed within the notion of widespread human rights deprivations. While this form of human rights deprivation as a basis for humanitarian intervention is probably less accepted than intervention to prevent human rights atrocities, it has served as at least a partial rationale for U.S. interventions in the Western Hemisphere, as seen in the following discussion of Panama and in the case study of Haiti in chapter 5.

10. The United States in Panama (1989–90)

General Manuel Noriega, the military strongman in Panama, was an ally of the United States during much of his career.[71] In the late 1980s, however, increased drug trafficking through Panama to the United States associated with Noriega strained relations. In February 1988, after Panamanian President Eric Arturo Delvalle attempted to fire him, Noriega managed to call a session of the Panama National Assembly, which impeached Delvalle and installed a new President. The United States imposed economic sanctions on Panama[72] and refused to recognize the new government,[73] which had important legal effects for Panama. For

69. G.A. Res. 38/7, U.N. GAOR, 38th Sess., Supp. No. 47, at 19, U.N. Doc. A/38/47 (1983).

70. MOORE, *supra* note 64, at 44, n.5.

71. This subsection is based largely on the following discussions of the intervention and the primary sources to which they refer: D. Alberts, Note, *The United States Invasion of Panama: Unilateral Military Intervention to Effectuate a Change in Government—A Continuum of Lawfulness*, 1 TRANSNAT'L L. & CONTEMP. PROB. 261 (1991); M. Hilaire, *The United States Intervention in Panama: Legal or Illegal under International Law*, 1990 R.D. INT'L SCI. DIPL. & POL. 241; J. Miller, *International Intervention: The United States Invasion of Panama*, 31 HARV. INT'L L.J. 633 (1990); J. Quigley, *The Legality of the United States Invasion of Panama*, 15 YALE J. INT'L L. 276 (1990); J. Terry, *The Panama Intervention: Law in Support of Policy*, 39 NAVAL L. REV. 5 (1990).

72. *See* M. Leich, *Contemporary Practice of the United States Relating to International Law*, 82 AM. J. INT'L L. 566 (1988).

73. White House Statement (Feb. 25, 1988), *in* DEP'T ST. BULL., May 1988, at 69.

example, the United States designated Delvalle's ambassador to the United States, Juan Sosa, as the only accredited representative of Panama entitled to withdraw extensive Panamanian funds from U.S. banks on behalf of the Republic of Panama.[74]

After two grand juries in Florida indicted Noriega on counts of drug trafficking, tensions between Panama and the United States grew even stronger. In an effort to regain international credibility, Noreiga allowed elections to be held in Panama in May 1989. International observers asserted that Guillermo Endara won the election over Noreiga's candidate, but Noriega's supporters publicly beat up Endara and his running mates, and Noriega purported to annul the election. The United States called for the Panamanian Defense Forces (PDF) to overthrow Noriega and, through the OAS, pursued bilateral and multilateral efforts to negotiate his resignation.[75] In October 1989, members of the PDF attempted a coup, but failed. The failure of U.S. forces in Panama to assist the coup leaders resulted in considerable criticism of U.S. President George Bush's Administration.

Relations between Noriega and the United States, including the 12,000 U.S. forces stationed in Panama as a part of the U.S.-Panama Canal Treaties,[76] quickly deteriorated further. On December 15, 1989, the Panamanian legislative body adopted a resolution declaring the country to be in a state of war with the United States and declaring Noriega as "Maximum Leader."[77] That same day, a U.S. Marine officer was killed by members of the PDF, another was wounded, and a third was stopped at a road block, where he was beaten and his wife threatened. In addition to U.S. forces stationed in Panama, some 15,000 U.S. citizens also lived in Panama.

On December 20, 1989 some 12,000 U.S. military forces landed in Panama, equipped with helicopter gunships and artillery. Along with other

74. This designation occurs under the Edge Act, 12 U.S.C. sec. 632 (1994). *See* Republic of Panama v. Citizens & Southern Int'l Bank, 682 F. Supp. 1544 (S.D. Fla. 1988); Republic of Panama v. Republic Nat'l Bank of N.Y., 681 F. Supp. 1066 (S.D.N.Y. 1988).

75. *See* U.S. Department of State Statements (May 8–12, 1989), *in* Dep't St. Bull., July 1989, at 67–71.

76. Treaty Concerning the Permanent Neutrality and Operation of the Panama Canal, Sept. 7, 1977, Pan.-U.S., 33 U.S.T. 1; Panama Canal Treaty, Sept. 7, 1977, Pan.-U.S., 33 U.S.T. 39.

77. Arguably, this resolution could have been considered an internal action by Panama equivalent to the declaration of a state of emergency and not an action directed toward the United States. *See* A. Rubin, *Reason and Law Reject Our Panama Invasion*, N.Y. Times, Jan. 2, 1990, A18 (letter to the editor). One commentator asserts that the resolution was Noriega's attempt "to cloak himself in the mantle of [former President] Torrijos" and that the characterization of being at war "had been a staple of the regime's rhetoric for months." J. Dinges, Our Man in Panama 306 (1990).

U.S. forces already stationed in Panama, they proceeded to rout the PDF, to force Noriega into hiding, and to install Endara as President of Panama. The United States recognized the new government and lifted its economic sanctions on Panama.[78] After turning himself in to the Papal Nunciate for diplomatic protection, Noriega was taken into custody by U.S. forces on January 3, 1990 and flown to Florida. On April 9, 1992 Noriega was convicted in a Miami federal court on eight counts of drug trafficking and narcotics-related charges. On July 10 he was sentenced to forty years in prison.[79]

The statements made by the United States at the time reveal a combination of reasons and motivations for conducting the intervention.[80] The U.S. Permanent Representative to the United Nations, Jeane Kirkpatrick, justified the U.S. action to the Security Council as follows:

In accordance with Article 51 of the United Nations Charter, United States forces have exercised their inherent right of self-defence under international law by taking action in Panama in response to armed attacks by forces under the direction of Manuel Noriega. The action is designed to protect American lives as well as to fulfil the obligations of the United States to defend the integrity of the Panama Canal Treaties.[81]

In addition, the United States asserted that it undertook the action after "consultation" with Endara and that he and his vice presidents welcomed and supported the intervention.[82] Two days later, the U.S. Permanent Representative asserted to the Security Council that the United States did not claim a right "to enforce the will of history by intervening in favor of democracy where we are not welcomed," but that the international community should welcome the restoration of democracy in

78. Address to the Nation Announcing United States Military Action in Panama, 25 WEEKLY COMP. PRES. DOC. 1974 (Dec. 20, 1989) [hereinafter Address to the Nation].

79. W. Booth, *Noriega Receives 40 Years; Panamanian Could Be Eligible for Parole After 10 Years*, WASH. POST, July 11, 1992, at A1.

80. For President Bush's initial statement, *see* Address to the Nation, *supra* note 78.

81. U.N. SCOR, 44th Sess., 2899th mtg. at 31, U.N. Doc. S/PV.2899 (1989). In his memoirs of his tenure as Secretary of State, James Baker emphasizes his support for the invasion due to a concern for the lives of U.S. citizens in Panama. J. BAKER, THE POLITICS OF DIPLOMACY: REVOLUTION, WAR & PEACE, 1989–92 188–89 (1995). Yet, Baker notes that his concern was based on a "hunch" and that a U.S. intelligence report that Noriega was actually planning on kidnapping U.S. soldiers was only received after President Bush ordered the invasion. *Id.* at 189 n. Further, Baker characterizes the December 16 murder of the U.S. soldier as the U.S. Government being "handed the reason for doing what we should have done in October," which suggests that the U.S. reasons for invading predated that time. *Id.* at 188.

82. Letter from the United States to the President of the Security Council (Dec. 20, 1989), U.N. Doc. S/21035 (1989).

Panama.[83] After General Noriega was taken into custody, President Bush stated that he ordered U.S. troops to Panama with four objectives: (1) to safeguard the lives of American citizens; (2) to help restore democracy; (3) to protect the integrity of the Panama Canal Treaties; and (4) to bring Noriega to justice.[84]

These statements prima facie indicate that the United States acted potentially on various legal bases: in self-defense; in the exercise of treaty rights; at the consent of the legitimate government of Panama; to enforce U.S. law; and to restore a particular type of human right in Panama, the right to free elections. Thus, the United States did not purport to act solely, or even primarily, on the basis of a legal right to protect Panamanian human rights. Looking behind these statements leads also to a conclusion that, for the United States, the primary purpose of the intervention was not to restore democracy to Panama. Rather, the primary purpose was more closely related to U.S. national interests; to eliminate a severe irritant in U.S. foreign relations with Latin America (Manuel Noriega); and in the process to emphasize to other countries in the region the seriousness with which the United States viewed international drug trafficking.

U.S. public opinion strongly supported the intervention, although reaction among U.S. scholars of international law was mixed.[85] For the most part, however, the international community did not support the legality of the intervention. In the debate at the Security Council, the Soviet Union declared the intervention to be "a flagrant violation of the elementary norms of international law and the United Nations Charter,"[86] China condemned the "aggressive action of the United States,"[87] and Brazil and Colombia "deplored" the U.S. intervention.[88] France commented that "recourse to force is always deplorable and cannot be approved *per se*, whatever the causes," but refrained from voicing either support or criticism of the intervention.[89] Finland recognized the right

83. U.N. SCOR, 44th Sess., 2902d mtg. at 8, 12, U.N. Doc. S/PV.2902 (1989).

84. Remarks Announcing the Surrender of General Manuel Noriega in Panama (Jan. 3, 1990), *in* I PUBLIC PAPERS OF THE PRESIDENTS: GEORGE BUSH, 1990, at 8 (1991).

85. *Compare* V. Nanda, *The Validity of United States Intervention in Panama Under International Law*, 84 AM. J. INT'L L. 494 (1990) (the U.S. acted unlawfully); T. Farer, *Panama: Beyond the Charter Paradigm*, 84 AM. J. INT'L L. 503 (the U.S. action cannot fit within traditional international law, but was undertaken in a good cause); A. D'Amato, *The Invasion of Panama Was a Lawful Response to Tyranny*, 84 AM. J. INT'L L. 516 (the U.S. acted lawfully).

86. U.N. Doc. S/PV.2899, *supra* note 81, at 17.

87. *Id.* at 21.

88. U.N. SCOR, 44th Sess., 2900th mtg. at 21, U.N. Doc. S/PV.2900 (1989); U.N. Doc. S/PV.2902, *supra* note 83, at 17.

89. U.N. Doc. S/PV.2899, *supra* note 81, at 23–25.

of self-defense but considered the U.S. use of force disproportionate to Panama's actions.[90] Only Canada and Britain voiced support during the debate for the intervention, the latter stressing that it was taken with the agreement and support of Endara.[91]

When the Security Council voted on a resolution critical of the U.S. action,[92] ten members supported the resolution, Finland abstained, and Britain, Canada, France, and the United States voted against.[93] Since three permanent members did not concur, the resolution failed. Comments made after the vote by Finland and France indicate not that they ultimately decided to support the U.S. intervention but that they found the language of the draft resolution unsatisfactory, particularly its failure to reference the right of the people of Panama to a democratically elected government.[94]

The General Assembly adopted a resolution on December 29 very similar to the one that failed in the Security Council. The resolution "strongly deplore[d]" the intervention as a "flagrant violation of international law" and demanded "the immediate cessation of the intervention and the withdrawal from Panama of the armed invasion forces of the United States."[95] Likewise, the OAS denounced the intervention.[96]

In sum, the United States did not assert that it was exercising a unilateral right of humanitarian intervention in Panama, although it did advance as one of the bases for the intervention the desire to restore democracy. The circumstances of the intervention do not point to this rationale as the unstated primary motivation for the intervention. Moreover, most members of the Security Council and the General Assembly denounced the intervention as a violation of international law. Thus, even if pro-democratic intervention is considered within the scope of humanitarian intervention, the intervention in Panama is not a strong precedent in support of its acceptance by the international community.

---

90. U.N. Doc. S/PV.2900, *supra* note 88, at 14–15.

91. U.N. Doc. S/PV.2899, *supra* note 81, at 26, 29–30. El Salvador, invited to address the Security Council as an interested state, expressed its support for "the legitimate Government of Panama presided over by Mr. Guillermo Endara" but refrained from expressly supporting the U.S. intervention. U.N. Doc. S/PV.2900, *supra* note 88, at 47.

92. The draft resolution would have stated that the Security Council "strongly deplores" the intervention as a "flagrant violation of international law" and "demands the immediate cessation of the intervention and the withdrawal of the United States armed forces from Panama." U.N. Doc. S/21048 (1989).

93. U.N. Doc. S/PV.2902, *supra* note 83, at 18–20.

94. *Id*. at 21–22.

95. G.A. Res. 44/240, U.N. GAOR, 44th Sess., Supp. No. 49, at 52, paras. 1–2, U.N. Doc. A/44/49 (1989).

96. O.A.S. Boletín de Noticias, Dec. 22, 1989, *cited in* Farer, *supra* note 85, at 507, n.5.

B. Developments at the United Nations During the Cold War

During the Cold War, the United Nations made impressive strides in developing the international law of human rights and otherwise promoting the protection of those rights. Various UN organs adopted important conventions and declarations regulating a wide range of human rights and developed procedures for implementing and supervising those rights.[97] At the same time, the Security Council only once authorized the use of armed force as a response to a situation that implicated predominantly internal, human rights issues—the authorization granted to Great Britain in 1966 to blockade oil-laden vessels supplying the racist regime in Southern Rhodesia. Even in that instance, the authorization was extended to the state that was seen under international law as responsible for Rhodesia and that itself voted for the resolution (Great Britain); moreover, the authorization was limited to the use of force outside the territory of the targeted entity. All other cases involving the use of force in response to human rights concerns occurred as a result of non-UN sanctioned force.[98] Nevertheless, the practice of the Security Council, the General Assembly, ECOSOC, the Human Rights Commission, and the International Court of Justice merits a brief review, since it is the foundation of much of our contemporary thinking about humanitarian intervention after the Cold War.

1. The Security Council

The Security Council rarely used its enforcement powers to authorize the deployment of armed forces during the Cold War. Indeed, on only two occasions did the Security Council deploy forces with the power to coerce peace and security from a recalcitrant government. In 1950 the Security Council determined that North Korea's attack on South Korea constituted a breach of the peace and recommended that states furnish "such assistance" to South Korea as may be necessary to repel the attack and to "restore international peace and security in the area."[99] Obvi-

97. At the same time, there are important weaknesses in the ability of the United Nations in this area. *See generally* T. MERON, HUMAN RIGHTS LAW-MAKING IN THE UNITED NATIONS: A CRITIQUE OF INSTRUMENTS AND PROCESS (1986); P. Alston, *The U.N.'s Human Rights Record: From San Francisco to Vienna and Beyond*, 16 HUM. RTS. Q. 375 (1994).

98. *E.g.*, France's intervention in the Central African Republic, discussed *supra* sec. A(8).

99. S.C. Res. 82, U.N. SCOR, 5th Sess., 473d mtg. at 4, U.N. Doc. S/INF/5/Rev.1 (1965); S.C. Res. 83, U.N. SCOR, 5th Sess., 474th mtg. at 5, U.N. Doc. S/INF/5/Rev.1 (1965); S.C. Res. 84, U.N. SCOR, 5th Sess., 476 mtg. at 6, U.N. Doc. S/INF/5/Rev.1 (1965). These resolutions were possible because the Soviet Union was temporarily absent from the Security

ously, this action related to overt aggression, not internal human rights issues.

In one other instance, however, coercive action by the Security Council was possible to advance human rights values. In the early 1960s, Southern Rhodesia (a "self-governing colony" of Britain) was dominated by a white racist government that prevented political participation by parties representing Southern Rhodesia's black majority and that engaged in other discriminatory practices. After Southern Rhodesia declared independence from Britain in November 1965, it became increasingly isolated from the global community. Because of British resistance, the Security Council could not agree to pursue armed intervention, but it did pass a resolution calling on states voluntarily to impose an oil embargo on, and to break diplomatic relations with, Southern Rhodesia.[100] The following year, when it became apparent that voluntary sanctions were not sufficient, Britain supported the Security Council in authorizing British naval forces to prevent the passage of oil tankers to Mozambique ports in support of Southern Rhodesia[101] and, for the first time under the UN Charter, the Security Council imposed selective mandatory sanctions.[102] This action, however, did not have the effect of deposing the Government of Southern Rhodesia, which remained in power until 1979.

The authorization of force against Southern Rhodesia was much more limited in scope and in intrusiveness than the Security Council's enforcement action in Korea; the British naval forces remained off the coast of Mozambique, and no military forces entered Rhodesian territory. Its significance lies in the willingness of the Security Council to view a predominantly internal human rights situation as one involving a "threat to the peace" under Chapter VII of the UN Charter. Indeed, it is in the practice of the Security Council in respect of southern Africa as a

---

Council in protest over the Council's refusal to seat the representatives from the People's Republic of China. However, the Security Council did not deploy the forces under its own command and control. Rather, it requested the United States to designate the commander of the forces and authorized the unified force "at its discretion" to use the United Nations flag in the course of its operations.

100. S.C. Res. 217, U.N. SCOR, 20th Sess., 1258th mtg. at 8, U.N. Doc. S/INF/20/Rev.1 (1965).

101. S.C. Res. 221, U.N. SCOR, 21st Sess., 1277th mtg. at 5, U.N. Doc. S/INF/21/Rev.1 (1966).

102. S.C. Res. 232, U.N. SCOR, 21st Sess., 1340th mtg. at 7, U.N. Doc. S/INF/21/Rev.1 (1966), *reprinted in* 3 WESTON, *supra* note 17, at III.T.2. Comprehensive and mandatory economic sanctions were imposed in 1968. S.C. Res. 253, U.N. SCOR, 23rd Sess., 1428th mtg. at 5, U.N. Doc. S/INF/23/Rev.1 (1968), *reprinted in* 3 WESTON, *supra* note 17, at III.T.5.

whole in the 1960s that one can see the beginning of an expansive interpretation to what constitutes a "threat to the peace."[103] There, the Security Council characterized two essentially internal situations of human rights abuses related to systematic racial discrimination as threatening international peace and security because of the potential for international conflict resulting from the existence and policies of white racist regimes surrounded or bordered by non-white states, first in South Africa where odious policies of apartheid had developed and then in Southern Rhodesia. In the case of South Africa, Resolution 181 (1963) (imposing a voluntary arms embargo)[104] and Resolution 418 (1977) (imposing a mandatory arms embargo)[105] found the policies and acts of South Africa to constitute a threat to international peace and security, although it should be noted that in Resolution 418 the Security Council was in part concerned with South Africa's "persistent acts of aggression against the neighboring states" (by which was meant South African military cross-border incursions taken against black South African resistance groups operating from neighboring countries). In the case of Southern Rhodesia, Resolution 216 (1965)[106] made no mention of a threat to the peace, but Resolution 217 (1965),[107] Resolution 221 (1966),[108] Resolution 232 (1966),[109] and Resolution 253 (1968)[110] made increasingly strong references to a threat to the peace by the proclamation of independence by white racist authorities in Southern Rhodesia.

Korea and Southern Rhodesia, therefore, represent the two precedents during the Cold War for the deployment of military forces by the Security Council to engage in coercive action. That is not to say these were the only times the United Nations deployed military forces. Along with the General Assembly, the Security Council on several occasions authorized the deployment of armed forces to maintain peace, with the

---

103. For a discussion of how the Security Council has "paved the way" for a more expansive application of the concept of "threats" to international peace and security, *see* J. Delbrück, *A Fresh Look at Humanitarian Intervention Under the Authority of the United Nations*, 67 IND. L.J. 887, 899 (1992).

104. S.C. Res. 181, U.N. SCOR, 18th Sess., 1056th mtg. at 7, U.N. Doc. S/RES/181 (1963).

105. S.C. Res. 418, U.N. SCOR, 32nd Sess., 2046th mtg. at 5, U.N. Doc. S/RES/418 (1977).

106. S.C. Res. 216, U.N. SCOR, 20th Sess., 1258th mtg. at 8, U.N. Doc. S/RES/216 (1965).

107. S.C. Res. 217, *supra* note 100.

108. S.C. Res. 221, *supra* note 101.

109. S.C. Res. 232, *supra* note 102.

110. S.C. Res. 253, *supra* note 102.

consent of the concerned states.[111] These "peacekeeping" missions were a major contribution to the maintenance of international peace and security during the Cold War, and it is ironic that the UN Charter does not specifically provide for them. Different peacekeeping missions served different functions, such as supervising ceasefires,[112] assisting in the return to peace through mediation efforts,[113] and patrolling a buffer zone.[114] Nevertheless, they all shared certain key elements: they were predicated upon the consent of those states in which they operated; they strove to maintain impartiality in whatever conflict arose; and, for the most part, they involved forces that were neither equipped nor authorized to engage in military action other than as necessary to protect themselves. While it is not possible in the constraints of this study to provide a detailed discussion of these peacekeeping operations,[115] one of the issues discussed in chapter 6 is the difficulty in applying principles

---

111. For a brief chronological survey of thirty-three instances of U.N. peacekeeping operations, from the Balkan conflict beginning in 1946 through the deployment of peacekeeping forces to Haiti in 1993, see THE CHARTER OF THE UNITED NATIONS: A COMMENTARY 576–87 (B. Simma ed., 1994).

112. This was the primary function of the United Nations Emergency Force in the Middle East (UNEF).

113. This was, at least initially, the primary function of the United Nations Force in the Congo (ONUC). Arguably, the deployment of UN forces to the Congo evolved into an enforcement action when the Security Council authorized the use of force in the last resort to end the secession of Katanga. For an excellent discussion of how the function of such an operation can change over time, see G. ABI-SAAB, THE UNITED NATIONS OPERATION IN THE CONGO 1960–1964 (1978).

114. This was the primary function of the United Nations Disengagement Observation Force (UNDOF), which operated between Israel and Syria, and of the United Nations Interim Force in Lebanon (UNIFIL), which operated between Israel and Lebanon.

115. There are numerous studies of UN peacekeeping. *See, e.g.*, BASIC DOCUMENTS ON UNITED NATIONS AND RELATED PEACE-KEEPING FORCES (R. Siekmann ed., 2d ed. 1989); THE BLUE HELMETS: A REVIEW OF UNITED NATIONS PEACE-KEEPING (U.N. pub. 1990); D. BOWETT, UNITED NATIONS FORCES (1964); J. BOYD, UNITED NATIONS PEACEKEEPING OPERATIONS: A MILITARY AND POLITICAL APPRAISAL (1971); THE EVOLUTION OF UN PEACEKEEPING: CASE STUDIES AND COMPARATIVE ANALYSIS (W. Durch ed., 1993); M. HARBOTTLE, THE BLUE BERETS: A STUDY OF PEACEKEEPING OPERATIONS (1971); R. HIGGINS, UNITED NATIONS PEACEKEEPING 1946–67 (4 vols. 1969–1981); F. LIU, UNITED NATIONS PEACEKEEPING AND THE NON-USE OF FORCE (1992); PEACE-KEEPING — APPRAISALS AND PROPOSALS (H. Wiseman ed., 1983); THE THIN BLUE LINE (I. Rikhye et al. eds., 1974); S. RATNER, THE NEW UN PEACEKEEPING: BUILDING PEACE IN LANDS OF CONFLICT AFTER THE COLD WAR (1995); UNITED NATIONS PEACE-KEEPING, LEGAL ESSAYS (A. Cassese ed., 1978); THE UNITED NATIONS AND PEACE-KEEPING: RESULTS, LIMITATIONS, AND PROSPECTS: THE LESSONS OF 40 YEARS OF EXPERIENCE (I. Rikhye ed., 1990). For a bibliography, see G. FERMANN, BIBLIOGRAPHY ON INTERNATIONAL PEACEKEEPING (1992).

developed for peacekeeping operations to UN operations constituting humanitarian intervention.

2. The General Assembly

One of the most striking constitutional developments of the Charter era came early on in the "Uniting for Peace Resolution." [116] Under this resolution, the General Assembly in 1950 asserted that it could take action in matters relating to international peace and security in the event that the Security Council was unable to discharge its "primary" responsibility in that area because of a lack of unanimity. Specifically, where there appeared to be a threat to the peace, breach of the peace, or act of aggression:

the General Assembly shall consider the matter immediately with a view to making appropriate recommendations to Members for collective measures, including in the case of a breach of the peace or act of aggression the use of armed force when necessary, to maintain or restore international peace and security. [117]

While the General Assembly used this authority in the 1950s during the Korean crisis and to establish the United Nations Emergency Force (UNEF) to secure and supervise the cessation of hostilities between Egypt and Israel in 1950, this arrogation of power never fully developed during the Cold War. [118] At bottom, it became obvious that the financial and military support of the major powers of the world were necessary to undertake enforcement action successfully and that those powers were not willing to see the General Assembly lead in this area; thus, the General Assembly simply could not go it alone.

Nevertheless, the General Assembly played a considerable role during this period in the generation of human rights norms. The absence of any definition of "human rights" and "freedoms" in the UN Charter prompted efforts by the General Assembly to provide greater content to these terms. The "Universal Declaration of Human Rights" adopted by the UN General Assembly in 1948 [119] sets out in some detail what is meant by fundamental rights and freedoms. These include not just "the right to life, liberty, and security of person" [120] and freedom from slavery and

---

116. G.A. Res. 377, U.N. GAOR, 5th Sess., Supp. No. 20, at 10, U.N. Doc. A/1775 (1950).

117. *Id.* para. 1.

118. *See* THE CHARTER OF THE UNITED NATIONS: A COMMENTARY, *supra* note 111, at 235. The resolution was used, however, on a number of occasions as the basis for discussion of issues in the General Assembly. *Id.* at 260–61.

119. G.A. Res. 217 A, U.N. Doc. A/810, at 71 (1948).

120. *Id.* art. 3.

torture,[121] but other less commonly discussed human rights and freedoms, such as "the right to marry and found a family,"[122] "the right to own property,"[123] and "the right to take part in the government of [one's] country."[124] The Universal Declaration was not intended to serve as a legally binding instrument, but over the years it has exercised considerable moral and political authority and is today considered by some scholars as having passed into customary international law, in whole or in part.[125]

The adoption of the Universal Declaration was the harbinger of other UN instruments designed to establish human rights through legally binding instruments. Among these instruments, the most significant are the 1948 Convention on the Prevention and Punishment of the Crime of Genocide,[126] the 1951 Convention Relating to the Status of Refugees,[127] the 1953 Convention on the Political Rights of Women,[128] the 1953 protocol and 1956 convention amending and supplementing the 1926 Slavery Convention,[129] the 1966 International Covenant on Economic, Social, and Cultural Rights,[130] the 1966 International Covenant on Civil and Political Rights,[131] the 1966 International Convention on

121. *Id.* arts. 4–5.

122. *Id.* art. 16.

123. *Id.* art. 17.

124. *Id.* art. 21.

125. *See, e.g., Assembly for Human Rights, Montreal Statement*, 9 J. INT'L COMM. JURISTS 94, 94–95 (1968). The Final Act of the United Nations International Conference on Human Rights at Teheran, May 13, 1968 (also known as the "Proclamation of Teheran") provides in paragraph 2: "The Universal Declaration of Human Rights states a common understanding of the peoples of the world concerning the inalienable and inviolable rights of all members of the human family *and constitutes an obligation for the members of the international community*" (emphasis added). *Reprinted in* 3 WESTON, *supra* note 17, at III.U.1.

126. Convention on the Prevention and Punishment of the Crime of Genocide, Dec. 9, 1948, 78 U.N.T.S. 277, *reprinted in* 3 WESTON, *supra* note 17, at III.J.1.

127. Convention Relating to the Status of Refugees, July 28, 1951, 189 U.N.T.S. 137, *reprinted in* 3 WESTON, *supra* note 17, at III.G.4. This convention has a protocol. Protocol Relating to the Status of Refugees, Jan. 31, 1967, 19 U.S.T. 6223, 606 U.N.T.S. 267, *reprinted in* 3 WESTON, *supra* note 17, at III.G.8.

128. Convention on the Political Rights of Women, Mar. 31, 1953, 193 U.N.T.S. 135, *reprinted in* 3 WESTON, *supra* note 17, at III.C.9.

129. Slavery Convention, Sept. 25, 1926, 46 Stat. 2183, 60 L.N.T.S. 253, *reprinted as amended in* 212 U.N.T.S. 18, *reprinted in* 3 WESTON, *supra* note 17, at III.H.1; Protocol Amending the Slavery Convention, Dec. 7, 1953, 7 U.S.T. 479, 182 U.N.T.S. 51; Supplementary Convention on the Abolition of Slavery, the Slave Trade and Institutions and Practices Similar to Slavery, Sept. 7, 1956, 18 U.S.T. 3201, 266 U.N.T.S. 3, *reprinted in* 3 WESTON, *supra* note 17, at III.H.3.

130. International Covenant on Economic, Social and Cultural Rights, Dec. 16, 1966, 993 U.N.T.S. 3, *reprinted in* 3 WESTON, *supra* note 17, at III.A.2.

131. International Covenant on Civil and Political Rights, Dec. 16, 1966, 999 U.N.T.S. 171, *reprinted in* 3 WESTON, *supra* note 17, at III.A.3. There is an optional protocol to this

the Elimination of All Forms of Racial Discrimination,[132] the 1973 International Convention on the Suppression and Punishment of the Crime of Apartheid,[133] the 1979 Convention on the Elimination of All Forms of Discrimination Against Women,[134] and the 1984 Convention Against Torture and Other Cruel, Inhuman or Degrading Treatment or Punishment.[135] These conventions develop definitions for human rights within their purview and establish reporting, and in some instances petition, systems to standing committees.

Neither the Universal Declaration nor any of these human rights conventions expressly recognizes the right of a state to use force against a state that fails to live up to the standards and obligations set forth in those instruments. Nevertheless, in some instances within a convention there may be a political, if not legal, implication that states will use such force. Article 1 of the 1948 Genocide Convention, for example, provides that the parties will "undertake to prevent and punish" the crime of genocide, and Article 8 provides that "any Contracting Party may call upon the competent organs of the United Nations to take such action under the Charter of the United Nations as they consider appropriate for the prevention and suppression of the act of genocide." Because of these provisions some states appear reluctant to label actions as genocide out of a concern that they then will be expected to intervene in some fashion.[136] Likewise, Article 6 of the International Convention on the Suppression and Punishment of the Crime of Apartheid confirms the parties' obligations to carry out decisions of the Security Council aimed at the elimination of apartheid. Other of these human rights conventions contemplate action by the United Nations, but stop short of indicating whether such action includes military enforcement.

At the same time these human rights conventions were being devel-

---

Covenant. Optional Protocol, Dec. 16, 1966, 999 U.N.T.S. 302, *reprinted in* 3 WESTON, *supra* note 17, at III.A.4.

132. International Convention on the Elimination of All Forms of Racial Discrimination, Mar. 7, 1966, 660 U.N.T.S. 195, *reprinted in* 3 WESTON, *supra* note 17, at III.I.1.

133. International Convention on the Suppression and Punishment of the Crime of Apartheid, Nov. 30, 1973, 1015 U.N.T.S. 243, *reprinted in* 3 WESTON, *supra* note 17, at III.I.2.

134. Convention on the Elimination of All Forms of Discrimination Against Women, Dec. 18, 1979, 1249 U.N.T.S. 13, *reprinted in* 3 WESTON, *supra* note 17, at III.C.13.

135. Convention Against Torture and Other Cruel, Inhuman and Degrading Treatment or Punishment, G.A. Res. 39/46, U.N. GAOR, 39th Sess., Supp. No. 51, at 197 (Annex), U.N. Doc. A/39/51 (1985), *reprinted in* 23 I.L.M. 1027, 24 I.L.M. 535, 3 WESTON, *supra* note 17, at III.K.2.

136. *See, e.g.,* T. Lippman, *Administration Sidesteps Genocide Label in Rwanda,* WASH. POST, June 11, 1994, at A1.

oped, the General Assembly passed three prominent resolutions on the general issue of intervention by states. Passed in an era when newly emerging states were reacting to the abuses of colonialism and to the fear of Cold War interference by the major powers, these resolutions express the aspirations of developing countries for continued decolonization, for freely chosen political and economic systems of their own, and for respect of their sovereignty. Consequently, for the most part the resolutions take the view that, among other things, armed intervention by a state or states *is directly contrary* to the promotion of fundamental human rights and self-determination. In so doing, the resolutions expressly link the promotion of fundamental human rights to the maintenance of international peace and security—however, from the presumption that intervention always denies and never promotes the rights of the peoples of a state.

Two of the resolutions, on the other hand, were crafted so as to contemplate assistance by states to people struggling for self-determination, although it is not clear that this assistance includes assistance in the form of armed intervention.

The General Assembly adopted the first resolution on December 21, 1965, just months after the interventions in the Congo and the Dominican Republic. The resolution includes a "Declaration on the Inadmissibility of Intervention in the Domestic Affairs of States and Their Independence and Sovereignty."[137] The Declaration states in its preamble that the "violation of the principle of non-intervention poses a threat to the independence, freedom, and normal political, economic, social and cultural development of countries, particularly those which have freed themselves from colonialism, and can pose a serious threat to the maintenance of peace." It then proceeds in the body of the Declaration to state that:

No State has the right to intervene, directly or indirectly, for any reason whatever, in the internal or external affairs of any other State. Consequently, armed intervention and all other forms of interference or attempted threats against the personality of the State or against its political, economic, and cultural elements are condemned. . . . The strict observance of these obligations is an essential condition to ensure that nations live together in peace with one another, since the practice of any form of intervention not only violates the spirit and letter of the Charter of the United Nations but also leads to the creation of situations which threaten international peace and security.[138]

137. G.A. Res. 2131, U.N. GAOR, 20th Sess., Supp. No. 14, at 11, U.N. Doc. A/6014 (1966), *reprinted in* 5 I.L.M. 374, 3 WESTON, *supra* note 17, at II.A.2 [hereinafter *Declaration on the Inadmissibility of Intervention*].

138. *Id.* paras. 1, 4, 5.

The Declaration then reaffirms: "Every State has an inalienable right to choose its political, economic, social, and cultural systems, without interference in any form by another State."[139]

About five years later, on October 24, 1970, the General Assembly adopted a resolution to which was annexed a "Declaration on Principles of International Law Concerning Friendly Relations and Cooperation Among States in Accordance with the Charter of the United Nations."[140] The Preamble of the Declaration states, among other things, that the "subjection of peoples to alien subjugation, domination and exploitation constitutes a major obstacle to the promotion of international peace and security" and that the effective application of "the principle of equal rights and self-determination of peoples . . . is of paramount importance for the promotion of friendly relations among States." The body of the Declaration contains seven fundamental principles, the third of which is the principle of nonintervention, which reads in part:

> No State or group of States has the right to intervene, directly or indirectly, for any reason whatever, in the internal or external affairs of any other State. Consequently, armed intervention and all other forms of interference or attempted threats against the personality of the State or against its political, economic and cultural elements, are in violation of international law.
>
> . . .
>
> Every State has an inalienable right to choose its political, economic, social and cultural systems, without interference in any form by another State.

During the negotiations of this Declaration, states split over whether the Declaration should address the subjugation of peoples by their own government (as opposed to subjugation by a foreign state). The Latin American and Western countries believed it should, while the African and Asian countries believed it should not.[141] The final text of the fifth principle, which relates to self-determination, provides, among other things, that:

139. *Id.* para. 5.
140. G.A. Res. 2625, U.N. GAOR, 25th Sess., Supp. No. 28, at 121 (Annex), U.N. Doc. A/8028 (1971) [hereinafter *Declaration on Principles of International Law*]. The resolution was adopted by the General Assembly without a vote. For commentary, see G. Arangio-Ruiz, the United Nations Declaration on Friendly Relations and the System of the Sources of International Law (rev. ed., Sijthoff & Noordhoff 1979); R. Rosenstock, *The Declaration of Principles of International Law Concerning Friendly Relations: A Survey*, 65 Am. J. Int'l L. 713 (1971); R. Witten, Note, *The Declaration on Friendly Relations*, 12 Harv. J. Int'l L. 509 (1971).
141. For a discussion of this debate, see A. Tanca, *The Prohibition of Force in the U.N. Declaration on Friendly Relations of 1970*, in The Current Legal Regulation of the Use of Force 397, 404–408 (A. Cassese ed., 1986).

Every State has the duty to refrain from any forcible action which deprives peoples . . . of their right to self-determination and freedom and independence. In their actions against, and resistance to, such forcible action in pursuit of the exercise of their right to self-determination, such peoples are entitled to seek and to receive support in accordance with the purposes and principles of the Charter.

This language suggests that peoples struggling for self-determination do have some standing under the Declaration, can resist action by a state that deprives them of self-determination, and can receive "support" from abroad in so doing. While the meaning is not certain, this "support" does not appear to include armed intervention by foreign forces; if it did, the Declaration presumably would have provided for it among the lawful uses of force expressly listed.[142]

On December 14, 1974 (three years after India's intervention in East Pakistan and midst the turmoil of the war in Indo-China), the General Assembly adopted a resolution entitled "Definition of Aggression,"[143] purportedly to provide basic principles for guidance in determining aggression. In the Preamble, the resolution recognizes "the duty of States not to use armed force to deprive peoples of their right to self-determination, freedom and independence, or to disrupt territorial integrity." As formulated, this clause does not appear to address the use of armed force by a government against its own people. After enumerating various acts that constitute "aggression," including the "invasion or attack by the armed forces of a State of the territory of another State,"[144] the Definition states that "No consideration of whatever nature, whether political, economic, military or otherwise, may serve as a justification for aggression."[145] Yet the definition also states that it does not prejudice the right of "peoples" to struggle for self-determination, freedom, and independence, or their right "to seek and receive support" to that end[146] Again, this clause was adopted in the context of concerns with colonialism and racism, but the actual language is not so restricted and accepts as lawful the provision of an unspecified type of support to persons struggling for self-rule and freedom. These resolutions are clearly directed at unilateral actions by states, undertaken without any authority from the UN Security Council or regional organizations. All three essen-

---

142. *Id.* at 407.

143. G.A. Res. 3314, U.N. GAOR, 29th Sess., Supp. No. 31, at 142 (Annex), U.N. Doc. A/9631 (1975) [hereinafter *Definition on Aggression*]. For a two-volume collection of materials leading to the adoption of this resolution, *see* B. FERENCZ, DEFINING INTERNATIONAL AGGRESSION: THE SEARCH FOR WORLD PEACE (1975).

144. *Definition on Aggression, supra* note 143, art. 3, para. (a).

145. *Id.* art. 5.

146. *Id.* art. 7.

tially state that they do not have any effect on actions that may be taken under UN Charter Chapters VI, VII, or VIII.[147] With respect to unilateral actions, these resolutions indicate a clear preference against intervention, but also a recognition that certain special situations may exist justifying foreign intervention, such as where a minority within a state seeks self-determination with the final goal of decolonization. While the resolutions need not be restricted to cases of decolonization, no clear consensus emerged within them delineating other circumstances of self-determination that could justify foreign intervention.[148]

3. ECOSOC and the Commission on Human Rights

Although ECOSOC is subordinate to the General Assembly, the lawmaking powers of the General Assembly and ECOSOC are largely concurrent.[149] During the Cold War, the suborgans of ECOSOC served as important engines for the development of international human rights law and its implementation. Two of these are of particular note: the UN Commission on Human Rights (the Commission), established as one of ECOSOC's first acts (as ECOSOC was charged to do under UN Charter Article 68); and the Sub-Commission on Prevention of Discrimination and Protection of Minorities (the Sub-Commission), established in turn by the Commission.

Both the Commission and the Sub-Commission have had a major role in the development of human rights law. The Commission prepared drafts for the General Assembly of the Universal Declaration on Human Rights and other human rights instruments and has advised and provided services for the General Assembly at its request. Further, it has undertaken various studies of human rights conditions in particular countries or on particular topics and, since 1970, has received and considered petitions regarding systematic abuses of human rights by a government. The Sub-Commission also has prepared drafts of human rights instruments and likewise has studied particular situations of human rights violations.

Both sub-organs have been important also in establishing the principle, referred to in chapter 1 of this study, that a state that engages in "gross violations of internationally recognized human rights" violates the state's UN Charter obligations, as set forth in Articles 55 and 56.

147. *Declaration on the Inadmissibility of Intervention, supra* note 137, para. 8; *Declaration on Principles of International Law, supra* note 140, para. 3; *Definition on Aggression, supra* note 143, pmbl.

148. *See* THE CHARTER OF THE UNITED NATIONS: A COMMENTARY, *supra* note 111, at 69–70, 121–22.

149. MERON, *supra* note 97, at 272.

The origins of this principle may be seen in two ECOSOC resolutions. ECOSOC Resolution 1235 authorized the Commission and Sub-Commission to examine information "relevant to gross violations of human rights and fundamental freedoms," as exemplified by apartheid and racial discrimination in southern Africa.[150] ECOSOC Resolution 1503 authorized the Sub-Commission to appoint a working group to consider communications that "appear to reveal a consistent pattern of gross and reliably attested violations of human rights and fundamental freedoms within the terms of reference of the Sub-Commission."[151] If such a pattern is found to exist, the Sub-Commission may refer the matter to the Commission, whereupon the Commission may undertake a study of the matter or, with the consent of the state concerned, conduct an investigation. While there are significant differences in the "1235" and "1503" processes (for instance, the latter is conducted in confidence until such time as recommendations are made to ECOSOC), together these processes represent machinery by which the United Nations separates out for UN scrutiny "gross violations of human rights," as opposed to other violations of human rights that do not rise to a level meriting UN attention. Neither the Commission nor the Sub-Commission has been involved in Security Council or General Assembly deliberations regarding whether a particular incident of human rights abuses constitutes a threat to international peace and security or whether armed intervention should be authorized by the United Nations to respond to that threat.

4. The International Court of Justice

The International Court of Justice has not had the opportunity to address squarely the issue of humanitarian intervention, either conducted under the authority of the United Nations or by states acting without such authorization. Nevertheless, in several of its cases during the Cold War, the International Court of Justice has touched upon issues related to humanitarian intervention that provide some guidance regarding the approach the Court might take should the occasion arise.

150. E.S.C. Res. 1235, U.N. ESCOR, 42d Sess., Supp. No. 1, at 17, para. 2, U.N. Doc. E/4393 (1967), *reprinted in* 3 WESTON, *supra* note 17, at III.T.3. The antecedents of this resolution may be seen in G.A. Res. 2144 A, U.N. GAOR, 21st Sess., Supp. No. 16, at 46, U.N. Doc. A/6316 (1967), in which the General Assembly noted the "that gross violations of the rights and fundamental freedoms set forth in the Universal Declaration of Human Rights continue to occur in certain countries." The General Assembly then called upon ECOSOC and the Commission to consider ways of improving the capacity of the United Nations to put a stop to violations of human rights.

151. E.S.C. Res. 1503, U.N. ESCOR 48th Sess., Supp. No. 1A, at 8, para. 1, U.N. Doc. E/4832/Add.1 (1970), *reprinted in* 3 WESTON, *supra* note 17, at III.T.6.

The Court has rarely addressed issues relating generally to the use of force; when presented with such issues, the Court's decisions have been hostile to the exercise of armed force by one state against another and skeptical of claims that the action is permissible as a matter of self-help or self-defense. In the *Corfu Channel* case,[152] for example, the Court was not sympathetic to Great Britain's claim that it could intervene in Albanian territorial waters to vindicate British rights.[153] The Court took the position that, regardless of the object of the action, it was a violation of Albanian territorial integrity. Thus, in considering whether Article 2(4) had been violated, the Court did not find relevant that the intervening state had "good motivation," that territory was not seized or occupied, or that there might be "defects in international organization" under the Charter. The Court stated:

The Court can only regard the alleged right of intervention as the manifestation of a policy of force, such as has, in the past, given rise to most serious abuses and such as cannot, whatever be the present defects in international organization, find a place in international law. Intervention is perhaps still less admissible in the particular form it would take here; for, from the nature of things, it would be reserved for the most powerful States, and might easily lead to perverting the administration of international justice itself.[154]

At the same time, the Court asserted that Albania was obligated to act in accordance with "elementary considerations of humanity,"[155] which in this context meant warning other states that it had laid mines in its waters. Moreover, this obligation was imposed on Albania even though it was not a party to the relevant Hague Convention on mines.[156] The Court's decision does not tell us whether this obligation to be a "good neighbor" might be stretched to include an obligation not to engage in inhumane acts that shock the sensibilities of neighbors or the world community. If the Court's reasoning is applied in the human rights context, the fact that a state is not a party to particular human rights conventions may nevertheless allow the Court to use such conventions as standards

---

152. Corfu Channel (U.K. v. Alb.), 1949 I.C.J. 4 (Apr. 9).

153. The United Kingdom had deployed naval ships into the Albanian waters to sweep for mines which had previously caused damage to U.K. vessels. The United Kingdom argued that the action was justified both to ensure the safety of navigation and in order to secure evidence of Albania's actions in laying the mines, evidence that would otherwise be lost.

154. 1949 I.C.J. at 35.

155. *Id.* at 22.

156. Hague Convention (No. VIII) Relative to the Laying of Automatic Submarine Contact Mines, Oct. 18, 1907, 36 Stat. 2332, 1 Bevans 669, *reprinted in* 2 WESTON, *supra* note 17, at II.B.5.

by which to judge the state's conduct. Finally, the Court found Albania's obligation to arise not from its own direct action but from the omission of an act. This approach would suggest that, to the extent humanitarian intervention is justified, it would be so in cases either where the severe and widespread deprivation of human rights arises from direct action of a government *or* from its failure to act to prevent such deprivations, at least where it is capable of doing so.

In the *Case Concerning Military and Paramilitary Activities in and Against Nicaragua*, the Court narrowly construed the ability of states to resort to armed force. The Court found that under customary international law (which it found to track the UN Charter in this respect) states do not have a right of collective armed response to acts that do not constitute an armed attack.[157] Although the United States had not argued that its conduct with respect to Nicaragua was justified as humanitarian intervention and the Court did not have to address the issue to reach its decision, the Court nevertheless rejected the idea that military force could be used to monitor or ensure respect for human rights.

[W]hile the United States might form its own appraisal of the situation as to respect for human rights in Nicaragua, the use of force could not be the appropriate method to monitor or ensure such respect. With regard to the steps actually taken, the protection of human rights, a strictly humanitarian objective, cannot be compatible with the mining of ports, the destruction of oil installations, or again with the training, arming and equipping of the *contras*. The Court concludes that the argument derived from the preservation of human rights in Nicaragua cannot afford a legal justification for the conduct of the United States, and cannot in any event be reconciled with the legal strategy of the respondent State, which is based on the right of collective self-defence.[158]

Some scholars have concluded that the Court's voluntary observation is a clear indication that the Court rejects the legality of humanitarian intervention.[159] The broad language used by the Court might lead to such a conclusion, but the actions actually at issue—the mining of ports, the destruction of oil installations, and the training, arming, and equipping

157. Military and Paramilitary Activities (Nicar. v. U.S.), 1986 I.C.J. 14, para. 249 (June 27). For jurisdictional reasons, the Court technically was not applying the rules on the use of force as required by the U.N. Charter, but rather customary rules of international law. The Court left open whether a state subject to a use of force by another state falling short of an armed attack could justify proportionate countermeasures against the originating state. *Id.* paras. 210, 249.

158. *Id.* para. 268.

159. *See, e.g.,* N. Rodley, *Human Rights and Humanitarian Intervention: The Case Law of the World Court,* 38 INT'L & COMP. L.Q. 321, 332 (1989) ("This language unmistakably places the Court in the camp of those who claim that the doctrine of humanitarian intervention is without validity."); TESÓN, *supra* note 37, at 241–44.

of the contras—were hardly of the type normally associated with humanitarian intervention. Of perhaps greater significance, the Court also found that the provision of humanitarian aid (food, clothing, medicine) was lawful intervention so long as it was limited to the prevention and alleviation of human suffering and was given without discrimination to all in need.[160]

With regard to actions of the United Nations in addressing issues tangentially related to humanitarian intervention, the International Court of Justice has been more receptive. For instance, in the *Peace Treaties Case*,[161] the Court was reluctant to conclude that the United Nations acted ultra vires (beyond powers) granted by the UN Charter when inquiring into the treatment by states of their own nationals. In that case, Bulgaria, Hungary, and Romania argued that the General Assembly could not request an advisory opinion from the Court on a matter that related to actions of those governments in their own territories against their own nationals.[162] The Court was careful to note that the advisory opinion requested was not on the issue of whether those persons were in fact being denied human rights and fundamental freedoms but, rather, on the applicability of the dispute settlement procedure found in the relevant peace treaties. The Court decided that "The interpretation of the terms of a treaty for this purpose could not be considered as a question essentially within the domestic jurisdiction of a State."[163] The implication of the decision is that questions of international law cannot be considered matters essentially within the jurisdiction of a state. Writing in his personal capacity, Judge Gerald Fitzmaurice commented:

This in turn implies that the concept of domestic jurisdiction is a relative one, depending on the state and content of international law at any given time, and that there is no inherently necessary or fixed category of matters which always are and must be matters of domestic jurisdiction.[164]

160. 1986 I.C.J. at 124–25, paras. 242–43. The Court may have been influenced by the fact that in this case the humanitarian aid was provided by other than military forces. The U.S. legislation authorizing the humanitarian aid prohibited doing so through either the Department of Defense or the Central Intelligence Agency. *Id.* para. 97.

161. Interpretation of Peace Treaties with Bulgaria, Hungary, and Romania, 1950 I.C.J. 65 (Mar. 30).

162. This issue arose in the context of the admission of Bulgaria, Hungary, and Romania to the United Nations under Article 4 of the U.N. Charter, which turned in part on their willingness to fulfill in good faith their obligations under international instruments and to promote the purposes of the United Nations.

163. 1950 I.C.J. at 70.

164. G. Fitzmaurice, The Law and Procedure of the International Court of Justice 104–05 (1986) (noting as well the dictum of the Permanent Court of International Justice in Advisory Opinion No. 4, Nationality Decrees Issued in Tunis and Morocco, 1923 P.C.I.J. (ser. B) No. 4, at 24).

Similarly, in his separate opinion in the *Norwegian Loans* case regarding reservations to the Court's jurisdiction, Judge Lauterpacht noted that practically every aspect of the conduct of a state may be prima facie within the domestic jurisdiction of the state, and yet numerous matters, including the treatment of citizens in national territory, are now the subject of treaties and customary rules of international law.[165] In light of the dramatic increase in the content and scope of human rights law in the Charter era, the Court's jurisprudence suggests that it is unlikely to find many issues of human rights abuse to be outside the scope of UN competence.

If many issues of human rights abuse are within its competence, how far may the United Nations go in protecting those rights? The Court has had no opportunity to address the issue squarely, but did have an opportunity to consider whether UN forces could be deployed in a manner not expressly provided for in the UN Charter. In *Certain Expenses of the United Nations*,[166] the Court was asked to give its opinion on whether certain expenditures which were authorized by the General Assembly to cover the costs of the United Nations peacekeeping operations in the Congo (ONUC) and of the peacekeeping operations of the United Nations Emergency Force in the Middle East (UNEF) "constitute expenses of the Organization" within the meaning of Charter Article 17(2). In that case, certain states argued that the General Assembly (as opposed to the Security Council) had no authority to require states to pay expenses incurred in implementing its recommendations. The Court found that the deployment of peacekeeping forces (forces not engaged in enforcement or coercive action) at the recommendation of the General Assembly was not ultra vires when it is for the fulfillment of one of the stated purposes of the United Nations. The Court asserted:

In the legal systems of States, there is often some procedure for determining the validity of even a legislative or governmental act, but no analogous procedure is to be found in the structure of the United Nations. Proposals made during the drafting of the Charter to place the ultimate authority to interpret the Charter in the International Court of Justice were not accepted; the opinion which the Court is in course of rendering is an *advisory* opinion. As anticipated in 1945, therefore, each organ must, in the first place at least, determine its own jurisdiction. If the Security Council, for example, adopts a resolution purportedly for the maintenance of international peace and security and if, in accordance with a mandate or authorization in such resolution, the Secretary-General incurs financial obligations, these amounts must be presumed to constitute "expenses of the Organization."[167]

165. Certain Norwegian Loans (Fr. v. Nor.), 1957 I.C.J. 9, 51–52 (July 6) (separate opinion of Judge Lauterpacht).
166. Certain Expenses of the United Nations, 1962 I.C.J. 151 (July 20).
167. *Id.* at 168.

The Court appears to have left open whether there is some "second place" which might determine that a resolution was not for the maintenance of international peace and security, and indeed speaks earlier in the text of a "presumption" that such action is not ultra vires.[168] In chapter 6, consideration will be given to whether the Court itself should function as a check on the actions of the Security Council when authorizing or undertaking humanitarian intervention.

With respect to the general development of human rights law, mention must be made of the Court's dicta in the *Barcelona Traction* case,[169] which drew a distinction between the obligations of a state regarding the investments and nationals of another state and the more absolute and unqualified obligations of a state toward the international community as a whole.[170] The Court stated that these important erga omnes (towards all) obligations

derive, for example, in contemporary international law, from the outlawing of acts of aggression, and of genocide, as also from the principles and rules concerning the basic rights of the human person, including protection from slavery and racial discrimination. Some of the corresponding rights of protection have entered into the body of general international law; others are conferred by international instruments of a universal or quasi-universal character.[171]

It is not clear whether the Court was elevating human rights generally above other international rights, or was carving out only certain human rights closely associated with the human person and human dignity.[172] If the latter, then the Court may be said to have expressed a normative hierarchy of human rights. Which rights would fall within the first tier of absolute, unqualified human rights, however, is not altogether clear from the Court's decision, and the Court itself has not had the opportunity to clarify fully its reasoning.[173] To do so, one must look to various sources that emerged during the Cold War for a listing of those rights.

168. *Id.*

169. Barcelona Traction, Light and Power Co. (Belg. v. Spain), 1970 I.C.J. 3 (Feb. 5).

170. *Id.* para. 33.

171. *Id.* para. 34 (citation omitted).

172. *See* MERON, *supra* note 97, at 185–86 ("The Court seems to suggest that, while basic rights of the human person give rise to obligations *erga omnes* and are appropriate for protection by States regardless of the nationality of the victim, other human rights, or ordinary human rights, can be espoused under the agreements embodying such rights, only by the State of the nationality of the victims.").

173. The Court, however, has taken a strong stand in favor of the right of self-determination. *See* East Timor (Port. v. Aus.), 1995 I.C.J. at para 29 (June 30) ("In the Court's view, Portugal's assertion that the right of peoples to self-determination, as it evolved from the Charter and from United Nations practice, has an *erga omnes* character, is irreproachable."); *see also* Legal Consequences for States of the Continued Presence of

For instance, the "non-derogable" human rights common to some of the more important human rights conventions are "the right to life, the right to be free from torture and other inhuman or degrading treatment or punishment, the right to be free from slavery or servitude, and the principle of non-retroactivity of penal laws." [174] Common Article 3 of the 1949 Geneva Conventions on the protection of victims of war, which addresses armed conflicts not of an international nature, contains an important list of prohibitions on state action, which in turn suggests certain core human rights that may have passed into customary international law.[175] It prohibits: (a) violence to life and person, in particular murder of all kinds, mutilation, cruel treatment, and torture; (b) taking of hostages; (c) outrages upon personal dignity, in particular, humiliating and degrading treatment; and (d) the passing of sentences and the carrying out of executions without previous judgment pronounced by a regularly constituted court affording all the judicial guarantees recognized as indispensable by civilized peoples.[176] The Restatement (Third) of the Foreign Relations Law of the United States asserts that states violate customary international law if, as a matter of state policy, they commit: "(a) genocide, (b) slavery or slave trade, (c) the murder or causing the disappearance of individuals, (d) torture or other cruel, inhuman, or degrading treatment or punishment, (e) prolonged arbitrary detention, (f) systematic racial discrimination, or (g) a consistent pattern of gross violations of internationally recognized human rights." [177] The Restatement (Third) Comments assert that (a) through (f) are "inherently

South Africa in Namibia (South West Africa) Notwithstanding Security Council Resolution 276 (1970), 1971 I.C.J. 31–32, paras. 52–53; Western Sahara, 1975 I.C.J. 31–33, paras. 54–59.

174. J. ORAÁ, HUMAN RIGHTS IN STATES OF EMERGENCY IN INTERNATIONAL LAW 96 (1992) (reviewing the 1966 International Covenant on Civil and Political Rights, the 1950 European Convention on Human Rights, and the 1968 American Convention on Human Rights).

175. M. Matheson, *The United States Position on the Relation of Customary International Law to the 1977 Protocols Additional to the 1949 Geneva Conventions*, 2 AM. U.J. INT'L L. & POL'Y 419, 430–31 (1987) ("The basic core of Protocol II is, of course, reflected in common article 3 of the 1949 Conventions and therefore is, and should be, a part of generally accepted customary law").

176. Geneva Convention (No. I) for the Amelioration of the Condition of the Wounded and Sick in Armed Forces in the Field, Aug. 12, 1949, 6 U.S.T. 3114, 75 U.N.T.S. 31; Geneva Convention (No. II) for the Amelioration of the Condition of the Wounded, Sick and Shipwrecked Members of Armed Forces at Sea, Aug. 12, 1949, 6 U.S.T. 3114, 75 U.N.T.S. 85; Geneva Convention (No. III) Relative to the Treatment of Prisoners of War, Aug. 12, 1949, 6 U.S.T. 3114, 75 U.N.T.S. 135; Geneva Convention (No. IV) Relative to the Protection of Civilian Persons in Time of War, Aug. 12, 1949, 6 U.S.T. 3114, 75 U.N.T.S. 287. These conventions are reprinted in 2 WESTON, *supra* note 17, at II.B.11–14.

177. RESTATEMENT (THIRD) OF THE FOREIGN RELATIONS LAW OF THE UNITED STATES sec. 702 (1987).

'gross' " violations of human rights, even if a pattern does not exist, and are jus cogens (peremptory norms).[178]

It is probably neither possible nor desirable to establish a definitive list of these absolute human rights. Nevertheless, there are commonalities to the various sources, and they provide a sense of those rights that the international community finds the most compelling. It must be noted that these lists generally assume the involvement of a state acting in its official capacity (the Restatement (Third) makes this explicit) rather than the lapse of a state into anarchy, during which the violation of such rights occurs not as a matter of directed policy.

C. Regional Organizations

During the Cold War, a number of regional and subregional organizations were established to address security, economic, and other issues. Some of these organizations were involved in incidents of intervention related to humanitarian concerns, such as the OAS in the Dominican Republic and the OECS in Grenada. For the most part, however, these organizations were not actively involved in military interventions. Indeed, the constituent documents of these organizations often express a principle of nonintervention. For instance, Article 18 of the Charter of the OAS provides:

No State or group of States has the right to intervene, directly or indirectly, for any reason whatever, in the internal or external affairs of any other State. The foregoing principle prohibits not only armed force but also any other form of interference or attempted threat against the personality of the State or against its political, economic and cultural elements.[179]

Article 18 is, of course, a response to a long history of foreign intervention in Latin and South America.[180]

At the same time, regional organizations were very active during the Cold War in the promotion of human rights within their regions.[181] The

178. *Id.* sec. 702 cmts. m–n.

179. Charter of the Organization of American States, Apr. 30, 1948, 2 U.S.T. 2394, 119 U.N.T.S. 3, amended by Protocol of Buenos Aires, Feb. 27, 1967, 21 U.S.T. 607, 6 I.L.M. 310, which entered into force in 1970; *reprinted in* 1 Weston, *supra* note 17, at I.B.14. Similar provisions may be found in the Charter of the Organization of African Unity, May 25, 1963, 479 U.N.T.S. 39, *reprinted in* 1 Weston, *supra* note 17, at I.B.1 and in the Pact of the League of Arab States, Mar. 22, 1944, 70 U.N.T.S. 238, *reprinted in* 1 Weston, *supra* note 17, at I.B.16.

180. *See, e.g.,* L. Gardner et al., Creation of the American Empire: U.S. Diplomatic History (1973).

181. *See, e.g.,* B. Weston et al., *Regional Human Rights Regimes: A Comparison and Appraisal,* 20 Vand. J. Transnat'l L. 585 (1987).

European machinery, via the European Commission for Human Rights and the European Court of Human Rights, tended to emphasize human rights litigation, both through applications by individuals and disputes between states. The inter-American machinery, via the Inter-American Commission on Human Rights and the Inter-American Court of Human Rights, emphasized both litigation and fact-finding investigations. The promotion and protection of these human rights, however, were not linked to forcible intervention by either the regional organization or its member states. Chapter 7 will explore the problems of and prospects for humanitarian intervention by regional organizations.

D. Interpretations by Scholars

The Reporters of the 1987 Restatement (Third) have commented: "Whether a state may intervene with military force in the territory of another state without its consent, not to rescue the victims but to prevent or terminate human rights violations, is not agreed or authoritatively determined." [182] Indeed, the debate among legal scholars during the Cold War regarding the legality of humanitarian intervention under the UN Charter was quite spirited. Interestingly, this debate was not unlike the debate among scholars in the pre-Charter era regarding the legality of humanitarian intervention under customary international law. In both instances, proponents of humanitarian intervention tended to emphasize non-positivist approaches while opponents emphasized a dearth of state practice confirming the existence of such a right. In both instances, the debate focused almost exclusively on the issue of the legality of undertaking the intervention and very little on the manner in which the intervention should be conducted. In both instances, the debate was clouded by differing notions as to what constitutes "humanitarian intervention," particularly as to whether the protection of one's own nationals is to be included. The debate over the legality of humanitarian intervention during the Cold War resulted in extensive writings. It can readily be understood by reviewing a few of the more articulate commentators on this topic.

182. RESTATEMENT (THIRD) OF THE FOREIGN RELATIONS LAW OF THE UNITED STATES, sec. 703 cmt. e (1987). The black-letter law of the *Restatement (Third)* does not address the issue. The Reporters' Notes state that "It is far more difficult [than in the situation of rescue of nationals] to justify an implied exception to Article 2(4) that would permit a use of force otherwise contrary to that Article on the ground that the purpose is to suppress or prevent violations of human rights." *Id.* sec. 703 rptrs. note 8. The *Restatement (Third)* has been criticized for not addressing the issue more fully. *See, e.g.*, R. Bernhardt et al., Book Review, 86 AM. J. INT'L L. 608, 620 (1992) ("one would have liked a much more detailed discussion of the relevant questions").

Most scholars asserted that unilateral humanitarian intervention was not lawful under the United Nations Charter.[183] States are obligated under Article 2(4) of the Charter to refrain in their international relations from the threat or use of force, the argument goes, unless as an exercise of self-defense against an armed attack under Article 51 or otherwise authorized by the Security Council under Chapter VII. Thus, force may not be used for humanitarian reasons. The essential position was not that a massive deprivation of human rights is lawful or acceptable but, rather, that the paramount concern of the Charter, as reflected in its text, its negotiating history, and in the practice of states, is to prevent the initiation of transboundary uses of force, and there is no exception even for forcible actions inspired by the noble objectives of humanitarian intervention. One of the most visible U.S. proponents of this view was Louis Henkin, who wrote in his widely read book *How Nations Behave*:

> To me, these pressures eroding the prohibition on the use of force are deplorable, and the arguments to legitimize the use of force in those circumstances are unpersuasive and dangerous. . . . Violations of human rights are indeed all too common, and if it were permissible to remedy them by external use of force, there would be no law to forbid the use of force by almost any state against almost any other. Human rights, I believe, will have to be vindicated, and other injustices remedied, by other, peaceful means, not by opening the door to aggression and destroying the principal advance in international law, the outlawing of war and the prohibition of force.[184]

Professor Henkin's views were particularly striking due to his extensive scholarship favoring the promotion and development of human rights. Opponents of unilateral humanitarian intervention also would note the

183. Scholars that take the traditional approach include: Akehurst, *supra* note 37, at 105–08; D. Bowett, Book Review, 59 Brit. Y.B. Int'l L. 263, 263–65 (1988); J. Brierly, The Law of Nations 427–28 (H. Waldock ed., 6th ed. 1963) (apparently limiting permissible action to securing the safe removal of one's threatened nationals); I. Brownlie, *Humanitarian Intervention, in* Law and Civil War in the Modern World 217, 218 (J. Moore ed., 1974); I. Brownlie, International Law and Use of Force by States 301, 338–42 (1963); Franck & Rodley, *supra* note 5, at 299–302; R. Gardner, *Sovereignty and Intervention: The Just Use of Force*, Freedom at Issue, Mar.-Apr. 1985, at 15, 21; L. Henkin, *Use of Force: Law and U.S. Policy, in* L. Henkin et al., Right v. Might: International Law and the Use of Force 37, 41–42, 61 (2d ed. 1991) (rejecting intervention by force to topple a government or occupy territory to terminate atrocities); L. Henkin, *International Law: Politics, Values and Functions*, 216 R.C.A.D.I. 9, 153–54 (1989-IV); V. Kartashkin, *Human Rights and Humanitarian Intervention, in* Law and Force in the New International Order 202, 206–07 (L. Damrosch & D. Scheffer eds., 1991); O. Schachter, *The Right of States to Use Armed Force*, 82 Mich. L. Rev. 1620, 1629 (1984); O. Schachter, *The Lawful Resort to Unilateral Use of Force*, 10 Yale J. Int'l L. 291, 293–94 (1985).

184. L. Henkin, How Nations Behave: Law and Foreign Policy 144–145 (2d ed. 1979).

impossibility of separating humanitarian objectives from other political objectives; an intervention will always inure to the benefit of one or more local factions at the expense of others.

Proponents of the view that unilateral humanitarian intervention was lawful under the Charter—the minority view—attacked the traditional view as unnecessarily rigid.[185] To the extent that these scholars approached the issue from a rule-based perspective, they advocated a narrow reading of the prohibition in Article 2(4), arguing that humanitarian intervention is not a use of force "against the territorial integrity or political independence of any state," so long as it is limited to its humanitarian purposes. They emphasized that, while one purpose of the Charter is to prevent war, the Charter and the human rights instruments it spawned accord great significance to the protection of human rights.[186] Consequently, Article 2(4) should be interpreted in a manner that does not undermine the protection of these rights.[187] Even if Article 2(4) as

185. Scholars who have favored viewing humanitarian intervention as lawful, at least in certain circumstances, include: D'AMATO, *supra* note 66, at 351; J. Fonteyne, *Forcible Self-Help by States to Protect Human Rights: Recent Views from the United Nations, in* HUMANITARIAN INTERVENTION AND THE UNITED NATIONS 197, 220–21 (R. Lillich ed., 1973); R. HIGGINS, PROBLEMS AND PROCESS: INTERNATIONAL LAW AND HOW WE USE IT 247–48 (1994); 1 OPPENHEIM'S INTERNATIONAL LAW (H. Lauterpacht ed., 8th ed. 1955); R. Lillich, *Forcible Self-Help by States to Protect Human Rights*, 53 IOWA L. REV. 325 (1967); R. Lillich, *Humanitarian Intervention: A Reply to Ian Brownlie and a Plea for Constructive Alternatives, in* LAW AND CIVIL WAR IN THE MODERN WORLD, *supra* note 183, at 229; J. Moore, *The Control of Foreign Intervention in Internal Conflict*, 9 VA. J. INT'L L. 205, 261–64, 338 (1969), *reprinted in* J. MOORE, LAW AND THE INDO-CHINA WAR 115, 182–86 (1972); W. Reisman, *Humanitarian Intervention to Protect the Ibos, in* HUMANITARIAN INTERVENTION AND THE UNITED NATIONS 167 (R. Lillich ed., 1973); C. ROUSSEAU, DROIT INTERNATIONAL PUBLIC 324–25 (1953); TESÓN, *supra* note 37.

186. In the preamble to the Charter there is a reaffirmation of faith "in fundamental human rights, in the dignity and worth of the human person, in the equal rights of men and women and of nations large and small." Article 1 states that one of the purposes of the United Nations is the achievement of "international cooperation . . . in promoting and encouraging respect for human rights and for fundamental freedoms for all without distinction as to race, sex, language, or religion." Article 55 provides that "the United Nations shall promote . . . universal respect for, and observance of, human rights and fundamental freedoms for all without distinction as to race, sex language or religion"; in Article 56, "[a]ll Members pledge themselves to take joint and separate action in cooperation with the [United Nations] for the achievement of the purposes set forth in Article 55."

Both the General Assembly (Article 13) and the Economic and Social Council (Article 62) are expressly charged with promoting human rights, while the Security Council is not. The Charter itself does not enumerate "human rights" or "fundamental freedoms," although one of the first tasks of the Economic and Social Council was to establish the Commission on Human Rights, from which emerged the 1948 Universal Declaration of Human Rights. G.A. Res. 217A (III), U.N. Doc. A/810, at 71 (1948), *reprinted in* 3 WESTON, *supra* note 17, at III.A.1.

187. For some scholars, the Charter should be construed as actively *obligating* states to undertake joint and separate action in defense of human rights. *See* Reisman, *Humanitarian*

originally drafted may have prohibited humanitarian intervention, subsequent events, such as the inability of the Security Council to act effectively in the face of widespread violations of human rights, warrant an interpretation of Article 2(4) as allowing humanitarian intervention.[188]

Yet many proponents of unilateral humanitarian intervention sought to downplay a rule-based interpretation of the Charter.[189] As a way of side-stepping the traditional rule-based interpretation of the Charter, Fernando Tesón placed great emphasis on a "substantive moral philosophy of international relations"—one that shows that the rights of states derive from the rights of their peoples—to support the legality of humanitarian intervention under the Charter. According to this view, when the government of a state abuses its own people, the government loses the protection accorded the state that prohibits foreign intervention.[190]

Several scholars advanced the McDougal/Lasswell construct (discussed in chapter 1) of international law, as a "process of authoritative

---

Intervention to Protect the Ibos, supra note 185, at 175. In the wake of the U.S. intervention in Grenada, Professor Reisman took his thesis further in asserting that unilateral intervention is also permissible for overthrowing a despotic government. Reisman, *supra* note 68; *see also* M. McDougal & W. Reisman, *Response,* 3 INT'L LAW. 438, 442–44 (1968–69). *But see* T. Franck, *The Emerging Right to Democratic Governance,* 86 AM. J. INT'L L. 46, 85 (1992) ("To obtain the general consent necessary to render the denial of democracy a cognizable violation of an international community standard, it must be understood that whatever countermeasures are taken must first be authorized collectively by the appropriate U.N. institutions.").

188. Bazyler, *supra* note 50, at 579–80 (1987); R. Lillich, *Forcible Self-Help by States to Protect Human Rights, supra* note 185, at 344–47 (1967) ("Surely to require a state to sit back and watch the slaughter of innocent people in order to avoid violating blanket prohibitions against the use of force is to stress blackletter at the expense of far more fundamental values.").

189. For a discussion about how one reaches different conclusions about the lawfulness of humanitarian intervention depending on whether you approach it as a "classicist" or as a "realist," see T. Farer, *An Inquiry into the Legitimacy of Humanitarian Intervention,* in LAW AND FORCE IN THE NEW INTERNATIONAL ORDER 185 (L. Damrosch & D. Scheffer eds., 1991). Professor Farer concludes the Charter does not support humanitarian intervention and that countries (if asked) would limit unilateral recourse to force in the defense of territorial integrity and political independence, but concedes that "behind the broad general preference, states evidence participation in complex, highly nuanced codes of mitigation . . . which . . . seem equally to exceed the Charter limits on legitimate use of force." *Id.* at 197–98.

190. TESÓN, *supra* note 37. This approach relies in part on the philosophy of Immanuel Kant, which presents some difficulty since Kant argued in substance that humanitarian intervention jeopardizes the autonomy of all states. I. KANT, PERPETUAL PEACE [1795] 6–7 (Columbia U. Press, New York 1932). *But see* F. Tesón, *The Kantian Theory of International Law,* 92 COLUM. L. REV. 53, 90–94 (1992) (arguing that Kantian theory should lead to a conclusion that liberal democratic states can intervene in nonliberal democratic states to prevent serious human rights deprivations).

and controlling decision." Under this approach, the legality of a state's asserted humanitarian intervention turns on the contemporaneous appraisal of the action by other states and the subsequent review that the organized community may exercise in light of preferred community policy.[191] The difficulty in this approach proved to be that each time an incident of intervention occurred, a systematic appraisal did not result in a clear conclusion that the reason for intervention was the protection of human rights or that the intervention was acceptable to the international community. This deficiency prompted proponents of a right of unilateral humanitarian intervention to move to a next step of simply arguing that declaring such intervention illegal, in the face of the moral imperative of addressing the widespread deprivation of human rights, undermined the credibility of international law and made it irrelevant in governing state behavior.

It should be noted that proponents of a right of humanitarian intervention usually did not argue that the "inherent right of individual and collective self-defense" in Article 51 preserved a pre-Charter right of self-defense that included the concept of protecting individuals against their own state.[192] Further, to prevent resort to humanitarian intervention becoming a pretext for unlawful uses of force, these scholars advanced certain criteria that must be met by the intervening state for the intervention to be lawful.[193] The International Law Association, a nongovernmental organization of international law scholars, established a subcommittee on the international protection of human rights, which considered not just the status of humanitarian intervention under international law but also the prospects for drafting a "Protocol of Procedure

191. As discussed in chapter 1, this approach reflects the "New Haven" public order school of jurisprudence, best expressed with respect to the use of force in M. McDougal & F. Feliciano, Law and Minimum World Public Order: The Legal Regulation of International Coercion 416 (1961).

192. D. Bowett, *The Interrelation of Theories of Intervention and Self-Defense, in* Law and Civil War in the Modern World, *supra* note 183, at 38, 41.

193. For instance, Professor Nanda would require that the intervention be: (1) for a specific limited purpose; (2) by a recognized government; (3) for a limited duration; (4) limited in its use of coercive measures; and (5) due to a lack of other recourse. Nanda (pt. 2), *supra* note 22, at 475–79. Lillich would judge the lawfulness of the intervention based on: (1) the immediacy of the violation; (2) the extent of the violation of human rights; (3) the existence of an invitation by an appropriate authority; (4) the degree of coercive measures employed; and (5) the relative disinterestedness of the state invoking the coercive measures. Lillich, *Forcible Self-Help by States to Protect Human Rights, supra* note 185, 347–51. *See also* Bazyler, *supra* note 50, at 597–611; J. Fonteyne, *The Customary International Law Doctrine of Humanitarian Intervention: Its Current Validity Under the U.N. Charter,* 4 Cal. W. Int'l L.J. 203, 258–268 (1974). The efficacy of such criteria will be considered in chapter 8 *infra*.

for Humanitarian Intervention."[194] Ultimately, however, the subcommittee was unable to reach a consensus on the proposed protocol.[195]

In assessing this scholarly debate, it is important to keep in mind the backdrop of the Cold War. The tension between the the United States and the Soviet Union and the ever-present threat of nuclear annihilation had a significant impact on the thinking of international legal scholars regarding the use of force; this impact carried over to the attitudes of those that favored humanitarian intervention and those that opposed it. Scholars such as Quincy Wright essentially argued that overriding considerations in a time of thermo-nuclear weapons and international tension required an interpretation of the Charter that maintained a maximum resistance to all forms of armed action.[196] Unless a state was the subject of an armed attack, the state was forbidden from resorting to the use of force. As discussed in chapter 3, the text of the UN Charter and its *travaux préparatoires* strongly supported this view. Wright believed that a strict interpretation of the UN Charter in conjunction with a clear definition of what was meant by "aggression" would serve as a foundation for securing voluntary compliance by states with the Charter's prohibitions on the use of force.

Other scholars, such as Julius Stone, conceded that Professor Wright's "extreme view" might be correct, but asserted that it led to absurd results and injustice, and therefore should be set aside.[197] Stone was particularly concerned with the fact that the machinery for collective security at the United Nations had proven ineffective, leaving states necessarily to fend for themselves but under restrictive UN Charter norms. He asked:

Even if the grand design of the United Nations *was* to substitute collective peace enforcement and peaceful change for the traditional role of war as a means (in part at least) of vindicating rights, and effecting adjustment of the *status quo* so as to secure a tolerable level of justice, are we to say that resort to force has been completely outlawed, even when no substitute means of relief is available? It is not believed that such a position makes either moral, political or even legal sense.[198]

In particular, the possibility of a nuclear first strike led Stone to believe that a state must be able to act in anticipatory self-defense.

194. International Law Association (ILA), Report of the Fifty-Fourth Conference 633, 641 (1971). For subsequent reports, see ILA, Report of the Fifty-Fifth Conference 608 (1974); ILA, Report of the Fifty-Sixth Conference 217 (1976); ILA, Report of the Fifty-Seventh Conference 519 (1978).

195. ILA, Report of the Fifty-Seventh Conference 519, 521 (1978).

196. *See* Q. Wright, *The Prevention of Aggression*, 50 Am. J. Int'l L. 514 (1956).

197. J. Stone, Aggression and World Order: A Critique of United Nations Theories of Aggression 97 (1958).

198. *Id.* at 100.

Stone's views, however, were not limited to the issue of anticipatory self-defense; they encompassed as well situations that are relevant to the issue of humanitarian intervention. For instance, Stone advanced the following hypothesis:

Suppose, for example, that a Great Power decided that the only way it could continue to control a satellite State was to wipe out the satellite's entire population and recolonize the area with "reliable" people. Suppose the satellite government agreed to this measure and established the necessary mass extermination apparatus for carrying out the plan. Would the rest of the Members of the United Nations be compelled to stand by and watch this operation merely because requisite decision of United Nations organs was blocked, and the operation did not involve an "armed attack" on any Member of the United Nations? [199]

That Professor Stone, writing in 1958, was heavily influenced by the Soviet intervention in Hungary is without question. He charged that the Soviet Union's rejection of the legality of anticipatory self-defense was consistent with Soviet interests, such as pressure tactics in Eastern and Central Europe.[200]

While the paralysis of the Security Council was used by supporters of unilateral intervention as a reason why states should be able to act on their own, opponents of unilateral humanitarian intervention drew the opposite conclusion. Paul Szasz, of the UN Legal Office, explained:

The United Nations did not deal with a situation like Bangladesh and Nigeria because to deal with it would have required the use of military or other force by that organization, which, assuming there was a disagreement among the great powers on the subject, would have threatened the peace. . . . Where you have this sort of conflict, the United Nations tends to become paralyzed, and human rights are subordinated to the obligations to keep the peace.[201]

In sum, since one of the permanent members was opposed to interventionary action, it had to be the case that such action could lead to an even greater conflict.

Common ground among most of these scholars was the preferability of humanitarian intervention under the authority of the United Nations rather than unilateral humanitarian intervention,[202] but there was little analysis of how to advance such action by the United Nations. Most schol-

---

199. *Id.* at 99.

200. *Id.* at 100 n.17.

201. P. Szasz, Statement at Symposium on Humanitarian Assistance and Intervention (Mar. 10–11, 1972), *in* THE UNITED NATIONS: A REASSESSMENT; SANCTIONS, PEACE-KEEPING, AND HUMANITARIAN ASSISTANCE (J. Paxman & G. Boggs eds., 1973).

202. Lillich, *Humanitarian Intervention: A Reply to Ian Brownlie and a Plea for Constructive Alternatives, supra* note 185, at 238; R. FALK, LEGAL ORDER IN A VIOLENT WORLD 166–67 (1968).

ars simply noted that action may be taken by the Security Council under Chapter VII when there is a threat to the peace.[203] Yet, even here, some scholars argued that the requirement under Chapter VII for "a threat to the peace, a breach of the peace, or an act of aggression" per se did not fit the concept of humanitarian intervention. In their view, nothing in the Charter's *travaux préparatoires* indicated that the founders envisioned threats by a state against its own nationals as the type of incident that would trigger a breach of the peace requiring Security Council action.[204] Absent this trigger, UN action recommending humanitarian intervention "would be an *ultra vires* recommendation, and would constitute an illegal act of intervention, for neither the organization nor its members may take forceful interventionary measures unless the act against humanity was found to constitute a threat to the peace."[205] Perhaps reflecting this uncertainty, the Restatement (Third), in one of its comments, would only go as far as to say that humanitarian intervention "might be acceptable if taken pursuant to resolution of a United Nations body or of a regional organization."[206]

The issue of humanitarian intervention by regional organizations received even less attention. Those scholars who focused on it, however, tended to see regional organizational action as having a greater legitimacy than unilateral humanitarian intervention, even though the Charter does not exempt action by regional organizations under Article 53 from the strictures of Article 2(4) (as discussed in chapter 3). Ian Brownlie, a forceful critic of those who viewed unilateral humanitarian intervention as lawful, noted that "The Security Council has shown itself to be tolerant and, indeed, supine in the face of regional initiatives or acts of political solidarity not easy to reconcile with the clear terms of Article 53 of the United Nations Charter."[207]

E. Summary

An analysis that begins and ends with the provisions and intent behind the UN Charter provides an incomplete picture of the norms operating in international society. The actions and reactions of states to conflicts as they arise, the attitudes of states as expressed through the organs of the

203. *E.g.*, Brownlie, *supra* note 183, at 226.

204. *See* J. Humphrey, *Forward* to Humanitarian Intervention and the United Nations viii (R. Lillich ed., 1973); *see also* Farer, *supra* note 189, at 190.

205. A. Thomas & A. Thomas, Jr., Non-intervention: The Law and Its Import in the Americas 385 (1956).

206. Restatement (Third) of the Foreign Relations Law of the United States sec. 703 cmt. e.

207. Brownlie, *supra* note 183, at 227.

United Nations system, and the views of scholars of international law and policy are sources of information that provide greater depth to these norms. During the Cold War, all of these sources (or lawmaking processes) were heavily influenced by the bipolar structure of international society.

Interventions by the superpowers occurred primarily in their own spheres of influence and were driven largely by a concern that unfolding events would inure to the benefit of the rival superpower. Interventions by other states were driven occasionally by humanitarian concerns (such as that of France in the Central African Republic), but most of the time the humanitarian benefits were overshadowed by geo-political motivations (such as that of India in East Pakistan and Vietnam in Cambodia). In virtually all instances, the intervening states characterized the intervention as justifiable on a basis other than a doctrine of humanitarian intervention, thus placing some doubt on the acceptance of such a doctrine by the international community. Moreover, the international community was highly critical of most of these interventions; and, when the issue was squarely addressed, the international community disfavored a humanitarian intervention exception relative to the general prohibition on the use of force. This rejection of the doctrine of humanitarian intervention was likely the product of various factors: a desire in the post-World War II era to achieve world order through the application of strict rules on the use of force; the dogmatic abhorrence of foreign intervention by states newly emerging from colonial rule; a belief that states were incapable of acting solely for altruistic reasons in a Cold War world; and the general fear of all transnational conflict in an age of nuclear weapons and superpower rivalry.

Since the UN Security Council was incapable of obtaining a consensus on the use of force to address threats to international peace, states and regional organizations were left on their own to develop coercive techniques for conflict management. At the same time, an impressive array of human rights instruments were developed within the UN system that had the gradual effect of transforming the treatment by a state of its nationals from a matter largely of national concern to a matter that in many situations was of international concern. Scholars wishing to see the protection of these human rights placed on the same level of importance as the self-defense of the state argued forcefully for confirmation of a doctrine of humanitarian intervention. Others saw no evidence of such a doctrine in the practice of states and doubted that acknowledging such a doctrine would enhance the maintenance of world order.

Although difficulties certainly remain, the end of the Cold War and the break-up of the former Soviet Union have developed new opportunities for humanitarian intervention under the authority of the Security

Council. Whereas previously a lack of concurrence by one or more of the permanent members stymied efforts under Chapter VII, the Security Council, since 1990, has invoked Chapter VII in resolutions that are unprecedented both in number and scope. On the basis of these resolutions, several incidents of foreign intervention have been authorized by the Security Council to address widespread deprivations of human rights. These incidents—the focus of the next chapter—reveal various means for forcibly addressing human rights deprivations, while at the same time highlighting the inherent difficulties in deploying such force effectively.

Chapter 5
Incidents of Intervention After the Cold War

This chapter addresses six post-Cold War incidents of what might be considered humanitarian intervention: Liberia, Iraq, Bosnia-Herzegovina, Somalia, Rwanda, and Haiti. Greater attention to detail and analysis is given to these incidents than was given to the incidents discussed in chapter 4 since these six incidents have not as yet received extensive scrutiny by scholars. Indeed, all of these interventions have only recently concluded or remain ongoing as of the date of this study, which is current as of October 1995.

These six incidents are presented roughly in chronological order, based on the year in which significant forcible action was taken by the international community (although other action may have existed in earlier or subsequent years). As will be seen, there are important differences among them. In some cases, the Security Council expressly authorized the intervention; in others the intervention was not authorized by the Security Council, or at best occurred with the implied authority of the Security Council. In some cases, the role of regional organizations was minimal, while in others the intervention occurred only with the political or military backing of a regional organization. In some cases, the human rights deprivations were in the nature of brutal atrocities that claimed the lives of hundreds of thousands of people, while in one case the rights at stake were largely political in nature. In some cases, the local government or factions vehemently opposed the intervention, while in others the de jure government favored intervention while the de facto government did not. In some cases, the objective of the intervention was simply to establish safe havens for the protection of displaced persons, while in others there existed a broader mission of stabilizing the conflict, disarming factions, and achieving political reconciliation.

Yet there are commonalities among these interventions from which at least themes, if not lessons, may be derived. All occurred after a significant loss of life or suffering by a civilian population and after significant flows of refugees began pouring out of the target state into neighboring states. With the exception of Haiti, all occurred in the context of violent civil war among factions within the target state. With the exception of Liberia, all were driven by the military and logistical capabilities of a major power, usually the United States. And, in all instances, the intervention had a positive effect in saving lives, although in no case did military intervention alone resolve the underlying problem afflicting the target state.

To analyze these incidents usefully, it is necessary first to consider the underlying facts involved and then to assess each set of facts by asking the following questions: Do actions by states or the United Nations in this incident suggest a use of force or intervention that implicates the prohibitions contained in Article 2(4) or 2(7) of the UN Charter? If so, was the use of force for purposes of self-defense or to restore international peace, or was it predominantly for the protection of human rights? Was there any direct authorization from the local governing authorities for the intervention? If not, was there authorization from the Security Council pursuant to a finding that there was a "threat to the peace" and, if so, what was the nature of that threat? Alternatively, was there authorization from a regional organization, or did the intervening states plead that they were authorized pursuant to customary rules of international law? Was there a general reaction by the international community as to the lawfulness of the actions taken by states or by the United Nations? What basic lessons might be learned from the incident? Common themes, successes, and failures of these incidents will be explored in subsequent chapters.

A. Liberia (1990)

1. Essential Facts

Unlike most African states, Liberia has had a lengthy national history. It was founded in 1822 by slaves freed in the United States with the aid of U.S. President James Monroe and gained its independence in 1847, thereby making it Africa's first independent republic. By 1958, it still was only one of nine independent states on the African continent.

Yet Liberia's lengthy independent history did not shield it from the political and economic turmoil that most African states experienced in the post-colonial era. In 1980, a violent coup by the Armed Forces of Liberia (AFL) resulted in the assassination of President William R. Tolbert and the ascension to power of a radical military officer, Samuel Doe. Doe's repressive rule made him unpopular and the subject himself of repeated coup attempts. In 1989 Charles Taylor, a former Liberian minister who had fallen out of favor with Doe and fled from Liberia, organized a rebel force in the neighboring francophone Ivory Coast, with the support of some of the citizens of that country. On December 24, 1989, Taylor's forces (known as the National Patriotic Front or NPFL) invaded Liberia. Although revolution against Doe was supported by most Liberians, the invasion sparked an all-out civil war among Doe's AFL, Taylor's NPFL, and a third rebel group, the Independent National Patriotic Front of Liberia (INPFL) led by Prince Johnson. Doe's AFL sought to suppress the insurgency through indiscriminate attacks on villages and people in the Nimba Province of Liberia entered by Taylor's NPFL forces, and this led to the movement of up to 10,000 refugees from Liberia into the Ivory Coast.[1] One Western diplomat stated: "The army started shooting and hacking at anyone they thought was a rebel. They didn't care if they were civilians or not. From all accounts, they were committing real atrocities."[2] By May 1990 some 200,000 of 270,000 persons residing in the Nimba Province had fled their homes, seeking sanctuary either in the capital city of Monrovia or in the neighboring countries of Guinea and the Ivory Coast.[3] The AFL, however, proved incapable of repulsing or destroying the NPFL, which throughout spring 1990 gained control of progressively larger portions of the country and summarily killed government officials and others considered to be supporters of Doe's government.[4]

By summer 1990, the rebel forces dominated the country: Doe's AFL was confined to a small part of Monrovia; Johnson's INPFL controlled the rest of Monrovia and its port; and Taylor's NPFL controlled the rest of Liberia. Thousands of people, mostly unarmed civilians, were dead and thousands more wounded.[5] In August, U.S. marines evacuated U.S. and other nationals by helicopter but took no action to address the overall crisis in the country.[6] Vicious fighting and brutal coercion continued among different ethnic and tribal clans supporting one or another of the

1. J. Perlez, *Refugees Report Liberian "Scorched Earth" Drive on Rebels*, N.Y. TIMES, Jan. 9, 1990, at A3.

2. K. Noble, *Masses of Liberian Refugees Flee Rebellion and Reprisal Killings*, N.Y. TIMES, Jan. 31, 1990, at A1.

3. K. Noble, *War of Quick but Brutal Clashes Unfolds in Liberia*, N.Y. TIMES, May 18, 1990, at A3.

4. AMNESTY INTERATIONAL REPORT, 1991 145, 145–46 (1991).

5. K. Noble, *Negotiations to Settle Liberian War End in Failure*, N.Y. TIMES, Aug. 23, 1990, at A11.

6. For a study of this rescue operation and its significance in international law for the issue of protection of nationals, *see* R. Lillich, *Forcible Protection of Nationals Abroad: The Liberian "Incident" of 1990*, 35 GERMAN Y.B. INT'L L. 205 (1992).

main factions;[7] combatants were not physically distinguishable from non-combatants, and targeting on all sides was indiscriminate. Civil administration, social services, and economic activities (including the banking system) throughout the country began to disintegrate, and shortages of foreign exchange virtually precluded the import of food, fuel, and other essential consumer goods. It was believed that eventually widespread disease would break out. Massive numbers of civilians continued to flee to Monrovia for protection, more than doubling its population, while others left the country. By March 1993, war-related casualties were estimated at as high as 150,000 (mostly civilians) and Liberian refugees in Guinea, the Ivory Coast, and Sierra Leone at 600,000 to 700,000.[8]

The Economic Community of West African States (ECOWAS), an organization of sixteen states (including Liberia)[9] that was established in 1975,[10] monitored the events in Liberia from their inception. The principal governing institution of ECOWAS is the Authority of Heads of State and Government (ECOWAS Authority), which meets annually. Its primary aim is to promote cooperation and development in all fields of economic activity, and in social and cultural matters, for the purpose of "raising the standard of living of its peoples, of increasing and maintaining economic stability, of fostering closer relations among its members and of contributing to the progress and development of the African continent."[11] ECOWAS represents the broadest, most comprehensive attempt yet at subregional organization in Africa and may be a foundation for Africa's future development; in 1991, the Organization of African

7. K. Noble, *From Liberian War, Tales of Brutality*, N.Y. TIMES, July 9, 1990, at A3; Reuter, *Fierce Fighting Erupts Near Monrovia*, N.Y. TIMES, Aug. 10, 1993, at A3.

8. *Report of the Secretary-General*, para. 8, U.N. Doc. S/25402 (1993).

9. The members of ECOWAS are Benin, Burkina Faso, Cape Verde, Ivory Coast, Gambia, Ghana, Guinea, Guinea-Bissau, Liberia, Mali, Mauritania, Niger, Nigeria, Senegal, Sierra Leone, and Togo.

10. Treaty of the Economic Community of West African States, May 28, 1975, 1010 U.N.T.S. 17, 14 I.L.M. 1200, *reprinted in* REGIONAL PEACE-KEEPING AND INTERNATIONAL ENFORCEMENT: THE LIBERIAN CRISIS 1 (M. Weller ed., 1994) [hereinafter THE LIBERIAN CRISIS].

For general information on ECOWAS, *see* M. Ajomo, *Regional Economic Organisations: The African Experience*, 25 INT'L & COMP. L.Q. 58 (1979); S. ASANTE, POLITICAL ECONOMY OF REGIONALISM IN AFRICA: A DECADE OF THE ECONOMIC COMMUNITY OF WEST AFRICAN STATES (1986); U. EZENWE, ECOWAS AND THE ECONOMIC INTEGRATION OF WEST AFRICA 126 (1983); S. Olofin, *ECOWAS and the Lomé Convention: An Experiment in Complementary or Conflicting Customs Union Arrangements?*, 16 J. COMMON MKT. STUD. 53 (1977); B. Zagaris, *The Economic Community of West African States (ECOWAS): An Analysis and Prospects*, 10 CASE W. RES. J. INT'L L. 93 (1978).

11. Treaty of the Economic Community of West African States, *supra* note 10, art. 2, para. 1.

Unity (OAU) concluded a treaty establishing the African Economic Community, which envisions such groupings for the entire continent.[12] Yet ECOWAS's powers are limited. For instance, unlike the European Union (EU), it does not have the power to require its members to adopt uniform legislation in accordance with community programs.[13]

In the late 1970s, the ECOWAS Authority decided that ECOWAS could not achieve its objectives without an "atmosphere of peace and harmonious understanding" among its members, and consequently developed both a 1978 Protocol on Non-Aggression and a 1981 Protocol Relating to Mutual Assistance on Defence.[14] The thrust of the two protocols was to generate trust and confidence among the member states and to shift from a reliance on foreign powers for their defense by building their own regional collective security mechanism. The 1981 Protocol requires member states to earmark military units for an "Allied Armed Forces of the Community" (AAFC) to be used: (1) to act as a buffer between two member states engaged in armed conflict; (2) to address an internal conflict in a member state that is actively maintained and sustained from outside ECOWAS when requested by that member state; and (3) to address an external armed threat or aggression against a member state when requested by that member state. The ECOWAS forces are not to intervene if a conflict remains "purely internal." [15]

At its annual meeting in May 1990, the ECOWAS Authority established a Standing Mediation Committee to investigate disputes and conflicts within the community.[16] The Standing Mediation Committee decided to focus its work on Liberia, and in June representatives of the Committee participated in negotiations with the Liberian factions in an effort to achieve a peaceful settlement. Those efforts failed, however. In July President Doe, whose forces were reeling from the NPFL advance, sent a letter to the Standing Mediation Committee stating that "it would seem most expedient at this time to introduce an ECOWAS Peace-keeping Force into Liberia to forestall increasing terror and tension and to assure

12. Treaty Establishing the African Economic Community, June 3, 1991, 30 I.L.M. 1241, *reprinted in* 4 INTERNATIONAL LAW AND WORLD ORDER: BASIC DOCUMENTS IV.B.2 (B. Weston ed., 1994) (hereafter WESTON).

13. *See* Treaty of the Economic Community of West African States, *supra* note 10, art. 3.

14. Protocol on Non-Aggression, Apr. 22, 1978, *reprinted in* THE LIBERIAN CRISIS, *supra* note 10, at 18; Protocol relating to Mutual Assistance on Defence, May 29, 1981, *reprinted in* THE LIBERIAN CRISIS, *supra* note 10, at 19.

15. Protocol relating to Mutual Assistance on Defence, *supra* note 14, arts. 4, 16, 17, 18.

16. ECOWAS, Authority of Heads of State and Government, Decision A/DEC.9/5/90 Relating to the Establishment of the Standing Mediation Committee, May 30, 1990, para. 24, *reprinted in* THE LIBERIAN CRISIS, *supra* note 10, at 38. Gambia, Ghana, Guinea, Nigeria, Sierra Leone, and Togo participated in the meeting.

a peaceful transitional environment."[17] By this point, the reports of human rights abuses indicated that they were being committed on a massive scale by both the AFL and the rebel forces.

In early August, the Committee met and found that:

The failure of the warring parties to cease hostilities has led to the massive destruction of property and the massacre by all the parties of thousands of innocent civilians including foreign nationals, women and children, some of whom had sought sanctuary in churches, hospitals, diplomatic missions and under Red Cross protection, contrary to all recognised standards of civilised behaviour. Worse still, there are corpses lying unburied in the streets of cities and towns, which could lead to a serious outbreak of an epidemic. The civil war has also trapped thousands of foreign nationals, including ECOWAS citizens, without any means of escape or protection.

The result of all this is a state of anarchy and the total breakdown of law and order in Liberia. Presently, there is a government in Liberia which cannot govern and contending factions which are holding the entire population as hostage, depriving them of food, health facilities and other basic necessities of life.

These developments have traumatised the Liberian population and greatly shocked the people of the sub-region and the rest of the international community. They have also led to hundreds of thousands of Liberians being displaced and made refugees in neighbouring countries, and the spilling of hostilities into neighbouring countries.[18]

To address this situation, the Committee decided, "on behalf of the ECOWAS Authority," to advance a plan for bringing peace to Liberia. First, it called on the warring parties in Liberia to observe an immediate ceasefire. Second, it established an ECOWAS Cease-fire Monitoring Group (ECOMOG) for the purpose of "keeping the peace, restoring law and order and ensuring that the cease-fire is respected" and called upon the UN Security Council to support this action. In establishing ECOMOG, however, the Committee did not implement the mechanism for a multinational force envisioned by the 1981 protocol. Third, it established a Special Emergency Fund for voluntary contributions to support ECOMOG. Finally, rather than call for the full reinstatement of Samuel Doe as President of the country, it called for him to step aside and for a national conference of all Liberian political parties and other interested groups to establish an interim government pending free and fair elections.[19]

17. Letter addressed by President Samuel K. Doe to the Chairman and Members of the Ministerial Meeting of the ECOWAS Standing Mediation Committee, July 14, 1990, *reprinted in* THE LIBERIAN CRISIS, *supra* note 10, at 60.

18. ECOWAS, Standing Mediation Committee, Final Communiqué of the First Session, Aug. 7, 1990, paras. 6–8, *reprinted in* THE LIBERIAN CRISIS, *supra* note 10, at 73.

19. *Id.* at paras. 10–14, 18; *see also* ECOWAS, Standing Mediation Committee, Decision A/DEC.1/8/90 on the Cease-fire and Establishment of an ECOWAS Cease-fire Monitoring

Shortly thereafter, Dr. Amos C. Sawyer, who was not the leader of any of the Liberian factions and who (it was agreed) would not stand for President when elections occurred, was elected "Interim President" at a national conference organized by ECOWAS. Then, on August 13, regulations were adopted to govern the operations of ECOMOG. In addition to providing for the wearing of a special uniform and the flying of a special flag, the regulations provided:

> The ECOWAS Cease-fire Monitoring Group is a subsidiary organ of the Community consisting of the Commander and all military personnel placed under his Command by Member States. The members of the Group, although remaining in their national service, are, during the period of their assignment to the Group, international personnel under the authority of ECOWAS and subject to the instructions of the Commander through the chain of command. The functions of the Group are exclusively international and members of the Group shall discharge these functions and regulate their conduct with the interest of ECOWAS only in view.[20]

ECOMOG consisted primarily of military units from Gambia, Ghana, Guinea, Nigeria, and Sierra Leone and was commanded by a Ghanian general, Arnold Quainoo.[21]

On August 24, 1990, after just two weeks of preparation, ECOMOG forces landed at Monrovia's port. The largest contingent of the initial ECOMOG forces of 3,000 was supplied by the most militarily-powerful state in the region, Nigeria.[22] Samuel Doe, still technically President but whose forces were largely confined to central Monrovia, opposed the intervention. While he had favored assistance from foreign forces to put

---

Group for Liberia, Aug. 7, 1990, *reprinted in* THE LIBERIAN CRISIS, *supra* note 10, at 67; ECOWAS, Standing Mediation Committee, Decision A/DEC.2/8/90 on the Constitution of an Interim Government in the Republic of Liberia, Aug. 7, 1990, *reprinted in* THE LIBERIAN CRISIS, *supra* note 10, at 69; ECOWAS, Standing Mediation Committee, Decision A/DEC.3/8/90 on the Establishment of a Special Emergency Fund for ECOWAS Operations in the Republic of Liberia, Aug. 7, 1990, *reprinted in* THE LIBERIAN CRISIS, *supra* note 10, at 70; ECOWAS, Standing Mediation Committee, Decision A/DEC.4/8/90 on the Establishment of an ECOWAS Observer Group for Presidential and General Elections in the Republic of Liberia, Aug. 7, 1990, *reprinted in* THE LIBERIAN CRISIS, *supra* note 10, at 71.

20. ECOWAS Regulations for a Cease-fire Monitoring Group (ECOMOG) in Liberia, Aug. 13, 1990, para. 6, *reprinted in* THE LIBERIAN CRISIS, *supra* note 10, 77 at 79.

21. *NPFL Tells ECOWAS No Cease-fire Till Doe Goes*, BBC MONITORING REP., Aug. 9, 1990, *reprinted in* THE LIBERIAN CRISIS, *supra* note 10, at 75. Troops from Mali and Senegal also initially participated, but Senegal withdrew its contribution in January 1993. Togo initially was supposed to participate, but later refused to do so. Burkina Faso initially did not participate, but then later did.

22. Associated Press, *West Africa Force Repels Attack by Liberia Rebels*, N.Y. TIMES, Aug. 26, 1990, sec. 1, at 13.

down the insurgency, he did not accept the basis for the ECOMOG intervention, which called for his resignation and replacement by an interim
government.[23] Charles Taylor, whose NPFL forces at this point occupied
most of Liberia, strongly opposed the ECOMOG intervention.[24] The
NPFL was reported to be particularly angry that Nigerian and Guinean
forces were participating in ECOMOG, since the NPFL believed those
countries were partial to President Doe.[25] The INPFL leader, Prince
Johnson, did not oppose the intervention and even met the ECOMOG
forces when they arrived.[26]

Within two days, ECOMOG clashed with Taylor's forces. The better-
trained and better-equipped ECOMOG forces were successful, however,
in keeping Taylor's forces out of Monrovia and in establishing a zone
for humanitarian assistance to be channeled to many of the victims
of the civil war. On September 9, 1990 President Doe left the heavily
fortified palace in which he had been barricaded and went to the
ECOMOG headquarters, reportedly to discuss a ceasefire agreement
with the INPFL. Fighting broke out between the factions, killing some
sixty people and resulting in Doe's capture by the INPFL.[27] The next day,
Doe either died from wounds sustained during his capture or was killed
by the INPFL. ECOMOG forces were present at the time of Doe's capture
but reportedly were unable to stop the fighting, prompting some charges
that they may have acted in collusion with the INPFL.[28]

Although ECOMOG was called a "peacekeeping" force, it was aggressive in responding to attacks by the NPFL. It was ECOMOG that used
aircraft for the first time in the civil war, to bomb NPFL positions
outside Monrovia.[29] The willingness of ECOMOG to pursue the NPFL
with heavy artillery and tanks undoubtedly helped ECOWAS to bring
representatives from all of the warring factions to the table for a series
of meetings. At an extraordinary session of the ECOWAS Authority in
November 1990, the Liberian factions agreed to establish a ceasefire
across Liberia.[30] The ceasefire agreement and the presence of the

---

23. K. Noble, *Liberia Leader, Rejecting Truce Offer, Won't Quit*, N.Y. TIMES, Aug. 21, 1990,
at A11.

24. *Report of the Secretary-General, supra* note 8, para. 25.

25. K. Noble, *West African Force Sent to Liberia*, N.Y. TIMES, Aug. 22, 1990, at A3.

26. Associated Press, *supra* note 22.

27. K. Noble, *Liberian President Captured by Rebels in a Fierce Gunfight*, N.Y. TIMES, Sept. 10,
1990, at A1.

28. K. Noble, *Liberian Insurgents Kill President, Diplomats and Broadcasts Report*, N.Y. TIMES,
Aug. 11, 1990, at A1.

29. K. Noble, *Ghana Is Said to Strike Liberian Rebels*, N.Y. TIMES, Sept. 17, 1990, at A3.

30. ECOWAS, Authority of Heads of State and Government, Decision A/DEC.1/11/90
Relating to the Approval of the Decision of the Community Standing Mediation Committee
Taken During its First Session from 6 to 7 August 1990, Nov. 28, 1990, *reprinted in* THE

ECOMOG forces in Liberia (which reached 15,000 persons) in a "peace-keeping" mode prevented widespread fighting for 21 months. The leader of the INPFL, Prince Johnson, surrendered to ECOMOG, and INPFL ceased to exist as a warring faction. Sporadic fighting, however, did continue in Liberia; moreover, Taylor provided support to rebels in neighboring Sierra Leone, sparking a war that would last several years in that country.[31]

After consultations within the Security Council, on January 22, 1991, the President of the Security Council stated that "The members of the Security Council commend the efforts made by the ECOWAS Heads of State and Government to promote peace and normalcy in Liberia" and called upon the parties to the conflict to respect the ceasefire agreement.[32] This statement, in essence, endorsed the intervention of ECOMOG. Countries outside ECOWAS also supported the ECOMOG intervention. The OAU voiced its support for ECOWAS and individual states provided financial support.[33]

Pursuant to a series of four meetings in Yamoussoukro, Ivory Coast, agreement was reached in October 1991 on specific steps to implement the ECOWAS peace plan (Yamoussoukro IV Accord).[34] These steps included the reshaping of the national forces provided to ECOMOG to reflect the West African community as a whole, the gathering of armed units at camps where they would be disarmed under the supervision of ECOMOG, and the monitoring of all entry points into Liberia by ECOMOG to prevent external influences. Further, ECOMOG was to create a process by which Interim Elections Commissioners and ad hoc Supreme Court judges would be appointed in anticipation of holding

---

LIBERIAN CRISIS, *supra* note 10, at 111; *see also* K. Noble, *Liberian Factions Agree to a Cease-fire*, N.Y. TIMES, Nov. 29, 1990, at A3.

31. K. Noble, *Liberian Conflict Engulfs Neighbor*, N.Y. TIMES, Apr. 16, 1991, at A7; H. French, *Refugees Starving in West Africa's Last Civil War*, INT'L HERALD TRIB., Oct. 3, 1995, at 2.

32. *Note by the President of the Security Council*, U.N. Doc. S/22133 (1991); *see also Note by the President of the Security Council*, U.N. Doc. S/23886 (1992) (supporting the Yamoussoukro IV Accord as the best possible framework for a peaceful resolution of the Liberian conflict).

33. During the thirty months following the intervention, the United States provided nearly $29 million in support to ECOWAS, in addition to more than $203 million in humanitarian assistance. H. Cohen, Peace-Keeping and Conflict Resolution in Africa, Statement Before the Subcommittee on Africa of the House Foreign Affairs Committee (Mar. 31, 1993), *in* 4 U.S. DEP'T ST. DISPATCH 270, 271 (1993) (Assistant Secretary of State for African Affairs). The United Kingdom provided £8.8 million in humanitarian relief both bilaterally and through the European Community. U.N. SCOR, 48th Sess., 3263d mtg. at 28, U.N. Doc. S/PV.3263 (1993).

34. Yamoussoukro IV Accord, Oct. 30, 1991, *reprinted in Letter Dated 30 April 1992 from Senegal to the Secretary-General*, Annex, para. 3, U.N. Doc. S/24815 (1992) and *in* THE LIBERIAN CRISIS, *supra* note 10, at 175.

elections.[35] A buffer zone would be created along the Liberia-Sierra Leone border. The process was to be completed within six months, by April 1992.

Although he signed the Yamoussoukro IV Accord, Charles Taylor resisted compliance with its encampment and disarmament provisions.[36] In July 1992, due to Taylor's intransigence, ECOWAS threatened to impose comprehensive sanctions against the territory held by the NPFL.[37] In August 1992 the ceasefire broke down and a new rebel force, the United Liberation Movement of Liberia for Democracy (ULIMO) led by Alhaji Kromah, impatient with the slow pace of the peace process, attacked Taylor's NPFL forces from their base in Sierra Leone, pushing them out of two southwestern counties. The NPFL remained undeterred, however, taking hostage some 600 ECOMOG troops deployed in its territory pursuant to the disarmament and encampment program. In mid-October, Taylor's NPFL forces attacked the ECOMOG forces in Monrovia, forcing ECOMOG to switch from a "peacekeeping" mode to a "peace enforcement" mode. The plan for elections was suspended, ECOMOG successfully reestablished a perimeter around Mogadishu and began striking at NPFL lines of supply, and fighting between the two forces resulted in extensive deaths and property damage over several months, including collateral civilian casualties.[38]

In late 1992 Charles Taylor told the United Nations that he did not regard ECOMOG as a "neutral" entity; he criticized Nigeria's dominant role in ECOMOG, asserted that ECOMOG was supporting the AFL and

35. *See* ECOWAS Committee of Five, Final Communique of the Informal Consultative Group, Apr. 7, 1992, *reprinted in Letter Dated 30 April 1992 from Senegal to the Secretary-General*, Annex, para. 3, U.N. Doc. S/23863 (1992) and *in* THE LIBERIAN CRISIS, *supra* note 10, at 189.

36. *See generally Crisis in Liberia: The Regional Impact; and a Review of U.S. Policy and Markup of H.R. 994, Hearing Before the Subcomm. on Africa of the House Comm. on Foreign Affairs*, 102d Cong., 1st Sess. (1991).

37. ECOWAS, Authority of Heads of State and Government, Decision A/DEC.8/7/92 Relating to Sanctions Against Charles Taylor and the National Patriotic Front of Liberia, July 27–29, 1992, *reprinted in* THE LIBERIAN CRISIS, *supra* note 10, at 206. The sanctions were actually imposed beginning in November 1992 on all warring factions after a meeting of the Authority of Heads of State and Government in Abuja. ECOWAS, First Meeting of the Committee of Nine on the Liberian Crisis, Final Communiqué, Nov. 7, 1992, *reprinted in* THE LIBERIAN CRISIS, *supra* note 10, at 241 [hereinafter ECOWAS Meeting of Nov. 7, 1992]; *see also* ECOWAS, First Joint Session of the ECOWAS Standing Mediation Committee and the Committee of Five, Decision A/DEC.1/10/92 Relating to the Implementation of Decision A/DEC.8/7/92 on Sanctions against Parties to the Liberian Conflict which Fail to Comply with the Implementation of the Yamoussoukro Accord of 30 October 1991, and Final Communique of the First Joint Summit Meeting of the ECOWAS Standing Mediation Committee and the Committee of Five, Oct. 30, 1992, *reprinted in* THE LIBERIAN CRISIS, *supra* note 10, at 232.

38. *See* K. Maier, *Air Raids on Liberia Intensify*, WASH. POST, Apr. 4, 1993, at A40.

ULIMO, and argued that the ECOWAS establishment of an Interim Government contravened the Liberian constitution. Further, he stated that, in light of the fate of Samuel Doe, he feared for his own security should he lay down his arms.[39]

On November 7, 1992 a "committee of nine" of the ECOWAS states declared that, because all the Liberian warring factions had failed to implement the terms of the Yamoussoukro IV Accord, economic sanctions would be imposed, with the exception of humanitarian goods.[40] ECOWAS sought (through the committee of nine) to have these sanctions made mandatory by the Security Council for the entire international community,[41] as did the Liberian Interim Government.[42] The Liberian Foreign Minister argued that Security Council sanctions were necessary to bring peace to the Liberian situation, which "has all the makings of one that could degenerate into a wider conflagration in West Africa."[43]

On November 19, 1992 the Security Council passed Resolution 788 in which it determined that "the deterioration of the situation in Liberia constitutes a threat to international peace and security, particularly in West Africa as a whole."[44] The Security Council called on all the Liberian factions to respect the ceasefire and again "commended" ECOWAS for its efforts to restore peace, security, and stability in Liberia. It further decided, under Chapter VII of the UN Charter, to impose a general and complete embargo on all deliveries of weapons and military equipment to Liberia, with the exception of weapons and military equipment destined for the sole use of ECOMOG.[45]

The discussion by the members of the Security Council indicated broad support for the ECOMOG intervention, without reservation. The United States asserted:

[W]e must not lose sight of what ECOWAS has accomplished through intervention and negotiation. The dispatch of a six-nation West African peace-keeping force in August 1990 demonstrated unprecedented African determination to

39. *Report of the Secretary-General, supra* note 8, at 28.

40. ECOWAS Meeting of Nov. 7, 1992, *supra* note 37. The Committee of Nine coordinated ECOWAS activities on Liberia and was composed of the foreign ministers of Burkina Faso, Gambia, Ghana, Guinea, Ivory Coast, Mali, Nigeria, Senegal, and Sierra Leone.

41. *Id*. para. 16.

42. *Letter Dated 18 November 1992 from Liberia to the President of the Security Council*, U.N. Doc. S/24825 (1992).

43. U.N. SCOR, 47th Sess., 3138th mtg. at 18, U.N. Doc. S/PV.3138 (1992) (statement of Gabriel Baccus Matthews, Minister of Foreign Affairs of the Interim Government of Liberia).

44. S.C. Res. 788, U.N. SCOR, 47th Sess., 3138th mtg. at 99, pmbl., U.N. Doc. S/INF/48 (1993).

45. *Id*. paras. 8–9.

take the lead in regional conflict resolution. ECOMOG ended the killing, separated the warring factions, allowed relief assistance to flow to avert starvation and established a cease-fire and framework for peaceful negotiations. . . .

Although the dispatch of peace-keeping forces to Liberia was a decision taken by the ECOWAS Governments on their own initiative, we have supported this effort from its inception.[46]

Statements by various other Security Council members suggested an appreciation for the capabilities of subregional organizations in addressing conflicts in their region and the need for Security Council support for those actions.

More active involvement of the United Nations proved necessary, though, due to the mistrust that had developed between ECOMOG and the NPFL. In Resolution 788, the Security Council requested the Secretary-General to dispatch a special representative to Liberia to evaluate the situation,[47] and in ensuing discussions with the local and regional leaders the special representative uncovered a belief that the United Nations should assume a greater role in the resolution of the Liberian conflict.[48] Consequently, the Security Council passed Resolution 813, in which it declared its "readiness to consider appropriate measures in support of [ECOWAS] if any party is unwilling to cooperate in implementation of the provisions of the Yamoussoukro Accords, in particular the encampment and disarmament provisions."[49] Further, the Security Council requested the Secretary-General, in consultation with ECOWAS, to consider the possibility of convening a meeting of the warring factions.[50]

Numerous meetings attended by UN and ECOWAS representatives occurred over the next eighteen months in an effort to achieve a negotiated settlement. Ultimately, a successful meeting of the various factions was held under the auspices of the United Nations in Geneva on July 10–17, 1993. The factions agreed to conclude a new peace agreement that provided for a new ceasefire, set forth steps for encampment, disarmament, and demobilization, and established procedures leading to general and presidential elections. To allay concerns of the NPFL regarding ECOMOG, it was agreed that ECOMOG would be expanded to include

46. U.N. Doc. S/PV.3138 (1992), *supra* note 43, at 74–76.

47. S.C. Res. 788, *supra* note 44, para. 7. The Secretary-General appointed Mr. Trevor Livingston Gordon-Somers, a national of Jamaica, as the special representative. Following his appointment, Gordon-Somers visited Liberia, Benin, Burkina Faso, Gambia, Guinea, Ivory Coast, Nigeria, Senegal, and Sierra Leone. Gordon-Somers was replaced by Anthony B. Nyaki, a national of Tanzania, on December 28, 1994.

48. *Report of the Secretary-General, supra* note 8, paras. 21–37.

49. S.C. Res. 813, U.N. SCOR, 48th Sess., 3187th mtg. at 108, para. 11, U.N. Doc. S/INF/49 (1994).

50. *Id.* para. 17.

additional forces from countries not already participating in ECOMOG (including countries outside the West African region, such as Tanzania and Uganda), and it was proposed that UN military observers monitor and verify the ceasefire as well as the implementation of the encampment, disarmament, and demobilization of the Liberian factions.[51] The resultant peace agreement was signed at an ECOWAS summit held at Cotonou, Benin, by the Interim Government of Liberia, the NPFL, and the ULIMO on July 25, 1993 (the Cotonou Agreement).[52]

In August 1993, the Security Council agreed in principle to the creation of a UN Observer Mission in Liberia (UNOMIL),[53] which was established in September.[54] Thereafter, ECOMOG sought to supervise the implementation of the Cotonou Agreement, including disarmament of Liberian forces, while the United Nations monitored and verified that ECOMOG's implementation was being conducted in an impartial manner. A special trust fund was established by the Secretary-General to furnish assistance to countries of the region that had contributed to the ECOWAS operation. This was the first time a UN peacekeeping mission was undertaken in cooperation with a peacekeeping operation already set up by another organization.

The commitment of the Liberian factions to a peaceful, national reconciliation proved elusive, however. Fighting among and within the factions continued, and efforts for disarmament and establishment of the transitional government initially stalled. Ultimately, agreement was reached on the composition of most of the positions for a new Council of State of a Transitional Government, which was installed on March 7, 1994, and disarmament purportedly commenced. Certain key positions in this Transitional Government, however, could not be agreed upon (Taylor felt his faction was underrepresented), and, in any event, it had little authority outside Monrovia. Consequently the fighting continued, making elections impossible.[55] In some instances, UN military observers and aid workers were captured in areas controlled by Taylor.[56]

In September 1994, another peace accord was signed in Akosombo,

51. For a report on the negotiations and a description of the Cotonou Agreement, *see Further Report of the Secretary-General*, U.N. Doc. S/26200 (1993).

52. Cotonou Agreement, July 25, 1993, *reprinted in Letter Dated 6 August 1993 from Benin to the Secretary-General*, Annex, U.N. Doc. S/26272 (1993).

53. S.C. Res. 856, U.N. SCOR, 48th Sess., 3263d mtg. at 110, U.N. Doc. S/INF/49 (1994).

54. S.C. Res. 866, U.N. SCOR, 48th Sess., 3281st mtg. at 110, U.N. Doc. S/INF/49 (1994).

55. C. Shiner, *In Battle and in Politics, Liberia's Motley Factions Fight On*, WASH. POST, Aug. 7, 1994, at A27 (reporting that only 3,300 of 60,000 fighters have been disarmed); H. French, *As War Factions Shatter, Liberia Falls into Chaos*, N.Y. TIMES, Oct. 22, 1994, sec. 1, at 4.

56. Reuters, *Fighting Flares in Liberia Despite Two-Day-Old Cease-Fire Accord*, WASH. POST, Sept. 15, 1994, at A33 (reporting continued fighting and seizing of U.N. monitors and aid workers).

Ghana, once again calling for disarmament and elections by October 1995[57] and then a further peace accord in Accra, Ghana, in December 1994.[58] But they too proved unable to prevent continued fighting, forcing UNOMIL to reduce its presence.[59] By the end of 1994, some 1.1 million Liberians remained internally displaced and some 785,000 Liberians were refugees: an estimated 420,000 in Guinea, 320,000 in Ivory Coast, 20,000 in Ghana, 20,000 in Sierra Leone, and 5,000 in Nigeria and other countries.[60] Efforts to repatriate these Liberians were futile given the ongoing civil violence, which saw periodic massacres of civilians by marauding armed militias.[61]

On August 19, 1995, a further peace accord was signed at Abuja, Nigeria, by the main warring factions.[62] Within weeks, the top positions in a new Liberian government had been agreed upon, with Charles Taylor's representatives taking the key foreign affairs, interior, and justice positions. Reportedly now satisfied with the power-sharing arrangements, Taylor pledged to allow ECOMOG to disarm his faction, once again potentially paving the way for a lasting peace in Liberia, after six years of war and some 150,000 deaths.[63]

2. Assessment of the Intervention

The deployment by five states of 3,000 armed forces into Liberia in August 1990 sought to suppress both the regular and irregular forces operating in Liberia. It was not limited to the protection of foreign na-

---

57. Reuters, *Liberian Warlords Sign Peace Accord*, WASH. POST, Sept. 13, 1994, at A17.

58. Agreement on the Clarification of the Akosombo Agreement, Dec. 21, 1994, *reprinted in Letter Dated 5 January 1995 from Ghana to the President of the Security Council*, Annex II, U.N. Doc. S/1995/7 (1994).

59. *See Seventh Progress Report of the Secretary General*, U.N. Doc. S/1994/1167 (1994); S.C. Res. 950, U.N. SCOR, 49th Sess., 3442d mtg., U.N. Doc. S/RES/950 (1994); *Eighth Progress Report of the Secretary-General*, S/1995/9 (1995); S.C. Res. 972, U.N. SCOR, 50th Sess., 3489th mtg., U.N. Doc. S/RES/972 (1995).

60. U.S. COMMITTEE FOR REFUGEES, WORLD REFUGEE SURVEY — 1995 63 (1995) [hereinafter WORLD REFUGEE SURVEY].

61. *See, e.g.*, H. French, *62 Slain in Raid on Village Near Liberia Port*, N.Y. TIMES, Apr. 19, 1995, at A5; H. French, *As Violence Mounts, Liberians Hope for Foreign Help*, N.Y. TIMES, May 3, 1995, at A3; H. French, *Long War Turns Liberia Into Core of a Spreading Blight*, N.Y. TIMES, May 25, 1995, at A11 ("In the countryside, instead of merely being the theater of constant small-scale skirmishes between poorly armed peasants, one village after another has been leveled and inhabitants slaughtered by the heavy firepower of tribally based militias that mark their territory with the skulls of their victims.").

62. Agence France-Presse, *Liberians Sign A New Peace Pact*, INT'L HERALD TRIB., Aug. 21, 1995, at 7.

63. *Liberians Agree on Top Posts in Cabinet*, INT'L HERALD TRIB., Sept. 4, 1995, at 7.

tionals. Consequently, the intervention was a use of force against a state by a group of states that raises questions under Article 2(4) of the UN Charter.

The reason for the intervention was multifaceted. The August 1990 statement of the ECOWAS Standing Mediation Committee asserted that thousands of non-Liberian West African nationals were trapped in Liberia. Furthermore, large numbers of refugees had fled to neighboring countries, causing considerable economic and political turmoil in the region. The turbulence in Liberia had the potential to expand into a much wider regional conflict. Indeed, in April 1991, neighboring Sierra Leone was attacked by rebels who received support from Liberia, and in 1992 ULIMO operations from its base in Sierra Leone actually pushed nearly 100,000 Sierra Leonean refugees into Liberia.[64] Reports circulated that some of the Liberian rebel groups were receiving support from external sources and that some of the NPFL rebels were not Liberian nationals but, rather, foreigners who were fighting due to a promise of future support for rebellion against the government of their country.[65] Consequently, the Liberian civil war contained elements that went beyond just internal conflict.

Nevertheless, the dominant concern expressed in the Standing Mediation Committee statement was for the plight of Liberian nationals that had been killed, wounded, or forced to flee their homes during the vicious nine-month civil war. Nigeria, whose forces dominated ECOMOG, characterized the goals of ECOMOG as follows:

None of the member States of ECOMOG has any territorial ambitions in Liberia. None of them has any objectives of hegemony. Our principal goals consist of

64. WORLD REFUGEE SURVEY, *supra* note 60, at 63, 73–74.

65. The OAU representative to the Security Council summarized:

All the harm that this crisis has done to Liberia is well known. But in addition it has many destabilizing factors for countries of the region. First, a huge quantity of weapons is now circulating in that part of Africa. Moreover, they are accompanied by a whole range of military experts of all types who are, more than ever before, selling themselves openly to the highest bidder in the international market. In addition, there are hundreds of thousands of refugees—more than a third of the population of Liberia—scattered about the various neighbouring countries, putting an increasingly intolerable burden on those countries, which have limited resources. Furthermore, the war has crossed the borders of Liberia, spreading to Sierra Leone. Perhaps tomorrow it will spread to other countries of the region.

U.N. Doc. S/PV.3138 (1992), *supra* note 43, at 22 (statement of the representative of Senegal, on behalf of the OAU). See also the various statements by governmental and ECOWAS representatives cited in K. Kufuor, *The Legality of the Intervention in the Liberian Civil War by the Economic Community of West African States*, 5 AFRICAN J. INT'L & COMP. L. 525 (1993).

ending the carnage, promoting peace between the various factions and ethnic groups and establishing a firm basis for democratic elections.[66]

These views were confirmed by the actions taken after the intervention. The ECOMOG intervention was neither limited to the rescue of foreign nationals nor to the establishment of buffer zones with neighboring states. Its primary mission was, first, to establish a zone around Monrovia to allow relief operations to proceed, and then to bring about a ceasefire among the warring factions and create a process that would lead to elections. As such, while other reasons also were present, the intervention was predominantly humanitarian in nature (although it is to be noted that not all the actions by the ECOMOG forces were altruistic; observers reported that ECOMOG officers undertook lucrative business ventures to exploit Liberia's timber, diamond, rubber, and gold resources and that ECOMOG forces looted Monrovia's suburbs for refrigerators, air conditioners, and other goods[67]).

The intervention was not authorized by the Liberian factions. Samuel Doe, the internationally recognized head of government at the time of the intervention, would have welcomed an intervention designed to suppress the rebel insurgency, but he opposed the ECOMOG intervention, which sought to replace him as President. Charles Taylor, whose rebel forces at the time of the intervention controlled all of Liberia outside Monrovia, opposed the intervention since he saw his forces on the verge of seizing control of the country and regarded ECOMOG as dominated by countries that supported Doe. The intervention was supported by the Interim President, Amos Sawyer, but this was a government created by and dependent upon the intervention forces themselves.

Authorization cannot be derived from the protocols on security adopted by ECOWAS to which Liberia was a party. There are no provisions in the 1978 Protocol that provide for intervention by ECOWAS. Moreover, Articles 2 and 3 of the 1978 Protocol provide:

2. Each Member State shall refrain from committing, encouraging, or condoning acts of subversion, hostility or aggression against the territorial integrity or political independence of the other Member States.

3. Each Member State shall undertake to prevent foreigners resident on its territory from using its territory as a base for committing the acts referred to in Article 2 against the sovereignty and territorial integrity of Member States.

66. U.N. Doc. S/PV.3138 (1992), *supra* note 43, at 46.

67. C. Shiner, *8-Nation African Force Is Peacekeeping Model in War-Torn Liberia*, Wash. Post, Apr. 1, 1994, at A26.

It might be said that Article 3 was relevant to the Liberian crisis, since Charles Taylor's forces initially launched their fight from the Ivory Coast. Yet this action would only implicate obligations of the Ivory Coast under Article 3, not the obligations of Liberia. By August 1990 there were extensive refugee flows out of Liberia, but there was at that time little evidence of acts of "subversion, hostility or aggression" by the Liberian factions against neighboring states.

The Ivory Coast asserted to the Security Council that the ECOMOG intervention had "its roots" in Article 4(b) of the 1981 Protocol.[68] Article 4(b) provides:

Member states shall also take appropriate measures such as specified in Articles 17 and 18 of the present Protocol in the following circumstances: . . . (b) In case of internal armed conflict within any Member State engineered and supported actively from outside likely to endanger the security and peace in the entire community. In this case the Authority shall appreciate and decide on this situation *in full collaboration with the authority of the Member State or States concerned.* (emphasis added)

The NPFL may have been receiving financial and military support from other West African states. Article 4(b), however, expressly contemplates as a response the "collaboration" of ECOWAS states with the authority of the relevant member state, which in this case would mean collaboration with (not replacement of) President Doe. Moreover, while the NPFL initially launched its rebellion from the Ivory Coast with some support from citizens of that state, the "outside support" in this case might actually be viewed as the ECOWAS intervention itself. It was *after* the ECOMOG intervention that the Government of Burkina Faso (which initially opposed the intervention out of concern that it would exacerbate the situation) reportedly began supporting the NPFL.[69] Indeed, the Government of Sierra Leone regarded the spillover of violence from Liberia to be directly related to Sierra Leone's support of the ECOMOG intervention.[70]

Even if violations attributable to Liberia may be found in the 1978 or 1981 Protocols,[71] the remedy for those violations should have been the measures set forth in the 1981 Protocol regarding the deployment of earmarked units from all of the ECOWAS states. These measures were

68. U.N. Doc. S/PV.3138 (1992), *supra* note 43, at 27.

69. K. Noble, *Civil War in Liberia Threatening To Divide West African Neighbors*, N.Y. TIMES, Aug. 29, 1990, at A1. Within several months, Burkina Faso purported to withdraw its support for the NPFL and provided troops to ECOMOG.

70. U.N. Doc. S/PV.3138 (1992), *supra* note 43, at 52.

71. *Supra* note 14.

not invoked. Instead, ECOWAS proceeded to create a Standing Mediation Committee of a limited number of countries, which on its own
decided to create and deploy ECOMOG without the Government of Liberia's express consent. There is nothing in the ECOWAS Treaty that
would support such a mandate for the ECOWAS Authority, let alone one
of its committees. Notably, in its August 1990 statement, the Standing
Mediation Committee did not explicitly invoke rights of the ECOWAS
member states under the 1978 or 1981 Protocols. Nor is there a basis for
the intervention in the Charter of the Organization of African Unity.[72]
Indeed, both the 1981 Protocol and the OAU Charter contain language prohibiting interventions except in conditions that essentially relate to self-defense. In short, ECOMOG was a subregional organization
designed to address economic affairs which, after enacting some instruments related to security, miraculously transformed itself into a collective
security organization with wide-ranging capabilities.

Since authorization from Liberia did not exist, upon what authority
did the intervention occur? The fact that ECOMOG was associated with
a regional organization (ECOWAS) does not remove it from the normal
constraints imposed on intervention by states under the UN Charter.
ECOWAS member states indicated to the Security Council that the
intervention was in accordance with Chapter VIII of the UN Charter.[73]
Yet, while Chapter VIII of the Charter promotes the peaceful settlement of disputes through regional arrangements, Article 53 expressly
says that "no enforcement action shall be taken under regional arrangements or by regional agencies without the authorization of the Security
Council. . . ."

The Security Council did not explicitly or implicitly authorize the
ECOMOG intervention. The first statement issued by the Security Council through its President was made in January 1991, five months after the
intervention occurred. At that time, the intervention had resulted in a
ceasefire and in the beginning of a national reconciliation process. In
light of this success, the President of the Security Council "commended"
the ECOWAS efforts, which perhaps gave a symbolic UN blessing to the
intervention. Only after the ceasefire broke down in November 1992 did
the Security Council itself declare by resolution that the "deterioration
of the situation in Liberia constitutes a threat to international peace and
security, particularly in West Africa" and then act under Chapter VII to
impose an arms embargo, without reference to Chapter VIII. Even at this
point, the Security Council did not authorize ECOMOG to "use all nec-

---

72. Charter of the Organization of African Unity, May 25, 1963, 479 U.N.T.S. 39, *reprinted
in* 1 WESTON, *supra* note 12, at I.B.I.

73. *See, e.g., id.*, at 32, 44–45 (statements of the Ivory Coast and Nigeria).

essary means" to implement the Yamoussoukro IV Accord or otherwise restore peace and security to Liberia, although it did continue to "commend" ECOWAS efforts.

The reaction of the international community to the intervention by ECOMOG was almost universally favorable. Statements made in the debates at the Security Council and in the General Assembly were highly critical of the Liberian warring factions but supportive of the ECOWAS actions. Admittedly, the international community's attention during the fall of 1990 was riveted on the dramatic events unfolding subsequent to Iraq's August invasion of Kuwait. Nevertheless, to the extent that attention was focused on the legality of the intervention in Liberia, it would appear that the intervention was not viewed as violative of international law. Particularly striking was the willingness to view the intervention as appropriate because it was conducted through the machinery of a subregional organization, without any scrutiny of the rules by which that organization was supposed to operate. This contrasts sharply with the United States intervention in Grenada,[74] where the participation of the Organization of Eastern Caribbean States did little to quell the intense criticism of the lawfulness of the U.S. action and where the OECS rules were claimed to be inconsistent with the action taken.

How legally significant was the intervention in Liberia? Refugee flows from Liberia initially prompted the concern of neighboring states, but there was the potential also for the armed conflict spilling over the border. As such, notwithstanding the presence of considerable human right deprivations, it is easy to identify a transboundary "threat to the peace" in the Liberian crisis. But of greater significance is that the intervention in Liberia occurred at the hands of states operating under the auspices of a subregional economic organization. Certainly Nigeria was the dominant state involved in the intervention; nevertheless, the intervention was conceived within the context of a subregional organization and was pursued and justified as an intervention on behalf of that organization. That the economic well-being of a sub-region should be linked to its overall stability is no surprise. The willingness of an economic organization to undertake military operations, however, is noteworthy. Moreover, in situations where the global community and even regional organizations are unwilling to address a humanitarian crisis, it may be left to subregional organizations to act. Although the mandate of ECOWAS to undertake such action is difficult to discern from its constituent documents, the intervention suggests that states cooperating within a subregional organization can engage in a successful intervention even without UN authorization and, further, that they may be thus more im-

74. Discussed *supra* chapter 4.

munized from international criticism than if any one state had proceeded to intervene on its own. At the same time those organizations must be willing to pay, or obtain support from the international community to pay, a high financial cost for maintaining an intervention force. In Liberia it is estimated that the intervention cost some $80 million annually from 1990 to 1994.[75]

A final legally significant factor in the Liberian case is found in the relationship that developed between the Security Council and ECOWAS. The Security Council's ex post facto support of the intervention and enthusiastic reception to ECOWAS's request for global sanctions indicates agreement with the Nigerian statement that the "collective self-help" undertaken by ECOWAS is "an important building-block in the new world order of shared responsibility for the maintenance of international peace and security which we seek to establish."[76] As the Secretary-General stated:

Liberia continues to represent an example of systematic and effective cooperation between the United Nations and regional organizations, as envisaged in Chapter VIII of the Charter. The role of the United Nations has been a supportive one. Closest contact and consultation have been maintained with ECOWAS, which will continue to play the central role in the implementation of the [Cotonou] peace agreement.[77]

Indeed, the ability of the United Nations to act as a disinterested broker allowed the Cotonou Agreement to be concluded and, in addition, allowed for the deployment of the UN monitoring force.[78]

The Liberian crisis, however, does not represent the best example of "systematic and effective cooperation" between the UN and a regional organization. The civil strife in Liberia lasted throughout 1990 without any significant attention by the United Nations; ECOWAS proceeded to intervene on its own in part through a realization that no one else would attend to West African affairs. It would have been preferable for the Security Council to authorize the ECOMOG intervention prior to its occurrence or, at a minimum, to declare the situation in Liberia a threat to international peace so as to acknowledge the existence of conditions that

75. C. Shiner, *supra* note 55. The cost to the United Nations of operating UNOMIL in 1994 was approximately $36.4 million. U.N. Department of Public Information Reference Paper, *The United Nations and the Situation in Liberia* (April 1995).

76. U.N. Doc. S/PV.3138 (1992), *supra* note 43, at 44–45.

77. *Further Report of the Secretary-General, supra* note 51, para. 17.

78. *See* U.N. Doc. S/PV.3263 (1993), *supra* note 33, at 8 (statement of representative of Benin) ("But I wish here to stress that the role of the United Nations has been decisive in introducing a climate of confidence between the parties without which we would not be speaking today of the Cotonou Agreement").

would merit intervention. Only after the intervention occurred and appeared successful did the Security Council become involved in a significant manner. Further, while the ECOMOG intervention may well have prevented a widespread massacre by Taylor's forces in Monrovia, neither UN nor regional action in Liberia proved capable of preventing a wholesale political deterioration in Liberia. Indeed, civil war raged for years after the ECOMOG intervention, and the intervening forces themselves became drawn into the conflict in such a manner as to compromise their ability to achieve a negotiated settlement.

B. Northern Iraq (1991) and Southern Iraq (1992)

1. Essential Facts

Iraq's Invasion of Kuwait

On August 2, 1990 Iraq invaded its neighbor to the south, Kuwait. Within a matter of hours, Iraq installed a new government in Kuwait, closed all Kuwaiti ports and its airport, banned foreign travel, imposed a curfew, and cut off telecommunications with the outside world.[79] Over the next several weeks, Iraq purported to annex Kuwait, detained foreign nationals, including diplomats, and engaged in the murder, rape, and torture of Kuwaiti nationals and residents.

An emergency session of the UN Security Council on August 2 determined in Resolution 660 that Iraq's invasion constituted a breach of international peace and security and demanded that Iraq withdraw immediately and unconditionally.[80] Throughout the fall of 1990, the Security Council progressively escalated its condemnation of Iraq through various resolutions, including the imposition of trade sanctions backed by a maritime interception operation by member states acting in defense of Kuwait.[81] On November 29, 1990 the Security Council took the extreme step, in Resolution 678, of authorizing member states cooperating with Kuwait "to use all necessary means to uphold and implement Security Council resolution 660 (1990) and all subsequent relevant resolutions and to restore international peace and security in the area," unless, on or before January 15, 1991, Iraq complied with the Council's resolu-

---

79. Various accounts of Iraq's invasion of Kuwait and subsequent expulsion in early 1991 have appeared in newspapers, periodicals, and books. *See, e.g.*, L. FREEDMAN & E. KARSH, THE GULF CONFLICT 1990–91: DIPLOMACY AND WAR IN THE NEW WORLD ORDER (1993); M. SIFRY & C. CERF, THE GULF WAR READER: HISTORY, DOCUMENTS, OPINIONS (1991).

80. S.C. Res. 660, U.N. SCOR, 45th Sess., 2932d mtg. at 19, U.N. Doc. S/INF/46 (1991), *reprinted in*, 2 WESTON, *supra* note 12, at II.D.22. The vote in the Security Council was unanimous, with Yemen abstaining.

81. S.C. Res. 665, U.N. SCOR, 45th Sess., 2938th mtg. at 21, U.N. Doc. S/INF/46 (1991).

tions.[82] Although in December 1990 Iraq had allowed foreign nationals to depart Iraq and Kuwait, it failed to withdraw from Kuwait by the deadline, thereby paving the way for a multinational coalition force to evict Iraq forcibly from Kuwait.

The assault on Iraq's military forces and facilities in both Kuwait and Iraq commenced with an air campaign and concluded 42 days later after ground forces swept through Kuwait and into southern Iraq, stopping well short of seizing Baghdad and capturing Iraq's President and military ruler, Saddam Hussein. The fighting between coalition and Iraqi forces ended with a February 28 provisional ceasefire, negotiated by the militaries on each side, and was followed by a UN ceasefire resolution, Resolution 687.[83] On April 6, 1991, in letters to the Security Council and the Secretary-General, Iraq accepted the terms of Resolution 687.[84]

Shortly after the provisional ceasefire, however, Hussein's regime was confronted with an internal breakdown of civil order. Cities in Iraq's southeastern region saw antigovernment demonstrations and religious unrest, particularly by Shiite Muslim fundamentalists who long had been suppressed by Hussein's Sunni Muslim regime.[85] Reports emerged that Iraqi Kurdish rebels in the north were also fighting Iraqi government forces and seizing various towns,[86] while the official Iranian news agency reported fighting in towns in the eastern part of the country, near the Iraq-Iran border.[87]

Iraq's Internal Repression

The Iraqi government immediately struck back, first in the south. The Iraqi-controlled *Al Thawra* newspaper said that "everybody who

82. S.C. Res. 678, U.N. SCOR, 45th Sess., 2963d mtg. at 27, U.N. Doc. S/INF/46 (1991), *reprinted in*, 2 WESTON, *supra* note 12, at II.D.23.

83. S.C. Res. 687, U.N. SCOR, 46th Sess., 2981st mtg. at 11, UN. Doc. S/INF/47 (1993), *reprinted in* 2 WESTON, *supra* note 12, at II.D.25.

84. *Identical Letters Dated 6 April 1991 from Iraq to the Secretary-General and the President of the Security Council*, U.N. Doc. S/22456 (1991). Iraq's acceptance letter is a bit obscure and lengthy, but ultimately concludes that Iraq "has no choice but to accept this resolution." *Id.* at 7; A. Cowell, *Baghdad Formally Agrees to "Unjust" U.N. Conditions for Permanent Ceasefire*, N.Y. TIMES, Apr. 7, 1991, sec. 1, at 1. On April 11, the Security Council informed Iraq that, in light of its acceptance, a formal ceasefire was in effect. *Letter Dated 11 April 1991 from the President of the Security Council to the Permanent Representative of Iraq*, U.N. Doc. S/22485 (1991) [hereinafter Letter Dated 11 April 1991].

85. N. Boustany, *Refugees Tell of Turmoil in Iraq: Troops Recount Allied Onslaught*, WASH. POST, Mar. 4, 1991, at A1.

86. N. Boustany, *Violence Reported Spreading in Iraq; Army Units Clash*, WASH. POST, Mar. 6, 1991, at A1.

87. L. Hockstader, *Baghdad Warns Insurrectionists "They Will Pay,"* WASH. POST, Mar. 8, 1991, at A1.

tries to undermine the security [of the Iraqi government] is a traitor and a mercenary. . . . All of them shall regret it. They will pay." [88] Iraq charged that "large numbers of armed and organized groups [that had] infiltrated into [Iraq] from a neighboring State" were engaged in "widespread acts of subversion, murder, destruction, arson and pillage." [89]

Refugees and opposition leaders began providing unconfirmed accounts of mass executions of rebels in the southern port city of Basra, including 400 people publicly executed in one day after an anti-Hussein protest.[90] Other refugees reported Iraqi government shelling in central and southern Iraq of families in their homes, on the streets, and in the fields, as well as summary executions of young Shiite males.[91] Concern that Hussein might use chemical weapons against the rebel forces prompted the United States to warn Iraq in Washington and at the United Nations that such action would be taken "seriously." [92]

Along with reports that Iraqi government forces were hanging rebels from utility poles and gun barrels of tanks, reports also emerged that the largely outgunned and disorganized Shiite rebels were themselves executing persons suspected of collaborating with the Iraqi Government.[93] *Al-Thawra* blamed "rioters" for many of the deaths in the south.[94] The Iraqi government deployed helicopter gunships to suppress the rebels, which highlighted the failure of the coalition forces in the ceasefire arrangements to prevent Iraq's use of such aircraft.[95] The United States then threatened to down the helicopters,[96] and coalition forces banned their use, although U.S. Secretary of State James A. Baker characterized the ban as intended only as a security measure in furtherance of the ceasefire arrangements, with the "collateral effect" of reducing the

88. *Id.*

89. *Identical Letters Dated 20 March 1991 from Iraq to the Secretary-General and President of the Security Council*, U.N. Doc. S/22371 (1991); *see also Letters Dated 3 April 1991 from Iraq to the Secretary-General*, U.N. Docs. S/22439, S/22440 (1991) (charging Iranian support of subversive activities).

90. Hockstader, *supra* note 87.

91. N. Boustany, *A Trail of Death in Iraq: Shiite Refugees Tell of Atrocities by Republican Guard*, WASH. POST, Mar. 26, 1991, at A1.

92. L. Hockstader, *Iraq Told Not to Use Chemicals: U.S. Issues Warning As Insurgents Fight Army Units in South*, WASH. POST, Mar. 10, 1991, at A1; P. Tyler, *U.S. Said to Plan Bombing of Iraqis if They Gas Rebels*, N.Y. TIMES, Mar. 10, 1991, at 1.

93. N. Boustany, *Iraqi Troops Reportedly Hang Rebels from Tanks: Refugees Say Opposition Losing Ground*, WASH. POST, Mar. 13, 1991, at A24.

94. J. Randal, *Iraq Says Rebellion Toll High*, WASH. POST, Mar. 18, 1991, at A1.

95. D. Balz, *Bush Criticizes Iraq's Use of Helicopters on Rebels*, WASH. POST, Mar. 15, 1991, at A37.

96. D. Hoffman & B. Gellman, *U.S. Threatens to Down Any Iraqi Combat Aircraft*, WASH. POST, Mar. 16, 1991, at A1.

ability of Hussein's forces to fight the rebellion.[97] Despite this warning, Iraq continued to use the helicopters without their being shot down.[98]

Developments in the north began differently, largely because the Iraqi Kurdish rebels were better organized than the southern Iraqi Shiites and because, after the war against Iraq on behalf of Kuwait, Iraqi government forces were concentrated in the south. By March 16, 1990, the Kurdish rebels claimed that they controlled 80 to 90 percent of the land in the northern Iraqi region of Kurdistan.[99] Once Iraqi military forces had largely quelled the rebellion in the south, however, Baghdad moved thousands of troops to the north.[100] By March 29, Iraqi government forces had launched intensive air, missile, and artillery attacks against the Kurds, with heavy casualties reported by Kurdish leaders.[101] These attacks resulted in hundreds of thousands of Kurds—rebel forces and civilians—retreating into the mountains of northern Iraq and southern Turkey, where they had little food and inadequate shelter against the cold.[102] After some 20,000 to 40,000 Kurds crossed the 8,000-foot mountains into lower-lying refugee camps in Turkey, Turkish military forces were deployed across the mountainous border into Iraq to prevent most Kurds from entering Turkey; within two weeks death rates in the mountains were estimated by international relief agencies at as many as 1,000 Kurds per day.[103] Lack of sanitation in the mountains posed acute threats

97. Randal, *supra* note 94.

98. E. Sciolino, *U.S. Warns Against Attack by Iraq on Kurdish Refugees*, N.Y. TIMES, Apr. 11, 1992, at A10.

99. Hoffman & Gellman, *supra* note 96.

100. J. Randal, *Kurds Seize Iraqi Base and Work to Demoralize Saddam's Army*, WASH. POST, Mar. 28, 1991, at A1.

101. J. Goshko, *Kurds Ousted from Kirkuk, Baghdad Says*, WASH. POST, Mar. 29, 1991, at A13. The Western press subsequently carried photographs of crippled and shoeless Kurds fleeing into the mountains, including children with napalm burns on their faces from Iraqi air attacks. *Hell in a Very Small Place*, WASH. POST, Apr. 18, 1991, at A35.

102. J. Goshko, *Rebel Urges West to Aid Iraqi Kurds: Millions Said to Flee Saddam's Offensive to Retake the North*, WASH. POST, Apr. 2, 1991, at A1. The head of the Kurdish Democratic Party initially estimated three million Kurds fled into the mountains, but in late April the U.S. State Department placed the number at 850,000. B. Harden, *U.S. Troops Order Iraqi Police Away; Marines Step Up Work on Tent Camps*, WASH. POST, Apr. 23, 1991, at A1.

103. *That Slippery Slope*, ECONOMIST, Apr. 13, 1991, at 39; *Cavalry to the Rescue*, ECONOMIST, Apr. 20, 1991, at 41; B. Harden, *GIs, Kurds Find Kinks in "Operation Comfort,"* WASH. POST, Apr. 18, 1991, at A1. In late April, U.S. White House spokesman Marlin Fitzwater said the number of deaths had declined and stabilized at about 510 per day. G. Frankel, *An Uphill Fight to Keep Kurds from Graveyard*, WASH. POST, Apr. 24, 1991, at A1.

Turkey wanted to avoid a repetition of the 1988 exodus of Iraqi Kurds to Turkey (prompted by Iraqi government attacks on the Kurds using chemical weapons); some estimates were that 60,000 Kurds fled Iraq in 1988 after Turkey opened its border, with 28,000 still remaining in Turkish camps as of April 1991. B. Gellman & W. Drozdiak, *U.S. Troops Enter Northern Iraq to Set Up Camps*, WASH. POST, Apr. 18, 1991, at A1.

of diarrhea (leading to dehydration), cholera, and measles epidemics; the UN Children's Fund warned that measles could kill more than fifty percent of the children, most of whom were not inoculated against the disease.[104] During the same time period, roughly 850,000 Iraqis fled Iraq into Iran, where they were sheltered in local communities and crude tents.[105] Middle East Watch reported that senior Arab diplomats were informed privately by Iraqi leaders that an estimated 250,000 people were killed during the uprisings, with most of the casualties in the south.[106]

The Intervention in Northern Iraq (April 1991)

On April 2, 1991 the Government of Turkey urgently sought a Security Council meeting, informing the Security Council that, due to actions taken by the Iraqi army, approximately 220,000 Iraqi nationals, many of them women and children, were massing along the Turkish border. Turkey charged that the pressing of these people toward the border constituted "an excessive use of force and a threat to the region's peace and security" and further noted that some Iraqi mortar shells had fallen on Turkish territory.[107] At the meeting of the Security Council, Turkey stated:

> The threat posed by these events to the security of the region needs no elaboration. In the chaotic conditions prevailing in northern Iraq, it is conceivable that a million people might be forced to move from that country to Turkey. No country can cope with such a massive influx of destitute people fleeing for their lives. Turkey will not allow its border provinces to be overwhelmed by such a flood of displaced persons.[108]

Iran also notified the Security Council that an estimated 500,000 Iraqi nationals were crossing into Iran and that, if it continued, the situation would have consequences that "threaten regional peace and security." [109] Both Turkey and Iran called on the international community to act.

104. Frankel, *supra* note 103.

105. *Misery in Iran*, ECONOMIST, Apr. 20, 1991, at 42.

106. *Mass Killings in Iraq: Hearing Before Senate Comm. on Foreign Relations*, 102d Cong., 2d Sess. 10 (1992) [hereinafter *Mass Killings in Iraq*] (statement of Mr. Andrew Whitley, Executive Director, Middle East Watch, New York).

107. *Letter Dated 2 April 1991 from Turkey to the President of the Security Council*, U.N Doc. S/22435 (1991); *see also* J. Goshko, *U.N. Action Urged on Crisis in Iraq*, WASH. POST, Apr. 3, 1991, at A1. In its presentation to the Security Council, Turkey estimated that 200,000 to 300,000 people were already driven toward the Turkey-Iraq border, 100,000 had crossed the border, and perhaps 600,000 more were on the move to the border. U.N. SCOR, 46th Sess., 2982 mtg. at 6, U.N. Doc. S/PV.2982 (1991).

108. U.N. Doc. S/PV.2982 (1991), *supra* note 107, at 6.

109. *Letter Dated 4 April 1991 from Iran to the Secretary-General*, U.N. Doc. S/22447 (1991); *see also Letter Dated 3 April 1991 from Iran to the Secretary-General*, U.N. Doc. S/22436 (1991).

The United Nations had been actively monitoring the plight of Iraqi nationals in the postwar period; on March 20, the UN Under-Secretary-General for Administration and Management had reported to the Secretary-General on humanitarian needs in both Iraq and Kuwait.[110] Yet the primary focus of the Security Council up to April 3 was establishing the terms of the ceasefire agreement with Iraq, embodied in Resolution 687.[111] Without waiting for the United Nations to act, France (on April 3) and Britain (on April 4) decided unilaterally to send emergency aid to the Kurdish refugees in northern Iraq.[112]

On April 5, having finished its work on Resolution 687, the Security Council passed Resolution 688 by a vote of 10 in favor, 3 against (Cuba, Yemen, and Zimbabwe), and 2 abstentions (China and India), noting its responsibility for the maintenance of peace and security and its concern that Iraq's repression had "led to a massive flow of refugees towards and across international frontiers and to cross border incursions, which threaten international peace and security." [113] The Security Council also condemned and demanded that Iraq end the repression of its nationals, and further stated that it:

2. *Demands* that Iraq, as a contribution to removing the threat to international peace and security in the region, immediately end this repression and expresses the hope in the same context that an open dialogue will take place to ensure that the human and political rights of all Iraqi citizens are respected;

3. *Insists* that Iraq allow immediate access by international humanitarian organizations to all those in need of assistance in all parts of Iraq and to make available all necessary facilities for their operations;

4. *Requests* the Secretary-General to pursue his humanitarian efforts in Iraq and to report forthwith, if appropriate on the basis of a further mission to the region, on the plight of the Iraqi civilian population . . . ;

5. *Requests* further the Secretary-General to use all the resources at his disposal, including those of the relevant United Nations agencies, to address urgently the critical needs of the refugees and displaced Iraqi population;

6. *Appeals* to all Member States and to all humanitarian organizations to contribute to these humanitarian relief efforts; . . .

Governments opposing the resolution did so primarily on the grounds that it transgressed the principle of nonintervention in the internal af-

Iran ultimately reported that some 900,000 refugees had crossed the border. *Letter Dated 11 April 1991 from Iran to the Secretary-General*, U.N. Doc. S/22482 (1991).

110. *Letter Dated 20 March 1991 from the Secretary-General to the President of the Security Council*, U.N. Doc. S/22366 (1991).

111. Resolution 687, *supra* note 83.

112. H. Fontanaud, *France Says World Must Re-examine "Non-Interference" Code*, Reuters, Apr. 4, 1991, *available in* LEXIS, Nexis Library, REUWLD File.

113. S.C. Res. 688, U.N. SCOR, 46th Sess., 2982d mtg. at 31, U.N. Doc. S/INF/47 (1993), *reprinted in* 3 WESTON, *supra* note 12, at III.F.3.

fairs of states, and that such questions were properly addressed only by organs of the United Nations other than the Security Council. Yemen noted that "there is no conflict or war taking place across the borders of Iraq with its neighbors," and since, therefore, there was no threat to international peace and security, the matter was "not within the Council's purview." [114] Zimbabwe asserted that "a domestic political conflict lies at the core of the situation" and, therefore, despite the humanitarian dimensions, should not be before the Security Council. [115] Cuba noted that the specific powers granted to the Security Council in Chapters VI, VII, VIII, and XII "do not include the questions of a humanitarian nature"; rather, Chapter IX, which addresses such questions, is the responsibility of the General Assembly. [116] Iraq's representative to the United Nations called the resolution "a flagrant, illegitimate interference in Iraq's internal affairs" and a violation of Article 2(7) of the Charter. Further, Iraq charged that the United States and Iraq's neighbors were fomenting dissent within Iraq in anticipation of its partition. [117]

The states that supported the resolution characterized it as necessary action to address a threat to international peace from the flows of refugees. [118] None of these states characterized the resolution as explicitly authorizing states to deploy military forces into Iraq, but the Security Council was aware that three states were planning on providing relief supplies to the Kurds through airdrops. In its statement, the United States noted that it had decided earlier that day, before the vote on Resolution 688, to use military aircraft to drop food, blankets, clothing, tents, and other relief-related items into northern Iraq. None of the speakers who followed the United States challenged this action. Great Britain noted that it too would be providing humanitarian relief and characterized Resolution 688 as giving "firm backing to the Secretary-General, to the United Nations specialized agencies and to all the *governmental* and non-governmental organizations whose efforts are now so urgently needed." [119] France, which also had decided previously to deliver relief supplies to the Kurds, saw the resolution as providing for no more than actually appeared in its wording: a condemnation of Iraqi repression, an

114. U.N. Doc. S/PV.2982 (1991), *supra* note 107, at 27.

115. *Id.* at 31.

116. *Id.* at 46.

117. *Id.* at 17; *see also Identical Letters Dated 8 April 1991 from Iraq to the Secretary-General and the President of the Security Council*, U.N. Doc. S/22460 (1991).

118. Some states offered additional justifications. For instance, Great Britain asserted that Iraq's obligations under common Article 3 of the 1949 Geneva Conventions to protect innocent civilians from violence also justified Security Council action. U.N. Doc. S/PV.2982 (1991), *supra* note 107, at 66.

119. *Id.* at 64–65 (emphasis added).

appeal for respect for human and political rights, and a demand that Iraq allow access by "international humanitarian organizations."[120]

Yet the action of states in the aftermath of Resolution 688 went beyond the literal wording of the resolution. The day after Resolution 688 was passed, the United States warned Iraq not to use any armed action in northern Iraq (whether by ground forces or by aircraft) since it would be a threat to relief operations and to the refugees. The United States declared a "no-fly" zone in northern Iraq, prohibiting all Iraqi flights north of the 36th parallel. The basis for this zone, according to U.S. officials, was Resolution 688, which gave the United States the mandate to do what was necessary to conduct relief operations.[121] With the cooperation of the Government of Turkey, British, French, and U.S. military units commenced an extensive relief operation, consisting of air dropping tons of food, water, coats, tents, blankets, and medicines into Iraq.[122] The decision was made in consultation with various states, including Kuwait, Turkey, Saudi Arabia, and the Soviet Union.

According to the statements of these countries, the motivation behind the airlift and the no-fly zone was to alleviate the plight of the Kurds. At the same time, various other motivations may also have been present. For instance, in the United States, various domestic groups (Congressional members, the media, human rights activists) placed pressure on the Bush Administration to act by accusing the President of having encouraged Iraqis to revolt against Saddam Hussein and then abandoning them when they did.[123] In Great Britain, it was speculated that Prime Minister John Major was motivated by a need to appear domestically more decisive in his leadership skills.[124] Further, there was pressure on these countries to help Turkey, a key NATO ally, whose support for the coalition efforts against Iraq during the war had been critical, particularly its decision to shut down the Iraqi oil pipeline to the port of Ceyhan.[125]

120. *Id.* at 53–55.

121. Sciolino, *supra* note 98.

122. C. Krauss, *U.S. Will Airdrop Food and Clothes to Kurds in Iraq*, N.Y. TIMES, Apr. 6, 1991, sec. 1, at 1; C. Haberman, *6 U.S. Planes Begin Airlifting Relief to Kurds in Iraq*, N.Y. TIMES, Apr. 8, 1991, at A1.

123. *See, e.g.*, HOUSE COMM. ON FOREIGN AFF., 102d CONG., CONGRESS AND FOREIGN POLICY 1991, at 27 (Comm. Print 1992) ("Many Members also believed that the United States, in calling on the Iraqi people to overthrow Saddam, had led the rebels to expect U.S. support and that the United States thereby incurred an obligation to help them when they were defeated."). On April 11, four days before Operation Provide Comfort was announced, the Senate passed S. Res. 99, 102d Cong., 1st Sess. (1991), which asserted a U.S. "moral obligation" to provide such relief.

124. J. Cassidy, D. Hughes & J. Adams, *Haven from the Hell-Holes*, SUNDAY TIMES (London), Apr. 21, 1991.

125. Before the war against Iraq, about half of Iraq's oil passed through Turkey; by shutting down its pipeline, Turkey contributed substantially to Iraq's economic isolation. *See*

Iraq protested the airdrops as an infringement of Iraqi sovereignty, a violation of the principles of international law, and a direct interference in the internal affairs of Iraq. In Iraq's view, any such relief operations could lawfully be conducted only "through the Iraqi authorities and the Iraqi Red Crescent Society."[126]

Within days of commencing the airdrops, it became clear that hundreds of thousands of Kurds were in difficult-to-reach mountain areas along the Turkish-Iraqi border and that the only way to supply them adequately would be to encourage them to move to less mountainous areas in northern Iraq. To allay Kurdish fears of further attacks from Iraqi forces, European Community (EC)[127] leaders, meeting in Luxembourg, called for the establishment of "enclaves" in northern Iraq where the Kurds would be safe.[128] The plan to create these protected enclaves reportedly was conceived by Britain, was raised at and agreed upon with modifications by the EC Council of Ministers, and then was accepted by the United States under the rubric of creating "safe havens," a term reportedly designed to avoid subsequent claims of statehood by the Kurds.[129] The United States dubbed the action "Operation Provide Comfort."

The original European idea was to use UN forces to guard the safe havens. British Prime Minister Major, who put forward the proposal to the EC, characterized it as "intended to build on Security Council Resolutions 687 and 688." He further stated that:

whether we will need a new Security Council resolution, we do not believe so. We believe the rubric exists within 688 to avoid the need for a separate resolution[,] but clearly we will need to discuss that in New York.[130]

China and the Soviet Union, however, reportedly expressed serious reservations about such a UN deployment even for humanitarian reasons,

---

DEPARTMENT OF DEFENSE, CONDUCT OF PERSIAN GULF WAR 22 (1992) (final report to U.S. Congress pursuant to Title V of the Persian Gulf Conflict Supplemental Authorization and Personnel Benefits Act of 1991 (P.L. 102–25)).

126. *Identical Letters Dated 8 April 1991 from Iraq to the Secretary-General and the President of the Security Council*, U.N. Doc. S/22459 (1991).

127. With the signing at Maastricht of the Treaty on European Union on February 7, 1992, the European Community changed its nomenclature to European Union (EU). "EC" will be used when referring to events prior to February 7, 1992, and "EU" will be used when referring to subsequent events.

128. A. Riding, *Europeans Urging Enclave for Kurds in Northern Iraq*, N.Y. TIMES, Apr. 9, 1991, at A1.

129. P. Tyler, *Bush Sees Accord on "Safe Havens" in Iraq*, N.Y. TIMES, Apr. 12, 1991, at A1; *Appeals by France, Britain and Turkey Prompted Bush to Deploy U.S. Troops*, WASH. POST, Apr. 18, 1991, at A37.

130. Transcript of Press Conference given by Prime Minister John Major in Luxembourg (Apr. 8, 1991), *reprinted in* IRAQ AND KUWAIT: THE HOSTILITIES AND THEIR AFTERMATH 714, 715 (M. Weller ed., 1993) [hereinafter IRAQ AND KUWAIT].

regarding it as infringing on the sovereignty of a UN member state. For this reason, it was reported that the United States and the Europeans did not seek additional authorization from the Security Council and instead pursued the matter on their own.[131]

The United States led the way in organizing the establishment of the safe havens, using airlifts and trucking of supplies into northern Iraq for distribution by military and relief workers.[132] By late April, approximately 2,000 U.S. Marines and several hundred British and French troops were in Iraq as part of an allied force.[133] Other states joined in the effort and, at the height of the operation, more than 20,000 forces from 13 different states were involved.[134]

The Secretary-General and UN agencies were willing to place UN personnel in Iraq only with Iraqi consent. Iraq, in turn, preferred UN involvement in any international relief operation scheme rather than involvement by the Western powers. Consequently, on April 18, 1991, a Memorandum of Understanding was signed between the United Nations and Iraq allowing the United Nations to have a "humanitarian presence" throughout Iraq, without any military component ("UN-Iraq MOU").[135] The UN-Iraq MOU permitted the United Nations to promote the voluntary return home of refugees and displaced persons. UN personnel and personnel of nongovernmental relief agencies were allowed to staff UN sub-offices and "humanitarian centers" to facilitate the provision of impartial humanitarian assistance. Although the UN-Iraq MOU stated that Iraq "has not accepted" Resolution 688, Iraq agreed to facilitate the UN efforts.

While Iraq heeded the warnings of the allied force that Iraqi military personnel should stay south of Iraq's 36th parallel,[136] Iraq categorically rejected the establishment of the allied safe havens as "a flagrant viola-

131. *Id.*

132. C. Haberman, *U.S. Military Takes Over Relief For Kurdish Refugees in Iraq*, N.Y. TIMES, Apr. 13, 1991, sec. 1, at 1; J. Kifner, *U.S. Marines Land in Northern Iraq to Set Up Camps*, N.Y. TIMES, Apr. 21, 1991, sec. 1, at 1.

133. B. Harden, *U.S. Expands Control of Refugee Zone*, WASH. POST, Apr. 24, 1991, at A1.

134. J. Brown, *Last Allies Pull Out of North Iraq*, FIN. TIMES, July 16, 1991, at 6.

135. Memorandum of Understanding Between Iraq and the United Nations, Apr. 18, 1991, para. 4, U.N. Doc. S/22663 (1991), *reprinted in* 30 I.L.M. 860. The Memorandum noted that the relief operation "shall be without prejudice to the sovereignty, territorial integrity, political independence, security and non-interference in the internal affairs of the Republic of Iraq." *Id.* para. 20. Efforts by Iraq in 1992 to block food shipments to the Kurds and to reduce the numbers of UN guards and relief workers by refusing to renew visas led to the conclusion of a new memorandum of understanding in November 1992.

136. B. Harden, *Marines Building Iraqi Refugee Sites*, WASH. POST, Apr. 21, 1991, at A1. Iraqi police forces periodically tested the will of the foreign forces. *See, e.g.*, Harden, *supra* note 102.

tion of Iraq's sovereignty and territorial integrity," particularly since the UN-Iraq MOU made it possible to pursue such relief operations in "an integrated and balanced manner" without the intervention of foreign forces.[137] Nevertheless, in light of the reality of the safe havens, Iraq called for the United Nations to assume responsibility for the relief centers established by the allied coalition in an effort to get foreign military forces out of northern Iraq.[138] Iraq demanded, however, that the UN operation be strictly civilian run and that Iraq be solely responsible for security in the region, which raised concerns by foreign relief workers.[139]

From the start, the coalition plan had been to withdraw from northern Iraq after UN and other humanitarian relief organizations assumed responsibility for the well-being of the Kurds, including protection for the Kurds from the Government of Iraq. Yet UN officials initially said that the coalition approach violated basic UN principles of setting up and operating relief programs, because the presence of the coalition's military forces was not pursuant to the consent of the Government of Iraq. Further, they contended that without Iraqi consent such a program would not succeed.[140]

After a meeting of the Security Council, however, Secretary-General Javier Pérez de Cuéllar indicated he would accept the eventual ceding of control of (and hence responsibility for protecting) the camps to the United Nations.[141] Iraq agreed in principle to the deployment of a UN "guard force," and the UN and Iraq negotiated an annex to the UN-Iraq MOU setting forth the terms of their presence.[142] Shortly thereafter, a

---

137. *Letter Dated 21 April 1991 from Iraq to the UN Secretary-General*, U.N. Doc. S/22513 (1991) [hereinafter Letter Dated 21 April 1991]; *see also Letter Dated 24 April 1991 from Iraq to the Secretary-General*, U.N. Doc. S/22531 (1991); *Letter Dated 27 April 1991 from Iraq to the Secretary-General*, U.N. Doc. S/22545 (1991); *Letter Dated 29 April 1991 from Iraq to the Secretary-General*, U.N. Doc. S/22550 (1991) (referring to "serious breaches and unprecedented violations of the sovereignty, independence and territorial integrity of Iraq by the United States of America and its allies").

138. *Letter Dated 21 April 1991, supra* note 137.

139. G. Frankel, *Relief Agencies Balk at U.S. Enclave Plan*, WASH. POST, Apr. 25, 1991, at A17.

140. *Id.* An unidentified U.N. official was quoted as saying:

You won't see a U.N. flag flying over the camps unless the Iraqi government agrees to it. The U.S. government basically wants us to go into northern Iraq as part of a military intervention force, and then it leaves and we run the camps. But the Iraqis will see us as part of an alien force. It's a formula for disaster.

Several U.N. officials also expressed concern about jeopardizing the relief projects their agencies hoped to undertake elsewhere in Iraq in the post-war period. *Id.*

141. *Id.*

142. Memorandum of Understanding Between Iraq and the United Nations, *supra* note 135, Annex.

UN guard force of approximately 500 lightly armed[143] troops was deployed in northern Iraq to serve as observers and to protect UN relief workers in northern and eastern Iraq. However, this UN force was not charged with protecting Iraqi civilians.[144]

By mid-July, most of the Kurds who fled to Turkey in March had returned to Iraq; foreign military forces had withdrawn across the border to Turkey to form a multinational rapid-deployment force to deter further actions by the Government of Iraq against the Kurds.[145] The coalition announced that it would continue to conduct periodic reconnaissance flights in the northern no-fly zone.[146] When, in mid-1992, Iraq sought to shut down the UN operation by refusing to renew the UN-Iraq MOU, the Security Council instructed the Secretary-General to continue the program anyway, although it stopped short of declaring Iraq's refusal to be a violation of Resolution 688.[147]

Free from Iraqi government repression due to the banishment of Iraqi military forces in the north and the presence of UN forces, Iraqi opposition groups held meetings in northern Iraq to broaden the base of an organized political opposition, known as the Iraq National Congress (INC).[148] Further, they opened negotiations with Hussein's government on greater autonomy for Kurds in northern Iraq. These negotiations were ultimately inconclusive and ran parallel to low-level violence between Iraqi forces and Kurdish guerillas. Over time, however, three Iraqi Kurdish groups (the Kurdistan Democratic Party, the Patriotic Union of Kurdistan, and the Islamic Movement of Iraqi Kurdistan) set up de facto governments in three sections of northern Iraq under the cover of Operation Provide Comfort. When Kurdish separatist guerrillas (the Kurdish Workers Party or PKK) established bases in northern Iraq from which to conduct attacks inside Turkey, Turkey, in both 1992 and 1995, launched major raids into northern Iraq to suppress the insur-

---

143. The UN forces were permitted to carry pistols and revolvers provided by Iraqi authorities. *Id.*, para. 6; *see also Report to the Secretary-General Dated 15 July 1991 on Humanitarian Needs in Iraq: Report of the Executive Delegate*, para. 12, *in* U.N. Doc. S/22799 (1991) (Annex).

144. *See* C. Haberman, *U.N. Takes Over From U.S. for Kurds in Iraq*, N.Y. TIMES, May 14, 1991, at A10.

145. A. Devroy, *U.S. to Join Force to Protect Kurds*, WASH. POST, July 11, 1991, at A1. For the United States, this border operation was dubbed "Operation Poised Hammer."

146. Brown, *supra* note 134.

147. P. Lewis, *U.N. Agencies Ordered to Continue Efforts in Iraq*, N.Y. TIMES, Sept. 3, 1992, at A10.

148. President Bush informed the Congress that he supported the efforts of the INC to rally Iraqis against Hussein's regime. Letter to Congressional Leaders Reporting on Iraq's Compliance with United Nations Security Council Resolutions, 28 WEEKLY COMP. PRES. DOC. 2308 (Nov. 16, 1992).

gency.[149] The existence of the Kurdish separatist movement in both Iraq and Turkey created a complicated situation, with Turkey supporting efforts to assist the Kurds in northern Iraq at the same time it was charged, by groups inside and outside Turkey, of itself committing human rights violations against Kurdish civilians within Turkey.[150]

Since 1992 the Kurdish region of northern Iraq has operated as an autonomous region of Iraq. During 1992 and 1993 more Kurds were displaced from armed skirmishes along the line dividing the Kurdish zone from the area controlled by the Government of Iraq. Further, the Government of Iraq maintained an internal embargo on the Kurdish zone, preventing basic foodstuffs and commodities from being transshiped through the government-controlled zone. By the end of 1994, an estimated 600,000 persons remained displaced within northern Iraq, of which some 400,000 could not return to their places of origin in government-controlled Iraq or along border areas out of concern for their safety.[151] At the same time, international contributions to relief efforts declined and the UN guard force present in northern Iraq was reduced to 100, a level below that estimated by the United Nations as necessary to maintain a sufficient presence.

The Intervention in Southern Iraq (August 1992)

Immediately after the war ended, coalition forces controlled a zone in southern Iraq but did not intervene outside this zone to protect Iraqi Shiites suffering from Iraqi government repression, including the use of attack helicopters. Thousands of refugees fled into the zone to escape Iraqi attacks. Kuwait refused to allow any of the refugees to cross into its territory, although Saudi Arabia allowed some 50,000 to encamp in Saudi Arabia. Coalition forces withdrew from southern Iraq in mid-April 1991 and allowed refugees who did not wish to stay in Iraq to pull back with them.[152]

The Government of Iraq basically regained control of its southern region by mid-1991 and effectively sealed off most access to the outside

149. K. Couturier, *Turkey Invades North Iraq to Battle Kurdish Guerrillas*, WASH. POST, Mar. 21, 1995, at A1. In 1992, Turkey deployed 20,000 troops into northern Iraq. In 1995, Turkey deployed 35,000 troops into northern Iraq.

150. *See, e.g.*, J. Darnton, *Rights Violations in Turkey Said to Rise*, N.Y. TIMES, Mar. 6, 1995, at A7.

151. WORLD REFUGEE SURVEY, *supra* note 60, at 114, 115.

152. M. Gordon, *Refugees in South Beg Army to Stay*, N.Y. TIMES, Apr. 13, 1991, sec. 1, at 5; M. Gordon, *G.I.'s in Iraq Start Moving to a Zone Bordering Kuwait*, N.Y. TIMES, Apr. 15, 1992, at A1.

world.[153] Iraqi government attacks continued against the Shiites for more than a year, with an estimated 50,000 to 100,000 Iraqi soldiers fighting some 10,000 lightly armed Shiite guerillas located mostly in the southern marshes or scattered among the southern cities.[154] The government's tactic of indiscriminately killing Shiite civilians prompted some 200,000 Shiites to flee into the southern marshes for protection, although it did not trigger a mass exodus out of Iraq.[155]

On August 7, 1992 the United States wrote to the President of the Security Council requesting an urgent meeting and referring to "the continuing repression of the Iraqi civilian population in many parts of Iraq, which threatens international peace and security in the region."[156] The Government of Iran also wrote to the Secretary-General, noting that the situation in Iraq was of concern, particularly in the south where "Various independent sources have confirmed the systematic campaign of elimination of the inhabitants in these areas."[157] On August 11, 1992 the Security Council heard a report from Max van der Stoel, the Special Rapporteur for Iraq appointed by the UN Commission on Human Rights. Van der Stoel had previously issued a report on the condition of human rights in Iraq, to which Iraq had objected in a letter to the Security Council.[158] Van der Stoel asserted that it was no coincidence that the Iraqi Government had invaded Kuwait and that Iraq was now attacking its own people.

Various Security Council members concurred that there is a link between a state's treatment of its own nationals and its propensity to engage in war. Austria noted: "From our own history, we know that peace was most threatened when human rights were abolished and minorities persecuted, and when democratic processes gave way to totalitarian practices."[159] Hungary complimented Van der Stoel for having enhanced:

153. *See Mass Killings in Iraq, supra* note 106, at 11.

154. *Confronting Baghdad*, N.Y. Times, Aug. 27, 1992, at A14 (chart/map).

155. C. Hedges, *Deep in the Marshes of Iraq, Flames of Rebellion Flicker*, N.Y. Times, Mar. 15, 1992, sec. 1, at 1.

156. *Letter Dated 7 August 1992 from the United States to the President of the Security Council*, U.N. Doc. S/24396 (1992).

157. *Letter Dated 10 August 1992 from Iran to the Secretary-General*, U.N. Doc. S/24414 (1992).

158. *Letter Dated 3 August 1992 from Belgium to the President of the Security Council*, Annex, U.N. Doc. S/24386 (1992), *reprinted in* Iraq and Kuwait, *supra* note 130, at 698 (Van der Stoel report); *Letter Dated 6 August 1992 from Iraq to the Security Council*, U.N. Doc. S/24388 (1992).

159. U.N. SCOR, 47th Sess., 3105th mtg., U.N. Doc. S/PV.3105 (1992), *reprinted in* Iraq and Kuwait, *supra* note 130, at 701.

awareness of the linkage between the way a Government treated its own citizens and the way it acted in the international arena, the linkage between enforcing respect for human rights and maintaining international peace and security. Resolution 688 had clearly recognized that relationship by keeping the question of repression in Iraq under review by the Council.[160]

The United States, Great Britain, and France accused Iraq of violating Resolution 688 by conducting a systematic military campaign against the Shiites; the United States, in particular, said it was concerned about the use of fixed-wing aircraft to bomb Shiite villages.[161] All three countries warned Iraq that they might come to the aid of the Shiites in the southern marshlands if Iraq continued its acts of oppression.[162]

Within days of this warning, the three countries decided to establish a zone in southern Iraq below the 32nd parallel into which Iraqi military and civilian planes could not fly. Any such flights by Iraqi aircraft, it was warned, risked being shot down by aircraft of the three-nation coalition, which would begin conducting surveillance operations of Iraqi troop movements (unlike in the north, the presence of Iraqi ground forces in this zone was not prohibited).[163] Iraq objected to this decision in a letter to the Secretary-General, asserting that the true objective of the operation was to divide Iraq on an ethnic basis.[164]

The ban on Iraqi flights and British, French, and U.S. coalition surveillance operations commenced in southern Iraq on August 27, 1992 without incident. Iraq had already pulled almost all of its aircraft and helicopters out of the southern zone and initially did not challenge coalition overflights of Iraqi territory.[165] The effect of the no-fly zone was to prevent an estimated thirty flights per day of Iraqi helicopters and fixed-wing aircraft that had been engaged in reconnoitering and attacking Shiite guerilla positions and to enable the coalition to monitor Iraqi military movements.[166] Iraq protested the imposition of the no-flight zone and the coalition surveillance operations as a violation of Iraqi sovereignty. When, in an attempt to forestall the action, Iraq offered to allow Security

---

160. *Id.*

161. M. Gordon, *U.S. Thinks Iraq Prepares for Big Push on the Shiites*, N.Y. TIMES, Aug. 18, 1992, at A6.

162. P. Lewis, *U.S., Britain, and France Warn Baghdad on Shiites*, N.Y. TIMES, Aug. 12, 1992, at A6.

163. M. Gordon, *British, French, and U.S. Agree to Hit Iraqi Aircraft in the South*, N.Y. TIMES, Aug. 19, 1992, at A1.

164. *Letter Dated 7 August, 1992, supra* note 156.

165. M. Wines, *U.S. and Allies Say Flight Ban in Iraq Will Start Today*, N.Y. TIMES, Aug. 27, 1992, at A1; W. Schmidt, *Iraq Fires Words, but No Missiles, at Allied Planes*, N.Y. TIMES, Aug. 28, 1992, at A8.

166. Gordon, *supra* note 163.

Council members to inspect the southern marshes, the offer was not accepted.[167]

On September 16, U.S. President George Bush reported to Congress that "As a result of the no-fly zone, Iraqi use of aircraft to conduct repression of the civilian population in the region, in particular the bombing of citizens around the marsh areas, has stopped,"[168] although he later acknowledged that the coalition monitoring "cannot detect lower level acts of oppression."[169] Press reports indicated that mass arrests, executions, and indiscriminate shelling of villages continued, as well as a systematic campaign to turn southern Iraq into a desert by draining and burning the marshes.[170] Access to the south by UN relief personnel was denied by Iraq beginning in October 1992.[171]

Enforcement of the no-fly zone was not passive. An Iraqi aircraft flew into the no-fly zone on December 27, 1992 and, according to the U.S. military, turned to confront U.S. aircraft after a U.S. radio warning was issued. The U.S. aircraft then shot down the Iraqi aircraft.[172] When Iraq moved surface-to-air missiles into the zone in late December, British, French, Russian, and U.S. officials provided Iraq with an ultimatum: move the missiles north of the 32nd parallel latitude or face "appropriate and decisive" retaliation. The United States asserted that the presence of the missiles violated Resolution 688, while Iraq claimed that its actions were "purely defensive, within its sovereign right." Further, Iraq questioned the right of the coalition forces to enforce the no-fly zone, arguing that it was not specifically supported by a UN resolution but, rather, was a coalition initiative growing out of the coalition's own interpretation of broad resolutions.[173]

In the closing days of the U.S. Bush Administration, Iraq threatened aerial surveillance operations in both northern and southern Iraq and relief operations in the north, by deploying missile batteries in the south, rearming air defenses in the north, and attacking relief convoys in the

167. Y. Ibrahim, *Iraq Says U.N. Can Inspect Shiites' Area in South*, N.Y. TIMES, Aug. 22, 1992, sec. 1, at 4; W. Schmidt, *Iraq Says It Is Ready to Fight Allies Over Air Zone*, N.Y. TIMES, Aug. 27, 1992, at A14.

168. Letter to Congressional Leaders Reporting on Iraq's Compliance with Security Council Resolutions, 28 WEEKLY COMP. PRES. DOC. 1668, 1669 (Sept. 16, 1992).

169. Letter to Congressional Leaders reporting on Iraq's Compliance with United Nations Security Council Resolutions, 29 WEEKLY COMP. PRES. DOC. 67, 67 (Jan. 19, 1993).

170. T. Lippman, *Iraq's War on "Marsh Arabs: Artillery, Bulldozers Assault Fragile Habitat*, WASH. POST, Oct. 18, 1993, at A1.

171. *To the Aid of Iraqis*, THE TIMES (London), Jan. 15, 1993, at 15 (editorial).

172. H. Dewar, *U.S. Fighter Downs Iraqi Military Jet in Flight-Ban Zone*, WASH. POST, Dec. 28, 1992, at A1.

173. M. Gordon, *Iraq Given Friday Deadline*, N.Y. TIMES, Jan. 7, 1993, at A8.

north.[174] At the same time, Iraq threatened the post-war UN activities relating to Iraq's disarmament and boundary demarcation with Kuwait. First, on January 7, 1993, Iraq informed the UN Office of the Special Commission in Baghdad (responsible for the post-war weapons destruction program) and the Headquarters of the UN Iraq-Kuwait Observation Mission (responsible for monitoring the Iraq-Kuwait border) that Iraq would no longer allow the United Nations to transport its personnel into Iraq's territory using its own aircraft. The next day, the President of the Security Council issued a statement declaring that:

Such restrictions constitute an unacceptable and material breach of the relevant provisions of resolution 687 (1991), which established the ceasefire and provided the conditions essential to the restoration of peace and security in the region.[175]

In the statement, he demanded that Iraq abide by its obligations and warned Iraq "of the serious consequences which would ensue from failure to comply with its obligations." [176] Second, Iraq engaged in unauthorized incursions over the newly drawn border with Kuwait to retrieve missiles and explosives left by Iraqi forces when retreating during the war. These incursions prompted a second statement by the President of the Security Council that Iraq was in material breach of its obligations under Resolution 687.[177]

On January 14, 1993, 110 coalition planes attacked four Iraqi surface-to-air missile sites and four air defense command bunkers in southern Iraq. The reason stated by the coalition forces for the attack was not Iraqi efforts to impede surveillance operations in the south but, rather, actions by Iraq that transgressed the Security Council's resolutions on disarmament and boundary demarcation. As such, the attack was supported by the members of the Security Council[178] and by the Secretary-General, who stated that the raid had a "mandate" from the Security Council in that it was in response to Iraq's violation of the ceasefire agreement.[179] A second attack on January 17 was even more closely associated with the

174. B. Gellman & A. Devroy, *U.S. Delivers Limited Air Strike on Iraq*, WASH. POST, Jan. 14, 1993, at A1.

175. U.N. SCOR, 48th Sess., 3161st mtg. at 6, U.N. Doc. S/PV.3161 (1993).

176. *Id.* at 7.

177. U.N. SCOR, 48th Sess., 3162d mtg. at 4, U.N. Doc. S/PV.3162 (1993).

178. J. Preston, *U.N. Members Support Allied Effort in Iraq*, WASH. POST, Jan. 14, 1993, at A17.

179. Statement Made by the Secretary-General of the United Nations in Paris (Jan. 14, 1993), *reprinted in* IRAQ AND KUWAIT, *supra* note 130, at 741; *see also* Letter to Congressional Leaders Reporting on Iraq's Compliance with United Nations Security Council Resolutions, *supra* note 169, at 67 (quoting statement of U.N. Secretary-General Boutros-Ghali).

weapons destruction aspect of Resolution 687 by targeting a nuclear fabrication facility near Baghdad, which resulted in collateral damage to a hotel in downtown Baghdad.[180] A third attack on January 18 targeted missile batteries in northern and southern Iraq. This series of military actions prompted a renewed debate (even among the members of the coalition itself) about the legality of the no-fly zones and about how far the coalition could go in enforcing the no-fly zones.[181]

While coalition efforts likely impeded Iraqi efforts to pacify the Shiites, the Iraqi government continued its tactics on the ground throughout 1994. Estimates of the number of persons killed remained difficult to estimate since UN and other relief agencies were not permitted access to the area; estimates of displaced persons were similarly difficult, and ranged from 40,000 to as many as 1,000,000.[182]

2. Assessment of the Interventions

The actions taken in both northern and southern Iraq involved the deployment of military forces from other states into Iraq in a manner that suppressed the activities of Iraqi military forces. Consequently it can be characterized as use of force by a state or group of states against Iraq that normally would implicate the prohibition on the use of force contained in Article 2(4) of the Charter.

The primary motivation for the interventions was to protect Iraqi nationals from a widespread denial of basic human rights. In the case of northern Iraq, the intervention sought to provide shelter, clothing, and medicine to Iraqi Kurds that had fled into the mountains along the Iraq-Turkey border to escape from Iraqi government military attacks. In southern Iraq, the intervention sought to prevent Iraqi government air attacks on Iraqi Muslim Shiites that had fled into the marshes of southern Iraq, to deny aerial reconnaissance for the Iraqi government's direction of attacks against the Shiites, and to monitor such attacks. In both instances, insurgent irregular forces were in rebellion against the Iraqi central government. In light of their limited nature, the interventions were primarily designed not to assist these insurgencies (although to a certain degree they had such a collateral effect) but, rather, to assist civilian populations exposed to indiscriminate and ruthless attacks that forced them to flee their homes.

180. *Id.* at 68; *see* N. Boustany, *Attack Jolts Iraqi Capital*, WASH. POST, Jan. 18, 1993, at A1.

181. *See, e.g.*, J. Bone, *Security Council Members Query the Legal Basis of "No-Fly" Zones*, THE TIMES (London), Dec. 28, 1992; N. Wood & A. Leathley, *Rifkind Faces Cross-Party Misgivings over Strategy*, THE TIMES (London), Jan. 19, 1993, at 1 (discussing dissension within British ruling party).

182. WORLD REFUGEE SURVEY, 1995, *supra* note 60, at 116.

Nevertheless, one cannot deny that there were other motivations at play during the interventions in northern and southern Iraq. The intervention in northern Iraq, in particular, certainly reflected a concern about the potentially destabilizing effect of flows of refugees into Turkey and Iran on those countries. Turkey had made it quite clear that it would not tolerate such an influx and even had deployed Turkish forces across its border with Iraq to stem the refugee flows. Had Iraq's repression of the Kurds not prompted those flows, the international community might not have acted at all.[183] Whether or not there was a feeling of responsibility by the three Western powers that they helped to create the conditions that led to the Iraqi insurgencies, these countries certainly were influenced by the relationship between the military defeat of Iraq by forces acting on behalf of Kuwait and the subsequent plight of the Iraqi nationals. Further, Britain, France, and the United States were in a NATO alliance with Turkey,[184] which had supported the Western-led response to Iraq's invasion of Kuwait and which was seeking to avoid a massive refugee problem. Finally, it must be noted that the intervention in southern Iraq occurred at a time when Iraq increasingly was challenging the implementation of its post-war obligations under the Security Council's resolutions; the attacks by coalition forces on Iraqi surface-to-air missile sites in the winter of 1992–93 were not characterized by the United States or the Secretary-General as flowing from Resolution 688 (the humanitarian aid resolution) but, rather, from Resolution 687 (the cease-fire resolution).

Despite these other motivations, the dominant motivation of the United Nations and those countries engaged in the interventions was to assist the people of Iraq. This is especially evident in the intervention in southern Iraq, which began a year after the cessation of the war, at a time when there were no significant new flows of refugees occurring as a result of Iraq's repression of the Shiites in the south. Yet it is also evident in the intervention in northern Iraq. That intervention responded to the

183. In 1987, Iraq initiated a campaign to depopulate Iraqi Kurdistan through the systematic destruction of Kurdish villages, the massive use of chemical weapons, deportation and execution. This military operation, code-named the "Al-Anfal" campaign, resulted in the death of at least 180,000 people (about five percent of the population of Iraqi Kurdistan) but did not result in action by other countries to protect the Kurds. *See Mass Killings in Iraq, supra* note 106, at 1–2 (statement of Senate Foreign Relations Committee Chairman Claiborne Pell). Considerable information on this campaign was uncovered in documents captured by Kurdish rebels in northern Iraq in 1991. *See* SENATE COMM. ON FOREIGN RELATIONS, SADDAM'S DOCUMENTS, S. REP. No. 111, 102d Cong., 2d Sess. (1992).

184. The North Atlantic Treaty, Apr. 4, 1949, 63 Stat. 2241, 34 U.N.T.S. 243, requires the parties to consult together whenever the territorial integrity, political independence, or security of any of the parties is threatened, *id.* art. 4, and to assist each other by action each deems necessary in the event of an armed attack, *id.* art. 5.

widespread sickness and death of persons trapped in mountainous regions who had been unable to cross into neighboring states.

The interventions in Iraq were without authorization from the Government of Iraq, the target state. Iraq vehemently protested the initial airdrops in the north and protested both the establishment by foreign forces of safe havens in northern Iraq and of no-fly zones in northern and southern Iraq. Iraqi government military forces were excluded from northern Iraq, and Iraqi aircraft were shot down when they flew into airspace over either northern or southern Iraq. Iraq consented to the presence of UN personnel engaged in relief operations, but never authorized the presence of foreign military forces or the presence of any forces (including UN personnel) charged with protecting Iraqi nationals.[185]

The interventions in northern and southern Iraq were not specifically debated or authorized by the Security Council. Resolution 688 established that there was a threat to international peace and security, which it characterized as arising not simply from the "repression of the Iraqi civilian population" but, rather, from the "massive flow of refugees towards and across international frontiers and to cross border incursions." Yet Resolution 688 does not contain any language explicitly authorizing states or UN forces "to use all necessary means" to establish safe havens for Iraqi nationals, to ensure the delivery of humanitarian relief supplies, or to establish no-fly zones. Rather, Resolution 688 merely "insisted" that Iraq allow access by "international humanitarian organizations," requested the Secretary-General to pursue humanitarian efforts in Iraq and "appealed" to states to contribute to these humanitarian relief efforts. Nor did Resolution 688 contain an explicit requirement that states acting under the resolution provide regular reports to the Security Council, a step taken in the two prior Iraq-related resolutions that clearly authorized the use of force, Resolution 665 (maritime enforcement of sanctions) and Resolution 678 (air and ground campaign on behalf of Kuwait). The explicit thrust of Resolution 688, then, was to demand that Iraq cease its repression, to encourage Iraq strongly to allow humanitarian relief efforts to go forward, and to promote international cooperation to this end.

One might argue that explicit support for the interventions is found in a combination of Resolution 688 (the humanitarian relief resolution)

---

185. Some commentators have argued that the conditions in northern Iraq, in which the Government of Iraq was incapable of addressing the problem, the world community was willing to act aggressively, and the Kurds were anxious for assistance, created an atmosphere of Iraqi consent. *See, e.g.*, P. Weckel, *Le Chapitre VII de la Charte et Son Application Par Le Conseil de Sécurité*, 37 ANNUAIRE FR. D. INT'L 165, 193–94 (1991) ("Ainsi, à la faible contrainte exercée par le Conseil de Sécurité, l'Iraq a répondu par une acceptation minimale de l'intervention étrangère à des fins humanitaires. Il a toléré celle-ci.").

and Resolution 678 (the original use of force resolution). Resolution 678 authorized states acting on behalf of Kuwait to use "all necessary means" to uphold and implement Security Council Resolution 660 "and all subsequent relevant resolutions" and to "restore peace and security in the area." Of course, Resolution 688 did not exist at the time Resolution 678 was passed, but it certainly was a "subsequent" Security Council resolution directly related to the immediate aftermath of the Iraq-Kuwait crisis. Furthermore, Resolution 688 made clear that Iraq's repression in northern and southern Iraq was a threat to international peace and security; if Resolution 678 authorized states to restore peace and security in the area, then efforts to curtail this repression were explicitly authorized.

The primary difficulty with this interpretation is the passage of Resolution 687 (the ceasefire resolution) and Iraq's acceptance of that resolution, which set forth the conditions for the cessation of hostilities against Iraq that were initiated by Resolution 678. Paragraph 33 of Resolution 687 stated that, once Iraq accepted the provisions of Resolution 687, "a formal cease-fire is effective between Iraq and Kuwait and the Member States cooperating with Kuwait in accordance with Resolution 678 (1990)." The President of the Security Council informed Iraq on behalf of the members of the Security Council that the conditions established in Resolution 687 "have been met and that the formal cease-fire referred to in paragraph 33 of that resolution is therefore effective." [186] The conditions set forth in Resolution 687, which were formulated at a time when the repression within Iraq was well known and which were finalized just three days before Resolution 688 was passed, did not include a promise by Iraq to refrain from widespread deprivation of human rights in Iraq. While it is easy to see why Iraq's failure to abide by the conditions of Resolution 687 might "revive" the authorization to use force provided in Resolution 678, it is less clear why such authorization is revived in other circumstances, such as a failure to abide by Resolution 688. Indeed, while the circumstances that gave rise to Resolution 688 were related to the aftermath of the Iraq-Kuwait war, Resolution 688 itself was not considered directly related to the war; this is reflected in the fact that the subject matter of Resolution 688 (humanitarian relief) was not included in Resolution 687 and that, unlike all the other resolutions relating to the war, Resolution 688 does not refer to any of the earlier resolutions, including Resolutions 678 and 687.[187] In January 1993, Iraq

186. *Letter Dated 11 April 1991, supra* note 84.

187. Some subsequent resolutions do group Resolution 688 with the earlier Security Council resolutions. *See* the first preambular paragraphs of S.C. Res. 706, U.N. SCOR, 46th Sess., 3004th mtg. at 21, U.N. Doc. S/INF/47 (1993) and S.C. Res. 712, U.N. SCOR, 46th Sess., 3008th mtg. at 24, U.N. Doc. S/INF/47 (1993). Resolutions 706 and 712 attempted to set up an exception to the embargo on exports by Iraq, in which oil sales by

was found by the members of the Security Council to be in material breach of Resolution 687, but this was long after the commencement of the interventions in both northern and southern Iraq. Moreover, to the extent that a material breach of Resolution 687 permitted action to terminate or suspend the ceasefire, it would appear to have been for the party to the ceasefire agreement—the Security Council—to take such action, not member states acting on their own initiative.

A further difficulty arises if Resolution 678 is regarded not as emanating from Article 42 or from Chapter VII as a whole but, rather, as an affirmation of Kuwait's right under Article 51 to engage in individual and collective self-defense.[188] If this interpretation is correct, then the whole concept of "reviving" Resolution 678 is misplaced, for it provides no authority beyond that which already would exist under a theory of self-defense. No states argued that the interventions in northern or southern Iraq were in the exercise of a right of self-defense.

Finally, prior to assuming responsibility for the relief operations in northern Iraq, UN officials believed that Iraqi consent was necessary; consequently, a memorandum of understanding was concluded between the UN and Iraq. Yet if intervention by states in Iraq was authorized under Resolution 688, presumably intervention by the Secretary-General (who is the dominant focus in Resolution 688 for the pursuit of humanitarian efforts) should have been permissible as well, and the UN resistance to engaging in relief operations without Iraqi consent misconceived.

Thus, it does not appear that Resolution 688 alone or in combination with Resolution 678 can be said to have explicitly authorized the interventions in Iraq. Whether the states that intervened in Iraq did so with implicit authorization from the Security Council is more difficult to say. That is, in the overall situation with respect to Iraq in April 1991 and August 1992, can it be said that authorization for intervention somehow emanated from the Security Council's resolutions notwithstanding the lack of explicit language to that effect? Nothing in the Security Council debate over Resolution 688 suggests this conclusion; indeed, the resis-

---

Iraq would finance the purchase of foodstuffs, medicines, and materials and supplies for essential civilian needs. This mechanism was never used by Iraq.

188. *See* O. Schachter, *United Nations Law in the Gulf Conflict*, 85 Am. J. Int'l L. 452 (1991). Regarding Resolution 678 as simply an affirmation of a right of self-defense is inconsistent with the development of the Security Council's resolutions during the Gulf conflict. Resolution 678 had its pedigree ("all necessary means") in Resolution 665, which was passed precisely because of disagreement among the Security Council members over whether states could enforce U.N. sanctions under the rubric of collective self-defense. The debate surrounding the passage of Resolution 665 indicates that those states were not affirming a preexisting right to engage in such collective action, but rather were providing the legal basis for it.

tance of some states to even the minimal action expressed in that resolution suggests otherwise. Yet the dramatic intrusiveness of coalition activities in the affairs of Iraq under the auspices of the Security Council in the post-war atmosphere, and the potential for further actions based on Resolution 688, could not have been lost on the members of the Security Council. Resolution 688 "internationalized" the plight of Iraqi nationals and labelled the consequences of that plight as a threat to international peace and security. The carefully worded resolution stopped short of explicitly authorizing humanitarian intervention by states, but was crafted midst an atmosphere in which states in fact were already intervening through the aerial delivery of foodstuffs.

The views of the states conducting the intervention were less than clear on this point. With respect to the intervention in northern Iraq, a leading British publication confidently stated that "Britain, France, and America argue that their action is covered by Security Council Resolution 688,"[189] while a leading U.S. editorialist with equal confidence asserted that the United States "begrudgingly followed the lead of the British and French into a 'duty to intervene' " under international law, unrelated to Security Council resolutions.[190] In fact, while some statements by the leaders of the intervening states suggested that a unilateral right to intervene for humanitarian purposes existed, other statements took the view that the interventions were either based on or "consistent" with Resolution 688. To understand whether there is any coherency to these views requires reviewing the positions of the British, French, and U.S. governments.

In Britain, the position was somewhat mixed. On the one hand, the statements of British government officials at the time of the intervention in northern Iraq pointed to Resolution 688 as though it provided the basis for the interventions. British Prime Minister John Major asserted that the safe haven plan was intended to "build on Security Council Resolutions 687 and 688" and that "the rubric exists within 688" for foreign forces to patrol within Iraq.[191] Further, Prime Minister Major stated that "in the light of the wording of UN Security Council resolution 688" it would be surprising for Iraq to reject the establishment of safe havens, but if Iraq did, then Britain "certainly would not be deterred in proceeding." [192] British Secretary of State for Foreign and Commonwealth Affairs Douglas Hurd informed the British Parliament that the efforts to establish a safe haven "are to help provide emer-

189. *Cavalry to the Rescue, supra* note 103.

190. W. Safire, *Duty to Intervene*, N.Y. Times, Apr. 15, 1991, at A17.

191. Transcript of Press Conference given by Prime Minister John Major in Luxembourg (Apr. 8, 1991), *supra* note 130, at 714–15.

192. *Id.* at 715.

gency aid, as authorised by Security Council resolution 688."[193] The next day, when asked whether a nonconsensual presence of UN personnel in northern Iraq would be a violation of Iraqi sovereignty, Hurd responded:

No, because the Security Council Resolution 688 insists—that's the word it uses—that the UN operation should be carried out in Iraq. So there's no violation of Iraqi sovereignty.[194]

Such an interpretation of Resolution 688 would serve also as a basis for interventions by individual states for protecting relief operations. An aggressive, expansive interpretation of Resolution 688 was not, however, the only British approach for justifying the interventions in Iraq. Various statements were made suggesting that Resolution 688, while relevant to the situation, was not the sole basis for the interventions. For instance, in formulating the safe haven plan, British Prime Minister Major also emphasized that the action was not interference in Iraq's internal affairs because it was "protection of a population from persecution."[195] In justifying the no-fly zone in southern Iraq, Secretary Hurd claimed:

Not every action that a British Government or an American Government or a French Government takes has to be underwritten by a specific provision in a UN resolution provided we comply with international law. International law recognises extreme humanitarian need. No-one [who] has looked at the report which the UN . . . received the other day from Mr Van der Stoel, its representative[,] can doubt [an] extreme humanitarian need.[196]

Perhaps most significantly, in late 1992, well after both interventions had occurred, the Legal Counsellor to the Foreign and Commonwealth Office informed the Foreign Affairs Committee of the House of Commons that:

Resolution 688 recognised that there was a severe human rights and humanitarian situation in Iraq and, in particular, northern Iraq; but the intervention in northern Iraq "Provide Comfort" was in fact, not specifically mandated by the United Nations, but the states taking action in northern Iraq did so in exercise of the customary international law principle of humanitarian intervention.[197]

193. Further Statement of Douglas Hurd, UK House of Commons Parliamentary Debates (Apr. 17, 1991), *reprinted in* IRAQ AND KUWAIT, *supra* note 130, at 720.
194. Interview with Foreign Secretary Douglas Hurd (Apr. 15, 1991), *reprinted in Hurd Interviewed on Saving Kurdish Refugees*, F.B.I.S. W. EUR. DAILY REP., Apr. 18, 1991, at 6.
195. Riding, *supra* note 128.
196. Interview with Secretary Douglas Hurd (Aug. 19, 1992), *reprinted in* IRAQ AND KUWAIT, *supra* note 130, at 723.
197. *The Expanding Role of the United Nations and its Implications for U.K. Policy: Minutes of Evidence, Hearing Before the Foreign Affairs Comm. of the House of Commons*, Sess. 1992–93, Dec. 2, 1992, at 84 (statement of Anthony Aust, Legal Counsellor, U.K. Foreign and Commonwealth Office).

When probed on the nature of this right under international law, he stated:

There is no agreement in the sense of rules which have been laid down by any international body, but the practice of states does show over a long period that it is generally accepted that in extreme circumstances a state can intervene in another state for humanitarian reasons. . . . Resolution 688 did not actually authorise it, but it did recognise there was a very serious situation in Iraq, particularly in North Iraq. Most of the precedents before that relate perhaps more to intervention in order to protect one's own nationals who are being mistreated or neglected by the territorial state. But international law in this field develops to meet new situations and that is what we are seeing now in the case of Iraq.[198]

Thus evidence may be found in British statements reflecting alternative interpretations.

For several years prior to the passage of Resolution 688, French leaders had advocated a right to take emergency humanitarian action inside states without their consent.[199] The origins of this initiative may lie in efforts by nongovernmental relief organizations, particularly those based in France, to provide humanitarian relief even without host government consent.[200] Some statements of French government officials at the time of the intervention in northern Iraq seemed to concede that the "right to intervene" had not yet fully developed in international law. Foreign Minister Roland Dumas dismissed the need for, and implicitly accepted the lack of, a legal basis by declaring: "Law is one thing, but the safeguard of a population is something at least as precious."[201] Yet many French officials, including Dumas, argued that just as Germany's murder of Europe's Jews brought about the concept of "crimes against humanity," so Saddam Hussein's mistreatment of the Kurds argued for a recognition of a "duty to intervene" to prevent gross violations of human rights.[202] President François Mitterrand, the most eloquent French advocate for such intervention, stated:

Les exigences pour le respect du droit se font aujourd'hui plus fortes dans le domaine des droits fondamentaux de l'homme. L'évolution des sociétés et une médiatisation croissante au niveau mondial y conduisent. Ce ne sont plus, là en-

---

198. *Id.* at 92.

199. For quotes by President Mitterrand, Foreign Minister Dumas, and Humanitarian Affairs Minister Kouchner from 1987–89, *see* Fontanaud, *supra* note 112.

200. J. Mann, *No Sovereignty for Suffering*, N.Y. TIMES, May 12, 1991, sec. 4, at 17 (editorial by President of U.S. affiliate of Doctors of the World). These nongovernmental relief organizations included Doctors of the World and Doctors Without Borders, which had been headed at one time by French Humanitarian Affairs Minister Bernard Kouchner.

201. P. Webster, *France: Humanitarian Aid Minister Rushes to Turkey to Assess Needs of Kurdish Refugees*, GUARDIAN, Apr. 4, 1991, at 24.

202. *That Slippery Slope, supra* note 103.

core, les principes qui ont changé. Mais la conscience internationale ne veut plus tolérer certaines situations qui, au nom de la non-ingérence dans les affaires intérieures d'un Etat, peuvent exister ici ou là. Aujourd'hui, lorsque nous constatons des violations flagrantes et massives des droits de l'homme, nous ne pouvons rester passifs. Notre devoir, c'est de fair cesser ces situations. Voilà ce que signifie le devoir d'assistance humanitaire.[203]

Mitterrand thus emphasized less the legal basis of a right to intervene by other states than he did *the loss by the target state* of its right to noninterference in its domestic affairs when it was engaged in massive human rights violations.

U.S. President George Bush, in his April 16, 1991 press conference announcing the safe haven plan, characterized the establishment of the safe havens as "[c]onsistent with United Nations Security Council Resolution 688,"[204] leaving ambiguous whether the action derived its authority from the resolution or from some other source. President Bush acknowledged that "some might argue that this is an intervention into the internal affairs of Iraq." Yet, in response, instead of emphasizing authorization from the United Nations, he suggested that "the humanitarian concern, the refugee concern is so overwhelming that there will be a lot of understanding about this."[205] This is an interesting initial statement; it conveys a sense that perhaps the intervention cannot be justified on the basis of UN authorization (and may even be inconsistent with the UN Charter), but that, nevertheless, circumstances justified it.

---

203. Interview with President Mitterrand (Sept. 7, 1991), *quoted in* J. Charpentier, *Pratique Francaise du Droit International*, 37 ANNUAIRE FR. D. INT'L 933, 939 (1991) (emphasis added). The author's English translation is as follows:

> Today there is a growing insistence on respect for the law in the area of fundamental human rights. Changing societies and increasing media attention at the world level have brought this about. There again, the principles are still the same, but the international conscience is no longer willing to tolerate certain situations which, in deference to noninterference in the internal affairs of a State, may exist here and there. Today, when we observe flagrant human rights violations on a massive scale, we cannot stand idly by. We have a duty to put a stop to these situations. This is what the duty of humanitarian assistance means.

204. The President's News Conference, 27 WEEKLY COMP. PRES. DOC. 444, 444 (1991). President Bush used this same formulation one month later in his report to the Congress on the situation in the region. Letter to Congressional Leaders on the Situation in the Persian Gulf, 27 WEEKLY COMP. PRES. DOC. 621, 622 (May 17, 1991) ("It is a humanitarian measure designed to save lives, consistent with Resolution 688.").

205. The President's News Conference, *supra* note 204, at 446; *see also* Letter to Congressional Leaders on the Situation in the Persian Gulf, 27 WEEKLY COMP. PRES. DOC. 966, 967 (July 17, 1991) ("[t]his effort was not intended as a permanent solution to the problem, nor as a military intervention in the internal affairs of Iraq. Rather, it was intended as a humanitarian measure to save lives").

President Bush noted that a new Security Council resolution might be necessary for UN forces to be deployed to Iraq,[206] implicitly suggesting that the existing resolutions were not sufficient, at least politically and perhaps legally, for intervention by UN forces.[207]

The day after President Bush's press conference, UN Secretary-General Javier Pérez de Cuéllar stated that for the establishment of safe havens to be lawful, Iraq's consent and a new UN Security Council resolution would be necessary.[208] White House officials were then reported as insisting that Resolution 688 itself gave the U.S. forces sufficient authority to enter Iraq for these purposes.[209] The U.S. State Department spokesperson stated that Resolution 688 "provides full authority for the President's plan to assist with the refugee situation."[210] Secretary of State Baker, meeting with his EC counterparts, stated somewhat more cautiously that the action was "fully consistent with Security Council Resolution 688."[211]

The same approach was taken with respect to the intervention in southern Iraq. In reporting to the U.S. Congress, President Bush justified the no-fly zone as "to implement Security Council Resolution 688."[212] At his press conference on the matter, he explained the relationship to Resolution 688 as follows:

> By denying access to UN monitors and other observers, Saddam has sought to prevent the world from learning of his brutality. It is time to ensure that the world does know.
>
> Therefore, the United States and its coalition partners have today informed the Iraqi Government that 24 hours from now coalition aircraft, including those of the United States, will begin flying surveillance missions in southern Iraq, south of 32 degrees north latitude, to monitor the situation there. This will provide coverage of the areas where a majority of the most recent violations of Resolution 688 have taken place.[213]

This interpretation suggests a U.S. view that, while Resolution 688 may not have expressly authorized intervention by individual states, such in-

206. The President's News Conference, *supra* note 204, at 445.

207. By mid-May, however, President Bush was quoted as saying authority for deployment of a UN force had been granted under existing resolutions. P. Tyler, *Bush May Seek U.N. Ruling for Force in Kurdish Zone*, N.Y. TIMES, May 16, 1991, at A16.

208. Gellman & Drozdiak, *supra* note 103.

209. *Id.*

210. N. Lewis, *Legal Scholars Debate Refugee Plan*, N.Y. TIMES, Apr. 19, 1991, at A8.

211. S. Greenhouse, *After the War: Baker Defends Refugee Plan at European Meeting*, N.Y. TIMES, Apr. 18, 1991, at A18.

212. Letter to Congressional Leaders Reporting on Iraq's Compliance with United Nations Security Council Resolutions, *supra* note 168, at 1669.

213. Remarks on Hurricane Andrew and the Situation in Iraq and an Exchange with Reporters, 28 WEEKLY COMP. PRES. DOC. 1512, 1512 (Aug. 26, 1992).

tervention was permissible for purposes of preventing Iraq's violations of Resolution 688. This might be characterized as a "self-help" doctrine in support of the United Nations; perhaps a reference to Article 2(5) of the UN Charter (requiring UN members to give the United Nations every assistance in any action it takes under the Charter) would have been appropriate. In any event, the U.S. government never indicated acceptance of a right of humanitarian intervention without UN authorization but instead related the interventions to Resolution 688. Whether it felt legally compelled to do this is not altogether clear, although it should be noted that the U.S. Government never has expressly endorsed a right of unilateral humanitarian intervention under the UN Charter.[214] The U.S. executive branch may have been concerned that the deployment of U.S. forces equipped for combat into Iraq be regarded as within the scope of the existing U.S. congressional authorization to use force, which was tied to implementation of Security Council resolutions.[215]

In sum, the statements of the three intervening states are not consistent and are at times vague, perhaps in order to avoid highlighting differences among them, although all three governments asserted that no further UN authority beyond Resolution 688 was necessary. For France and perhaps Britain, this conclusion apparently derived from the view that UN authority was not necessary for the interventions at all, while for the United States this conclusion derived from the view that Resolution 688 itself provided authority for the interventions.

214. Such sweeping statements invariably prove overbroad. For instance, in 1976 a U.S. State Department attorney-adviser, in the context of foreign military assistance provided to Angolan rebels, assessed the impact of various instruments, such as the U.N. Charter and General Assembly resolutions, on the principle of nonintervention, and concluded:

> The position of the United States that emerges from its participation in the development and refinement of the nonintervention principle in contemporary international law is as follows . . . The broad language prohibiting all forms of intervention was fully acknowledged as no greater a prohibition than had already been accepted by the United States in its treaty relations with Latin America, but that it did not affect the right to intervene in other states for purposes that were sanctioned under customary international law, *i.e.*, protection of a state's own nationals; protection of the lives of other nationals *or humanitarian intervention*; and for legitimate collective self-defense.

1976 Digest of United States Practice in International Law 3, 5 (emphasis added).

215. The Congressional authorization to use force, however, did not expressly include force to implement Resolution 688. The Authorization for Use of Military Force Against Iraq Resolution of January 14, 1991, Pub. L. No. 102–1, H.J. Res. 77, 102d Cong., 1st Sess., 105 Stat. 3 (1991), authorized the President to use U.S. forces "pursuant to" Security Council Resolution 678 "in order to achieve implementation of" the Security Council resolutions leading up to Resolution 678, which were explicitly listed. The Congress did not provide an authorization that covered the use of U.S. forces to implement unspecified future Security Council resolutions.

While the intervening states regarded their interventions as lawful, the reaction among other states was mixed. Obviously Iraq rejected the legality of all aspects of the interventions and maintained that the coalition's actions were a pretext for partitioning Iraq. Those members of the Security Council that voted against Resolution 688 on the grounds that it interfered with Iraq's sovereignty did not support the legality of the interventions. Many states supported (or at least were silent regarding) the initial airdrops into northern Iraq. Some, such as Japan, supported the airdrops under Resolution 688 by arguing that, since access for international relief organizations had not been granted, the airdrops were justified.[216] Yet several countries supportive of the intervention in the north were less supportive of the intervention in the south, including some members of the Security Council.[217] Several states in the Middle East were also wary of the intervention in southern Iraq, although perhaps more on political than legal grounds. Syria reportedly opposed the no-fly zone because it threatened Iraq's territorial integrity; Egyptian officials and Egypt's semi-official press criticized the plan as setting a dangerous precedent.[218] Other countries in the Persian Gulf region, such as the United Arab Emirates and Oman, expressed reservations regarding the coalition plan out of concern for the possible partitioning of Iraq.[219]

Some states spoke out against the intervention in the General Assembly in December 1991, arguing that it could not be justified either on the basis of a unilateral right of intervention or on the basis of Security Council authorization. At the same time, several states spoke out in favor. In any event, no General Assembly resolution emerged condemning the interventions in either northern or southern Iraq.[220] Reactions by nongovernmental organizations were mixed. Some nongovernmental observers that regarded the coalition actions in the north as legitimately based on Resolution 688 doubted that action in the south—sixteen

216. *Letter Dated 12 April 1991 from Japan to the Secretary-General*, U.N. Doc. S/22499 (1991).

217. *See, e.g.*, Bone, *supra* note 181.

218. W. Schmidt, *Iraq Aircraft Ban Arouses Arab Ire*, N.Y. TIMES, Aug. 23, 1992, sec. 1, at 15.

219. Y. Ibrahim, *Iraq Vows to Resist Western Flight Ban*, N.Y. TIMES, Aug. 21, 1992, at A6.

220. Resolutions passed in 1991 and 1992 by the General Assembly focused on Iraq's treatment of its nationals without reference to the interventions in northern or southern Iraq. G.A. Res. 46/134, U.N. GAOR, 46th Sess., Supp. No. 49, at 206, U.N. Doc. A/46/49 (1992) (adopted 129 to 1 with 17 abstentions); G.A. Res 47/145, U.N. GAOR, 47th Sess., Supp. No. 49, at 221, U.N. Doc. A/47/49 (1993) (adopted 126 to 2 with 26 abstentions). Likewise, the UN Commission on Human Rights condemned Iraq's human rights violations without comment on the interventions. E.S.C. Res. 1992/71, U.N. ESCOR, 48th Sess., Supp. No. 2, at 166, U.N. Doc. E/1992/22 (1992).

months after the passage of the resolution and at a time when there were no refugee flows—could be based on that resolution.[221]

Sifting through the various statements made by governments and nongovernmental entities over an extended time leads to a conclusion that, while many governments and others expressed serious reservations, ultimately the interventions in Iraq were regarded by the world community as somehow emanating from authority granted by the Security Council. Why? With respect to northern Iraq, the intervention occurred in the immediate aftermath of a war conducted pursuant to Security Council authorization, at a time when the Security Council was imposing extensive requirements on a defeated Iraq that radically intruded into Iraqi internal affairs. It would have been very odd to condemn coalition forces in northern Iraq as unlawfully interfering in Iraq's "domestic affairs" at a time when the Security Council had authorized the presence of such forces in southern Iraq, as well as extensive destruction of Iraqi weapons, seizure of Iraqi assets, continued economic sanctions, and even the demarcation of Iraq's boundary with Kuwait, all in an effort to restore peace and security to the region. In addition, the intervention was directly linked to Security Council action in that Turkey had specifically approached the Security Council seeking assistance and that the Security Council had asserted the situation in northern Iraq was a threat to the peace. Resolution 688 made the treatment by Iraq of its citizens an issue of international concern warranting action by the international community. At the same time, it made clear the view of the international community that Iraq must permit foreign relief organizations access to Iraq. Though military protection for these relief organizations to help create the conditions for delivery of relief supplies was outside the explicit terms of Resolution 688, it is more in the nature of an extrapolation than a contradiction. Simply put, the coalition airdrop, which then expanded into the creation of "safe havens," was the blossom of a seed planted by the Security Council in Resolution 688.

221. For instance, the editors of the New York Times asked:

> On what authority does [President Bush] proceed? Every U.S. military move against Iraq so far has been explicitly authorized by U.N. resolutions. To justify the no-fly zone the White House cites Resolution 688, demanding that Iraq halt repression and authorizing continued monitoring of human rights issues.
>
> That resolution's clear concern was the surge of Kurdish refugees across international borders, threatening the peace. . . . Fighter jets bristling with missiles are not obvious weapons for protecting a human rights monitoring mission. The real goal, surely, is to shield Shiite rebels from Iraqi air attack. But on what authority?

No Fly in Iraq. Why?, N.Y. TIMES, Aug. 28, 1992, at A24 (editorial).

The intervention in southern Iraq was less temporally linked to Resolution 688, but it was also an effort to address the humanitarian concerns that gave rise to the threat to peace identified in Resolution 688. Further, at the time of the intervention in August 1992, intrusive efforts of the Security Council to identify and destroy Iraqi weapons, demarcate the Iraq-Kuwait boundary, use Iraqi assets to pay claims, and maintain economic sanctions still were taking place. Indeed, the aerial flights by the allied forces over both northern and southern Iraq ultimately led to attacks on Iraqi missile sites and facilities that were variously characterized as related to Resolution 688 and as related to the overall ceasefire arrangement between the UN and Iraq.

Thus the lack of global condemnation of the interventions was most likely not based on a perception that states have a unilateral right to intervene for humanitarian purposes. Rather, it was based on a perception that authority to intervene for these purposes emanated in some fashion from Security Council authorization. On the one hand, this could be attributable to the overall post-war situation; this is the view that many observers, including opponents of a unilateral right to humanitarian intervention, would likely take. On the other hand, it could be attributable to an acceptance of humanitarian intervention by a state or states acting on their own initiative subsequent to a Security Council identification of a threat to peace and security from a widespread deprivation of human rights, even where the Security Council does not expressly authorize intervention. In either case, it might be said that the interventions, while not explicitly authorized, were "legitimized" by the overall involvement of the Security Council in Iraq.

Assuming that the interventions were based in some fashion on Resolution 688, can the basis in the UN Charter for that resolution be determined? In Resolution 688, the Security Council did not refer to specific chapters or articles of the Charter, although it did refer to its "duties and responsibilities under the Charter of the United Nations for the maintenance of international peace and security." These duties and responsibilities are conferred by Article 24 of the Charter; the powers to discharge these duties and responsibilities are set forth in Chapters VI, VII, VIII, and XII. However, since Resolution 688 was not related either to regional action or to the trusteeship system, it had to arise from either Chapter VI or Chapter VII. As a Chapter VI action, Resolution 688 would be characterized as a recommendation for an appropriate method for resolving a situation that threatened international peace and security. As such, it would not provide a basis for authorizing enforcement action. Support for this view may exist in the omission of any reference to Chapter VII, which was explicitly mentioned in virtually every other preceding resolution relating to Iraq.[222]

In Resolution 688, however, the Security Council stated that it was "gravely concerned" about circumstances that it considered to "threaten international peace and security in the region."[223] This language is not well suited to Chapter VI, which is oriented toward resolving situations (particularly disputes between states) prior to the time that they are "likely to endanger the maintenance of international peace and security."[224] Rather, it is suited to Chapter VII, which is oriented toward action with respect to threats to or breaches of the peace. Within Chapter VII, the resolution could be characterized as simply a recommendation issued pursuant to Article 39, as provisional measures pursuant to Article 40, as nonforcible measures under Article 41, or as an authorization for forcible intervention under Article 42 or under the Security Council's general powers to restore peace and security.

Like many of the resolutions relating to the Iraq crisis, the text of the resolution provides few clues as to the exact basis within Chapter VII. Iraq and the Secretary-General's delegate entered into a memorandum of understanding in which they noted that Iraq had not "accepted" Resolution 688, implying that the resolution was not a binding decision but, rather, in the nature of a recommendation. Obviously, persons inclined toward the view that the resolution did not authorize forcible intervention would likely regard the resolution as arising from Articles 39, 40, or 41 and would note that, rather than explicitly decide upon specific enforcement measures, the Security Council decided "to remain seized of the matter."

Yet the resolution did not request—it demanded—that Iraq cease its repression and allow access by humanitarian organizations. It then requested states to contribute to these humanitarian relief efforts. This ap-

222. Chapter VII was explicitly invoked in Security Council Resolutions 660, 661, 664, 666, 667, 670, 674, 677, 678, 686, and 687. The Security Council did not mention Chapter VII in Resolutions 662, 665 (authorizing forcible naval interception operations in support of the economic sanctions), and 669.

223. Preambular paragraph 3 in Resolution 688 reads:

Gravely concerned by the repression of the Iraqi civilian population in many parts of Iraq, including most recently in Kurdish-populated areas, which led to a massive flow of refugees towards and across international frontiers and to cross-border incursions which threaten international peace and security in the region.

S.C. Res. 688, *supra* note 113. The formulation in Resolution 688 was not as strong as the formulation used in the very first resolution against Iraq, Resolution 660, which "determined" that there existed a breach of international peace and security. S.C. Res. 660, *supra* note 80.

224. *See* U.N. CHARTER arts. 33, para. 1, 34, 37, para. 2.

proach bears some similarity to the approach taken in other resolutions that arguably provided for enforcement action against Iraq under Article 42 (e.g., in Resolution 665 and its preceding resolutions), where the Security Council first demanded action from Iraq and "called upon" states to use "measures" to insure implementation of these demands.

Those persons inclined to the view that Resolution 688's demand to Iraq and request to other states authorized forcible intervention by states pursuant to Article 42 are exposed to the criticism that the requirements of Article 42 were not met. Prior to taking measures under Article 42, Article 39 provides that the Security Council "determine" that there exists a threat to the peace. As discussed above, such a determination seems implicit in the Preamble to Resolution 688, but the magical word "determines" is not evident (as it was in other Iraq-related resolutions). Further, Article 42 provides that the Security Council "consider" nonforcible measures to be inadequate to maintain or restore international peace and security; nothing in the resolution or the Security Council debate on the resolution indicates that the members of the Security Council regarded nonforcible measures as inadequate to address the threat. Indeed, Resolution 688 expresses the "hope" of the Security Council that "an open dialogue will take place to ensure that the human and political rights of all Iraqi citizens are respected." This would leave supporters of the view that the intervention was based on Resolution 688 arguing that it arose not from Article 42 but, rather, from the Security Council's general powers to maintain and restore international peace and security. A liberal construction of the Security Council's authority under Chapter VII finds support within the international legal community,[225] although such a construction, in essence, eviscerates whatever limitations on Security Council powers that might otherwise be found in analyzing the specific provisions of Chapter VII.

Finally, the discussions at the Security Council during the passage of

---

225. *See, e.g., Schachter, supra* note 188, at 461. In support of a liberal construction, Schachter cites to Certain Expenses of the United Nations, 1962 I.C.J. 151, 167 (July 20). In that case, however, the Court was not stating that the Security Council, when deploying armed forces, may act on a basis other than Article 42. Rather, the Court was speaking more narrowly to the issue of whether the Security Council could take such measures in the absence of agreements between states and the United Nations concluded pursuant to U.N. Charter Article 43. The Court's unwillingess to find the Security Council "impotent" due to the nonexistence of Article 43 agreements provides support for the view that the Security Council may proceed without such agreements (presumably under Article 42, THE CHARTER OF THE UNITED NATIONS: A COMMENTARY 633 (B. Simma ed., 1994)), but does not address the issue of the Security Council using armed force outside the context of Article 42. In any event, the actions at issue in that case, which involved U.N. forces deployed with the consent of the host countries, were found by the Court not to be enforcement actions within the "compass" of Chapter VII.

Resolution 688 and the subsequent intervention in Iraq evidence a belief among states that there is a fundamental link between the manner
in which governments treat their own people and their propensity to
threaten or use force against other states. Where governmental control
is highly centralized in an elite class which is capable of exercising power
with relative impunity (i.e., without public and judicial scrutiny and restraint), then the government is more easily capable of either inflicting
human rights violations on it own people or undertaking military action
abroad.

C. Bosnia-Herzegovina (1992)

1. Essential Facts

Unlike the other Central and Eastern European countries, Yugoslavia
successfully broke with the Soviet Union as early as 1948, pursuing its
own brand of "market socialism." That one man, Marshal Josip Broz
Tito, could maintain control over a unified Yugoslav state throughout
the Cold War (until his death in 1980) was a remarkable feat. For Yugoslavia as a state was in many respects an artificial twentieth-century construct of six republics whose peoples were divided ethnically, culturally,
and religiously and by centuries of deep-seated animosities.[226]

   After Tito's death, an eight-member federal collective presidency operated successfully until 1991. Yugoslavia could not escape, however, the
shock waves of a collapsed Soviet Union that reverberated throughout
Central and Eastern Europe. On June 25, 1991, the Yugoslav republics
of Slovenia and Croatia declared independence from the Yugoslav federation. Shortly thereafter, tanks of the Serb-dominated federal Yugoslav
People's Army (JNA) rolled into Slovenia, marking the beginning of a
civil war that ultimately would engulf much of the country, causing tens
of thousands of deaths, hundreds of thousands of refugees, and billions

---

226. For general background on the war in the former Yugoslavia, *see* R. DONIA & J.
FINE JR., BOSNIA AND HERCEGOVINA: A TRADITION BETRAYED (1994); M. GLENNY, THE FALL
OF YUGOSLAVIA: THE THIRD BALKAN WAR (rev. ed. 1994); N. GNESOTTO, LEÇONS DE LA
YOUGOSLAVIE (1994); R. KAPLAN, BALKAN GHOSTS: A JOURNEY THROUGH HISTORY (1993);
D. VERNET & J. GONIN, LE RÊVE SACRIFIÉ: CHRONIQUE DES GUERRES YOUGOSLAVES (1994).
Describing the exact causes of the war is difficult. For a discussion of why the initial out-
break of war in the former Yugoslavia between Serbs and Croats is attributable primarily to
contemporary ideological and political differences rather than ancient animosities or reli-
gious differences, *see* I. Banac, *The Fearful Asymmetry of War: The Causes and Consequences of
Yugoslavia's Demise*, DAEDALUS, Spring 1992, at 141. For a refutation of the Serb argument
that Muslims in Bosnia are fundamentalists bent on establishing a radical Islamic state, *see*
Y. Sadowski, *Bosnia's Muslims: A Fundamentalist Threat?*, BROOKINGS REV., Winter 1995, at 10.

of dollars in property damage.[227] With the assistance of diplomatic intervention by the EC and the Conference on Security and Cooperation in Europe (CSCE),[228] the JNA forces withdrew from, and peace was established in, Slovenia in July 1991. An EC-CSCE observer mission was deployed to Slovenia to monitor the peace with the consent of the Yugoslav parties.

At the same time, fighting broke out in Croatia. Whereas in Slovenia the fighting was between Slovenian forces and the JNA, in Croatia the fighting was between three parties: Croatian defense forces, local Serbian irregular forces, and the Serb-dominated JNA. Before long, Serb forces took control of about one-third of Croatia (which they called the Krajina); in doing so, JNA forces extensively shelled the Croatian cities of Vukovar and Dubrovnik.

In September 1991, the Security Council determined that the continuation of the fighting in Yugoslavia was a threat to international peace and security and imposed a general embargo on all deliveries of weapons and military equipment to Yugoslavia.[229] On December 17, the EC decided to recognize Slovenia and Croatia as independent states. As winter set in, thousands were homeless and exposed to starvation, prompting the United Nations to organize a humanitarian relief effort lead by the UN High Commissioner for Refugees. Special UN envoys managed in January 1992 to secure a ceasefire in Croatia that, at least temporarily, froze the military and political status quo.[230]

The focal point of the civil war then shifted to the Republic of Bosnia-Herzegovina. Bosnia-Herzegovina contained a majority Muslim population, but with significant Serbian and Croatian minorities. In 1992, Serbia and Croatia began providing extensive assistance to those minorities against the Bosnian army. The support of Serbia was particularly significant, for Serbia inherited the firepower of the JNA and was capable of drawing on extensive stockpiles unavailable to the poorly equipped

227. For an account by the U.S. Ambassador to Yugoslavia recounting the origins of the conflict, *see* W. Zimmermann, *The Last Ambassador: A Memoir of the Collapse of Yugoslavia*, FOREIGN AFF., Mar.-Apr. 1995, at 2.

228. On January 1, 1995, the CSCE became the Organization for Security and Co-operation in Europe (OSCE), as provided in CSCE Budapest Summit Declaration, Dec. 6, 1994, para. 3, and in CSCE, Budapest Decisions, ch. 1, para. 1, *reprinted in* 34 I.L.M. 764 (1995).

229. S.C. Res. 713, U.N. SCOR, 46th Sess., 3009th mtg. at 42, U.N. Doc. S/INF/47 (1993), *reprinted in* 2 WESTON, *supra* note 12, at II.D.15.

230. *See Report of the Secretary-General*, U.N. Doc. S/23363 & Add.1 (1992). Sporadic fighting continued in Croatia leading to a "permanent ceasefire" agreement signed on March 29, 1994 between the Government of Croatia and the Croation Serb rebels. Croatian Government forces then attacked the rebels in May 1995, as discussed *infra*.

army of Bosnia-Herzegovina. Indeed, Bosnia's inability to obtain arms to defend itself was subsequently a part of a suit it brought against Serbia and Montenegro before the International Court of Justice.[231]

In April 1992, a few days before the United States and other NATO countries recognized the Republic of Bosnia-Herzegovina as an independent state, Serb forces launched an attack against Bosnia-Herzegovina from Serbia. The fighting that followed was brutal, involving indiscriminate, vicious attacks on and torture of civilians, sieges of cities sheltering starving civilians, rape as an instrument of warfare, and inhumane treatment of prisoners. The term "ethnic cleansing" came to mean the elimination by an ethnic group exercising control over a given territory of members of other ethnic groups either by forced expulsion or death. While none of the warring factions in Bosnia-Herzegovina conducted themselves with clean hands, the vast majority of these atrocities were committed by the Serbs,[232] acts that ultimately prompted the Security Council to establish an international criminal tribunal in The Hague to prosecute persons responsible for violations of international humanitarian law in the former Yugoslavia after January 1, 1991.[233] In addition to people trapped in their villages or cities by the fighting, the United Nations High Commissioner for Refugees estimated that there were 1.2

---

231. Bosnia-Herzegovina's Application was filed on March 20, 1993, alleging violations by Serbia and Montenegro of the Convention on the Prevention and Punishment of the Crime of Genocide, Dec. 9, 1948, 78 U.N.T.S. 277 (which entered into force Jan. 12, 1951 and to which the former Socialist Federal Republic of Yugoslavia was a party), *reprinted in* 3 WESTON, *supra* note 12, at III.J.1. The Application also charged violations of the UN Charter, the Geneva and Hague Conventions respecting the laws of war, the Universal Declaration of Human Rights, and customary rules of international law. The jurisdiction of the Court was based on Article IX of Genocide Convention. On April 8, 1993, the International Court issued a provisional order demanding that Serbia and Montenegro take measures to prevent the crime of genocide in Bosnia-Herzegovina, but did not rule on Bosnia's request to be exempted from the Security Council's arms embargo. Application of the Convention on the Prevention and Punishment of the Crime of Genocide (Bosnia and Herzegovina v. Yugo. (Serbia and Montenegro)), 1993 I.C.J. 3 (Order of Apr. 8); E. Robinson, *World Court Orders Belgrade to Prevent "Genocide" in Bosnia*, WASH. POST, Apr. 9, 1993, at A19.

232. *See* R. Cohen, *C.I.A. Report on Bosnia Blames Serbs for 90% of the War Crimes*, N.Y. TIMES, Mar. 9, 1995, at A1.

233. S.C. Res. 808, U.N. SCOR, 48th Sess., 3175th mtg. at 28, U.N. Doc. S/INF/49 (1994); S.C. Res. 827, U.N. SCOR, 48th Sess., 3217th mtg. at 29, U.N. Doc. S/INF/49 (1994). *See* M. BASSIOUNI & P. MANIKAS, THE LAW OF THE INTERNATIONAL CRIMINAL TRIBUNAL FOR THE FORMER YUGOSLAVIA (1996); J. O'Brien, *The International Tribunal for Violations of International Humanitarian Law in the Former Yugoslavia*, 87 AM. J. INT'L L. 639 (1993). Despite the complications it might create for attaining a peace, the Tribunal proceeded to indict as war criminals dozens of persons in the former Yugoslavia, including Radovan Karadzic, the leader of the Bosnian Serbs, and Ratko Mladic, the commander of the Bosnian Serb army. *Peace, Justice, Warring Angels*, ECONOMIST, Apr. 29, 1995, at 62.

million displaced persons within the former Yugoslavia and that more than 230,000 had fled the region entirely.[234]

In February 1992 the Security Council established a UN Protection Force (UNPROFOR). While UNPROFOR was headquartered in Bosnia's Sarajevo, its initial mandate was to undertake patrolling functions in Croatia between government forces and the Croatian Serbs in Krajina.[235] After the outbreak of fighting in Bosnia-Herzegovina, UNPROFOR was forced to relocate its headquarters to Belgrade and then to Zagreb. Between 1992 and 1995, the Security Council gradually expanded UNPROFOR's mandate to reflect changing conditions in the republics of the former Yugoslavia. This mandate was expanded geographically (such as establishing a presence in Macedonia)[236] and functionally (such as protecting convoys of released detainees,[237] reopening the Sarajevo airport,[238] and monitoring of "pink zones," meaning Serb-controlled areas lying outside UN protected areas).[239]

In May 1992, Bosnia-Herzegovina was admitted as a member of the United Nations (along with Croatia and Slovenia).[240] Serbia-Montenegro proclaimed the dissolution of the former "Socialist Federated Republic of Yugoslavia" in April 1992 and purported to establish a new state, the "Federal Republic of Yugoslavia." The Security Council, however, decided that new state could not claim UN membership based on the prior UN membership of the Socialist Federal Republic of Yugosla-

---

234. *See Yugoslavia: The Question of Intervention: Hearing Before Subcomm. on European Affairs of the Senate Comm. on Foreign Relations*, 102d Cong., 2d Sess. 9 (1992) (prepared statement of Ralph Johnson, U.S. Deputy Assistant Secretary of State).

235. S.C. Res. 743, U.N. SCOR, 47th Sess., 3055th mtg. at 8, U.N. Doc. S/INF/48 (1993). For documentation leading to the creation of this peacekeeping force, *see Further Report of the Secretary-General*, U.N. Doc. S/23592 & Add.1 (1992); S.C. Res. 740, U.N. SCOR, 47th Sess., 3049th mtg. at 7, U.N. Doc. S/INF/48 (1993); S.C. Res. 724, U.N. SCOR, 46th Sess., 3023d mtg. at 45, U.N. Doc. S/INF/47 (1993); *Report of the Secretary-General*, U.N. Doc. S/23280 (1991) (especially Annex III).

236. S.C. Res. 795, U.N. SCOR, 47th Sess., 3147th mtg. at 37, U.N. Doc. S/INF/48 (1993).

237. S.C. Res. 776, U.N. SCOR, 47th Sess., 3114th mtg. at 33, U.N. Doc. S/INF/48 (1993).

238. S.C. Res. 758, U.N. SCOR, 47th Sess., 3083d mtg. at 17, U.N. Doc. S/INF/48 (1993); S.C. Res. 761, U.N. SCOR, 47th Sess., 3087th mtg. at 19, U.N. Doc. S/INF/48 (1993).

239. S.C. Res. 779, U.N. SCOR, 47th Sess., 3118th mtg. at 34, U.N. Doc. S/INF/48 (1993).

240. G.A. Res. 46/237, U.N. GAOR, 46th Sess., Supp. No. 49A, at 5, U.N. Doc. A/46/49/Add.1 (1993) (Bosnia-Herzegovina admission); G.A. Res. 46/236, U.N. GAOR, 46th Sess., Supp. No. 49A, at 5, U.N. Doc. A/46/49/Add.1 (1993) (Slovenia admission); G.A. Res. 46/238, U.N. GAOR, 46th Sess., Supp. No. 49A, at 5, U.N. Doc. A/46/49/Add.1 (1993) (Croatia admission).

via.[241] Although it participated in diplomatic efforts to resolve the conflict, Serbia-Montenegro, by providing economic and military support to the Bosnian Serbs, came to be viewed by the international community as the primary culprit in the conflict. The Secretary-General reported on May 12, 1992:

> All international observers agree that what is happening is a concerted effort by the Serbs of Bosnia-Herzegovina, with the acquiescence of, and at least some support from, [the Yugoslav People's Army], to create "ethnically pure" regions in the context of negotiations on the "cantonization" of the Republic [of Bosnia-Herzegovina] in the EC Conference on Bosnia-Herzegovina.[242]

For this reason, the Security Council demanded that JNA forces (as well as Croatian Army forces) and all other support be withdrawn from Bosnia-Herzegovina.[243] When Serbia-Montenegro failed to comply, the Security Council condemned this failure and, on May 30, 1992, imposed a general embargo on the import to and export from Serbia-Montenegro of all commodities and products (including transfers of funds for such

241. S.C. Res. 777, U.N. SCOR, 47th Sess., 3116th mtg. at 34, U.N. Doc. S/INF/48 (1993). The Security Council previously had noted that Serbia and Montenegro's claim to continue automatically the UN membership of the former Yugoslavia "has not been generally accepted." S.C. Res. 757, U.N. SCOR, 47th Sess., 3082d mtg. at 13, pmbl., U.N. Doc. S/INF/48 (1993), *reprinted in* 2 WESTON, *supra* note 12, at II.D.17a. Based on the Security Council's recommendation, the General Assembly decided that Serbia and Montenegro could not continue automatically the UN membership of the former Socialist Federal Republic of Yugoslavia, and would have to apply for membership before it could participate in the work of the General Assembly. G.A. Res. 47/1, U.N. GAOR, 47th Sess., Supp. No. 49, at 12, U.N. Doc. A/47/49 (1993). *See* Y. Blum, *UN Membership of the "New" Yugoslavia: Continuity or Break?*, 86 AM. J. INT'L L. 830 (1992); *see also* associated commentary at *Correspondents' Agora: UN Membership of the Former Yugoslavia*, 87 AM. J. INT'L L. 240 (1993).

242. *Further Report of the Secretary-General*, U.N. Doc. S/23900 (1992), para. 5. The NATO Foreign Ministers in late 1992 similarly laid blame with the Serbs:

> Primary responsibility for the conflict in Bosnia-Herzegovina lies with the present leadership of Serbia and the Bosnian Serbs. They have sought territorial gains by force and engaged in systemic gross violations of human rights and international humanitarian law, including the barbarous practice of "ethnic cleansing." There is the systematic detention and rape of Muslim women and girls. Relief convoys are being harassed and delayed.

Statement on Former Yugoslavia by the NATO Foreign Ministers, Dec. 17, 1992, FOREIGN POL'Y BULL., Jan.-Apr. 1993, at 85, para. 2.

243. S.C. Res. 752, U.N. SCOR, 47th Sess., 3075th mtg. at 12, paras. 3, 4, U.N. Doc. S/INF/48 (1993). While Serbia claimed it had withdrawn all JNA forces, some 80,000 remained in Bosnia-Herzegovina on the pretext that they were now soldiers in the Bosnian Serb Army, along with the tanks, equipment, and supplies that belonged to the JNA. *See* 1 HELSINKI WATCH, WAR CRIMES IN BOSNIA-HERZEGOVINA 35–36 (1992).

purposes), with the exception of medical supplies and foodstuffs.[244] In addition, it sanctioned Serbia-Montenegro by ordering states to freeze Serbian and Montenegran assets abroad, to prohibit services related to its aircraft and weapons, to prohibit flights of aircraft to and from it, to ban its participation in official cultural and sporting events, to suspend scientific and technical cooperation with it, and to reduce diplomatic personnel assigned to Belgrade.[245]

These steps, however, did not stop the fighting. The trade sanctions proved porous; Serbia-Montenegro had too many means of overland and waterway access to the outside world. As the casualties mounted, Bosnian Muslims became increasingly isolated in small portions of what was once Bosnia-Herzegovina. Relief convoys found it difficult to gain consent to reach communities of Muslims through Bosnian Serb lines. Although the warring factions reached agreement in London in July 1992 on a ceasefire,[246] which was to include supervision by UNPROFOR of heavy weapons possessed by the factions, the ceasefire did not hold, and reports of widespread violations of international humanitarian law continued.[247] As winter approached, it became apparent that military force would be necessary to avert a disaster of genocidal proportions.

In August 1992, the Security Council called upon states to take "all measures necessary" to facilitate the delivery of humanitarian assistance

244. S.C. Res. 757, *supra* note 241 para. 4. When it became apparent that transshipments of goods (shipments ostensibly destined for some third state) through Serbia and Montenegro were being diverted and kept in Serbia and Montenegro, the Security Council tightened the sanctions by banning transshipments of certain key products (crude oil, coal, metals, chemicals, rubber, and motors) unless authorized by the sanctions committee on a case-by-case basis. S.C. Res. 787, U.N. SCOR, 47th Sess., 3137th mtg. at 29, para. 9, U.N. Doc. S/INF/48 (1993). When sanctions violations persisted, the Security Council banned the transport of all commodities and products across the Serbia and Montenegro borders (with limited exceptions, such as humanitarian supplies) and ordered neighboring states to prevent the passage of all freight vehicles and rolling stock except at certain locations. It also ordered neighboring states to seize modes of transport owned by persons in Serbia and Montenegro or used in violation of the sanctions. S.C. Res. 820, U.N. SCOR, 48th Sess., 3200th mtg. at 7, U.N. Doc. S/INF/49 (1994) (the resolution also prohibited the provision of all services, financial or nonfinancial, to persons in Serbia and Montenegro, again with limited exceptions).

245. S.C. Res. 757, *supra* note 241.

246. *Letter Dated 17 July 1992 from Belgium, France and Britain to the President of the Security Council*, U.N. Doc. S/24303 (1992).

247. At the London Conference on the Former Yugoslavia, held Aug. 26–27, 1992, states established a permanent negotiating forum co-chaired by the United Nations and the European Community and developed an international plan of action to deal with the crisis. For relevant documents, *see Material Relating to the London Conference (August 26– 27, 1992) and the Crisis in the Former Yugoslavia*, 3 U.S. Dep't St. Dispatch, Supp. No. 7 (1992).

to Bosnia-Herzegovina[248] and demanded immediate access to detention centers for the International Committee of the Red Cross.[249] The formulation "all measures necessary" was similar to the "all necessary means" language used in Resolution 678 of November 1990 to authorize the use of force against Iraq on behalf of Kuwait, and was much broader than the language used in Resolution 688 of April 1991 to deal with the humanitarian crisis in Iraq.[250] In the case of Bosnia-Herzegovina, the formulation was capable of serving as the basis for military intervention by one or more states should they choose to do so to facilitate the delivery of humanitarian assistance by military means. Such intervention might have been well received; at this point, most states were appalled at the atrocities being committed against Muslims in Bosnia-Herzegovina and attributed them in large part to units of Serbia-Montenegro's JNA and elements of the Croatian Army.[251] Thus, by a vote of 136−1−5, the General Assembly adopted a resolution calling on the Security Council to take "further appropriate measures" under Chapter VII to end the war in Bosnia-Herzegovina and to restore the unity and territorial integrity of Bosnia-Herzegovina.[252] While plans were made for thousands of NATO troops to be deployed to Bosnia to protect humanitarian convoys, the step ultimately taken in September 1992 was only to expand the mandate of UNPROFOR forces to protect those delivering relief supplies.[253] Unlike the international response to Somalia later that year, no state or states undertook to organize and deploy a multinational intervention force for Bosnia.

In October 1992, to ensure the safety of humanitarian flights and to assist in the cessation of hostilities, the Security Council established a ban on all military flights in the airspace over Bosnia-Herzegovina.[254] Imposing this ban was a source of tension among the Security Council

248. S.C. Res. 770, U.N. SCOR, 47th Sess., 3106th mtg. at 24, U.N. Doc. S/INF/48 (1993).

249. *Id.*; S.C. Res. 771, U.N. SCOR, 47th Sess., 3106th mtg. at 25, U.N. Doc. S/INF/48 (1993). A similar demand was made by the UN Commission on Human Rights. UNHCR Res. 1992/S-1/1, U.N. ESCOR, 1st Special Sess., Supp. No. 2A, at 2, U.N. Doc. E/1992/22/Add.1, E/CN.4/1992/84/Add.1/Rev.1 (1992).

250. S.C. Res. 678, *supra* note 82; S.C. Res. 688, *supra* note 113.

251. For a description of the "massive and systematic violations of human rights" in Bosnia-Herzegovina in 1992, *see Human Rights Questions: Human Rights Situations and Reports of the Special Rapporteurs and Representatives—Situation of Human Rights in the Territory of the Former Yugoslavia*, U.N. Doc. A/47/666, S/24809 (1992) (report by Special Rapporteur of the Commission on Human Rights).

252. G.A. Res. 46/242, U.N. GAOR, 46th Sess., Supp. No. 49A, at 6, para. 5, U.N. Doc. A/46/49/Add.1 (1993), *reprinted in*, 3 WESTON, *supra* note 12, at III.J.3.

253. S.C. Res. 776, *supra* note 237.

254. S.C. Res. 781, U.N. SCOR, 47th Sess., 3122d mtg. at 27, U.N. Doc. S/INF/48 (1993); S.C. Res. 786, U.N. SCOR, 47th Sess., 3133d mtg. at 28, U.N. Doc. S/INF/48 (1993).

members; some believed that it would create difficulties for UNPROFOR relations with the competing factions in fulfilling its relief functions. Initially, the ban was implemented simply through a monitoring system associated with the UN peacekeeping operation, UNPROFOR. A Monitoring Coordination and Control Centre (MCCC) established at UNPROFOR headquarters in Zagreb received technical monitoring information from NATO; unless the flights had received prior approval from MCCC, they were reported to the Security Council. Subsequently, however, when it was apparent that Serb aircraft had violated the ban hundreds of times,[255] the Security Council extended the ban to cover nonmilitary aircraft as well and authorized member states, acting nationally or through regional organizations (i.e., NATO) to take "all necessary measures" to ensure compliance with the flight ban, "proportionate to the specific circumstances and the nature of the flights."[256] NATO's North Atlantic Council agreed to provide NATO air support to enforce the ban, beginning in mid-April 1993.[257] The rules of engagement for the flights called for identifying aircraft violating the ban, escorting them out of the zone, and only as a last resort shooting them down;[258] but even with threatened NATO enforcement of the no-fly zone, the warring factions in Bosnia regularly violated the ban with impunity.[259]

In November 1992, the Security Council called upon all states, acting nationally or through regional agencies or arrangements, to "use such measures commensurate with the specific circumstances as may be necessary under the authority of the Council to halt all inward and outward maritime shipping in order to inspect and verify their cargoes and destinations" in implementation of the sanctions.[260] Based on this resolution,

255. *See, e.g., Note Verbale Dated 25 February 1993 from the Secretary-General to the President of Security Council,* U.N. Doc. S/24900/Add.22 (1993).

256. S.C. Res. 816, U.N. SCOR, 48th Sess., 3191st mtg. at 4, U.N. Doc. S/INF/49 (1994). The resolution passed 14–0, with China abstaining. For information on its implementation, see *Letter Dated 9 April 1993 from the Secretary-General to the President of the Security Council,* Annex, U.N. Doc. S/25567 (1993).

257. NATO designated the action "Operation Deny Flight." *See* Letter to Congressional Leaders Reporting on the No-Fly Zone Over Bosnia, Apr. 13, 1993, 29 WEEKLY COMP. PRES. DOC. 586 (Apr. 13, 1993).

258. A. Riding, *NATO Agrees to Enforce Flight Ban over Bosnia Ordered by U.N.,* N.Y. TIMES, Apr. 3, 1993, sec. 1, at A5; W. Drozdiak, *NATO to Patrol Bosnian Skies Starting Monday,* WASH. POST, Apr. 9, 1993, at A1. This operation represented the first time German soldiers were allowed to take part in combat operations since 1945 and was unsuccessfully challenged before Germany's federal constitutional court. M. Fisher, *High Court Allows German Participation in U.N. Balkan Mission,* WASH POST, Apr. 9, 1993, at A19.

259. B. Crossette, *United Nations Reports Serbian Helicopter Sorties in Bosnia, a Violation of Flight Ban,* N.Y. TIMES, Feb. 8, 1995, at A12; J. Pomfret, *NATO, U.N. Squabble Over Bosnia: "No-Fly" Zone Violations at Issue,* WASH. POST, Feb. 21, 1995, at A1.

260. S.C. Res. 787, *supra* note 244, para. 12.

NATO and Western European Union (WEU, the defense-oriented affiliate of the EU) forces moved to stop trafficking with Serbia-Montenegro through Adriatic ports. Most of the sanctions violations, however, occurred through smuggling along the Danube River (which connects many European countries, including Serbia-Montenegro, to the Black Sea). Preventing those violations proved difficult because of Serbia-Montenegro's ability to retaliate against the transport of other states' commerce.[261]

Throughout the first half of 1993, the United Nations and the EU tried to gain adherence to a peace plan that would divide Bosnia into ten semiautonomous provinces dominated by different ethnic groups. This "Vance-Owen" plan (named after the UN and EC mediators) called for a weak central government located in Sarajevo consisting of representatives from Bosnia's Muslim, Croatian, and Serb factions. The plan ultimately was rejected by the Bosnian Serbs, and the violence in Bosnia dragged on.

In March 1993, U.S. forces (in coordination with the United Nations) began air-dropping food and medicine to Muslim enclaves in Bosnia-Herzegovina which could not be reached by land.[262] In April and May 1993, the Security Council carved out six of these enclaves as "safe areas" for the protection of the Bosnian civilians,[263] and subsequently it expanded the mandate of UNPROFOR to enable it to deter attacks against those areas, to occupy certain key points on the ground to this end, and to reply to bombardments against the safe areas.[264] Thus, UNPROFOR was granted the ability to use force to accomplish its mission, which suggested a more aggressive application of traditional UN peacekeeping principles. Further, the Security Council authorized member states, acting nationally or through regional organizations, to take "all necessary measures, through the use of air power," in and around the six safe havens established to protect Bosnian Muslims and in support of

261. D. Ottaway, *Embargo Leaks at Danube; Serbs' Threats on River Erode U.N. Sanctions*, WASH. POST, Mar. 4, 1993, at A21.

262. *See* Statement Announcing Airdrops Providing Humanitarian Aid to Bosnia-Herzegovina, 29 WEEKLY COMP. PRES. DOC. 318 (Feb. 25, 1993) (announcement of President Clinton that the United States would begin airdrops in coordination with the United Nations); J. Lancaster & A. Devroy, *U.S. Accuses Serbs of New Attacks; Contradicting Aspen, Clinton Says Airdrops to Muslims Continue*, WASH. POST, Mar. 4, 1993, at A1.

263. S.C. Res. 819, U.N. SCOR, 48th Sess., 3199th mtg. at 6, U.N. Doc. S/INF/49 (1994); S.C. Res. 824, U.N. SCOR, 48th Sess., 3208th mtg. at 11, U.N. Doc. S/INF/49 (1994). The six safe areas were Bihac, Gorazde, Sarajevo, Srebrenica, Tuzla, and Zepa. Both resolutions were by a vote of 15–0.

264. S.C. Res. 836, U.N. SCOR, 48th Sess., 3228th mtg. at 13, paras. 5, 9, U.N. Doc. S/INF/49 (1994). The vote was 13–0, with Pakistan and Venezuela abstaining.

UNPROFOR.[265] The Secretary-General subsequently estimated that to perform these additional functions, UNPROFOR would need an additional 34,000 troops at a cost of $250 million for the first six months and $26 million per month thereafter.[266] In August 1993, the Secretary-General reported that procedures were in place for the use of air power in support of UNPROFOR in Bosnia-Herzegovina.[267]

The United States sought agreement with its European allies both to remove the embargo on weapons to the Bosnian Government so that it could arm itself and to conduct air strikes against Serb artillery sites. During 1993, it was unsuccessful in both cases. The European states expressed concern that allowing more weapons into the region would exacerbate the conflict and that air strikes would imperil UNPROFOR forces on the ground. Instead, they pressed for a negotiated settlement on the basis of a new EU plan that would divide Bosnia into three republics along ethnic lines (Croatian, Muslim, and Serb).

By 1994, however, the EU plan had failed to win Muslim support, and the use of airstrikes became seen as the only way to prevent further catastrophic Bosnian Serb attacks on the UN-protected enclaves. On February 5, 1994, a mortar shell landed in a crowded open-air market in Sarajevo, killing at least 66 people and wounding more than 200.[268] Secretary-General Boutros Boutros-Ghali sent a two-page letter to NATO Secretary Manfred Woerner requesting that NATO decide whether to use air power as a response to the shelling,[269] which the United States endorsed.[270] A special meeting of NATO was held in Brussels to address the issue and resulted in a NATO warning to the Bosnian Serbs either to withdraw their artillery twelve miles from the center of Sarajevo, to turn them over to UN forces by February 21, or to face airstrikes.[271] The tactic worked; Bosnian Serb forces withdrew or abandoned their artillery around Sarajevo, and the bombardment ended. Thereafter, some sem-

---

265. *Id.* para. 10. The same authority was later granted with respect to support of UNPROFOR in Croatia. S.C. Res. 958, U.N. SCOR, 49th Sess., 3461st mtg. U.N. Doc. S/RES/958 (1994).

266. *Report of the Secretary-General*, U.N. Doc. S/25939 & Add.1 (1993).

267. *Letter Dated 18 August 1993 from the Secretary-General to the President of the Security Council*, U.N. Doc. S/26335 (1993). These procedures were noted by the Security Council. S.C. Res. 859, U.N. SCOR, 48th Sess., 3269th mtg. at 16, para. 5, U.N. Doc. S/INF/49 (1994).

268. J. Kifner, *66 Die As Shell Wrecks Sarajevo Market*, N.Y. TIMES, Feb. 6, 1994, sec. 1, at 1.

269. W. Claiborne & D. Williams, *U.N. Chief Prods NATO on Bosnia Airstrikes*, WASH. POST, Feb. 7, 1994, at A1.

270. D. Williams, *U.S. Backs U.N. Plan for Bosnia Airstrikes*, WASH. POST, Feb. 8, 1994, at A1.

271. D. Ottaway, *NATO Gives Serbs Airstrike Deadline*, WASH. POST, Feb. 10, 1994, at A1.

blance of normalcy returned to Sarajevo, although occasional incidents of Serb shelling and NATO responses occurred.[272]

On March 13, NATO authorized airstrikes for the first time against Serb artillery positions near the besieged town of Maglaj in northern Bosnia. French UNPROFOR forces had wanted to enter the town but had been prevented by Serb fire, and so requested NATO support. When two NATO jets flew low over the area, the Serb fire stopped, allowing the UNPROFOR forces to enter Maglaj without airstrikes actually occurring.[273]

In early April 1994, it appeared that the Muslim enclave of Gorazde, containing some 65,000 people, many from surrounding Serb-held parts of eastern Bosnia, would fall to the Bosnian Serbs unless NATO forces challenged the Bosnian Serb tanks and artillery that were constantly shelling the town. On April 10, UNPROFOR peacekeepers requested NATO intervention, and two U.S. Air Force F-16s launched from Italy dropped bombs on a Serb command post outside Gorazde. While Serb forces were far from disabled from continuing their attack on Gorazde, the airstrike worked; within 18 minutes all Serb shelling of Gorazde stopped.[274] There continued to be a concern for the safety of UNPROFOR forces should the Serb forces choose to respond aggressively to the NATO intervention, but it was believed that the UNPROFOR forces were already at risk from the relentless Serb shelling.

In early 1994, Bosnian Muslims and Croats agreed on a constitution for a common confederation, thereby ending the fighting between them that had broken out in April 1993. This cooperation allowed the Muslim-led Bosnian Government army to focus its efforts on defeating the Bosnian Serbs. Further, a "contact group" of five powers—Britain, France, Germany, Russia, and the United States—threw their weight behind developing a partition plan for Bosnia. The plan would require the Bosnian Serbs to relinquish about one-third of the territory they controlled, leaving them in control of slightly less than half of Bosnia. The Muslim-Croatian Bosnians would control the rest of Bosnia, except for an area around Sarajevo that would be under UN control. While the Bosnian Government supported the plan, the Bosnian Serbs rejected it, notwithstanding efforts by Russia and Serbia to convince them otherwise.[275] On

272. *See, e.g.*, J. Pomfret, *U.S. Jets Hit Serbs After Raid on Arms*, WASH. POST, Aug. 6, 1994, at A1; C. Sudetic, *Serbs Launch More Shells at Sarajevo*, N.Y. TIMES, Aug. 7, 1994, sec. 1, at 9.

273. K. Schork, *NATO Warplanes Protect U.N. Unit*, WASH. POST, Mar. 14, 1994, at A13.

274. J. Randal, *U.S. Jets Strike Serb Forces Near Bosnian Town*, WASH. POST, Apr. 11, 1994, at A1.

275. *See* D. Ottaway, *Bosnian Serbs Again Reject Peace Plan, List Issues for Negotiation*, WASH. POST, July 29, 1994, at A32; Associated Press, *Bosnian Serbs Again Reject Peace Plan*, N.Y. TIMES, Aug. 4, 1994, at A11.

August 5, Serbian President Slobodon Milosevič, under pressure from the United Nations, NATO, and the EU, announced that Serbia was cutting all political and economic ties with the Bosnian Serbs (with the exception of humanitarian aid) in an effort to persuade them to accept the international plan.[276] In response, the Security Council lifted some of the sanctions previously imposed on Serbia and Montenegro.[277]

By the winter of 1994–95, however, it remained unclear whether the Serbian blockade was holding.[278] Further, Croatian Serbs in the Krajina launched attacks into Bosnia-Herzegovina, further pinning down Bosnian Government forces in their fight against the Bosnian Serbs. Former U.S. President Jimmy Carter brokered a four-month ceasefire agreement among the Bosnian factions beginning January 1, 1995,[279] which held until the end of March. At that point, perhaps sensing fatigue on the part of Bosnian Serbs with a war that had now lasted three years, the Bosnian Government undertook offenses against Bosnian Serbs in central and northern Bosnian and won significant victories.[280] Thereafter, the Bosnian Government refused to renew the ceasefire and reports emerged that Iran was supplying the Bosnian Government with weapons in violation of the UN embargo.[281]

In neighboring Croatia, Croatian President Franjo Tudjman grew impatient with the failure of UNPROFOR forces in Croatia to prevent military support from Serbia to Croatian Serbs. In January 1995, Tudjman threatened to withdraw Croatia's consent to the presence of UNPROFOR after March 31, charging that UNPROFOR was simply perpetuating the rebel Serbs' control of the areas they had seized.[282] In re-

276. J. Pomfret, *Yugoslavia Orders End of Ties to Bosnian Serbs*, WASH. POST, Aug. 5, 1994, at A23.

277. S.C. Res. 943, U.N. SCOR, 49th Sess., 3428th mtg., U.N. Doc. S/RES/943 (1994); S.C. Res. 970, U.N. SCOR, 50th Sess., 3487th mtg., U.N. Doc. S/RES/970 (1995); S.C. Res. 988, U.N. SCOR, 50th Sess., 3522d mtg., U.N. Doc. S/RES/988 (1995).

278. B. Crossette, *U.N. Suspects Serbia of Aiding Serbs in Bosnia*, N.Y. TIMES, Feb. 9, 1995, at A10; J. Pomfret, *Serbia Suspected of Aiding Bosnian Allies*, WASH. POST, Dec. 9, 1994, at A37; *Letter Dated 4 January 1995 from the Secretary-General to the President of the Security Council*, U.N. Doc. S/1995/6 (1995).

279. S. Kinzer, *Bosnian Muslims and Serbs Agree to Four-Month Truce*, N.Y. TIMES, Jan. 1, 1995, sec. 1, at 8.

280. R. Cohen, *Bosnian Serb Crossroad: Win Soon or Seek Peace*, N.Y. TIMES, Mar. 26, 1995, sec. 1, at 3.

281. The reports stated that the United States knew of the violations but chose to ignore them since U.S. Congressional support for the weapons embargo against the Bosnian Government had evaporated. D. Williams & T. Lippman, *U.S. Is Allowing Iran To Arm Bosnia Muslims*, WASH. POST, Apr. 14, 1995, at A1; D. Jehl, *U.S. Looks Away as Iran Arms Bosnia*, N.Y. TIMES, Apr. 15, sec. 1, at 3. By August 1995, both houses of the U.S. Congress had voted to lift the embargo on Bosnia.

282. C. Spolar, *U.N. Deal on Croatia Fuels Hope for Peace*, WASH. POST, Apr. 2, 1995, at A34.

sponse, the Security Council agreed to reduce and rearrange the deployment of UNPROFOR forces in Croatia so as to emphasize more the monitoring of personnel, equipment, and weapons that cross the border between Croatia and Serbia.[283] In fact, the Security Council passed a series of resolutions that divided the existing UNPROFOR into three separately named units: one for Croatia, known as the United Nations Confidence Restoration Operation in Croatia (UNCRO);[284] one for Bosnia-Herzegovina, which would continue to be called UNPROFOR and which would receive those UNPROFOR assets from Croatia not needed to support UNCRO;[285] and one for Macedonia, known as the United Nations Preventative Deployment Force (UNPREDEP).[286] (The names of the two new forces were of some significance: the Government of Croatia believed that stating "Croatia" in UNCRO recognized Government's sovereignty over the territory held by the Croatian Serbs;[287] and that not mentioning "Macedonia" in UNPREDEP avoided a controversy with Greece over the use of that name.[288]) Efforts by members of the Security Council to further strengthen the monitoring of Serbia's borders with both Croatia and Bosnia-Herzegovina, however, fell victim to Russia's veto, which claimed that Serbia was cooperating with the UN sanctions.[289]

In early May, the Croatian Government forces stormed across the ceasefire lines to attack the Croatian Serb rebels in an enclave in central Croatia.[290] Although an arrangement was made whereby Serb rebels would surrender their weapons to UN forces and then be allowed to return to Serb-held territory in Bosnia, the Croation Government changed its mind after the weapons were surrendered and took the rebels captive.[291]

The offensive pursued by the Bosnian Government in spring 1995 prompted the Bosnian rebels to move their heavy artillery back into the UN exclusion zone around the beseiged city of Sarajevo and for both

---

283. J. Pomfret, *International Force Blocks Serb Effort To Resupply Rebels*, WASH. POST, Apr. 19, 1995, at A28.

284. S.C. Res. 981, U.N. SCOR, 50th Sess., 3512th mtg., U.N. Doc. S/RES/981 (1995).

285. S.C. Res. 982, U.N. SCOR, 50th Sess., 3512th mtg., U.N. Doc. S/RES/982 (1995).

286. S.C. Res. 983, U.N. SCOR, 50th Sess., 3512th mtg., U.N. Doc. S/RES/983 (1995).

287. L. Meixler, *U.N. Council Votes New Mandate for Balkan Peacekeeping Forces*, WASH. POST, Apr. 1, 1995, at A18.

288. *See* R. Bonner, *Balkan Conflict's Spread to Macedonia is Feared*, N.Y. TIMES, Apr. 9, 1995, sec. 1, at 12.

289. B. Crossette, *Russia Balks at a U.N. Move to Tighten Serbia Border Ban*, N.Y. TIMES, Apr. 21, 1995, at A8.

290. R. Cohen, *Croatia Hits Area Rebels Hold, Crossing U.N. Lines*, N.Y. TIMES, May 2, 1995, at A1.

291. J. Pomfret, *Croatia Holds 1,000 POWs*, WASH. POST, May 6, 1995, at A17.

sides, after a fifteen-month hiatus, to resume their shelling.[292] In turn, UNPROFOR threatened to conduct airstrikes if either side did not desist;[293] when the Serb rebels failed to do so, NATO jets were dispatched to bomb the arms depot at the rebels' headquarters.[294] Instead of backing down, the Serb rebels proceeded to shell five of the six UN-designated safe areas and seize more than 300 UNPROFOR soldiers, chaining many at strategic locations as human shields against further NATO bombing.[295] The Serb rebels incrementally released the hostages,[296] but the action prompted the United Nations to consolidate and relocate the UNPROFOR forces so that they would be less vulnerable to Serb rebel attacks and prompted NATO and European Union countries to deploy a rapid reaction force to Bosnia-Herzegovina to help protect them.[297] That force, however, could not stem the tide of the Bosnian Serb attacks; on July 11, 1995, they overran the UN-designated safe area of Srebrenica, forcing nearly 30,000 civilians to flee and trapping some 430 Dutch UNPROFOR forces.[298] Within two weeks, they overran a second UN-designated area, Zepa, again forcing out the Muslim population.[299]

Fearing that the enclave of Bihac would be next, Western governments "played the Croatian card" by tacitly acknowledging to the Croatian Government that an offensive against Croatian Serbs would be helpful in

292. J. Brand, *Worst Fighting in 15 Months Leaves Five Dead in Sarajevo*, WASH. POST, May 17, 1995, at A25.

293. J. Brand, *NATO Strikes Threatened in Sarajevo*, WASH. POST, May 25, 1995, at A33.

294. R. Cohen, *NATO Jets Bomb Arms Deport at Bosnian Serb Headquarters*, N.Y. TIMES, May 26, 1995, sec. 1, at 1.

295. *Id.*; R. Cohen, *After a 2d Strike from NATO, Serbs Detain U.N. Forces*, N.Y. TIMES, May 27, 1995, sec. 1, at 1; R. Cohen, *2 French Killed as Sarajevo Battle Takes New Course*, N.Y. TIMES, May 28, 1995, sec. 1, at 1; C. Whitney, *Serbs Kill a Bosnian Leader and Take More Hostages*, N.Y. TIMES, May 29, 1995, sec. 1, at 1.

296. *See, e.g.*, B. Graham & C. Spolar, *Bosnian Serbs Free 108 More Hostages*, WASH. POST, June 7, 1995, at A1.

297. W. Drozdiak & B. Graham, *European Force Set for Bosnia*, WASH. POST, June 4, 1995, at 1.

298. S. Power, *Bosnian Serbs Seize "Safe Area,"* WASH. POST, July 12, 1995, at A1. The expulsions from Srebrenica brought further reports of executions, abductions, and other atrocities by the Serb rebels. J. Pomfret, *Witnesses Allege Abuses by Serbs*, WASH. POST, July 16, 1995, at A1; E. Schmitt, *Spy Photos Indicate Mass Grave At Serb-Held Town, U.S. Says*, N.Y. TIMES, Aug. 10, 1995, sec. 1, at 1; M. Dobbs & C. Spolar, *12,000 Muslims and a Trek Through Serb Killing Fields*, INT'L HERALD TRIB., Oct. 27, 1995, at 1; M. Dobbs & R. Smith, *U.S. Has New Evidence of Serb Crimes in Bosnia*, INT'L HERALD TRIB., Oct. 30, 1995, at 1.

299. J. Pomfret, *Bosnian Serbs Claim Fall of 2nd U.N. "Safe Area,"* WASH. POST, July 20, 1995, at A1; J. Pomfret, *Bosnian Muslims Flee As Serbs Seize Town*, WASH. POST, July 26, 1995, at A1; J. Pomfret, *Serbs Burn Zepa, Reportedly Kill Bosnian Commander*, WASH. POST, July 30, 1995, at A22.

reducing Serb pressure on nearby Bihac.[300] On August 4, Croatian Government forces invaded the Krajina, shattering the rebels' control of the region and unleashing their own form of "ethnic cleansing." [301] The Government of Serbia-Montenegro did not intervene, and before long some 200,000 Croatian Serbs had been displaced from their homes and fled into Serbia-Montenegro and Bosnia-Herzegovina.[302]

Whatever the merits of promoting a Croatian Government offensive, it set the stage for a new round of peace talks, this time launched by the United States. The initiative pursued a "carrot and stick" approach, promising the Bosnian Serbs better territorial concessions than previously had been offered, while at the same time promising a six-month NATO bombing campaign and a rearming of the Bosnian Government if the Bosnian Serbs did not negotiate.[303] At first, the Bosnian Serbs wavered, and so NATO airstrikes commenced across rebel territory.[304] In mid-September, however, peace talks commenced in Geneva and led to agreement on a set of principles for pursuing an enduring peace. These principles provided that: (1) Bosnia-Herzegovina would remain as one state in its existing borders; (2) Bosnia-Herzegovina would consist of two entities, the Muslim-Croation Federation (comprising 51 percent of the territory) and a Serbian Republic (comprising the rest); (3) both entities may have "special relationships" with neighboring countries, such as Croatia and Serbia-Montenegro; (4) the two entities would hold elections under international supervision and would observe international human rights standards; and (5) displaced persons could move freely between the two entities.[305] By the end of September, agreement was reached in New York providing for elections in Bosnia-Herzegovina and the basic workings of a parliament and presidency.[306]

300. *See, e.g.*, D. Priest, *U.S. Hoping Military Move Will Ease Pressure on Bihac*, WASH. POST, Aug. 3, 1995, at A24. Prior to this time, Western governments were concerned that a Croatian Government offensive would draw Serbian Government forces back into the conflicts in Croatia or Bosnia-Herzegovina.

301. J. Rupert, *Croatia Launches Invasion of Region Held by Serb Rebels*, WASH. POST, Aug. 5, 1995, at A1; J. Pomfret & J. Rupert, *U.N. Reports Attacks on Serb Civilians*, WASH. POST, Aug. 10, 1995, at A1.

302. J. Perlez, *Croatian Serbs Blame Belgrade For Their Rout*, N.Y. TIMES, Aug. 11, 1992, sec. 1, at 1.

303. S. Greenhouse, *U.S. Warns Of Air Strikes Unless Serbs Negotiate*, INT'L HERALD TRIB., Aug. 28, 1995, at 1.

304. R. Cohen, *NATO Warns Bosnian Serbs Raids Will Go On*, INT'L HERALD TRIB., Aug. 31, 1995, at 1; R. Cohen, *Bombing the Serbs Toward Talks*, INT'L HERALD TRIB., Sept. 1, 1995, at 1.

305. W. Drozdiak, *Warring Factions in Bosnia Reach Accord on Key Issues*, INT'L HERALD TRIB., Sept. 9–10, 1995, at 1.

306. *Agreement Forged on Principles for Settling Bosnia War*, INT'L HERALD TRIB., Sept. 27, 1995, at 1.

On October 6, 1995, a country-wide ceasefire was reached after nearly four years of bloodshed in Bosnia-Herzegovina; in most parts of the country the ceasefire held. Over the course of three weeks of "proximity talks" at a U.S. military base outside Dayton, Ohio, the principles agreed upon at Geneva were developed into a lengthy agreement of complex rules, which was initialed at Dayton on November 23 and then signed in Paris on December 14 by or on behalf of the representatives of all the relevant factions ("Paris Agreement"). In accordance with the Paris Agreement, some 60,000 NATO troops deployed to Bosnia-Herzegovina in late 1995, forming the backbone of an Implementation Force (IFOR) charged with enforcing the agreement. On December 15, the Security Council passed Resolution 1033, which authorized states acting through or in cooperation with NATO to establish such a multinational force under unified, non-UN command and control. Among other things, Resolution 1033 authorized states to take all necessary measures, at the request of IFOR, either in defense of IFOR or to assist IFOR in carrying out its mission.[307]

By the beginning of 1996, the prospects for an enduring peace in Bosnia-Herzegovina remained uncertain. Some deadlines set forth in the Paris Agreement for the return of prisoners and the transfer of control over territory had slipped and the relationship between the IFOR forces and the local factions was precarious, complicated in part by continuing efforts of the International Criminal Tribunal for the former Yugoslavia to bring to justice the primary perpetrators of war crimes in the region.

2. Assessment of the Intervention

In the case of Bosnia-Herzegovina, various actions undertaken by states prior to the conclusion of the Paris Agreement implicated the UN Charter Article 2(4) prohibition on the use of force: (1) the military enforcement by states of a no-fly zone over Bosnia-Herzegovina and a heavy weapons exclusion zone around Sarajevo; (2) the military enforcement by states of comprehensive arms and economic sanctions; (3) the airdropping of food and medicine to Muslim-held enclaves; and (4) the threat and use of force to ensure the six safe havens established to protect Bosnian Muslims. In addition, the authorization of those actions by the Security Council, along with the protection by UNPROFOR forces of relief convoys and safe havens, implicated the Charter Article 2(7) prohibition on UN intervention in affairs essentially within the jurisdiction of a state.

307. S.C. Res. 1033, U.N. SCOR, 50th Sess., 3610 mtg., U.N. Doc. S/1995/1033 (1995). The Paris Agreement, formally known as the General Framework Agreement for Peace in Bosnia and Herzegovina, along with its annexes, is reprinted at U.N. Doc. S/1995/999, annex (1995).

One purpose of these actions was certainly to provide assistance to Bosnian civilians suffering from widespread deprivations of internationally recognized human rights. In light of the horrifying television and print images of civilians dying in Bosnia-Herzegovina, there was a tremendous desire to maintain humanitarian aid to these victims and protect them from wanton violence. Nevertheless, the context in which these actions were taken suggests two other purposes that dominated the response of the international community and, thus, that the actions taken in Bosnia-Herzegovina do not fit easily within the concept of humanitarian intervention.

First, the conflict in Bosnia-Herzegovina was not simply an internal conflict involving deprivations of human rights; from its inception, an essential element of the conflict was the economic and military support provided by other states to the Bosnian Serb rebels (primarily by Serbia-Montenegro, but also by Croatia), support that constituted armed aggression against Bosnia-Herzegovina in violation of UN Charter Article 2(4). The General Assembly declared Bosnia-Herzegovina to be the subject of armed aggression, triggering its right of self-defense under Article 51.[308] While that conclusion was never expressly stated by the Security Council, the Security Council implicitly recognized this right early on during the conflict when it said, in May 1992, that it:

3. *Also demands* that all forms of interference from outside Bosnia and Herzegovina, including by units of the Yugoslav People's Army as well as elements of the Croatian Army, cease immediately, and that Bosnia and Herzegovina's neighbours take swift action to end such interference and respect the territorial integrity of Bosnia and Herzegovina;

4. *Demands also* that those units of the Yugoslav People's Army and elements of the Croatian Army now in Bosnia and Herzegovina must either be withdrawn, or be subject to the authority of the Government of Bosnia-Herzegovina, or be disbanded and disarmed with their weapons placed under effective international monitoring . . . . [309]

By 1995, both Serbia-Montenegro and Croatia may have withdrawn most overt support for the Bosnian Serbs and Croats. They had set in train, however, an insurgency that continued and to which the international community could properly respond as a matter of assisting Bosnia-Herzegovina in the exercise of its inherent right of self-defense. Obviously, Bosnia-Herzegovina would have preferred greater assistance than it in fact received from the international community, such as the ability to receive weapons and military equipment from other states and more extensive NATO suppression of Bosnian Serb artillery. Nevertheless, the actions that the international community did undertake—enforcement

308. G.A. Res. 46/242, *supra* note 252, pmbl.
309. S.C. Res. 752, *supra* note 243, paras. 3, 4.

of sanctions, a weapons exclusion zone and a no-fly zone, creation and protection of safe havens, and airdropping of food—can all be characterized as assisting Bosnia-Herzegovina to defend itself.[310] As such, these actions do not fit well the concept of humanitarian intervention as traditionally understood or as more specifically defined in chapter 1.

Second, to the extent that the actions of the international community seemed to fall short in assisting Bosnia-Herzegovina in exercising a right of self-defense (e.g., by denying the Bosnian Government itself the ability to obtain arms), the reason for those actions was the fear of wider war in the Balkans and beyond. Indeed, there was—and remains—an overall, driving concern by the intervening states, as well as by the United Nations, that the conflict in Bosnia-Herzegovina might spread to other parts of the former Yugoslavia (e.g., Kosovo and Macedonia) and thereby draw interventions by countries such as Albania, Bulgaria, Greece, and Turkey. Throughout the crisis, complex ties of religion, ethnicity, and nationalism had the potential for spinning out of control, as they did in the first part of this century. The danger of such instability in the Balkans represented a direct threat to the national security of several states, and more generally to international peace and security in Central, Eastern, and Southern Europe. The actions taken by the Security Council represented primarily an effort to address that threat; again, this motivation suggests that the actions taken are not properly classified as humanitarian intervention.

Understanding the international community's response in Bosnia-Herzegovina as an effort primarily to address a threat to international peace and security aids in understanding why so little was done to assist Bosnian Muslims from suffering human rights atrocities. Between September 25, 1991 and April 28, 1995, the Security Council adopted 73 resolutions directly related to the situation in the former Yugoslavia, and the President of the Security Council issued 70 statements on the crisis.[311] Yet during this period neither the global community nor the European

310. Virtually all of these actions were taken with the consent of the Government of Bosnia-Herzegovina. The Bosnian Government did not agree with the application of an arms embargo on all factions in Bosnia-Herzegovina, which sought to prevent weapons from being supplied to the Bosnian Government as well. With respect to all the other actions taken by the international community, only in early 1995 did the Bosnian Government indicate that it might withdraw consent to U.N. action in Bosnia-Herzegovina when the issue of renewing UNPROFOR's mandate arose. Undoubtedly frustrated that the United Nations was not doing enough to enforce weapons exclusion zones, to maintain safe areas, to prevent violations of no-flight zones, and to keep open relief lines, the Bosnian Government's step was viewed as a tactic to encourage the Security Council to strengthen UNPROFOR's mandate. B. Crossette, *Bosnia Seeks Short Extension of Operations of U.N. Force*, N.Y. Times, Mar. 24, 1995, at A2.

311. U.N. Department of Public Information Reference Paper, *The United Nations and the Situation in the Former Yugoslavia* v (April 1995).

regional organizations forcibly intervened in the conflict so as to bring a halt to the widespread violence and atrocities, despite a general recognition that the violence represented a modern-day "holocaust" in Europe. Rather, for months, the international community sought to mediate an end to the crisis and to conduct humanitarian operations only in accordance with traditional peacekeeping principles, including consent of all the warring factions. Only three years into the conflict did military airstrikes first occur for the purpose of protecting designated safehavens, and only then when it was apparent that the safety of the peacekeepers themselves was at risk. Ultimately, three of those safehavens were attacked and overtaken.

The conflict in Bosnia-Herzegovina thus exemplified how neither the international community nor states acting in their individual capacity perceive a legal or perhaps even moral obligation or duty to act in situations in which there are widespread and severe human rights atrocities, at least where there are broader security concerns at stake. Of course, there were also practical concerns that weighed against conducting an extensive intervention to protect human rights. Unlike the intervention in Iraq, U.S. analysts officially saw Bosnia as a situation in which the local Serb forces were well armed, loosely organized, and very familiar with the geography of the land, which was conducive to guerilla warfare.[312] Therefore, absent the consent of all the relevant factions (such as was achieved at Dayton), any deployment of ground forces would either sustain significant casualties or would have to be so massive as to entail significant political and economic costs. Moreover, the ethnic ties of Russia to Serbia-Montenegro made it difficult for Russia to support an aggressive use of Chapter VII to combat Bosnian Serb forces. These political and economic constraints carried the day and made clear that neither the United Nations nor its member states perceived a duty to act.

Some early lessons may be derived from the experience in Bosnia-Herzegovina. First, the fact that there are now, after the Cold War, greater possibilities for action by or under the authority of the Security Council does not mean that such action in fact will be forthcoming. While in the immediate aftermath of the Cold War there were some concerns expressed within the international community about the Security Council being too activist and even abusive of its powers, the efforts undertaken in Bosnia-Herzegovina highlight a different, perhaps more serious problem—the failure of the Security Council to exercise fully its powers in appropriate situations. Of course, the problem arises not with the Security Council itself as an institution, but rather with its members.

---

312. *See, e.g.,* B. Gellman, *Defense Planners Making Case Against Intervention in Yugoslavia,* WASH. POST, June 13, 1992, at A16.

The Bosnian crisis shows that, absent the support of a major power for committing the military and economic resources necessary to conduct an intervention, it is quite difficult for such an intervention to occur even where significant human rights values are at stake.

Second, failure to act in such situations creates a danger of sending a signal that future human rights atrocities will not necessarily be addressed by the United Nations or by regional organizations (at least not in a timely, effective fashion). The failure of the international community to take significant enforcement action throughout 1992 undoubtedly encouraged the continuation of atrocities in Bosnia-Herzegovina during 1993–94. Further, while it is difficult to gauge collateral effects, it is likely that the inaction of the Security Council was subsequently read in other parts of the world, such as Somalia and Haiti, as a signal that the Security Council will tolerate human rights atrocities where the costs of preventing those atrocities are deemed high.

Third, there is a fundamental incompatibily in the United Nations and regional organizations playing the role of neutral mediator and peacekeeper at the same time they are considering undertaking forcible military action. Many of the statements and initiatives of the United Nations, NATO, the EU, and the CSCE toward the factions operating in Bosnia-Herzegovina were cautious and strained toward evenhandedness in order not to prejudice hopes for a peaceful resolution of the conflict. Efforts by some states, such as the United States, to promote air attacks on Bosnian Serb positions were for many crucial months rejected by other states and UN officials who were concerned that UNPROFOR forces on the ground would bear the brunt of Bosnian Serb retaliation and that UNPROFOR's ability to gain consent to its relief activities would be prejudiced.[313] On the other hand, once it is agreed that military force is necessary against one of the warring factions, the United Nations and an organization such as NATO can be effective in launching military actions that have a direct, immediate, and positive effect in saving lives.

D. Somalia (1992)

1. Essential Facts

The Somali Civil War

In 1988, civil war broke out in Somalia, with various factions and clans seeking the ouster of President Mohamed Siad Barre. After Barre was

---

313. *See, e.g.*, B. Crossette, *U.N. Overrules New Calls For Air Strikes Against Serbs*, N.Y. TIMES, May 9, 1995 at A8. NATO and the United Nations had agreed upon a "dual key" arrangement for conducting airstrikes, in which approval had to exist from both NATO and the United Nations before such strikes could commence.

overthrown in January 1991, these factions and clans turned on each other, killing thousands of people, uprooting hundreds of thousands more from their homes, destroying the country's infrastructure, and crippling its economy. Even in the best of times, Somalia—a country of some 6.7 million people—was subject to recurring droughts, overgrazing, and desertification and qualified as one of the poorest and least developed countries in the world. As reports and images of massive starvation mounted, various countries and private organizations sent emergency food shipments and other assistance, but the lack of a central government and the continuing civil strife prevented effective distribution of relief. By December 1992, the United Nations estimated Somali deaths at more than 300,000; furthermore, 900,000 Somalis had fled to neighboring Kenya, Ethiopia, and Djibouti, and to Yemen and Saudi Arabia.[314]

International efforts to address the situation in Somalia moved very slowly. On January 20, 1992, the Permanent Mission of Somalia forwarded to the President of the UN Security Council a letter the mission had received from Omer Arteh Qhalib, the "Interim Prime Minister" of Somalia. The mission noted that Mr. Arteh had been appointed as the Interim Prime Minister pursuant to arrangements agreed on by the Somali political parties that had participated in a national reconciliation conference in Djibouti in July 1991. Mr. Arteh's letter requested the mission to "present to the United Nations Security Council the deteriorating situation in Somalia particularly the fighting in Mogadishu." Mr. Arteh stated that he was confident "the United Nations Security Council

---

314. *Fact Sheet: Somalia—Operation Restore Hope*, 3 U.S. DEP'T ST. DISPATCH 898, 899 (1992). For information on the state of Somalia in early 1992, see *The Situation in Somalia: Report of the Secretary-General*, U.N. Doc. S/23829 & Add.1–2 (1992). During the course of 1992, leading up to the authorization of an extensive deployment of forces in December, the Secretary-General made a series of reports to the Security Council on the situation in Somalia. *See The Situation in Somalia: Report of the Secretary-General*, U.N. Doc. S/23693 & Corr.1 (1992); *Letter Dated 23 June 1992 from the Secretary-General to the President of the Security Council*, U.N. Doc. S/24179 (1992) [hereinafter *Letter Dated 23 June 1992*]; *Report of the Secretary-General on the Situation in Somalia*, U.N. Doc. S/24343 (1992); *The Situation in Somalia: Report of the Secretary-General*, U.N. Doc. S/24480 (1992); *Letter Dated 24 November 1992 from the Secretary-General to the President of the Security Council*, U.N. Doc. S/24859 (1992) [hereinafter *Letter Dated 24 November 1992*]; *Letter Dated 29 November 1992 from the Secretary-General to the President of the Security Council*, U.N. Doc. S/24868 (1992) [hereinafter *Letter Dated 29 November 1992*]. For views of the U.S. State Department on the situation in Somalia just prior to the decision to deploy U.S. forces, *see U.N. Peacekeeping in Africa: The Western Sahara and Somalia: Hearing Before Subcomm. on African Affairs of the Senate Comm. on Foreign Relations*, 102d Cong., 2d Sess. 2–12 (1991) (testimony of John R. Bolton, Assistant Secretary of State for International Organizations, and Robert Houdek, Deputy Assistant Secretary of State for African Affairs).

will come up with a programme of effective action to end the fighting and contribute to cementing peace and stability in the country."[315]

In addition, certain regional organizations appealed to the Security Council to take action. The League of Arab States expressed concern that developments in Somalia "pose an increasing threat to the national unity and territorial integrity of Somalia" and reaffirmed its determination to "preserve the national unity and territorial integrity of Somalia."[316] The League neither significantly emphasized humanitarian concerns with the situation in Somalia nor mentioned the issue of refugees. In its submission to the Security Council, the Organization of African Unity (OAU) expressed humanitarian concerns, called upon the main factions in Mogadishu to cease fighting, and requested the international community to use "influence" to "encourage" the parties to seek peaceful resolution of the conflict and to respond to the urgent needs of the Somali people by providing assistance, especially food and medicine.[317]

On January 23, 1992, the UN Security Council unanimously passed Resolution 733, stating that it was "concerned" that the continuation of the situation in Somalia constituted a threat to international peace and security.[318] The Security Council requested the Secretary-General to increase UN humanitarian assistance to the Somali population, in liaison with other international organizations, and to appoint a coordinator to oversee the effective delivery of the assistance. Invoking its Chapter VII authority, the Security Council decided that all states must embargo the delivery of weapons and military equipment to Somalia. Further, the Security Council called upon the Somali warring factions to cooperate with the Secretary-General and to help ensure the safety of personnel sent to provide humanitarian assistance.

The United Nations initially favored a course of deploying observers and forces based on the consent of the local factions; the standard peacekeeping approach used during the Cold War. On March 3, 1992, cease-

---

315. *Letter Dated 20 January 1992 from Somalia to the President of the Security Council*, Annex I, U.N. Doc. S/23445 (1992).

316. *Letter Dated 21 January 1992 from Morocco to the President of the Security Council*, Annex, U.N. Doc. S/23448 (1992).

317. *Letter Dated 23 January 1992 from Guinea to the President of the Security Council*, Annex, U.N. Doc. S/23469 (1992).

318. S.C. Res. 733, U.N. SCOR, 47th Sess., 3039th mtg. at 55, U.N. Doc. S/INF/48 (1993), *reprinted in* 2 WESTON, *supra* note 12, at II.D.5. Although the Security Council was aware of the movement of refugees out of the country to neighboring countries, this fact is not expressly recognized in the resolution; rather the preamble simply notes alarm at the "heavy loss of human life and widespread material damage" in Somalia and its "consequences on stability and peace in the region."

fire agreements were signed under UN auspices by the two warring factions in Mogadishu, which allowed in principle the establishment of a UN observer mission aimed at stabilizing the ceasefire.[319] In his report to the Security Council, the Secretary-General stated that, while not expressly provided in the agreements, it was understood that an objective of the observer mission would be to assist in the delivery of humanitarian assistance in and around Mogadishu. Realizing that assisting in the delivery of humanitarian assistance was qualitatively different than just a monitoring mission, the Secretary-General added that "I am aware that this exercise represents an innovation that may require careful consideration by the Security Council." [320]

The Security Council seized upon the opportunity to establish an observer mission for these purposes and, on March 17, unanimously passed another resolution authorizing the dispatch of a technical team to Somalia to work out the details.[321] The Secretary-General provided a plan of action to the Security Council, but cautioned that such a plan assumes that "security measures, including United Nations security personnel, will be quickly put in place to protect relief workers and relief supplies." [322] Indeed, a theme of the Secretary-General's reports throughout 1992 was that the deteriorating security conditions (looting and hijacking of food supplies, death and injury to relief workers) were a major impediment to the commencement of effective relief operations.

While the primary focus of the Secretary-General in his reports and the Security Council in its debates was on the plight of Somalis in Somalia, the external effects of the situation were also at issue. As stated by the Secretary-General, just prior to the authorization of the UN monitoring mission:

As already evidenced by the flow of refugees from Somalia into Kenya, Djibouti and Ethiopia, the crisis has regional consequences and there are grave concerns

319. The ceasefire agreements appear at Annex III to U.N. Doc. S/23693 (1992), *supra* note 314. The operative part of the agreements states that the leaders of each faction:

Hereby agree to take immediate steps, personally as well as through the persons under my command, for the implementation of measures aimed at stabilizing the cease-fire by means of a United Nations monitoring mechanism. The measures will be formulated by a United Nations technical team that will arrive in Mogadiscio shortly.

Shortly thereafter, various Somali leaders and elders signed a Letter of Agreement addressed to the United Nations committing themselves to work for peace and stability in Somalia. U.N. Doc. S/23829 (1992), *supra* note 314, Annexes I-IV.

320. U.N. Doc. S/23693 (1992), *supra* note 314, para. 74.

321. S.C. Res. 746, U.N. SCOR, 47th Sess., 3060th mtg. at 56, U.N. Doc. S/INF/48 (1993).

322. U.N. Doc. S/23829/Add.1 (1992), *supra* note 314, para. 48.

about the effects such population movements will have on the Horn of Africa. Measures to encourage Somalis who also might seek refuge in neighboring countries to stay in their homeland need to be explored as a matter of urgency.[323]

Thus, on April 24, 1992, the Security Council unanimously adopted Resolution 751 establishing a UN Operation in Somalia (UNOSOM) and asked the Secretary-General to deploy 50 UN observers to monitor the ceasefire in Mogadishu. Further, in paragraphs 4 and 5, the Security Council agreed "in principle" to establish a 500-person UN security force to be deployed as soon as possible after the Secretary-General consulted with the Somali factions and provided recommendations to the Security Council.[324] The functions of this security force were to provide security for UN personnel, equipment, and supplies in Mogadishu and to escort deliveries of humanitarian supplies to distribution centers in Mogadishu and its immediate environs. The security force was not to serve any law and order functions.[325]

After considerable wrangling, the principal factions in Mogadishu agreed to the deployment of the uniformed and unarmed observers[326] but not to an armed security force. After the failure of satisfactory consultations with the warring factions, the Security Council, on July 27, passed a resolution that appeared to up the ante slightly. After "recognizing" that the provision of humanitarian assistance was an important element in restoring international peace and security in the area, the Security Council requested the Secretary-General to mount an urgent airlift operation, and called upon:

all parties, movements and factions in Somalia to cooperate with the United Nations with a view to the urgent deployment of United Nations security personnel called for in paragraphs 4 and 5 of its resolution 751 (1992), and otherwise assist in the general stabilization of the situation in Somalia, without which cooperation the Security Council does not exclude other measures to deliver humanitarian assistance to Somalia.[327]

Whether this veiled threat had the effect intended is unclear, but on August 12 the two factions in Mogadishu agreed to the deployment

323. *Id.* para. 46. Likewise, in his report of August 24, 1992, the Secretary-General noted: "The absence of food is a significant cause of the large-scale population movements that are taking place from Somalia into Kenya, Ethiopia and Djibouti." U.N. Doc. S/24480 (1992), *supra* note 314, para. 11. The Secretary-General estimated that along the Kenyan border alone there were 280,000 refugees, with approximately 2,000 arriving daily. *Id.* para. 22.

324. S.C. Res. 751, U.N. SCOR, 47th Sess., 3069th mtg. at 57, U.N. Doc. S/INF/48 (1993).

325. U.N. Doc. S/23829 (1992), *supra* note 314, paras. 27–29.

326. *Letter Dated 23 June 1992, supra* note 314.

327. S.C. Res. 767, U.N. SCOR, 47th Sess., 3101st mtg. at 59, para. 4, U.N. Doc. S/INF/48 (1993). The vote was unanimous.

of a 500-person armed UN security force, and similar agreements were reached with factions in two other parts of Somalia.[328]

At the same time that the United Nations was pursuing consent to the deployment of a security force, it had organized a joint World Food Program/United Nations Children's Fund airlift which, beginning in March 1992, transported food by two flights a day from Kenya to three Somali cities.[329] Yet, since many of the most destitute Somalis were located in the interior of the country, the Secretary-General urged[330] and the Security Council endorsed[331] a more comprehensive airlift operation. In August 1992, the United States commenced an emergency airlift of food supplies from Kenya into Somalia, using both Department of Defense aircraft and civilian aircraft.[332] Similar airlifts by military forces of other countries followed. These airlifts met no resistance from the Somali factions and were not condemned as unlawful intervention by the world community.

On August 28, the Security Council authorized the deployment of armed forces to Mogadishu,[333] and by September 14 Pakistani infantry troops began arriving, totalling 500 by the end of the month. These forces, however, were never deployed outside the city's seaport and airport because the Somali faction leaders could not agree on their placement. During October and November, Somalia's two largest seaports, Mogadishu and Kismayu, were closed by the warring factions, dramatically reducing foreign relief to Somali citizens. Armed gangs shot and seriously wounded one of the Pakistani soldiers; the Pakistanis themselves had ultimately to hire about 1,000 young Somali gunmen as "security guards" to help keep control of the airport.[334]

On November 24, the Secretary-General reported to the Security Council that the cooperation which had been developing with the key Somali clan leaders was breaking down. One leader based in Mogadishu, Mohammed Farah Aideed, had declared that the Pakistani battalion would no longer be tolerated in the streets of Mogadishu and warned that any forcible UNOSOM deployment would be met with violence. Followers of another Mogadishu leader, Ali Mahdi, reportedly hijacked and robbed two patrol vehicles driven by unarmed UNOSOM military ob-

328. U.N. Doc. S/24480 (1992), *supra* note 314, para. 24.

329. U.N. Doc. S/24343 (1992), *supra* note 314, para. 33.

330. *Id.* at para. 61.

331. S.C. Res. 767, *supra* note 327, para 2.

332. *Chronology: Background to Operation Restore Hope, January 1991-December 8, 1992*, U.S. DEP'T ST. DISPATCH 900, 901 (1992).

333. S.C. Res. 775, U.N. SCOR, 47th Sess., 3110th mtg. at 61, U.N. Doc. S/INF/48 (1993).

334. K. Richburg, *Pakistanis Work to Charm Somalis*, WASH. POST, May 14, 1993, at A33.

servers. Pakistani forces in control of the Mogadishu airport had come under heavy fire on November 13, although they remained in control of the airport. Widspread looting of aid supplies, robbery, armed banditry, and general lawlessness were pervasive, endangering relief workers as well as those they sought to help. Relief ships were prevented from docking, and some were shelled. As humanitarian supplies actually reaching beneficiaries dropped to barely a trickle, the Secretary-General reported that additional UNOSOM battalions were needed to address the problem, but that consent by Somali authorities had only been secured for deployment of a Canadian battalion at the town of Bosasso.[335]

The Intervention Under UNITAF

On November 25, 1992, the United States offered to provide some 20,000 troops to help ensure distribution of food and aid in Somalia and as part of a multinational force authorized by the United Nations. In light of this offer, the Secretary-General on November 29 reported to the Security Council that "Somalia has become a country without a government or other political authorities with whom the basis for humanitarian activities can be negotiated." Consequently, the Secretary-General recommended that the Security Council resort to use of its enforcement authority under Chapter VII of the Charter, since UNOSOM's experience in Somalia showed that delivery of relief supplies "cannot be achieved by a United Nations operation based on the accepted principles of peacekeeping." The purposes of the operation would be (1) to create conditions in which relief operations could be delivered to those in need, including the disarming of irregular forces; and (2) to promote national reconciliation to remove the main factors that created the humanitarian emergency. As one option, the Secretary-General proposed a country-wide enforcement operation undertaken by a group of member states authorized by the Security Council.[336]

On December 3, 1992, the Security Council passed Resolution 794 authorizing a U.S.-led force to enter Somalia to safeguard relief work.[337] The resolution, which merits quoting at some length, stated in part the following:

Recognizing the unique character of the present situation in Somalia and mindful of its deteriorating, complex and extraordinary nature, requiring an immediate and exceptional response,

335. *Letter Dated 24 November 1992, supra* note 314.
336. *Letter Dated 29 November 1992, supra* note 314.
337. S.C. Res. 794, U.N. SCOR, 47th Sess., 3145th mtg. at 63, U.N. Doc. S/INF/48 (1993), *reprinted in* 2 WESTON, *supra* note 12, at II.D.6.

Determining that the magnitude of the human tragedy caused by the conflict in Somalia, further exacerbated by the obstacles being created to the distribution of humanitarian assistance, constitutes a threat to international peace and security,

. . .

Expressing grave alarm at continuing reports of widespread violations of international humanitarian law occurring in Somalia, including reports of violence and threats of violence against personnel participating lawfully in impartial humanitarian relief activities; deliberate attacks on non-combatants, relief consignments and vehicles, and medical and relief facilities; and impeding the delivery of food and medical supplies essential for the survival of the civilian population,

Dismayed by the continuation of conditions that impede the delivery of humanitarian supplies to destinations within Somalia, and in particular reports of looting of relief supplies destined for starving people, attacks on aircraft and ships bringing in humanitarian relief supplies, and attacks on the Pakistani UNOSOM contingent in Mogadishu,

. . .

Sharing the Secretary-General's assessment that the situation in Somalia is intolerable and that it has become necessary to review the basic premises and principles of the United Nations effort in Somalia, and that UNOSOM's existing course would not in present circumstances be an adequate response to the tragedy in Somalia, . . .

Determined further to restore peace, stability and law and order with a view to facilitating the process of a political settlement under the auspices of the United Nations, aimed at national reconciliation in Somalia, and encouraging the Secretary-General and his Special Representative to continue and intensify their work at the national and regional levels to promote these objectives, . . .

7. *Endorses* the recommendation by the Secretary-General in his letter of 29 November 1992 (S/24868) that action under Chapter VII of the Charter of the United Nations should be taken in order to establish a secure environment for humanitarian relief operations in Somalia as soon as possible;

8. *Welcomes* the offer by a Member State described in the Secretary-General's letter to the Council of 29 November 1992 (S/24868) concerning the establishment of an operation to create such a secure environment;

9. *Welcomes* offers by other Member States to participate in that operation;

10. *Acting* under Chapter VII of the Charter of the United Nations, authorizes the Secretary-General and Member States cooperating to implement the offer referred to in paragraph 8 above to use all necessary means to establish as soon as possible a secure environment for humanitarian relief operations in Somalia;

11. *Calls* on all Member States which are in a position to do so to provide military forces and to make additional contributions, in cash or in kind, in accordance with paragraph 10 above and requests the Secretary-General to establish a fund through which the contributions, where appropriate, could be channelled to the States or operations concerned;

12. *Authorizes* the Secretary-General and the Member States concerned to make the necessary arrangements for the unified command and control of the forces involved, which will reflect the offer referred to in paragraph 8 above;

. . .

19. *Requests* the Secretary-General and his Special Representative to continue their efforts to achieve a political settlement in Somalia.

U.S. Marines arrived in Mogadishu on December 8 and immediately seized control of the airport, seaport, and surrounding areas.[338] Some 19 other states supported the intervention with personnel, equipment, and funding.[339] As foreseen in Resolution 794, these states assumed the operational responsibilities for the mission, with the United States providing a report directly to the Security Council on the early stages of the operation of what became known as the Unified Task Force (UNITAF).[340]

By late January 1993, 24,000 U.S. marines had been deployed throughout southern Somalia, largely ending the civil strife that had prevented relief efforts in that area for so many months;[341] total UNITAF forces peaked in early 1993 at 38,300.[342] The deployment was the largest humanitarian-military relief operation in UN history; between December 9, 1992 and February 19, 1993, 70,000 tons of food and medical supplies were delivered to Somalia.[343] The success of the operation in this first stage was attributable to the massive deployment (which easily overwhelmed the unorganized armed Somali factions), the participation of multiple states ensuring global political support, and the desert terrain that allowed few hiding places for armed resistance (at least outside the major cities). The financial cost of the operation, however, was high. Pursuant to Resolution 794, the Secretary-General established a "Trust Fund for Somalia-Unified Command," with an initial target of $400 million to fund certain costs of the operation from voluntary contributions of member states.[344] The human cost of the operation also was signifi-

338. K. Richburg & W. Claiborne, *Marines, Navy Land in Somalia's Capital*, WASH. POST, Dec. 9, 1992, at A1; J. Lancaster, *Hitting the Beach in the Glare of the Night*, WASH. POST, Dec. 9, 1992, at A1.

339. *Intervention in Somalia; International Contributions*, WASH. POST, Dec. 19, 1992, at A15.

340. *Letter Dated 17 December from the United States to the President of the Security Council*, Annex, U.N. Doc. S/24976 (1992); *Letter Dated 19 January 1993 from the United States to the President of the Security Council*, Annex, U.N. Doc. S/25126 (1993).

341. J. Lancaster, *Mogadishu's "Green Line" Is Erased—in Theory*, WASH. POST, Jan. 20, 1993, at A23. As early as January 1993, U.S. forces began redeploying to the United States, as contributions from other states increased. By early February, there were 32,000 UNITAF troops, of which 18,000 were from the United States. R. Houdek, Statement Before the Subcommittee on Africa of the House Foreign Affairs Committee (Feb. 17, 1993), *in* 4 U.S. DEP'T ST. DISPATCH 99 (1993) (Deputy Assistant Secretary of State for African Affairs).

342. K. Richburg, *supra* note 334.

343. M. Albright, Current Status of U.S. Policy on Bosnia, Somalia, and U.N. Reform, Statement before the Subcommittee on Foreign Operations, Export Financing, and Related Programs of the House Appropriations Committee (Mar. 12, 1993), *in* 4 U.S. DEP'T ST. DISPATCH 207, 209 (1993) (U.S. Permanent Representative to the United Nations).

344. *Report of the Secretary-General*, para 10, U.N. Doc. S/24992 (1992). As of mid-March 1993, $115 million had been raised in donations, mostly from Japan. The purpose of the

cant; by May 1993, when the UNITAF phase ended, over 100 Somalis were thought to have been killed by foreign forces, along with seventeen foreign soldiers (eight of them U.S. soldiers).[345]

On its face, Resolution 794 left various matters unanswered, such as the exact command and control of the forces, whether they would carry UN insignia, and what degree of force would be used against the Somali factions. With respect to the use of force, one Somali faction leader asserted: "We expect the Americans to behave as a friendly force, not as an occupation force." [346] Notwithstanding that expectation, the U.S. forces considered themselves authorized to use armed force against the Somali factions to protect themselves; U.S. Secretary of Defense Richard Cheney stated that U.S. forces would also be able to take "preemptive action" against anyone posing a threat to the safety of U.S. forces or relief workers.[347]

A further ambiguity related to the exact mission of the intervening forces. Everyone agreed that creating a secure environment for humanitarian relief operations was the basic objective, but numerous peripheral issues arose as to how that objective might be achieved. For instance, it was unclear whether the mission of the forces included the disarming of the Somalian factions. The Secretary-General maintained that the forces operating under Resolution 794 were supposed to disarm the Somali factions to bring about national reconciliation;[348] he had called for such disarming in his letter to the Security Council,[349] and the resolution "endorsed" (paragraph 7) his recommendation that action (including disarming of the factions) under Chapter VII be taken to "establish a secure environment for humanitarian relief operations in Somalia as soon as possible." However, the Security Council's "authorization" for states to "use all necessary means" to establish a secure environment was to implement the U.S. offer. Thus, the relevant issue was whether the U.S. offer included disarming of the Somali factions to bring about national

---

fund was not to reimburse all states for the costs of their deployments, but rather to cover expenses associated with the transport and in-country operations of forces from developing countries unable to finance their own operations.

345. D. Schemo, *Declare Victory, Hand Off, Slip Out, Cross Fingers*, N.Y. Times, May 2, 1993, sec. 4, at 1 (editorial). These deaths included traffic accidents and one suicide. K. Richburg, *Forces Leaving Somalia See Job Well Done*, Wash. Post, May 4, 1993, at A1.

346. J. Perlez, *Powerful Somalian Objects to U.S. Disarming Fighters*, N.Y. Times, Dec. 6, 1992, at 14; *see also* K. Richburg, *The Guns of Mogadishu: Somali Warlords' Arms Pose Challenge for U.S. Force*, Wash. Post, Dec. 6, 1992, at A1 (interview with Mr. Osman Ato, aide to General Mohammed Farah Aideed).

347. Richburg, *supra* note 346.

348. P. Lewis, *U.N. Says Somali Clans Must Disarm Before Peace*, N.Y. Times, Dec. 6, 1992, sec. 1, at 15.

349. *Letter Dated 24 November 1992, supra* note 314, at 3.

reconciliation. The United States initially skirted the issue of disarming the factions; once deployed, U.S. forces proceeded by disarming gunmen openly displaying weapons but not seeking to seize caches held by factional leaders. Nevertheless, U.S. forces ultimately began seeking out, seizing, and destroying certain weapons where feasible[350] and requiring that other weapons be placed in stockpiles subject to UN inspection.[351] In this way, UNITAF sought to dilute the power of the leaders of the factions.

Yet it was unclear from Resolution 794 to what extent the intervening forces were to assist in the reconstruction of Somalia, politically and economically. Although months later some would deride the involvement of U.S. forces in "nation-building," it was clear early on in the intervention that simply protecting relief operations would not be adequate to resolve the overall problem. For this reason, shortly after the intervention, U.S. officials began helping to create dialogues among local civic leaders, and the U.S. military was involved in infrastructural and rehabilitation projects as well as cleaning up debris.[352] Supporting women, intellectuals, clerics, and elders as voices of the Somali people was seen as a further way of diluting the power of the faction leaders. Eventually, U.S. forces began helping Somalis organize a Mogadishu police force of up to 3,500 men, in part to help curtail their own exposure to sniper fire.[353]

The United Nations was also involved in efforts to achieve national reconciliation. After convening a preliminary meeting in January 1993, the Secretary-General organized a peace conference in Ethiopia on March 15, 1993 in order to bring together some 250 persons from a broad cross section of Somalia, representing political movements, community, religious and women's groups, civic and nongovernmental organizations, and elders and eminent persons. After thirteen days of bargaining, a comprehensive agreement was reached on issues of disarmament and security, reconstruction and rehabilitation, restoration of property, the peaceful settlement of disputes, and the establishment of an interim government. That interim government was to consist of a three-tiered, federal-style Transitional National Council (TNC) com-

---

350. *See, e.g.*, J. Lancaster & K. Richburg, *Marines Seize Tons of Weapons in Raid on Mogadishu Bazaar*, WASH. POST, Jan. 12, 1993, at A12.

351. The Somali faction leaders signed a pact on January 15, 1993, agreeing to disarm their militias.

352. K. Richburg, *Broader U.S. Role Developing in Somalia*, WASH. POST, Dec. 31, 1992, at A16.

353. K. Richburg, *Top Marine Calls Somalia Mission Done*, WASH. POST, Jan. 30, 1993, at A18. Efforts to maintain a Somali police force continued when the operation was transferred to the United Nations. K. Richburg, *Somali Police Force Back on the Beat*, WASH. POST, May 17, 1993, at A15.

posed of centralized administrative departments, 18 regional councils, and 92 district councils. The plan was for the TNC to operate as the prime political authority in Somalia for two years (with legislative functions), after which elections would be held and thereafter a constitution drafted. The 74-member TNC was to consist of representatives from each of the regions and factions, with at least 15 percent of the seats set aside for women.[354]

The UN Takes Over from UNITAF

In March 1993, the Secretary-General proposed that, by May 1, UNITAF transfer command to a UN force to consist of up to 28,000 troops under a UN commander.[355] This second phase of UN operations in Somalia (known as UNOSOM II) was authorized unanimously by the Security Council in Resolution 814 of March 26, 1993,[356] marking the first time "blue helmets" were to be deployed with the power to engage in combat to enforce their mandate, as opposed to simply "keep the peace" by their presence. Although many would continue to refer to it as a "peacekeeping" operation, it was well understood that UNOSOM II's mandate was unlike that of any peacekeeping force previously deployed. UNOSOM II was given extensive authority to control heavy weapons of the Somali factions, to seize small arms, to de-mine various areas,[357] to protect relief workers, and to aid in the return and resettlement of displaced persons. Whereas UNITAF had operated in only approximately 40 percent of Somalia and had focused primarily on protecting relief operations, UNOSOM II would operate throughout the country and would increase the emphasis on disarmament of the factions. The total annual cost of the operation was estimated at $1.5 billion, a considerable sum since it represented roughly half the amount the United Nations was spending on its peacekeeping operations at that time.[358] Whereas UNITAF was a voluntary undertaking with the contributing members absorbing most of the costs of their deployment, UNOSOM II operated on the basis of the UN peacekeeping scale of assessments. The mandate for UNOSOM II was limited to seven months, with the expec-

354. J. Parmelee, *Somalis Reach Peace Accord*, WASH. POST, Mar. 28, 1993, at A22; *Further Report of the Secretary-General*, paras. 23–26, U.N. Doc. S/26317 (1993).

355. J. Preston, *Shift to U.N. Targeted for May 1*, WASH. POST, Mar. 4, 1993, at A14.

356. S.C. Res. 814, U.N. SCOR, 48th Sess., 3188th mtg. at 80, U.N. Doc. S/INF/49 (1994); *see also* J. Preston, *U.N. Establishes Force for Somalia*, WASH. POST, Mar. 27, 1993, at A13.

357. By some estimates, there were up to one million mines planted in Somalia. Their presence was a major obstacle to the return of refugees and the resumption of agricultural and livestock production. *Further Report of the Secretary-General, supra* note 354, para. 19.

358. P. Lewis, *U.N. Will Increase Troops in Somalia*, N.Y. TIMES, Mar. 27, 1992, sec. 1, at 3.

tation that it would be renewed by the Security Council at the end of that time if necessary.

The unprecedented enforcement mandate of UNOSOM II was noted by the members of the Security Council, who were worried that it would lead to intrusive actions of the United Nations elsewhere without regard to the consent of the affected states. To limit the precedent, several states linked the UNOSOM II mandate to the absence of governmental authority and institutions in Somalia and urged that it return as soon as possible to a force deployed and operating with the consent of the local factions. The representative of China stated:

Authorizing UNOSOM II to take enforcement action under Chapter VII of the Charter in order to implement its mandate has made it the first operation of its kind in the history of United Nations peace-keeping. It is our understanding that this authorization is based on the needs of the unique situation in Somalia and should not constitute a precedent for United Nations peace-keeping operations. . . . UNOSOM II should promptly resume its normal peace-keeping operations.[359]

As will be seen, this initial appreciation of the unprecedented mandate given UNOSOM II unfortunately did not generate new thinking about how a UN force must operate to implement such a mandate successfully.

The effective transfer of authority from UNITAF to UNOSOM II took place on April 28, 1993 with the transfer of the last regional command from the United States to the United Nations.[360] At the core of the UNOSOM II forces were 4,000 Pakistani forces, all operating under more expanded rules of engagement than existed for UNOSOM I.[361] Many of the forces deployed under UNITAF—particularly from Australia, Canada, and the United States—departed; by July 1993, UNOSOM had just over 20,000 troops from 27 countries.[362] A United States "Quick Reaction Force" remained on standby for support of UNOSOM II but was not a part of the UN force.

At the time of the transfer of control to UNOSOM II, the intervention by foreign forces in Somalia was considered by the international community and many Somalis to be a tremendous success, at least in terms of reducing violence in Somalia and preventing widespread starvation.

359. U.N. SCOR, 48th Sess., 3188th mtg. at 22, U.N. Doc. S/PV.3188 (1993).

360. M. Fineman, *U.S. Troops Hand Off Last Somali Area to U.N. Forces*, L.A. TIMES, Apr. 29, 1993, at A1. The official transfer of authority from the United States to the United Nations took place on May 4, 1993. K. Richburg, *U.N. Takes Command of Troops in Somalia*, WASH. POST, May 5, 1993, at A23. Some 3,625 U.S. servicemen, mostly in logistics and support roles, were placed under UN command, complete with blue berets and patches. *Id.*

361. K. Richburg, *supra* note 334.

362. *Further Report of the Secretary-General, supra* note 354, para. 6.

Schools were being reopened, food-for-work programs were underway rather than just free food distribution, and commercial enterprises were being encouraged. The question was whether this success could continue and be built upon by UN-led forces under UNOSOM II.

Before long it was clear that maintaining such success would be difficult. At the end of July 1993, the Secretary-General stated:

> From the outset [of UNOSOM II], a major difficulty was created by the administrative and logistical requirements of supporting and deploying this very large number of troops from many countries within a relatively short time-frame. Administrative, financial and logistical procedures sometimes caused delays, impeding rapid deployment. . . . Some troop-contributing countries, especially those having recently joined UNOSOM, were not in a position to provide the troops within scheduled time-frames. Others found it difficult to provide their soldiers with adequate weapons and equipment. In some cases, the provision of weapons and equipment from third countries had to be arranged, causing further delays.[363]

The sheer logistical difficulty for the United Nations in coordinating such a large operation thus itself proved to be a major problem.

An even more serious problem arose with respect to the cooperation of the Somali faction leaders. Two days after UNOSOM II formally took over, a Somali faction leader named Ahmed Omar Jess launched an attack on the port city of Kismayo which was repulsed by UNOSOM II Belgian forces.[364] The worst of the local resistance, however, occurred in Mogadishu. In press conferences and radio broadcasts, Mohammed Farah Aideed (perhaps the most powerful of the faction leaders prior the intervention of foreign forces) accused the United Nations of interfering in Somalia's internal affairs by fostering new local government councils and a temporary judicial system outside the control of leaders such as himself.[365] At the same time, Aideed traveled to neighboring countries seeking money and support, purportedly for "democratic" reasons.[366]

On June 5, violence broke out in Mogadishu, leaving 24 UN Pakistani forces dead and 56 wounded[367]—the highest casualty toll suffered by UN forces in a single incident since 1961 in the Congo—as well as scores of Somalis, both combatants and noncombatants. The violence consisted

363. *Id.* paras. 8–9.

364. *Id.* para. 12.

365. K. Richburg, *Americans in Somalia Face Threat*, WASH. POST, May 14, 1993, at A36.

366. K. Richburg, *Somali Warlords Shift Roles*, WASH. POST, May 11, 1993, at A12.

367. For information on the attack, *see Report of the Secretary-General*, U.N. Doc. S/26022 (1993), and the executive summary of the report of an independent expert, Professor Tom Farer, who carried out a more comprehensive investigation on the behalf of the United Nations. *Report Pursuant to Paragraph 5 of Security Council Resolution 837*, Annex, U.N. Doc. S/2o351 (1993) [hereinafter *Executive Summary*].

of running battles in various parts of southern Mogadishu between Somali gunmen and UN forces. The immediate provocation of the Somali
gunmen, who were reportedly loyal to Aideed, was said to be a rumor
that the United Nations intended to take over a radio station operated
by Aideed. The United Nations, in fact, never seized the radio station
and denied that it ever intended to do so. At the time of the attacks, UN
forces were engaged in food distribution, efforts to inspect stockpiles of
weapons, including those of Aideed, which had been established under
UNITAF, and rescue efforts after the initial attacks began.[368] In one major incident, Pakistani forces were pinned down by a three-sided ambush
that lasted several hours. The investigations by the United Nations indicate that the attacks were a calculated, premediated series of actions designed to challenge and intimidate the UNOSOM II forces. Although
Aideed disclaimed responsibility for the attacks, the United Nations investigation determined that his authorization of the attacks was supported by "clear and convincing evidence." [369]

The Security Council responded by passing a resolution condemning
the attacks and affirming that the Secretary-General was authorized under Resolution 814 to "take all measures necessary against all those responsible for the armed attacks [and] to establish the effective authority
of [UNOSOM II] throughout Somalia, including to secure the investigation of their actions and their arrest and detention for prosecution,
trial, and punishment." [370] Additional UN forces from France and the
United States, including attack planes, were deployed to Somalia.

Beginning on June 12, UNOSOM II and national forces in support of
it conducted air and ground military actions designed to disable or destroy ordnance, weapons, and equipment located in the previously authorized weapons sites in southern Mogadishu.[371] The objective of the
UN actions was to commence the effective disarmament of Mogadishu,
which invariably involved attacks on targets in civilian areas, thereby
causing collateral civilian deaths.[372] The position of the United Nations
was that disarmament was essential to end the intimidation and terroriza-
tion by the Somali factions; if they refused to disarm voluntarily, then it

368. *Executive Summary, supra* note 367. For newspaper accounts, see Associated Press,
26 U.N. Troops Reported Dead in Somalia Combat, N.Y. TIMES, June 6, 1993, sec. 1, at 6; K.
Richburg, *Mogadishu Erupts in Violence,* WASH. POST, June 6, 1993, at A29.

369. *Executive Summary, supra* note 367, para. 24.

370. S.C. Res. 837, U.N. SCOR, 48th Sess., 3229th mtg. at 83, para. 5, U.N. Doc. S/INF/
49 (1994).

371. UNOSOM II also disabled the radio system operated by Aideed. The forces involved in these operations were from Pakistan, France, Italy, Morocco, and the United
States. *Report of the Secretary-General, supra* note 367, paras. 19–22.

372. K. Richburg, *U.N. Presses Somalia Attacks As New Role Is Questioned: Mogadishu Civilians Reportedly Injured in U.S. Daytime Raid,* WASH. POST, June 15, 1993, at A1.

was up to UNOSOM II to disarm them through compulsion.[373] This need for disarmament, as noted above, was the view that the Secretary-General consistently had held even prior to the time of the UNITAF intervention.[374] Yet, after this point, the UN mission began to look to the Somali people and the global community more like a low-level military campaign against urban guerillas than a mission that was humanitarian in nature.

After the June 5 attacks, virtually all of the international relief workers operating in Mogadishu and nonessential UN staff left Somalia, with distribution of food and medical supplies halting in Mogadishu and in those areas dependent on supplies dispatched from Mogadishu. Relief efforts in other parts of Somalia were not affected. By June 21, UNOSOM II forces were capable of again providing adequate protection to some of the workers in Mogadishu so that limited relief operations there could recommence. The streets of Mogadishu, however, remained plagued with violence.

On June 13, gunfire again broke out between Pakistani UN forces and Somali gunmen in southern Mogadishu. Some witnesses stated that the Pakistani forces were the first to fire, while the UN forces asserted that Somali gunmen fired first and used civilian crowds as a screen for their fire.[375] More than a dozen civilians (including children) were killed, either as a result of fire by UNOSOM II forces or possibly (according to some witnesses) because the Somali gunmen themselves were firing upon civilians to produce bodies for the international media.[376]

On June 17, UNOSOM II forces attacked and seized Aideed's headquarters in an action that cost the lives of five UN troops and at least 60 Somalis. One aspect of the raid included UN forces opening fire on a Mogadishu hospital to which Aideed gunmen had fled and where, according to U.S. military officials, they used some patients as human shields to fire upon UN forces.[377] On the same day, the Secretary-General's Special Representative to Somalia called for the arrest and detention of Aideed under the authority of the Security Council's resolutions.[378] Aideed eluded the UN forces, despite a UN offer of $25,000 for any information leading to his arrest.[379] The UN special envoy as-

373. *Further Report of the Secretary-General, supra* note 354, para. 15.
374. *See supra* notes 348–49 and accompanying text.
375. K. Richburg, *U.N. Unit Kills 14 Somali Civilians*, WASH. POST, June 14, 1993, at A1.
376. *Report of the Secretary-General, supra* note 367, para. 23; *Executive Summary, supra* note 367, para. 8.
377. K. Richburg, *U.N. Troops Battle Somalis*, WASH. POST, June 18, 1993, at A1.
378. *Id.*
379. D. Lorch, *U.N. Troops Begin an Effort to Take Over Somali Streets*, N.Y. TIMES, July 11, 1993, sec. 1, at 14.

serted that the search for Aideed was secondary to efforts to secure relief aid in Somalia,[380] yet for several months the search was to become the most visible aspect of UNOSOM II.

Some countries contributing to UNOSOM II were disturbed that the mission had shifted from humanitarian effort to military enforcement.[381] Tension over the conduct of the operation between the United Nations and the Italian forces assigned to UNOSOM II ultimately resulted in UN efforts to remove the commander of the Italian forces.[382] Reports also emerged that UN staff members were dissatisfied with the military campaign being pursued by UNOSOM II and critical of certain tactics, such as firing upon buildings without first warning their occupants.[383]

Throughout the summer of 1993, the UNOSOM II forces largely remained garrisoned in their compounds, enduring nightly attacks from snipers using grenades, mortars, and small arms, and venturing out only during the day to engage in selected military strikes against positions held by Aideed's supporters. On August 9, four U.S. soldiers assigned to UNOSOM II were killed by a land mine, the first U.S. deaths since the initiation of UNOSOM II.[384] On September 5, seven Nigerian soldiers assigned to UNOSOM II were gunned down in a predawn ambush.[385] On September 9, U.S. and Pakistani forces opened fire on Somali men, women, and children, who U.S. officials maintained had attacked with grenades and gunfire; some 60 Somalis were killed.[386]

In late August, the United States had sent to Somalia 400 members of an elite light-infantry force trained in special operations (known as Army "Rangers") whose mission was to assist in capturing Aideed. Aideed was known to move about frequently in southern Mogadishu, often in disguise. After several unsuccessful efforts to capture him, the Rangers tried once again on October 3, only to find themselves caught in a 16-hour battle that left 12 U.S. forces killed, 80 wounded, and one captured.[387]

380. K. Richburg, *Aideed "No Longer Part of Process,"* WASH. POST, June 19, 1993, at A14.

381. K. Richburg, *Criticism Mounts over Somali Raid*, WASH. POST, July 15, 1993, at A21.

382. The tension apparently arose when the Italian forces pursued diplomatic initiatives with Somali leaders on their own rather than carry out military actions ordered by the U.N. commander. *See* J. Preston, *U.N. Removes Italian General Impeding Somalia Operation*, WASH. POST, July 15, 1993, at A20; D. Lorch, *Disunity Hampering U.N. Somalia Effort*, N.Y. TIMES, July 12, 1992, at A8; W. Drozdiak, *Italy Seeks Tighter Somalia Rules*, WASH. POST, July 25, 1993, at A21.

383. K. Richburg, *U.N. Report Criticizes Military Tactics of Somalia Peace Keepers*, WASH. POST, Aug. 5, 1993, at A22.

384. K. Richburg, *4 U.S. Soldiers Killed in Somalia*, WASH. POST, Aug. 9, 1993, at A1.

385. K. Richburg, *7 Peace Keepers Killed in Somalia*, WASH. POST, Sept. 6, 1993, at A1.

386. K. Richburg, *U.S. Helicopters Fire on Somalis*, WASH. POST, Sept. 10, 1993, at A1.

387. R. Atkinson, *Deliverance From Warlord's Fury: Rangers Pinned Down in Mogadishu Recall Harrowing Rescue*, WASH. POST, Oct. 7, 1993, at A1.

Television cameras caught startling images of the body of a dead U.S. soldier being dragged through the streets of Mogadishu (while Somali onlookers cheered) and of the frightened, bruised, and wounded prisoner of war. Diplomatic efforts led to the release of the captured American, reportedly without conditions,[388] but soon thereafter the United States adopted a more conciliatory approach to Aideed, and within days the Rangers had left Somalia with their mission incomplete.[389]

The intensity of military activities in Mogadishu obscured many of the achievements of UNOSOM elsewhere in Somalia, ranging from cooperative disarmament of various factions, to the fostering of police and judicial systems, to the first steps of establishing local governing bodies.[390] Starvation in Somalia had been largely eradicated. Immunization and nutrition programs had stemmed the widespread deaths of children. Schools were steadily reopening. Prospects for the Somali harvest were good.[391] On September 22, 1993, the Security Council unanimously adopted Resolution 865, which announced that UNOSOM II would seek to complete its mission by March 1995.[392] Although the resolution continued to support the arrest of Aideed and the disarmament of the Somali factions, it proclaimed as the mission's "highest priority" the promotion of national reconciliation and the rebuilding of political institutions in Somalia.[393]

The violence in Mogadishu, however, had taken its toll on the enthusiasm of states to support UNOSOM II. The United States announced that U.S. combat personnel in Somalia would temporarily be increased, but would depart no later than March 1994.[394] Other Western states indicated that they too would pull out their troops, leaving in doubt whether UNOSOM II could continue.[395] Further, practical problems of maintaining the UN operation proved troubling, such as the detention

---

388. K. Richburg, *Somali Faction Frees U.S. Pilot*, WASH. POST, Oct. 15, 1993, at A1.

389. J. Lancaster, *Mission Incomplete, Rangers Pack Up*, WASH. POST, Oct. 21, 1993, at A1.

390. K. Richburg, *Somalia's First Step: U.N. Forms Councils As Test in Democracy*, WASH. POST, Sept. 25, 1993, at A1.

391. *Further Report of the Secretary-General, supra* note 354, para. 45.

392. S.C. Res. 865, U.N. SCOR, 48th Sess., 3280th mtg. at 84, para. 4, U.N. Doc. S/INF/ 49 (1994).

393. *Id.* pmbl.

394. R. Marcus & A. Devroy, *Clinton to Double Force in Somalia*, WASH. POST, Oct. 8, 1993, at A1. The violence in Mogadishu became so bad the United States decided in August 1994 to withdraw from Somalia all twenty-two of its diplomats remaining in the country, along with the Marines protecting them. J. Harris, *Official Presence of U.S. in Somalia Ends Sept. 15*, WASH. POST, Aug. 27, 1994, at A11.

395. J. Preston, *Italy, Germany Confirm Pullout from Somalia*, WASH. POST, Dec. 21, 1993, at A19.

without charge of captured Somalis,[396] reports of excessive force against Somali civilians, including torture,[397] and outbreaks of violence spawned by efforts to organize local councils.[398] In mid-November, the Security Council suspended its order authorizing the arrest of Aideed and established an independent commission to investigate the June 24 ambush of the UN peacekeeping forces.[399] In a confidential report leaked to the press in mid-1994, that commission accused UNOSOM II of provoking Aideed by "overstepping" its mandate.[400]

On November 28–December 1, 1993, a Humanitarian Conference on Somalia was convened in Addis Ababa, Ethiopia under the auspices of the United Nations. About 90 delegates from Somalia's 18 regions attended. Many criticized the United Nations for deviating from its original humanitarian goals toward military confrontation.[401] Aideed boycotted the talks but did participate with rival Somali leaders in subsequent political talks not held under the auspices of the United Nations.[402]

With the departure of Western forces from UNOSOM II imminent, the Security Council voted on February 4, 1994, to alter UNOSOM II's mandate and to reduce the force from more than 30,000 to no more than 22,000.[403] Resolution 897 restricted UNOSOM II to protection of humanitarian aid deliveries, primarily outside Mogadishu. Aware that efforts to round up heavy weapons in Mogadishu had led to the conflict with Aideed, the Security Council decided that UNOSOM II itself would no longer seek to disarm the Somali factions and would fight only if they themselves came under attack. Further, UNOSOM II would only "assist" the ongoing political process in Somalia, which "should culminate" in a

396. K. Richburg, *Somalis' Imprisonment Poses Questions About U.N. Role*, WASH. POST, Nov. 7, 1993, at A45.

397. C. Farnsworth, *Torture by Army Peacekeepers in Somalia Shocks Canada*, N.Y. TIMES, Nov. 27, 1994, sec. 1, at 14 (recounting a Canadian unit's torture to death of a Somali teenager accused of looting).

398. K. Richburg, *Clashes in Somali Town Blamed on U.N.*, WASH. POST, Nov. 21, 1993, at A29.

399. Matthew S.W. Ngulube, Chief Justice of Zambia, was selected to head an international commission of jurists to investigate the incident. R. Atkinson, *Wide Look at Somalia Violence Vowed*, WASH. POST, Dec. 1, 1993, at A20.

400. P. Lewis, *Report Faults Commanders of U.N. Forces in Somalia*, N.Y. TIMES, May 20, 1994, at A10.

401. R. Atkinson, *Mogadishu Calm As Attention Turns to Talks*, WASH. POST, Nov. 28, 1993, at A33; J. Parmelee, *Shift Urged in U.N. Role in Somalia*, WASH. POST, Dec. 2, 1993, at A42.

402. Ironically, in light of months of efforts during 1993 by the United States to locate and apprehend Aideed, Aideed was flown to the talks on a U.S. military transport plane. J. Parmelee, *U.S. Military Plane Flies Aideed to Ethiopia for Talks on Somalia*, WASH. POST, Dec. 3, 1993, at A31.

403. S.C. Res. 897, U.N. SCOR, 49th Sess., 3334th mtg., U.N. Doc. S/RES/987 (1994).

democratically elected government. The effect of the resolution was to leave to the Somali factions themselves the primary responsibility for establishing a lasting peace or "nation-building." [404]

On March 24, 1994, Aideed and his primary rival, Ali Hahdi Mohamed—who led an alliance of 12 anti-Aideed Somali factions—signed a peace pact in Nairobi establishing a ceasefire among the factions and calling for a reconciliation conference for the establishment of a new government. The pact provided for a "[r]epudiation of any form of violence as a means of resolving conflicts and implementation of [a] ceasefire and voluntary disarmament throughout Somalia." [405] The factions failed to honor this pledge, however, and sporadic fighting continued in Mogadishu. Outside Mogadishu, on the other hand, clan warfare largely subsided, and harvests throughout the country were strong throughout 1994 and 1995.

After considering reports from the Secretary-General about the condition of Somalia, [406] the Security Council decided on November 4, 1994 to proceed with orderly withdrawal of all UNOSOM II military forces and assets from Somalia. [407] As the UNOSOM II forces prepared for their departure, the Mogadishu faction leaders Aideed and Mahdi met and managed to conclude agreements in February 1995 calling for transition to a democratic state based on a principle of power-sharing and the peaceful settlement of disputes, and for the removal of roadblocks, reopening of markets, and management of the airport and seaport at Mogadishu.

In late February 1995, 14,000 troops from seven nations were deployed to Mogadishu to form a protective cordon around the 2,400 UNOSOM troops as they withdrew from Somalia. [408] On March 3, 1995, after two years of elaborate attempts at "nation-building," including a yearly UN budget of $1 billion and the presence at its height of 18,000 UN soldiers, the last foreign forces were withdrawn from Somalia. [409]

2. Assessment of the Intervention

The December 1992 intervention in Somalia by military forces of the United States, thereafter joined by military forces of several other states,

---

404. J. Preston, *U.N. Moves Toward New Role in Somalia*, WASH. POST, Feb. 5, 1994, at A14.

405. *Further Report of the Secretary-General*, Annex I, para. 1(b), U.N. Doc. S/1994/614 (1994); Reuters, *Somalia's Warring Factions Sign Peace Accord*, WASH. POST, Mar. 25, 1994, at A26.

406. *Report of the Secretary-General*, U.N. Doc. S/1994/1068 (1994); *Report of the Secretary-General: Part Two*, U.N. Doc. S/1994/1166 (1994).

407. S.C. Res. 954, U.N. SCOR, 49th Sess., 3447th mtg., U.N. Doc. S/RES/954 (1994).

408. R. Atkinson, *Marines Launch Final Phase of Somalia Pullout*, WASH. POST, Feb. 28, 1995, at A12. The extraction operation was dubbed "Operation United Shield."

409. R. Atkinson, *Marines Close Curtain on U.N. in Somalia*, WASH. POST, Mar. 3, 1995, at A1.

sought to suppress irregular Somali military forces. Consequently, the intervention was a use of force against a state by a group of states that would normally implicate Article 2(4) of the UN Charter. The May 1993 assumption of responsibility by UN forces for this action likewise sought to suppress irregular Somali military forces. As such, it would normally implicate the prohibition in Article 2(7) of the Charter against intervention in matters essentially within the domestic jurisdiction of a state.

The reason for the interventions was not self-defense but, rather, to create the conditions under which relief operations could prevent widespread death from civil violence, starvation, and lack of basic medical supplies. The primary impetus for the initial intervention was the offer by the United States to provide military forces to conduct the intervention; it generally was recognized that the United States had no strategic or economic interest in Somalia.[410] In explaining the U.S. purpose in proposing UN intervention, U.S. President George Bush characterized the deployment as "necessary to address a major humanitarian calamity, avert related threats to international peace and security, and protect the safety of Americans and others engaged in relief operations."[411] The impetus toward international action in Somalia was generally credited to U.S. public and governmental concern over the fate of the Somali people, generated in large part by extensive televised and photographic images in the United States of widespread violence, starvation, and sickness in Somalia.

If one looks for secondary motivations in conducting the intervention, it is certainly possible to find them. There was a public relations benefit for the United States vis-à-vis the rest of the world, for the U.S. military vis-à-vis its domestic U.S. constituencies (including the Congress), and for President Bush in the last weeks of his Presidency. After leaving the government, a national security aide to President Bush stated that the U.S. action was "a good signal to the Muslim world" since Somalia was both an African and Muslim country.[412] Moreover, since the Horn of Africa had been a major staging ground of Cold War tensions, with both the United States and the Soviet Union providing extensive weaponry to the states in the region, there may have been a sense that the United States was morally obligated to help states such as Somalia remain stable in a post-Cold War environment. Finally, some charged that U.S. national

410. D. Oberdorfer, *The Path to Intervention: A Massive Tragedy "We Could Do Something About,"* Wash. Post, Dec. 6, 1992, at A1.

411. Letter to Congressional Leaders on the Situation in Somalia, 28 Weekly Comp. Pres. Doc. 2338, 2338–39 (Dec. 10, 1992).

412. Richburg, *supra* note 346 (statement of Jonathan Howe, a retired U.S. Navy admiral, national security aide to President George Bush, and the Secretary-General's special envoy to Somalia during UNOSOM II).

security interests were directly at stake; an unstable Horn of Africa could provide an opening for Iranian military and political power in the region, as well as Islamic fundamentalism, which in turn could destabilize the United States' close ally and oil supplier, Saudi Arabia.[413]

In Somalia, there was no central government capable of authorizing the intervention of foreign forces. The initial Security Council resolutions all referred to the request by the Somalia "Interim Prime Minister" for Security Council action, but Resolution 794 (issued ten months later) authorizing the deployment of U.S. and other foreign forces to Somalia, and Resolution 814 authorizing the deployment of UN forces under UNOSOM II, do not contain this reference, signalling that these actions were not undertaken pursuant to that request. While there was no central government in control of Somalia, there were leaders of factions that the United Nations considered in control of various portions of Somalia and with whom agreements were initially negotiated in 1992 to permit the deployment of certain limited UN military forces (UNOSOM I). Agreement could not be reached with these leaders for a more extensive UN deployment, but a key issue is whether such consent was even possible; the chaotic situation in Somalia suggests that the faction leaders did not exercise effective authority over all the armed elements in areas they claimed to control. When no authorities exist capable of governing a country, the values of political independence and sovereignty normally at stake during an intervention would seem to be minimized. In the case of Somalia, the overwhelming humanitarian values, when weighed against the values of political independence and sovereignty, were found compelling and led to the authorization of foreign forces to intervene. Had there been authorities fully in control of Somalia, it is not clear that the international community would have viewed the decision to intervene in the same way.

The December 1992 intervention in Somalia by U.S. military forces in conjunction with forces from other countries was expressly debated and authorized by the Security Council. The Security Council had before it options that included deployment of a force under UN command, but chose instead to authorize individual states to conduct the intervention. Resolution 794 specifically stated in operative paragraph 10 that the Security Council was acting under Chapter VII of the Charter in authorizing states to "use all necessary means" to provide a secure environment for relief operations. The transfer of control to UNOSOM II in May 1993 was also expressly debated and authorized by the Security Council. The significance of Resolution 814 is that it marked the first time that the

413. *See, e.g.*, C. Whalen, *In Somalia, the Saudi Connection*, WASH. POST, Oct. 17, 1993, at C2 (editorial).

United Nations itself deployed an armed force with specific orders to use all the force necessary to accomplish its mission.

Resolution 794 does not indicate the exact basis within Chapter VII upon which the Security Council was acting; presumably it would be either Article 42 or the Security Council's general powers under Chapter VII as a whole to maintain international peace and security. In light of the progression of events relating to Somalia, Article 42 is the likely basis. First, the Security Council expressly "determined" that the "human tragedy caused by the conflict in Somalia" constituted a threat to international peace and security. Second, during 1992, nonforcible efforts by the United Nations to ensure the delivery of relief shipments and to bring about national reconciliation failed. Finally, Resolution 794 contained various provisions relating to military forces directly under the command and control of the United Nations, the situation naturally associated with an Article 42 action. For instance, Resolution 794 expanded the personnel of UNOSOM I, authorized not just member states but also the Secretary-General himself to "use all necessary means" to create a secure environment for humanitarian relief, and contemplated UNOSOM taking over the operation upon the withdrawal of the military forces of the intervening states.

Although the Secretary-General took the position that any intervention in Somalia *had* to be based on the Security Council's enforcement powers in Chapter VII,[414] it is not clear that this position was correct. When the Security Council fails to act to address a threat to the peace, the General Assembly is competent under the Uniting for Peace Resolution to make recommendations to Member States for collective, forcible measures.[415] The measures, however, cannot be in the nature of "enforcement action" or the matter must be left to the Security Council under Article 11(2).[416] The measures will clearly be enforcement action

---

414. In his November 29, 1992, letter to the Security Council outlining potential options in Somalia, the Secretary-General stated:

At present no government exists in Somalia that could request and allow such use of force. It would therefore be necessary for the Security Council to make a determination under Article 39 of the Charter that a threat to the peace exists, as a result of the repercussions of the Somali conflict on the entire region, and to decide what measures should be taken to maintain international peace and security. The Council would also have to determine that non-military measures as referred to in Chapter VII were not capable of giving effect to the Council's decisions.

Letter Dated 29 November 1992, supra note 314, at 3.

415. *Uniting for Peace Resolution*, G.A. Res. 377, U.N. GAOR, 5th Sess., Supp. No. 20, at 10, U.N. Doc. A/1775 (1950), *reprinted in* 2 WESTON, *supra* note 12, at II.D.1.

416. *See* Certain Expenses of the United Nations, 1962 I.C.J. 151, 163 (July 20).

when the consent of the targeted state has not been provided. However, in the case of Somalia, where the consent of a central government of the targeted state was not possible because there was no recognized central government, arguably intervention by foreign states would not constitute "enforcement action." If so, the action need not occur under Chapter VII. On the other hand, under Article 12(1) of the Charter,[417] the General Assembly cannot make recommendations regarding a situation when the Security Council is exercising functions assigned to it with respect to that situation. Since the situation in Somalia remained under active review by the Security Council, arguably the General Assembly was precluded from action.

The Security Council asserted that it was taking action against a "threat to international peace and security." It is notable, however, that Resolutions 794 and 814 do not refer to the effects of the Somali crisis on neighboring countries, such as the flow of refugees. There were in fact significant flows of refugees to neighboring countries, but the dominant issue discussed by the Security Council members when passing Resolutions 794 and 814 was not the threat of these flows (which had existed for some time) but, rather, the need to address immediately the internal catastrophe of violence and starvation inflicted on the Somali people. Indeed, at the point the United Nations decided to withdraw its forces from Somalia in late 1994, there were still some 460,000 Somali refugees in neighboring countries.[418] The sense of the debate over Resolution 794 was that the domestic situation alone warranted action, and would anywhere that it might occur globally. At the same time, states participating in that debate were conscious that such a situation has external repercussions. The duality of the concern was captured by the representative from Cape Verde:

What is occurring in Somalia is a threat to the very existence of Somali society; but at the same time it represents one of the most serious challenges to the full establishment of a new international order on Earth within which the United Nations has a role of capital importance to play.

Moreover, we have no doubt that the national conflict has a second dimension—an international dimension—in view of the fact that, because of its reper-

---

417. Article 12(1) states:

While the Security Council is exercising in respect of any dispute or situation the functions assigned to it in the present Charter, the General Assembly shall not make any recommendation with regard to that dispute or situation unless the Security Council so requests.

U.N. CHARTER, art. 12, para. 1

418. WORLD REFUGEE SURVEY, 1995, *supra* note 60, at 74.

cussions on neighboring States, it is imperilling the stability and security of the whole region.[419]

Although the situation in Somalia was very different from that which presented itself in Iraq in 1991 and Bosnia-Herzegovina in 1992, the Security Council was conscious of a linkage to the pathbreaking steps taken by the Security Council to authorize the use of force to protect humanitarian efforts in those countries.[420] In voting for the resolution, the U.S. representative noted that the mission was to resolve the Somali crisis, but stated that "the international community is also taking an important step in developing a strategy for dealing with the potential disorder and conflicts of the post-cold-war world."[421] He noted: "[I]n the case of Somalia, and in other cases we are sure to face in the future, it is important that we send this unambiguous message: the international community has the intent and will to act decisively regarding peace-keeping problems that threaten international stability."[422]

The statements of governments and nongovernmental groups during 1992–93 indicate acceptance of the legality of the intervention, although at various times there was criticism of the conduct of the operation. There is no indication in the debates or statements by the relevant political actors of an acceptance that the United States or other states could have proceeded to intervene in Somalia without Security Council authorization. The desire of the United States for Security Council authorization prior to intervening could be regarded simply as political prudence; the United Nations was already involved in Somalia with UNOSOM I, and the United States expected the United Nations to take over the operation from UNITAF. Yet, the U.S. approach also suggests a lack of confidence in the widespread acceptance by the world community of a right to unilateral forcible action, absent such authorization, even in dire humanitarian circumstances. As such, the U.S. behavior may reflect a paradox regarding humanitarian intervention; the more the intervention is purely humanitarian, the less the intervening state regards its own vital interests at stake, the less likely it will act if there are political and economic costs from international criticism of the action, and thus the more likely it will regard UN authorization and the participation by other states as necessary and desirable.

The fate of the UNOSOM II operation stands as a stark warning that interventions conducted under the command and control of the United Nations are not immune to the problems that afflict interventions by

---

419. U.N. SCOR, 47th Sess., 3145th mtg. at 19–20, U.N. Doc. S/PV.3145 (1992).
420. *See, e.g., id.*, at 31 (statement by Austria).
421. *Id.* at 36.
422. *Id.* at 38.

individual states. Those that have criticized the conduct of the intervention fall roughly into two camps. One view holds that the United Nations proved too reluctant to follow through aggressively in its campaign against Aideed, the chief culprit of the attacks on the UN forces. This was the view of, among others, Brigadier General Ikram ul-Hasan, the commander of the UNOSOM II Pakistani forces, who charged that on many occasions UN forces were close to demolishing Aideed's military capability but were held back by UN officials concerned about public opinion.[423] Another view holds that the biggest UN mistake was entering into conflict with local leaders such as Aideed. This was the view of the chief U.S. representative to Somalia, Robert B. Oakley, who took the position that UNOSOM II violated "the first axiom of peacekeeping: Don't make enemies."[424] Those opposing views highlight two perhaps irreconcilable problems with humanitarian intervention; conducting forcible intervention cannot be done on the basis of traditional peacekeeping principles since consent is not present, yet that lack of consent over time will present serious obstacles to national reconciliation and can erode local and international support for the intervention.

Regardless of how one assesses the nature of the problems encountered by UNOSOM II, all would agree that the financial costs of such an operation are tremendous. From December 1992 to June 1994, the United Nations spent close to $2 billion dollars on its humanitarian activities in Somalia.[425] This, too, presents a serious problem for humanitarian intervention. To address a humanitarian crisis on the scale of what happened in Somalia requires a massive deployment of forces and relief, which entails very high financial costs that the United Nations and its members are likely to accept only in exceptional circumstances.

The intervention in Somalia serves as a precedent for UN Security Council authorization of states to intervene for humanitarian purposes, at least in situations where there has been a collapse of the local government. The ultimate transfer of responsibility from U.S.-led to UN-led forces serves as a precedent for the UN Security Council itself undertaking intervention for humanitarian purposes, even though China expressed concerns about the departure from the UN's traditional peacekeeping approach. Thus, the intervention in Somalia is a marked advance in the state of UN practice, which has always been wary of intervening in the internal affairs of a state without that state's consent. After the Cold War, in the absence of strategic global rivalries infused into every regional or local conflict, it appears that the United Nations

423. K. Richburg, *Pakistani Says U.N. Bungled on Aideed*, WASH. POST, Nov. 3, 1993, A11.
424. T. Lippman, *Clinton Envoy Cites Lessons of Somalia*, WASH. POST, Dec. 18, 1993, at A8.
425. *Further Report of the Secretary-General, supra* note 405, at Annex II; J. Preston, *U.N. Adds 4 Months in Somalia*, WASH. POST, June 1, 1994, at A21.

is less inclined to allow concern for human rights to stop at territorial borders. Nevertheless, the political difficulties and economic costs of military interventions may serve as considerable constraints on the deployment of UN forces for this purpose.

E. Rwanda (1994)

1. Essential Facts

The small, land-locked African country of Rwanda was a German colony that was placed under a Belgium-administered, League of Nations mandate after the First World War. Rwanda's population consists primarily of the Hutu—a Bantu tribe—and the Tutsi—Amharic warriors that arrived in the region in the sixteenth century, establishing themselves as a ruling caste.[426] Belgium ruled Rwanda largely through Tutsi overlords, but in 1961 the Belgian mandate was terminated and Rwanda became an independent republic. With the creation of the Rwandan Republic, the Tutsis lost power (they comprised only about 15 percent of the 7.7 million population). Many fled the country and many others were killed through sporadic pogroms by the Hutus. Periodic clashes between the groups became a feature of Rwandan affairs, and in 1990 civil war broke out between the Hutu government forces and the Tutsi-led rebel Rwandan Patriotic Front (R.P.F.), which launched an invasion from neighboring Uganda. In August 1993, a truce was negotiated between the two forces in Arusha, Tanzania, which called for an interim administration and new elections (the Arusha Accords).

On April 6, 1994, Rwanda's moderate Hutu President, Juvénal Habyarimana, was killed in a plane crash outside the Rwandan capital, Kigali.[427] The circumstances of the crash were unclear; some believed that Tutsi rebels shot down the plane, while others suspected that Hutu government military forces themselves shot down the plane due to their disdain for the moderate Habyarimana's efforts to reconcile with the Tutsis. Militant ethnic Hutus then seized control of the government (killing Habyarimana's Prime Minister) and charged that Habyarimana was assassinated by Tutsi rebels using surface-to-air rockets, which in turn provoked rampages against the Tutsis by gangs of Hutu youths as well as by paramilitary groups and militias.[428] These militant Hutus indiscriminately attacked both Tutsis and moderate Hutus associated with the Habyari-

426. P. Calvocoressi, World Politics Since 1945, at 461 (1987).

427. Habyarimana had seized power in 1973 in a coup d'état. Burundi's President, Cyprien Ntaryamira, was also killed in the plane crash.

428. These militias—known as Interahamwe (Those Who Stand Together) and Impuza Mugambi (The Single-Minded Ones)—were created, armed, and trained by the Hutu

mana Government, using machetes, pangas (machete-like weapons), and sharpened sticks. On a much lesser scale, the Tutsis responded in kind,[429] and Hutu government military forces were re-engaged by the Tutsi-led rebel force, led by Paul Kagame. By the end of April, it appeared that some 200,000 people were dead from the civil war and ethnic massacres, with another 250,000 having fled the country.[430] The atrocities committed were brutal, vivid, and ultimately numbing. Ugandan officials reported that as many as 10,000 bodies had floated down the Kagera River into Lake Victoria.[431] In one incident, 500 Tutsis seeking refuge in a church compound were shot or hacked to death by Hutu soldiers over a two-day period.[432] Thousands of women and girls were raped.[433] By mid-summer 1994, UN estimates of the number dead had been revised upward to 500,000. Some relief organizations operating in Rwanda placed the number as high as one million.[434]

The United Nations' efforts to respond to the crisis were halting, confused, and ineffective. At the time of Habyarimana's death, a UN peacekeeping force had been in Rwanda since October 1993, among other things, to monitor the ceasefire between the Hutu Government and the R.P.F. under the Arusha Accords.[435] In the wake of Habyarimana's

---

Government, but throughout the Rwandan crisis it was not clear that they were in fact being directed by the rump Hutu Government. K. Richburg, *Rwanda's Final Killing Ground*, WASH. POST, June 9, 1994, at A1.

429. Reuters, *U.N. Accuses Tutsi Rebels of Atrocities*, WASH. POST, May 18, 1994, at A16; D. Lorch, *In a Bleak Camp, Rwanda Refugees Say Each Tribe Is Joining in the Kill*, N.Y. TIMES, May 18, 1994, at A6.

430. J. Preston, *250,000 Flee Rwanda for Tanzania*, WASH. POST, Apr. 30, 1994, at A1; K. Richburg, *Bodies Clog Rwandan River: Officials Count Hundreds of Corpses Per Day Floating into Tanzania*, WASH. POST, May 2, 1994, at A12.

431. The *New York Times* quoted one Ugandan farmer who pulled bodies out of Lake Victoria as follows:

"One time, I found a woman," he said. "She had five children tied to her. One on each arm. One on each leg. One on her back. She had no wounds."

D. Lorch, *Bodies from Rwanda Cast a Pall on Lakeside Villages*, N.Y. TIMES, May 28, 1994, sec. 1, at 1.

432. D. Lorch, *Heart of Rwanda's Darkness: Slaughter at a Rural Church*, N.Y. TIMES, June 3, 1994, at A1; *see generally* R. Winter, *Journey into Genocide: A Rwanda Diary*, WASH. POST, June 5, 1994, at C1 (account of three-day journey through Rwanda by director of U.S. Committee for Refugees, a private humanitarian agency).

433. D. Lorch, *Wave of Rape Adds New Horror To Rwanda's Trail of Savagery*, N.Y. TIMES, May 15, 1995, sec. 1, at 1.

434. K. Richburg, *The World Ignored Genocide, Tutsis Say*, WASH. POST, Aug. 8, 1994, at A1 (reporting that the International Committee of the Red Cross—the only relief agency operating throughout Rwanda during the massacres—estimated that one million may have been killed).

435. This peacekeeping force was authorized under S.C. Res. 872, U.N. SCOR, 48th Sess., 3288th mtg. at 102, U.N. Doc. S/INF/49 (1994). Just prior to Habyarimana's death,

death, this peacekeeping force—the UN Assistance Mission for Rwanda (UNAMIR)—was unable to prevent the outbreak of widespread violence despite adjustments to its mandate[436] and was reduced by the Security Council to fewer than 300 Ghanaian soldiers when UNAMIR's own safety became at risk.[437] UN humanitarian relief flights into Rwanda commenced, but had to be suspended after the aircraft came under fire[438] and could only be resumed sporadically. A ceasefire was negotiated between the warring factions, but the rebel force continued to fight and threatened to take control of the capital, Kigali.[439]

On April 29, UN Secretary-General Boutros Boutros-Ghali urged the deployment of additional, all-African UN peacekeeping forces to Rwanda, and submitted a plan on May 13 that called for sending 5,500 soldiers to Kigali under an expanded UNAMIR mandate that would protect refugees and assist relief workers there and in the countryside.[440] At first, the Security Council could not agree on moving forward with this plan, in large part due to resistance by the United States, which pointed out that, despite the Secretary-General's efforts, no state had made a firm offer to send their forces to Rwanda and that the Rwandan factions had not given unconditional consent to the UN operation. The United States argued for more detailed planning before going into Kigali, since the active fighting placed both UN forces and UN prestige at risk, which in turn could jeopardize U.S. funding for UN peacekeeping operations.[441] On May 17, the other Security Council members prevailed on the United States to drop some of its objections, and thereupon the Security Council unanimously approved the deployment of 500 more Ghanaian peacekeeping soldiers under the expanded UNAMIR mandate, with the ex-

---

the Security Council extended UNAMIR's mandate until July 29, 1994. S.C. Res. 909, U.N. SCOR, 49th Sess., 3358th mtg., U.N. Doc. S/RES/909 (1994). The functions of UNAMIR were to assist in ensuring the security of Kigali, to monitor the ceasefire agreement, to monitor the transition to elected government, and to assist with mine clearance.

436. S.C. Res. 912, U.N. SCOR, 49th Sess., 3368th mtg., U.N. Doc. S/RES/912 (1994). In the bloodshed that followed Habyarimana's death, ten Belgian soldiers were killed, prompting Belgium to withdraw its battalion from UNAMIR.

437. Reuters, *U.N. Force Nears Collapse in Chaotic Rwanda*, WASH. POST, Apr. 21, 1994, at A26; J. Preston, *Death Toll in Rwanda Is Said to Top 100,000*, WASH. POST, Apr. 22, 1994, at A1.

438. News Services, *U.N. Suspends Aid Flights to Rwanda; Cease-Fire Negotiated*, WASH. POST, May 6, 1994, at A32.

439. Associated Press, *Rwandan Rebels Shell Capital and Army Units*, N.Y. TIMES, May 11, 1994, at A9.

440. *Report of the Secretary-General*, U.N. Doc. S/1994/565 (1994); P. Lewis, *U.S. Opposes Plan for U.N. Force in Rwanda*, N.Y. TIMES, May 12, 1994, at A9.

441. P. Lewis, *U.N. Backs Troops for Rwanda but Terms Bar Any Action Soon*, N.Y. TIMES, May 17, 1994, at A1. The United States pays for approximately one-third of all U.N. peacekeeping operations; in 1995, it sought to reduce that proportion to one-fourth.

pectation of more to follow.[442] Fourteen African nations offered to contribute additional forces to the peacekeeping operation[443] and, on June 8, 1994, the Security Council passed Resolution 925 authorizing the deployment of the full 5,500 soldiers to Rwanda.[444] In subparagraphs 4(a) and (b) of Resolution 925, the Security Council called upon UNAMIR to provide security and protection for displaced persons and security and support for the distribution of relief.[445] However, difficulties in obtaining logistical support (particularly from the United States) severely impeded the deployments and made it unlikely that the additional forces could be deployed for some time.[446]

The slowness in deploying forces was not the only UN failure in Rwanda. On May 31, the Vatican requested that the Security Council declare a "safe area" around a large religious complex in the town of Kabgayi to prevent any armed forces from entering it. Some 38,000 persons had sought refuge in the complex.[447] Although "safe havens" had previ-

442. S.C. Res. 918, U.N. SCOR, 49th Sess., 3377th mtg., U.N. Doc. S/RES/918 (1994). Ironically, Rwanda had a seat on the Security Council at this time, which was occupied by a representative of the rump Hutu Government. Moreover, Rwanda was due to take over the Presidency of the Council in September 1994.

443. Ghana, Ethiopia, and Senegal were the first nations to offer peacekeeping forces. P. Lewis, *3 African Lands Offer Troops for Rwanda*, N.Y. TIMES, May 25, 1994, at A12. Shortly thereafter, eleven more African nations also pledged to provide peacekeeping forces. Reuters, *Africans Pledge Troops for Rwanda*, WASH. POST, June 4, 1994, at A15 (the additional eleven were Angola, Benin, Botswana, Cameroon, Eritrea, Mali, Mozambique, Tanzania, Uganda, Zambia, and Zimbabwe).

444. S.C. Res. 925, U.N. SCOR, 49th Sess., 3388th mtg., U.N. Doc. S/RES/925 (1994). This resolution also called for the establishment of a special trust fund for the support of UNAMIR, to which states could contribute on a voluntary basis.

445. The text of paragraph 4 reads as follows:

Reaffirms that UNAMIR, in addition to continuing to act as an intermediary between the parties in an attempt to secure their agreement to a cease-fire, will:

   (a) Contribute to the security and protection of displaced persons, refugees and civilians at risk in Rwanda, including through the establishment and maintenance, where feasible, of secure humanitarian areas; and

   (b) Provide security and support for the distribution of relief supplies and humanitarian relief operations.

Id. para. 4.

446. The United States said it would take at least a month to send to Rwanda fifty U.S. armored vehicles needed by the UN peacekeeping forces, which the United States offered to lease to the United Nations for $10 million. M. Gordon, *U.N.'s Rwanda Deployment Slowed by Lack of Vehicles*, N.Y. TIMES, June 9, 1994, at A10. The Ghanian soldiers also had to be trained to use the vehicles. The Security Council eventually passed a resolution calling on states to provide the necessary logistical support to allow UNAMIR to fulfill its mandate. S.C. Res. 929, U.N. SCOR, 49th Sess., 3392d mtg., U.N. Doc. S/RES/929 (1994).

447. P. Lewis, *Vatican Asks U.N. for "Safe Area" in Rwanda*, N.Y. TIMES, June 1, 1994, at A11.

ously been declared by the Security Council in Bosnia-Herzegovina, [448] the Security Council ignored the Vatican's request. On June 8, Tutsi soldiers entered the complex and massacred the Archbishop of Kigali, two other bishops, and ten priests. [449]

The Security Council condemned the violence in Rwanda and took steps to hold accountable those who committed the atrocities. As was done for the conflict in Bosnia-Herzegovina, concern with the level of the atrocities prompted the Security Council to request the Secretary-General to establish an impartial commission of experts to examine information regarding grave violations of international humanitarian law, including genocide. [450]

By the end of May, the rebels occupied northern and eastern Rwanda and large parts of Kigali (including the airport) and were advancing to the west on the Hutu government headquarters at Gitarama. [451] When the Hutu leaders abandoned Gitarama, it appeared that an outright victory for the rebels might be imminent. [452] On June 6, the Hutu government forces, increasingly concentrated and entrenched in the west, launched a major counterattack against the increasingly stretched Tutsi rebels. [453] The counterattack failed and it was thought that the fighting might continue indefinitely. [454] Even if the Tutsi rebels prevailed, it was unclear whether they could control a majority Hutu population.

On June 15, French Foreign Minister Alain Juppé announced that France was prepared, "along with its main European and African partners," to intervene in Rwanda to protect groups threatened with "extinction." [455] The willingness of France to take the lead in such an

448. *Supra* section C.

449. P. Lewis, *Rebels in Rwanda Said to Slay 3 Bishops and 10 Other Clerics*, N.Y. TIMES, June 10, 1994, at A1; A. Hartley, *Rwanda Rebels Kill Archbishop, Priests*, WASH. POST, June 10, 1994, at A22; *see also* M. Ignatieff, *Alone With The Secretary-General*, NEW YORKER, Aug. 14, 1995, 33, 34–36 (massacre at Nyarubuye missionary compound); S. Buckley, *Skulls of Nyamata a Reminder of Rwanda's "Horrible History,"* WASH. POST, July 16, 1995, at A24 (massacre at Nyamata church). On the day of the massacre, S.C. Res. 925, U.N. SCOR, 49th Sess., 3400th mtg., U.N. Doc. S/RES/935 (1994), decided that UNAMIR should establish and maintain secure humanitarian areas where possible.

450. S.C. Res. 935, U.N. SCOR, 49th Sess., 3400th mtg., U.N. Doc. S/RES/935 (1994). The vote was unanimous.

451. Associated Press, *Soldiers Join the Flight from Rwanda's Capital*, N.Y. TIMES, May 27, 1994, at A5; K. Richburg, *Rebel Victory Called Path to Ending Rwandan Slaughter*, WASH. POST, May 29, 1994, at A48.

452. K. Richburg, *Rwandan Leaders Flee Rebel Advance*, WASH. POST, May 30, 1994, at A1.

453. Associated Press, *Rwandan Army Attacks Rebels in Southwest*, N.Y. TIMES, June 7, 1994, at A13.

454. K. Richburg, *U.N. General Sees No End in Rwanda*, WASH. POST, June 11, 1994, at A18.

455. Reuters, *France May Move In to End Rwanda Killing*, N.Y. TIMES, June 16, 1994, at A12; Associated Press, *Cease-fire Fails to Silence Artillery Duels in Rwanda*, WASH. POST, June 16,

intervention was met by other states with some misgivings; France had played a major role in arming and training the Hutu-dominated Rwandan government forces, which were responsible for many of the killings in Rwanda.[456] While most of the atrocities had been inflicted on the Tutsis, France appeared mostly concerned that well-armed Tutsis, as they took control of western Rwanda, would commit atrocities against defenseless Hutu civilians. Moreover, there were concerns that the French might seek to bolster the Hutu government forces in their fight against the Tutsi rebels. The leaders of the Tutsi rebels immediately declared their opposition to any intervention by France.[457] Their military chief declared: "Nous considérons les Français comme une force hostile que nous combattrons par tous les moyens."[458]

Juppé sought to allay concerns that France was intervening in support of the Hutu-dominated government forces, contending that France was acting impartially and was "not going to Rwanda to engage in war but to save a population. . . . This is not a political intervention to separate belligerents but to protect civilians."[459] In a lengthy article in the Paris-based *Libération*, Juppé declared that there was a "real duty to intervene in Rwanda" to halt the massacres and that "It is no longer time to deplore the massacres with our arms folded, but to take action."[460]

France initially insisted that it would not act alone, but it soon became clear that none of its allies intended to join in the intervention.[461] The WEU met, and while some members offered to provide equipment for the intervention, none offered to provide troops.[462] The United States

---

1994, at A27. France is the only ex-colonial power to keep troops in Africa; the largest French overseas base, with about 5,000 marines, is in Djibouti. J. Darnton, *Intervening With Élan and No Regrets*, N.Y. TIMES, June 26, 1994, sec. 4, at 3.

456. The deceased President Habyarimana was reportedly a close personal friend of France's President Mitterrand; even the plane carrying Habyarimana that was shot down was a gift to him from France. M. Simons, *France's Rwanda Connection*, N.Y. TIMES, July 3, 1994, sec. 1, at 6.

457. The military chief of the rebel group stated:

France trained the militias and the army, and it did not condemn the murderers. France is clearly partial, and the return of its soldiers would only complicate the situation.

W. Drozdiak, *No Rescue for Rwanda*, WASH. POST, June 18, 1994, at A17.

458. S. Smith, *L'Armee Française Malvenue au Rwanda*, LIBÉRATION, June 20, 1994, at 12 (author's translation: "We consider the French to be a hostile force that we will combat by all means.").

459. W. Drozdiak, *supra* note 457.

460. *Cited in* A. Riding, *France Seeks Partners for Rwandan Venture*, N.Y. TIMES, June 17, 1994, at A8.

461. *Id.*

462. W. Drozdiak, *France Presses Plan for Rwanda Mission*, WASH. POST, June 20, 1994, at A9.

supported the idea as a means of bridging the gap before arrival of the 5,500 planned UN peacekeepers, but also declined to provide its own forces for the intervention.[463] Three of Rwanda's neighbors—Burundi, Tanzania, and Uganda—denied France permission to stage operations from their territory.[464]

French President François Mitterrand declared that, regardless of whether other states responded positively, France would act, but French Defense Minister François Léotard asserted that France would not "go it alone." Léotard declared that it was necessary to "get a mandate from the international community and the help of African countries." [465] Similarly, Juppé declared "Nous ne ferons rien sans un feu vert des Nations unies pour monter cette opération à but strictement humanitaire," [466] and even asserted that the intervening force would be under the flag and support of the United Nations.[467] By June 21, 1,000 French troops were positioned to intervene from Zaire and the Central African Republic, but France wanted express Security Council authorization before intervening.[468] As the Security Council considered a draft French resolution, the rebel Tutsi force vowed to "do all we can to resist this French invasion" and urged the Security Council not to authorize it.[469]

On June 22, the Security Council passed Resolution 929 authorizing the use of "all necessary means to achieve the humanitarian objectives" that had been established for UNAMIR in paragraph 4 of Resolution 925.[470] Among other things, the resolution stated:

> *Determined* to contribute to the resumption of the process of political settlement under the Arusha Peace Agreement and *encouraging* the Secretary-General and his Special Representative for Rwanda to continue and redouble their efforts at the national, regional and international levels to promote these objectives, . . .
> *Taking into account* the time needed to gather the necessary resources for the

---

463. J. Preston, *U.S. Endorses French Initiative for Military Mission in Rwanda*, WASH. POST, June 21, 1994, at A10.

464. *Few Allies Help France*, N.Y. TIMES, June 24, 1994, at A8.

465. D. Crary, *Mitterrand Readies French Troops for Rwanda*, WASH. POST, June 19, 1994, at A25; Reuters, *France Says It Will Send Intervention Force to Rwandan Border*, N.Y. TIMES, June 19, 1994, sec. 1, at 11 (France unwilling to wait for UN deployment of peacekeepers).

466. *Une "question d'heures et de jours,"* LE FIGARO, June 20, 1994, at B3 (author's translation: "We will do nothing without a United Nations green light for mounting this strictly humanitarian operation.").

467. Crary, *supra* note 465.

468. *Letter Dated 21 June 1994 from France to the President of the Security Council*, U.N. Doc. S/1994/738 (1994); J. Follain, *French Set to Intervene in Rwanda, Await Word from U.N.*, WASH. POST, June 22, 1994, at A16.

469. Follain, *supra* note 468.

470. S.C. Res. 929, *supra* note 446, para. 3. For the text of sub-paragraphs 4(a) and (b) of S.C. Res. 925, *see supra* note 445.

effective deployment of UNAMIR, as expanded in resolutions 918 (1994) and 925 (1994),

Noting the offer by Member States to cooperate with the Secretary-General towards the fulfillment of the objectives of the United Nations in Rwanda (S/1994/734), and *stressing* the strictly humanitarian character of this operation which shall be conducted in an impartial and neutral fashion, and shall not constitute an interposition force between the parties, . . .

Deeply concerned by the continuation of systematic and widespread killings of the civilian population in Rwanda,

Recognizing that the current situation in Rwanda constitutes a unique case which demands an urgent response by the international community,

Determining that the magnitude of the humanitarian crisis in Rwanda constitutes a threat to peace and security in the region,

1. *Welcomes* the Secretary-General's letter dated 19 June 1994 (S/1994/728) and *agrees* that a multinational operation may be set up for humanitarian purposes in Rwanda until UNAMIR is brought up to the necessary strength;

2. *Welcomes also* the offer by Member States (S/1994/734) to cooperate with the Secretary-General in order to achieve the objectives of the United Nations in Rwanda through the establishment of a temporary operation under national command and control aimed at contributing, in an impartial way, to the security and protection of displaced persons, refugees and civilians at risk in Rwanda, on the understanding that the costs of implementing the offer will be borne by the Member States concerned;

3. *Acting* under Chapter VII of the Charter of the United Nations, *authorizes* the Member States cooperating with the Secretary-General to conduct the operation referred to in paragraph 2 above using all necessary means to achieve the humanitarian objectives set out in sub-paragraphs 4(a) and (b) of resolution 925 (1994);

4. *Decides* that the mission of Member States cooperating with the Secretary-General will be limited to a period of two months following the adoption of the present resolution, unless the Secretary-General determines at an earlier date that the expanded UNAMIR is able to carry out its mandate.

The resolution thus authorized France to use "all necessary means" to protect Rwandan civilians, but called for a "strictly humanitarian" and "impartial, neutral" operation that would not interfere in the fighting between the rebel and the government forces. Further, the resolution kept the troops under French (not UN) command and stated that the duration of the intervention would be limited to two months. This duration reportedly was less than the three months sought by the Secretary-General, apparently due to a need to ease French domestic concerns about being involved in a prolonged conflict.[471]

The Security Council vote was ten in favor (including the rump Hutu government representative of Rwanda), none opposed, and five absten-

---

471. J. Preston, *U.N. Supports France on Force for Rwanda*, WASH. POST, June 23, 1994, at A24; R. Lyons, *French Offer Is First Step Toward a Multinational Force*, N.Y. TIMES, June 23, 1994, at A8.

tions (Brazil, China, New Zealand, Nigeria, and Pakistan). To the Security Council, France asserted:

The goal of the French initiative is exclusively humanitarian: the initiative is motivated by the plight of the people, in the face of which, we believe, the international community cannot and must not remain passive. It will not be the mission of our soldiers in Rwanda to interpose themselves between the warring parties, still less to influence in any way the military and political situation. Our objective is simple: to rescue endangered civilians and put an end to the massacres, and to do so in an impartial manner.[472]

Those who voted in favor of the resolution saw it as necessary due to the delays experienced in providing sufficient support to UNAMIR. The United States noted that there was skepticism "in some quarters" that France would play a truly impartial role in Rwanda. Consequently the United States noted that the resolution "has been narrowed to address exactly that concern, and that the mandate of the force is limited to addressing humanitarian needs." [473] The delegations that abstained voiced concern about the intervention going forward at the same time that UN peacekeeping forces were in Rwanda. New Zealand explained its abstention as a concern that "Trying to run two separate operations in parallel with different command arrangements does not work and, in the long run, those whom we set out to save can be those who suffer." [474] Brazil asserted that the Security Council should avoid using its extraordinary Article VII powers in such cases and noted the difficulty in simultaneously operating peacekeeping and "peace-forcing" operations in the same state.[475]

On June 23, a few hundred French troops in armored vehicles and helicopters crossed from Zaire sixty miles into western Rwanda. The Tutsi rebels reacted by ordering French aid workers, medical personnel, and journalists to leave areas under Tutsi control, an order subsequently retracted.[476] Within days, the French forces were joined by a small contingent of Senegalese troops, and both forces made contact with Hutu civilians.[477] The French forces made efforts to show that their tactics were evenhanded by going after the Hutu irregular militias, dismantling their

472. U.N. SCOR, 49th Sess., 3392d mtg., at 5–6, U.N. Doc. S/PV.3392 (1994).
473. *Id.* at 6.
474. *Id.* at 7.
475. *Id.* at 2–3.
476. M. Simons, *French Troops Enter Rwanda in Aid Mission*, N.Y. TIMES, June 24, 1994, at A1; M. Simons, *French Soldiers in Rwanda Report Finding Mass Graves*, N.Y. TIMES, June 25, 1994, at sec. 1, at 5.
477. J. Randal, *Hailed by Hutus, French Visit Camp in Rwanda*, WASH. POST, June 26, 1994, at A26.

roadblocks, disarming them, and telling them to go home.[478] Reportedly surprised to find that widespread killings of Tutsi civilians, not Hutu civilians, was ongoing, they also acknowledged that this killing needed to be stopped.[479] Yet the French operations were limited to the western portion of Rwanda and, in any event, were not adequate for ensuring the protection of civilians or relief operations throughout Rwanda. French Defense Minister François Léotard candidly admitted: "We cannot evacuate everybody. We've only got hundreds of people here; there are hundreds of thousands who need help."[480]

The rump Hutu government urged the French to assist it in preventing a rebel victory and then asserted that it had been manipulated when that assistance was not forthcoming.[481] At the same time, French efforts to assist Rwandan civilians resulted in armed clashes with the Tutsi rebels.[482] As the rebels continued to advance on western Rwanda, France requested that the Security Council authorize the creation of a safe haven in southwestern Rwanda, but the Tutsi rebels rejected the proposal, arguing that France was seeking to bolster the rapidly weakening Hutu government forces located in western Rwanda.[483]

On July 4, the Tutsi rebels gained control of Kigali and Rwanda's second largest city, Butare. Without waiting for UN approval, France declared a safe zone in southwestern Rwanda (the Cyangugu-Kibuye-Gikongoro triangle), covering about one-fifth of Rwandese territory, for the protection of Rwandan civilians. France's military commander in Rwanda stated that any Tutsi rebel forces entering the zone would be fired upon "without any hesitation" if they threatened the population.[484] Most of the population in the safe zone were Hutu, including some 250,000 refugees from parts of Rwanda controlled by the rebels.[485]

French forces withdrew from the rest of western Rwanda into this safe zone, which led to a routing of the Hutu government forces in western

478. Reuters, *French Paratroopers Disarm Rwanda Militias, Saying They are Allies of Neither Tribe*, N.Y. TIMES, June 26, 1994, sec. 1, at 10.

479. R. Bonner, *Grisly Discovery in Rwanda Leads French to Widen Role*, N.Y. TIMES, July 1, 1994, at A1; J. Randal, *French Troops Race to Rescue of Tutsis*, WASH. POST, July 1, 1994, at A27.

480. R. Bonner, *Tutsi Refugees Reported Trapped in Rwanda*, N.Y. TIMES, June 30, 1994, at A11.

481. R. Bonner, *As French Aid the Tutsi, Backlash Grows*, N.Y. TIMES, July 2, 1994, sec. 1, at 5; Associated Press, *Rwanda Asks France to Help Hold Off Rebels*, N.Y. TIMES, July 3, 1994, sec. 1, at 6.

482. R. Bonner, *French Force in Skirmish in Rwanda*, N.Y. TIMES, July 4, 1994, sec. 1, at 2; J. Randal, *French Troops, Rebels Clash*, WASH. POST, July 4, 1994, at A14.

483. Randal, *supra* note 482.

484. J. Randal, *Rebels Take Chief Cities in Rwanda*, WASH. POST, July 5, 1994, at A1; R. Bonner, *French Establish a Base in Rwanda to Block Rebels*, N.Y. TIMES, July 5, 1994, at A1.

485. Randal, *supra* note 484; Bonner, *supra* note 484.

Rwanda by the rebels and to the collapse of the rump Hutu government. Within days, a quarter million Hutus, fearful that the advancing Tutsi rebels would extract revenge upon them, fled across the western Rwandan border into Zaire.[486] Many of these fears were unfounded and were fueled by rumors spread by Hutu militants, but by the time the rebels announced a ceasefire on July 18, more than a million Hutus had fled into Zaire while another million had sought refuge inside the French safe zone.[487] The influx of refugees into Zaire caught the international relief community offguard; before long, cholera and dysentery became rampant in the refugee camps, killing thousands and sparking new emergency relief efforts by the United Nations and its member states, along with efforts to convince the refugees they would be safe if they returned to Rwanda.[488]

On July 19, the rebels announced the formation of a government of national unity, composed of both Tutsi and Hutu (both the President, Pasteur Bizimungu, and the Prime Minister, Faustin Twagiramungu, were moderate Hutus).[489] This government was subsequently recognized as the legitimate government of Rwanda by most states and gained representation at the United Nations.[490] On July 29, although it was generally recognized by the international community that the refugee crisis could be resolved only by encouraging Rwandans that it was safe to return to their homes in Rwanda, France announced that it was commencing the withdrawal of its now-2,500 forces from the safe zone Rwanda, to be completed by the two-month deadline of August 22. While the new Rwandan government agreed that the French forces could be replaced by 2,200 forces from Ethiopia and other African countries, UN officials and some states expressed alarm that the French withdrawal would spark another exodus of Hutus and urged the French to

486. K. Richburg, *Rwandan Army Routed; Refugees Engulf Zaire*, WASH. POST, July 15, 1994, at A1; R. Bonner, *Rwandan Refugees Flood Zaire as Rebel Forces Gain*, N.Y. TIMES, July 15, 1994, at A1.

487. J. Randal & K. Richburg, *Rebels Declare Victory, Cease-Fire in Rwanda*, WASH. POST, July 19, 1994, at A1.

488. T. Lippman & R. Fowler, *U.S. and U.N. Rush Relief to Rwandans*, WASH. POST, July 22, 1994, at A1; R. Bonner, *Cholera's Spread Raises Fear of Toll of 40,000 Rwandans*, N.Y. TIMES, July 24, 1994, sec. 1, at 1; K. Richburg, *Dysentery Strikes Rwandans As Cholera Deaths Ebb*, WASH. POST, July 31, 1994, at A28 (the U.N. estimated death rates at 1,000 to 2,000 daily). Despite the French presence, health conditions in the safe zone in southwestern Rwanda were also poor. R. Bonner, *Starvation Threatens a "Safe Haven" in Rwanda*, N.Y. TIMES, Aug. 7, 1994, sec. 1, at 3.

489. R. Bonner, *Rwandan Rebels Name Cabinet of Hutu and Tutsi, but Those Fleeing Are Still Fearful*, N.Y. TIMES, July 20, 1994, at A6.

490. R. Lyons, *New Rwandan Government Welcomed to U.N.*, N.Y. TIMES, Sept. 1, 1994, at A14.

stay.[491] The new Rwandan Government, however, favored French withdrawal by the August 22 deadline.[492]

As the deadline approached, the fear of another exodus proved partially well founded, as thousands more Rwandans fled from the safe zone into Zaire.[493] Nevertheless, as planned, all French forces left Rwanda by August 22.[494] In a joint statement, French President Mitterrand and Prime Minister Edouard Balladur declared that "France has fulfilled its duty. . . . It is now up to the Rwandan authorities and the international community to assume, as of today, all of their responsibilities."[495] In the wake of the French withdrawal, disturbing reports emerged both about the new Tutsi government's treatment of ethnic Hutus[496] and about the violence in refugee camps outside Rwanda committed by soldiers of the former Hutu government.[497] While the UN Secretary-General appealed to sixty countries for an international force to be sent to the camps in Zaire to control the violence, none of those countries responded positively, leaving the task to Zairian and Tanzanian troops.[498] The United Nations supported those efforts, however, by establishing a peacekeeping operation in Zaire consisting of Zairian troops charged with keeping order in the refugee camps—the first operation in the history of the United Nations in which a nation's troops were used as peacekeepers on their own soil.[499]

Further, the Security Council took some steps to encourage refugees to believe they would be safe were they to return to Rwanda. UNAMIR maintained its presence in Rwanda, charged with contributing to the se-

491. W. Drozdiak, *France Begins Troop Withdrawal from Rwanda*, WASH. POST, July 30, 1994, at A12.

492. P. Taylor, *Rwanda's New Tutsi Leaders Seek Swift Genocide Trials for Ousted Hutus*, WASH. POST, Aug. 3, 1994, at A21.

493. K. Richburg, *New Tide of Refugees Heads Out of Rwanda*, WASH. POST, Aug. 20, 1994, at A1. In the ten days surrounding the French withdrawal, about 70,000 refugees fled the safe zone. K. Richburg, *Rwanda's Feared Wave of Refugees Turns Out to Be a Trickle*, WASH. POST, Aug. 26, 1994, at A17.

494. K. Richburg, *French Troops Withdraw from Rwanda Safe Zone*, WASH. POST, Aug. 22, 1994, at A14.

495. K. Richburg, *New Tide of Refugees Heads out of Rwanda, supra* note 493.

496. *E.g.*, R. Bonner, *U.N. Stops Returning Rwandan Refugees*, N.Y. TIMES, Sept. 28, 1994, at A7 (report issued by U.N. consultant that there was a pattern of killings and reprisals by Rwandan government soldiers against returning refugees). Eventually, the United Nations resumed assisting in the repatriation of Rwandan refugees. R. Bonner, *U.N. Will Help Rwandan Refugees Return to Rwanda*, N.Y. TIMES, Dec. 20, 1994, at A7.

497. *See, e.g.*, R. Bonner, *Rwandans Who Massacred Now Terrorize Camps*, N.Y. TIMES, Oct. 31, 1994, at A1.

498. *Force to Aid Rwandans Abandoned*, WASH. POST, Jan. 24, 1995, at A12.

499. Reuters, *Zairians Begin a U.N. Mission for Rwandans*, N.Y. TIMES, Feb. 13, 1995, at A6.

curity and protection of displaced persons and providing support for relief operations.[500] As a means of demonstrating that those responsible for the widespread killings in Rwanda would be brought to justice in an orderly fashion, rather than indiscriminately punished by the new Rwandan government, the United Nations established an international tribunal to prosecute persons responsible for genocide and other serious violations of international humanitarian law committed in Rwanda during 1994. As in the case of the former Yugoslavia, the Security Council adopted a statute governing the jurisdiction and procedure of the tribunal.[501] Separately, Rwandan courts proceeded to prosecute persons suspected of genocide[502] amid criticisms that its nascent penal system was incapable of dispensing justice to the vast number of persons in custody.[503] In the last half of 1994, an estimated 100,000 Hutu refugees repatriated to Rwanda.[504]

By 1995, there remained some 250,000 Rwandans, primarily Hutu, located at nine camps within Rwanda's border, fearful of returning to their homes and intimidated by Hutu militants in the camps themselves. The presence of the Hutu militants in the camps was regarded by the new Rwandan government as a threat; consequently, in April 1995, the government began a campaign to close the camps and force the dislocated Hutus to return to their homes. In doing so, chaos ensued at the largest camp at Kibeho, when hundreds of Hutus died either by being trampled to death or by being shot by government forces, in part because they were used as human shields by the Hutu militants.[505] Within a few weeks, however, the camps had been closed, and the vast majority returned home without incident.[506] Similarly, in August 1995, the government of Zaire undertook a campaign of forced repatriation of Rwandan and Bu-

---

500. *See* S.C. Res. 965, U.N. SCOR, 49th Sess., 3473d mtg., U.N. Doc. S/RES/965 (1994).

501. S.C. Res. 955, U.N. SCOR, 49th Sess., 3453d mtg., U.N. Doc. S/RES/955 (1994); *see also* S.C. Res. 978, U.N. SCOR, 50th Sess., 3504th mtg., U.N. Doc. S/RES/978 (1995).

502. D. Lorch, *As Rwanda Trials Open, a Nation Struggles*, N.Y. TIMES, Apr. 7, 1995, sec. 1, at 1; Reuters, *One Year Later, Rwandans on Trial*, WASH. POST, Apr. 7, 1995, at A33.

503. D. Lorch, *Rwanda Jails: No Space, No Food, No Justice*, N.Y. TIMES, Apr. 15, 1995, sec. 1, at 1.

504. WORLD REFUGEE SURVEY, *supra* note 60, at 71.

505. Associated Press, *22 Killed at Rwandan Refugee Site*, WASH. POST, Apr. 22, 1995, at A22; S. Buckley, *Rwandan Troops Said to Kill Hundreds in Largest Refugee Camp*, WASH. POST, Apr. 23, 1995, at A26; S. Buckley, *At Least 2,000 Refugees Die in Rwandan Violence*, WASH. POST, Apr. 24, 1995, at A1; *From Awful to Worse*, ECONOMIST, Apr. 29, 1995, at 50. The Rwandan government prosecuted nine government soldiers implicated in the massacre at Kibeho. Reuters, *Rwanda Opens The Trial of 14 In the Military*, N.Y. TIMES, May 3, 1995, at A12.

506. Associated Press, *Last Hutu Refugees Leave Dreaded Camp*, N.Y. TIMES, May 10, 1995, at A3.

rundi refugees located at camps in Zaire; some 130,000 were forced out of the camps within a matter of days.[507]

On June 9, 1995, the Security Council voted to cut by more than half the UNAMIR forces, reflecting a desire by the Rwandan government that the forces be reduced and even withdrawn.[508] Ultimately, despite the continuing fear of Hutu refugees that returning to Rwanda would subject them to reprisals, the Rwandan government insisted that UNAMIR forces leave Rwanda entirely, which occurred in early 1996.

2. Assessment of the Intervention

The deployment of French military forces into Rwanda in June 1994 was a use of force that normally would implicate Article 2(4) of the UN Charter. The reason given for the intervention was neither self-defense nor the protection of French nationals but, rather, the creation of conditions for the protection of Rwandan nationals and of relief operations being conducted for their benefit. The highest leaders of the French government declared that they were motivated by a concern with the atrocious massacres inflicted on Rwandans by government-led forces and paramilitary units and by the rebel forces. These leaders denied any objective to achieve gains for France or to support one of the Rwandan factions over the other.

By intervening only in the western part of Rwanda, where the Hutu government forces were on the run, France initially gave the appearance of favoring the Hutus; it is possible that some French leaders in fact intended to aid the Hutu government forces but miscalculated France's ability to do so. Various French leaders made statements to the effect that it was impossible for the Tutsis to rule the country because of their minority status and that the best solution would be for the Hutus and Tutsis to fight to a standstill so as to create the conditions for a negotiated settlement. Moreover, France had over the course of many years developed a close relationship with Habyarimana's Hutu government; ranging from extensive French foreign aid and arms sales to extensive use of French "advisers" to assist the government in its clash with the R.P.F., to personal friendships between the children of both states' highest leaders.[509]

507. *85,000 Flee, Zaire Drives Refugees Out of UN Camps*, INT'L HERALD TRIB., Aug. 23, 1995, at 1; Reuters, *Fleeing Rwandan Refugees Now Number 130,000*, INT'L HERALD TRIB., Aug. 24, 1995, at 1.

508. C. Wren, *U.N. to Withdraw Over Half Of Military Force in Rwanda*, N.Y. TIMES, June 10, 1995, sec. 1, at 5; B. Crossette, *Send the Peacekeepers Home, A Ravaged Rwanda Tells U.N.*, N.Y. TIMES, June 8, 1995, at A9.

509. A. Shoumatoff, *Gallic Mischief: Why is France in Rwanda?*, NEW YORKER, July 18, 1994, at 4. Shoumatoff speculates that France itself might have been involved in Habyarimana's

On balance, however, the actions of the French forces ultimately confirmed an overall humanitarian motivation. France was appalled by the atrocities being committed and believed it was in a position to assist in ending the bloodshed. As such, the French intervention fits the concept of humanitarian intervention.

The Hutu-dominated government forces welcomed the French intervention, but their status as the internationally recognized government capable of authorizing foreign intervention is at best dubious. After the death of Juvénal Habyarimana and the murder of his Prime Minister, the militant government forces proclaimed themselves as the rump government of Rwanda, and while they were represented throughout this time on the Security Council itself, they seized power in a manner inconsistent with Rwandan internal processes. Moreover, they had unleashed a brutal slaughter of the Rwandan people that was condemned by the international community and that had resulted in a rebellion through which the government forces lost control of two-thirds of Rwanda. Many of the rebels (including Paul Kagame) were veterans of the Ugandan army, and Uganda likely provided some support for the rebels, although that support appears to have been minimal.[510]

A fair reading of the situation at the time of the intervention, then, would regard the Hutu-dominated government and the rebel National Patriotic Front as co-belligerents. As such, authorization for foreign intervention by the Hutu-dominated government alone cannot provide a sufficient legal basis for foreign intervention. For its part, the rebel Royal Patriotic Front did not consent to the intervention by the French. The rebel forces did not trust France due to its close relationship in the past with the Hutu-dominated government, and they believed the French would impede an outright rebel victory. They requested the Security Council not to authorize the intervention and warned the French that they would treat them as invaders if they came into contact with them.

As was the case for Somalia, the intervention was expressly authorized by the Security Council. Even before the French intervention, the Security Council had declared the civil strife in Rwanda as constituting a threat to the peace, and had done so with emphasis more on the slaughter of Rwandan nationals than on their flight to neighboring countries. As also done in Somalia, the Security Council placed various conditions on the intervention regarding its operation and duration.

The international community provided little support for the French intervention; some of Rwanda's neighbors even denied French use of

---

death to end his efforts at reconciling with the the the R.P.F. (which would have undercut France's influence in Rwanda) and that the intervention might have served the function of retrieving incriminating evidence.

510. R. Bonner, *How Minority Tutsi Won the War*, N.Y. Times, Sept. 6, 1994, at A6.

bases in their countries for the staging of forces. While the French asserted that they had a "duty to intervene" in Rwanda due to the atrocities being committed, no other state asserted that such a duty existed. Indeed, many states (including the United States) not only refused to participate in the humanitarian intervention but declined to participate in the UN peacekeeping operation undertaken with the consent of the warring factions. No European nation offered to provide forces for the enhanced UN peacekeeping operation in Kigali, let alone to assist France in its humanitarian intervention.[511] Likewise, guidelines issued by the U.S. Clinton Administration during the crisis called for the deployment of U.S. forces for UN peacekeeping only when U.S. national interests were at stake,[512] and Rwanda did not present such a situation. When U.S. Ambassador to the United Nations Madeleine Albright testified before a House Foreign Affairs subcommittee on why the United States opposed the deployment of UN forces to Rwanda, no member of Congress challenged the position. From the U.S. Government perspective, neither the United States nor the United Nations had a legal or apparently even moral obligation to take such action.[513]

The difference between Western concern with the killing in Rwanda and the killing in Bosnia-Herzegovina has not gone unnoticed. One commentator observed:

. . . Bosnia has a vocal, articulate constituency. Rwanda has none. Bosnians are white, European, familiar. Rwandans are black, African, foreign. For Western intellectuals, Sarajevo evokes Spanish Civil War romance. Kigali evokes nothing more than Heart of Darkness nihilism.

It is a curious humanitarianism, however, that advocates humanitarian intervention on grounds of familiarity, race and romance. What counts is the scale of the violence and the suffering. Rwanda is the unequivocal case of genocide occurring in the world today, and genocide demands intervention.[514]

Of course, France did intervene in Rwanda, but its intervention may have been influenced by its sense of responsibility for arming and advising Hutu-dominated government military forces that proceeded to massacre

511. S. Kinzer, *European Leaders Reluctant to Send Troops to Rwanda*, N.Y. TIMES, May 25, 1994, at A1 (resistance to enhanced peacekeeping operation).

512. U.S. Policy on Reforming Multilateral Peace Operations, Presidential Decision Directive 25, signed May 3, 1994, *edited and reprinted in* 2 A.B.A. SEC. WORLD ORDER UNDER LAW REP. Spring/Summer 1994, at 9. For the White House announcement, see Statement by the Press Secretary on Reforming Multilateral Peace Operations, 30 WEEKLY COMP. PRES. DOC. 998 (May 5, 1994).

513. *See* D. Jehl, *U.S. is Showing a New Caution on U.N. Peacekeeping Missions*, N.Y. TIMES, May 18, 1994, at A1.

514. C. Krauthammer, *Stop the Genocide in Rwanda*, WASH. POST, May 27, 1994, at A25 (editorial).

or promote the massacre of hundreds of thousands of people. Thus it may be seen that wholly disinterested states perhaps feel no need to intervene in crises such as Rwanda, whereas those states that have some form of connection to the crisis (and as such may be perceived by one or more of the factions as other than neutral) do intervene.

Part of the success of the French operation was its recognition of the importance of *using* military force to achieve *limited* goals while at the same time acting as *impartially* as possible with respect to the local warring factions. France did not hesitate to use military force when it saw its objectives threatened; those objectives, however, were limited in geographic scope. The zone established by France primarily affected one side's ability to advance (the Tutsi rebels), but France refused the other side's efforts to use French forces for military gain. Indeed, when the French forces initially intervened, the Hutu rump government Foreign Minister noted: "We would like this operation to go beyond a humanitarian intervention. We would like to see the French force the R.P.F. to accept a cease-fire."[515] But France did not let itself be drawn into the conflict in such a manner, nor did it see the pursuit of a process of national reconciliation as one of its objectives. Instead, it used military force in a limited, effective fashion to address human rights concerns. The UNAMIR forces in Rwanda had no such mandate and, as such, their influence was far less than that of the French. As the French forces were withdrawing from Rwanda, the director of relief operations for Concern (an Irish relief organization) lamented the lack of respect for the authority of the UN forces: "The French were a protection force and drew the line, and everyone knew not to cross it. Everyone knows that the U.N. has no spine, that's the bottom line."[516]

At the same time, part of the weakness of the French operation arose from the desire by the intervening force (as also seen in Somalia) to minimize its involvement both in the scope of activities undertaken in the country and the duration of the operation. By establishing a safe zone in just the southwestern part of Rwanda and declaring that it would be present in Rwanda for only two months, the impact of the intervention on the protection of civilians and the creation of conditions for national reconciliation were significantly reduced. France left Rwanda at a time when millions of Rwandans remained displaced, when the newly recognized government had yet to establish effective mechanisms for peace and stability in Rwanda, and when the Hutu military forces and militant groups had fled into the mountains or to neighboring countries

515. Reuters, *supra* note 478.

516. R. Bonner, *As French Leave Rwanda, Critics Reverse Position*, N.Y. TIMES, Aug. 23, 1994, at A6 (comments of Mike McDonagh).

while remaining a potent guerilla threat. Not only was the humanitarian crisis far from over, but the French withdrawal itself fostered a greater sense of insecurity among a million-some Rwandans that had sought shelter in the French zone; it also prompted another wave of refugees into neighboring countries.

F. Haiti (1993–94)

1. Essential Facts

Haiti—by most estimates the poorest country in the Western hemisphere—was ruled dictatorially for decades during the twentieth century by the Duvalier family. When "Baby Doc" Duvalier was overthrown in 1986, the country stumbled toward a democracy midst widespread poverty. In December 1990, Jean-Bertrand Aristide became Haiti's President after an internationally monitored election in which he gained some 70 percent of the vote. A liberal Roman Catholic priest, Aristide had achieved a wide following among the Haitian poor through promises of radical reform. In advancing his program, however, Aristide failed to develop allies among the economic and military elites of the country; his fiery rhetoric about the "struggles between the classes" particularly alienated the Haitian business community. On September 30, 1991, less than eight months after Aristide assumed office, the Haitian military forces, led by Lieutenant General Raoul Cédras, and police forces, led by Lieutenant Colonel Michel François, overthrew Aristide and imposed military rule.

The overthrow of the democratically elected Aristide was denounced by the international community.[517] On October 8, the Organization of American States (OAS) recommended that its members adhere to a regional trade embargo on Haiti that, among other things, would cut off oil exports to Haiti from Colombia, Mexico, the United States, and Venezuela.[518] The effect of the embargo was to raise the price of food and fuel in Haiti, thereby wrecking the meager Haitian economy, yet without visibly shaking the resolve of Haiti's de facto leaders. Haitian military and police forces (along with plainclothed gunmen known as "attachés")

517. See G.A. Res. 46/7, U.N. GAOR, 46th Sess., Supp. No. 49, at 13, paras. 1–2, U.N. Doc. A/46/49 (1993), in which the General Assembly condemned the "attempted illegal replacement of the constitutional President of Haiti" and "affirm[ed] as unacceptable any entity resulting from that illegal situation."

518. For resolutions of the OAS Foreign Ministers, see OAS Doc. MRE/RES.1/91, OAS Doc. MRE/RES.2/91, OAS Doc. MRE/RES.3/92, and OAS Doc. MRE/RES.4/92; for resolutions and declarations of the OAS Permanent Council, see OAS Doc. CP/RES.594 (923/92), OAS Doc. CP/Dec.8 (927/93), OAS Doc. CP/Dec.9 (931/93), and OAS Doc. CP/Dec.10 (934/93).

proceeded to commit acts of violence and intimidation against those believed to be supporters of Aristide.

Political and economic conditions in Haiti grew so bad that in 1992, tens of thousands of Haitians tried to flee to the United States by boat, prompting U.S. President George Bush, in May 1992, to send U.S. Coast Guard cutters to interdict and forcibly repatriate the Haitian refugees.[519] Human rights groups estimated at that time that between 500 and 3,000 people had been killed by the military since the coup.[520]

After taking office in January 1993, President Bill Clinton maintained the Bush approach of forcibly repatriating the Haitians but also enlisted increased UN support for resolving the crisis in Haiti. Until this point, Haitian matters had been handled by the UN General Assembly, which authorized the deployment, in April 1993, of a joint UN-OAS mission to Haiti charged with monitoring human rights violations.[521] The Clinton Administration urged greater involvement by the Security Council, arguing that the risk of massive refugee exodus was a threat to the peace.[522] On February 26, the Security Council issued a statement noting with concern that the "humanitarian crises" in Haiti, including mass displacements of population, were "becoming or aggravating threats to international peace and security."[523] The UN-OAS special mediator, Dante Caputo, renewed his efforts to find common ground between Aristide and the military, but to no avail.

On June 7, 1993, Aristide's representative to the United Nations requested the imposition of a universal and mandatory UN trade embargo on Haiti.[524] On June 16, the Security Council unanimously passed Reso-

---

519. *See* Exec. Order No. 12807, 57 Fed. Reg. 23,133 (1992). The legality of the President's executive order was upheld by the U.S. Supreme Court in Sale v. Haitian Centers Council, Inc., 113 S. Ct. 2549 (1993).

520. H. French, *Haitian Military and Aristide Sign Pact to End Crisis*, N.Y. TIMES, July 4, 1993, sec. 1, at 1; *see also* D. Farah, *Repression Still Rife in Rural Haiti*, WASH. POST, May 30, 1993, at A37.

521. The mission was known as the International Civilian Mission (MICIVIH). *See* G.A. Res. 46/7, *supra* note 517; G.A. Res. 46/138, U.N. GAOR, 46th Sess., Supp. No. 49, at 211, U.N. Doc. A/46/49 (1992); G.A. Res. 47/20 A, U.N. GAOR, 47th Sess., Supp. No. 49, at 21, U.N. Doc. A/47/49 (1993); G.A. Res. 47/143, U.N. GAOR, 47th Sess., Supp. No. 49, at 219, U.N. Doc. A/47/49 (1993); and G.A. Res. 47/20 B, U.N. GAOR, 47th Sess., Supp. No. 49 (II) at 1, U.N. Doc. A/47/49 (Vol. II) (1994). The human rights mission was headquartered in Port-au-Prince, with 14 regional offices and suboffices across Haiti. U.N. Department of Public Information Reference Paper, *The United Nations and the Situation in Haiti* 4 (1995).

522. J. Preston, *U.N. Votes to Clamp Oil Embargo on Haiti*, WASH. POST, June 17, 1993, at A1.

523. *Note by the President of the Security Council*, U.N. Doc. S/25344 (1993).

524. *Letter Dated 7 June 1993 from the Permanent Representative of Haiti to the President of the Security Council*, U.N. Doc. S/25958 (1993).

lution 841 imposing economic sanctions on Haiti.[525] In determining that
the Haitian situation threatened international peace and security, the
Security Council recalled its February 26 statement and said that it was:

> *Deploring* the fact that, despite the efforts of the international community, the
> legitimate Government of President Jean-Bertrand Aristide has not been rein-
> stated; [and]
> *Concerned* that the persistence of this situation contributes to a climate of fear
> of persecution and economic dislocation, which could increase the number of
> Haitians seeking refuge in neighbouring Member States, and *convinced* that a
> reversal of this situation is needed to prevent its negative repercussions on the
> region.[526]

In its resolution, the Security Council noted the provisions of Chapter
VIII of the Charter and the need for effective cooperation between the
United Nations and regional organizations. The Security Council also
noted that the request by Aristide for economic sanctions, made in the
context of prior OAS and General Assembly action, created a "unique
and exceptional situation" warranting "extraordinary measures" by the
Security Council.

Resolution 841 provided that the sanctions would enter into force on
June 23 unless a diplomatic solution was reached. No such solution being reached, the sanctions were imposed. The sanctions were limited
in scope; they prevented the sale to Haiti of petroleum and petroleum
products (with the exception of small quantities for essential human
needs), arms of all types, military and police vehicles and equipment,
and associated spare parts. The sanctions also froze Haitian government
assets abroad. The importance of the sanctions was that, unlike the OAS
sanctions, they were global in nature, and thus Haiti was prevented from
importing oil from outside the OAS region. For once, it appeared economic sanctions were highly successful; shortly after they were imposed,
the Haitian military came to the negotiating table purportedly willing to
make significant concessions.

On July 3, 1993, an agreement was signed on Governors Island in New
York by Aristide and Cédras.[527] The agreement contained a ten-point
plan for resolving the Haitian crisis. Aristide would return to Haiti by
October 30, 1993, after steps were taken to reconstitute the Haitian Parliament and install a new Prime Minister picked by Aristide. Before Aristide returned, Cédras and his principal associates would step aside in

---

525. S.C. Res. 841, U.N. SCOR, 48th Sess., 3238th mtg. at 119, pmbl., U.N. Doc. S/INF/
49 (1994), *reprinted in* 3 WESTON, *supra* note 12, at III.T.3.

526. *Id.* pmbl.

527. J. Preston, *Aristide, Officer Sign Haiti Pact*, WASH. POST, July 4, 1993, at A1; the agreement is attached to *Report of the Secretary-General*, S/26063 (1993).

exchange for political amnesty for the crime of undertaking the coup, although this amnesty would not shield them from criminal charges brought for acts of violence against individuals. During the transition period, the United Nations would send experts to Haiti to begin training a new professional army and police force, removed from politics and disassociated from each other. An extensive international aid program would be instituted to rebuild the Haitian infrastructure and create thousands of jobs.

It appeared, initially, that the plan would work. The Haitian Parliament was reconstituted, and it confirmed a new Prime Minister picked by Aristide, Robert Malval. Once this occurred, and in accordance with the Governors Island Agreement, the United Nations and the OAS, on August 27, lifted their economic sanctions.[528] Thereafter, however, the agreement started to break down. Cédras' supporters began criticizing the anticipated deployment of foreign forces under UN auspices. In response, Malval was quoted as saying that the UN force would "enter as civilians on regular airline flights . . . they will not come in armed. The authorization for them to carry guns will come from the Haitian authorities."[529] In the following weeks, a campaign of murder and intimidation took place in the form of armed gangs terrorizing the population and attacking Aristide's allies.

Despite the violence, however, plans proceeded for the deployment of a UN Mission in Haiti (UNMIH), a 1,300-member multilateral force charged with helping to retrain Haiti's military and police forces and to rebuild the country's infrastructure.[530] On September 23, the Security Council authorized the dispatch of UNMIH,[531] and the United Nations received written commitments from Haitian military and port authorities that they would not obstruct the deployment. Nevertheless, on October 11, the military leaders, using armed civilian gangs and small boats, blocked the arrival at Port-au-Prince of a U.S. vessel, *USS Harlan County*, carrying 218 U.S. and Canadian troops.[532] Efforts to obtain assurances from the military that these forces would be protected and that the Haitian military still intended to step aside were unsuccessful. Since the U.S.

528. S.C. Res. 861, U.N. SCOR, 48th Sess., 3271st mtg., at 121, U.N. Doc. S/INF/49 (1994).

529. M. Tarr, *Embargoes on Haiti Set to Be Lifted*, WASH. POST, Aug. 27, 1993, at A27.

530. S.C. Res. 862, U.N. SCOR, 48th Sess., 3272d mtg. at 121, U.N. Doc. S/INF/49 (1994) (authorizing the dispatch of an advance team to prepare for UNMIH); *Report of the Secretary-General*, U.N. Doc. S/26480 (1993).

531. S.C. Res. 867, U.N. SCOR, 48th Sess., 3282d mtg. at 122, U.N. Doc. S/INF/49 (1994).

532. D. Farah & M. Tarr, *Haitians Block U.S. Troop Arrival*, WASH. POST, Oct. 12, 1993, at A1.

vessel had no combat capability and the forces were not equipped to handle violence, President Clinton on October 12 ordered the ship returned to the United States and cancelled the voyage of another.[533] The withdrawal of the vessel was perceived as a major victory for the Haitian military and engendered controversy at the United Nations since it was done by the United States without consultation.[534]

The violence in Haiti continued. On October 14, paramilitary forces in Haiti assassinated Guy Malary, Aristide's Minister of Justice. The Security Council voted unanimously on October 13 to reimpose the limited economic sanctions,[535] a step which took effect on October 19. In the resolution, the Security Council declared that it was acting under Chapter VII of the Charter and that the failure of the Haitian military forces to "fulfil obligations under the [Governors Island] Agreement constitutes a threat to peace and security in the region." In addition, on October 16, the Security Council voted unanimously to enforce the sanctions by calling on states:

acting nationally or through regional agencies or arrangements, cooperating with the legitimate Government of Haiti, to use such measures commensurate with the specific circumstances as may be necessary under the authority of the Council to ensure strict implementation of [the sanctions], and in particular to halt inbound maritime shipping as necessary in order to inspect and verify their cargos and destinations.[536]

The Security Council reaffirmed that, "in these unique and exceptional circumstances," the failure of the Haitian military to abide by the Governors Island Agreement constituted a threat to peace and security in the region and declared that it was acting under Chapter VII and Chapter VIII. Aristide's representative to the United Nations supported the measure, noting that strict application of the sanctions would help "put an end to the suffering of a people that has already made so many sacrifices for the sake of democracy."[537] Many other Security Council members also spoke in favor of restoring democracy to Haiti through military enforcement of the sanctions.

To that end, President Clinton and Canadian Prime Minister Kim Campbell ordered naval warships to patrol the waters off Haiti. In his

533. D. Farah & R. Marcus, *U.S. Pulls Troop Ship Back from Haiti*, WASH. POST, Oct. 13, 1993, at A1.

534. J. Preston, *Haiti Embargo Revived*, WASH. POST, Oct. 14, 1993, at A1.

535. S.C. Res. 873, U.N. SCOR, 48th Sess., 3291st mtg. at 125, U.N. Doc. S/INF/49 (1994). For the Security Council debate, *see* U.N. SCOR, 48th Sess., 3291st mtg., U.N. Doc. S/PV.3291 (1993).

536. S.C. Res. 875, U.N. SCOR, 48th Sess., 3293d mtg. at 125, para. 1, U.N. Doc. S/INF/49 (1994).

537. U.N. SCOR, 48th Sess., 3293d mtg. at 4, U.N. Doc. S/PV.3293 (1993).

news conference, President Clinton stated that this enforcement of economic sanctions was "to ensure the safety of the Americans in Haiti and to press for the restoration of democracy there through the strongest possible enforcement of these sanctions."[538] Ultimately, about a dozen ships from Argentina, Canada, France, and the United States engaged in the search-and-seizure operation, and in some cases fired warning shots against suspected vessels.[539] Between October 1993 and May 1994, the U.S. Navy queried 7,585 vessels and boarded 1,103, of which it diverted 101 and cleared 1,002.[540] The flag states of the diverted vessels were notified through diplomatic channels, with a request that the flag country undertake an investigation and other appropriate action.

Unlike the cases of Liberia, Iraq, Bosnia-Herzegovina, Somalia, and Rwanda, thousands of Haitians were not dying daily as a result of a breakdown in civil order or the repression of their government. Human rights abuses certainly occurred under the Haitian military regime; the joint UN-OAS mission monitoring human rights in Haiti filed periodic reports recounting repression inflicted on Aristide's followers in Haiti, including arbitrary arrests, abductions, and dozens of politically motivated rapes.[541] The overriding concern of the international community, however, seemed to turn more on the fact that a democratically elected leader had been ousted and replaced by a militant group bent on consolidating and maintaining their power.

Ironically, the sanctions themselves, over several months, imposed considerable hardship on the people of Haiti, resulting in (or at least aggravating) malnutrition, deteriorating health care, and hunger that in some areas approached starvation. One study found that about 1,000 more children were dying monthly with the sanctions in place than had been previously the case, and that the sanctions helped create 100,000 new cases of moderate or severe malnutrition.[542] While the sanctions did not prohibit shipment of humanitarian supplies to Haiti, they nevertheless had concomitant effects on the ability of hospitals and relief organi-

538. R. Marcus & B. Gellman, *U.S. Sends Ships to Enforce Embargo*, WASH. POST, Oct. 16, 1993, at A1.

539. *See* J. Preston, *U.N. Widens Sanctions Against Haiti*, WASH. POST, May 7, 1994, at A1; T. Lippman, *U.S. Navy Ships Fire Warning Shots off Haiti*, WASH. POST, May 25, 1994, at A28; T. Lippman, *U.S. Patrol Craft to Tighten Haiti Embargo*, WASH. POST, May 27, 1994, at A31.

540. J. Harris, *From Sailing 7 Seas to Sealing 1 Coastline*, WASH. POST, June 19, 1994, at A23.

541. *See Reports of the International Civilian Mission to Haiti, reprinted in Notes by the Secretary-General*, Annex, U.N. Docs. A/47/960 (1993), A/48/532 & Add.2 (1993); *Report of the Secretary-General*, U.N. Doc. A/48/931 (1994); *Report of the Secretary-General*, U.N. Doc. S/1994/742 (1994); *Report of the Secretary-General*, U.N. Doc. S/1994/765 (1994); *see also* D. Farah, *Aristide's Backers: Latest Plan Falls Short*, WASH. POST, May 2, 1994, at A1; J. Reitman, *Political Repression by Rape Increasing in Haiti*, WASH. POST, July 22, 1994, at A10.

542. D. Farah, *Rural Haitians Reeling*, WASH. POST, Nov. 27, 1993, at A1.

zations to function (e.g., arising from a lack of fuel); and the de facto Haitian leaders at times withheld such supplies to place pressure on the international community.[543] At the same time, Haiti's military rulers and their wealthy backers were avoiding significant hardship by smuggling sufficient supplies for themselves from the neighboring Dominican Republic.

Nevertheless, the United States sought—and on May 6, 1994, the Security Council approved—more comprehensive economic sanctions designed to affect Haiti's ruling elite. Taking effect May 20,[544] the expanded sanctions retained exemptions for food, medicine, and cooking fuel but banned private flights in and out of Haiti except for those delivering humanitarian aid.[545] All military and police officers, and their civilian supporters, were barred from traveling outside Haiti, and states were "urged" to freeze Haitian assets.[546] The prohibitions on travel out of the country became so comprehensive that even those persons who would have been accepted as political refugees by the United States could not leave Haiti.[547] This step was taken with the knowledge that if sanctions did not work, the only alternatives left for the United Nations would be to authorize a military intervention or give up.

In May 1994, U.S. officials began hinting at the possibility of a U.S. military intervention in Haiti. On May 20, U.S. President Clinton himself stated at a White House press conference that he was considering military intervention in Haiti.[548] From the President's remarks, it was not clear whether he meant intervention only under the authority of the United Nations or the OAS, or whether the United States would proceed unilaterally. He listed six reasons for why it would be in the U.S. interest to intervene: (1) Haiti was "in our backyard"; (2) Haiti had been used as a staging area for drug shipments bound for the United States; (3) Haiti was the only Western Hemisphere country where military leaders had seized power from an elected leader; (4) several thousand U.S. nationals live in Haiti; (5) one million Haitian-Americans live in the United States;

543. *See, e.g.*, R. Bragg, *Haiti Rulers Hold Relief Fuel, Endangering Lives*, N.Y. TIMES, Aug. 22, 1994, at A3.

544. S.C. Res. 917, U.N. SCOR, 49th Sess., 3376th mtg., U.N. Doc. S/RES/917 (1994).

545. The United States and Canada subsequently banned all commercial flights and virtually all financial transactions between their countries and Haiti. S. Greenhouse, *U.S. Bars Flights and Money Deals with the Haitians*, N.Y. TIMES, June 11, 1994, sec. 1, at 1.

546. This ban affected approximately 600 persons with assets in the United States. *See* J. Preston, *supra* note 539; A. Devroy & D. Williams, *U.S. Freezes Haitian Assets to Put Pressure on Leaders*, WASH. POST, June 23, 1994, at A18.

547. R. Bragg, *Cleared by the U.S., 800 Are Trapped in Haiti*, N.Y. TIMES, Aug. 15, 1994, at A1.

548. The President's News Conference with Prime Minister Rao of India, 30 WEEKLY COMP. PRES. DOC. 1117, 1122 (May 19, 1994); D. Jehl, *Clinton Spells Out Reasons He Might Use Force in Haiti*, N.Y. TIMES, May 20, 1994, at A1.

and (6) continued military rule could result in massive refugee flows to the United States. The President's statement sought to clarify for the U.S. public why it was important to restore democracy in Haiti; at the same time, it served as a warning to the Haitian military rulers that a failure to step down might be met with military intervention.[549] The primary emphasis of the statement was on the restoration of democracy; human rights abuses in Haiti were not on the President's list of reasons why the United States might militarily intervene in Haiti.

The prospect of U.S. military action met with mixed reaction in the United States.[550] Outside the United States, several Latin American states publicly opposed the use of force in Haiti. When the OAS considered a resolution condemning Haiti's military, language proposed by Antigua and Argentina noting the option of using military force was dropped due to the strong opposition of Brazil, Ecuador, Peru, and Uruguay. Canada, Cuba, and Mexico also publicly stated their opposition to the use of force.[551] On the other hand, U.S. officials claimed that in private discussions a majority of Western Hemisphere states said they were prepared to support military intervention in Haiti if the sanctions failed.[552]

The attitude of exiled Haitian President Aristide regarding military intervention was unclear. On the one hand, Aristide asserted that under the Haitian Constitution he was barred from formally inviting foreign military intervention in Haiti. Yet on June 3, 1994, Aristide told the *New York Times* that the United States should be "moving toward a surgical action" to remove Haiti's military leadership and asked why the United States could not act in Haiti as it did in Panama in 1989.[553] This was the strongest statement made by Aristide inviting military intervention, in light of his concern regarding the Haitian Constitution.

Haitian refugees continued to stream out of Haiti on boats in an effort to reach the United States. The United States continued to turn back the

549. *See also* M. Gordon, *Weighing Options, U.S. Aides Assess Invasion of Haiti*, N.Y. TIMES, May 30, 1994, sec. 1, at 1.

550. *Compare* J. Kerry, *Make Haiti's Thugs Tremble*, N.Y. TIMES, May 16, 1994, A17 (editorial by U.S. Senator advocating a U.S.-led international force) *with* J. Bolton, *The Case for Not Invading Haiti*, WASH. POST, May 17, 1994, at A17 (former Assistant Secretary of State opposing such intervention).

551. H. French, *U.S. Hint of Force to End Haiti Crisis Draws Opposition*, N.Y. TIMES, May 13, 1994, at A1; H. French, *Hands Off Haiti, Say Dominicans*, N.Y. TIMES, May 15, 1994, sec. 1, at 9 (detailing Dominican opposition to intervention).

552. S. Greenhouse, *A Haiti Invasion Wins Hemispheric Support*, WASH. POST, June 13, 1994, at A10.

553. H. French, *Doubting Sanctions, Aristide Urges U.S. Action on Haiti*, N.Y. TIMES, June 3, 1994, at A3; *see also* H. French, *U.S. Hint of Force to End Haiti Crisis Draws Opposition, supra* note 551 (reporting that while stating that the Constitution bars him from requesting intervention, Aristide also said that the Haitian people would welcome any effort to rescue them from military rule).

boats. In early July 1994, the Clinton Administration embarked on a policy of establishing temporary refugee camps in neighboring Caribbean countries, where Haitian refugees picked up at sea would be taken. While the negotiation of agreements with various countries to this end met with mixed success (some 14,000 were taken to the U.S. base at Guantánamo Bay, Cuba), the approach had a real effect in discouraging Haitians from fleeing Haiti.

On July 11, the government established by the Haitian military authorities ordered the joint UN-OAS mission monitoring human rights in Haiti to leave within two days because it was involved in "gratuitous accusations which put in peril the credibility of the Government and the country's institutions."[554] Shortly thereafter, the Clinton Administration began seeking explicit UN authorization for military intervention in Haiti. Senior Administration officials were reported as saying that President Clinton was uneasy about taking unilateral military action, even though the intervention was within the Western Hemisphere.[555] Certain Latin American states on the Security Council reportedly insisted that Aristide request such intervention. In a letter dated July 29, 1994, to Secretary-General Boutros Boutros-Ghali, Aristide called for the international community "to take swift and determined action" to help Haiti, but stopped short of expressly calling for military intervention.[556]

On July 31, by Resolution 940, the Security Council authorized military intervention in Haiti.[557] Resolution 940 states, inter alia:

Condemning the continuing disregard of [the agreements to transition back to democracy] by the illegal de facto regime, and the regime's refusal to cooperate with efforts by the United Nations and the Organization of American States (O.A.S.) to bring about their implementation,

Gravely concerned by the significant further deterioration of the humanitarian situation in Haiti, in particular the continuing escalation by the illegal de facto regime of systematic violations of civil liberties, the desperate plight of Haitian refugees and the recent expulsion of the staff of the International Civilian Mission, which was condemned in its Presidential statement of 12 July 1994, . . .

Taking note of the letter dated 29 July 1994 from the legitimately elected President of Haiti and the letter dated 30 July 1994 from the Permanent Representative of Haiti to the United Nations, . . .

Reaffirming that the goal of the international community remains the restoration of democracy in Haiti and the prompt return of the legitimately elected

554. G. Pierre-Pierre, *Haiti Orders Out Foreign Monitors of Human Rights*, N.Y. TIMES, July 12, 1994, at A1.

555. D. Jehl, *Clinton Seeks U.N. Approval of Any Plan to Invade Haiti*, N.Y. TIMES, July 22, 1994, at A1.

556. *Letter Dated 29 July 1994 from Haiti to the Secretary-General*, Annex, U.N. Doc. S/1994/905 (1994); *see also Letter Dated 30 July 1994 from Haiti to the President of the Security Council*, U.N. Doc. S/1994/910 (1994).

557. S.C. Res. 940, U.N. SCOR, 49th Sess., 3134th mtg., U.N. Doc. S/RES/940 (1994).

President, Jean-Bertrand Aristide, within the framework of the Governors Island Agreement, . . .

Determining that the situation in Haiti continues to be a threat to peace and security in the region, . . .

4. *Acting* under Chapter VII of the Charter of the United Nations, authorizes Member States to form a multinational force under unified command and control and, in this framework, to use all necessary means to facilitate the departure from Haiti of the military leadership, consistent with the Governors Island Agreement, the prompt return of the legitimately elected President and the restoration of the legitimate authorities of the Government of Haiti, and to establish and maintain a secure and stable environment that will permit implementation of the Governors Island Agreement, on the understanding that the cost of implementing this temporary operation will be borne by Member States;

5. *Approves* the establishment upon the adoption of this resolution, of an advance team of UNMIH of not more than sixty personnel, including a group of observers, to establish the appropriate means of coordination with the multinational force, to carry out the monitoring of the operations of the multinational force and other functions described in paragraph 23 of the report of the Secretary-General of 15 July 1994, and to assess requirements and to prepare for the deployment of UNMIH upon completion of the mission of the multinational force; . . .

8. *Decides* that the multinational force will terminate its mission and UNMIH will assume the full range of its functions described in paragraph 9 below when a secure and stable environment has been established and UNMIH has adequate force capability and structure to assume the full range of its functions; the determination will be made by the Security Council, taking into account recommendations from the Member States of the Multinational Force, which are based on the assessment of the commander of the multinational force and from the Secretary-General;

9. *Decides* to revise and extend the mandate of the United Nations Mission in Haiti for a period of six months to assist the democratic Government of Haiti in fulfilling its responsibilities in connection with:

a. sustaining the secure and stable environment established during the multinational phase and protecting international personnel and key installations; and

b. the professionalization of the Haitian armed forces and the creation of a separate police force;

10. *Requests* also that UNMIH assist the legitimate constitutional authorities of Haiti in establishing an environment conducive to the organization of free and fair elections to be called by those authorities and, when requested by them, monitored by the United Nations, in coordination with the Organization of American States (O.A.S.); . . .

The vote on the resolution was twelve to zero, with abstentions by Brazil and China. During the Security Council debate, those countries favoring intervention recounted the human rights violations in Haiti and the need to restore democracy. China asserted that the resolution set a "dangerous precedent." Several Latin American countries not represented on the Security Council (Cuba, Mexico, and Uruguay) were permitted to participate in the debate and expressed strong reservations about military intervention.

When asked at a press conference on August 4 why he sought approval for military intervention from the United Nations, President Clinton replied:

[L]et me say I think all Americans should be pleased that the United Nations stated, with a strong firm voice that includes many voices from our own area, that we should keep on the table the option of forceably [sic] removing the dictators who have usurped power in Haiti and who have trampled human rights and murdered innocent people. Let me remind you all of what our interests are there: We have Americans living and working there, several thousand of them. We have a million Haitian-Americans in this country who have family and friends there. We have an interest in promoting democracy in our hemisphere. We have an interest in stabilizing those democracies that are in our hemisphere.

For the first time ever, 33 of the 35 nations in the Caribbean and Central and South America are governed by popularly elected leaders but many of those democracies are fragile. As we look ahead to the next century, we need a strong and democratic Latin America and Central America and Caribbean with which to trade and grow.

So those are our fundamental interests.[558]

Thus President Clinton avoided commenting on why UN approval was sought, and instead focused on the fact of UN support and why U.S. interests were at stake.

After the passage of Resolution 940, the United States undertook an extensive public relations campaign in which it provided extensive details about an impending invasion, in the hope of frightening the Haitian military authorities into stepping down. In late August, the United States obtained commitments from Antigua and Barbuda, Barbados, Belize, Jamaica, and Trinidad and Tobago to provide a nominal number (266) of noncombatant forces to be used several days after an invasion by some 10,000 to 20,000 U.S. troops; by mid-September, similar pledges were received from twelve other nations, for a total of 1,500 troops.[559] At the same time, the thirteen-member Caribbean Community and Common Market indicated its support for an invasion of Haiti as a last resort,[560] while the United States announced the dispatch of twelve large transport ships to waters off the coast of Haiti laden with weapons and supplies for Army and Marine forces. It also announced the deployment to the area of the aircraft carriers *USS America* and *USS Eisenhower* for use in helicop-

558. News Conference of President Clinton (Aug. 3, 1994), *reprinted in* N.Y. TIMES, Aug. 4, 1994, at A16.

559. E. Schmitt, *U.S. Backed on Possible Invasion of Haiti*, N.Y. TIMES, Aug. 31, 1994, at A8; R. Smith, *Multinational Forces Fly to Puerto Rico for Peacekeeping Training*, WASH. POST, Sept. 13, 1994, at A16.

560. E. Schmitt, *U.S. Pessimistic About Avoiding Invasion of Haiti*, N.Y. TIMES, Sept. 4, 1994, sec. 1, at 1.

ter operations.[561] U.S. military planes dropped leaflets over Haiti with a drawing of Aristide and a message in Creole promoting his return.[562]

Faced with significant opposition to an invasion in the U.S. Congress and among the U.S. public, President Clinton explained, on September 15, in a nationally televised address why "the United States is leading the international effort to restore democratic government in Haiti." He stated:

> [T]he United States must protect interests, to stop the brutal atrocities that threaten tens of thousands of Haitians, to secure our borders, and to preserve stability and promote democracy in our hemisphere, and to uphold the reliability of the commitments we make and the commitments others make to us.[563]

For the first time, President Clinton raised and emphasized the human rights violations committed by the military and police regime in Haiti. He graphically asserted that the regime had conducted a "reign of terror" by raping the wives and daughters of political dissidents, killing priests, slaying orphans (because Aristide once ran an orphanage), leaving body parts of those slain as warnings to others, and forcing children "to watch as their mothers' faces are slashed with machetes." President Clinton called upon the Haitian authorities to "[l]eave now or we will force you from power."

With the invasion apparently imminent, President Clinton dispatched to Haiti a U.S. delegation lead by former U.S. President Jimmy Carter with a mandate to negotiate the manner in which the military authorities would leave power.[564] The Carter delegation met with the Haitian military authorities on September 17–18 and, in a dramatic breakthrough, reached an agreement shortly after President Clinton ordered the commencement of the invasion; sixty-one U.S. Army transport and refueling planes launched from North Carolina had to be recalled. The agreement,[565] signed by former President Carter and the military-appointed President of Haiti, Émile Jonassaint, read as follows:

561. M. Gordon, *U.S. Hopes Talk of War Forces Out Haiti Army*, N.Y. TIMES, Sept. 10, 1994, sec. 1, at 4; J. Harris, *USS Eisenhower to Sail Toward Haiti Next Week*, WASH. POST, Sept. 10, 1994, at A19; M. Gordon, *Top U.S. Officials Outline Strategy for Haiti Invasion*, N.Y. TIMES, Sept. 14, 1994, at A1.

562. H. Dewar & A. Devroy, *Clinton, in Talk Thursday, to Explain Policy on Haiti*, WASH. POST, Sept. 14, 1994, at A1. In English, the leaflets read: "The sun of democracy, the light of justice, the warmth of reconciliation. With the return of President Aristide."

563. Speech of President Clinton (Sept. 15, 1994), *reprinted in* N.Y. TIMES, Sept. 16, 1994, at A10 *and* WASH. POST, Sept. 16, 1994, at A31.

564. R. Marcus & A. Devroy, *Clinton Sends Carter, Powell and Nunn to Haiti*, WASH. POST, Sept. 17, 1994, at A1.

565. Text of Agreement, Sept. 18, 1994, *reprinted in* WASH. POST, Sept. 19, 1994, at A17 *and* N.Y. TIMES, Sept. 20, 1994, at A12.

1. The purpose of this agreement is to foster peace in Haiti, to avoid violence and bloodshed, to promote freedom and democracy, and to forge a sustained and mutually beneficial relationship between the governments, people, and institutions of Haiti and the United States.

2. To implement this agreement, the Haitian military and police forces will work in close cooperation with the U.S. Military Mission. This cooperation, conducted with mutual respect, will last during the transitional period required for insuring vital institutions of the country.

3. In order to personally contribute to the success of this agreement, certain military officers of the Haitian armed forces are willing to consent to an early and honorable retirement in accordance with U.N. Resolutions 917 and 940 when a general amnesty will be voted into law by the Haitian Parliament, or Oct. 15, 1994, whichever is earlier. The parties to this agreement pledge to work with the Haitian Parliament to expedite this action. Their successors will be named according to the Haitian Constitution and existing military law.

4. The military activities of the U.S. Military Mission will be coordinated with the Haitian military high command.

5. The economic embargo and the economic sanctions will be lifted without delay in accordance with relevant U.N. Resolutions and the need of the Haitian people will be met as quickly as possible.

6. The forthcoming legislative elections will be held in a free and democratic manner.

7. It is understood that the above agreement is conditioned on the approval of the civilian governments of the United States and Haiti.

(The "certain military officers" were understood to be Lieutenant General Cédras, his chief of staff, Brigadier General Philippe Biamby, and Lieutenant Colonel François.) The next morning, September 19, the first 3,000 of what would become nearly 20,000 (primarily U.S.) forces landed in Haiti without opposition and took control of its airfields and ports.[566]

Fears that there would be riots by the Haitian poor against Haitian police and military authorities proved unfounded, but the cooperative nature of the intervention led to some misgivings. Haitian police—on hand to maintain crowd control of Haitians celebrating the arrival of U.S. forces—in several instances beat Haitian civilians, causing at least one death by clubbing.[567] Additionally, pro-military gunmen on several occasions fired upon Haitian civilians celebrating the impending return of President Aristide.[568] Instructions to U.S. forces were therefore modi-

566. L. Rohter, *3,000 U.S. Troops Land Without Opposition and Take Over Ports and Airfields in Haiti*, N.Y. TIMES, Sept. 20, 1994, at A1; D. Farah, *U.S. Troops Find Haiti Calm, Military Cooperative*, WASH. POST, Sept. 20, 1994, at A1. U.S. forces suffered their first death only four months later, when a U.S. soldier was killed after a gun battle near a road checkpoint. B. Graham, *U.S. Soldier Is Killed in Haiti Battle*, WASH. POST, Jan. 13, 1995, at A25.

567. *See, e.g.*, J. Kifner, *Haitian Police Crush Rally as American Troops Watch*, N.Y. TIMES, Sept. 21, 1994, at A1.

568. *See, e.g.*, W. Booth & D. Farah, *Haiti on Knife's Edge; At Least 5 Killed in Clashes as GIs Stand Aside*, WASH. POST, Oct. 1, 1994, at A1.

fied to allow action to prevent such abuses, and U.S. forces proceeded to dismantle certain key Haitian military and police units of their weapons and authority[569] as well as those of the paramilitary "attachés."[570] On September 24, U.S. marines shot and killed nine armed Haitians outside a Cap-Haitien police station, apparently after one of the Haitians pointed a weapon at the Marines.[571] This prompted hundreds of unarmed Haitians two days later to storm Cap-Hatien police stations and army barracks to commandeer weapons, which were then turned over to U.S. Marines.[572]

On September 29, the Haitian Parliament convened in a special session to consider the amnesty to be provided for the military and police authorities. After a week of discussion, a law was passed allowing President Aristide to provide amnesty for "political" acts but not for crimes under the Haitian penal code, such as murder, rape, and corruption.[573] On October 4, Lieutenant Colonel François left Haiti for the Dominican Republic.[574] On October 10, Lieutenant General Cédras and Brigadier General Biamby surrendered their commands, and on October 13 fled to Panama.[575]

On October 15, President Aristide returned to Haiti after three years in exile.[576] While the road to recovery for Haiti would be a long one, the UN and OAS economic sanctions were lifted,[577] extensive relief aid began flowing into Haiti, and plans commenced for the reconstruction of civilian rule through new parliamentary elections. The United States and

569. J. Kifner, *U.S. Soldiers Begin Dismantling Elite Haitian Military Company*, N.Y. TIMES, Sept. 23, 1994, at A1; D. Farah, *Haitians Cheer U.S. Takeover of Police Station*, WASH. POST, Sept. 27, 1994, at A1.

570. B. Graham, *U.S. Troops to Disarm Haitians; Soldiers Plan to Target Paramilitary "Attaches" Tied to Cedras Regime*, WASH. POST, Oct. 2, 1994, at A1; D. Farah, *GIs Arrest Members of Notorious Haitian Militia*, WASH. POST, Oct. 4, 1994, at A1.

571. W. Booth & J. Rupert, *Marines Kill 9 Haitians in Battle at Police Station*, WASH. POST, Sept. 25, 1994, at A1.

572. W. Booth, *Crowds Ransack Barracks in Haitian City; Weapons Turned Over to American Marines*, WASH. POST, Sept. 26, 1994, at A1.

573. W. Booth, *Haiti Completes Limited Amnesty Bill for Aristide to Extend to Military*, WASH. POST, Oct. 8, 1994, at A10.

574. W. Booth & D. Farah, *Feared Police Chief Quits, Flees Haiti*, WASH. POST, Oct. 5, 1994, at A1.

575. D. Farah & W. Booth, *Last Two of Haiti's Military Triumvirate Quit*, WASH. POST, Oct. 11, 1994, at A1; J. Kifner, *Not Looking Back, Cédras Flies to Panama Exile*, N.Y. TIMES, Oct. 14, 1994, at A6.

576. D. Farah, *Aristide Returns to Acclaim in Haiti*, WASH. POST, Oct. 16, 1994, at A1. The Security Council welcomed the return of President Aristide, commended the efforts of the multinational force deployed to Haiti, and noted that UNMIH would replace that force once a secure and stable environment had been established. S.C. Res. 948, U.N. SCOR, 49th Sess., 3437th mtg., U.N. Doc. S/RES/948 (1994).

577. S.C. Res. 944, U.N. SCOR, 49th Sess., 3430th mtg., U.N. Doc. S/RES/944 (1994).

other states undertook extensive efforts to train a new, corruption-free police force that would be supportive of civilian rule.[578] At the same time, the United States began repatriating Haitian refugees whether they wished to return to Haiti or not.[579]

The United States saw its mission in Haiti as narrowly defined: to return Aristide to power and to give Haitians a short period of time to begin rebuilding their nation. With memories of Somalia still fresh, the United States did not engage in systematic disarming of Haitain civilian paramilitary groups, or pursue extensive infrastructure rebuilding, or anything else that suggested "nation-building."[580] So in January 1995, the Security Council determined that Haiti had become a sufficiently secure and stable environment to allow a transfer of military authority from the multinational, U.S.-led forces to UNMIH by the end of March.[581] To that end, UNMIH recruited additional military contingents, civilian police, and other civilian personnel to assume the responsibilities that previously had been envisaged for it after the signing of the Governors Island Agreement, as well as those envisaged after the authorization for a multinational force to intervene.[582] The augmented UNMIH consisted of approximately 6,000 forces under UN command, about 2,400 of which were from the United States, plus some 570 civilian police forces and 450 civilian staff. At the insistence of the United States, the military component of the force was commanded by a U.S. general officer for the first time in the history of UN forces. The expectation was that UNMIH would remain in Haiti until the inauguration of a successor to Aristide in February 1996.[583]

Conditions in Haiti, of course, were far from stable throughout 1995. Crime and political tensions were high and economic conditions poor.[584] Nevertheless, the largest election in the history of Haiti, from parliamen-

---

578. *Haiti Pins Future on Police, Courts*, WASH. POST, Feb. 1, 1995, at A15.

579. L. Rohter, *U.S. Starts the Return of Haitians from Guantanamo*, N.Y. TIMES, Jan. 7, 1995, sec. 1, at 3.

580. D. Farah, *To Clinton, Mission Accomplished; to Haitians, Hopes Dashed*, WASH. POST, Mar. 30, 1995, at A1. The U.S. Embassy spokesman in Haiti stated:

> We learned a lot from Somalia. . . . That includes not getting sucked into a morass of things better left to an internal police structures (sic). . . . We took a narrow view of creating a "safe and secure environment." We were determined that what went wrong in Somalia would not go wrong here.

Id.

581. S.C. Res. 975, U.N. SCOR, 50th Sess., 3496th mtg., U.N. Doc. S/RES/975 (1995).

582. S.C. Res. 867, *supra* note 531; S.C. Res. 940, *supra* note 557.

583. L. Rohter, *U.N. Force Takes Up Duties in Haiti*, N.Y. TIMES, Apr. 2, 1995, sec. 1, at 14.

584. L. Rohter, *Many Haitians Fearful Despite U.N. Presence*, N.Y. TIMES, Apr. 3, 1995, at A8.

tary posts down to municipal council posts, were held in June 1995,[585] and Haiti appeared back on track as a democratic state.

2. Assessment of the Intervention

Three of the actions taken by the international community fall within the scope of "intervention" as defined in this study. First, the imposition of comprehensive economic sanctions on Haiti, already the poorest state in the Western Hemisphere, was a highly coercive step that sought to dictate a political result. Second, the deployment of warships off the coast of Haiti beginning in October 1993 to enforce those sanctions was a use of force by states against Haiti that would normally implicate Article 2(4) of the UN Charter, and thus constitutes a form of intervention. Blockade of the ports of a foreign state was considered an act of war under pre-Charter customary international law and, in "Charter" language, constitutes a use of force against the political sovereignty of a state. Third, the statements made by U.S. President Clinton and his representatives in the beginning of May 1994, and leading up to the visit of the Carter delegation, regarding a military invasion of Haiti constituted a threat of force by the United States that implicates Article 2(4) of the Charter as well. That threat ultimately resulted in the capitulation of the Haitian military and police authorities to the deployment of thousands of U.S. forces to Haiti and the restoration of President Aristide.

The reasons stated for the economic sanctions, the naval blockade, and the threat of military invasion were not self-defense. The members of the Security Council generally agreed that these steps were all necessary for alleviating the violence taking place in Haiti and restoring Haiti's democratically elected President. They believed that Haiti's best chance for future development rested in a return to democracy. In particular, the United States, the driving force behind the Security Council's resolutions, saw itself as committed to resisting threats to democracy in its hemisphere.[586] More parochially, the United States also wanted to avoid a flood of illegal immigrants to its shores provoked by continued repression and poverty in Haiti. There was also considerable domestic pressure on the U.S. Administration, such as from the Congressional Black Caucus, to take meaningful action on Haiti as a showing of U.S. moral leadership on racial matters.[587]

While President Clinton also mentioned stemming the drug trade, the presence of U.S. nationals in Haiti, and a desire to enhance economic

585. L. Rohter, *Testing Fragile Democracy, Haiti Votes*, N.Y. TIMES, June 26, 1995, sec. 1, at 1.

586. J. Goshko, *Pullback Is New Setback for Clinton*, WASH. POST, Oct. 14, 1993, at A24.

587. J. Goshko & B. Graham, *Escalating U.S. Pressure on Haiti Is a Two-Edged Sword*, WASH. POST, June 12, 1994, at A9.

trade as reasons for U.S. action with respect to Haiti, these concerns do not seem to have played much of a role in the U.S. involvement in the crisis. Even with respect to human rights concerns, President Clinton did not emphasize human rights atrocities until the eve of the planned invasion; prior to that time he avoided focusing attention on the human rights violations in Haiti, perhaps partly out of a concern that it would highlight the United States' own unwillingness to allow those fleeing Haiti to enter the United States. Ultimately, in his speech to the nation shortly before the planned invasion, President Clinton did emphasize the human rights violations as one of several reasons why the United States must act to "restore democratic government to Haiti."

Overall, it would appear that the actions of the United Nations and of the United States were driven partly by a concern with human rights atrocities and partly by a concern for refugee flows, but more dominantly driven by a desire to restore democracy to Haiti (which would have, of course, a consequential effect in stemming the human rights atrocities and refugee flows). The United States even dubbed the military blockade of Haiti "Operation Support Democracy."[588] While this form of human rights deprivation is considerably different from those seen in the other case studies examined in this chapter, it nevertheless falls within a broad definition of "widespread and severe deprivation of human rights." In sum, the imposition of economic sanctions, the military blockade, and the threat of military invasion in Haiti constitute examples of humanitarian intervention.

These steps by the international community were taken without the authorization of the military and civilian authorities in de facto control of Haiti, as those authorities opposed such actions even though ultimately they accepted the deployment of military forces to Haiti in September 1994 as inevitable and even though they cooperated with those forces when they arrived. As such, under the traditional rule of international law, one cannot find authorization for the foreign intervention based on the consent of the local governing authorities. Haiti, however, presented a unique situation from the other case studies in this chapter, having an internationally recognized, democratically elected head of government, President Aristide, who essentially authorized these steps in exile. President Aristide explicitly favored the economic embargo and the enforcement of that embargo and also, at least impliedly, the threat of military invasion (although the evidence for the latter is mixed because Aristide felt that politically he could not publicly request an invasion). Arguably, President Aristide's consent alone was not regarded by the United States or the other members of the United Nations as a suffi-

588. Harris, *supra* note 540.

cient legal basis for these actions; rather, states treated the steps as "enforcement action" under Chapter VII undertaken to address a threat to international peace. Yet the relevant Security Council resolutions[589] each take note of requests from President Aristide or his representative, and the invocation of Chapter VII can be explained as a necessary element for undertaking steps that all UN member states would be obliged to support. Thus, while the actions taken by states in this incident are consistent with the traditional rule of international law, it may be that the extreme emphasis throughout this incident on the illegitimacy of a government de facto in control of a state at the expense of a government de jure elected pursuant to an internationally supervised election suggests a basis for altering the traditional rule. The altered rule would provide that, where a civil war has broken out within a state whereby the rebelling faction has achieved the status of a co-belligerent, foreign intervention cannot rely solely on authorization from the de jure government unless that government was democratically elected by a process that was recognized by the international community.

In any event, the actions by the international community in the case of Haiti were undertaken with the express authorization of the UN Security Council, acting under both Chapter VII and Chapter VIII with respect to the blockade and under only Chapter VII with respect to the imposition of economic sanctions and the threat of invasion. The nature of the "threat" to the peace identified by the Security Council, however, is somewhat elusive. When UN economic sanctions were first imposed in Resolution 841, the Security Council considered the threat to peace and security to be the *possibility* of refugee flows to neighboring countries, which in turn existed because the failure to reinstate Aristide contributed to a "climate of fear and persecution and economic dislocation" in Haiti. Further, in the resolutions reimposing the economic sanctions on Haiti and imposing the military blockade, the Security Council did not declare the flow of refugees (or widespread human rights abuses, repression, or starvation) as the basis for the threat to peace and security in the region but, rather, the Security Council found the failure of Haiti's de facto leaders to abide by the Governors Island Agreement as the threat to international peace and security. Thus the threat to peace shifted from the *consequences* of failing to reinstate Aristide to simply the *failure* to abide by an international commitment to reinstate Aristide, regardless of the consequences. After months went by and the deadline for the military authorities to step down under the Governors Island Agreement had long passed, the Security Council shifted back (in Resolution 940 autho-

589. S.C. Res. 841, *supra* note 525, pmbl.; S.C. Res. 875, *supra* note 536; S.C. Res. 940, *supra* note 557, pmbl.

rizing the invasion of Haiti) to defining more broadly the threat to peace and security in Haiti as the "deterioration of the humanitarian situation in Haiti"—in particular, "systematic violations of civil liberties" and the "desperate plight of Haitian refugees"—even though these violations and refugee flows were on a far lesser scale than seen in the other incidents discussed in this chapter.

As noted above, the overriding goal seen throughout the crisis was the "restoration of democracy" in Haiti. Linking that goal to a cognizable "threat to the peace" under Chapter VII, however, is difficult. The *New York Times* observed in an editorial:

> To justify the use of U.N. force [to invade Haiti], Washington recklessly stretched the boundaries of what constitutes a threat to international peace and security under Chapter Seven of the U.N. Charter. General Raoul Cédras's violation of the pledges he made in the Governors Island agreements last year is legitimately an international issue. So is the tide of refugees and systematic violation of human rights. But none of those issues now rise to the threshold necessary to justify invasion. On many of the same grounds, Cuban émigrés might well lobby the Clinton Administration to seek U.N. authorization for invading Cuba.[590]

Cuba, of course, was the only other country in the Western Hemisphere in 1994 that was not under a democratic form of government; like Haiti, Cuba had a poor human rights record and was a source of some refugee flows to the United States. Thus, the "threat to the peace" from the Haitian crisis was very similar to that present vis-à-vis Cuba. The only real difference between them was that Fidel Castro, Cuba's military strongman, had come to power three decades earlier and did not usurp a democratically elected government.

The reaction of the international community to the military blockade and the threat of invasion was supportive, but not overwhelmingly so. The Security Council resolution authorizing the blockade passed unanimously, but few states provided vessels to enforce the blockade. Brazil and China abstained on the Security Council resolution authorizing an invasion, and several Latin American countries expressed strong reservations. A nominal number of non-U.S. forces were committed to the invasion, but many states (including Canada) refused to join the invasion forces. Whereas in the cases of Bosnia-Herzegovina, Somalia, and Rwanda, there was pressure brought by the international community on the United States to act, in the case of Haiti pressure was brought by the United States on the United Nations to authorize U.S. action. Once agreement was reached with the Haitian military authorities for a cooperative deployment of forces to Haiti, the reaction of the international

590. *A U.N. License to Invade Haiti*, N.Y. Times, Aug. 2, 1994, at A20 (editorial).

community was very favorable, both in Latin American and elsewhere.[591]

There are some immediate lessons to be learned from the Haitian crisis. Five are particularly noteworthy.

First, military enforcement of economic sanctions imposed on a state as a means for preventing repression can itself have serious effects on the well-being of the nationals of that country. Those advocating humanitarian intervention in the form of an economic blockade would do well to weigh the likelihood of achieving the humanitarian objectives against the negative effects on those it seeks to assist.

Second, the interplay between the United Nations, the OAS, and the United States was an important element of the intervention in Haiti. The OAS led the way in initiating economic sanctions against Haiti and in seeking to mediate a resolution. The General Assembly also condemned the coup, called upon the Haitian military authorities to step aside, and sought to foster a peaceful resolution of the crisis. After two years, the Security Council became involved through the imposition of mandatory, global sanctions modeled on the OAS sanctions. Those sanctions had an immediate and positive affect in bringing the Haitian military leaders to the negotiating table and in the signing of the Governors Island Agreement. The implementation of that agreement, of course, was a failure, but it suggests that cooperation between the Security Council and a regional organization can have powerful effects. Behind both international organizations, of course, stood the diplomatic, economic, and military power of the United States; its support ultimately proved crucial to Aristide's successful restoration. Although Security Council approval was by no means assured, the United States was unwilling to undertake military intervention without its authorization, a striking departure from actions taken by the United States during the Cold War when Security Council approval would have been highly unlikely. At the same time, coordination between the United States, the OAS, and the United Nations was uneven and certainly was dominated by the United States. This may be seen in the United States' decision to withdraw the *USS Harlan County* without consulting the United Nations and in the highly visible role taken by U.S.-appointed mediators throughout the crisis at the expense of those of the Secretary-General and the OAS. Indeed, in a stark contrast to the success in the peaceful deployment of U.S. forces to Haiti on September 19, the United Nations on that same day made public the resignation of the UN envoy to Haiti, Dante Caputo. Mr. Caputo asserted that "In effect the total absence of consultation and information

591. W. Drozdiak, *Allies Hail Haiti Pact, Pledge Aid*, WASH. POST, Sept. 20, 1994, at A14; J. Brooke, *Latin America Breathes a Half-Sigh of Relief Over Haiti*, N.Y. TIMES, Sept. 20, 1994, at A11.

from the United States Government makes me believe that this country has in fact taken the unilateral decision of acting on its own in the Haitian process."[592] In other words, while the United States was eager to obtain UN approval for military intervention and to develop nominal, symbolic cooperation with other states, in the end it alone would decide whether, how, and when to intervene.

Third, while the Security Council resolution authorizing military invasion left open the exact timing for doing so, it nevertheless contained some important restrictions that affected the ultimate deployment of forces to Haiti. The resolution authorized invasion only by a "multinational force," so the United States was obliged to seek support from other states. With respect to deposing the de facto authorities, the resolution authorized using all necessary means only to "facilitate the departure from Haiti of the military leadership, consistent with the Governors Island Agreement." With respect to a new government, the resolution authorized only the restoration of the Aristide government, which is important since Aristide was viewed with suspicion by many conservatives in the United States. Further, the resolution established a UN observer force to monitor the operations of the multinational force and to lay the groundwork for the transition from the multinational force to a UN peacekeeping force once a secure and stable environment was established.

Fourth, the tension between seeking all possible nonforcible means for ending a crisis and effectively addressing that crisis was readily apparent in the case of Haiti. The last-minute success of the Carter delegation in averting a military invasion undoubtedly saved lives of both foreign and Haitian forces. At the same time, however, it resulted in a recognition of the "honor" of, and a general amnesty for, the Haitian military authorities who just days earlier had been branded by President Clinton as thugs and murderers. Thus, the less forcible the intervention, the greater is the sense that the international community is not intruding excessively into the sovereign nature of the target country; but by the same token, the greater must be the compromises made to accommodate the local authorities who necessitated the intervention in the first place.

Finally, Haiti continued the pattern of an initial intervention led by a major power (once again, the United States) to be followed by a UN-commanded force charged with assisting in establishing national reconciliation. As in the case of Somalia, a key concern of the United Nations was that the initial force take steps to disarm local militants for fear that a UN-commanded force would be ill-equipped to undertake such a task

592. C. Sims, *Former U.N. Envoy Deplores Haiti Accord*, N.Y. TIMES, Sept. 22, 1994, at A15.

on its own.[593] Unlike Somalia, the will of the Haitian people to achieve national reconciliation existed, thereby providing a sound basis for the international community to provide useful assistance and resources to Haiti in recovering from the crisis.

In the end, Resolution 940 on Haiti stands as a striking precedent for a very expansive view of what can constitute a threat to international peace, and in the future may be used as support by those who favor Security Council action to promote the development (or at least the preservation) of democracies worldwide.

593. J. Preston, *U.N., U.S. Clash on Disarming Haitians*, WASH. POST, Oct. 20, 1994, at A31.

Chapter 6
The United Nations and Humanitarian Intervention

As is evident in the responses of the Security Council to recent events in Liberia, Iraq, Somalia, Rwanda, and Haiti, the possibilities for intervention under the authority of the United Nations by states seeking to prevent widespread deprivations of human rights are greater now than ever before under the UN Charter. At the same time, it is quite clear that the willingness of the Security Council to pursue such intervention is limited; indeed, there are considerable problems and inherent limitations in the capacity of the United Nations and its member states to conduct these interventions.[1]

Various steps can and should be taken to increase the likelihood of UN intervention when appropriate occasions arise, such as the provision of adequate funding and other support for UN activities and the "reen-

---

1. Already the literature on the relevance of the United Nations after the Cold War (and its problems) is vast. *See, e.g.*, P. BAEHR & L. GORDENKER, THE UNITED NATIONS IN THE 1990s (2d ed. 1994); M. BEDJAOUI, THE NEW WORLD ORDER AND THE SECURITY COUNCIL: TESTING THE LEGALITY OF ITS ACTS (1995); Y. BLUM, ERODING THE UNITED NATIONS CHARTER (1993); THE CHALLENGING ROLE OF THE UN SECRETARY-GENERAL: MAKING "THE MOST IMPOSSIBLE JOB IN THE WORLD" POSSIBLE (B. Rivlin & L. Gordenker eds., 1993); B. FERENCZ, NEW LEGAL FOUNDATIONS FOR GLOBAL SURVIVAL: SECURITY THROUGH THE SECURITY COUNCIL (1994); W. GORDON, THE UNITED NATIONS AT THE CROSSROADS OF RE-FORM (1994); M. JAKOBSON, THE UNITED NATIONS IN THE 1990s — A SECOND CHANCE? (1993); J. LEE ET AL., TO UNITE OUR STRENGTH: ENHANCING THE UNITED NATIONS PEACE AND SECURITY SYSTEM (1992); R. RIGHTER, UTOPIA LOST: THE UNITED NATIONS AND WORLD ORDER (1995); J. ROCHESTER, WAITING FOR THE MILLENNIUM: THE UNITED NATIONS AND THE FUTURE OF WORLD ORDER (1993); UNITED NATIONS, DIVIDED WORLD: THE UN'S ROLE IN INTERNATIONAL RELATIONS (A. Roberts & B. Kingsbury eds., 2d ed. 1993); THE UNITED NATIONS IN THE NEW WORLD ORDER: THE WORLD ORGANIZATION AT FIFTY (D. Bourantonis & J. Wiener eds., 1995); B. URQUHART & E. CHILDERS, A WORLD IN NEED OF LEADERSHIP: TOMMORROW'S UNITED NATIONS (1990); R. WILLIAMSON, THE UNITED NATIONS: A PLACE OF PROMISE AND OF MISCHIEF (1991); Symposium, *Preferred Futures for the United Nations*, 4 TRANSNAT'L L. & CONTEMP. PROB. 309 (1994).

gineering" of the UN bureaucracy to enhance efficiency and encourage such support. Moreover, when UN interventions do occur, their success will depend in large part on whether such action is at least perceived as grounded on powers granted by the UN Charter and, concomitantly, whether the legitimacy of the United Nations authority is accepted by the international community. This chapter explores a series of questions relating to humanitarian intervention and the United Nations, with the purpose of both analyzing trends to date and assessing desirable future steps.

A. The Evolving Nature of "Threats to the Peace"

As discussed in chapter 3, the primary organ for the maintenance of international peace and security in the UN system is the Security Council. The Security Council's enforcement powers are premised on the existence of a threat to international peace and security.

The negotiating history of the UN Charter, however, provides little guidance as to what was meant by a "threat to the peace." Some states at San Francisco favored defining the term "aggression" or at least explicating it by example, believing that the Security Council then would be more likely to act in appropriate circumstances. Other states feared granting the Security Council powers that were too wideranging or might be used to intrude on national sovereignty. Both views were overtaken by a general sense that the Security Council must be provided wide discretion in determining and addressing "threats to the peace, breaches of the peace, and acts of aggression." Attempting to provide greater definition to terms such as "aggression" would not only be difficult but could fail to capture the complex situations in which aggression arises, and thus inadvertently limit the ability of the Security Council to act. The Chairman of the U.S. delegation at San Francisco, Secretary of State Edward R. Stetinius, Jr., reported that "an overwhelming majority of the participating governments were of the opinion that the circumstances in which threats to the peace or aggression might occur are so varied that [Article 39 of the Charter] should be left as broad and as flexible as possible." [2] Nevertheless, at that time, states believed there *were* limits on the scope of the Security Council's power; some "threat to the peace" was necessary before action under Chapter VII of the Charter was permissible. Situations where a threat to the peace was not present precluded enforcement action and, "if the matter was essentially within the domes-

2. U.S. DEPARTMENT OF STATE, CHARTER OF THE UNITED NATIONS: REPORT TO THE PRESIDENT ON THE RESULTS OF THE SAN FRANCISCO CONFERENCE (1945) (Greenwood Press 1969); *see also* Doc. 881, III/3/46, 12 U.N.C.I.O. Docs. 505 (1945).

tic jurisdiction of any state," precluded any "intervention" by the United Nations per Article 2(7) of the Charter.

Yet international community expectations regarding the sanctity of national sovereignty and the limited role of the United Nations have steadily changed from the early years of the Charter to the present. The adoption of human rights instruments and the increasing consideration of human rights issues at the United Nations whittled away at the limitation on "intervention" in Article 2(7). As Thomas Franck notes, it "is no longer arguable that the United Nations cannot exert pressure against governments that oppress their own peoples" in a variety of ways.[3]

This development of human rights law had a natural effect on the international community's expectations of what constitutes a threat to the peace. Having placed human rights on its agenda, it is not surprising that the United Nations would consider and pursue the ultimate forms of pressure on human rights violators through sanctions and enforcement of those sanctions. While the Cold War ordinarily stymied the Security Council in this realm, when action was possible (as it was during the 1960s and 1970s with respect to Rhodesia and South Africa) the Security Council found "threats to the peace" in essentially internal situations. Some questioned the appropriateness of this development, but it generally was accepted that it was for the Security Council to make such determinations. The Security Council's practice reflected a continuing belief that a "threat to the peace" was a necessary predicate for Security Council action while at the same time it expanded the traditional conception of what constitutes a "threat."

The practice of the United Nations after the Cold War continues this expansive attitude regarding "threats to the peace," allowing the United Nations, when member states (and particularly the major powers) have the political will to do so, to authorize or legitimate the use of military force to prevent widespread deprivations of human rights. The interventions in Iraq, Somalia, Rwanda, and Haiti reflect a continuing belief that a "threat to the peace" is necessary for Security Council action; while the Security Council's involvement in the intervention in Liberia was after the fact, the same is true in that case. At the same time, the essence of the "threat" in all of these cases did not lie in the transboundary effects of the human rights deprivations but, rather, in the deprivations themselves.

In all of these cases, there were transboundary effects of human rights deprivations in the flow of refugees to neighboring states. In all of these cases (with the possible exception of Haiti), solid arguments can be

---

3. T. Franck, *The Emerging Right to Democratic Governance*, 86 AM. J. INT'L L. 46, 85 (1992).

made that political relations within the region were destabilized by these refugee flows. Massive movements of people into neighboring countries can be destabilizing to those countries in the maintenance of their economic and political systems, with the neighboring countries being forced to allocate potentially scarce resources to provide food, water, medicine, and shelter to the refugees. Further, reports by the refugees of human rights deprivations may engender civil unrest among the people of a neighboring state, particularly if they share ethnic, religious, or cultural ties with the refugees. If the economic and political turmoil created in the neighboring states is serious, those states may regard the refugee flows as a threat that must be responded to, if possible, through action against the state originating the flows, action that might take the form of either a use of force[4] or some other form of counterintervention, but in any event action that would confirm the existence of a threat to international peace.

Yet, while the transboundary effects that arose with respect to Iraq, Somalia, Liberia, Rwanda, and Haiti were an element of the intervention in those cases, they were *not* the central focus of the Security Council's deliberations or the Secretary-General's reports on those cases, nor were they the central focus of the interventions. Indeed, as noted in chapter 5, in several cases the refugees remained outside the target state at the time the intervening forces were withdrawn. A candid assessment of the interventions leads to the conclusion that the "threats to the peace" identified had much less to do with transboundary effects than with a concern for the rights of the civilian populations of those countries. Consider each case in turn.

In Liberia, the movement of refugees was a feature of the Security Council's actions but cannot be regarded as the fundamental aspect of the "threat to the peace." The initial refugee flows from Liberia were the product of President Doe's military tactics; yet ECOMOG's intervention into Liberia prevented the Taylor faction from successfully deposing Doe. The predominant reason for ECOMOG's intervention was to prevent what might have been, under a Taylor-led government, an internal ethnic bloodbath in Monrovia. When, in Resolution 788 of November 1992,[5] the Security Council posited a "threat to the peace" from a "de-

---

4. The use of force against the originating state to respond to flows of refugees presumably would be a violation of Charter Article 2(4) under the jurisprudence of the International Court, since the flows of refugees would not rise to the level of "armed attack" sufficient to trigger a right of self-defense under Article 51. *See* Military and Paramilitary Activities (Nicar. v. U.S.), 1986 I.C.J. 14, paras. 195, 211 (June 27).

5. S.C. Res. 788, U.N. SCOR, 47th Sess., 3138th mtg. at 99 pmbl., U.N. Doc. S/INF/48 (1993).

terioration of the situation in Liberia," it had in mind the possibility that
ECOMOG would fail in its goal of national reconciliation and thus fail
to prevent further and greater human rights atrocities.

Resolution 688 on Iraq[6] characterized the internal deprivation of human rights as a threat to international peace in the context of the transboundary effects of internal repression. Formally, the Security Council
found that repression leading to the flow of refugees "toward and across
international frontiers" and "cross border incursions" constituted a
threat to international peace. Yet the threat to the peace was not so much
related to the national security of Turkey or Iran as it was to the images
of destitute civilians, including children, dying by the thousands from
starvation and disease. Had the security of Turkey or Iran been the fundamental issue, the Security Council might have called upon states to
help Turkey and Iran prevent Iraqi nationals from entering Turkish and
Iranian territory. In fact, Turkey had successfully accomplished this task,
which is why the Iraqi Kurds were trapped in the mountains in the first
place. The fundamental issue for the Security Council was whether the
global community could tolerate the death and suffering that was occurring from the consequences of Iraq's repression. To address this issue,
Resolution 688 condemned Iraq's repression, demanded that the Iraqi
government enter into a dialogue with its people, and insisted that Iraq
open its borders to international humanitarian organizations. The interventions by Britain, France, and the United States were not designed
simply to protect the security of Iraq's neighbors but to eliminate the
conditions that gave rise to the plight of Iraq's nationals. Subsequent
actions by those states in southern Iraq were conducted particularly in
response to internal repression, since by August 1992 the issue was no
longer prevention of further flows of refugees.

In Resolution 794 on Somalia,[7] the Security Council found that the
"magnitude of the human tragedy caused by the conflict in Somalia, further exacerbated by the obstacles being created to the distribution of
humanitarian assistance, constituted a threat to international peace and
security." While this catastrophe created a massive flow of refugees, the
Security Council's resolution made no mention of refugees, and the subsequent intervention was not designed simply to repatriate those refugees. The primary focus of the intervention under UNITAF was, rather,
to open food relief lines into Somalia so as to prevent widespread star-

6. S.C. Res. 688, U.N. SCOR, 46th Sess., 2982d mtg. at 31, U.N. Doc. S/INF/47 (1993), *reprinted in* 3 INTERNATIONAL LAW & WORLD ORDER: BASIC DOCUMENTS III.F.3 (B. Weston ed., 1994) [hereinafter WESTON].
7. S.C. Res. 794, U.N. SCOR, 47th Sess., 3145th mtg. at 63, U.N. Doc. S/INF/48 (1993), *reprinted in* 2 WESTON, *supra* note 6, at II.D.6.

vation and disease among Somalis *in Somalia*. The primary focus of UNOSOM II was the disarmament of the warring factions in Somalia and the nurturing of a process of national reconciliation. One benefit of these actions was the creation of conditions for the repatriation of Somali refugees, but to cast the intervention as designed wholly or predominantly to address that issue would be incorrect.

Resolution 929 authorizing the French intervention in Rwanda[8] provided only a passing reference to refugees, and even then only to refugees *in Rwanda*. The concern of the international community that led to the French intervention was the brutal massacres of Tutsis by unrestrained Hutu militias, that over a two-month period led to the death of as many as a half million people. This slaughter was of genocidal proportions and lies at the heart of what the Security Council considered as constituting a threat to the peace.

Finally, the flight of Haitian refugees to the United States in the first half of 1992 gave greater urgency to resolving the crisis in Haiti, yet the United States on its own initiative successfully stemmed that flow of refugees. The imposition, the maintenance, and ultimately the military enforcement of economic sanctions were fundamentally related to the restoration of democratic rule in Haiti. The threat identified in Resolution 875[9] (authorizing force to halt maritime shipping) and in Resolution 940[10] (authorizing military invasion) was the failure of Haitian military authorities to abide by the Governors Island Agreement. That agreement provided for transition from military rule to rule by the democratically elected Aristide; it did not, at least directly, address the violence and intimidation inflicted by the Haitian military against the Haitian people. Thus, while the Haitian military authorities did commit human rights deprivations, albeit not to the widespread degree seen in Liberia, Iraq, Somalia, Bosnia, or Rwanda, these abuses were not the focus of the Security Council's decisions. The action of the Security Council was, rather, in response to the widespread deprivation of a very different type of human right, the right to democratic representation in public affairs. In this sense, Haiti represents the "outer envelope" of what the international community, to date, has considered threats to the peace justifying UN-authorized enforcement actions.

The view that purely internal armed conflict can constitute a "threat to the peace" under Article 39 is now regarded as "settled practice of the Security Council and the common understanding of the United Nations

---

8. S.C. Res. 929, U.N. SCOR, 49th Sess., 3392d mtg., U.N. Doc. S/RES/929 (1994).

9. S.C. Res. 875, U.N. SCOR, 48th Sess., 3293d mtg. at 125, para. 1, U.N. Doc. S/INF/49 (1949).

10. S.C. Res. 940, U.N. SCOR, 49th Sess., 3413th mtg., U.N. Doc. S/RES/940 (1994).

membership in general."[11] In theory, a wide range of conditions appear ripe for classification by the United Nations as "threats to the peace." When the Security Council met at its historic January 1992 meeting (for the first time, all its members were represented by heads of government), they discussed prospects for the United Nations after the Cold War. Through the President of the Security Council, they declared:

> The absence of war and military conflicts amongst States does not in itself ensure international peace and security. The non-military sources of instability in the economic, social, humanitarian and ecological fields have become threats to peace and security. The United Nations membership as a whole, working through the appropriate bodies, needs to give the highest priority to the solution of these matters.[12]

The report of the Secretary-General, entitled "An Agenda for Peace," which resulted from the Security Council meeting, took a similarly expansive interpretation of "threats to peace and security." It stated that:

> Poverty, disease, famine, oppression and despair abound, joining to produce 17 million refugees, 20 million displaced persons and massive migrations of peoples within and beyond national borders. These are both sources and consequences of conflict that require the ceaseless attention and the highest priority in the efforts of the United Nations. A porous ozone shield could pose a greater threat to an exposed population than a hostile army. Drought and disease can decimate no less mercilessly than the weapons of war. So at this moment of renewed opportunity, the efforts of the Organization to build peace, stability and security must encompass matters beyond military threats in order to break the fetters of strife and warfare that have characterized the past.[13]

Thus, flush with the success of expelling Iran from Kuwait, and apparently eager to build a "new world order," the members of the Security Council and the Secretary-General in 1992 saw possibilities for UN action well beyond what had been intended when the United Nations was established and well beyond anything it had achieved to date.

11. Prosecutor v. Dusko Tadic, Decision on the Defence Motion for Interlocutory Appeal on Jurisdiction, U.N. Doc. IT-94-1-AR72 before the Appeals Chamber of the International Tribunal for the Prosecution of Persons Responsible for Serious Violations of International Humanitarian Law Committed in the Territory of Former Yugoslavia since 1991, para. 30 (Oct. 2, 1995) [hereinafter Tribunal on War Crimes in Former Yugoslavia, Decision of October 1995] ("It can thus be said that there is a common understanding, manifested by the 'subsequent practice' of the membership of the United Nations at large, that the 'threat to the peace' of Article 39 may include, as one of its species, internal armed conflicts.").

12. U.N. SCOR, 47th Sess., 3046 mtg. at 143, U.N. Doc. S/PV.3046 (1992).

13. *An Agenda for Peace: Preventative Diplomacy, Peacemaking and Peace-Keeping*, U.N. GAOR, 47th Sess., Agenda Item 10, para. 13, U.N. Doc. A/47/277, S/24111 (1992) [hereinafter *An Agenda for Peace*], *reprinted in* 2 WESTON, *supra* note 6, at II.D.4.

Will such an expansive view of "threat to the peace" withstand the test of time? The interventions in Liberia, Iraq, Somalia, Rwanda, and Haiti do not stand for the proposition that the Security Council can and will regard as threats to the peace widespread deprivations of human rights in which there are absolutely no transboundary effects. Nevertheless, in most instances of such deprivations, there will be discernible transboundary effects that would seem to fit the patterns of these cases, whether in the flow of refugees or the agitation of neighboring states. However, it remains to be seen how far the Security Council will go in finding threats to the peace from human rights deprivations. Is the massive migration of peoples solely "within borders" really enough to constitute a threat to the peace? Is famine without any displacement of a population enough? The Secretary-General's views are even more provocative: can the failure of a state to prevent the emission of chlorofluorocarbons really be considered a threat to international peace, thereby allowing enforcement action under Chapter VII?

Recent reports of the death of the nation-state may be somewhat exaggerated, but there can be little doubt that the past century has seen an astounding change in the centrality of the nation-state as a means for organizing global behavior. In the economic sphere, communications among private actors (including consumers) increasingly control the movement of capital, corporations, goods, and services across national borders, while governmental policies are increasingly disciplined by the actions of the private sector and the currency markets.[14] In the political sphere, the global agenda is increasingly driven by private persons and nongovernmental organizations on a range of issues from sustainable development to the rights of women to health and nutrition. These changes, no doubt fuelled by the rapid development of information technologies, reflect in part the inherent limitations of government control in the "information age" and in part an increasing dissatisfaction with states and governments as the vehicle for assessing global problems and the means for dealing with them. Communities are reaching across borders to other communities, by-passing their governments, and, in so doing, challenging the norms upon which the international legal system is built. One of these norms is the traditional concept of "domestic jurisdiction," which tends to characterize any action that does not have tangible external effects as being domestic in character. In a 1968 article on the situation in Southern Rhodesia, Myres McDougal and Michael Reisman offered the following explanation for why actions appearing to occur solely within a state in fact have external effects:

14. *See, e.g.*, K. OHMAE, THE END OF THE NATION STATE: THE RISE OF REGIONAL ECONOMIES (1995).

In the contemporary intensely interdependent world, peoples interact not merely through the modalities of collaborative or combative operations but also through shared subjectivities—not merely through the physical movements of goods and services or exercises with armaments, but also through communications in which they simply take each other into account. The peoples in one territorial community may realistically regard themselves as being affected by activities in another territorial community, though no goods or people cross any boundaries. Much more important than the physical movements are the communications which peoples make to each other.[15]

If the trends of the past few decades continue, it seems likely that significant disturbances in the status quo within one national community will nevertheless be perceived by external communities as of such significance to them that the continuance of those disturbances constitutes a "threat." If so, depending on the magnitude of the perceived threat, it may be incumbent upon the United Nations to play a role in addressing the threat, if necessary through enforcement action.

B. Premises and Problems in the Security Council's New Role

The further the Security Council goes in finding threats to international peace from human rights violations, the more it may face questions about the basis within Chapter VII for its actions. If the drafters of the Charter intended to provide limited powers to the Security Council to address only threats to international peace and security, how can it be justified extending those powers to cover situations where the nexus to international peace and security is highly attenuated?

One response to this challenge is that the fundamental object in maintaining international peace and security is not for the sake of peace itself but, rather, "to save succeeding generations from the scourge of war"[16] and thereby, hopefully, to advance the well-being of people. There is evidence that numerically the well-being of people is far more threatened by widespread deprivations of human rights (particularly mass murder by governments of their own people) than by international or even civil armed conflicts. By some accounts, in this century, fifteen states alone have killed over 151 million of their own people through genocide, political executions, and mass murder (excluding deaths from war).[17] If

15. M. McDougal & W. Reisman, *Rhodesia and the United Nations: The Lawfulness of International Concern*, 62 AM. J. INT'L L. 1, 12 (1968).

16. U.N. CHARTER pmbl.

17. R. RUMMEL, DEATH BY GOVERNMENT 1–28 (1994). The fifteen states, during the relevant time periods and in descending order of number of persons killed, were: the USSR (1917–87); China under the People's Republic of China (1949–87); Germany (1934–45);

correct, these deaths represent almost four times the number of deaths resulting from all of the international and civil wars of this century.[18] As our appreciation of the real threats to the well-being of peoples develops, along with the development of human rights law generally, there may be a convergence between the rudimentary objective sought by those who champion a strict interpretation of Chapter VII (seeking to preserve life by restricting uses of transnational force) and the rudimentary objective sought by those who advocate a more flexible interpretation that allows for UN humanitarian intervention (seeking to preserve life through the use of transnational force). Our understanding of the maintenance of international peace and security will be remarkably unattuned to the violence inflicted on people if it remains narrowly focused on the issue of violence arising from transnational war.

A second response to the charge that the Security Council is exceeding its authority is to note that there may be a correlation between those states engaged in the widespread deprivation of human rights and their propensity to undertake aggression against their neighbors. Empirical evidence developed by political theorists indicates that liberal demo-

---

China under the Kuomintang (1928–49); Japan (1936–45); China under the Mao Soviet guerrillas (1923–49); Cambodia (1975–79); Turkey (1915–18); Vietnam (1945–87); Poland (1945–48); Pakistan (1958–87); Yugoslavia (1944–87); North Korea (1948–87); Mexico (1900–20); Russia (1900–17). Rummel's figures are based on his own research, much of which has been previously published in books on the USSR, on China, and on Nazi Germany.

18. *Id.* at 3. Statistics now emerging regarding deaths during and after the Iraq-Kuwait war may support this observation. Although there were early estimates of Iraqi casualties during the Gulf War of 100,000 dead and 300,000 wounded, these appear to have been grossly exaggerated. A former military analyst with the U.S. Defense Intelligence Agency provides the following estimate:

If the maximum estimates [of Iraqi troops in the Kuwait/Southern Iraq theater of operation or KTO] are to be believed, the Iraqi military suffered up to 9,500 dead and 26,500 wounded throughout the KTO for a total of 36,000 casualties, of which three-quarters occurred during the ground offensive. Since those estimates are largely derived from equipment losses, however, they are rather unreliable. . . . If the minimum estimates of Iraqi casualties are correct—and that appears to be the case—then the real toll of Iraqi dead and wounded from Desert Storm was smaller still. Those estimates place Iraqi dead in the KTO at 1,500. The figure for Iraqi wounded probably numbered around 3,000, of which 2,000 were captured while another 1,000 or so managed to escape.

J. Heidenrich, *The Gulf War: How Many Iraqis Died?* 90 FOREIGN POL'Y 108, 123–24 (1993). These figures can be compared with the vastly higher numbers of casualties that occurred in the aftermath of the war, inflicted by the Government of Iraq on its own people, as discussed in chapter 5.

cratic states do not go to war with one another[19] and are less prone to engage in the widespread deprivations of human rights than their non-liberal counterparts (although deprivations do occur).[20] Non-liberal states, characterized by high concentrations of power in regime elites, have a greater capacity for autonomous behavior in their economic and political action; they are not limited by democratic accountability, economic interdependence, and well-functioning judicial systems insulated from direct political influence.[21] As such they are more capable of resorting to war externally and to widespread violations of human rights internally.[22] On a theory of "where there is smoke there is fire," efforts by the Security Council to address the widespread deprivation of human rights through humanitarian intervention may assist in stripping from non-liberal state regime elites their sense of autonomy in pursuing force against either their own people or their neighbors. Put another way, by engaging in humanitarian intervention against a non-liberal state government, costs are imposed on the government that it would otherwise

19. *See* M. Doyle, *Kant, Liberal Legacies, and Foreign Affairs*, 12 PHIL. & PUB. AFF. 205, at 209–212 (1983) (conducting a survey of all wars fought in the past two centuries); *see also* Z. Maoz & N. Abdolali, *Regime Types and International Conflict, 1816–1976*, 33 J. CONFLICT RESOL. 3 (1989); S. Chan, *Mirror, Mirror on the Wall . . . Are the Freer Countries More Pacific?*, 28 J. CONFLICT RESOL. 617 (1984); B. Russett, *Politics and Alternative Security: Toward a More Democratic, Therefore More Peaceful World*, in ALTERNATIVE SECURITY: LIVING WITHOUT NUCLEAR DETERRENCE 107 (B. Weston ed. 1990).

20. RUMMEL, *supra* note 17, at 7–10.

21. For a discussion of the ramifications of this theory of liberal internationalism on approaches to international law, *see* A. Burley, *Toward an Age of Liberal Nations*, 33 HARV. INT'L. L.J. 393 (1992). *See also* R. Gardner, *The Comeback of Liberal Internationalism*, WASH. Q., Summer 1990, at 23. Obviously, there is a continuum in the degree to which states are or are not democracies. Some theorists have argued out that while mature democracies may be peaceful, states transitioning from authoritarian regimes to democratic regimes may actually be more aggressive and war-prone than they were prior to the transition. *See, e.g.*, E. Mansfield & J. Snyder, *Democratization and War*, FOREIGN AFF., May-June 1995, at 79. The result of this argument, however, is not to discourage the process of democratization, but rather to seek to manage its unwanted side effects. *Id.* at 94–97.

22. In the case of Somalia, the widespread deprivation of human rights during 1991 and 1992 was not the direct result of actions by a highly centralized nonliberal government. Nevertheless, it appears very much to have been the indirect result of one. Somalia was created from the merger of British and Italian colonies in 1960, and relative democracy survived until Major General Mohamed Siad Barre seized power in 1969. It was his efforts in favor of "scientific socialism" that helped erode the clan system and led to the large-scale imports of advanced weaponry and military advisers that ultimately led to undermining the nation's stability. Moreover, Barre's support for guerrillas in the Ogaden (a border region controlled by Ethiopia) after 1974 led to full-scale war between Somalia and Ethiopia, which ultimately unleashed serious domestic discontent against Barre's regime, and in turn Barre's repression of certain clans. J. Clark, *Debacle in Somalia*, 72 FOREIGN AFF., AMERICA AND THE WORLD 1992/93, at 109, 110.

not internalize. In doing so, the intervention may serve to deter or inhibit aggressive, external behavior by the non-liberal regime.

If true, UN humanitarian intervention may serve the purpose of reducing, not increasing, the likelihood of international armed conflict over the long run. For instance, had the United Nations intervened to stop the Iraqi Government from its unfettered killing of at least 180,000 Kurds in 1987 and 1988, Iraq's enthusiasm for invading Kuwait in 1990 might have been considerably tempered. This possibility, however, may serve as a questionable basis for justifying UN humanitarian intervention in that not all nondemocratic states engage in military aggression even if they do engage in widespread deprivations of human rights. Further, given the presence of a large number of nondemocratic states in the United Nations (roughly half), including on the Security Council, reaching an operational consensus on the promotion of democracy as an acceptable justification for UN humanitarian intervention seems remote.

Certain concerns arise from an expansive view of "threats to the peace," such as whether it will unleash a new era of "just wars." Efforts to refine and then to discredit the just war theory, as discussed in chapter 2, were in large part a reaction to the brutal and widespread religious wars that afflicted Europe during the sixteenth and seventeenth centuries. Likewise, the decline of the right to resort to war except in self-defense is a response to the calamitous wars of this century. Having reached a point where warfare is generally prohibited, is the international community now seeing a return to warfare for "right reasons" that ultimately it may regret? One might have confidence that the political pressures and relative diffusion of power present within the Security Council make it an unlikely crusader; nevertheless, many countries continue to view the Security Council as an "imperialist" tool of "colonial-minded" powers.[23] Little noticed in the political bartering by the United States toward securing Security Council authorization for the invasion of Haiti was the U.S. agreement to support Russia's desire for UN authorization of its peacekeeping deployment in Georgia.[24] Arguably, the United Nations is tolerating patterns that originated during the Cold War by recognizing the right of major powers to stabilize crises in states that fall within their spheres of influence, a notion far different from an ideal of UN collective security.

Another concern is that the more open-ended the activities of the Security Council, the more difficult it may be for states to cede power to it,

23. *See Open the Club*, ECONOMIST, Aug. 29, 1992, at 14.
24. D. Williams, *Powers Assert Influence in Peacekeeping Roles*, WASH. POST, July 30, 1994, at A12.

for example, by providing it with a standing force, by providing it with adequate financing, or by altering its constitutional structure, such as the relinquishment by the permanent members of the veto power. If in deciding to deploy military forces the Security Council were to remain narrowly focused on whether there existed some type of transnational aggression, then states might be willing to commit significant military and financial resources to the United Nations, knowing that these resources would be used rarely and only in obvious and grave circumstances. Yet an activist Security Council willing to pursue intervention in a range of circumstances may inhibit the commitment of such resources, due to a perception that the Security Council is overly involved in "policing" the world at the expense of member state funds and the lives of its soldiers.

A final concern is that loosening the concept of "threat to the peace" may influence the attitudes of states in their own unilateral projection of military force. If the flow of refugees or other nontraditional events can constitute threats to the peace but the Security Council does not act to address those threats, states individually may feel less inhibited in conducting unilateral intervention than previously was the case. Indeed, it may lead to a loosening of normative behavior across-the-board in uses of force such as self-defense. Whether this outcome is a desirable result will be discussed in chapters 7 and 8; it is sufficient here to note that the effects of an expanded role for the Security Council in addressing threats to the peace may not easily be limited to actions by that organ.

C. A Duty to Intervene?

It has been suggested that the United Nations has not only the right to intervene to prevent human rights deprivations but also a *legal* duty to do so in extreme cases.[25] The existence of a legal duty for the United Nations to intervene echoes similar arguments advanced during the

---

25. *See, e.g.*, H. Schermers, *The Obligation to Intervene in the Domestic Affairs of States*, in Humanitarian Law of Armed Conflict: Challenges Ahead (Essays in Honour of Frits Kalshoven) 583, 592 (A. Delissen & G. Tanja eds., 1991); N. Rodley, *Collective Intervention to Protect Human Rights and Civilian Populations: The Legal Framework*, in To Loose the Bands of Wickedness: International Intervention in Defence of Human Rights 14, 35 (N. Rodley ed., 1992). The idea of a "duty to intervene" recently has been associated with actions of nongovernmental organizations, such as the French group Médicins sans Frontières (Doctors Without Frontiers). It should be noted, however, that important nongovernmental groups such as the International Committee for the Red Cross (ICRC), do not accept this concept and continue to seek the consent of the host government. The ICRC's fundamental principles of operation continue to be used by most nongovernmental organizations. *See* Y. Beigbeder, The Role and Status of International Humanitarian Volunteers and Organizations 384 (1991).

Cold War regarding the duty of states to intervene.[26] Several European national systems contain the notion of a duty for persons to act when another person is endangered,[27] as do some of the laws of the states of the United States.[28] Common factors necessary for this duty to exist are: (1) some form of immediate or imminent danger to life; (2) a rescuer that is near to and aware of the danger; and (3) an ability of the rescuer to act effectively at minimal risk. On the international scene, this duty might arise from these national laws as a general principle of international law and be applied to the United Nations, regional organizations, or states acting in their individual capacities. Alternatively, an international duty to intervene might be seen as a corollary to the obligation of states under customary international law to punish those states or individuals that commit "crimes against humanity," and to punish those states or individuals that commit grave breaches of the 1949 Geneva Conventions,[29] including common Article 3 on internal conflicts.

To date, however, the notion of a "duty to intervene" by the United Nations, regional organizations, or states does not appear present in international law. While this duty exists in the national laws of many coun-

26. *See, e.g.,* the arguments advanced by W. Michael Reisman and Fernando Tesón, recounted in chapter 4, *supra.*

27. F. Feldbrugge, *Good and Bad Samaritans: A Comparative Survey of Criminal Law Provisions Concerning Failure to Rescue,* 14 AM. J. COMP. L. 630 (1965–66) (appendix contains English translations of a number of relevant criminal code provisions of European countries and Ethiopia). *See, e.g.,* Article 63 of the French Penal Code, which imposes criminal sanctions upon one "who voluntarily abstains from giving assistance to a person which he could, without risk to himself or to third persons, give either by his personal action or by securing assistance." French legal treatises assert that one who fails to perform this duty of assistance is subject to civil liabilities under Articles 1382 and 1383 of the French Civil Code.

28. *See, e.g.,* the State of Vermont's "Duty to Aid the Endangered Act":

> (a) A person who knows that another is exposed to grave physical harm shall, to the extent that the same can be rendered without danger or peril to himself or without interference with important duties owed to others, give reasonable assistance to the exposed person unless that assistance or care is being provided by others.
>   . . .
> (c) A person who willfully violates subsection (a) shall be fined not more than $100.00.

VT. STAT. ANN. tit. 12, sec. 519 (1973).

29. Geneva Convention (No. I) for the Amelioration of the Condition of the Wounded and Sick in Armed Forces in the Field, Aug. 12, 1949, 6 U.S.T. 3114, 75 U.N.T.S. 31; Geneva Convention (No. II) for the Amelioration of the Condition of the Wounded, Sick and Shipwrecked Members of Armed Forces at Sea, Aug. 12, 1949, 6 U.S.T. 3114, 75 U.N.T.S. 85; Geneva Convention (No. III) Relative to the Treatment of Prisoners of War, Aug. 12, 1949, 6 U.S.T. 3114, 75 U.N.T.S. 135; Geneva Convention (No. IV) Relative to the Protection of Civilian Persons in Time of War, Aug. 12, 1949, 6 U.S.T. 3114, 75 U.N.T.S. 287 [hereinafter 1949 Geneva Conventions]. These conventions are reprinted in 2 WESTON, *supra* note 6, at II.B.11–14.

tries, it does not exist in all of the principal legal systems of the world. Further, among common-law states, the general rule is that there is no duty to rescue an endangered person absent some special relationship between that person and the potential rescuer (e.g., husband-wife, shipmaster-crew, carrier-passenger).[30] In light of these disparities, it cannot be said that there is a general principle of law "recognized by civilized nations."[31] Further, there is no consensus among states that the United Nations, regional organizations, or states have such a legal duty under customary international law, nor does the practice of these organizations and states reflect such a duty. The list of places in which the international community has not forcibly intervened in recent years, despite widespread starvation and/or extensive internal violence against civilians, is quite long (and likely incomplete): Afghanistan, Algeria, Angola, Bhutan, Burundi, Chad, Cuba, Djibouti, El Salvador, Equitorial Guinea, Eritrea, Ethiopia, Ghana, Guatemala, Indonesia (East Timor), Iran, Mali, Mauritania, Mozambique, Myanmar (Burma), Niger, Sierra Leone, Sri Lanka, Sudan, Tibet, Togo, Western Sahara, Yemen, and Zaire. Indeed, due to the experience of the League of Nations, the drafters of the UN Charter purposefully avoided placing within it automatic obligations on UN members to act.

As national laws and international law develop, there may come a time when a "duty to intervene" will exist in international law. If so, it should be kept in mind that the duty in these national laws is qualified by key factors that will make the existence of the duty problematic under international law. The duty under these national laws does not attach unless the rescuer can act with minimal risk; yet in virtually all instances of humanitarian intervention by the United Nations, regional organizations, or states, there will be a substantial risk of death and danger to the intervening forces. Further, the duty under these national laws does not attach unless the rescuer is "near" to the rescuee; yet humanitarian intervention often involves deployment of military forces from around

---

30. P. Keeton et al., PROSSER AND KEETON ON THE LAW OF TORTS sec. 56, at 338–43 (4th ed. 1971). Several commentators have criticized the traditional rule and noted that there are an increasing number of exceptions applied by courts. *See, e.g.*, E. Weinrib, *The Case for a Duty to Rescue*, 90 YALE L.J. 247, 248, 293 (1980) (arguing that the "adoption of a duty of easy rescue in emergencies would fit a common-law pattern, found principally in contract law, that gives expression to the law's understanding of liberty"); M. SHAPO, THE DUTY TO ACT: TORT LAW, POWER, AND PUBLIC POLICY 3–73 (1977) (arguing that the duty should be seen as a function of the power of the rescuer over the rescuee, and therefore that in some situations even a complete bystander should be viewed by courts as having a duty when he can perform the rescue at minimal risk); J. Ames, *Law and Morals*, 22 HARV. L. REV. 97, 113 (1908–09).

31. Statute of the International Court of Justice, June 26, 1945, art. 38, para. 1(c), 59 Stat. 1031, T.S. No. 993, *reprinted in* 1 WESTON, *supra* note 6, at I.H.2.

the world to a target state, not just from neighboring states. Finally, the duty under these national laws is too broad for international law by speaking to *all* situations where life is endangered; it would only make sense as a general principle of international law if it applied to situations of a widespread and severe threat to the lives of a civilian population. At a minimum, if the duty present in national laws becomes a general principle of international law, it probably should be limited to situations where the rescue is based on the widespread endangerment of life (thus, the situation in Haiti would appear not to qualify) and where the risks to the intervening forces are minimal or nonexistent.

A more compelling argument might be made that the international community has a moral duty to intervene and that the soundest means of fulfilling it is through the use of the United Nations. Michael Walzer has analyzed the way societies and people argue about war, which he believes reveals a comprehensive view of war and a more or less systematic moral doctrine.[32] Under this doctrine, the "just war theory" is "alive and well," and it explains and can morally justify intervention to protect against human rights deprivations.[33] Walzer does not, however, seek to interpret positive international law in light of these moral principles.

D. The Structure of the Security Council and the Role of Other UN Organs

The increased activism of the Security Council after the Cold War has led to an inevitable questioning of whether all of the actions pursued by the Security Council are within its competence under the Charter. Moreover, questions have arisen as to whether such actions, even if within the Security Council's legal competence, should be considered legitimate in light of the structure of the Security Council, which gives considerable weight to the views of a limited number of powerful states.[34]

Many of the criticisms regarding the legitimacy of the Security Council's actions fail to take account of the objectives sought in the creation of the Security Council. The founders of the UN Charter were not inter-

32. M. WALZER, JUST AND UNJUST WARS: A MORAL ARGUMENT WITH HISTORICAL ILLUSTRATIONS (2d ed. 1992).

33. *Id.* at 101–08.

34. *See, e.g.*, D. Caron, *The Legitimacy of the Collective Authority of the Security Council*, 87 AM. J. INT'L L. 552 (1993) (see Caron's footnote 19 for citations to the issue of "legitimacy" generally in international relations and international law); B. Weston, *Security Council Resolution 678 and Persian Gulf Decision Making: Precarious Legitimacy*, 85 AM. J. INT'L L. 516 (1991). On the issue of what constitutes "legitimacy" in international law, *see* T. FRANCK, THE POWER OF LEGITIMACY AMONG NATIONS (1990); J. Alvarez, *The Quest for Legitimacy: An Examination of The Power of Legitimacy Among Nations by Thomas M. Franck*, 24 N.Y.U.J. INT'L L. & POL. 199 (1991) (book review).

ested in creating an ideal system of collective security in which all states could participate and which would react equally in all situations of international conflict. Based on the experience of the League of Nations, the founders knew that widespread participation by states, involving decision by consensus, was a recipe for inaction and that purportedly automatic sanctions led inexorably to an erosion of credibility. Further, they knew that unless the special interests of major powers were taken into account, those powers would not participate in the system, thereby eliminating an essential element of the system's success. Thus, the founders were interested in "the practical problem of managing postwar relationships more systematically than alliance systems had done in the past." [35] For them, achievement of the essential goal of a collective security system required that special status and special responsibilities be given to those states that, upon the basis of their overall power, were capable of coercing behavior (which to be done credibly requires the projection of military force) or that were capable of thwarting the actions of the system. Widespread participation of other states in the decision to apply power was seen as an appropriate secondary consideration, but one that could not be allowed to undermine the need for an efficient organ—one capable of acting quickly to address threats to international peace and security as they arose. Under this system, placing weight on the views of the major powers might not be ideal, but it was unavoidable and was a sensible approach to accommodating inescapable power differentials.

There is no reason to regard the concerns motivating the founders of the UN Charter to be any different than collective security concerns of today.[36] The most powerful states of the world are expected to do the "heavy lifting" of conflict management. These states will continue to insist that no actions proceed without their support and that the process leading to action not be frustrated by overly broad participation of states. These states are not granted carte blanche in their domination of the Security Council. The requirements of the concurring votes of all the

35. J. Lorenz, *The Case for Collective Security, in* Two Views on the Issue of Collective Security 19 (U.S. Institute of Peace, 1992).

36. There is, of course, always room for debating and pursuing reforms of the UN Charter system that advance the "practical problem" of international relationships. The most important reform may be the recomposition of the permanent members of the Security Council to reflect contemporary power differentials. Such reform will entail difficulties in the standard applied for such membership, the politics of changing the status quo, and the speed with which such reform can be achieved. The General Assembly has considered the issue of equitable representation on, and the increase in, the membership of the Security Council. *See Question of Equitable Representation on and Increase in the Membership of the Security Council*, U.N. Doc. A/48/264 (1993). Detailed discussion of this problem is beyond the scope of this study.

permanent members and a special majority of all members act as procedural safeguards against arbitrary or spurious decisions that benefit any one state. Indeed, the permanent members themselves hardly proceed lockstep in their approach to the maintenance of international peace and security; differences invariably exist and, absent persuasive reasons for bridging those differences, a consensus will not emerge and the action will not proceed. Moreover, as seen in the case studies in chapter 5, to obtain political support for a Security Council decision, it often is necessary to build safeguards (regarding timing, duration, and objectives of an intervention) into the resolution itself, as well as provision for the participation and monitoring by representatives of the United Nations itself. Changes to the composition of the Security Council can and should be made to support these rudiments of effective collective security, but not to dilute them.[37]

The arguments for "major power" involvement in collective security decisions, however, may be less compelling in situations of UN humanitarian intervention. In those situations, the national security interests of the major powers or their allies are not the central focus of the intervention; the predominant issue is, rather, the protection of the nationals of the target state. The salient issue is whether the human rights deprivations occurring within the target state are so severe and widespread that they "shock the conscience of humankind," not whether they shock the conscience of just a few powerful states. If there is a case for engaging the views of a wide range of states in the process of determining the conditions for UN intervention, such as through the General Assembly, or the view of a "nonpolitical" forum such as the International Court of Justice in its advisory capacity, the situation of humanitarian intervention would be an obvious candidate.

Through the Uniting for Peace Resolution,[38] the General Assembly has had limited experience recommending actions to maintain or restore international peace and security. The General Assembly also has been involved in the deployment of UN forces for peacekeeping operations. Were the Security Council incapable of agreeing upon humanitarian intervention in a particular case, the General Assembly, through

37. In 1993, the General Assembly established an open-ended working group to consider increasing the membership of the Security Council and other matters. G.A. Res. 48/26, U.N. GAOR, 48th Sess., Supp. No. 49, at 29, U.N. Doc. A/48/49 (1994). *See also* B. Crossette, *At the U.N., a Drive for Diversity*, N.Y. TIMES, Oct. 24, 1994, at A6; S. Murphy, *The Security Council, Legitimacy, and the Concept of Collective Security After the Cold War*, 32 COLUM. J. TRANSNAT'L L. 201, 246–69 (1994).

38. G.A. Res. 377, U.N. GAOR, 5th Sess., Supp. No. 20, at 10, U.N. Doc. A/1775 (1950), *reprinted in* 2 WESTON, *supra* note 6, at II.D.1.

the Uniting for Peace Resolution or some other (as yet nonexistent) resolution,[39] might seek to assert authority in this area. Under UN Charter Article 11(2), the General Assembly may discuss questions and issue recommendations relating to international peace and security brought before it by states or the Security Council; before issuing any recommendations, the General Assembly would have to find that the Security Council had ceased to deal with the matter, in accordance with UN Charter Article 12(1). There are, however, at least two problems with the General Assembly acting to recommend humanitarian intervention under the Uniting for Peace Resolution.

First, under the Uniting for Peace Resolution, the General Assembly may recommend the use of armed force only in cases where there is "a breach of the peace or act of aggression." By not including "threat to the peace" in this formulation, the Uniting for Peace Resolution contains a higher standard for General Assembly action than exists for the Security Council in exercising its powers under Chapter VII of the Charter. Situations calling for humanitarian intervention that rise to the level of a "breach of the peace or act of aggression" would seem to lose their internal, "humanitarian" character and become a situation of international armed conflict.

Second, the legality of the General Assembly issuing "recommendations" for humanitarian intervention by states is by no means free from doubt. The status of the Uniting for Peace Resolution always has been somewhat tenuous; its basis within the Charter is not clear, and its limited contextual use casts some doubt on its continued vitality. More important, the structure of the UN Charter suggests that recommendations are appropriate in situations implicating international peace and security where either the General Assembly (under Article 11) or the Security Council (under Chapter VI or Article 39) is pursuing measures *short of* "enforcement action"—that is, short of action that forcibly imposes a result on a target state. Article 11(2) draws a distinction between General Assembly "recommendations" and "actions" on issues of international peace and security; "actions" require referral by the General Assembly to the Security Council. Thus, for states to be authorized to engage in enforcement actions, it would appear that something more than a "recommendation" is needed; the appropriate UN organ would need actually to decide upon such measures (Article 39). The structure of Article 2(7) also suggests that enforcement action was not envisioned outside Security Council action under Chapter VII.

Most UN practice is consistent with this interpretation of the Charter,

39. *See,* e.g., the proposals of Frank Newman in HUMANITARIAN INTERVENTION AND THE UNITED NATIONS 123–24 (R. Lillich ed., 1973).

although in the case of the Korean conflict the Security Council "recommended" that states assist South Korea,[40] which was then followed by recommendations by the General Assembly under the Uniting for Peace Resolution on the management of that conflict. The more recent instances of enforcement action by the Security Council, however, have all "decided," "authorized" or "called upon" states to take action. Although the issue was not squarely before it, the International Court of Justice in the *Certain Expenses* case interpreted the term "action" in Article 11(2) as meaning "enforcement action," implying that the General Assembly could not undertake enforcement action on its own (even through the use of recommendations).[41]

The point may seem excessively formalistic, but, as a normative proposition, restricting the role of the General Assembly in this manner is appropriate. Situations where the General Assembly would be used to authorize humanitarian intervention most likely would arise when one of the Permanent Members has strong policy reasons for disfavoring intervention (and therefore would veto any decision by the Security Council). If reasons exist, then the Permanent Member's national security interests are likely to be at stake, and one must seriously question whether the value gained from the General Assembly authorizing the intervention outweighs the risk consequently incurred. It cannot be assumed that the Permanent Member will stand idly by as the intervention takes place; the risk of a counterintervention could be high, and the whole matter might escalate into a more serious international conflict.

Furthermore, the experience of intervention in Iraq, Somalia, Rwanda, Haiti, and even Bosnia suggests that in most instances humanitarian intervention will be preceded by a process of diplomatic and economic sanctions and that ultimately support by one of the major powers will be necessary for an effective intervention (although, as seen in the case of Liberia, major power involvement may not always be necessary). If so, for the General Assembly to proceed on its own without fully engaging the Permanent Members risks a failure to create those conditions most likely to prevent the need for the intervention and to ensure a successful intervention if one proves necessary.

This approach does not leave the General Assembly without a role. As a general matter, the General Assembly and its committees are more actively engaged in the consideration of human rights issues than is the Security Council. Through the General Assembly, it is possible for egregious situations of human rights deprivations to be placed on the global

40. S.C. Res. 83, U.N. SCOR, 5th Sess., 474th mtg. at 5, U.N. Doc. S/INF/5/Rev.1 (1965).

41. Certain Expenses of the United Nations, 1962 I.C.J. 151, 163–66 (July 20).

agenda and hence on the Security Council agenda. Further, if the Security Council is deadlocked on whether to authorize humanitarian intervention due to the recalcitrance of one or a few Security Council members, a widely supported General Assembly resolution recommending such action could tip the scales in favor of intervention. Conversely, to the extent that one or more states are viewed as dominating the Security Council in pressing for UN humanitarian intervention, a General Assembly resolution calling for restraint could assist in restraining Security Council behavior. Finally, if there is a right of regional organizations or states to engage in humanitarian intervention without UN authorization, characterization by the General Assembly of a situation as involving or as not involving a widespread and severe human rights deprivations is not without value.

As discussed in Chapters 3 and 4, the International Court of Justice was not granted and has not developed a significant role in decisions to deploy force under UN command or authority. Were the Security Council to authorize humanitarian intervention in a state, the International Court of Justice would not have jurisdiction to hear a case by that state against the Security Council since the Security Council is not itself a state.[42] It would be possible, however, for the Court to render a decision in a case brought by a targeted state against a state that conducted an intervention under the authority of the Security Council, thereby indirectly addressing the issue of the Security Council's authority. The Court indirectly reviewed the validity of a Security Council decision under Chapter VII in the cases brought by Libya against Britain and the United States relating to the downing of a Pan Am airliner over Lockerbie, Scotland.[43]

42. Only states may be parties in contentious cases before the International Court. Statute of the International Court of Justice, *supra* note 31, art. 34, para. 1.

43. Questions of Interpretation and Application of the 1971 Montreal Convention arising from the Aerial Incident at Lockerbie (Libya v. U.K.; Libya v. U.S.), 1992 I.C.J. 114 (Order of Apr. 14). In that case, Libya claimed that efforts of the United States and the United Kingdom to obtain custody of the two Libyans violated Libya's right to extradite or to prosecute those individuals under the Montreal Convention for the Suppression of Unlawful Acts Against the Safety of Civil Aviation, Sept. 23, 1971, 24 U.S.T. 564, 974 U.N.T.S. 177 ("Montreal Convention"). The two Libyans had been indicted in the United States and Scotland for causing the destruction of a U.S. airliner over Lockerbie, Scotland. Prior to the Court's decision on whether to grant interim measures of protection to Libya, the Security Council had recommended, S.C. Res. 731, U.N. SCOR, 47th Sess., 3063rd mtg. at 51, U.N. Doc. S/INF/48 (1993), and then ordered, S.C. Res. 748, U.N. SCOR, 47th Sess., 3063rd mtg. at 52, U.N. Doc. S/INF/48 (1993), Libya to surrender for trial the two Libyan officials implicated in the bombing. The Court found that the passage of Security Council Resolution 748 was a "decision" taken under UN Charter Chapter VII and creates an obligation on states under UN Charter Article 25 that prevails over obligations of states under

Alternatively, the Court might be asked by a competent UN body to render an advisory opinion on whether a UN-authorized deployment was in accordance with the Charter,[44] as occurred in the *Certain Expenses* case.[45] The Security Council itself (and particularly its members who are major powers) is unlikely to see any advantage in crafting a role for the International Court in this area. When the Security Council wishes to act, preliminary use of the International Court would be seen as an unnecessary impediment, as a surrendering of the Security Council's plenary power in this area, and as potentially creating an atmosphere of uncertainty in the legal and moral basis of the Security Council's action, even if a favorable opinion is rendered by the Court. When the Security Council does not wish to act, reference of a matter to the International Court would inevitably serve to highlight that inaction. Whether some other UN organ or international legal body would have the competence to seek such an advisory opinion from the Court would turn on the constitutional nature of that organ or body and the circumstances of the request.

In the end, it must be noted that the International Court never has declared an action by the Security Council under Chapter VII as ultra vires, or otherwise in violation of international law, but, rather, has given effect to such actions. Indeed, were it to do so it might be costly to the Court itself. The Court has limited abilities for gathering facts about ongoing conflicts and, if it were to issue an unfavorable opinion regarding pursuit of an intervention, the Court would be tainted if the intervention either proceeded and failed, or did not proceed and the situation within the target state continued or worsened. The Court has never served as an instrument for restraining or unleashing military power by the United Nations and would appear better suited for addressing disputes among

---

other international agreements (*e.g.*, the Montreal Convention), pursuant to UN Charter Article 103. The Court in essence refused to second-guess the Security Council's decision that a threat to the peace existed. The Court, however, was not issuing a final decision, but rather was declining to issue provisional measures. It stated that it was "not at this stage called upon to determine definitively the legal effect" of the resolution. 1992 I.C.J. 114, para. 43. Professor Franck argues that the Court in this decision actually asserted its right to second-guess the Security Council by not deciding outright that no relief would be forthcoming to Libya at any stage of the proceedings. T. Franck, *The "Powers of Appreciation": Who is the Ultimate Guardian of UN Legality?* 86 AM. J. INT'L L. 519 (1992); *but see* W. Reisman, *The Constitutional Crisis in the United Nations*, 87 AM. J. INT'L L. 83, 93–94 (1993) (noting that the absence of standards within the Charter delimiting the Security Council's power to determine that a threat to the peace exists suggests that a judicial review function would be difficult). For a cogent discussion, *see* J. Alvarez, *Judging the Security Council*, 90 AM. J. INT'L L. 1 (1996).

44. U.N. CHARTER art. 96.
45. *Supra* note 41.

states that might arise after an incident of UN humanitarian intervention occurs. It seems likely that the Court would come to the same conclusion reached by a subsidiary organ of the Security Council in deciding that Chapter VII could be used to establish a war crimes tribunal for the prosecution of serious violations of international humanitarian law committed in the former Yugoslavia.

Article 39 leaves the choice of means and their evaluation to the Security Council, which enjoys wide discretionary powers in this regard; and it could not have been otherwise, as such a choice involves political evaluation of highly complex and dynamic situations.[46]

Thus, as a practical matter, the Security Council is the UN body best positioned to determine authoritatively whether there exists a situation justifying the resort to humanitarian intervention.

E. The Means for UN Humanitarian Intervention

Chapter VII of the UN Charter envisages the negotiation of agreements under Article 43 by which states commit to provide military forces and logistical support to the United Nations when called upon to do so. Since no such agreements exist, the United Nations has developed different means for conducting humanitarian intervention.

Only rarely will the United Nations deploy forces under its own command for an enforcement action. After April 1993 in Somalia, the United Nations deployed military forces under UN command (UNOSOM II). The forces were provided to the United Nations under ad hoc voluntary arrangements between the United Nations and several states and were supported by voluntary financial contributions from states. Part of the difficulties experienced in UNOSOM II are attributable to the ad hoc nature of the deployment of the forces. The United Nations nominally has a Military Staff Committee, but does not have the ability to undertake significant contingency planning (e.g., lift arrangements) and has no facilities for the training of officers and troops regarding UN command and control, rules of engagement, or critical tasks such as civic reconstruction. When the Security Council decides to deploy forces, they must be hastily recruited and often are of uneven quality. As occurred in Somalia, the allegiance of national forces to the United Nations, as opposed to their own domestic constituency, is not always guaranteed, and their withdrawal is not within the control of the United Nations. Further, forces from various countries rarely have had the opportunity to train

---

46. Tribunal on War Crimes in Former Yugoslavia, Decision of October 1995, *supra* note 11, para. 39.

with each other and often suffer logistical and linguistic difficulties in communicating among themselves and with the local population.

The more likely means for conducting humanitarian intervention is through Security Council authorization of states to deploy forces under their own command in support of Security Council resolutions. This form of authorization was the nature of the interventions in northern and southern Iraq in 1991 and 1992 (to the extent that those interventions may be considered authorized by the Security Council), in Somalia by UNITAF from December 1992 through April 1993, the intervention in Rwanda by France in June 1994, and the naval enforcement of sanctions against Haiti beginning in October 1993 and the threatened intervention in 1994. This authorization may extend to states acting through a regional organization, as was the case with ECOMOG in Liberia, although in that case the "authorization" occurred ex post facto.[47] In these instances, there were far fewer difficulties of command and control, rules of engagement, and logistical cooperation than existed for the UN-led intervention force in Somalia, UNOSOM II. In the cases of Iraq, Somalia, and Haiti, one or more major NATO powers dominated the command structure of the intervention and dictated the rules of engagement. For the most part, the officers of the primary forces engaged in the intervention had trained with their counterparts and could draw on experiences of interoperability gained from NATO training exercises.

While there is an understandable uneasiness with the United Nations undertaking intervention by authorizing states to act in their national capacity, particularly where the major powers are involved, this will likely remain the only viable option for such intervention for some time to come.[48] Indeed, the case studies in chapter 5 suggest that the best chance for encouraging such intervention may be to promote the ability of major powers and other states concerned with the crisis (perhaps because it is in their sphere of interest) to undertake such intervention. One benefit of this approach is that it allows the United Nations to avoid placing its own prestige on the line at the riskiest point of the intervention and

47. While this study does not consider Bosnia to be a good example of humanitarian intervention, it is worth noting that, to the extent that the UN actions in that case can be considered intervention, they involved a mixture of authorizations for UN peacekeeping forces, states acting through regional organizations, and states acting on their own to enforce UN Security Council resolutions.

48. Of course, having the United Nations deploy the forces itself is no guarantee of impartiality. In the case of the former Yugoslavia, the United Nations was forced to dismiss one of its officers, a Russian, in part because he was conniving with Russia's traditional allies, the Serbs. The United Nations claimed he had allowed the Serbs to receive U.N. gasoline, as well as allowed artillery guns and anti-tank vehicles to cross the Danube into Serbian-held Croatia, all in violation of U.N. economic sanctions. R. Cohen, *U.N. Dismisses Russian From Croatia Peacekeeping Post*, N.Y. TIMES, Apr. 12, 1995, at A16.

instead allows it to assume control of the operation some months after the intervention has occurred. Another benefit is that it helps preserve the ability of the Secretary-General to act as an impartial mediator in the crisis, which plays to the strengths of the office of the Secretary-General and away from its weaknesses.[49]

Nevertheless, over time, opportunities for the negotiation and conclusion of Article 43 agreements should be explored. The existence of such agreements between member states and the United Nations for the provision of military forces, assistance, and facilities on UN call could expedite the ability of the UN to deploy well-trained and impartial forces in humanitarian situations and could facilitate burden-sharing and planning.[50] As noted in chapter 3, Article 43 contemplates the negotiation of agreements between member states and the Security Council for the contribution of "armed forces, assistance, and facilities, including rights of passage" whenever called upon by the Security Council. The agreements are to govern the "numbers and types of forces, their degree of readiness and general location, and the nature of the facilities and assistance to be provided." Under Article 47, a Military Staff Committee is to advise and assist the Security Council on the "employment and command of forces placed at its disposal" and is to be responsible for the "strategic direction" of those forces.

In the early years of the Charter era, efforts to establish Article 43 agreements foundered on Cold War distrust.[51] As Secretary-General Boutros Boutros-Ghali asserted in his "Agenda for Peace," however, "Under the political circumstances that now exist for the first time since the Charter was adopted, the long-standing obstacles to the conclusion of such special agreements should no longer prevail."[52] In November 1992,

49. *See generally* G. Picco, *The U.N. and the Use of Force*, FOREIGN AFF., Sept.-Oct. 1994, at 14.

50. *See, e.g.*, R. Johansen, *Reforming the United Nations to Eliminate War*, 4 TRANSNAT'L L. & CONTEMP. PROBS. 455, 476–483 (1994).

51. In 1946, the Security Council asked the Military Staff Committee to examine the issue of Article 43 agreements. The report of the Committee indicated disagreement on several key issues, such as the size and composition of the forces to be contributed, the location of the forces, and the conditions for their use and withdrawal. *See Report of the Military Staff Committee*, U.N. SCOR, 2d Sess., Special Supp. No. 1, U.N. Doc. S/336 (1947), *discussed in* L. GOODRICH, THE UNITED NATIONS IN A CHANGING WORLD 113–14 (1974) ("Generally speaking, the United States favored a large force with great striking power, flexibly composed, and so organized and located as to be readily available. The Soviet Union, on the other hand, saw no need of a large force, insisted that the principle of equality should govern contributions, and demanded clear definition of the conditions under which the force could be used.").

52. An Agenda for Peace, *supra* note 13, para. 43. The Secretary-General recommended that the Security Council initiate negotiations supported by the Military Staff Committee. In the United States, some members of the U.S. Senate have spoken out in favor of, and

the Secretary-General considered the option of a countrywide enforcement operation in Somalia to be carried out under United Nations command and control. He concluded, however, that the Secretariat did not "at present have the capability to command and control an enforcement operation of the size and urgency required by the present crisis in Somalia."[53]

Conclusion of Article 43 agreements could allow for coordination and training of a multinational force in advance of a humanitarian crisis, along with resolution of command and control issues and rules of engagement. While such agreements have never previously been achievable, states may find it more politically acceptable to pursue them if limited to humanitarian intervention, since the nature and scope of the intervention usually is (although not always) of a lesser order than action to repel aggression. Some of the states likely to shoulder the primary responsibility for forces, facilities, and assistance (Britain, France, and the United States) should find it politically acceptable to enter into these agreements because they are protected from being pulled unwillingly into humanitarian interventions by their status as permanent members of the Security Council. Other states willing to commit significant financial assistance in advance (Germany, Japan) might be eager to obtain access to Security Council deliberations if they could be given the opportunity to participate in the decision to intervene through Article 43 agreements.

One misconception about Article 43 is that it contemplates the possibility of a "standing army" under the control of the Security Council. The concept of a standing force—particularly an air force—maintained directly under the Security Council's control was discussed at length at

---

held hearings on, the idea of an Article 43 agreement by which U.S. forces would be placed at the disposal of the United Nations. *See Arming the United Nations Security Council: Hearing on The Collective Security Participation Resolution, S.J. Res. 325, Before the Senate Comm. on Foreign Relations*, 102d Cong., 2d Sess. (1992) [hereinafter *Arming the United Nations*]. Under the 1945 U.N. Participation Act, 22 U.S.C. secs. 287–287e (1988 & Supp.V 1993), the President was granted the statutory authority to negotiate Article 43 agreement(s) with the Security Council which, once approved by the Congress, would permit the President at future times to make U.S. forces available to the Security Council in accordance with the agreement(s) and without further Congressional authorization. The President, however, has never negotiated such an agreement.

Moreover, it is not clear whether, even with the approval of Congress, the President constitutionally *can* conclude a treaty that provides for the deployment of U.S. forces for combat without a contemporaneous declaration of war by the Congress under Article I, Section 8 of the Constitution. Even those constitutional scholars who assert that such a treaty is possible admit that there are doubts. *See, e.g.*, J. ELY, WAR AND RESPONSIBILITY: CONSTITUTIONAL LESSONS OF VIETNAM AND ITS AFTERMATH 14–15 (1993).

53. *Letter Dated 29 November 1992 from the Secretary-General to the President of the Security Council* 5, U.N. Doc. S/24868 (1992).

the Dumbarton Oaks Conference and ultimately rejected. The direction taken in Article 43 was not to create the possibility of a separate standing UN force but, rather, to establish a mechanism whereby national forces would be made available to the Security Council at the time of a crisis pursuant to prior agreement.[54] Consequently, while the creation of such a standing force under the overall Chapter VII powers of the Security Council might be possible, it would not appear to be within the scope of Article 43.

An ambitious approach to the use of Article 43 agreements would be to seek commitments from a large number of states for the use of significant numbers of their national forces upon call of the Security Council for humanitarian intervention. The advantages of such an approach would be to engage widespread support for UN humanitarian intervention, to spread the costs of undertaking such action, to enhance capabilities in this area through periodic joint training and exercises, and to aspire to fulfill the clear legal obligation under Article 43 of "all" members to enter into Article 43 agreements. Efforts to "go global" with large national contingents under Article 43 agreements, however, are bound to encounter difficulties, even if limited to humanitarian intervention. Many states will be reluctant to commit large numbers of their forces in advance for political and economic reasons, particularly where no vital interests are at stake. The negotiation and conclusion of such agreements could be time consuming. In addition, coordination of large numbers of forces from many countries for the purpose of training and exercises, let alone actual combat, would be very difficult and expensive for the United Nations. As the Secretary-General himself has noted, "it would be folly to attempt to do so at the present time when the Organization is resource-starved and hard pressed to handle the less demanding peacemaking and peace-keeping responsibilities entrusted to it."[55]

A less ambitious approach would be to seek contingents from a moderate number of states of a limited number of forces for use in humanitarian intervention. A limited pool of forces (e.g., 10,000 to 20,000) might prove less than is needed for particularly difficult crises or if multiple crises are occurring simultaneously. Yet a smaller force would be easier to fund, easier to train, and if readily available for deployment (i.e., a rapid reaction force) it could serve as a means of preventing an internal crisis from developing to a point where a larger force is neces-

54. Article 43 was the product of a U.S. compromise in the face of a strong desire of the Soviet Union to establish an international air corps maintained directly under the control of the Security Council. R. HILDERBRAND, DUMBARTON OAKS: THE ORIGINS OF THE UNITED NATIONS AND THE SEARCH FOR POSTWAR SECURITY 146–49 (1990).

55. *Supplement to An Agenda for Peace: Report of the Secretary-General*, para. 77, U.N. Doc. A/50/60, S/1995/1 (1995).

sary.[56] To address some of the concerns about placing national military forces under a UN command for an indefinite period, persons could be assigned to this force solely on a volunteer basis.[57] Volunteers may be more likely to accept the downsides to UN force deployments (including the command structure) and more willing to engage in the training with foreign forces necessary for a successful UN action. Further, use of persons who specifically volunteered for such a UN force may deflect some of the anxieties produced domestically when that force is placed in situations of danger.

For purposes of enhancing deterrence, there is considerable attraction to the idea of a rapidly deployable UN force because it would permit the Security Council to engage in humanitarian intervention without the need for lengthy domestic legislative approval processes, whether by the U.S. Congress or the Russian Parliament. Even if the forces are not deployed, informal communications, formal declarations, and nonforcible sanctions of the Security Council would have greater likelihood of deterring human rights abuses if it is known that a ready option for military deployment is available.[58] Deploying a force under UN command would present the local authorities with increased political costs in committing or tolerating the human rights abuses, particularly if the force is comprised of contingents from a broad number of countries.

There are, however, serious concerns with the establishment of Article 43 agreements for humanitarian intervention. First, states may *not* find it more palatable to enter into these agreements for purposes of humanitarian intervention; a lesser order of force may be involved, but at the same time lesser interests of states are involved. Moreover, the Security Council does not categorize its actions as "humanitarian intervention" as opposed to some other kind of intervention; all actions are in response to some threat to the peace. Even if a distinction could be developed for using a highly trained UN force in situations considered "humanitarian intervention," there would be a tendency to so characterize a situation whenever a UN force is needed.

Other concerns arise with respect to Article 43 agreements as a whole. Article 43 agreements may make it too easy for the United Nations to deploy military forces without sufficient deliberation both at the United Nations and within member states, whose support is essential for any military operation to succeed. There are certain "brakes" that exist in

56. *Id.* para. 44.

57. *See* B. Urquhart, *For a UN Voluntary Military Force*, N.Y. Rev. Books, June 10, 1993, at 3 (former Undersecretary-General of the United Nations).

58. *See An Agenda for Peace, supra* note 13, para. 43 ("The ready availability of armed forces on call could serve, in itself, as a means of deterring breaches of the peace since a potential aggressor would know that the Council had at its disposal a means of response.").

the current approach to UN deployments that serve a function in preventing imprudent actions. Also, since most states do not enjoy permanent member status they may be reluctant to enter into Article 43 agreements for the deployment of even small numbers of forces. If they did, they might be ordered to make available their forces for use by the United Nations against their own historical, religious, or ethnic allies, and even conceivably against themselves. Even a major power may not wish to face situations where it has to veto the deployment of UN forces to avoid its Article 43 agreement obligations.

Perhaps the most serious concern, however, is whether the placing of various national contingents under a single UN command is logistically and tactically feasible. During the Cold War, the lack of Article 43 agreements was rightly attributed largely to bipolar tensions. Yet even in the 1940s, when Article 43 agreements were first discussed, many logistical difficulties surfaced that were not resolved. These difficulties are even more pronounced in today's high technology environment, where the intelligence capabilities, communications, rules of engagement, and general training of different militaries vastly diverge. Some issues that prove difficult to resolve might be left open; for instance, command responsibility could be determined on an ad hoc basis for each enforcement action based on which countries were providing the most significant levels of forces. Yet most issues must be resolved in advance; establishing a multilateral UN force capable of expeditious deployment should not be done if that force ultimately is not capable of being organized and operated as effectively and efficiently as would be done under national commands. If it is not so capable, support will quickly evaporate and its credibility in both deterring and responding to humanitarian crises will be undermined.

It would be unfortunate if the concerns regarding deployment of military forces under Article 43 agreements precluded pursuit of other possibilities for Article 43 agreements. Article 43 speaks not just of placing military forces on call but of providing assistance and facilities as well, including rights of passage. Since one of the advantages often noted with Article 43 agreements is the ability to burden-share, it would seem reasonable to pursue agreements that allowed a standardized arrangement for states to provide funds to the United Nations for humanitarian intervention by the Security Council. An Article 43 burden-sharing agreement might be compulsory (which may assist some states under their domestic processes in the expeditious provision of funds) or, if that is not possible, might simply provide a mechanism for the orderly collection of funds. A standardized mechanism would seem preferable to an ad hoc approach, although ad hoc approaches can work both within and outside the UN system. In the case of funding for UNITAF in Somalia, an ad hoc trust fund was established by the Security Council and administered by the Secretary-General to receive funds for supporting military contingents provided by lesser developed countries.

Another possibility would be to negotiate Article 43 agreements that provide ready access to airfields, ports, railroads, and roads for forces engaged in humanitarian intervention. A third possibility would be Article 43 agreements that provide for the pre-positioning of ammunition, equipment (lethal or non-lethal), or other supplies (e.g., food) in a state for use in humanitarian situations. Many states are reluctant to engage in such stockpiling because it typically involves an association with one of the major powers, which can cause domestic or regional difficulties. Stockpiling pursuant to an association with the Security Council for humanitarian intervention, however, might be regarded as an entirely different matter. The benefit for the host country, of course, is both the existence of a relationship with the Security Council and the existence of materials that would help maintain regional stability. If necessary, the Article 43 agreement could provide the host government with the ability to veto the use of the materials in the region if the host state believed doing so would threaten its vital interests. At a minimum, the stockpiling of medical supplies and foodstuffs should pose a minimum of difficulty to the host state.

F. The Limits of UN Humanitarian Intervention

On the assumption that the Security Council has determined that a threat to the peace exists and has authorized the intervention of military forces under UN command or otherwise, how far may that intervention go in addressing the threat to the peace? The facile answer is that the force used must be "necessary and proportionate" to the threat at issue.[59] While this standard does not appear in Chapter VII, commentators and states appear to accept the application of this customary rule of in-

---

59. The rule constraining the use of force to that which is necessary and proportionate to the threat or aggression at hand can be traced back centuries. Under contemporary international law theory, reference is typically made to the August 6, 1842 letter of U.S. Secretary of State Daniel Webster to Lord Ashburton in the U.S.-U.K. Caroline incident:

> Undoubtedly it is just, that, while it is admitted that exceptions growing out of the great law of self-defense do exist, those exceptions should be confined to cases in which the "necessity of that self-defense is instant, overwhelming, and leaving no choice of means, and no moment for deliberation."

J. MOORE, 2 INTERNATIONAL LAW DIGEST 412 (1906).

ternational law to actions taken by or on behalf of the Security Council under Chapter VII.[60] Ironically, this standard owes much of its heritage to the just war doctrine of the Middle Ages: as discussed in chapter 2, the central feature of that doctrine was whether the use of force was for a "just cause." As the just war doctrine became secularized under Grotius and Vattel, the standard became one of whether the overall evil that a war would cause was balanced by the good that would be achieved.[61] That standard may underlie the modern standard of "necessary and proportionate" uses of force, but these standards are not congruent. Today's standard is influenced by the UN Charter's general prohibition on the use of the force except in limited circumstances and by the norms that have developed within international humanitarian law (such as the provisions contained within the 1949 Geneva Conventions[62] and their 1977 Protocols[63] for the protection of persons involved in armed conflict).

The exact requirements of the contemporary "necessary and proportionate" standard are far from clear. Presumably one must assess the justifiable ends of the use of force and then assess whether the actions taken further those ends without impinging excessively on other values. In the context of humanitarian intervention, the justifiable end is the cessation of widespread and severe deprivation of human rights. One might argue that action in furtherance of that end is limited to the simple protection of the civilian population (e.g., through the creation of enclaves) or the reopening of food relief lines. Any intervention of military forces, however, must contemplate the eventual removal of those forces from the target country. If the human rights deprivations will likely recommence upon removal of those forces, then the steps taken were not sufficient to achieve the justifiable end.

In Rwanda, the scope of the intervention was limited to the creation of a safe zone for the protection of refugees and displaced persons and the provision of relief to them. French forces withdrew two months after

60. *See, e.g.*, J. Gardam, *Proportionality and Force in International Law*, 87 AM. J. INT'L L. 391, 392 (1993) (noting in the context of the Iraq-Kuwait war the general acceptance that states acting under the authority of the Security Council were constrained by the proportionality and necessity rule).

61. *Id.* at 394–95.

62. 1949 Geneva Conventions, *supra* note 29.

63. Protocol Additional (No. I) to the Geneva Conventions of 12 August 1949, and Relating to the Protection of Victims of International Armed Conflict, June 8, 1977, 1125 UNTS 3, *reprinted in* 2 WESTON, *supra* note 6, at II.B.20; Protocol Additional (No. II) to the Geneva Conventions of 12 August 1949, and Relating to the Protection of Victims of Non-International Armed Conflicts, June 8, 1977, 1125 UNTS 609, *reprinted in* 2 WESTON, *supra* note 6, at II.B.21.

their arrival. The scope of the interventions in Liberia, Iraq, and Somalia ultimately went much further than simply protecting foreign relief personnel and ensuring the ability to provide humanitarian relief such as food, medicine, and shelter. A catalogue of forcible actions undertaken in one or more of those interventions, listed in increasing level of intrusiveness, would be as follows:

1. aerial reconnaissance of the movements of the targeted state's military or warring factions;
2. airdropping of foodstuffs, medicine, tents, and blankets to the civilian population;
3. prohibiting flights by the targeted state's military and civilian aircraft, both fixed and non-fixed wing;
4. prohibiting ground movements of the targeted state's military forces;
5. prohibiting emplacement of surface-to-air missiles in areas where intervening state aircraft are conducting reconnaissance flights;
6. deploying military forces, under either UN command or the command of states, into the targeted state to protect relief workers and assist in the distribution of humanitarian supplies;
7. disarming military forces within the targeted state, including the seizure and destruction of caches of stored weaponry;
8. shooting down the targeted state's military aircraft;
9. attacking and destroying surface-to-air missile sites;
10. shooting both armed forces and civilians in the targeted state perceived as threats to the forces of the intervening state;
11. permitting local insurgent groups to operate de facto governments in a protected zone;
12. creating a local police force; and
13. creating a process of national reconciliation and political settlement.

In principle, all these actions potentially could be for the purpose of preventing the widespread and severe deprivation of human rights.

At the same time, one can envision significant collateral damage to the target state's civilian population from the pursuit of several of these actions. Indeed, ECOMOG came under considerable criticism for its bombing tactics against Taylor's forces because of the collateral damage caused to the civilian population. Both UNITAF and UNOSOM forces likewise were criticized for firing upon Somali civilians. The nature of humanitarian intervention is such that unintended harm both to the intervening forces and the civilians they seek to protect is to be expected.

At some point, however, that harm may rise to a level at which the international community would regard the actions of the intervening forces (and perhaps the intervention as a whole) to be disproportionate or unnecessary for preventing the human rights deprivation.

Actions that appear to favor certain insurgent groups and that strive to achieve national reconciliation through democratic processes are perhaps the most susceptible to criticism. In theory, UN humanitarian intervention would not seek to favor insurgent groups over an established government, would not favor one faction over another in a civil war, or would not seek to alter the governing structure of the target state. The intervening states in Iraq and Rwanda went to some lengths to avoid characterizing their interventions as having such purposes. In contrast, the intervening forces in Somalia, Liberia, and Haiti were quite frank in their goals of reconstituting the target state's government. In the case of the widespread deprivation of human rights, it is difficult to see how the intervening states can effectively and permanently eliminate the threat to international peace and security without somehow altering the governing structure of the targeted state, which necessarily will favor certain political groups over others. The intervention in Iraq continued long after it commenced precisely because of a failure to alter the nature of the central government, thereby removing the source of the threat. The only alternative to altering the governing structure forcibly would be to reach an accommodation with the government by which it agreed to alter its behavior. For example, an accommodation of sorts was reached with the Government of Iraq; Iraq allowed UN forces to replace the forces of the intervening states and ceased aggressive action against the Kurds in the north. Aggressive action against the Shiites in the south, however, did not cease, and the ultimate fate of both the Kurds and the Shiites as of this writing is uncertain.

Likewise, in the case of a complete breakdown in civil order, or "failed state," the establishment of a governing structure may be the most necessary, albeit the most difficult, means for bringing an end to the disorder. In both Somalia and Liberia, it was deemed essential to engage the warring factions in efforts to reached a settlement leading to national reconciliation. Although both the Cotonou Agreement on Liberia and the Addis Ababa Accords on Somalia proved incapable of successful implementation, the intervening forces believed they had no choice but to try to develop a process of national reconciliation so as to permit an orderly withdrawal of the intervening forces.

In any event, actions that have the effect of altering the governing structure of the targeted state cannot per se be considered disproportionate or unnecessary.

G. Key Difficulties Encountered To Date

As has been noted, the international community is experiencing the product of a reinvigorated Security Council engaged in various actions, including action that fits the doctrine of humanitarian intervention. There are good things to say about this action. Before British, French, and U.S. forces intervened in northern Iraq in April 1991, 1,000 Iraq Kurds were dying each day. After that intervention, Kurdish deaths dropped dramatically. In the twelve months preceding the intervention by the UNITAF forces, some 300,000 Somalis died of starvation and violence. In the months following the intervention, pockets of suffering remained, but large-scale starvation had been eliminated and death rates dropped dramatically.[64] While withspread deaths occurred in Rwanda without any UN intervention, once intervention did occur a protective zone was established that likely helped end further deaths, and for now Rwanda has stabilized. Haiti today is a free democracy. While the Security Council was not initially involved in the ECOWAS intervention, that intervention is generally credited with preventing a bloodbath in Monrovia. These positive results are the reason why in egregious situations of human rights violation, if communicated by the media throughout the world, there will continue to be pressures on the United Nations to act.

Unfortunately, not all of the results of the UN experience in conducting humanitarian intervention are positive; indeed, they are decidedly mixed. The intervention in Iraq made great strides in protecting the Iraqi Kurds, but left the Iraqi Shiites subject to a vicious and effective campaign of human rights abuse. The intervention in Somalia did not succeed in addressing the root causes of the widespread starvation and violence in that country. The intervention in Rwanda had a limited success in protecting certain civilians, but came after as many as 500,000 had died in a two-month period and was limited in scope. The blockade on Haiti enforced economic sanctions on an already destitute civilian population, but neither it nor the threat of military invasion deposed an entrenched military elite. As discussed, Bosnia is more than just a situation of internal human rights abuses, but the interventions that did occur to protect Bosnian Muslims failed to prevent upwards of 250,000 deaths in a two-year period.

There are many reasons for these failures and it is dangerous to generalize too much in looking for common threads. Nevertheless, there are certain elements in the operation of the United Nations and its relation-

---

64. *See U.S. Policy in Somalia: Hearing Before the Senate Comm. on Foreign Relations*, 103d Cong., 1st Sess. 305 (1993).

ship to its member states that shed some light on these failures. It is important to identify these elements if we are to probe for ways to improve future UN humanitarian intervention.

- Collective Intervention Is Not Insulated from the Problems
Faced by Unilateral Intervention

Action by the United Nations is not inherently wiser or more efficient than action by a regional organization, which in turn is not necessarily better than action by a few states or even a single state. There is a value in collective decisionmaking because it allows various perspectives to be aired and can engender useful support from a wide variety of countries for a proposed action. However, decisions made by many states are not, because of their collective origin, necessarily superior to decisions made by individual states, and at times they may be worse, especially as to the amount of force to be used.[65] For instance, it is not readily apparent that the European Union's approach to handling the situation in Bosnia in 1993 was inherently better than the U.S. preference for arming the Bosnian Muslims and providing them air support in their fight against Bosnian Serbs. Indeed, the arguments are strong that the reverse may have been true. These are difficult issues at any level of decisionmaking, but the politics of collective decisionmaking may move states to the lowest common denominator of potential options, which often favors little or no action. If so, that minimal action may prove less effective in saving lives and creating the conditions for a negotiated peace than more aggressive action favored by one or a few states. Further, collective decisionmaking, while capable of expeditious action in certain circumstances, generally favors inertia, which in the context of human rights deprivations can have serious, irretrievable consequences.

There is no reason to believe that decisions regarding UN humanitarian intervention will be any easier or less controversial than UN decisions to address breaches of the peace or acts of aggression. Somalia was an easy case; large numbers of people were dying, the central government had crumbled, and the deployment of forces led by the United States promised great benefits with little likelihood of aggravating the situation. Consequently, the Security Council could expressly and expeditiously authorize intervention with the same ease that it imposed sanctions and ultimately authorized the use of force against Iraq's overt invasion of Kuwait of August 1990. Yet most cases of either aggression or humanitarian intervention will not be easy ones. As in Bosnia, the hu-

---

65. *See* I. CLAUDE, SWORDS INTO PLOWSHARES: PROBLEMS AND PROGRESS OF INTERNATIONAL ORGANIZATION 28 (4th ed. 1971).

man rights deprivations may be high, but the potential costs of intervening may be high as well. As in Haiti, the potential costs of intervention may be low, but the compelling nature of the human rights deprivations may be low also. As in Liberia and Rwanda, there may be difficulties in securing the attention of the Security Council. The decision to proceed with UN humanitarian intervention, as is the case when addressing aggression, inevitably is a decision to deploy large numbers of forces in a manner that can potentially lead to significant violence. Easy cases will be rare, hard cases will be controversial, and obscure cases will languish.

• UN Humanitarian Intervention Is Not Peacekeeping

If the United Nations is going to engage in humanitarian intervention, it needs to separate such action from the fundamental principles that guide it in peacekeeping operations. Peacekeeping operations are predicated on the consent of the host government; the forces deployed by the United Nations usually are small in number, lightly armed, and have limited rules of engagement. They seek not to alter conditions so much as to maintain a status quo, perhaps in order to allow for a peaceful transition to an orderly situation. By contrast, humanitarian intervention often requires the large-scale deployment of military forces capable of suppressing the regular or irregular forces of a country. Whether called "peacemaking," "peace-enforcing" or "new peacekeeping," what is necessary is essentially an armed invasion of a country to impose a change in conditions. Expectations about the requirements for, and the ease of, such a mission must be radically different from that of a peacekeeping operation.

Unfortunately, the Secretary-General's 1992 "Agenda for Peace" [66] did not advance such distinctions. In that document, four categories of UN action are set forth: preventive diplomacy, peacemaking, peacekeeping, and peace-building.[67] The concept of "peacemaking" would seem the appropriate one for deployment of UN forces to halt aggression as well as for humanitarian intervention and, in fact, under its "peacemaking" section, the Agenda for Peace discussed the use of force under Article 42 of the Charter.[68] Yet, "peacemaking" is defined as "action to bring hostile parties to agreement, *essentially through such peaceful means as those foreseen in Chapter VI* of the Charter of the United Nations." [69] Thus, the

66. *See generally, An Agenda for Peace, supra* note 13.
67. *Id.* para. 20.
68. *Id.* paras. 42–43.
69. *Id.* para. 20 (emphasis added); *see also id.* para. 34 ("Between the tasks of seeking to prevent conflict and keeping the peace lies the responsibility to try to bring hostile parties to agreement by peaceful means.").

"Agenda for Peace" thoroughly blurred the key distinction between actions by the United Nations undertaken in its traditional "peace-keeping" mode and those more aggressive actions now possible by the Security Council to "make" peace where there is internal or external conflict. In the 1995 "Supplement to An Agenda for Peace," this lapse was somewhat corrected by the addition of a section on "enforcement action" and by the recognition that "the logic of peace-keeping flows from political and military premises that are quite distinct from those of enforcement; and the dynamics of the latter are incompatible with the political process that peace-keeping is intended to facilitate." [70]

Somalia is the perfect example of the problem of failing to distinguish between peacekeeping functions and actions necessary to undertake humanitarian intervention. The initial deployment of a 500 person peacekeeping force to Somalia (UNOSOM I) with limited capabilities was a complete disaster. It served no function except to highlight the impotence of the United Nations to address the breakdown in Somalia. The humanitarian intervention under UNITAF, however, was successful in curtailing the widespread starvation and violence that was crippling the country. UNITAF differed quantitatively and qualitatively from UNOSOM; it consisted of thousands of heavily armed forces capable of firing upon Somali irregular forces, not just in self-defense but also to achieve certain objectives, such as the opening of relief lines. When control passed from UNITAF to UNOSOM II, this more aggressive approach to the intervention was maintained. Yet many states and the United Nations bureaucracy were uncomfortable with the UN forces undertaking such a role and at times confused the principles by which UNOSOM II was operating with those that operate for peacekeeping forces. This confusion ultimately served to undermine support for efforts to disarm and demobilize aggressively the Somali factions. In situations where a widespread deprivation of human rights presents itself, the United Nations cannot expect a consensual peacekeeping operation to provide an adequate means of addressing the problem unless it is already convinced that the principle actors in the country have decided to change the conditions that led to those deprivations.

Deployment of forces in a "peacekeeping" mode when in fact humanitarian intervention is called for also risks lending UN support to the human rights deprivations. The presence of an ineffective peacekeeping force can enhance the domestic status of local authorities if it appears they are capable of manipulating the international community. Further, impotent peacekeepers may create the appearance of purposeful international action when in reality none exists. Of course, this dilemma

---

70. *Supplement to An Agenda for Peace, supra* note 55, paras. 35, 77–80.

may also be true if humanitarian intervention is undertaken that is very limited in scope. For instance, the imposition of a no-fly zone over southern Iraq may have had an initial effect on Iraqi oppression of the Shiites, but in the long run it may have served as simply a substitute for meaningful international action. Likewise, the limited French intervention in Rwanda relieved the pressure on the international community to act in that crisis. In extreme cases, the presence of peacekeeping forces may serve to preclude more forceful humanitarian intervention; several of the European countries argued against UN-authorized attacks on Bosnian Serb positions out of concern for the safety of UNPROFOR peacekeepers.

The United Nations, of course, has fifty years of experience in peace-keeping operations and virtually no experience in the use of force to address aggression by states, let alone aggression by governing authorities against their own people through the widespread deprivation of human rights. This lack of experience and lack of contingency planning leads to complications that tarnish the image of the United Nations and, hence, its effectiveness. For instance, when UNOSOM II forces took Somali irregulars as prisoners, there was no established means for charging the prisoners with violations of Somali or international law and granting them rights of due process. This lacunae, in turn, led to criticisms that the United Nations itself was committing human rights violations in Somalia. In Bosnia, there were reports that UN forces seeking to alleviate starvation, such as by opening roads, were inadvertently aiding local factions engaged in warfare,[71] and even reports that UN troops took advantage of Muslim and Croat women forced into prostitution.[72]

- When It Comes to Intervention, the United Nations
  Is Mostly the Sum of Its Parts

The United Nations may be something more than the sum of its parts, but it is very dependent on those parts in undertaking humanitarian intervention. Like most international organizations, the United Nations experiences great difficulties in developing on its own effective, coherent strategies for resolution of crises; indeed, it has little independent political leverage, and hence its promises and threats often lack credibility.[73] Yet, if the United Nations is deficient in the field of humanitarian intervention, it is largely due to the schizophrenia of its member states, particularly the major powers upon which these interventions depend. On

---

71. J. Pomfret, *U.N. Aid Could Extend Bosnian War*, Wash. Post, Nov. 24, 1993, at A1.

72. R. Gutman, *U.N. Forces Accused of Using Serb-Run Brothel*, Wash. Post, Nov. 2, 1993, at A12.

73. S. Touval, *Why the U.N. Fails*, Foreign Aff., Sept.-Oct. 1994, at 44, 45.

the one hand, member states in theory support the use of the United Nations to address cases of widespread human rights deprivations. On the other hand, they are unwilling to provide the United Nations with mechanisms for calling up military forces when needed to address those cases, and to command, train, and equip those forces. On the one hand, member states will take steps on an ad hoc basis to assuage consciences shocked by human rights deprivations. On the other hand, these steps are usually of a short-term character; member states resist committing the resources necessary to root out the causes of those human rights deprivations. Because the advantage gained by member states in conducting humanitarian intervention is low, their actions will be a function of the political, economic, and military costs incurred. The nature of humanitarian intervention is such that the costs—political, economic, military—are usually high, particularly if the root causes of the problem are addressed. That the deployment of thousands of troops to Somalia would ultimately lead to the deaths of some of those troops and to the taking of prisoners of war should have come as no surprise to the intervening forces; yet it did, and led to a crumbling of support for the intervention by key member states, especially the United States.

This schizophrenia may be due to a lack of definition in the objectives sought by humanitarian intervention. The ambiguity in the "threat to the peace" in these cases, as well as the ad hoc (and sometimes ex post facto) character of the UN authorization, carry over to an ambiguity in the objectives sought. There is a very great difference between ending widespread human rights deprivations in the short term, and rooting out and eliminating their causes so as to create stability in the long term. The latter in many instances will require the disarmament of local factions, perhaps at great loss of life to the intervening forces, and the reconstitution of a government in the state. There also is a great difference between seeking to restore order in a country and seeking to bring to justice those that have committed heinous offenses in the past, whether against their own people or against UN forces. Restoring order may require the brokering of deals with leaders of factions with blood on their hands, at least so long as they command sufficient support within the country to block an enduring peace. In Cambodia, the United Nations shook hands with the Khmer Rouge in its largely successful effort at rebuilding that country. In Somalia, the failure of UNOSOM II to draw all factions into a process of national reconciliation ultimately proved its downfall.

Consequently, the United Nations and its member states would do well to consider steps to clarify international community expectations and objectives when engaging in humanitarian intervention. After the Cold War, we are now asking much more of the United Nations than ever has been asked of it before, and we are scrutinizing the conduct of its humanitarian interventions in ways that humanitarian intervention never was scrutinized in the pre-Charter era. Absent well-understood expectations and objectives, that scrutiny risks inhibiting UN action, which in turn invites failure. It will require patience, persistence, and perseverance on the part of the United Nations and its member states to establish acceptable expectations and objectives, and, on the basis of these expectations and objectives, to see humanitarian interventions through to their end.

H. Improvements for Future Interventions

Despite the serious questions that arise regarding UN humanitarian intervention, circumstances calling for such intervention undoubtedly will continue to occur in various parts of the world. As such, international lawyers and policymakers must strive to improve the ability of the United Nations to undertake or authorize states to undertake such intervention.

• Take Threats to the Peace Seriously

The heightened activity of the Security Council in the area of humanitarian intervention should be thoroughly reviewed to ensure that it is proceeding down a path that will not damage its capabilities. Classifying widespread deprivations of human rights as threats to international peace and security has a compelling moral quality to it. Yet unless the Security Council is capable of addressing such threats without exhausting its resources, this new development could have adverse consequences for its capability to resolve other threats to the peace.

Likewise, the Security Council's credibility is at stake. The interventions in Iraq in 1991 and 1992, in Somalia after December 1992, and in Haiti in 1994 gave credibility to the decisions of the Security Council because they involved the effective enforcement of the Security Council's humanitarian objectives. Conversely, the Security Council's actions in Liberia, Bosnia, Somalia before December 1992, and Rwanda were largely ineffective and therefore not credible. Another dimension to its credibility is the willingness to act consistently in the face of widespread deprivations of human rights. While the interventions were occurring in Iraq and Somalia, thousands of people in a wide variety of other African states, from the Sudan (next door to Somalia) to Zaire and Burundi (next door to Rwanda), and in certain republics of the former Soviet Union, were suffering similar circumstances. Yet, no significant Security Council action (let alone interventions) occurred with respect to these states, prompting some states to take matters into their own hands (such as occurred in Liberia) but more often to do nothing at all. The United Nations as presently constituted is not by itself capable of intervening at all times to address all situations. By treating like cases alike, however, the international community would help create standards of permissible and impermissible behavior that would assist in deterring human rights deprivations and in generating support for interventions when deemed necessary.

• Pursue Ad Hoc but Principled Action

The desire by scholars and commentators to see clear guidelines developed for the United Nations in pursuing humanitarian intervention is matched only by the resistance of the United Nations and member states to such criteria. UN actions in this area are destined to remain ad hoc, which may be preferable at least until experience is gained in how best to pursue such action.[74]

Nevertheless, it is appropriate to develop some general principles to guide the Security Council when authorizing, and to guide the Secretary-General when conducting, UN humanitarian intervention. These principles might be embodied in a Security Council or General Assembly resolution or in a statement by the President of the Security Council or the Secretary-General. Those principles that guided the United Nations for decades in the conduct of its peacekeeping operations were largely the product of statements by Secretary-General U Thant at the time of the first peacekeeping operations in the Middle East and the Congo.[75] Based on the interventions studied in chapter 5, however, the following principles would appear to be relevant:

1. the intervention should be based on the existence of a widespread deprivation of human rights, such as occurs from systematic and indiscriminate attacks on civilians by a central government or a system-wide breakdown in law and order producing the starvation and dislocation of the civilian population;

2. the intervention should be preceded by serious (but not necessarily

---

74. *See, e.g.*, O. Schachter, Commentary Before the 86th Annual Meeting of the American Society of International Law (Apr. 3, 1992), 86 Am. Soc'y Int'l L. Proc. 320 (1992) (warning against a "tendency on the part of those seeking to improve the United Nations to prescribe sets of rules for future cases, usually over-generalizing from past cases").

75. *See generally* D. Bowett, United Nations Forces: A Legal Study (1964); R. Higgins, United Nations Peace-Keeping: Documents and Commentary (4 vols. 1969–1981). For recent efforts at enhancing the capacity of UN peacekeeping, see *Report of the Secretary-General*, U.N. Doc. A/48/403, S/24650 (1994).

lengthy) diplomatic efforts to bring about the cessation of the widespread deprivation of human rights;

3. the intervention should be limited in scope to actions necessary and proportionate to end the widespread deprivation of human rights, which may include creating the conditions necessary for national reconciliation;

4. the intervening forces should withdraw as soon as possible after securing the conditions for ending the human rights deprivations; if a lengthy presence is necessary, it may be useful for the intervening forces to be under the command and control of the United Nations if the United Nations is provided sufficient financial and military resources;

5. the intervention should preserve the territorial integrity of the target state, by which is meant that the state's boundaries should not be redrawn except in the most unusual of circumstances; and

6. the intervention should interfere with the ruling structure of the target state only as necessary to provide for an enduring peace.

These principles, of course, are at a very general level and leave considerable room for interpretation in practice.

One of the key principles advanced by Antoine Rougier[76] and other scholars who favored humanitarian intervention early in this century was that the intervening forces should be "disinterested," meaning that the intervening state or states should not gain politically or economically from the intervention. This principle is of dubious value, particularly in the context of UN humanitarian intervention. So long as the dominant reason for the intervention is the protection of persons from widespread and severe human rights deprivations, it is not self-evident why the accrual of some political or economic benefits to an intervening state should disqualify it from participating in the intervention. At a minimum, it is likely that any intervening state will anticipate and welcome political benefits from its participation in the intervention, if nothing else by being considered a "good citizen" of the global community. Further, assuming that the intervention results in the reconstitution of a democratic government, it seems likely that government would look favorably on the intervening states as it establishes its external relations, whether in trade or other matters. To assert that states must be wholly "disinterested" in participating in humanitarian intervention ignores rudimentary aspects of geo-political behavior and may discourage any interventions from occurring at all. The central point is that the inter-

76. *See supra* chapter 2, Section D.

vention should be limited to those measures necessary to bring to an enduring end widespread deprivations of human rights; so long as that principle is followed, the concern with overreaching by the intervening states should take care of itself. Moreover, in the context of UN humanitarian intervention, there already are checks in place, especially the collective nature of the decision to intervene. As Rougier himself acknowledged, powerful states with personal interests are checked by more "disinterested" powers when operating within a collective system; if the powers collectively decide to proceed, the fact that one of them has greater interests at stake need not be relevant.

• Clarify the Type and Level of Human Rights Deprivations

Those skeptical of the legality and legitimacy of UN humanitarian intervention will prefer greater clarity regarding the type and level of human rights violations that justify such action. For the purpose of this study, a working definition of humanitarian intervention referred to "severe and widespread deprivation of human rights." That or a similar standard appears to fit the extensive loss of life and infliction of violence that occurred in the cases of Liberia, Iraq, Somalia, Bosnia, and Rwanda; the emergence of such a standard may be regarded as clarifying in part what is meant when UN Charter Articles 55 and 56 require states to take action, in conjunction with the United Nations, for the realization of "human rights and fundamental freedoms." As UN humanitarian intervention occurs in the future, such a standard undoubtedly will be refined.

Further, chapter 6 recounted a number of the human rights and law of war instruments that have emerged since the enactment of the Charter, as well as certain practices within UN suborgans and certain decisions of the International Court of Justice, that assist in elaborating a normative hierarchy of human rights. In particular, under Articles 62 and 68, the UN Economic and Social Council (ECOSOC) is mandated to promote respect for such rights and freedoms, including through the establishment of commissions. In anticipation of such action, the United Nations was deluged (from early in its existence) with petitions from individuals claiming violation of their human rights and freedoms. Initially, ECOSOC found that it had no power to take any action in regard to complaints concerning human rights.[77] Yet two exceptions were

---

77. For the two key ECOSOC resolutions on this subject, E.S.C. Res. 75, U.N. ESCOR, 5th Sess., Resolutions at 21, U.N. Doc. E/573 (1947) and E.S.C. Res. 728 F, U.N. ESCOR, 28th Sess., Supp. No. 1, at 19, U.N. Doc. E/3290 (1959), *reprinted in* 3 WESTON, *supra* note 6, at III.T.1.

carved out by ECOSOC with respect to "gross violations" of "human rights and fundamental freedoms." ECOSOC Resolution 1235[78] authorized the Human Rights Commission and its Sub-Commission on the Prevention of Discrimination and Protection Against Minorities "to examine information relevant to gross violations of human rights and fundamental freedoms, as exemplified" by South African apartheid and Southern Rhodesian racial discrimination. ECOSOC Resolution 1503[79] authorized the Sub-Commission to identify among petitions submitted by individuals those that "appear to reveal a consistent pattern of gross and reliably attested violations of human rights and fundamental freedoms" within the terms of reference of the Sub-Commission. The usefulness of this petition process has been questioned[80] and the secrecy of the deliberations by the Commission and Sub-Commission hinders full appreciation of the operative standards under the ECOSOC resolutions. Nevertheless, the distinction drawn between occasional violations of human rights and freedoms, and other more systematic patterns of gross violations, may also be instructive in crafting a standard for UN humanitarian intervention. The standard set by ECOSOC represents a minimum threshold for UN humanitarian intervention, a standard that may further evolve over time as UN human rights practice evolves.[81]

As noted earlier, the conduct of the Haitian authorities against their people is not on the same level of human rights deprivations as occurred in the other cases. The deprivation of human rights that sparked Security Council action involved the deprivation of the right to political participation through freely chosen representatives. As such, arguably the intervention in Haiti stands for the proposition that nondemocratic states may always be the target for UN humanitarian intervention or, more narrowly, that they may be the target where there is a reversion from democratic status to nondemocratic status accompanied by low levels of violence against those that support democracy. Advocates of this view might point to earlier interventions by the United States in Grenada and Panama as also evidencing a trend in favor of intervention in support of democracy. A more cautious view, however, would not read the intervention in Haiti as standing for quite so broad a proposition. While the UN-

78. E.S.C. Res. 1235, U.N. ESCOR 42d Sess., Supp. No. 1, at 17, U.N. Doc. E/4393 (1967), *reprinted in* 3 WESTON, *supra* note 6, at III.T.3.

79. E.S.C. Res. 1503, U.N. ESCOR, 48th Sess., Supp. No. 1A, at 8, U.N. Doc. E/4832/Add.1 (1970), *reprinted in* 3 WESTON, *supra* note 6, at III.T.6.

80. *See, e.g.*, T. Farer, *The United Nations and Human Rights: More than a Whimper, Less than a Roar*, 9 HUM. RTS. Q. 550 (1987).

81. For data on those 30 governments subject to Human Rights Commission review under Resolution 1503 from 1978 to 1986, see H. TOLLEY, JR., THE U.N. COMMISSION ON HUMAN RIGHTS 127–132 (1987).

authorized intervention in Haiti is a remarkable precedent, it does not appear to reflect a general recognition that deprivation of this form of human right serves generally as a basis for UN humanitarian intervention. Certainly other practice does not confirm such proposition; while such political rights are protected in human rights instruments[82] they heretofore have not by themselves served as a basis for UN condemnation, let alone UN intervention, and, indeed, the interventions by the United States in Grenada and Panama were condemned by the United Nations. Further, there are a large number of nondemocratic governments in the world today, including several that serve on the Security Council as permanent and non-permanent members, who would not support such a proposition. Rather, the intervention in Haiti will probably be regarded as an anomalous confluence of certain key factors: a strikingly poor, fledgling democracy that experienced a sudden internal coup by military elites; the location of this coup in the Western Hemisphere on the doorstep of the United States, which did not particularly want to intervene but was inexorably drawn to intervention for various reasons, including its perception of its special role in support of democracy in neighboring countries; and the status of the United States as a major power uniquely positioned to obtain Security Council authorization to intervene for this purpose.

- Improve the Capabilities of the Secretary-General and the Specialized Agencies

The Secretary-General served as a critical catalyst in the intervention in Somalia, a situation reminiscent of the Secretary-General's role in the UN operations in the Congo in the 1960s. Under Article 99 of the Charter, the Secretary-General may bring to the attention of the Security Council matters which in his opinion may threaten international peace and security. If the Security Council is to serve as the source of humanitarian intervention, this activism is useful and should be encouraged and coordinated.

Similar activism and coordination should be fostered among the different UN agencies. Prior to 1992, whenever emergency assistance and relief situations arose, several UN agencies were involved, including: the UN Disaster Relief Office (UNDRO); the Office of the UN High Commissioner for Refugees (UNHCR); the UN Development Program (UNDP); the UN Children's Fund (UNICEF); the UN World Food Program (WFO); and the World Health Organization (WHO). In theory,

---

82. *E.g.*, International Covenant on Civil and Political Rights, Dec. 16, 1966, art. 25, 993 U.N.T.S. 171, *reprinted in* 3 WESTON, *supra* note 6, at III.A.3.

UNDRO's primary mission was to coordinate UN assistance in disaster relief operations (UNDRO was active in both Iraq and Somalia) and to develop programs such as the UN International Emergency Network (UNIENET), which provides background and operational disaster-related information to subscribers around the world, including governments and nongovernmental organizations. Yet for years these UN agencies experienced difficulties in coordinating their operations;[83] in particular, UNDRO was criticized for failing to carry out its primary mission.[84]

In April 1992, during its forty-sixth session, the General Assembly passed by consensus Resolution 46/182, which sought to strengthen the coordination of all UN humanitarian emergency assistance.[85] The resolution recommended designation by the Secretary-General of a high-level coordinator, answerable only to the Secretary-General, whose functions include: (1) processing requests for emergency assistance requiring a coordinated response; (2) coordinating early warning systems; (3) organizing needs assessments missions; (4) facilitating access by operational organizations to emergency areas; (5) managing a Central Emergency Revolving Fund (CERF, to be established at a level of $50 million through voluntary contributions); (6) serving as a central focal point with governments and nongovernmental organizations; and (7) promoting a smooth transition from relief to rehabilitation and reconstruction programs. Thus was created the new UN Department of Humanitarian Affairs (DHA).

If implemented properly, the DHA would be a welcome advance in gathering information on and assisting in coordinating responses to natural and manmade emergencies, including widespread deprivation of human rights. Unfortunately, the task has proved to be a formidable one for many of the reasons UNDRO experienced difficulties. The high-level coordinator of the DHA is second only to the Secretary-General, but nevertheless is just one of many under-secretaries-general, and so has limited ability to impose coordination mechanisms on other agencies.

---

83. *See generally* R. Kent, Anatomy of Disaster Relief: The International Network in Action (1987).

84. *See, e.g., Evaluation of the Office of the United Nations Disaster Relief Coordinator, Joint Inspection Report Unit*, U.N. Doc. JIU/REP/80/11 (1980); U.S. Department of State, United States Participation in the United Nations, 1992, at 103–04 (1994) (report by the President to the Congress, available through the U.S. Government Printing Office); *see also* Righter, *supra* note 1, at 290 ("In practice, UNDRO rarely managed to act even as a traffic policeman, let alone the focus for action. While voluntary organizations welcomed and actively assisted the creation of UNDRO, the established UN agencies resented it as an interloper, and gave it a cold shoulder.").

85. G.A. Res. 46/182, U.N. GAOR, 46th Sess., Supp. No. 49, at 49, U.N. Doc. A/46/49 (1992).

Indeed, at least for the time being, the DHA in New York is heavily reliant on the same UNDRO infrastructure based in Geneva. In December 1993, Jan Eliasson, a Swedish diplomat appointed as coordinator by the Secretary-General, resigned, stating that he was frustrated with the difficulties he faced.

On a separate track, the 1993 Vienna Conference on Human Rights called for the establishment of a UN High Commissioner to protect and promote human rights. The General Assembly followed through on this recommendation on December 20, 1993 and created the new position to be based in Geneva.[86] The primary impetus for this new Commissioner was the belief that victims of human rights abuse need a place of ultimate recourse when institutions fail to act; presumably an individual can pursue investigations more expeditiously than entities such as the UN Commission on Human Rights and its Sub-Commission. The mandate set for the High Commissioner, however, was vague, in part due to conflicting views between the United States and China about the nature of the position. References to fact-finding missions, for example, were removed from the General Assembly's resolution, but the language retained enough breadth that such action by the High Commissioner remained possible.[87] To be successful, it will be essential that the Commissioner be absolutely independent, take a universal approach in investigating human rights abuses, and receive strong support from the Secretary-General to establish clearly the Commissioner's authority within the UN system. The Secretary-General appointed Ecuadorean diplomat José Ayala Lasso to be the first High Commissioner for Human Rights.

It would be very useful if this new Commissioner would provide regular "trouble shooter" reports to the Security Council on states' practices that are or may amount to widespread deprivations of human rights.[88] One means of achieving that objective would be to restructure the UN Centre for Human rights, also based in Geneva, and the relationship between the Centre and other UN agencies so as to allow the Commissioner to conduct fact-finding missions through the Centre and with the support of other UN agencies as well as regional organizations and nongovernmental organizations. An analogy for such reporting in the United States is the statutory requirement for the Department of State to provide the Congress with an annual report on the status of human

86. G.A. Res. 48/141, U.N. GAOR, 48th Sess., Supp. No. 49, at 261, U.N. Doc. A/48/49 (1994), *reprinted in* 3 WESTON, *supra* note 6, at III.T.14.

87. *See* J. Preston, *U.N. Acts to Establish Commissioner for Rights*, WASH. POST, Dec. 17, 1993, at A36.

88. *See, e.g.*, B. Ramcharan, *Reforming the United Nations to Secure Human Rights*, 4 TRANSNAT'L L. & CONTEMP. PROB. 503, 517–18 (1994).

rights in all member countries of the United Nations.[89] To avoid over-burdening the system and to ensure support for such reporting in its early stages, "trouble shooter" reports to the Security Council would best focus on only those countries engaged in widespread and serious violations.

Alternatively, states, international organizations, or nongovernmental organizations could be invited through a Security Council resolution to provide the UN Secretary-General with information on widespread human rights abuses that come to their attention. This request would be similar to the Security Council's request that states provide it with information on the mistreatment of civilians by Iraq in Resolution 674 (1990)[90] and its request to states and international organizations[91] to provide it with information on violations of humanitarian law in the territory of the former Yugoslavia in Resolution 771 (1992) and in Rwanda in Resolution 935 (1994),[92] but could be a standing request for information on which the Secretary-General could make periodic reports. States, of course, are already free to bring such matters to the attention of the Security Council, but a resolution calling upon states to do so might provide a better political basis for them to come forward with information. The resolution also could establish a basis for international organizations and nongovernmental organizations (which increasingly are becoming important sources of information) to provide information.

These channels of information could serve as an early warning system by which the Security Council as a routine matter could anticipate widespread human rights deprivations at an early stage in their development. If appropriate, warnings by the President of the Security Council could then be issued to authorities of the target state. This form of preventive diplomacy might deter the target state from persisting in conduct giving rise to the deprivations and avoid the need for intervention. If the deprivations persist, the Security Council could determine whether there exists a threat to international peace and security and authorize states or

89. 22 U.S.C. sec. 2151n(d) (1988).

90. S.C. Res. 674, U.N. SCOR, 45th Sess., 2951st mtg. at 25, para. 2, U.N. Doc. S/INF/46 (1991).

91. In many instances of widespread human rights violations, international organizations have served as early critics and sources of useful information, either in their function as monitoring groups or as relief organizations. These organizations would include the International Committee for the Red Cross, the International Medical Corps, the British-based Save the Children, Médecins sans Frontières, Amnesty International, and Middle-East Watch.

92. S.C. Res. 771, U.N. SCOR, 47th Sess., 3106th mtg. at 25, para. 5, U.N. Doc. S/INF/ 48 (1993), *reprinted in* 2 WESTON, *supra* note 6, at II.E.8; S.C. Res. 935, U.N. SCOR, 49th Sess., 3400th mtg., U.N. Doc. S/RES/935 (1994).

the United Nations itself to intervene. Such a system for gathering information would also be useful in the event that the Security Council later wished to pursue war crimes initiatives against the target state.[93] War crimes normally arise in the context of inter-state armed conflict; in the humanitarian intervention context, however, they may arise also under rules relating to conflicts not of an international character.

In the event the Security Council is to authorize states to intervene under their own command, another way of enhancing the role of the Secretary-General and the Security Council itself is to consider appropriate ways of structuring the authorizing resolution. For instance, the resolution could:

1. establish a role for the Secretary-General in the intervention process through a liaison office to the operational headquarters of the intervening states;
2. contemplate ultimate transfer of the operation to a United Nations force;
3. be limited to a specific period of time or area within the target state;
4. call for periodic reports by the intervening states to the Security Council on the progress of the intervention;
5. make clear the extent to which the intervening states can disarm local forces, establish a local police force, and otherwise affect the governing structure, if any, of the target state.

In the aftermath of Resolution 688 on Iraq, some countries may have felt that they had written a blank check for intervening states, and consequently consideration of these types of constraints may be necessary in the future to obtain enough votes in the Security Council. On the other hand, as occurred with Resolution 794 on Somalia, the desperate situation there, and the fact that the United States appeared to be the only country capable of remedying the situation expeditiously, provided greater opportunity for a broad resolution imposing limited constraints on the primary intervening state. Such methods and others for enhancing UN-authorized humanitarian intervention could be considered and reported on to the Secretary-General by a UN panel of experts drawn from diplomatic and relief communities.

Obviously, even if the legal authority and structure exists to conduct UN humanitarian intervention, there will continue to be situations in which the international community finds itself unwilling to authorize the deployment of forces in situations that would appear to call for them,

---

93. As noted in chapter 5, *supra*, the Security Council established UN war crimes tribunals to address violations of the laws of war in the former Yugoslavia and in Rwanda.

or unwilling to do so expeditiously. The failure to intervene to protect Muslim Shiites in southern Iraq in 1991 is such a case. Likewise, one critic of the humanitarian response to Somalia argues that, while U.S. funding and its ultimate deployment were praiseworthy, in the early stages "a lack of U.S. resolve in the Security Council only prolonged the Somali crisis and contributed to UN balking at both humanitarian and peace-keeping opportunities."[94] Nevertheless, the greater the ability to understand the nature of humanitarian crises and the ease to react expeditiously to them may promote the willingness of states and the United Nations to do so.

Finally, there are serious deficiencies in the current UN bureaucracy surrounding the Secretary-General. Too little attention has been paid to the ethics, transparency, efficiency, control, and accountability of UN officials in the performance of their duties.[95] Yet the United Nations cannot afford to be inept in the management of its own affairs; corruption and incompetence tarnish its image and ultimately undercut its ability to gain the trust and confidence of states and warring factions necessary to mediate effectively in crises. Further, the fundamental structure of the United Nations poses chronic difficulties in its ability to coordinate and deploy resources. From its inception, the United Nations has developed agencies to address sectoral problems but has not found a way to integrate and coordinate these agencies. Brian Urquhart and Eskine Childers note:

> The effect of these basic structural decisions on the Secretary-General's capacity to lead and coordinate has generally been underestimated. There is indeed an Administrative Committee on Coordination (ACC) which brings together the executive heads of the system two or three times yearly. The Secretary-General chairs this body, but it is nothing like a substantive cabinet for the UN system. A specialized agency director-general can at any time and on any issue invoke his autonomy and decline to cooperate in a measure of coordination—and legally be perfectly in order in doing so. Other executive heads, even if appointed by the Secretary-General, have their own governing bodies behind them.
>
> It can be imagined how effectively national governments might function if Ministers turned up to Cabinet meetings only twice a year, were responsible to their own separate parliaments (of bankers, agronomists, public health chiefs, educators, etc.), had their own separately authorized budgets, policies and pro-

---

94. J. Clark, *supra* note 22, at 119. Clark is also highly critical of the professionalism and competence of the UN relief agencies and UN diplomats engaged in conflict mediation in Somalia.

95. *See generally* M. SAHNOUN, SOMALIA: THE MISSED OPPORTUNITIES (1994) (memoir by the head of UNOSOM I); *see also* J. Preston, *Waste in Somalia Typifies Failings of U.N. Management*, WASH POST, Jan. 3, 1995, at A11; J. Preston, *Massive World Body Resists Shaping Up: Reform Efforts at U.N. Meet Opposition*, WASH. POST, Jan. 3, 1995, at A1.

grammes, and yet were supposed to be led and coordinated by a Prime Minister responsible to another parliament altogether.[96]

How best to redress this problem is beyond the scope of this study; it might involve radically restructuring the United Nations, including centralization of functions, or it might involve less radical steps, such as developing a cabinet-style culture among existing agency heads so as to promote better teamwork.[97] In either event, it will be up to the member states of the United Nations to ensure that the problem is addressed, first by insisting that reforms are necessary, then by reaching consensus on what those reforms should be, and finally by implementing that consensus through their representatives to the various UN agencies. In September 1995, a step was made in this direction by the establishment of an open-ended, high-level working group of the General Assembly charged with thoroughly reviewing studies and reports of relevant UN bodies and submissions of member states and other entities on revitalization and reform of the UN system. The objective of the group is to "specify by consensus those ideas and proposals drawn [from such studies and reports] that it concludes are appropriate for the purpose of revitalization, strengthening and reform of the United Nations system in fulfillment of the principles and purposes of the Charter of the United Nations."[98] Whether consensus can be achieved and, if so, acted upon effectively remains to be seen.

- Deter Human Rights Atrocities to Obviate the Need for Forcible Intervention

This study focuses predominantly on forcible intervention as a means of preventing serious and widespread deprivations of internationally recognized human rights. There are, however, nonforcible measures that the United Nations can pursue to seek to deter human rights atrocities before they even begin, and, given the uncertainty as to whether states will forcibly intervene to protect human rights, such measures should be seriously considered. This chapter has discussed already certain means of deterrence, such as simply having available a UN rapid deployment force and an activist, well-informed UN Secretariat capable of engaging in preventive diplomacy. There are other measures available as well that should be pursued to help obviate the need for forcible UN intervention.

As discussed in chapter 5 with respect to the interventions in Bosnia-

---

96. Urquhart & Childers, *supra* note 1, at 70.

97. *Id.* at 75.

98. G.A. Res. 49/252, U.N. GAOR, 49th Sess., 107th plenary mtg., U.N. Doc. A/49/L.68 (1995).

Herzegovina and Rwanda, the Security Council has established the first international war crimes tribunals ever under the UN Charter. These tribunals, staffed by highly qualified jurists and by experienced prosecutors and investigators, are methodically proceeding to piece together cases against the perpetrators of violations of international humanitarian law in Bosnia-Herzegovina and Rwanda and ultimately may convict persons highly placed in the leadership of the relevant factions in those conflicts. If so, the most enduring effect of these tribunals may not be the punishment they impose on particular individuals, or even the contribution they make to the process of national reconciliation and healing within those countries, but rather the clarion message sent to all those would-be instigators of such atrocities that they too may be subject to criminal sanctions. While those tribunals do not conduct trials when the defendant is in absentia, in many crises, such as Rwanda, the ability to obtain custody of defendants may not pose a problem depending on how the crisis resolves itself. Even in situations where the defendant is not in custody, an indictment by the tribunal serves as a means of limiting the movement of the individual to only those places safe from an international arrest warrant. Further, the simple identification of the individual by the United Nations as an accused war criminal, the international approbation that follows, and the public revelation of the acts committed by the individual would be unwelcome by all but the most hardened of persons, particularly those who envision themselves becoming regime elites welcomed in other capitals of the world. In this respect, it should be noted that the tribunal on war crimes in the former Yugoslavia has developed a proceeding whereby, even if the defendant is not in custody, the evidence against him or her can be placed before the tribunal (including the oral testimony of witnesses) for purposes of confirming the indictment, issuing a tribunal international arrest warrant, and potentially referring the matter to the Security Council if the arrest warrant cannot be effected.[99] Thus, the possibility of criminal sanctions, if sufficiently publicized, may serve as a powerful deterrent to the leaders throughout the world that their conduct may not go unchallenged. Obviously, such deterrence would be enhanced by establishment of a

99. This procedure, undertaken pursuant to Rule 61 of the tribunal's rules of procedure and evidence, was first used in the case of Dragan Nikolic in October 1995. During a one-week hearing broadcast worldwide, some thirteen witnesses provided oral testimony against Nikolic, the first person to be indicted by the tribunal, who was charged with violations of international humanitarian law while serving as the commander of a camp at Susica, in northeastern Bosnia-Herzegovina. The tribunal confirmed the indictment and issued a tribunal international arrest warrant. Le Procureur v. Dragan Nikolic, Examen de l'Acte D'Accusation dans le Cadre de l'Article 61 du Reglement de Procedure et de Preuve, U.N. Doc. IT-94-2-R61 (1995).

permanent international criminal tribunal, which is now under consideration by the United Nations.

In the same vein, further consideration should be given to imposing economic sanctions that are targeted at the individuals most likely to instigate human rights atrocities. Comprehensive economic sanctions against a state are a blunt tool and typically do not affect the relevant regime elites in that state. As was seen in the cases of Iraq and Haiti, the individuals in control of those states were quite capable of maintaining their standard of living notwithstanding comprehensive sanctions; indeed, ironically, the imposition of such sanctions can provide the conditions for the establishment of a black market in goods that can benefit the regime elites. Midway through the Haiti crisis, however, it became apparent there were steps that could be taken against the assets of private individuals who were either in a leadership role within Haiti or were in a position strongly to influence that leadership. Such sanctions should be seriously considered when all such crises arise. The effectiveness of targeted sanctions will turn on whether regime elites have significant assets abroad, such as in Europe or the United States, and whether such assets can be identified. Steps should be pursued within the United Nations to develop means of cooperation among states whose banks maintain significant foreign assets so as to allow for the ready identification and control of such assets. If so, and if sanctions against such assets were sufficiently automatic in the event human rights atrocities were to be committed, the relevant regime elites may be deterred from instigating them.

Finally, the United Nations should commit extensive resources to assist troubled states in establishing and nurturing institutions that foster the rule of law. Many of the internal conflicts of the world have their origins in the inability of the domestic institutions of a state to take account of and resolve inequities and differences of view among its nationals in a fair and just manner. The lack of such institutions in turn fosters a lack of respect for those institutions that do exist, which in turn breeds violence against them. "Democracy" can come in many forms, but basic rule-of-law institutions would provide for a government that is accountable to the people, operating under a constitutional system that includes an independent judiciary, and where laws are not applied in an arbitrary or ex post facto fashion. The United Nations is uniquely positioned to promote such institutions through its developmental and educational programs. Of course, not all states have such institutions and undoubtedly some would resist initiatives in this area by the United Nations. Yet the seeds of transnational and internal conflict do have their origins in the manner in which power is controlled and respected within states, and the international community would do well to pay attention to this fact.

Chapter 7
Regional Organizations and Humanitarian Intervention

In some ways, the problems of, and prospects for, humanitarian intervention under the auspices of regional organizations are no different from those associated with the United Nations. In both instances, the Charter contemplates a decision by the Security Council before forcible measures may be taken. In both instances, the measures are intended for the maintenance of international peace and security, though that concept has proven an elastic one. In both instances, the authorization may be granted to military forces operating under the command of the international organization or to states acting under their own command. In both instances, the credibility and perceived legitimacy of the intervention is enhanced because it is undertaken by a multilateral organization. In both instances, as discussed in chapter 6, there appears to be nothing about collective decisionmaking that is inherently wiser than decisionmaking by individual states, and opportunities for abuse and mistakes remain. Further, the impetus for the intervention may derive exclusively or predominantly from the interests of a particular global or regional power, in which case the legitimacy and credibility of the intervention—notwithstanding the multilateral authorization—still may be challenged.[1]

---

1. Writing in 1969, Ellen Frey-Wouters asserted:

> The primary role of Latin American members of the OAS in most collective security cases has been to provide a multilateral legitimacy for essentially unilateral U.S. action. The OAS serves to carry out the extracontinental objectives of the U.S., free from any control by the UN. It can be expected that the OAS will continue, at least in the immediate future, to be misused as a means to intervene against regimes of states which do not meet with the approval of the U.S.

E. Frey-Wouters, *The Prospects for Regionalism in World Affairs, in* 1 THE FUTURE OF THE INTERNATIONAL LEGAL ORDER: TRENDS AND PATTERNS 463, 533 (R. Falk & C. Black eds., 1969).

Although certainly susceptible to abuse, humanitarian intervention under the auspices of regional organizations is significant in that it presents a second layer of international organization—one presumably more closely associated with the underlying conflict—through which decisions may be made regarding the threat posed by widespread deprivations of human rights. At the same time, it preserves at least the perception of impartiality and evenhandedness associated with interventions conducted by a group of states as opposed to one or a few states acting alone. Regional organizations may be better situated for apprehending the beginnings of a human rights crisis than the United Nations, and, at least in theory, more capable of acting swiftly to address that crisis. Regional organizations also may be more apt to find it in their interest to expend the military and economic resources necessary for addressing the crisis.

Unfortunately, to date the role of regional organizations in addressing threats to international peace under Chapter VIII of the Charter has been marginal. Certain organizations, such as the Organization of American States (OAS), are relatively well-developed structures significantly involved in conflict management, if not in military deployments. Most regional organizations, however, are not so well developed and lack both the resources and the will to engage in significant conflict management, let alone engage in situations requiring the use of military force.

After the Cold War, the need for regional organizations to play a greater role in conflict management will likely increase. Notwithstanding greater potential for Security Council action, the Security Council will be neither willing nor able to address all conflicts, let alone all humanitarian crises. As groups of states become aware of the precariousness of relying on the Security Council to address violence, and aware that, with the proliferation of arms, even low levels of violence have a propensity to escalate, there will be opportunities to develop more capable and effective regional security mechanisms. Experience suggests, however, that coercive military action, including humanitarian intervention, will remain beyond the capabilities of regional organizations in the near term. Consequently, while efforts should be made to develop those capabilities, attention also should be paid to other ways regional organizations can play a role in this area, such as helping to define the norms of intervention after the Cold War and to distinguish between permissible and impermissible types of intervention. Thus, regional organizations could encourage United Nations humanitarian intervention in appropriate circumstances and restrain it in others.

A. Regional Arrangements Under the Charter

The UN Charter specifically recognizes regional organizations as entities for maintaining peace and security on the regional level. Chapter VIII of the Charter on "Regional Arrangements" consists of three articles: Article 52 (on peaceful settlement of disputes), Article 53 (on enforcement action), and Article 54 (on reports to the Security Council).

Article 52[2] states that regional "arrangements or agencies" are permitted under the Charter "for dealing with matters relating to the maintenance of international peace and security as are appropriate for regional action" so long as they "and their activities" are consistent with the purposes and principles of the United Nations. A contentious issue at the San Francisco Conference was whether it was necessary first to exhaust opportunities for conflict resolution at the regional level before resorting to the Security Council. Article 52(2) provides that UN members first shall use (and the Security Council shall encourage the use of) these regional arrangements and agencies for the peaceful settlement of disputes before referring a matter to the Security Council. At the same time, Article 52(4) provides that nothing in Article 52 impairs the authority of the Security Council to investigate or have placed before it disputes or situations that might lead to "international friction." Thus, the hierarchical relationship between the Security Council and regional organizations in addressing disputes and crisis situations is unclear.

Article 53[3] envisions the use of regional arrangements or agencies

2. Article 52 reads as follows:

1. Nothing in the present Charter precludes the existence of regional arrangements or agencies for dealing with such matters relating to the maintenance of international peace and security as are appropriate for regional action, provided that such arrangements or agencies and their activities are consistent with the Purposes and Principles of the United Nations.

2. The Members of the United Nations entering into such arrangements or constituting such agencies shall make every effort to achieve pacific settlement of local disputes through such regional arrangements or by such regional agencies before referring them to the Security Council.

3. The Security Council shall encourage the development of pacific settlement of local disputes through such regional arrangements or by such regional agencies either on the initiative of the states concerned or by reference from the Security Council.

4. This Article in no way impairs the application of Articles 34 and 35.

U.N. CHARTER art 52.

3. Article 53 reads as follows:

1. The Security Council shall, where appropriate, utilize such regional arrangements or agencies for enforcement action under its authority. But no enforcement action shall be

for "enforcement action." Here, too, controversy has arisen. First, the meaning of "enforcement action" ("mesures coercitives" in the French and "medidas coercitivas" in the Spanish text) is not entirely clear; on the one hand, it might include all forcible and nonforcible coercive actions taken against a state (thus paralleling Articles 41 and 42 of the Charter) or it might be limited only to forcible coercive actions.[4] In any event, as defined in chapter 1, humanitarian intervention typically involves forcible action and thus falls within either meaning of "enforcement action" in Article 53. Second, when undertaking such enforcement action at the regional level, the relationship of the United Nations vis-à-vis the regional organizations is unclear. The proposals that emerged from the Dumbarton Oaks Conference favored requiring authorization by the Security Council for all enforcement actions, including actions taken by regional organizations. Several states, including several associated with the inter-American collective security system,[5] feared that such

---

taken under regional arrangements or by regional agencies without the authorization of the Security Council, with the exception of measures against any enemy state, as defined in paragraph 2 of this Article, provided for pursuant to Article 107 or in regional arrangements directed against renewal of aggressive policy on the part of any such state, until such time as the Organization may, on request of the Government concerned, be charged with the responsibility for preventing further aggression by such a state.

2. The term enemy state as used in paragraph 1 of this Article applies to any state which during the Second World War has been an enemy of any signatory of the present Charter.

Id. art. 53.

4. The Chairman of Committee 4 of Commission III at the San Francisco Conference (which dealt with "regional arrangements"), Dr. Alberto Lleras Camargo, apparently did not regard nonforcible coercive action as "enforcement action." *See* M. CANYES, THE ORGANIZATION OF AMERICAN STATES AND THE UNITED NATIONS 54–56 (5th ed. 1960) (OAS publication). Even if originally intended otherwise, some commentators see the construction of Article 53 over time as favoring a gradual narrowing of its scope so as to exclude coverage of nonforcible coercion, largely due to a realization that, since states may undertake such coercion in their individual capacity, it would be odd to require them to obtain Security Council authorization when acting collectively. Further, it is argued that regional organizations must have such automony to have any significant role in the maintenance of international peace and security. *See, e.g.*, A. Levin, *The Organization of American States and the United Nations, in* REGIONALISM AND THE UNITED NATIONS 147, 169–70 (B. Andemicael ed., 1979) (article by a UNITAR research associate in a UNITAR publication).

5. Western Hemispheric security cooperation was expressly recognized in Article 21 of the Covenant of the League of Nations, which stated:

Nothing in this Covenant shall be deemed to affect the validity of international engagements, such as treaties of arbitration or regional understandings like the Monroe doctrine, for securing the maintenance of peace.

LEAGUE OF NATIONS COVENANT art. 21. The Monroe doctrine, announced by U.S. President James Monroe in his message to Congress on December 2, 1823, declared that the contian approach would bring undesirable extra-regional interference in regional affairs, such as the veto by an extra-regional power of regional enforcement action. A somewhat ambiguous compromise resolved the issue: under Article 53 no enforcement action may be taken by regional organizations without Security Council authorization,[6] but states may collectively engage in their inherent right of self-defense under Article 51 even without Security Council authorization when an armed attack occurs.[7]

Under Article 54, the Security Council must be kept informed of activities pursued under regional arrangements or agencies for the maintenance of international peace and security.[8] The OAS has been the most consistent in providing such reports.

Various instances of cooperation among states could qualify as either "regional arrangements" or "regional agencies" (the latter apparently referring to some form of institutional infrastructure) covered by UN Charter Chapter VIII. Yet there is no definition of "arrangement" or "agency" within the Charter that provides guidance about the scope of these terms,[9] and neither the Security Council nor the General Assembly has established such a definition.[10] Regional organizations may vary considerably in their primary focus—regional economic integration or community-building (e.g., the European Union or the Association of South East Asian Nations), regional defense against external threats (e.g., the North Atlantic Treaty Organization), or regional defense against internal threats (e.g., the OAS)—and yet at the same time

---

nents of the Western Hemisphere "are henceforth not to be considered as subjects for future colonization by any European powers." 1 Documents of American History 235, 236 (H. Commager & M. Cantor eds., 10th ed. 1988).

By the time of the San Francisco Conference, the inter-American system had developed the Pan-American Union, the forerunner to the 1948 Organization of American States. *See generally* A. Thomas & A. Thomas, Jr., The Organization of American States (1963).

6. Article 53 contains an exception for measures against those states that were the "enemy" in World War II. Today this exception would appear to be a historical anomaly.

7. For a lucid discussion of this compromise, see I. Claude, Jr., *The OAS, the UN, and the United States*, Int'l Conciliation No. 547, Mar. 1964, at 3–15.

8. Article 54 reads as follows:

The Security Council shall at all times be kept fully informed of activities undertaken or in contemplation under regional arrangements or by regional agencies for the maintenance of international peace and security.

U.N. Charter art. 54.

9. Efforts at San Francisco to define regional arrangements were not successful. *See* Doc. WD 70, III/A/4/11, 12 U.N.C.I.O. Docs. 857 (1945) (proposal of the Egyptian delegation).

10. Some decisions have been taken that imply recognition of certain organizations as regional organizations for purposes of Article 52(1). Frey-Wouters, *supra* note 1, at 533.

have multiple functions. Thus, it is not always clear when these organizations should be considered within the scope of Chapter VIII.

The best means for ascertaining whether a particular arrangement or agency in fact is covered by Chapter VIII would appear to be whether the states involved claim such status and whether this claim is accepted in UN practice.[11] The Charter of the OAS expressly states that "Within the United Nations, the Organization of American States is a regional agency."[12] The Charter of the Organization of African Unity[13] is not explicit on this issue, but its *travaux préparatoires* suggest that the OAU is also covered by Chapter VIII.[14] The provisions of the Pact of the Arab League[15] indicate that it operates both as a regional arrangement under Chapter VIII[16] and as a organization for collective self-defense under Article 51 of the Charter. The North Atlantic Treaty Alliance, however, is structured as only a defensive alliance and has not been regarded by its members as a regional agency under Chapter VIII. Nevertheless, in principle, there is no reason why an agency primarily designed to assist in collective self-defense cannot in some instances engage in other activities for the maintenance of international peace and security, such as fostering the peaceful settlement of disputes. In those instances, the agency may be subject to Chapter VIII.[17]

Further, there would appear to be a number of modalities for enforcement action under Chapter VIII. The Security Council could authorize the use of military force under the command of a regional organization to uphold decisions of the Security Council. Alternatively, the Security

---

11. M. Akehurst, *Enforcement Action by Regional Agencies, with Special Reference to the Organization of American States*, 42 BRIT. Y.B. INT'L L. 175, 178 (1967).

12. CHARTER OF THE ORGANIZATION OF AMERICAN STATES, Apr. 30, 1948, art. 1, 2 U.S.T. 2394, 119 U.N.T.S. 3, *reprinted in* 1 INTERNATIONAL LAW AND WORLD ORDER: BASIC DOCUMENTS I.B.14 (B. Weston ed., 1994) [hereinafter WESTON]. The OAS Charter is more elaborate in establishing its relationship to the United Nations and arrangements for cooperation with the United Nations than any other regional organization charter. The Preamble reaffirms the principles and purposes of the United Nations, and Article 4 sets forth certain purposes of the OAS in fulfillment of its regional obligations under the U.N. Charter.

13. CHARTER OF THE ORGANIZATION OF AFRICAN UNITY, May 25, 1963, 479 U.N.T.S. 39, *reprinted in* 1 WESTON, *supra* note 12, at I.B.1.

14. J. Antonio de Yturriaga, *L'Organisation de l'Unité Africaine et les Nations Unies*, 69 REV. GÉN. D. INT'L PUB. 370, 378 (1965).

15. PACT OF THE LEAGUE OF ARAB STATES, Mar. 22, 1944, 70 U.N.T.S. 238, *reprinted in* 1 WESTON, *supra* note 12, at I.B.16.

16. *See* M. Khadduri, *The Arab League as a Regional Arrangement*, 40 AM. J. INT'L L. 756 (1946).

17. *See* J. Moore, *The Role of Regional Arrangements in the Maintenance of World Order*, *in* 3 THE FUTURE OF INTERNATIONAL LEGAL ORDER: CONFLICT MANAGEMENT, *supra* note 1, at 122, 124 ("it seems preferable to recognize that regional organizations are located on a series of functional continuums").

Council could authorize the use of such force to uphold decisions of the regional organization itself. In the latter case, the regional organization would appear to have considerable control over the enforcement action if it could alter the decisions being enforced. The Security Council also could authorize states who are members of the regional organization to undertake enforcement action in their individual capacities to enforce decisions of the Security Council or of the regional organization. If so, it is less clear in what sense the Security Council is "utilizing" the regional organization for the enforcement action; this approach may be necessary, however, if the regional organization is not capable of operating through an integrated command structure. Finally, the Security Council could provide an ex post facto blessing of an enforcement action undertaken by a regional or subregional organization, which occurred in the case of the ECOWAS intervention in Liberia, discussed in chapter 5.

The OAS "quarantine" of Cuba in 1962 is the primary example of a use of force by a regional organization purportedly under the authority of Article 53. On October 23, the OAS "recommended" that member states:

take all measures, individually and collectively including the use of armed force, which they may deem necessary to ensure that the Government of Cuba cannot continue to receive from the Sino-Soviet powers military material and related supplies which may threaten the peace and security of the Continent and to prevent the missiles in Cuba with offensive capability from ever becoming an active threat to the peace and security of the Continent.[18]

Naval vessels from the United States plus Argentina, the Dominican Republic, and Venezuela turned back vessels headed to Cuba with arms. Eventually, the Soviet Union agreed to withdraw the missiles from Cuba in return for a promise from the United States not to invade Cuba.

The United States argued that the quarantine did not violate Article 2(4) of the Charter because it was permissible under Chapter VIII.[19] The problem with this argument is that the Security Council never authorized the quarantine, as would be expected under Article 53. The United States sought to obscure the issue by arguing, alternatively, that such action was consistent with earlier OAS practice (which, however, dealt with

18. *Resolution on the Adoption of Necessary Measures to Prevent Cuba from Threatening the Peace and Security of the Continent*, OAS Council, Acts, Annex A, OEA/Ser. G/V/C-d-1024 Rev.2 (Oct. 23, 1962).

19. L. Meeker, *Defensive Quarantine and the Law*, 57 Am. J. Int'l L. 515, 518–24 (1963); A. Chayes, *The Legal Case for U.S. Action on Cuba*, 47 Dep't St. Bull. 763 (1962); A. Chayes, *Law and the Quarantine of Cuba*, 41 Foreign Aff. 550, 553–57 (1963); *see also* A. Chayes, The Cuban Missile Crisis (1974). The U.S. Government's position did not go unchallenged. *See, e.g.,* J. Halderman, *Regional Enforcement Measures and the United Nations*, 52 Geo. L.J. 89 (1963).

nonforcible sanctions), that the quarantine was "recommended" not "required" by the OAS (a distinction that confounds logic), and that the action was implicitly authorized by the Security Council by the failure to pass an opposing resolution (which would have been impossible due to the US veto). In any event, the debates before the Security Council largely ignored the legal niceties of Chapter VIII in favor of simply trying to avoid a nuclear confrontation.[20]

The action of the OAS in this crisis stands either as an anomalous (perhaps illegal) event of the Cold War era or as a precedent for a willingness to interpret the requirement of Article 53 loosely. The concern expressed at San Francisco that the Security Council must have control over the enforcement actions of regional organizations or else the United Nations would be weakened seems to have dissipated with the realization that regional organizations are not particularly energetic enforcers and certainly not a threat to the functioning of the United Nations.

A loose interpretation of Article 53 is tolerable in situations where a regional organization is pursuing enforcement action against one of its own members in accordance with the constituent instruments of the organization. In such a case, the member state voluntarily enters into a regional arrangement that cedes certain elements of its sovereignty to the decisionmaking of the regional organization when taken in accordance with the rules and procedures of that organization. An important aspect of obtaining the authorization of the Security Council under Article 53, however, relates to actions by regional organizations that are outside the regional organization's competence. For instance, a regional organization will not have competence under its constituent instruments to take enforcement action against a state that is not a member of the regional organization (and perhaps not even within the "region"). This situation may arise where the nonmember state itself is a threat to the peace or where the vessels of that state seek to violate regional sanctions imposed on another state (which may be a member of the regional organization) that is the threat to the peace. Obviously, if the nonmember state engages in what may be construed as an "armed attack" for purposes of Article 51, then the regional organization may use force in the exercise of a collective right of self-defense even without Security Council authorization. It is when the action of the nonmember state does not rise to the level of an armed attack yet nevertheless threatens the peace that Security Council authorization under Article 53 is presumably

20. *But see* U.N. SCOR, 17th Sess., 1024th mtg., paras. 107–10, U.N. Doc. S/PV.1024 (1962) (Ghanaian delegate arguing that the quarantine constituted "enforcement action" under Article 53, which required express Security Council authorization).

needed. In such a case, an interpretation of Article 53 that denies the need for Security Council authorization, or that liberally construes an implied authorization, is less desirable.

The ambiguities that emerged from the San Francisco Conference regarding the powers of regional organizations vis-à-vis the United Nations remain today, but they have not themselves posed a problem for action by regional organizations. The weaknesses that exist with regional organizations are attributable less to defects in the UN Charter than to the unwillingness of member states, particularly the major powers, to cede significant control over matters of peace and security to those organizations. In addition, regional organizations often lack the necessary financial and human resources to play a major role in conflict management. Nevertheless, regional and subregional organizations (such as ECOWAS in Liberia) have exhibited important capabilities of conflict management in certain situations, including those that implicate humanitarian intervention. Even the Organization of African Unity, for example, which was criticized as largely ineffective in dealing with the situation in Somalia in 1991 through 1993 and Rwanda in 1994, has played a modest role in some internal conflicts with external implications, such as that of the Congo during 1964 through 1968 and Nigeria during 1967 through 1970.[21] For this reason, it is important to consider the application of Chapter VIII to humanitarian intervention both under past practice and as may occur in the future.

B. Applying Chapter VIII to Humanitarian Intervention

Humanitarian intervention by regional organizations, as defined in chapter 1, falls within the scope of Article 53 of Chapter VIII. Since humanitarian intervention is not defense against an armed attack, it does not rest on Article 51. Since it typically involves the threat or use of force by intervening forces, it does not fit with the pacific settlement of disputes envisaged by Article 52. As is the case for the Security Council itself when acting under Chapter VII, it must be argued that, in undertaking the humanitarian intervention, the regional organization is acting to maintain international peace and security. If humanitarian intervention by a regional organization is covered by Article 53, then according to that article such action should be preceded first by efforts to achieve a pacific settlement of the "dispute" and then by authorization from the Security Council. The remainder of this chapter examines the limited practice of

---

21. *See* B. ANDEMICAEL, THE OAU AND THE UN: RELATIONS BETWEEN THE ORGANIZATION OF AFRICAN UNITY AND THE UNITED NATIONS 65–83 (1976).

humanitarian intervention by regional organizations and prospects for such intervention in the future.

1. Practice

During the Cold War era, there were no good examples of humanitarian intervention by a regional organization. As discussed in chapter 4, the 1965 intervention in the Dominican Republic was not primarily motivated by human rights concerns as conventionally understood. Further, when the OAS took command of military operations from the United States, neither it nor the United States argued that the operation was an enforcement action under Article 53. The operation was viewed by the OAS, rather, as a consensual one to restore "normal conditions" to the Dominican Republic, and thus was seen to be within the scope of Article 52. This interpretation was challenged by Cuba, Jordan, and the Soviet Union but otherwise passed muster at the Security Council.[22] Interpreting the OAS operation as falling within the scope of Article 52 might be viewed as anomalous or as evidence of a willingness to interpret the scope of Article 52 loosely so as to cover military operations that seek to quell civil unrest in a "failed state."

The post-Cold War practice of humanitarian intervention by regional organizations is also limited. When the Security Council authorized the military blockade of Haiti,[23] it was acting expressly "under Chapters VII and VIII" of the UN Charter, and it called on states acting nationally "or through regional agencies or arrangements" to halt maritime shipping. Those states that proceeded to impose the blockade, however, acted nationally and not as part of an OAS force. Further, while the Security Council noted the OAS resolutions that imposed sanctions on Haiti,[24] the Security Council's authorization was for enforcement of the Security Council's own sanctions.[25] Resolution 940 authorizing invasion spoke only in terms of a multinational force formed by "Member States."

This study does not regard the military actions taken by the international community in Bosnia-Herzegovina during 1992 and 1993 to constitute humanitarian intervention because of the international character of that conflict. Nevertheless, it should be noted that those actions did involve the use of regional organizations to assist the Security Council. The Security Council referenced both Chapter VII and Chapter VIII in

22. Akehurst, *supra* note 11, at 211.

23. S.C. Res. 875, U.N. SCOR, 48th Sess., 3293d mtg. at 125, U.N. Doc. S/INF/49 (1994).

24. *Id.*, pmbl.

25. The Security Council's sanctions appear at S.C. Res. 873, U.N. SCOR, 48th Sess., 3291st mtg. at 125, U.N. Doc. S/INF/49 (1994) and S.C. Res. 841, U.N. SCOR, 48th Sess., 3238th mtg. at 119, U.N. Doc. S/INF/49 (1994).

granting authorization to states "acting nationally or through regional organizations" to use force to enforce a no-fly zone over Bosnia-Herzegovina,[26] to enforce the Security Council's economic sanctions,[27] and to protect six "safe havens" established to protect Bosnian Muslims.[28] As discussed in chapter 5, these actions were undertaken by states operating through NATO and Western European Union (WEU) command structures and are an indication of how regional organizations may operate outside their primary mission of collective self-defense.

The military intervention by ECOWAS in Liberia was not authorized in advance by the Security Council, although it was subsequently supported by statements of the President of the Security Council and implicitly by Security Council resolutions. Those resolutions (which imposed a weapons embargo and dispatched a special UN representative to Liberia) did not invoke Chapter VIII. Had the Security Council authorized the military intervention ex post facto, the logical basis for doing so would have been Article 53 of Chapter VIII; at the same time, such an authorization would have created a precedent for regional organizations to act under Article 53 prior to Security Council authorization, which is certainly not the sequence envisioned by that Article. The Security Council's resolutions essentially ignored the military intervention and instead focused on ECOWAS's diplomatic efforts at national reconciliation. Here, too, a reference to Chapter VIII would have been appropriate, either as an acknowledgment of a regional effort at dispute settlement under Article 52 or as an ongoing enforcement action under Article 53. Ultimately, the Secretary-General heralded the Liberian case as an example of cooperation under Chapter VIII. Certainly, Liberia stands as a example of the impact regional organizations can have upon humanitarian intervention as well as upon conflict management generally. Yet, the UN-ECOWAS "cooperation" fell short of that envisioned under Chapter VIII; the enforcement action was not expressly authorized under Article 53, and there is no record of ECOWAS reports to the Security Council pursuant to Article 54 of the Charter.

The ECOWAS intervention may be yet another example of the United Nations unwillingness to stand on a rigorous interpretation of Article 53, but instead to allow regional institutions to proceed without Security Council involvement, at least in some circumstances. This development would be consistent with the minimal practice during the Cold War (recounted above), although with the increased involvement of the Security Council in such crises one might also have predicted an effort by the

26. S.C. Res. 816, U.N. SCOR, 48th Sess., 3191st mtg. at 4, U.N. Doc. S/INF/49 (1994).
27. S.C. Res. 787, U.N. SCOR, 47th Sess., 3137th mtg. at 29, U.N. Doc. S/INF/48 (1993).
28. S.C. Res. 836, U.N. SCOR, 48th Sess., 3228th mtg. at 13, U.N. Doc. S/INF/49 (1994).

Security Council to consolidate powers as originally granted in the Charter. If such practice continues, at some point it may be said that a gloss on Article 53 exists, although at this stage the practice is too episodic. A less-than-rigorous interpretation of Article 53 may be benign in situations, like East Africa, where the Security Council does not act out of simple neglect. It is more troubling in situations where the failure to obtain Security Council authorization is due to the opposition of one or more permanent members of the Security Council or to the opposition of a majority of the members of the Security Council. For a regional organization to proceed with the intervention in those situations risks the matter escalating into a wider conflict and likely means that the humanitarian basis for the conflict is not readily apparent.

Oscar Schachter believes that the Liberian case may "suggest an interpretation of peacekeeping by regional bodies that allows for a collective military intervention to help end an internal conflict when a government has been deposed or no longer has effective authority."[29] Presumably this form of "peacekeeping" by regional bodies is permissible even without the consent of the local factions, on a theory that consent by a recognized government effectively in control of its territory is not possible. If so, the ECOWAS intervention in Liberia would be regarded as based on Article 52, and one might expect further interventions in the future without Security Council authorization in cases of "failed states" (e.g., Somalia, Liberia) but not in cases where recognized governments, with effective control of their territories, are directing the widespread and severe human rights abuses.

While collective military intervention may take this course, the result may not be particularly satisfying. As discussed in chapter 1, the lack of a centralized authority capable of providing consent cannot be equated with consent; in most situations, there will be key factions capable of granting consent just as effectively as in normal circumstances.[30] If constructive consent to intervention by regional organizations exists in the case of failed states, there does not appear to be any basis in the Charter or otherwise for denying the legality of intervention in such situations by states operating outside regional organizations, collectively or individually. Finally, the distinction between situations where a government is

---

29. O. Schachter, *Authorized Uses of Force by the United Nations and Regional Organizations*, in LAW AND FORCE IN THE NEW INTERNATIONAL ORDER 65, 88 (L. Damrosch & D. Scheffer eds., 1991).

30. For support on this point in the context of consent to the deployment of the OAU force in the Dominican Republic in 1965, *see* Akehurst, *supra* note 11, at 212 (arguing that consent to the deployment by the local factions served as the basis for the operation, "for does not consent given by both sides in a civil war represent the national will just as effectively as consent given by a government in more normal conditions?").

"deposed" or not in "effective control" and other situations may reso-
nate more in theory than in practice, at least in situations where there
are severe and widespread human rights deprivations. In none of the
cases discussed in chapter 5 was there a recognized government in effective control of all of its territory at the time of the intervention, with the
possible exception of the intervention on behalf of the Shiites in southern Iraq in August 1992. Yet there were unrecognized factions, such as
the Haitian military, the Tutsi rebels in Rwanda, or the rebel Taylor
forces in Liberia, that effectively controlled all or virtually all the territory
of the country. Accepting collective military intervention in all such situations on a basis that it is not "enforcement action" virtually writes Article 53 out of the Charter whenever internal conflicts arise.

Notwithstanding the asserted preference in UN Charter Chapter VIII
for addressing threats to the peace involving states within a region
through regional arrangements or agencies, there is little evidence from
the recent interventions in Liberia, Iraq, Bosnia-Herzegovina, Somalia,
Rwanda, or Haiti that states or the Security Council felt bound to encourage (let alone exhaust) use of regional agencies in addressing the
deprivations of human rights. Rather, it would appear that regional arrangements or agencies were used in some instances (Liberia, Bosnia-
Herzegovina, Haiti), while in others they were perceived as ineffective,
irrelevant, or even as an impediment in resolving the underlying problem (Iraq, Somalia, Rwanda). For example, in northern Iraq, part of the
difficulty with action by a regional organization was that the conditions
giving rise to the humanitarian intervention affected two regions; in
theory, both the Arab League and the institutions of Europe (as well as
NATO) could have acted. Politically (and probably militarily), however,
the Arab League could not move against the Government of Iraq, while
the flow of refugees into Turkey was not an "armed attack" triggering an
obligation of assistance by the NATO alliance. Another part of the problem in northern Iraq was the severe logistical difficulties in conducting
the humanitarian intervention. Today, Britain, France, and the United
States remain among the few countries capable of launching massive relief programs on short notice. In Somalia and Rwanda, the OAU was politically incapable of organizing and deploying military forces, even with
offers of assistance from out-of-region states. Regional organizations
simply do not have such capabilities and likely will not in the near future.

Even when a regional organization is engaged in the underlying crisis
in a meaningful manner, member states do not necessarily pursue humanitarian intervention through that regional organization. As noted
above, the 1993 authorization from the Security Council to proceed with
a military blockade of Haiti was not limited to action by the OAS. Rather,
the Security Council's authorization included states *acting nationally* to

enforce the sanctions and it was through states acting in their national capacity that the sanctions were in fact enforced. In Bosnia, authorization was provided to states acting through regional organizations or in their national capacity. The airstrikes conducted in early 1994 were within the NATO integrated command, but they consisted solely of U.S. jets flown from Aviano Air Base in Italy.

Whether greater involvement of regional organizations in the conduct of humanitarian intervention is desirable depends on policy and other considerations. Arguably, by waiting in vain for regional organizations to organize themselves and deploy forces, hundreds of thousands died in Bosnia-Herzegovina, Somalia, and Rwanda. If regional organizations are expected to take action in such cases, they must be provided the institutional and logistical capabilities well in advance of crises rather than be expected to develop them when a crisis occurs. In the case of Haiti, the OAS had been involved in sanctioning Haiti long before the Security Council, and it would have enhanced OAS involvement in the crisis for the Security Council to authorize enforcement action by military forces operating within an OAS command structure. Greater OAS involvement might also have defused arguments by the Haitian military that it was the target of U.S. imperialism. On the other hand, the United States and Canada were expected to contribute the primary forces to the naval blockade and preferred to maintain their own command structure. Further, the United States may have preferred not to augment OAS capabilities in this area since the United States does not have the same veto power in the OAS framework as it does in the Security Council.

Liberia and Haiti represent examples where both the United Nations and regional organizations are capable of working in tandem to address an underlying conflict. Particularly in the case of Liberia, it is clear that one or the other organization may be able to intercede at a certain point to act as an impartial mediator after an intervention has occurred. This concurrence of jurisdiction over a matter is possible due to the ambiguous role of the United Nations vis-à-vis regional organizations contained in the Charter, and it may serve as a useful means for creative dispute resolution in the future.

2. Prospects

One of the goals of the international community should be to encourage action by regional organizations under Article 53 when conditions arise calling for humanitarian intervention. Doing so could yield benefits that would not exist if the intervention were conducted by states acting under their own authority and could even yield benefits that would not exist if all such interventions were conducted under the authority of Chapter VII.

First, as a general matter, use of Article 53 rather than Chapter VII would enhance the development of conflict management tools on a regional level. Preventive diplomacy undertaken by regional organizations would be backed by an institutionalized means of enforcement measures, which might deter certain human rights atrocities from ever occurring. By engaging the Security Council in the process of pursuing those enforcement measures, both in the authorization under Article 53 and the reporting requirements of Article 54, a more symbiotic relationship between the regional organization and the Security Council could develop, playing to their respective strengths and weaknesses. Regional organizations are best situated to sound an early warning regarding the potential outbreak of human rights deprivations and to provide information on their causes and possible solutions. Yet regional organizations often are weak in the diplomatic, economic, and military pressure they can bring to bear on a potential aggressor, either because of a lack of their own resources or because of the political difficulty in acting against a state that is relatively powerful within the region. A closer relationship with the Security Council could enhance the ability of a regional organization to bring pressure on the human rights violator, while at the same time keep on the front line the organization best equipped to resolve the problem. More systematic linkage might include the conclusion of an agreement between the Security Council and the regional organization regarding information sharing, emergency consultation, periodic joint meetings, participation in Security Council meetings on issues related to the region, or placement of issues on the agenda of one entity by the other. The lack of systematic linkage might be resolved on an ad hoc basis as human rights crises arise, but this will invariably lead to confusing, perhaps over-bureaucratic, handling of a crisis. For instance, while the Security Council and NATO worked out a system for bombing Bosnian Serb targets, the requirement of prior authorization by UN commanders on the ground and UN officials in New York proved cumbersome.[31]

Second, use of regional organizations rather than reliance on Chapter VII may be the most likely means for achieving a successful intervention. A humanitarian intervention, if it is to occur, should occur in sufficient time to have a significant effect in stemming human rights deprivations; in the case of both Liberia and Haiti, the respective sub-

---

31. B. Gellman & T. Rowe, *U.S. Agrees to U.N. Veto on Bombing*, WASH. POST, Aug. 7, 1993, at A1.

regional and regional organizations perceived a threat and acted much more quickly than did the United Nations. Further, the military forces of states within a region usually are better positioned to handle difficulties that will arise regarding language, culture, and religion in conducting the intervention.[32] For instance, the intervention by ECOWAS in Liberia was not encumbered by the charges of renewed Western colonialism levied when the United States led forces into Somalia and when France intervened in Rwanda. Moreover, states within the region are more apt to appreciate the political sensitivities in "rebuilding" the nation so as to ensure long-term stability. On the other hand, familiarity *can* breed contempt; there may be times when the only forces that will be perceived as neutral or impartial in conducting an intervention will be those deployed from outside the region. Further, use of regional organizations does not guarantee constraints on major-power diplomacy; the regional organization itself may be dominated by a regional power seeking to use the organization for its own ends.

Third, greater use of Article 53 in lieu of Chapter VII plays to the spheres of influence that always have existed in international affairs. More powerful states in a region may find humanitarian intervention through a regional organization a useful way of spreading the political and economic costs of the intervention. Smaller powers in a region may find Article 53 useful precisely to push regional powers into some form of collective arrangement that can act as a constraint on that power's behavior, thereby decreasing the likelihood of interventions that are not truly humanitarian in nature. Smaller powers might also see greater use of regional organizations as a way to create precedents that discourage intervention by powers outside the regional bloc.

Use of Article 53 also yields benefits over humanitarian intervention by states in their individual capacities. As will be discussed in greater detail in the next chapter, it avoids a strained interpretation of Article 51 of the Charter, in which the right of self-defense against armed attack is transformed into a right to maintain international peace and security which may be invoked either by states collectively or individually without any oversight through the Security Council. Moreover, placing the humanitarian intervention in a regional forum may provide more credibility to the intervention than if it is conducted by states acting in their individual capacities. Credibility is enhanced because the intervention is the product of a decision by a group of several states collectively. Of course, as was seen in the "decision" by the Warsaw Pact to intervene in

---

32. This will not always be the case. In Somalia, the local Muslim population had closer affinity in religion and traditions with the Islamic world than with other parts of Africa, and thus countries such as Pakistan played a major role in the intervention.

Czechoslovakia in 1968, the fact that an intervention is conducted by a multilateral organization does not immunize it from abuses.

Indeed, placing humanitarian intervention in a regional forum may provide more credibility than intervention either by individual states or by the United Nations, for there may be regional instruments or institutions operating under the auspices of the regional organization that assist in clarifying the nature and existence of human rights deprivations.[33] For instance, an intervention in Somalia by African nations could have pointed to the African Charter on Human and Peoples' Rights[34] as one basis for assessing whether intervention was justified. The Preamble of that Charter recognizes that "fundamental human rights stem from the attributes of human beings, *which justifies their national and international protection*," while Article 23 provides that "All peoples shall have the right to *national* and international peace and security."[35] Admittedly, the African Charter does not expressly authorize military intervention to enforce these rights, but it does establish a Commission on Human and Peoples' Rights that could have provided an authoritative report on human rights deprivations, which in turn could have served as the basis for an intervention. Similarly, the Inter-American Commission on Human Rights now has more than thirty years of experience in promoting and protecting human rights within the inter-American system and might serve as a useful means of assessing the need for humanitarian intervention in that region. Where regional humanitarian intervention is possible, that intervention should be initiated and monitored closely by the Security Council.

As a general matter, however, the prospects for greater use of regional organizations for the conduct of humanitarian intervention are not favorable. The capacity of regional organizations to conduct humanitarian intervention is inextricably tied to their capacity to maintain international peace and security generally. As is the case for the United Nations itself, many states remain unwilling to place their forces under the command of regional organizations for enforcement actions. While states wish to maximize the rewards of a regional system, they also prefer not to transfer such a core attribute of their sovereignty to regional organizations, knowing that such organizations invariably may conduct military interventions that are antithetical to any given state's national interests.

33. For a discussion of the instruments of regional human rights regimes and their effectiveness, see B. Weston et al., *Regional Human Rights Regimes: A Comparison and Appraisal*, 20 VANDERBILT J. TRANSNAT'L L. 585 (1987).

34. African Charter on Human and Peoples' Rights, June 26, 1981, 21 I.L.M. 58, *reprinted in* 3 WESTON, *supra* note 12, at III.B.1. Most African nations including Somalia, are parties to the Charter.

35. *Id.* pmbl., art. 23 (emphasis added).

States that do not have significant military capabilities may in some instances band together to further their security interests, as was the case
for ECOWAS, but by and large even these states are fearful of a regional
organization with the capability to intervene.

Much of the difficulty in fostering regional approaches to humanitarian intervention is attributable to the lack of a stable consensus among
the states of most regional organizations about the means for handling
intra-regional and extra-regional affairs and the means for addressing
conflicts as they arise. Regional organizations, such as the League of
Arab States and the Organization of African Unity, contain members
whose views range from moderate to extremist. This not only weakens
the ability of the regional organization to respond in any given situation,
it also weakens the ability to create structures for future responses. Even
the most highly developed of regional organizations, the European
Union, as yet has not created a common security policy and does not
operate as a regional organization under Chapter VIII of the Charter.

Recent events suggest that states are unlikely to invoke Article 53
of the Charter as the basis for conducting humanitarian intervention
through regional organizations or arrangements. Where Security Council authorization can be readily obtained, the states may prefer to ground
their actions on Chapter VII to provide maximum flexibility in their actions, particularly if the intervention is to be conducted by states acting
in their individual capacities. Where Security Council authorization cannot be readily obtained, states may prefer to ground their intervention
on collective self-defense under Article 51 of the Charter rather than on
a contorted interpretation of Article 53. Alternatively, states may find it
convenient to ground their intervention on Article 52; humanitarian intervention will often involve confusing situations of a breakdown in governmental authority, such that the intervention may be cast as an effort
at "pacific settlement of a dispute" among local factions and not an "enforcement action." That approach is simply another way of arguing that
the intervention is not really an "intervention" at all, because there is no
centralized authority whose rights are being trampled. Whether this is
correct will be appraised by the international community on a case-by-
case basis.

For these reasons, coercive military action by regional organizations
(including humanitarian intervention) likely will remain, in the near
term, beyond the capabilities of regional organizations. Nevertheless,
regional organizations can play a role in the development of the norms
of humanitarian intervention in a post–Cold War world. The United
Nations, including the Security Council, currently is grappling with
when, where, and how humanitarian intervention should occur. It will
be driven by the views of its member states, which in turn will be driven

by perceptions as to how such intervention affects their own security, particularly on a regional level. Regional organizations can play a key role in shaping these views and perceptions, particularly as they develop from experiences with humanitarian crises over time.

As these crises arise, regional organizations can be active in establishing what nonforcible actions must first be taken to try to resolve the crisis before forcible action is considered. They can seek to engage the United Nations in such mediation efforts, which may run parallel to efforts by the regional organization, as occurred in the crisis in Haiti. They can undertake fact-finding missions to clarify the nature of the crisis and to indicate what level of human rights deprivations exist. If the results of these steps call for humanitarian intervention, the regional organization can encourage United Nations humanitarian intervention by passing appropriate resolutions and by sending communications to the Security Council through their own representatives and those of their member states. Such resolutions and communications can clarify the threat to international peace and the means by which an intervention should be conducted to address that threat. Conversely, they can discourage such action when they perceive an impermissible basis for the intervention. Regional organizations can participate in the intervention directly, particularly in efforts to obtain national reconciliation or otherwise "rebuild" the target state.

The ability of any given regional organization to undertake such actions to influence UN behavior will depend on the internal dynamics of that organization and its relationship to the United Nations. While to date the OAU has not played a role in the conduct of interventions, the resolutions of its Heads of States and Governments and its Assembly have provided a means for developing a consensus within the African community, which in turn have assisted in organizing instructions for their representatives to the United Nations.[36] The influence of the League of Arab States at the United Nations has been complicated in the past since most issues that arose related to Arab-Israeli differences; if current developments lead to a resolution of those differences, the League may be able to play a more influential role with the United Nations regarding crises within the Arab community. The OAS undoubtedly will continue to be dominated by the views of its most powerful member, the United States, but it still should be in a position to influence the initiation and conduct of UN humanitarian interventions if any occur in the Western Hemisphere. Other regional and subregional organizations can also serve as vehicles for conditioning UN behavior.

In sum, despite their weaknesses, "Regional organizations have an or-

36. *See* Frey-Wouters, *supra* note 1, at 540.

dering role to play in the present international system because of the nature of the system and the limitations it imposes upon both the UN and individual states to promote international order."[37] Prospects for humanitarian intervention by regional organizations serving as agents of the Security Council at this time would appear low, even though the benefits of such a role to world order would appear high. Greater prospects, however, may exist for regional organizations to condition the behavior of the United Nations in conducting or authorizing humanitarian intervention.

37. *Id.* at 543.

Chapter 8
Unilateral Humanitarian Intervention

During the Cold War, the attitudes, expectations, and values of states, international organizations, and scholars regarding the unilateral use of force were heavily influenced by two principal developments.

The first development was the defining feature of the Cold War: an intense ideological competition between the East and the West which, combined with the emergence of nuclear weapons, placed a very high premium on finding a way of maintaining minimum world public order. For some, achieving minimum world public order meant adhering strictly to universal norms that restrained the unilateral use of force in the hope that by fostering such norms transnational conflict would be minimized. Unless force was used only as a matter of self-defense or as authorized under Chapter VII, it was not permissible. The fact that the East-West competition left the Security Council paralyzed was an unfortunate circumstance, but could not be used to justify a state's resort to self-help measures other than as an exercise of self-defense. From this general perspective, minimum world public order could not condone as permissible distinctions between uses of force based on the ideological goals of the state conducting the coercive action; to do so in the climate of East-West competition was to threaten the nuclear peace and to abdicate any hope of universal adherence to international norms on the use of force. For others, achieving minimum world public order meant accepting the realities of the East-West competition and consequent Security Council paralysis, which played out less through classic transnational aggression than through "sub-aggression"—coercive behavior pursuant to which the East and West sought to draw states into their orbits through the manipulation of internal conflicts. The realities argued in favor of developing norms that accounted for such coercive behavior by regarding it as lawful when undertaken as a matter of reciprocity. In the West, advancing values of human rights and human dignity were fundamental to maintaining minimum world public order and provided a means for appraising coercive behavior on a basis other than simply whether an action was taken in self-defense.

The second principal development was the transition from a Western-oriented construct of international law to one that took account of the newly emerging states mostly of the southern Hemisphere. The Cold War coincided with the final collapse of the colonial empires of several of the Western states and the subsequent emergence of newly independent states. By the 1960s, these new states rose to a number and status whereby they could influence significantly the attitudes of the international community regarding the development of international legal norms. With respect to the use of force, these states advanced a somewhat contradictory agenda in which they condemned the intervention by states (especially the Western states) in the affairs of other states while at the same time carving out an exception according to which intervention was permissible to assist those suffering under colonial rule to achieve self-determination. The contradiction lay in the fact that the oppression of peoples during the Cold War was far from a product of only colonial rule; many of the newly independent states themselves operated authoritarian regimes that denied their peoples fundamental human rights, including rights to choose their government through free elections. The influence on international norms regarding the use of force was to implant uncertainties in their meaning; intervention was broadly condemned, but some kind of loophole existed for advancing certain causes deemed just, to wit, the throwing off of colonial rule.

After the Cold War, both of these developments are much less significant. The intense ideological competition between East and West is gone, and with the fragmentation of the Soviet Union and the change in governments of its satellite states has come a decrease in concern with global nuclear war. The prospect for rapid integration of the East into a community of liberal democratic states seems low, but so does the prospect of a return to a Cold War-type rivalry. At the same time, the states of the Southern Hemisphere are no longer considered the newly independent states of the world; their colonial antecedents continue to drift further into the past. While these states still advance claims for a new international economic order based on the premise that the Western, wealthier states have obtained their status partially at their expense, the clamor for international norms that permit coercive behavior in favor of self-determination has dimmed.

Other developments will now play a greater role in conditioning the growth of, and attitudes toward, international legal norms, among them: the globalization of capital flows and emergence of multinational economic entities having control and influence that transcend borders; the development of low-cost communications technologies permitting information to flow easily across borders without government control; the potential for wider proliferation of technology relating to weapons of mass destruction; the pervasive influence of narcotics trafficking; access to energy and other natural resources; the perils of global environmental degradation; and population growth and the transnational movement of persons. Of course, the demise of the Cold War, too, is affecting international norms regarding the use of force. Inevitably, fragmentation of societies previously bound together as a part of Cold War rivalries and concomitant efforts by the international community to promote human rights and democratic institutions in these societies are making themselves felt. The former Soviet Union and the states of Eastern and Central Europe are the obvious examples of this fragmentation, but others (such as Somalia and Haiti) exist as well; and this development points to shifting attitudes about the sanctity of states and territorial boundaries and challenges traditional notions of sovereignty that form the basis for international rules on the use of force.

An important consequence of this early post-Cold War normative development regarding the use of force has been the emergence of the UN Security Council as a potential option for assisting in the management of conflict; and it is partly in recognition of this consequence that the primary focus of this study so far has been with the role of the Security Council in using (or authorizing the use of) force on its own and in relation to regional organizations to prevent widespread and severe deprivations of human rights. Yet humanitarian intervention by a state or states without authorization by the United Nations or a regional organization—unilateral humanitarian intervention—remains a significant issue for international law. Notwithstanding the reawakening of the Security Council, at times the Security Council will fail to act, and states may be inclined to conduct humanitarian intervention on their own initiative, perhaps pointing to recent incidents as authority for their action.

This chapter assesses the problems of, and prospects for, unilateral humanitarian intervention after the Cold War. Consideration is given to a classical, traditional interpretation of whether such intervention may be considered lawful in light of the rules of the UN Charter and incidents of state practice since the creation of the Charter. Thereafter, consideration is given to two broader conceptions of international law. The first conception views international law as a process of authoritative decisionmaking whereby states use international law to advance certain fundamental values. Under this approach, attention is given first to the value of human dignity and then to that of systemic stability. The second conception views international law as derivative of a substantive moral philosophy that accords supremacy to the protection and enforcement of the natural rights of persons. Both conceptions are then considered in light of the post-Cold War emergence of the Security Council as an authoritative decisionmaker. Finally, in the event that unilateral humanitarian intervention is—or becomes—regarded as a permissible use of force, consideration is given to the efficacy of establishing criteria for the conduct of such intervention.

A. Rules-Oriented Approach

As discussed in chapter 1, international law may be conceived as a system of rules emanating primarily from textual agreement among states and the customary practice of states accompanied by their conviction that such practice is required by international law (*opinio juris*). As such, international law is seen as a restraint system on the conduct of states, albeit a relatively decentralized one. Under this approach, rule-oriented norms on the permissibility of unilateral humanitarian intervention derive primarily from the UN Charter, which may be interpreted in light of the intent of states in crafting the Charter and their subsequent interpretation of the Charter as incidents of intervention arise.

Chapter 3 explored the origins and text of the UN Charter as it related to provisions on the use of force by states. While arguments may be made that Article 2(4) of the Charter did not prohibit humanitarian intervention, the counterarguments are stronger that Article 2(4) was meant to be comprehensive in scope.[1] Greater ambiguity exists as to whether Article 51, which states that the UN Charter does not impair the inherent right of individual or collective self-defense if an armed attack occurs, includes a right by states to resort to unilateral humanitarian intervention. An initial reading of Article 51 seems to foreclose such a possibility; Article 51 preserves an *inherent* right of *self-defense* if an *armed attack* occurs against a *member of the United Nations*. Humanitarian intervention, as commonly understood and as defined for purposes of this study, is not a

---

1. Oscar Schachter analyzes the array of claims for exceptions to Article 2(4) and concludes that:

> [I]nternational law does not, and should not, legitimize the use of force across national lines except for self-defense (including collective defense) and enforcement measures ordered by the Security Council. Neither human rights, democracy or self-determination are acceptable legal grounds for waging war, nor for that matter, are traditional just war causes or righting of wrongs. This conclusion is not only in accord with the U.N. Charter as it was originally understood; it is also in keeping with the interpretation adopted by the great majority of States at the present time. When governments have resorted to force, they have almost invariably relied on self-defense as their legal justification.

O. SCHACHTER, INTERNATIONAL LAW IN THEORY AND PRACTICE 128 (1991).

defensive use of force by one state in response to another state, let alone an "armed attack" by another state. To the extent that there is an attack, that attack is occurring by the other state against its own nationals, who themselves are not a "Member of the United Nations." Further, even if one regards Article 51 as leaving unimpaired the exercise of self-defense as permitted under customary international law,[2] the doctrine of humanitarian intervention was manifestly different from the doctrine of *self*-defense under customary international law.[3] And even if these doctrines are viewed as vague and overlapping under customary international law, and thus may be lumped together under some overarching doctrine of self-defense/self-help, it is far from settled that the doctrine of humanitarian intervention survived the pre-World War II trend toward restricting uses of force (such as evidenced by the Kellogg-Briand Pact[4]) and further doubtful that after the German, Italian, and Japanese interventions in the name of protecting the rights of foreign nationals, the drafters of the UN Charter were anxious to retain such a doctrine.[5]

Highly restrictive interpretations of Articles 2(4) and 51, however, have not withstood the test of time. On various occasions since 1945 states have used force to protect their own nationals from danger in another state which the other state cannot or will not prevent.[6] It will be recalled that many of the incidents discussed in chapter 4 involved a state arguing, among other things, that it was entitled to intervene unilaterally in another state to protect its own nationals. In most of these incidents, the intervening state characterized its action as a lawful exercise of its right of self-defense. The language of Article 51 ("self-defense if an armed attack occurs against a Member of the United Nations"), however, does not seem to account for such a right to use force.[7] Neverthe-

2. D. BOWETT, SELF-DEFENCE IN INTERNATIONAL LAW 188 (1958).

3. *See* I. Brownlie, *Humanitarian Intervention, in* LAW AND CIVIL WAR IN THE MODERN WORLD 217, 219 (J. Moore ed., 1974).

4. General Treaty for the Renunciation of War as an Instrument of National Policy, Aug. 27, 1928, 94 LNTS 57, *reprinted in* 2 INTERNATIONAL LAW AND WORLD ORDER: BASIC DOCUMENTS II.A.1 (B. Weston ed., 1994).

5. *See* I. BROWNLIE, INTERNATIONAL LAW AND THE USE OF FORCE BY STATES 342 (1963); Q. Wright, *The Legality of Intervention Under the United Nations Charter,* 51 PROC. AM. SOC. INT'L L. 79, 88 (1957).

6. *See* 1 OPPENHEIM'S INTERNATIONAL LAW (PEACE) 440–42 (R. Jennings & A. Watts eds., 9th ed. 1992); *see also* THE CHARTER OF THE UNITED NATIONS: A COMMENTARY 125 (B. Simma ed., 1994) ("It can be said in summary that state practice is characterized by a considerable reluctance to qualify rescue operations involving the use of force as in any case unlawful").

7. Judge Jessup, at the outset of the U.N. Charter era, writes:

Traditional international law has recognized the right of a state to employ its armed forces for the protection of the lives and property of its nationals abroad in situations

less, many states and some scholars have come to the view that such intervention constitutes a "defense of nationals" that is, in effect, a "defense of the state" itself.[8] Other scholars, and in some instances officials of a state, have also characterized the action as a permissible exception to Article 2(4) of the Charter.[9]

---

where the state of their residence, because of revolutionary disturbances or other reasons, is unable or unwilling to grant them the protection to which they are entitled. Such action is not properly classified as self-defense, and it may fall short of intervention as that term is narrowly defined.

P. JESSUP, A MODERN LAW OF NATIONS 169 (Archon Books 1968) (1946) (quoting C. HYDE, 1 INTERNATIONAL LAW, CHIEFLY AS INTERPRETED AND APPLIED BY THE UNITED STATES sec. 69 (2d rev. ed. 1945)).

Although the issue of rescue of nationals was not squarely before the International Court of Justice in the case brought by Nicaragua against the United States, the Court's decision regards an "armed attack" as the movement of regular armed bands across an international frontier; lesser measures, such as the supply of arms across borders, do not constitute an "armed attack." Military and Paramilitary Activities (Nicar. v. U.S.), 1986 I.C.J. 4, at paras. 195, 230, 247 (June 27). The only possible exception to this noted by the Court was action taken in anticipation of an armed attack, which the Court chose not to address. *Id.*, para. 194. Under this approach, it would seem that the taking of another state's nationals as hostage would not constitute an "armed attack" on that other state. Moreover, other statements by the Court regarding the treatment of persons by a state suggest that it regards such actions as of a different status than transfrontier aggression. The Court cited with apparent agreement a listing of various uses of force from the Declaration on Friendly Relations, discussed *supra* chapter 4, which the Court said do not amount to "aggression," including forcible action depriving peoples of the right of self-determination, freedom, and independence. *Id.* para. 191. *See also* United States Diplomatic and Consular Staff in Tehran (U.S. v. Iran), 1980 I.C.J. 3, 52–54, 56, 64–65 (May 24) (dissenting opinions of Judges Morozov and Tarazi) (critical of U.S. effort to rescue hostages in Tehran).

8. Some of these scholars also support unilateral humanitarian intervention. Nevertheless, there appears considerable evidence that states themselves regard the use of force to protect or rescue their nationals as permissible self-defense under Article 51. *See* chapter 4 *supra*; *see also* R. Lillich, *Forcible Protection of Nationals Abroad: The Liberian "Incident" of 1990*, 35 GERMAN Y.B. INT'L L. 205, 217 n.86 (1992); D. Bowett, *The Use of Force for the Protection of Nationals Abroad, in* THE CURRENT LEGAL REGULATION OF THE USE OF FORCE 39 (A. Cassese ed., 1986); BOWETT, *supra* note 2, at 91, 93–96; T. Farer, *Panama: Beyond the Charter Paradigm*, 84 AM. J. INT'L L. 503, 505–06 (1990); SCHACHTER, *supra* note 1, at 126, 128, 144; C. Waldock, *The Regulation of the Use of Force by Individual States in International Law*, 81 R.C.A.D.I. 451, 466–67 (1952-II).

Not all scholars, however, regard the rescue of nationals as lawful under the U.N. Charter. *See, e.g.,* N. Ronzitti, RESCUING NATIONALS ABROAD THROUGH MILITARY COERCION AND INTERVENTION ON GROUNDS OF HUMANITY 62–64 (1985); BROWNLIE, *supra* note 5, at 301; M. Akehurst, *Humanitarian Intervention, in* INTERVENTION IN WORLD POLITICS 95 (H. Bull ed., 1984). Lillich points out, however, that even those scholars that regard the rescue of nationals as inconsistent with the U.N. Charter seem willing to in some fashion condone or rationalize such action. Lillich, *supra*, at 219–20.

9. A notable example is the statement of U.S. Ambassador Jeane Kirkpatrick following the U.S. invasion of Grenada. Ambassador Kirkpatrick Statement (Oct. 27, 1983), *in* DEP'T

As explained in chapter 1, the protection by a state of its own nationals is qualitatively different from the protection of the nationals of the target state. There is an essential juridical link between a state and its own nationals, and an international norm precluding a state from acting to protect its nationals from danger in another state simply cannot be sustained. Yet, while accepting that there is a great difference between the protection of one's own nationals and the protection of another state's nationals, it must be asked in what sense that difference is dictated by the Charter. Why is it that states regard the deployment of forces to another state for the protection of their nationals as consistent with the notion of "self-defense if an armed attack occurs against a Member State?" The answer may lie in a belief by states that such protection of nationals is a permissible form of self-help under pre-1945 customary international law which survived the Charter, notwithstanding the apparently restrictive language of Article 51. The answer may also lie in a belief that an "attack" on one's state includes an "attack" on one's nationals abroad. Yet another way of explaining this development, which this study submits is likely closer to the beliefs held by key decisionmakers in states, is a fundamental unwillingness of state A to stand by idly when state B commits or permits the infliction of violence against persons whose well-being state A regards as important to its national interests. These persons may be the armed forces of state A or the citizens of state A located abroad. If this latter explanation is what drives a more expanded interpretation of Article 51, it must be asked whether such reasoning is that far from a position that can encompass unilateral humanitarian intervention as well. One can imagine other

---

ST. BULL., Dec. 1983, at 74 (language of Article 2(4) provides ample justification for the use of force "in pursuit of other values also inscribed in the charter—freedom, democracy, peace"); *see also* Lillich, *supra* note 8, at 216 (and authorities cited therein); L. HENKIN, HOW NATIONS BEHAVE: LAW AND FOREIGN POLICY 145 (2d ed. 1979); L. Henkin, *International Law: Politics, Values and Functions*, 216 R.C.A.D.I. 9, 153–54 (1989-IV); RESTATEMENT (THIRD) OF THE FOREIGN RELATIONS LAW OF THE UNITED STATES sec. 703 cmt. e, rptrs. note 8 (1986) ("Missions strictly for rescue . . . were commonly thought not to violate Article 2(4), either because they did not involve the 'use of force' or were not against 'the territorial integrity or political independence' of the target state, within the meaning of Article 2(4)"). Henkin is more comfortable fitting the rescue of nationals under Article 2(4) than under Article 51, apparently due to a belief that a full-scale conflict is more likely to result if the intervention is considered a lawful response to "armed attack" under Article 51.

As explained in chapter 3, *supra*, this study regards the language of Article 2(4) and the travaux préparatoires of the Charter as expressing a broad prohibition on the use of force. In assessing the practice of states, this study finds that this view of Article 2(4) has not changed; when states have intervened in other states to protect their nationals, they usually have not claimed that they acted on the basis of an exception embodied in Article 2(4) but, rather, that they acted in self-defense.

categories of persons that might also be important to the national interests of the intervening state. For instance, one of the arguments made by
President Clinton in justifying U.S. military intervention in Haiti was that
there were a large number of U.S. nationals who were of Haitian origin,
and who presumably had familial connections with Haitian nationals.

This latter explanation for an expanded view of Article 51 may help
explain why it is generally accepted that state A may rescue not only its
own nationals but those of state C as well who happen to be at risk in the
target state B.[10] There is no juridical link between state A and the nationals of state C, yet it is generally accepted that state A may rescue state C's
nationals. Of course, this might be explained as an act of collective self-
defense under Article 51 whereby state C has requested state A to rescue
its nationals, but such an interpretation truly begins to strain Article 51.

The basis in the UN Charter for justifying the rescue of the nationals
of a third state is perhaps less problematic if one regards the rescue of
nationals as a permissible exception to Article 2(4). One adherent of
that view, Louis Henkin, acknowledges a right of a state to protect its own
nationals as well as the nationals of another state (perhaps including the
nationals of the target state, although he is not clear on this point); both
constitute an exception to Article 2(4) and, as such, there is no need to
consider the juridical relationship of the rescuee to the rescuing state.
Rather, in construing the nature of this exception, Henkin sees a distinction between the permissible liberation of "hostages" and impermissible
intervention "by force to topple a Government or occupy its territory
even if that were truly necessary to terminate atrocities or to liberate
detainees." [11]

Yet if one is willing to accept within the scope of Article 2(4) or Article 51 an ability to protect one's own nationals and the nationals of
others abroad, it would appear that the lines being drawn are dictated
less by the language of the Charter than by the manner in which states
perceive their fundamental national interests. As such, the rules of the
UN Charter on the use of force appear more ambiguous than might
otherwise be thought. As states move down the road of an expanded interpretation of the Charter's key provisions restraining the use of force,
there may be no principled basis within the language of the Charter itself
for regarding unilateral humanitarian intervention as impermissible.

The question becomes, then, whether state practice since the inception of the Charter indicates that states accept a right of unilateral
humanitarian intervention. As discussed in chapter 4, unilateral hu-

10. *See, e.g.*, U.N. SCOR, 31th Sess., 1939th mtg., at 13, U.N. Doc. S/PV.1939 (1976) (self-
defense argument advanced by Israel to justify its rescue operation at Entebbe, Uganda,
involving non-Israeli nationals).

11. Henkin, *supra* note 9, at 153–54.

manitarian intervention did not achieve widespread acceptance as an exception to the prohibitions on the use of force contained in the UN Charter during the Cold War. In cases where the doctrine might have been applied, states did not advance it as a legal basis for their action. Some scholars argued that even if states did not advance unilateral humanitarian intervention as a basis for their actions, it was nevertheless the underlying reason for certain interventions and therefore should be considered lawful. Many other scholars, however, noted the lack of approval by the international community of interventions that could have been characterized as humanitarian; these scholars adhered to a view that unilateral humanitarian intervention could not be reconciled with the restraints embodied in the UN Charter.

The statements and conduct of relevant political actors in the interventions since the end of the Cold War are unlikely to resolve this debate. The interventions in Liberia, Iraq, Bosnia-Herzegovina, Somalia, Rwanda, and Haiti contain evidence that may be used by both proponents and opponents of a right of unilateral humanitarian intervention. Proponents of such a right will focus on the lack of explicit authorization in Resolution 688 for states to intervene in Iraq and on the explanations of France and Great Britain which gave a very strong sense that those two countries believed intervention was justified solely on humanitarian grounds even without UN approval. In particular, the intervention in southern Iraq occurred sixteen months after the "threat" was identified in Resolution 688, at a time when the flows of Iraqi refugees out of Iraq had long stopped. Consequently, it will be argued, the interventions in northern and southern Iraq cannot be regarded as based on Security Council authorization but, instead, on a unilateral right to intervene to hinder widespread human rights abuses. The intervention by ECOWAS in Liberia clearly was not authorized by the United Nations; yet, rather than condemn the intervention as contrary to the provisions of the Charter, the Security Council in essence condoned the intervention. Although the intervention occurred under the auspices of a subregional organization, a close review of the constituent documents of that organization indicates that the intervention was not within its competence. Even in Somalia, Rwanda, and Haiti, where the interventions were expressly authorized by the Security Council, proponents will argue that the authorizations were essentially a recognition by the international community that the maintenance of international peace and security justifies intervention by one state (perhaps accompanied by token contingents from other states) to curtail internal strife, starvation, or other human rights deprivations in another state; for, in each of these instances, the intervention was not conducted (at least at the outset) by UN forces operating under UN command but, rather, by the forces of individual states operating largely independently of the United Nations.

Opponents of a right of unilateral humanitarian intervention will dissect each incident and show why it cannot stand as a pure example of unilateral humanitarian intervention. For Liberia, the intervention was conducted not by states operating in their individual capacities but by a subregional organization, acting with the knowledge and eventually the support of the Security Council. ECOWAS may have acted inconsistently with the provisions of Chapter VIII and with its own constituent instruments, but it still was a collective action within the framework of a regional organization and cannot stand as a precedent for unilateral humanitarian intervention. For Iraq, explicit UN authorization may not have existed, but authorization implicitly existed either in Resolution 688 or in the overall intrusion of the United Nations in Iraqi internal affairs in a postwar environment. In Bosnia, all the actions were taken with the consent of the internationally recognized government of Bosnia in response to aggression by another state, and therefore cannot be considered intervention at all, let alone humanitarian intervention. For Somalia, Rwanda, and Haiti, explicit UN authorization existed; consequently, they, too, cannot stand as precedents for unilateral humanitarian intervention. Further, opponents of a right of unilateral humanitarian intervention will emphasize the difference between situations where there has been a complete breakdown in governmental authority (Somalia, Liberia, Rwanda) and other situations where this is not the case, noting that in the former there is no government capable of providing consent to an intervention. As such, interventions in those countries are not precedents for humanitarian intervention in situations where a government is in full control of its country and is conducting human rights atrocities.

Based on the post-Cold War practice to date, the opponents of a unilateral right of humanitarian intervention probably have the stronger hand. For the most part, the interventions in Liberia, Iraq, Bosnia-Herzgovina, Somalia, Rwanda, and Haiti are not persuasive in demonstrating a unilateral right of humanitarian intervention under international law. In each of these instances, the intervention related in some fashion to the authority of the Security Council or a regional organization, which best explains the overall acceptance by the international community of the interventions. Moreover, one of the most striking features of the case studies explored in chapter 5 was the pursuit by France of Security Council authorization prior to intervening in Rwanda and the pursuit by the United States of Security Council authorization prior to intervening in Haiti. Seeking Security Council authorization is politically a prudent course of action, particularly if a state wishes to extract itself from the target state and replace its forces with UN forces. Yet the concept of France seeking UN approval before intervening in francophone

Africa and of the United States seeking UN approval before intervening in its Caribbean sphere of influence is a remarkable development in world public order and cannot be easily discounted. It evidences a lack of confidence in the ability of a state to proceed on its own initiative in conducting such intervention and a belief that the expectations of the global community in a post-Cold War environment require benediction by the Security Council.

This expectation of Security Council involvement, however, is not applied to all potential forms of humanitarian intervention. Based on the incidents discussed in chapter 5, there appears to be at least one exception to the conclusion that unilateral humanitarian intervention remains outside the scope of permissible behavior under the UN Charter. Gleaned from the various post–Cold War case studies can be found an acceptance of the least intrusive form of unilateral humanitarian intervention: the airdropping of food and supplies by a state to provide urgent relief to the civilian population of the target state. There is evidence in both the interventions in northern Iraq and in Somalia that the world community does not regard such airdrops as unlawful unilateral intervention.[12] In the case of northern Iraq, France, the United Kingdom, and the United States all announced they would undertake such airdrops to provide relief to the Kurds *even before Resolution 688 was passed*. During the debate before the Security Council on Resolution 688,[13] none of the members of the Security Council, and not even Iraq, charged that such airdrops, even when conducted by military aircraft, were unlawful. Likewise, in August 1992, before Resolution 794[14] was passed, the United States and other countries announced airdrops of food and supplies in Somalia by military and civilian aircraft, and this, too, was not condemned as unlawful. Of course, in the case of Somalia, the lack of a central government and the existence of a UN airlift program undoubtedly mitigated the likelihood of such condemnation.

The permissibility of airdropping food and supplies leads to more difficult questions about how far a state can go in protecting aircraft engaged in the airdrops, such as prohibiting the movement of the target state's aircraft and attacking the target state's aircraft and missile batteries. To date, there is insufficient state practice to clarify whether

12. In addition to the Iraq and Somalia case studies provided in chapter 5, see P. Costa & P. Evans, *The Indian Supply Drop Into Sri Lanka: Non-Military Humanitarian Aid and the Troubling Idea of Intervention*, 3 CONN. J. INT'L L. 417 (1988) (recounting the 1987 incident in which five Indian jets escorted a number of cargo planes carrying food and medical supplies into Sri Lankan airspace so as to provide assistance to beleaguered Tamil Sri Lankan civilians under attack from Sri Lankan troops).

13. U.N. SCOR, 46th Sess., 2982d mtg., U.N. Doc. S/PV.2982 (1991).

14. S.C. Res., U.N. SCOR, 47th Sess., 3145th mtg. at 63, U.N. Doc. S/INF/48 (1993).

such steps are within the scope of a unilateral right to humanitarian intervention.

In sum, the rules embedded in the UN Charter do not allow for unilateral humanitarian intervention in general. The practice of states during the Cold War does not evidence a belief that such intervention is generally permissible under the Charter, but it does evidence a belief by states and scholars that the rules of the Charter are not to be strictly applied in certain situations where the fundamental interests of states are at stake, such as in the rescue of nationals. This may provide an opening for rules on the use of force to accommodate unilateral humanitarian intervention.

The post-Cold War interventions discussed in chapter 5 also do not yet demonstrate the acceptance of a general right of unilateral humanitarian intervention. Rather, they confirm the power of the Security Council to legitimate or itself to undertake humanitarian intervention under Chapter VII of the Charter and the ability of the Security Council to construe broadly its Chapter VII powers to address widespread deprivations of human rights. There are, however, some ambiguities. It might be argued that the international community will regard unilateral humanitarian intervention as lawful under the rules of the UN Charter if there is some link to legitimization by the Security Council or a regional organization, even if that link is tenuous (Liberia, Iraq). Furthermore, there may be some gaps in the overall disapproval of unilateral humanitarian intervention; the airdropping of foodstuffs may be just one form of humanitarian intervention deemed permissible by states as further incidents arise in the future.

B. Policy-Oriented Approach

As discussed in chapter 1, international law on the use of force consists of more than just an objective application of the "rules" codified in the UN Charter; it consists of processes for authoritative decisionmaking that exist within wider contexts of morality and politics. The specific rules that exist on the use of force are ambiguous and lacking in detailed development; one must look to broad principles and purposes to apply those rules in given situations. Yet these broad principles and purposes are themselves often opposing in character, not because the law is defective but because there are complex social realities underlying such principles and purposes.[15]

With respect to unilateral humanitarian intervention, general prin-

15. Schachter, *supra* note 1, at 21.

ciples favoring political independence and territorial integrity are in conflict with other principles favoring justice, human dignity, and self-determination. In any given instance of potential unilateral humanitarian intervention, national decisionmakers must decide whether international law allows for a choice about whether to proceed with an intervention and, if so, what facts and conditions are important to afford that choice. Whether the intervention is in fact permissible under international law will then turn on whether the intervention is found to be in conformity with international community values and expectations.

A decisionmaker faced with whether to engage in unilateral humanitarian intervention would first assess accumulated past decisions by states about the lawfulness of such intervention. The prior subsection suggests that those decisions, as embodied in the "rules" of international law, appear to disfavor unilateral humanitarian intervention but, in the end, are in fact somewhat ambiguous and may be evolving. Under a policy-oriented approach, a decisionmaker would then proceed to consider whether the context in which those past decisions were articulated has now changed and make a choice about intervention based on community interests and the promotion of common values. Two sets of community interests/common values are discussed below: those relating to the promotion of human dignity and justice and those relating to the promotion of systemic stability.

1. Favoring Intervention to Promote Human Dignity and Justice

In their classic 1961 treatise on the use of force,[16] Myres McDougal and Florentino Feliciano set forth as the basic principle of minimum world public order "that force and intense coercion are not to be used for the expansion of values."[17] At the same time, they recognized that, in a decentralized international legal order, the ambiguities present in characterizing an action as unlawful coercion or lawful self-defense required reliance on a governing norm of "reasonableness." The reasonableness of any particular instance of coercion would turn on its operational and functional significance for community goals;[18] thus, for example, in all instances of unilateral coercion, it would be unreasonable to use more force than was necessary to achieve one's goal. As a benchmark for assessing the reasonableness of coercive behavior, McDougal and many of his associates argue that the patterns of behavior in the international

16. M. MCDOUGAL & F. FELICIANO, LAW AND MINIMUM WORLD PUBLIC ORDER: THE LEGAL REGULATION OF INTERNATIONAL COERCION (1961).
17. *Id.* at 377.
18. *Id.* at 218.

community reveal an aspiration of the "overwhelming numbers of the peoples of the globe" for law that accords with the values of "human dignity."[19]

In their treatise, McDougal and Feliciano accept the classical view that the UN Charter prohibits forcible measures by states other than those taken in self-defense. They argue that the "overwhelming common interest in basic order" and the potential costs of using force in a nuclear era mitigated against allowing states to act against "lesser wrongs" even where no other remedies existed.[20] McDougal, however, later recanted this position and claimed the classical view to be too rigid.[21] In collaboration with one of his protégés, Michael Reisman, McDougal argued that unilateral humanitarian intervention is justifiable action to promote human dignity; in their view, rigid prohibitions in the UN Charter on self-help measures falling short of self-defense were not sustainable in light of the paralysis of the Security Council.[22] Instead, such restraints on the use of force must be interpreted so as to take into account the protection of human rights as one of the most fundamental, peremptory norms of the UN Charter. Reisman writes more recently:

Insofar as [humanitarian intervention] is precipitated by intense human rights deprivations and conforms to the general international legal regulations governing the use of force—economy, timeliness, commensurance, lawfulness of purpose, and so on—it represents a vindication of international law and is, in fact, substitute or functional enforcement.[23]

The protection of human rights and the maintenance of peace are to be accorded equal weight under the Charter; absent some alternative means for enforcing the protection of human rights, states may exercise a prerogative of self-help.

Several objections may be raised to this position. The primary objection is that under this approach the legality of an intervention seems to depend upon whether it implements notions of human dignity or justice as interpreted by Western moral and political traditions.

19. M. McDougal et al., Studies in World Public Order 39 (1960); *see generally* Toward World Order and Human Dignity (W. Reisman & B. Weston eds., 1976).

20. McDougal & Feliciano, *supra* note 16, at 207–08 n.193.

21. M. McDougal, *Authority to Use Force on the High Seas*, 20 Naval War College Rev. 19, 28–29 (1967) ("I'm ashamed to confess that at one time I lent my support to the suggestion that Article 2(4) and the related articles did preclude the use of self-help less than self-defense").

22. *See, e.g.*, M. McDougal & W. Reisman, *Rhodesia and the United Nations: The Lawfulness of International Concern*, 62 Am. J. Int'l L. 1 (1968).

23. W. Reisman, *Humanitarian Intervention to Protect the Ibos, in* Humanitarian Intervention and the United Nations 167, 177 (R. Lillich ed., 1973); *see also* W. Reisman, Nullity and Revision 848–49 (1971).

Suppose, for instance, that there is a military coup in state B whereby a constitutionally elected president is ousted by military authorities. The ousted president had sought to develop a liberal, democratic state in which a free-market economy operated, but his reforms had created an unstable economic situation (rampant inflation and a concentration of wealth in certain elites at the expense of others), soaring crime rates, and a breakdown in traditional fabric of the society, in the form of increased prostitution, divorce rates, and the disintegration of the family structure. The military coup leaders proceed to operate an authoritarian state where freedom of the press, assembly, and other civil and political rights are severely curtailed, but inflation stabilizes, gross national product increases, and the distribution of goods and services among the populace becomes more regularized. If international law is driven by notions of "human dignity" and "justice," it is not clear whether one should regard an intervention by state A to restore the deposed president as lawful. If Western political and moral traditions are applied to these notions, then it would appear that the intervention would be considered lawful, inasmuch as those traditions regard liberal democracy as the basis for promoting human dignity and justice. Yet if the political and moral traditions of other parts of the world are applied to these notions (for instance, traditions present in East Asia or in the Middle East), the legality of the intervention is less clear.[24] In *Law, Morality, and the Relations of States*,[25] Terry Nardin criticizes the idea that shared values and common purposes should serve to guide international law in areas where the law is uncertain, for the law is uncertain precisely because of a lack of such shared values and common purposes. Rather, where international society cannot agree on specific rules of conduct, a "purposive" approach should give way to an approach that supports rules of "accommodation" or "coexistence." For Nardin:

24. Consider the following comment on U.S. society by Lee Kuan Yew, who presided over Singapore's "soft" authoritarian government for three decades, during which Singapore experienced explosive economic growth:

> [A]s a total system, I find parts of [the American system] totally unacceptable: guns, drugs, violent crime, vagrancy, unbecoming behavior in public—in sum the breakdown of civil society. The expansion of the right of the individual to behave or misbehave as he pleases has come at the expense of orderly society. In the East the main object is to have a well-ordered society so that everybody can have maximum enjoyment of his freedoms. This freedom can only exist in an ordered state and not in a natural state of contention and anarchy.

F. Zakaria, *Culture is Destiny: A Conversation with Lee Kuan Yew*, 73:2 FOREIGN AFF. 109, 111 (1994).

25. T. NARDIN, LAW, MORALITY, AND THE RELATIONS OF STATES (1983).

Law understood as an instrument for the pursuit of shared purposes is clearly dependent upon the existence of such purposes. But law understood as a framework of restraint and coexistence among those pursuing divergent purposes presupposes diversity and the toleration of this diversity. Given the existence in our world of significant differences of belief, value, and interest, the expectation of global unity on the basis of shared purposes is sure to be disappointed. The basis of international association lies in deference to practices that embody recognition of the fact that we must coexist on this planet with others with whom we sometimes share little beyond a common predicament.[26]

On the other hand, if unilateral humanitarian intervention is restricted to situations where a state is engaged in the widespread deprivation of basic human rights—atrocities that "shock the conscience of humankind"—the argument is stronger that there exists global condemnation of such actions as contrary to community notions of "justice" and "human dignity." The development of human rights law since the inception of the Charter, as discussed in chapter 4, indicates that there are certain core human rights values (such as the prohibition on genocide) that states of all traditions agree upon. In this respect, international lawyers make reference to the jus cogens, by which is meant fundamental norms of law from which no state may derogate,[27] and make further reference to obligations that are erga omnes, by which is meant obligations of a state that are so offensive they are owed to all other states. Even so, the issue is not simply whether states agree that they share an adherence to these core human rights values but whether they share a belief in the enforcement of those values by means of unilateral humanitarian intervention; indeed, one of the least controversial examples of jus cogens is the prohibition on the use of force.[28] At this stage, the less powerful states of the world are deeply distrustful of the prospect of enforcing human rights by means of forcible intervention.

This tension is readily apparent in the outcome of the 1993 UN Conference on Human Rights mentioned at the beginning of chapter 1.[29] It also is apparent in the manner by which the General Assembly addressed the issue of humanitarian emergencies in the aftermath of the interven-

26. *Id.* at 323–24; *see also* R. FALK, LEGAL ORDER IN A VIOLENT WORLD 88 (1968):

[I]s it proper to base a social order of diverse normative systems upon the presumed superiority of one's own system? Is not such self-validating assurance itself a defection from one of the prime discoveries of those seeking to promote the values of human dignity in the West? We have come a long way from the lethal certitude that provided a moral underpinning for the Inquisition and the Crusades. Or have we?

27. I. BROWNLIE, PRINCIPLES OF PUBLIC INTERNATIONAL LAW 512–15 (4th ed. 1990).
28. *Id.* at 513.
29. *Supra* ch. 1 at 8–10.

tion in northern Iraq.[30] In that case, the General Assembly considered the issue of how to strengthen coordination of humanitarian emergency assistance within the United Nations, due to a perception that the United Nations had been ineffective in addressing crises in Iraq, Liberia, and the Horn of Africa. The debate focused on a variety of relief issues, and resulted in a resolution containing a lengthy annex.[31] Notably, the "Guiding Principles" in the Annex state, inter alia:

3. The sovereignty, territorial integrity and national unity of States must be fully respected in accordance with the Charter of the United Nations. In this context, humanitarian assistance *should be provided with the consent of the affected country* and in principle on the basis of an appeal by the affected country.

4. Each State has the responsibility first and foremost to take care of the victims of natural disasters and other emergencies occurring on its territory. Hence *the affected State has the primary role* in the initiation, organization, coordination, and implementation of humanitarian assistance within its territory.

5. The magnitude and duration of many emergencies may be beyond the response capacity of many affected countries. International cooperation to address emergency situations and to strengthen the response capacity of affected countries is thus of great importance. *Such cooperation should be provided in accordance with international law and national laws.* Intergovernmental and non-governmental organizations working impartially and with strictly humanitarian motives should continue to make a significant contribution in supplementing national efforts.

The resolution, an initiative of the developed states, succeeded in creating conditions for pressuring countries into accepting humanitarian assistance. Nevertheless, the developing states strenuously resisted any language that would imply a right to unilateral humanitarian intervention. The language of the resolution indicates that humanitarian assistance should be provided with the "consent" of the host country, that the host country has the "primary" role in coordinating such assistance, and that international cooperation should be in accordance with international and national laws.[32]

30. *Supra* ch. 5, sec. B.
31. G.A. Res. 46/182, U.N. GAOR, 46th Sess., U.N. Doc. A/RES/46/182 (1991).
32. The record of the debate reinforces this view. Speaking on behalf of the Group of 77, the representative from Ghana warned that "respect for sovereignty is not an idle stipulation which can be rejected outright in the name of even the most noble gestures." U.N. Doc. A/46/PV.41–42 (1991). *But see* D. Scheffer, *Toward a Modern Doctrine of Humanitarian Intervention*, 23 U. TOL. L. REV. 253, 281 (1992). Scheffer argues that the resolution leaves the door open to nonconsensual assistance because it says that consent "should" (as opposed to "must" or "shall") be provided. The language of the resolution, however, does not compel such an interpretation. The resolution states that *humanitarian assistance* (not consent) "should" be provided; the absence of "must" or "shall" is explainable on the basis that no delegation believed there was a duty to provide such assistance, even if the host state consented.

A second objection to the use of "human dignity" and "justice" for the application of international law to humanitarian intervention lies in the difficulty in applying the concept to actual incidents of intervention. One might concede that if a government is engaged in killing a large number of its people, and if an intervention could alter, with minimal loss of life, the government so that the killings would end, then the intervention advances values of human dignity and justice. It is submitted, however, that such situations rarely present themselves. In practice, various complicating factors arise: the human rights abuses may be a response to a uprising by internal forces that themselves may not be representative of a majority (or even minority) of the population; the crisis may be the product of external meddling, such as the encouragement of rebellion, the supply of arms, the imposition of sanctions, or an external unwillingness to accept refugees; and any intervention may have the effect of prolonging the conflict and even directly causing significant loss of life.

Take, for instance, the case studies explored in chapter 5. The intervention in northern Iraq was undertaken on behalf of a minority group, the Kurds, who were fleeing indiscriminate attacks by the Iraqi Government and were dying by the thousands in the mountainous region along the Turkish border. The Kurds, however, were trapped in the mountains due only indirectly to the Iraqi Government; the direct cause was the refusal of the Government of Turkey to allow the Kurds to cross the border. Advancing the values of human dignity and justice could have been achieved by forcing the Turks to allow the Kurds to enter Turkey rather than by intervening militarily in Iraq. Indeed, as has been seen in some instances, the "threat to peace" perceived from the internal human rights violations is associated with flows of refugees which neighboring states do not wish to accept. These restrictions may be rational, but it is unclear why any shared conception of public dignity or justice is not seen as requiring the amelioration of such restrictions. At the other extreme, would not advancing values of human dignity and justice favor more aggressive support of the Kurds in their struggle to be free of Iraqi control? If so, it would favor intervention to conduct a bloody war for the purpose of establishing an independent Kurdistan, which ultimately may or may not prove to be democratic.

In situations like Somalia, Liberia, and Rwanda, the human rights violations arose less from the actions of a central government than from a breakdown in civil order. To advance a value of human dignity, presumably any intervention should have occurred to reestablish order in the most effective, expeditious manner. Arguably, this could have taken the form of intervening on behalf of the most powerful faction within the society to assist it in ending the civil strife, while at the same time conditioning support for that faction on the just treatment of the other, less powerful factions. Thus, in Liberia, support could have been given by ECOWAS to Taylor's forces; in Somalia, support could have been given to one of the powerful warlords in Mogadishu, perhaps Mohammed Aideed; and in Rwanda, support could have been given by France to the RFP. Instead, these interventions did the exact opposite; they essentially supported weaker factions in the target state for the purpose of attempting to create pluralist societies. As an ultimate goal, the creation of a pluralist society may be seen as advancing values of human dignity and justice, but in Liberia and Somalia it may have prolonged the conflict and has yet to prove achievable. In Haiti, it requires rather strained logic to argue that values of human dignity and justice were advanced by the military enforcement of comprehensive economic sanctions on the poorest country in the Western Hemisphere. True advancement of those values might have called either for immediate military intervention after the coup occurred or no action by the international community.

It might be argued that the difficulty of applying these values is no different than the difficulty in applying other universal values, such as those embedded in the concept of self-defense. The point is, however, that while in theory intervention to prevent human rights atrocities would seem to advance values of human dignity and justice, in practice it is not at all clear that such intervention, and the manner and form in which it is conducted, does advance those values. And if this is true, promotion of those values as a guide for decisionmakers in determining the legality of any given intervention appears questionable.

2. Favoring Intervention to Promote Systemic Stability

As an alternative to the promotion of values of human dignity and justice, one might posit that, in a decentralized international legal order, the ambiguities present in characterizing an action as unlawful coercion or lawful self-defense require promotion of values associated with systemic stability.[33] That is, the reasonableness of any particular instance of

---

33. "Systems theorists" in the field of international relations have developed sophisticated typologies of "international systems" in order to explain the behavior of states. Thus, they study the interaction of states within a particular structure to ascertain established patterns of behavior. Norms develop within these systems when they promote the reciprocal interests of most states most of the time. Conversely, norms break down or lose their effectiveness when they no longer promote such interests. For a comprehensive effort to show how characteristics of different systems are reflected in international law, see generally M. KAPLAN & N. KATZENBACH, THE POLITICAL FOUNDATIONS OF INTERNATIONAL LAW (1961); for critiques, see R. FALK, THE STATUS OF LAW IN INTERNATIONAL SOCIETY 486–95 (1970); K. WALTZ, THEORY OF INTERNATIONAL POLITICS 38–59 (1979).

coercion would turn not on whether that action promotes ideological values favored by decisionmakers but, rather, on whether the action is consistent with common legal norms and procedures accepted by decisionmakers with different ideological orientations. With respect to the use of force, common legal norms and procedures acceptable to diverse states have at their core the desire to prevent coercive expansion by aggressive states and to avoid nuclear war and other warfare that would result in mass destruction of persons and property. Upon this core, states build other norms and procedures where it is mutually advantageous. These horizontal ordering techniques are necessary due to the decentralized nature of international society and are driven and adhered to by notions of reciprocity and self-interest.

One can argue that, after the Cold War, it should be possible to develop common norms and procedures to allow for unilateral humanitarian intervention. First, human rights deprivations of the type that occurred in Iran, Somalia, Liberia, and Rwanda have a destablilizing effect on neighboring countries. As discussed in more detail in chapter 6, the flows of refugees into neighboring states, as well as the awareness by those and other states that widespread harm is occurring to nationals with whom they may have an affinity, surely represent a threat to the peace and thus a threat to stable international relations. Further, regime elites engaged in the most flagrant of human rights violations may be regarded (due to their internal autonomy) as likely candidates for conducting external aggression. As such, it may be possible for states to adopt a common norm that permits intervention to prevent the most flagrant of human rights violations and to provide security for insular social groups in situations where not to act will lead to regional instability. This norm would recognize that there is a diversity of views among the states of the world, but that in an interdependent world it is not possible to tolerate all forms of intolerance that may exist within any given state. In other words, to use Nardin's terminology, the norm would seek to provide for coexistence among states in a world where the conduct of widespread atrocities by one state simply cannot be ignored by other states. The norm would illuminate a threshold of permissible intervention; actions taken beyond this threshold would be ones that threaten a widening of the conflict and, thus, a fostering of greater instability.

Second, even states skeptical about unilateral humanitarian intervention may perceive widespread human rights deprivations as a threat to international stability because they threaten the current mode by which the international system is organized. That is, a system built upon state sovereignty that fails to address flagrant abuses of human rights may tend toward a revolutionary transformation of that system; states such as

China, which commit their own human rights violations, nevertheless may realize that denying other states any international legal basis for conducting humanitarian intervention in egregious cases (e.g., France in Rwanda), even in limited circumstances, risks forcing those other states to develop an even less reliable system of international order.

The problem with this approach is that there is little evidence that states regard widespread human rights deprivations as such a significant threat to international stability that it justifies a norm favoring *unilateral* humanitarian intervention. In certain situations, a particular state may find it important to intervene—such as the United States in Somalia or France in Rwanda—but recent incidents suggest that such states regard UN authorization as an important means for legitimizing the intervention. It simply cannot be said that the international community as a whole regards unilateral intervention as a necessary step in maintaining systemic stability. In fact, as discussed in the prior section, there is a significant sense among the less powerful nations and even certain powerful nations, such as China, that intervention for the purpose of advancing human rights values itself threatens systemic stability. Stability is threatened due to the impossibility of developing norms and standards to guide such intervention, because any such norms and standards are open to abuse by states acting for other than altruistic reasons, and because even in cases of true humanitarian intervention the end results are often equivocal at best.

C. Philosophy-Oriented Approach

The policy-oriented approach to international law championed by Myres McDougal and his associates maintains a central focus on the attitudes of national policymakers in states. A decision to use force against another state, if taken in conformity with community expectations about proper decisionmaking (as opposed to decisions based on naked power) is an "authoritative" decision. However, one may share the overall assessment that a rules-oriented, "value-free" approach is an inaccurate, or at least incomplete, approach to international law without accepting that those values are to be found in the attitudes and assessments of national policymakers. One could postulate, instead, that the values used to ascertain and apply international law are to be derived from a comprehensive theory of moral philosophy, such as one that accords supremacy to the protection and enforcement of the natural rights of persons. Whether national policymakers agree with the dictates of this moral philosophy is not relevant, since the "community goals and expectations" central to the policy-oriented approach may be morally wrong.

In his 1988 treatise on humanitarian intervention,[34] Fernando Tesón takes such an approach, arguing that the ambiguities present in the international rules on the use of force should be resolved through reliance on a substantive moral philosophy of international relations that commits itself to normative individualism. Under this theory, the primary normative unit is no longer the state, but the individual, since the end for which states should strive (and hence for which international law should strive) is the well-being and protection of individuals, not of the state itself. Seen in this light, the principle of state sovereignty derives from a need to protect the individuals of a state from aggression by other states. Yet when the government of a state commits human rights abuses against its own people, the basis upon which the principle of state sovereignty is built crumbles and other states are permitted to intervene to protect those people. Consequently, Tesón argues, international law permits "the proportionate transboundary help, including forcible help, provided by governments to individuals in another state who are being denied basic human rights and who themselves would be rationally willing to revolt against their oppressive government."[35]

Tesón's position has roots in both the natural law tradition discussed in chapter 2, which drew upon notions of morality in developing international law, and upon more modern theorists and moral philosophers.[36] He believes that moral philosophy is inextricably related to the articulation of legal propositions,[37] that one can identify moral principles to which all rational agents would give allegiance,[38] and that if a moral theory based on these principles is correct then it is universally correct, not just within particular constitutional societies (e.g., Western democracies) but other societies as well.[39] The thesis is an extremely interesting one and a very useful contribution to the debate on the legality of unilateral humanitarian intervention.

Ultimately, however, it fails to bridge gaps in the analysis. First, Tesón is forced to concede at the outset that regarding human rights as univer-

34. F. Tesón, Humanitarian Intervention: An Inquiry into Law and Morality (1988).

35. *Id.* at 5.

36. Although he often draws different conclusions, Tesón is particularly influenced by the link between morality and international relations explored by theorists Michael Walzer and Charles Beitz and the emphasis on the rights of individuals explored by philosophers John Rawls and Ronald Dworkin. *See* M. Walzer, Just and Unjust Wars: A Moral Argument with Historical Illustrations (2d ed. 1992); C. Beitz, Political Theory and International Relations (1979); J. Rawls, A Theory of Justice (1971); R. Dworkin, Taking Rights Seriously (1977).

37. Tesón, *supra* note 34, at 6.

38. *Id.* at 9.

39. *Id.* at 10.

sal and as having moral supremacy over state sovereignty "ultimately rests on a deep conviction" which is both an "act of faith" and a "tribute to reason."[40] Second, although Tesón struggles admirably to prove otherwise, moral philosophy simply does not compel the conclusion that an injustice imposed on one party grants a second party the right to remedy that injustice. Moral philosophy in the Lockean/contractarian natural rights tradition only goes so far as to justify the revolt of the people against their own regime; it does not support intervention by foreign states.[41] Indeed, theorists such as John Rawls and Michael Walzer draw the exact opposite conclusion from that of Tesón; moral philosophy argues strongly in favor of a principle of nonintervention so as to allow a people to settle their own affairs without the interference of foreign powers.[42]

Tesón seeks to circumvent this difficulty by presuming an invitation and consent to foreign intervention by a rational local population. Thus, humanitarian intervention is conceived of as support for an oppressed peoples seeking to exercise their right of self-determination, to revolt against their renegade government in order to force it to comply with its contractual obligations to its people. In an ideal scenario of a minority government regime inflicting human rights abuses on the majority of the people of a state, Tesón's inherent presumption is coherent. Yet, in practice, this presumption appears questionable (or at least of limited utility), even in situations where there exists a genocidal regime. Consider, for example, the massacres promoted by the rump Hutu government against the minority Tutsis in Rwanda. Arguably, the vast majority of Rwandans supported the slaughter, or at least were indifferent to it; while some Hutus sought to protect the Tutsis, many more were them-

---

40. *Id.* at xv.

41. *See* J. Donnelly, *Human Rights, Humanitarian Intervention and American Foreign Policy: Law, Morality and Politics,* 37 J. INT'L AFF. 311, 319 (1984):

> Violation of A's right by B in no way entails a right of C to enforce A's right; simply because a wrong is committed, we cannot assume that anyone has a right to rectify it— let alone a third party. If a people has a right to be ruled by a government that respects basic human rights, a nation under the domination of a genocidal tyrant has a right to revolt; this view, which lies at the heart of the Lockean/contractarian natural rights tradition, is widely accepted. Foreign actors, however, would seem to lack similar authority to overthrow a tyrant.

42. RAWLS, *supra* note 36, at 378; WALZER, *supra* note 36, *passim.* Note, however, that Walzer maintains an intermediate position; he views moral philosophy as sustaining a general principle of nonintervention to protect human rights, except in situations of "massive violations of human rights." *Id.* at 101. Thus, Tesón and Walzer are in agreement in extreme situations of human rights violations but differ at lower levels of human rights violations.

selves caught up in the fervor of the slaughter. If one were to have taken a countrywide vote in Rwanda in early 1994 as to whether it was desirable to revolt against the rump Hutu government, and a further vote as to whether foreign intervention was desired to prevent the slaughter of Tutsis, the likely outcome of both would have been a decisive "no." A similar result might have occurred with respect to the interventions on behalf of the Kurds in Iraq; most Iraqis have no affinity for the Kurds and in all likelihood do not favor intervention by Western powers. Similarly, in situations of civil war where a number of factions are vying for control of a country, such as occurred in Somalia or Liberia, it might be said that a majority of the population were rebelling against their de jure government, but the human rights concerns at issue may well relate to the rebelling factions themselves. Further, support by the local population for foreign intervention in that situation often will be as fragmented as the factions themselves. Perhaps Tesón would apply his analysis to a minority group within a state; if that minority group rationally would be willing to revolt, then humanitarian intervention is morally and legally justifiable on behalf of that minority. Yet, in most instances, it would be demonstrably *irrational* for a small minority of a population to seek to revolt against a majority-supported oppressive government; the rational choice would be to leave the country, precisely the step that other states are unwilling to support through liberal refugee policies.

Finally, even if one accepts Tesón's moral philosophy, the nexus between that philosophy and international law is murky. International legal order is not built upon the moral philosophy espoused by Tesón; notwithstanding the tremendous advances in human rights law during this century, states and the general principle of state sovereignty remain at the core of international law. Persons remain, for the most part, at the periphery of international law as conceived of and practiced by the world community. None of the interventions assessed by Tesón—Tanzania in Uganda, France in the Central African Republic, India in Bangladesh, and the United States in Grenada—evidence a belief by states or peoples within states that the international legal order is or should be organized otherwise. By moving from positivism and from the expectations of the international community, Tesón leads one into a utopian world order that compares poorly with how states behave in fact. Even if taken as a call for a new international order based upon Tesón's substantive moral philosophy, left unanswered are a range of questions about how an order that gave primacy to the individual would fare overall. Contemporary trends toward the fragmentation of states and the atomization of societies raise serious questions about whether such a world order itself, premised on individual rights of self-determination, would lead to widespread regional and ethnic conflicts, and perhaps even to anarchy.

D. The Security Council as Authoritative Decisionmaker

States (and many scholars) resist recognizing a right of unilateral humanitarian intervention due to a fear of abuse by unscrupulous states. Whether such fears are well-founded is not clear. Certainly history is adorned with incidents of state intervention for the wrong reasons; recognizing in principle another "right reason" (to stand beside self-defense and collective security measures) might help erode restraints on the use of force generally. On the other hand, even if a right of unilateral humanitarian intervention were recognized, states presumably would still fear its abuse and therefore might be reluctant to use it as an excuse for intervention unless the circumstances were quite clear. Indeed, fear of abuse does not reside solely in smaller states that are the likely targets of intervention; larger states, such as the United States, are undoubtedly also concerned about opening a floodgate of interventions that could create worldwide conditions of instability. Furthermore, assessing and determining the legality of unilateral humanitarian intervention in principle is no more difficult than assessing and determining the legality of self-defense. Both are certainly subject to abuse, but the question is whether the marginal value of permitting each exceeds the costs of not having it. Certainly the value of allowing states to determine the circumstances in which they may exercise their inherent right of self-defense is considered to outweigh the costs of its abuse. The question is whether the same can be said of humanitarian intervention. If it is true that a far greater number of lives is lost through widespread deprivation of human rights than through armed conflict involving typical aggression/defense, then the value of permitting humanitarian intervention notwithstanding the possibility of abuse would appear high.

During the Cold War, concerns with the possible abuse of a right of unilateral humanitarian intervention existed because states were left to self-judge their actions. There was no entity to which states could turn for authoritative guidance on whether a particular situation merited humanitarian intervention and, if so, how it should be conducted. Indeed, the paralysis of the Security Council was a central element of the arguments deployed during the Cold War by policy-oriented theorists for why unilateral humanitarian intervention is a permissible use of force under the UN Charter. The view was that the prohibitions contained in the UN Charter on the use of force were conditioned on the operation of a Security Council itself capable of addressing threats to international peace and security. Without that mechanism for enforcement of the rights of states, it was necessary for states to engage in self-help against the lawless behavior of other states. Thus Myres McDougal's *volte-face* was directly related to a concern that the collective enforcement machinery of the

United Nations had proven defective.[43] The same is true also of Reisman.[44] Their views echo those of other, less process-oriented theorists. Richard Lillich, one of the earliest and most eloquent advocates of a right to unilateral humanitarian intervention, posited that the failure to develop effective international machinery to facilitate humanitarian interventions arguably permits a state to intervene unilaterally in appropriate situations.[45] Similarly, Judge Philip Jessup asserted in the context of protection of nationals that unilateral action might be permissible if the United Nations failed to act quickly enough.[46]

Whether the failure of the Security Council to act in a manner intended by the drafters of the UN Charter vitiates the use of force norms embedded in the Charter is far from accepted and, indeed, is rejected by a number of scholars.[47] In the wake of the Cold War, however, it is apparent that, for the time being, the previous dissension among the permanent members no longer exists. From 1990 to 1995, the Security Council passed approximately 350 resolutions, more than half the number of resolutions passed from 1945 to 1990. Many of those resolutions are actively directed at the management of international peace and security, including the deployment of fact-finding missions, deployment of numerous peacekeeping operations, the condemnation of aggression, the imposition of economic sanctions, the military enforcement of economic sanctions, "no-fly zones" and (in the case of Iraq) expulsion of an aggressor, and the creative use of commissions and tribunals to determine international boundaries, war crimes, and war reparations.[48] Chapter 5 alone recounts the various incidents in which the Security Council has been an active participant in efforts to address humanitarian crises.

Thus, whereas during the Cold War the Security Council was unable to act due to ideological differences among the permanent members, that simply is no longer is the case. Rather than acting unilaterally, states

43. McDougal, *supra* note 21, at 28–29 ("In the absence of collective machinery against attack and deprivation, I would suggest that the principle of major purposes requires an interpretation which would honor self-help against prior unlawfulness.").

44. REISMAN, *supra* note 23, at 848–49; W. Reisman, *Coercion and Self-Determination: Construing Charter Article 2(4)*, 78 AM. J. INT'L L. 642 (1984).

45. R. Lillich, *Humanitarian Intervention: A Reply to Ian Brownlie and a Plea for Constructive Alternatives, in* LAW AND CIVIL WAR IN THE MODERN WORLD 229, 247 (J. Moore ed., 1974).

46. JESSUP, *supra* note 7, at 170–71. Not all scholars predicated their views on the absence of effective security machinery. *See, e.g.*, J. STONE, AGGRESSION AND WORLD ORDER: A CRITIQUE OF UNITED NATIONS THEORIES OF AGGRESSION 43 (1958); TESÓN, *supra* note 34, at 140–41.

47. *See, e.g.*, Henkin, *supra* note 9, at 146; O. Schachter, *The Right of States to Use Armed Force*, 82 MICH. L. REV. 1620 (1984).

48. *See* S. Murphy, *The Security Council, Legitimacy, and the Concept of Collective Security After the Cold War*, 32 COLUM. J. TRANSNAT'L L. 201 (1994).

now have an option of petitioning the Security Council for action. Consequently, arguments that favor unilateral humanitarian intervention, on the grounds that the Security Council does not work, themselves no longer work. If once "caducuous,"[49] the original construction of the Charter now regenerates.

Of course, there is no guarantee that the Security Council will act upon a petition by a state seeking UN humanitarian intervention. If the requesting state wishes the intervention to occur through use of military forces under the command and control of the United Nations, the lack of forces at the disposal of the United Nations (discussed in chapter 6) will make approval of such request unlikely. It must be assumed, however, that the requesting state itself has the capability of conducting the intervention, otherwise the issue of unilateral humanitarian intervention does not arise. Even if the Security Council is not in a position to deploy forces under the command and control of the United Nations, it is in a position to authorize the requesting state to conduct the intervention with whatever restrictions it deems appropriate, including monitoring the intervention through the offices of the Secretary-General and transfering the operation to the United Nations after a period of time. Based on recent incidents, authorization of states to conduct such intervention appears the likely mode of UN humanitarian intervention. There are, of course, numerous concerns with whether the Security Council, as currently structured, is a satisfactory forum for authoritative decisionmaking in this area (as discussed in chapter 6). Nevertheless, it is submitted that, notwithstanding those defects, it remains a better entity for decision-making than states acting unilaterally.

There still may be times, of course, when the Security Council is unwilling to authorize such intervention. This unwillingness may be based upon any number of factors, including: the human rights deprivations are not of a sufficient magnitude to justify intervention; intervention by the petitioning state would exacerbate rather than ameliorate the crisis; and other, less intrusive means of resolving the crisis have not yet been pursued. The refusal to authorize humanitarian intervention in such circumstances cannot be regarded as a basis for resorting to unilateral humanitarian intervention on a theory that the Security Council mechanism is "defective," even if some members of the Security Council favor the intervention while others do not. Rather, by not acting, the Security Council is acting as an authoritative decisionmaker; the decentralized system of international law for once is centralized in an organ capable of weighing the factors for and against intervention and providing a decision that other states are compelled to accept. Since true cases of hu-

49. REISMAN, *supra* note 23, at 849.

manitarian intervention do not involve the national security interests of states wishing to intervene, arguments in favor of unilateral action as a matter of state prerogative appear weak.

E. Toward Criteria for the Conduct of Unilateral Humanitarian Intervention

It is certainly possible that, at some future time, the ideological differences that stymied Security Council action during the Cold War could return. If so, the arguments in favor of allowing unilateral humanitarian intervention will be stronger. Moreover, the composition of the Security Council, which places great weight upon the views of certain major powers at the expense of other powers while at the same time providing limited representation for the international community as a whole, may lead some states to reject the view that Security Council authorization is necessary before conducting an intervention. Finally, as was seen in the case of Liberia, failure of the Security Council to act may arise more from preoccupation with other matters than from a determination that the action is not warranted. For these reasons, it is well to consider whether there are conditions or criteria that might be developed by the international community to serve as a guide in assessing such intervention.

A critical concern for opponents of a unilateral right to humanitarian intervention is that the existence of such a right could be subject to abuse. States might begin forcibly intervening in the domestic affairs of another state claiming the target state is engaging in deprivations of human rights when in fact the intervening states are simply seeking to advance their own interests by altering the political or economic structure of the target state. One way of addressing this concern is to seek acceptable and authoritative methods of allowing unilateral humanitarian intervention to proceed. As noted above, allowing states themselves to determine whether situations calling for humanitarian intervention exist could be predicated on their first requesting action by the Security Council. If the Security Council failed to act, either due to the exercise of the "veto power" or otherwise, states might then be expected to pursue alternative methods for authoritative decisionmaking. Depending on the circumstances, an authoritative decision regarding *the existence of conditions* calling for humanitarian intervention might reside in the General Assembly[50] or in a regional organization, although neither entity may be

50. If the General Assembly is to become significantly active in this area, it would be useful to identify which of its committees should take the lead. The Third Committee of the General Assembly is responsible primarily for cultural, humanitarian, and social affairs and regularly considers issues related to human rights. The Second Committee, however,

capable of authorizing enforcement action.[51] The diminished role of regional organizations in crisis situations (discussed in chapter 7) is a particularly unfortunate contemporary reality, since such organizations are best placed to identify human rights abuses at an early stage and have the most at stake in regional stability. On the other hand, the tendency of states to seek support from regional organizations, as in the cases of Liberia and Haiti, reinforces the sense that regional organizations can serve as authoritative decisionmakers. Finally, some other form of international organization might serve as a basis for authoritative, collective decisionmaking (e.g., NATO), on the theory that collective action is less susceptible to abuse.[52]

Absent a United Nations or regional organization determination of a threat to the peace from the widespread deprivation of human rights, a state may be inclined to intervene on its own authority. Various scholars have developed criteria for assessing the legality of unilateral humanitarian intervention. Richard Lillich has set forth the following criteria[53]:

1. *Immediacy of violation of human rights* (intervention is permissible "only on those rare occasions when the danger to the individuals concerned is imminent" and the target state is unable or unwilling to protect them);

2. *Extent of violation of human rights* (intervention is permissible "only when a substantial deprivation of human rights values has occurred or is threatened");

3. *Invitation to use forcible self-help* (intervention is permissible if the de jure government requests it);

4. *Degree of coercive measures employed* (the amount of force used and its duration is relevant to its legality);

5. *Relative disinterestedness of acting state* (the presence of other motives does not invalidate the intervention "if the overriding motive is the protection of human rights").

John Norton Moore[54] offers supplements and variants to these criteria, which presumably could be adopted in the form of a resolution by the

---

is active on issues related to increased assistance to countries experiencing difficult economic circumstances. The Sixth Committee is responsible for legal matters.

51. U.N. CHARTER arts. 11, para. 2, 53, para. 1.

52. *See* J. Chopra & T. Weiss, *Sovereignty Is No Longer Sacrosanct: Codifying Humanitarian Intervention*, 6 ETHICS & INT'L AFF. 114 (1992).

53. R. Lillich, *Forcible Self-Help by States to Protect Human Rights*, 53 IOWA L. REV. 325, 347–51 (1967).

54. Moore offers the following criteria for determining the legitimacy of interventions which go beyond pre-insurgency assistance:

Security Council or the General Assembly, although there appears little support for such action at this time.[55]

The efficacy of developing criteria must be questioned. First, as a general matter, and for the same reason that governments might decide to proceed unilaterally in the conduct of humanitarian intervention, states are likely to resist the development of, and adherence to, criteria that purport to control such intervention. Second, developing criteria might serve less to restrain unilateral humanitarian intervention and more to provide a pretext for abusive intervention. That is, by establishing a list of factors that if checked off justify an intervention, states otherwise inclined not to intervene because it is generally disfavored may seek to exploit vague criteria as a cover for intervention. Indeed, for this reason, some scholars would prefer to regard unilateral intervention as a violation of international law, which the international community can choose to ignore in situations where the intervention is truly humanitarian and

1. an immediate and extensive threat to fundamental human rights, particularly a threat of widespread loss of human life;
2. a proportional use of force which does not threaten greater destruction of values than the human rights at stake;
3. a minimal effect on authority structures;
4. a prompt disengagement, consistent with the purpose of the action;
5. immediate full reporting to the Security Council and appropriate regional organizations.

J. MOORE, LAW AND THE INDO-CHINA WAR 186 (1972).

55. For other efforts to develop criteria, see T. Behuniak, *The Law of Unilateral Humanitarian Intervention by Armed Force: A Legal Survey*, 79 MIL. L. REV. 157, 186–90 (1978); W. Verwey, *Humanitarian Intervention Under International Law*, 32 NETH. INT'L L. REV. 357, 413–18 (1985); M. Bazyler, *Reexamining the Doctrine of Humanitarian Intervention in Light of the Atrocities in Kampuchea and Ethiopia*, 23 STAN J. INT'L L. 547, 597–607 (1987); V. Nanda, *Tragedies in Northern Iraq, Liberia, Yugoslavia, and Haiti—Revisiting the Validity of Humanitarian Intervention Under International Law—Part I*, 20 DENV. J. INT'L L. & POL'Y 305, 330 (1992) (citing A. MACINTYRE, AFTER VIRTUE 62–66 (2d ed. 1984)); D. Scheffer, *supra* note 32, at 290–91. Scheffer's criteria are

1. The Security Council is deadlocked indefinitely on the issue and has not explicitly prohibited intervention to meet the humanitarian crisis. . . .
2. Alternative peaceful remedies, including economic sanctions, have been exhausted within the period of time during which the humanitarian crisis has not reached crisis dimensions.
3. The severity of human rights violations is apparent.
4. Every effort is made to diversify the intervening forces among many nations. . . .
5. The humanitarian purpose and objective of the intervention is paramount.
6. The intervention will have a convincingly positive effect on human rights in the target country. In other words, more good than harm will come of the intervention.
7. The long-term political independence and territorial integrity of the target state will not be imperiled by the intervention.

morally justifiable.[56] Finally, the criteria that have been suggested by various scholars, when measured against recent incidents of intervention, can be seen as lacking.

For instance, most criteria that have been proposed include in some fashion a requirement that the intervening state be "disinterested," by which is meant that the intervening state obtain no benefit or gain. This requirement traces its pedigree to the doctrine of humanitarian intervention under customary international law and, as discussed in chapter 2, appears in the writings of various scholars at the beginning of this century, such as Antoine Rougier. Yet, as seems apparent from recent incidents of intervention, if the rudimentary objective in allowing the action is to promote human rights values, requiring that a state seeking to intervene be "disinterested" may not be desirable. The interventions in Somalia, Liberia, Rwanda, and Haiti can be characterized as "far too little, far too late"; significant intervention in Bosnia has never occurred at all. If such interventions are to occur in a timely, effective fashion, it may be that the intervening state needs more than just altruistic reasons for its action.

Similarly, some lists of criteria promote the exhaustion of alternative means of coercion prior to intervention, such as the imposition of economic sanctions. Yet, the imposition of economic sanctions on Bosnia and Haiti suggest that such measures can be blunt instruments that harm the very people they seek to protect with little effect in inducing the local authorities and factions to curtail human rights abuses. Criteria that favor minimization of coercive force and no alteration in the political structures of the target state are also difficult to sustain. Respectable arguments may be made that the only means for effectively ending widespread human rights deprivations is to engage in a massive invasion that ousts the local government and installs a new government more sensitive to human rights concerns. The intervention in southern Iraq is a good example of how minimalist coercive techniques bring marginal benefits in the short run but prove largely deficient in the long run.

Most lists of criteria favor no long-term effect on the political independence of the target state, which includes the prompt withdrawal of the intervening forces. This notion appears to coincide with the desires of

---

56. *See* P. Malanczuk, Humanitarian Intervention and the Legitimacy of the Use of Force 30–31 (1993); *see also* Schachter, *supra* note 1, at 126 ("I believe it is highly undesirable to have a new rule allowing humanitarian intervention [without U.N. approval], for that could provide a pretext for abusive intervention. It would be better to acquiesce in a violation that is considered necessary and desirable in the particular circumstances than to adopt a principle that would open a wide gap in the barrier against unilateral use of force").

the intervening states in recent incidents; consider, for example, the withdrawal of U.S. forces from Somalia after six months and the withdrawal of French forces from Rwanda after two months. Yet, in both those instances, it generally was recognized by the international community that such withdrawals were not in the best interests of maintaining stability and creating the conditions for national reconciliation within the target state. Recent incidents suggest that the intervening state often will be under domestic pressure to withdraw quickly and that it will do so by foisting the responsibility it has undertaken onto a less-than-capable United Nations. Consequently, at least in some instances, the concern for ensuring a prompt withdrawal of the intervening forces, so as to maintain the long-term political independence of the target state, may be overstated.

Finally, most lists attempt to characterize the degree of human rights abuse that can justify unilateral humanitarian intervention. This study has used the phrase "widespread deprivations of internationally recognized human rights" as a part of its working definition for humanitarian intervention. Similar phrases, such as "immediate and extensive threat to fundamental human rights" or "widespread atrocities" may be used as conditions for assessing the legality of the intervention. Yet, as chapter 5 indicates, the type and level of human rights for which the international community is willing to act can vary considerably. Restricting unilateral humanitarian intervention to "widespread atrocities" would appear to preclude intervention of the type authorized by the Security Council in Haiti. Such a restriction may be a good thing if one believes there should be a narrower category of human rights violations for which unilateral humanitarian intervention is permissible than there is for UN-authorized humanitarian intervention. It is doubtful, however, whether it is possible to sustain such a distinction; indeed, chapter 6 cautions that the expansive treatment by the Security Council as to what constitutes a "threat to peace" may have spillover effects upon states in respect of how they view the application of use of force norms to them.

This study regards such lists of criteria as useful exercises in attempting to clarify factors that must be weighed by the international community when assessing humanitarian intervention, whether they occur on a unilateral basis or otherwise. On balance, however, it seems unlikely that the international community can or should at this time agree upon such criteria; there is too much resistance to the legality of unilateral humanitarian intervention and too much variance in the conditions under which such interventions occur. At best, it might be said that certain general principles should guide states when conducting and assessing such intervention, such as those set forth in chapter 6 with respect to UN humanitarian intervention [57] or, more generally, the "principles of humanity, neutrality, and impartiality" identified by the General Assembly in considering the provision of humanitarian assistance by states.[58] Such principles may be vague, but they seem to be present in the conduct of the UN-authorized interventions discussed in chapter 5 and are probably the most that can be said about how unilateral humanitarian interventions should be conducted pending future developments.

In conclusion, unilateral humanitarian intervention finds little support in the rules of the UN Charter and in state practice in the post-Charter era, including those incidents discussed in chapter 5. Over time, as states have interpreted those rules, an exception has developed for forcible action in the protection by a state of its own nationals. Trends of this type may provide an opening for a general acceptance by the international community of unilateral humanitarian intervention in the future. Under a process-oriented approach to international law, values of human dignity and justice suggest that such a development may be warranted, but countervailing arguments may be made that there is an inherent indeterminacy and difficulty in applying such values to justify intervention. Similarly, values of systemic stability might support unilateral humanitarian intervention if the destruction of human rights values is seen as a threat to an orderly international society, but here, too, a comparable (and perhaps even greater) threat to order by allowing unilateral humanitarian intervention casts doubt on such a position. In a post-Cold War environment, process-oriented theorists who justified unilateral humanitarian intervention largely on the basis of a defective Security Council apparatus, have lost that core element of their argument. The reemergence of the Security Council as an authoritative decisionmaker creates a significant hurdle for those who would continue to advance arguments in favor of the legality of unilateral humanitarian intervention. While such interventions may nevertheless occur, the crafting of definitive criteria for use in assessing and conducting such interventions appears, at worst, unsuited to the variety of situations in which such interventions occur, and, at best, premature.

57. *See supra* ch. 5, sec. H, at 322–23.
58. G.A. Res. 46/182, U.N. GAOR, 46th Sess., Supp. No. 49, at 49, Annex, para. 2, U.N. Doc. A/46/49 (1992).

Conclusion

Over the centuries, civilizations (and then states) developed an appreciation for the destructive nature of war. For this reason, moral and legal constraints emerged regarding the resort to military force and the conduct of hostilities once begun. At the same time, national decisionmakers, nobles, philosophers, theologians, and jurists retained a belief in the use of military force for noble causes; the value of maintaining international peace and order did not displace values of justice emanating from God or from right reason. The questionable character of these noble causes (e.g., the Crusades) was troublesome and prompted continuing efforts to clarify the source and content of the "just war."

The rise of legal positivism in the nineteenth century marked a turning from universal norms of justice as a guide to state behavior. Instead, international law looked to state practice as the font of international legal norms. At first, this practice favored norms that only loosely sought to control resort to war by force; interventions were tolerated for various reasons, including collective actions by states acting in concert. By the twentieth century, when modern warfare proved the costs of such permissive norms to be unacceptably high, a new norm emerged calling for the absolute maintenance of international peace and order. This development crystallized first in the 1928 Kellogg-Briand Pact[1] and became ascendant in the proposals of the Four Powers that emerged from Dumbarton Oaks.[2] Although concepts of justice and human rights were inserted in the UN Charter at San Francisco, the core features formulated by the major powers on the use of force remained unchanged by the Charter: all uses of force against the territorial integrity or political in-

1. General Treaty for the Renunciation of War as an Instrument of National Policy, Aug. 27, 1928, 94 LNTS 57, *reprinted in* 2 INTERNATIONAL LAW AND WORLD ORDER: BASIC DOCUMENTS II.A.1 (B. Weston, ed. 1994).

2. Proposals for the Establishment of a General International Organization, Oct. 7, 1944, 11 DEP'T ST. BULL. 368 (1944).

dependence of a state were forbidden, absent self-defense or collective responses by the United Nations to address threats to, or breaches of, the peace and acts of aggression.

This development, also embodied in various regional collective security agreements, is so far the high-water mark of international legal efforts to create world order through international agreement—an effort to foreclose, once and for all, armed aggression by states against other states. While aggression has by no means been eliminated from states' behavior, the international community's expectations expressed in the UN Charter have had an enduring effect. The resort to international war today is no longer acceptable to the international community; the international community usually imposes intense political, economic, and military costs on those states that resort to international war. Yet, in two respects, the UN Charter's approach to the use of force proved unsatisfactory.

First, in restricting the ability of states to resort to force, considerable reliance was placed in the UN Charter on the role of the UN Security Council to maintain international peace and security. During the Cold War, as discussed in chapter 4, this reliance on an effective collective security mechanism proved a dismal failure. While it was recognized that the Security Council would not be able to address *all* threats to peace and security, particularly those in which the national security interests of the Permanent Members were at stake, it was not envisioned that political polarization would paralyze the Security Council from taking *any* actions to maintain international peace and security.

Second, while the maintenance of international peace and security represents a dominant (perhaps the predominant) interest of the community of states, time has shown that it is not the sole interest of the international community writ large (states, organizations, individuals). From the emergence at Nuremberg of "crimes against humanity," to the imposition of sanctions against South African apartheid, to the overall and increasing intrusiveness of human rights laws and instruments into affairs previously considered within the "domestic jurisdiction" of states, there can be little question that the value of justice in the way states behave toward their own citizens is an accepted and dynamic element of inter-state behavior under the UN Charter. Newspapers and television images beamed worldwide capture the injustice of brutal civil wars in which modern technology, mines, and weapons are turned on innocent civilians by power-hungry militants. The images also capture the suffering of thousands of desperate persons fleeing their homes and across borders, seeking refuge from civil war and starvation. Such situations shock the conscience of the global community and, despite the well-worn principle of "sovereignty," create political pressure to act in situations where action can ameliorate intense suffering. This action may involve diplomatic efforts, food relief shipments, or refuge for those that flee their country. Yet it may also involve the transboundary projection of military force. The UN Charter's failure specifically to permit forcible action by the United Nations, regional organizations, or individual states to address even the most egregious of human rights violations denies an inescapable feature of inter-state relations. The aspiration for international peace and order is understandable, but such an order is destined not to endure unless it is also just.

During the Cold War, many instances of human rights violations and deprivations went unaddressed, even by states acting unilaterally. Any interventions by the major powers tended to be driven by their distrust of one another. Interventions by other states sometimes had, as one motivation, the desire to end human rights abuses, but typically were characterized by the intervening states as actions taken in self-defense, evidencing a lack of confidence that humanitarian intervention per se was an acceptable feature of state behavior under the UN Charter.

As the world moves into the twenty-first century, the collective security mechanism of the United Nations appears finally to be coming of age. The demise of Cold War tensions has brought an unprecedented (albeit imperfect) ability to use the Security Council to address a wide range of issues relating to international peace and security. At the same time, the disappearance of Cold War alliances has unleashed well-armed former "client" states and groups around the world that use religious, ethnic, cultural, or political hatreds to create new political structures. These new conflicts do not reflect classic cases of armed aggression; typically they involve internal strife or civil war by competing factions. They do not always raise apparent issues of international peace and security, at least not as the concept has been understood traditionally. Nevertheless, states are seeking UN (or UN-authorized) action to address these issues. The prevention of transnational aggression is not alone a sufficient end in establishing world order; states believe that military intervention can and should be used to prevent widespread human rights violations and deprivations.

Recent interventions in Liberia, Iraq, Somalia, Rwanda, and Haiti, and to a certain extent in Bosnia, reveal evolving attitudes about the use of military force to protect human rights. Despite the variety in the objectives and successes of these interventions, much can be learned from the manner in which they were conducted and the difficulties they encountered. The United Nations is viewed as a desirable forum for blessing such intervention; it provides cover for those states wishing to intervene but not wishing to incur political costs in doing so unilaterally. The United Nations can serve as an adjunct to regional efforts in the imposition of effective economic sanctions (including arms embargoes) and can assist in mediation and monitoring in the event a regional entity is not perceived as sufficiently impartial. The United Nations also provides a means for intervening states to spread the economic costs of intervention and to extricate their forces after an intervention has succeeded in its primary task, as occurred in Iraq, Somalia, and Haiti.

Although the Security Council is now politically capable of acting, questions arise as to whether and how under the UN Charter it is competent to do so and whether in the long run this new capability is a desirable development in UN practice. By considering essentially internal human rights violations and deprivations to be "threats to the peace," the Security Council is expanding the scope of its authority beyond that originally envisioned in Chapter VII of the Charter. This development may be explained in part as recognizing a link between the propensity of a government to inflict violence on its own people and the propensity of that government to inflict violence on its neighbors, and that the Security Council should be prepared to act in either situation. Yet the statements by the members of the Security Council do not reveal a belief that such a linkage must be established prior to acting. Indeed, in the case of Haiti, the Security Council was willing to authorize intervention in a situation where the human rights values at stake were of a quite different order and magnitude than that seen in Liberia, Iraq, Bosnia, Somalia, or Rwanda, and where the capability (let alone the propensity) of the local government to inflict violence on its neighbors was hardly apparent. It remains unclear how expansively the Security Council will interpret "threats to the peace"; one can postulate a variety of nontraditional issues (drug trafficking, environmental degradation) that could serve as a basis for Security Council action.

Whereas in theory an activist Security Council is appealing, in practice there are difficulties. The composition and decisionmaking process of the Security Council is open to criticism; it favors the views of major powers at the expense of the international community as a whole, and at present it is particularly dominated by the most powerful state, the United States. While the Security Council is far more active now than it was during the Cold War, its actions nevertheless are subject to political constraints in the event its members cannot agree on how to proceed in a particular crisis, as was the case for much of the time with respect to Bosnia. Further, the United Nations is not well equipped to undertake functions of monitoring or itself undertaking military interventions. Member states have not provided the Security Council the ability to draw upon their military and economic resources for the conduct of military interventions or to assume responsibility for such interventions when conducted initially by forces under national command. Failure to provide such resources risks undermining the credibility of the Security Council and the United Nations as a tool for international conflict management.

Greater activism by the Security Council in authorizing or undertaking humanitarian intervention may have the effect of loosening normative restraints on the use of force generally; history is replete with instances where states have abused doctrines favoring uses of force for just causes. For this reason, greater use of regional organizations could serve as a second layer of authoritative decisionmaking that would avoid the difficulties inherent in unilateral action. Unfortunately, the prospects for action by regional organizations in this area are uncertain.

Recent events show a striking willingness of states to forego unilateral humanitarian intervention in favor of Security Council authorization, thereby reinforcing the views of those that regard unilateral humanitarian intervention as unlawful. Nevertheless, the possibility of unilateral intervention remains and, if undertaken, should be guided by the same principles of humanity, impartiality, and neutrality that pervade UN-authorized interventions.

Law serves as a conditioning factor in the behavior of states. It encompasses certain general rules developed through prior state practice and institutional processes for authoritative decisionmaking. Within that law, values of order and justice compete in an effort to establish an enduring peace. The emergence of the Security Council as an active player in international conflict management is a promising means by which account may be taken of these values. It is likely that the most contentious steps taken by the Security Council over the next several years will be forcible interventions in the affairs of states for the purpose of protecting the nationals of those states. Yet, as world order evolves, the use of the Security Council in this fashion must be approached carefully. Attention must be paid to the bases upon, and means by, which the Security Council pursues humanitarian intervention, the conditions that merit such interventions, and the practice that develops over time as these interventions are pursued. Unless the Security Council is perceived as acting in a lawful fashion, its effectiveness will be diminished and the credence given by states to international rules on the use of force severely strained.

Appendix: United Nations Documents

The documents issued by UN organs that are cited in this study are too numerous to reproduce here. Persons wishing to review these documents are directed to the official records series of the United Nations, which is arranged under the name of the relevant organ associated with that document, such as the Security Council Official Records (SCOR). Each organ's official records typically are arranged in separate parts that are issued for each year (or session) during which the organ sits. Ordinarily, one part contains verbatim or summary reports of what took place at the organ's meetings during a given year and a second part contains decisions and resolutions passed by the organ during those meetings. A third part also may contain materials gathered for consideration by that organ in anticipation of its meetings.

Security Council resolutions are published in a yearly compilation entitled "Resolutions and Decisions of the Security Council 19___— Security Council Officials Records: ___ Year." This yearly compilation is assigned the UN document symbol "S/INF." Thus, for example, S/INF/ 49 is the symbol associated with "Resolutions and Decisions of the Security Council 1993—Security Council Official Records: Forty-Eighth Year." If one goes to that volume knowing at which meeting a particular resolution was passed and the page number on which it may be found, then the text of the resolution may be readily located.

UN official records can be found at many university and law school libraries. In addition, the United Nations maintains an information center at its headquarters in New York and at numerous other locations throughout the world, primarily in capitals such as Washington, D.C. Researchers also should be aware that, recently, the UN Department of Public Information has begun to issue lengthy reference papers on crises in which the United Nations is involved and which contain a brief description of the crisis, the nature of the UN involvement, and reprints of selected UN resolutions and statements that are associated with the crisis in question.

To assist a reader wishing to do further study of the most recent interventions of the United Nations discussed in Chapter 5, here follows a list of the most important Security Council resolutions or statements associated with those interventions. This selection demonstrates the various means, forcible and non-forcible, by which the Security Council seeks to coerce behavior by recalcitrant local authorities.

Liberia

Note by the President of the Security Council, S/22133 (1991)
Note by the President of the Security Council, S/23886 (1992)
S.C. Res. 788, U.N. SCOR, 47th Sess., 3138th mtg. at 99, U.N. Doc. S/INF/48 (1993)
S.C. Res. 813, U.N. SCOR, 48th Sess., 3187th mtg. at 108, U.N. Doc. S/INF/49 (1994)
S.C. Res. 856, U.N. SCOR, 48th Sess., 3263d mtg. at 110, U.N. Doc. S/INF/49 (1994)
S.C. Res. 866, U.N. SCOR, 48th Sess., 3281st mtg. at 110, U.N. Doc. S/INF/49 (1994)
S.C. Res. 950, U.N. SCOR, 49th Sess., 3442d mtg., U.N. Doc. S/INF/950 (1994)
S.C. Res. 972, U.N. SCOR, 50th Sess., 3489th mtg., U.N. Doc. S/INF/972 (1995)

Iraq

S.C. Res. 688, U.N. SCOR, 46th Sess., 2982d mtg. at 31, U.N. Doc. S/INF/47 (1993)

Bosnia-Herzegovina

S.C. Res. 713, U.N. SCOR, 46th Sess., 3009th mtg. at 42, U.N. Doc. S/INF/47 (1993)
S.C. Res. 743, U.N. SCOR, 47th Sess., 3055th mtg. at 8, U.N. Doc. S/INF/48 (1993)
S.C. Res. 752, U.N. SCOR, 47th Sess., 3075th mtg. at 12, U.N. Doc. S/INF/48 (1993)
S.C. Res. 757, U.N. SCOR, 47th Sess., 3082d mtg. at 13, U.N. Doc. S/INF/48 (1993)
S.C. Res. 770, U.N. SCOR, 47th Sess., 3106th mtg. at 24, U.N. Doc. S/INF/48 (1993)
S.C. Res. 781, U.N. SCOR, 47th Sess., 3122d mtg. at 27, U.N. Doc. S/INF/48 (1993)
S.C. Res. 787, U.N. SCOR, 47th Sess., 3137th mtg. at 29, U.N. Doc. S/INF/48 (1993)
S.C. Res. 816, U.N. SCOR, 48th Sess., 3191st mtg. at 4, U.N. Doc. S/INF/49 (1994)
S.C. Res. 820, U.N. SCOR, 48th Sess., 3200th mtg. at 7, U.N. Doc. S/INF/49 (1994)

S.C. Res. 824, U.N. SCOR, 48th Sess., 3208th mtg. at 11, U.N. Doc. S/INF/49 (1994)

S.C. Res. 836, U.N. SCOR, 48th Sess., 3228th mtg. at 13, U.N. Doc. S/INF/49 (1994)

S.C. Res. 859, U.N. SCOR, 48th Sess., 3269th mtg. at 16, para. 5, U.N. Doc. S/INF/49 (1994)

S.C. Res. 1033, U.N. SCOR, 50th Sess., 3610 mtg., U.N. Doc. S/1995/1033 (1995)

Somalia

S.C. Res. 733, U.N. SCOR, 47th Sess., 3039th mtg. at 55, U.N. Doc. S/INF/48 (1993)

S.C. Res. 751, U.N. SCOR, 47th Sess., 3069th mtg. at 57, U.N. Doc. S/INF/48 (1993)

S.C. Res. 794, U.N. SCOR, 47th Sess., 3145th mtg. at 63, U.N. Doc. S/INF/48 (1993)

S.C. Res. 814, U.N. SCOR, 48th Sess., 3188th mtg. at 80, U.N. Doc. S/INF/49 (1994)

S.C. Res. 837, U.N. SCOR, 48th Sess., 3229th mtg. at 83, U.N. Doc. S/INF/49 (1994)

S.C. Res. 865, U.N. SCOR, 48th Sess., 3280th mtg. at 84, U.N. Doc. S/INF/49 (1994)

S.C. Res. 897, U.N. SCOR, 49th Sess., 3334th mtg., U.N. Doc. S/RES/987 (1994)

S.C. Res. 954, U.N. SCOR, 49th Sess., 3447th mtg., U.N. Doc. S/RES/954 (1994)

Rwanda

S.C. Res. 872, U.N. SCOR, 48th Sess., 3288th mtg. at 102, U.N. Doc. S/INF/49 (1994)

Statement by the President of the Security Council, S/PRST/1994/16 (1994)

S.C. Res. 912, U.N. SCOR, 49th Sess., 3368th mtg., U.N. Doc. S/RES/912 (1994)

Statement by the President of the Security Council, S/PRST/1994/21 (1994)

S.C. Res. 918, U.N. SCOR, 49th Sess., 3388th mtg., U.N. Doc. S/RES/925 (1994)

S.C. Res. 925, U.N. SCOR, 49th Sess., 3388th mtg., U.N. Doc. S/RES/925 (1994)

S.C. Res. 929, U.N. SCOR, 49th Sess., 3392d mtg., U.N. Doc. S/RES/929 (1994)

Haiti

S.C. Res. 841, U.N. SCOR, 48th Sess., 3238th mtg. at 119, U.N. Doc. S/INF/49 (1994)

S.C. Res. 861, U.N. SCOR, 48th Sess., 3271th mtg., at 121, U.N. Doc. S/INF/49 (1994)

S.C. Res. 867, U.N. SCOR, 48th Sess., 3282d mtg. at 122, U.N. Doc. S/INF/49 (1994)

S.C. Res. 873, U.N. SCOR, 48th Sess., 3291st mtg. at 125, U.N. Doc. S/INF/49 (1994)

S.C. Res. 875, U.N. SCOR, 48th Sess., 3293d mtg. at 125, U.N. Doc. S/INF/49 (1994)

S.C. Res. 917, U.N. SCOR, 49th Sess., 3376th mtg., U.N. Doc. S/RES/917 (1994)
S.C. Res. 940, U.N. SCOR, 49th Sess., 3134th mtg., U.N. Doc. S/RES/940 (1994)
S.C. Res. 944, U.N. SCOR, 49th Sess., 3430th mtg., U.N. Doc. S/RES/944 (1994)
S.C. Res. 948, U.N. SCOR, 49th Sess., 3437th mtg., U.N. Doc. S/RES/948 (1994)
S.C. Res. 975, U.N. SCOR, 50th Sess., 3496th mtg., U.N. Doc. S/RES/975 (1995)

Bibliography

Primary Sources

I. United Nations Documents

S.C. Res.	Resolutions of the Security Council
G.A. Res.	Resolutions of the General Assembly
SCOR	Security Council Official Records
GAOR	General Assembly Official Records
S/	Documents Pertaining to the Security Council
A/	Documents Pertaining to the General Assembly
E/CN.4	Documents Pertaining to the Human Rights Commission
I.C.J.	Publications of the International Court of Justice
U.N.C.I.O	Documents Pertaining to the United Nations Conference on International Organization, San Francisco, 1945 (22 vols.)
U.N.T.S.	United Nations Treaty Series

II. Collections of Documents

BRITISH AND FOREIGN STATE PAPERS (1812–1943)
Commager, H. & Cantor, M. eds. DOCUMENTS OF AMERICAN HISTORY (10th ed. 1988)
FOREIGN RELATIONS OF THE UNITED STATES, DIPLOMATIC PAPERS (1932–present)
Goach, G. & Temperley, H. eds. BRITISH DOCUMENTS ON THE ORIGINS OF THE WAR, 1898–1914 (1927) (11 vols.)
PAPERS RELATING TO THE FOREIGN RELATIONS OF THE UNITED STATES (1861–1931)
Sohn, L. ed. INTERNATIONAL ORGANIZATION AND INTEGRATION: ANOTATED BASIC DOCUMENTS OF INTERNATIONAL ORGANIZATIONS AND ARRANGEMENTS (1986)
Weston, B. ed. INTERNATIONAL LAW AND WORLD ORDER: BASIC DOCUMENTS (1994) (5 vols.)

III. Media Reports

F.B.I.S.	Foreign Broadcast Information Service, U.S. Government, Washington, D.C.

LE FIGARO   Le Figaro, Paris
GUARDIAN   The Guardian, London
INT'L HERALD TRIBUNE   International Herald Tribune, Paris
LIBÉRATION   Libération, Paris
N.Y. TIMES   New York Times, New York
THE TIMES   The Times, London
WASH. POST   Washington Post, Washington, D.C.

Secondary Sources

I. Books

A. INTERNATIONAL LAW

1. Humanitarian Intervention

Damrosch, L. ed. ENFORCING RESTRAINT: COLLECTIVE INTERVENTION IN INTERNAL CONFLICTS (1993)
Lillich, R. ed. HUMANITARIAN INTERVENTION AND THE UNITED NATIONS (1973)
Ronzitti, N. RESCUING NATIONALS ABROAD THROUGH MILITARY COERCION AND INTERVENTION ON GROUNDS OF HUMANITY (1985)
Reed, L. & Kaysen, C. EMERGING NORMS OF JUSTIFIED INTERVENTION (1993)
Rodley, N. ed. TO LOOSE THE BANDS OF WICKEDNESS: INTERNATIONAL INTERVENTION IN DEFENCE OF HUMAN RIGHTS (1992)
Tesón, F. HUMANITARIAN INTERVENTION: AN INQUIRY INTO LAW AND MORALITY (1988)

2. Use of Force Generally

Arend, A. & Beck, R. INTERNATIONAL LAW AND THE USE OF FORCE: BEYOND THE UN CHARTER PARADIGM (1993)
Best, G. HUMANITY IN WARFARE: THE MODERN HISTORY OF THE INTERNATIONAL LAW OF ARMED CONFLICT (1983)
Bowett, D. SELF-DEFENCE IN INTERNATIONAL LAW (1958)
Brownlie, I. INTERNATIONAL LAW AND THE USE OF FORCE BY STATES (1963) (reprinted 1991)
Bull, H. ed. INTERVENTION IN WORLD POLITICS (1984)
Cassese, A. ed. THE CURRENT LEGAL REGULATION OF THE USE OF FORCE (1986)
Damrosch, L. & Scheffer D. eds. LAW AND FORCE IN THE NEW INTERNATIONAL ORDER (1991)
Dinstein, Y. WAR, AGGRESSION AND SELF-DEFENCE (1988)
Ely, J. WAR AND RESPONSIBILITY: CONSTITUTIONAL LESSONS OF VIETNAM AND ITS AFTERMATH (1993)
Falk, R. LEGAL ORDER IN A VIOLENT WORLD (1968)
Ferencz, B. DEFINING INTERNATIONAL AGGRESSION: THE SEARCH FOR WORLD PEACE (1975)
Henkin, L. et al. RIGHT V. MIGHT: INTERNATIONAL LAW AND THE USE OF FORCE (2d ed. 1991)
Hodges, H. THE DOCTRINE OF INTERVENTION (1915)

Jaquet, L. ed. INTERVENTION IN INTERNATIONAL POLITICS (1971)

McDougal, M. & Feliciano, F. LAW AND MINIMUM WORLD PUBLIC ORDER: THE REGULATION OF INTERNATIONAL COERCION (1961)

Moore, J. ed. LAW AND CIVIL WAR IN THE MODERN WORLD (1974)

Moore, J. LAW AND THE INDO-CHINA WAR (1974)

Sicilianos, L. LÉS RÉACTIONS DÉCENTRALISÉES A L'ILLICITE: DES CONTRE MESURES A LA LÉGITIME DÉFENSE (1990)

Singh, J. USE OF FORCE UNDER INTERNATIONAL LAW (1984)

Stone, J. AGGRESSION AND WORLD ORDER: A CRITIQUE OF UNITED NATIONS THEORIES OF AGGRESSION (1958)

Stowell, E. INTERVENTION IN INTERNATIONAL LAW (1921)

Thomas, A. & Thomas Jr., A. NON-INTERVENTION: THE LAW AND ITS IMPORT IN THE AMERICAS (1956)

Vincent, R. NONINTERVENTION AND INTERNATIONAL ORDER (1974)

Weston, B. ed. ALTERNATIVE SECURITY: LIVING WITHOUT NUCLEAR DETERRENCE (1990)

3. Human Rights

Beigbeder, Y. THE ROLE AND STATUS OF INTERNATIONAL HUMANITARIAN VOLUNTEERS AND ORGANIZATIONS (1991)

Cahill, K. ed. A FRAMEWORK FOR SURVIVAL: HEALTH, HUMAN RIGHTS, AND HUMANITARIAN ASSISTANCE IN CONFLICTS AND DISASTERS (1993)

Claude, R. & Weston, B. eds. HUMAN RIGHTS IN THE WORLD COMMUNITY: ISSUES AND ACTION (2d ed. 1992)

Delissen, A. & Tanja, G. eds. HUMANITARIAN LAW OF ARMED CONFLICT: CHALLENGES AHEAD (1991)

Ganji, M. INTERNATIONAL PROTECTION OF HUMAN RIGHTS (1962)

Lauterpacht, H. INTERNATIONAL LAW AND HUMAN RIGHTS (1950)

Lillich, R. INTERNATIONAL HUMAN RIGHTS: PROBLEMS OF LAW, POLICY, AND PRACTICE (2d ed. 1991)

Meron, T. HUMAN RIGHTS LAW-MAKING IN THE UNITED NATIONS: A CRITIQUE OF INSTRUMENTS AND PROCESS (1986)

Oraá, J. HUMAN RIGHTS IN STATES OF EMERGENCY IN INTERNATIONAL LAW (1992)

Robinson, J. HUMAN RIGHTS AND FUNDAMENTAL FREEDOMS IN THE CHARTER OF THE UNITED NATIONS: A COMMENTARY (1946)

Sohn, L. & Buergenthal, T. INTERNATIONAL PROTECTION OF HUMAN RIGHTS (1973)

U.S. Committee for Refugees, WORLD REFUGEE SURVEY — 1995 (1995)

4. General Legal Treatises

American Law Institute, RESTATEMENT (THIRD) OF THE FOREIGN RELATIONS LAW OF THE UNITED STATES (1987) (2 vols.)

Bhatia, H. INTERNATIONAL LAW AND PRACTICE IN ANCIENT INDIA (1977)

Borchard, E. THE DIPLOMATIC PROTECTION OF CITIZENS ABROAD (1915) (reprinted 1970)

Brierly, J. THE LAW OF NATIONS (6th ed. 1963) (H. Waldock ed.)

Brownlie, I. PRINCIPLES OF PUBLIC INTERNATIONAL LAW (4th ed. 1990)

Bull, H. et al. eds. HUGO GROTIUS AND INTERNATIONAL RELATIONS (1992)
Combacau, J. & Sur, S. DROIT INTERNATIONAL PUBLIC (1993)
Carty, A. THE DECAY OF INTERNATIONAL LAW? A REAPPRAISAL OF THE LIMITS OF LEGAL IMAGINATION IN INTERNATIONAL AFFAIRS (1986)
D'Amato, A. INTERNATIONAL LAW: PROCESS AND PROSPECT (2d ed. 1995)
Falk, R. THE STATUS OF LAW IN INTERNATIONAL SOCIETY (1970)
Falk, R. & Black, C. eds. THE FUTURE OF THE INTERNATIONAL LEGAL ORDER (1969–82) (5 vols.)
Fisher, R. POINTS OF CHOICE (1978)
Franck, T. THE POWER OF LEGITIMACY AMONG NATIONS (1990)
Friedmann, W. THE CHANGING STRUCTURE OF INTERNATIONAL LAW (1964)
Grotius, H. DE JURE BELLI AC PACIS LIBRI TRES (ON THE LAW OF WAR AND PEACE) [1646] (1925) (F. Kelsey trans.)
Henkin, L. HOW NATIONS BEHAVE: LAW AND FOREIGN POLICY (2d ed. 1979)
Higgins, R. PROBLEMS AND PROCESS: INTERNATIONAL LAW AND HOW WE USE IT (1994)
Hyde, C. INTERNATIONAL LAW, CHIEFLY AS INTERPRETED AND APPLIED BY THE UNITED STATES (2d rev. ed. 1945)
Jennings, R. & Watts, A. eds. OPPENHEIM'S INTERNATIONAL LAW (9th ed. 1992) (2 vols.)
Jessup, P. A MODERN LAW OF NATIONS (1946) (reprinted 1968)
Kelsen, H. PRINCIPLES OF INTERNATIONAL LAW (1952)
Kennedy, D. INTERNATIONAL LEGAL STRUCTURES (1987)
Khadduri, M. WAR AND PEACE IN THE LAW OF ISLAM (1955)
Koskenniemi, M. FROM APOLOGY TO UTOPIA: THE STRUCTURE OF INTERNATIONAL LEGAL ARGUMENT (1989)
Lasswell, H. & McDougal, M. JURISPRUDENCE FOR A FREE SOCIETY: STUDIES IN LAW, SCIENCE AND POLICY (1992) (2 vols.)
Lauterpacht, H. ed. OPPENHEIM'S INTERNATIONAL LAW (7th ed. 1952) (8th ed. 1955) (2 vols.)
Macdonald, R. & Johnson, D. eds. THE STRUCTURE AND PROCESS OF INTERNATIONAL LAW: ESSAYS IN LEGAL PHILOSOPHY, DOCTRINE AND THEORY 17 (1983)
Mensah-Brown, A. ed. AFRICAN INTERNATIONAL LEGAL HISTORY (1975)
McDougal, M. et al. STUDIES IN WORLD PUBLIC ORDER (1960)
Nussbaum, A. A CONCISE HISTORY OF THE LAW OF NATIONS (rev. ed. 1954)
Oppenheim, L. INTERNATIONAL LAW, A TREATISE (1st ed. 1905) (2d ed. 1912) (2 vols.)
Phillimore, R. COMMENTARIES UPON INTERNATIONAL LAW (3d ed. 1879) (2 vols.)
Phillipson, C. THE INTERNATIONAL LAW AND CUSTOM OF ANCIENT GREECE AND ROME (1911) (2 vols.)
Reisman, W. NULLITY AND REVISION: THE REVIEW AND ENFORCEMENT OF INTERNATIONAL JUDGMENTS AND AWARDS (1971)
Reisman, W. & Willard, A. eds. INTERNATIONAL INCIDENTS: THE LAW THAT COUNTS IN WORLD POLITICS (1988)
Reisman, W. & Weston, B. eds. TOWARD WORLD ORDER AND HUMAN DIGNITY: ESSAYS IN HONOR OF MYRES S. MCDOUGAL (1976)
Rousseau, C. DROIT INTERNATIONAL PUBLIC (1971–83) (5 vols.)
Ruddy, F. INTERNATIONAL LAW IN THE ENLIGHTENMENT (1975)
Schachter, O. INTERNATIONAL LAW IN THEORY AND PRACTICE (1991)
Shapo, M. THE DUTY TO ACT: TORT LAW, POWER, AND PUBLIC POLICY (1977)
Singh, N. INDIA AND INTERNATIONAL LAW (1969)

Stowell, E. INTERNATIONAL LAW (1931)

Vattel, E. THE LAW OF NATIONS OR THE PRINCIPLES OF NATURAL LAW APPLIED TO THE CONDUCT AND TO THE AFFAIRS OF NATIONS AND OF SOVEREIGNS [1758] (1916) (C. Fenwick trans.)

Westlake, J. INTERNATIONAL LAW (1910) (2 vols.)

Wheaton, H. ELEMENTS OF INTERNATIONAL LAW [1836] (1936) (G. Wilson ed.)

B. INTERNATIONAL RELATIONS

Albrecht-Carrié, R. A DIPLOMATIC HISTORY OF EUROPE SINCE THE CONGRESS OF VIENNA (1973)

Baker, J. THE POLITICS OF DIPLOMACY: REVOLUTION, WAR & PEACE, 1989–1992 (1995)

Beitz, C. POLITICAL THEORY AND INTERNATIONAL RELATIONS (1979)

Bodin, J. THE SIX BOOKES OF A COMMONWEALE [1576] (1962) (K. McRae trans.)

Boyle, F. WORLD POLITICS AND INTERNATIONAL LAW (1985)

Butterfield, H. & Wight, M. eds. DIPLOMATIC INVESTIGATIONS: ESSAYS IN THE THEORY OF INTERNATIONAL POLITICS (1966)

Calvocoressi, P. WORLD POLITICS SINCE 1945 (5th ed. 1987)

Dobrynin, A. IN CONFIDENCE: MOSCOW'S AMBASSADOR TO AMERICA'S SIX COLD WAR PRESIDENTS (1995)

Forsythe, D. THE POLITICS OF INTERNATIONAL LAW: U.S. FOREIGN POLICY RECONSIDERED (1990)

Gardner, L. et al. CREATION OF THE AMERICAN EMPIRE: U.S. DIPLOMATIC HISTORY (1973)

Heckscher, A. WOODROW WILSON (1991)

Hobbes, T. LEVIATHAN, OR THE MATTER, FORME AND POWER OF A COMMONWEALTH ECCLESIASTICALL AND CIVIL [1651] (1962) (M. Oakeshott ed.)

Holbraad, C. THE CONCERT OF EUROPE: A STUDY IN GERMAN AND BRITISH INTERNATIONAL THEORY 1815–1914 (1970)

Hoffmann, S. DUTIES BEYOND BORDERS: ON THE LIMITS AND POSSIBILITIES OF ETHICAL INTERNATIONAL POLITICS (1981)

Kaplan, M. & Katzenbach, N. THE POLITICAL FOUNDATIONS OF INTERNATIONAL LAW (1961)

Kennan, G. AMERICAN DIPLOMACY 1900–1950 (1951)

Kent, R. ANATOMY OF DISASTER RELIEF: THE INTERNATIONAL NETWORK IN ACTION (1987)

Kissinger, H. DIPLOMACY (1994)

Machiavelli, N. THE PRINCE [1513] (1948) (W. Marriot trans.)

Medlicott, W. BISMARK, GLADSTONE, AND THE CONCERT OF EUROPE (1956)

Morgenthau, H. POLITICS AMONG NATIONS: THE STRUGGLE FOR POWER AND PEACE (4th ed. 1967)

Mowat, R. A HISTORY OF EUROPEAN DIPLOMACY 1815–1914 (1933)

Ohmae, K. THE END OF THE NATION STATE: THE RISE OF REGIONAL ECONOMIES (1995)

Rosecrance, R. THE RISE OF THE TRADING STATE: COMMERCE AND CONQUEST IN THE MODERN WORLD (1986)

Rummel, R. DEATH BY GOVERNMENT (1994)

Shultz, G. TURMOIL AND TRIUMPH: MY YEARS AS SECRETARY OF STATE (1993)

Waltz, K. THEORY OF INTERNATIONAL POLITICS (1979)

C. The United Nations and International Organization

Alston, P. ed. The United Nations and Human Rights: A Critical Appraisal (1992)
Andemicael, B. The OAU and the UN: Relations between the Organization of African Unity and the United Nations (1976)
Andemicael, B. ed. Regionalism and the United Nations (1979)
Asher, R. et al. The United Nations and Promotion of the General Welfare (1957) (reprinted 1980)
Baehr, P. & Gordenker, L. The United Nations in the 1990s (2d ed. 1994)
Bailey, S. The Procedure of the UN Security Council (2d ed. 1988)
Bedjaoui, M. The New World Order and the Security Council: Testing the Legality of its Acts (1994)
Bennett, A. International Organizations: Principles and Issues (1984)
Blum, Y. Eroding the United Nations Charter (1993)
Bourantonis, D. & Wiener, J. eds. The United Nations in the New World Order: The World Organization at Fifty (1995)
Bowett, D. United Nations Forces (1964)
Bowett, D. The Law of International Institutions (4th ed. 1982)
Boyd, J. United Nations Peace-keeping Operations: A Military and Political Appraisal (1971)
Cassese, A. ed. United Nations Peace-keeping, Legal Essays (1978)
Canyes, M. The Organization of American States and the United Nations (5th ed. 1960)
Claude Jr., I. Swords into Plowshares: Problems and Progress of International Organization (4th ed. 1971)
Cot, J. & Pellet, A. eds. La Charte des Nations Unies, Commentaire Article Par Article (2d ed. 1991)
Durch, W. ed. The Evolution of UN Peacekeeping: Case Studies and Comparative Analysis (1993)
Ehrlich, T. Cyprus 1958–1967 (1974)
Fenwick, C. The Organization of American States: The Inter-American Regional System (1963)
Ferencz, B. New Legal Foundations for Global Survival: Security Through the Security Council (1994)
Fitzmaurice, G. The Law and Procedure of the International Court of Justice (1986) (2 vols.)
Goodrich, L. et al. Charter of the United Nations: Commentary and Documents (3d ed. 1969)
Goodrich, L. The United Nations in a Changing World (1974)
Gordon, W. The United Nations at the Crossroads of Reform (1994)
Gross, L. Essays on International Law and Organization (1976) (2 vols.)
Harbottle, M. The Blue Berets: A Study of Peacekeeping Operations (1971)
Higgins, R. United Nations Peacekeeping: Documents and Commentary (1969–81) (4 vols.)
Higgins, R. The Development of International Law Through the Political Organs of the United Nations (1963)
Hilderbrand, R. Dumbarton Oaks: The Origins of the United Nations and the Search for Postwar Security (1990)
Jakobson, M. The United Nations in the 1990s—A Second Chance? (1993)

Kay, D. ed. THE UNITED NATIONS POLITICAL SYSTEM (1967)

Kelsen, H. THE LAW OF THE UNITED NATIONS (1950)

Kirgis, F. INTERNATIONAL ORGANIZATIONS IN THEIR LEGAL SETTING (2d ed. 1993)

Lee, J. et al. TO UNITE OUR STRENGTH: ENHANCING THE UNITED NATIONS PEACE AND SECURITY SYSTEM (1992)

Lissitzyn, O. THE INTERNATIONAL COURT OF JUSTICE: ITS ROLE IN THE MAINTE- NANCE OF INTERNATIONAL PEACE AND SECURITY (1951)

Liu, F. UNITED NATIONS PEACEKEEPING AND THE NON-USE OF FORCE (1992)

Luard, E. A HISTORY OF THE UNITED NATIONS: THE YEARS OF WESTERN DOMI- NATION, 1945–1955 (1982)

Murphy, J. THE UNITED NATIONS AND THE CONTROL OF INTERNATIONAL VIO- LENCE: A LEGAL AND POLITICAL ANALYSIS (1982)

Nicholas, H. THE UNITED NATIONS AS POLITICAL INSTITUTION (1975)

Paxman, J. & Boggs, G. eds. THE UNITED NATIONS: A REASSESSMENT; SANCTIONS, PEACEKEEPING, AND HUMANITARIAN ASSISTANCE (1973)

Rajan, M. THE EXPANDING JURISDICTION OF THE UNITED NATIONS (1982)

Ratner, S. THE NEW UN PEACEKEEPING: BUILDING PEACE IN LANDS OF CONFLICT AFTER THE COLD WAR (1995)

Righter, R. UTOPIA LOST: THE UNITED NATIONS AND WORLD ORDER (1995)

Rikhye, I. ed. THE UNITED NATIONS AND PEACEKEEPING: RESULTS, LIMITATIONS, AND PROSPECTS (1990)

Rikhye, I. et al. THE THIN BLUE LINE (1974)

Rivlin, B. & Gordenker, L. eds. THE CHALLENGING ROLE OF THE UN SECRETARY- GENERAL: MAKING "THE MOST IMPOSSIBLE JOB IN THE WORLD" POSSIBLE (1993)

Roberts, A. & Kingsbury, B. eds. UNITED NATIONS, DIVIDED WORLD: THE UN'S ROLES IN INTERNATIONAL RELATIONS (2d ed. 1993)

Rochester, J. WAITING FOR THE MILLENNIUM: THE UNITED NATIONS AND THE FUTURE OF WORLD ORDER (1993)

Ruda, J. THE PURPOSES AND PRINCIPLES OF THE UNITED NATIONS CHARTER (A LEGISLATIVE HISTORY OF THE PREAMBLE, ARTICLE 1 AND ARTICLE 2) (1983)

Schermers, H. INTERNATIONAL INSTITUTIONAL LAW (1980)

Siekmann, R. ed. BASIC DOCUMENTS ON UNITED NATIONS AND RELATED PEACE- KEEPING FORCES (2d ed. 1989)

Simma, B. ed. THE CHARTER OF THE UNITED NATIONS: A COMMENTARY (1994)

Thomas, A. & Thomas Jr., A. THE ORGANIZATION OF AMERICAN STATES (1963)

Tolley Jr., H. THE U.N. COMMISSION ON HUMAN RIGHTS (1987)

United Nations, THE BLUE HELMETS: A REVIEW OF UNITED NATIONS PEACE- KEEPING (1990)

United Nations, THE UNITED NATIONS AND THE MAINTENANCE OF INTERNA- TIONAL PEACE AND SECURITY (1987)

Urquhart, B. & Childers, E. A WORLD IN NEED OF LEADERSHIP: TOMORROW'S UNITED NATIONS (1990)

U.S. Dept. of State, CHARTER OF THE UNITED NATIONS: REPORT TO THE PRESI- DENT ON THE RESULTS OF THE SAN FRANCISCO CONFERENCE (1945) (reprinted 1969)

U.S. Institute of Peace, TWO VIEWS ON THE ISSUE OF COLLECTIVE SECURITY (1992)

Walters, F. A HISTORY OF THE LEAGUE OF NATIONS (1952) (2 vols.)

Williamson, R. THE UNITED NATIONS: A PLACE OF PROMISE AND OF MISCHIEF (1991)
Wiseman, H. ed. PEACE-KEEPING — APPRAISALS AND PROPOSALS (1983)

D. PHILOSOPHY, THEOLOGY, AND JUST WAR THEORY

Aquinas, T. ST. THOMAS AQUINAS ON POLITICS AND ETHICS (1988) (P. Sigmund ed. & trans.)
Aristotle. THE POLITICS (rev. ed. 1992) (T. Sinclair trans., T. Saunders ed.)
Augustine of Hippo. THE CITY OF GOD (1950) (M. Dods trans.)
Austin, J. THE PROVINCE OF JURISPRUDENCE DETERMINED (1955) (H. Hart ed.)
Cicero, M. THE BASIC WORKS OF CICERO (1951) (M. Hadas ed.)
Dworkin, R. TAKING RIGHTS SERIOUSLY (1977)
Hart, H. THE CONCEPT OF LAW (1961)
Johnson, J. & Weigel, G. JUST WAR AND THE GULF WAR (1991)
Johnson, J. JUST WAR TRADITION AND THE RESTRAINT OF WAR: A MORAL AND HISTORICAL INQUIRY (1981)
Johnson, J. IDEOLOGY, REASON, AND THE LIMITATION OF WAR: RELIGIOUS AND SECULAR CONCEPTS 1200–1740 (1975)
Kant, I. PERPETUAL PEACE [1795] (1939)
Melzer, Y. CONCEPTS OF JUST WAR (1975)
Mill, J. ESSAYS ON POLITICS AND CULTURE (1962) (reprinted 1973) (G. Himmelfarb ed.)
Nardin, T. LAW, MORALITY, AND THE RELATIONS OF STATES (1983)
O'Brien, W. THE CONDUCT OF JUST AND LIMITED WAR (1981)
Parkinson, F. THE PHILOSOPHY OF INTERNATIONAL RELATIONS: A STUDY IN THE HISTORY OF THOUGHT (1977)
Plato. THE REPUBLIC OF PLATO (1945) (F. Cornford ed.)
Rawls, J. A THEORY OF JUSTICE (1971)
Russell, F. THE JUST WAR IN THE MIDDLE AGES (1975)
Schacht, J. AN INTRODUCTION TO ISLAMIC LAW (1964)
Toynbee, A. CIVILIZATION ON TRIAL (1948)
Voegelin, E. ORDER AND HISTORY: ISRAEL AND REVELATION (1957)
Walzer, M. JUST AND UNJUST WARS: A MORAL ARGUMENT WITH HISTORICAL ILLUSTRATIONS (2d ed. 1992)
Weber, M. ANCIENT JUDAISM (1952)

E. STUDIES OF SPECIFIC INTERVENTIONS

1. Pre-U.N. Charter Interventions

O'Toole, G. THE SPANISH WAR: AN AMERICAN EPIC 1898 (1984)
Trask, D. THE WAR WITH SPAIN IN 1898 (1981)

2. Cambodia

Burchett, W. THE CHINA-CAMBODIA-VIETNAM TRIANGLE (1981)
CAMBODIA: RENDEZVOUS WITH DEATH (K. Jackson ed., 1989)

Chanda, N. BROTHER ENEMY: THE WAR AFTER THE WAR (1986)
Klintworth, G. VIETNAM'S INTERVENTION IN CAMBODIA IN INTERNATIONAL LAW (1989)
Shawcross, W. THE QUALITY OF MERCY: CAMBODIA, HOLOCAUST, AND MODERN CONSCIENCE (1984)

3. Central African Republic

O'Toole, T. THE CENTRAL AFRICAN REPUBLIC: THE CONTINENT'S HIDDEN HEART (1986)
Zoctizoum, Y. HISTOIRE DE LA CENTRAFRIQUE: VIOLENCE DU DÉVELOPPEMENT, DOMINATION AND INÉGALITÉS (1983)

4. Congo

Abi-Saab, G. THE UNITED NATIONS OPERATION IN THE CONGO 1960–1964 (1978)
Epstein, H. ed. REVOLT IN THE CONGO, 1960–64 (1965)

5. Cuba

Allison, G. ESSENCE OF DECISION: EXPLAINING THE CUBAN MISSILE CRISIS (1971)
Chayes, A. THE CUBAN MISSILE CRISIS (1974)

6. Czechoslovakia

Bergmann, P. SELF-DETERMINATION: THE CASE OF CZECHOSLOVAKIA 1968–1969 (1972)
Dawisha, K. THE KREMLIN AND THE PRAGUE SPRING (1984)
Golan, G. THE CZECHOSLOVAK REFORM MOVEMENT: COMMUNISM IN CRISIS 1962–68 (1971)
Skilling, G. CZECHOSLOVAKIA'S INTERRUPTED REVOLUTION (1976)
Valenta, J. SOVIET INTERVENTION IN CZECHOSLOVAKIA, 1968: ANATOMY OF A DECISION (1979)

7. Dominican Republic

Corey, J. ed. THE DOMINICAN REPUBLIC CRISIS 1965 (1967)
Kurzman, D. SANTO DOMINGO: REVOLT OF THE DAMNED (1965)
Lowenthal, A. THE DOMINICAN INTERVENTION (1972)
Slater, J. INTERVENTION AND NEGOTIATION: THE UNITED STATES AND THE DOMINICAN REVOLUTION (1970)
Szulc, T. DOMINICAN DIARY (1965)

8. East Pakistan

International Commission of Jurists, THE EVENTS IN EAST PAKISTAN: A LEGAL STUDY (1972)

Misra, K. THE ROLE OF THE UNITED NATIONS IN THE INDO-PAKISTANI CONFLICT (1973)

Rizvi, H. INTERNAL STRIFE AND EXTERNAL AGGRESSION: INDIA'S ROLE IN THE CIVIL WAR IN EAST PAKISTAN (1981)

9. Grenada

Gilmore, W. THE GRENADA INTERVENTION: ANALYSIS AND DOCUMENTATION (1984)

Moore, J. LAW AND THE GRENADA MISSION (1984)

Payne, A. et al. GRENADA: REVOLUTION AND INVASION (1984)

10. Hungary

International Commission of Jurists, THE HUNGARIAN SITUATION AND THE RULE OF LAW (1957)

Szikszoy, J. THE LEGAL ASPECTS OF THE HUNGARIAN QUESTION (1963)

11. Iraq

Freedman, L. & Karsh, E. THE GULF CONFLICT 1990–91: DIPLOMACY AND WAR IN THE NEW WORLD ORDER (1993)

Weller, M. ed. IRAQ AND KUWAIT: THE HOSTILITIES AND THEIR AFTERMATH (1993)

12. Lebanon

Dawisha, A. SYRIA AND THE LEBANESE CRISIS (1980)

Hiro, D. LEBANON FIRE AND EMBERS: A HISTORY OF THE LEBANESE CIVIL WAR (1993)

Mackey, S. LEBANON: DEATH OF A NATION (1989)

Weinberger, N. SYRIAN INTERVENTION IN LEBANON: THE 1975–76 CIVIL WAR (1986)

13. Liberia

Weller, M. ed. REGIONAL PEACE-KEEPING AND INTERNATIONAL ENFORCEMENT: THE LIBERIAN CRISIS (1994)

14. Somalia

Makinda, S. SEEKING PEACE FROM CHAOS: HUMANITARIAN INTERVENTION IN SOMALIA (1993)

Sahnoun, M. SOMALIA: THE MISSED OPPORTUNITIES (1994)

15. Suez

Bowie, R. Suez 1956 (1974)

16. Yugoslavia

Bassiouni, M. & Manikas, P. The Law of the International Criminal Tribunal for the Former Yugoslavia (1996)
Donia, R. & Fine Jr., J. Bosnia and Hercegovina: A Tradition Betrayed (1994)
Glenny, M. The Fall of Yugoslavia: The Third Balkan War (rev. ed. 1994)
Gnesotto, N. Leçons de la Yougoslavie (1994)
Helsinki Watch. War Crimes in Bosnia-Herzegovina (1992)
Kaplan, R. Balkan Ghosts: A Journey Through History (1993)
Vernet, D. & Gonin, J. Le Rêve Sacrifié: Chronique des Guerres Yougoslaves (1994)

II. Articles

A. International Law

1. Humanitarian Intervention Generally

Aaron, A. *Humanitarian Intervention, Nationality, and the Rights of Refugees*, 26 Harv. Int'l L.J. 585 (1985)
Aroneau, E. *La guerre internationale d'intervention pour cause d'humanite*, 19 Revue Int'l de Droit Penal 173 (1948)
Bazyler, M. *Reexamining the Doctrine of Humanitarian Intervention in Light of the Atrocities in Kampuchea and Ethiopia*, 23 Stan. J. Int'l L. 547 (1987)
Behuniak, T. *The Law of Unilateral Humanitarian Intervention by Armed Force: A Legal Survey*, 79 Mil. L. Rev. 157 (1978)
Benjamin, B. *Unilateral Humanitarian Intervention: Legalizing the Use of Force to Prevent Human Rights Atrocities*, 16 Fordham Int'l L.J. 120 (1992–93)
Bogen, D. *The Law of Humanitarian Intervention: U.S. Policy in Cuba (1898) and in the Dominican Republic (1965)*, 7 Harv. Int'l L. Club J. 296 (1966)
Cabranes, J. *Human Rights and Non-Intervention in the Inter-American System*, 65 Mich. L. Rev. 1147 (1967)
Chandrahasan, N. *Use of Force to Ensure Humanitarian Relief: A South Asian Precedent Examined*, 42 Int'l & Comp. L.Q. 664 (1993)
Chopra, J. & Weiss, T. *Sovereignty is No Longer Sacrosanct: Codifying Humanitarian Intervention*, 6 Ethics & Int'l Aff. 114 (1992)
Clark, R. *Humanitarian Intervention: Help to Your Friends and State Practice*, 13 Ga. J. Int'l & Comp. L. 211 (1983)
Claydon, J. *Humanitarian Intervention and International Law*, 1:3 Queen's Intramural L.J. 36 (1969)
Corten, O. & Klein, P. *L'autorisation de recourir a la force a des fins humanitaires: Droit d'ingérence ou retour aux sources?* 4 Eur. J. Int'l L. 506 (1993)

Costa, P. & Evans, P. *The Indian Supply Drop Into Sri Lanka: Non-Military Humanitarian Aid and the Troubling Idea of Intervention*, 3 CONN. J. INT'L L. 417 (1988)

Delbrück, J. *A Fresh Look at Humanitarian Intervention Under the Authority of the United Nations*, 67 IND. L.J. 887 (1992)

De Schutter, B. *Humanitarian Intervention: A United Nations Task*, 3 CAL. W. INT'L L. REV. 21 (1972)

Domestici-Met, M. *Aspects juridiques recents de l'assistance humanitaire*, 35 ANNUAIRE FRANÇAISE DE DROIT INT'L 117 (1989)

Fairley, H. *State Actors, Humanitarian Intervention and International Law: Reopening Pandora's Box*, 10 GA. J. INT'L & COMP. L. 29 (1980)

Farer, T. *Human Rights in Law's Empire: The Jurisprudence War*, 85 AM. J. INT'L L. 117 (1991)

Fonteyne, J. *The Customary International Law Doctrine of Humanitarian Intervention: Its Current Validity Under the U.N. Charter*, 4 CAL. W. INT'L L.J. 203 (1974)

Goehel, C. *Population Transfer, Humanitarian Law, and the Use of Ground Force in U.N. Peacemaking*, 25 N.Y.U.J. INT'L L. & POL. 627 (1993)

Jhabvala, F. *Unilateral Humanitarian Intervention and International Law*, 21 INDIAN J. INT'L L. 208 (1981)

Levitin, M. *The Law of Force and the Force of Law: Grenada, the Falklands, and Humanitarian Intervention*, 27 HARV. INT'L L.J. 621 (1986)

Lillich, R. *Forcible Self-Help by States to Protect Human Rights*, 53 IOWA L. REV. 325 (1967)

Lillich, R. *Intervention to Protect Human Rights*, 15 McGILL L.J. 205 (1969)

Lillich, R. *Humanitarian Intervention through the United Nations: Towards the Development of Criteria*, 53 ZEITSCHRIFT FUR AUSLANDISCHES OFFENTLICHES RECHT & VOLKERRECHT 557 (1993)

Lopez, F. *The Lawfulness of Humanitarian Intervention*, J. LEGAL STUD. ANN. 97 (1991)

Malanczuk, P. *Humanitarian Intervention and the Legitimacy of the Use of Force*, INAUGURAL LECTURE, UNIVERSITY OF AMSTERDAM, JANUARY 22, 1993 (reprint distributed by Martinus Nijhoff International) (1993)

Mandelstam, A. *La protection des minorités*, 1 RECUEIL DES COURS D'ACADEMIE DE DROIT INT'L (R.C.A.D.I.) 367 (1923)

Maurice, F. *Humanitarian Ambition*, 32 INT'L REV. RED CROSS 363 (1992)

McDougal, M. & Reisman, W. *Rhodesia and the United Nations: The Lawfulness of International Concern*, 62 AM. J. INT'L L. 1 (1968)

McDougal, M. & Reisman, W. *Response*, 3 INT'L LAW. 438 (1968–69)

Nafziger, J. *Self-Determination and Humanitarian Intervention in a Community of Power*, 20 DENV. J. INT'L L. & POL'Y 9 (1991)

Nanda, V. *Tragedies in Northern Iraq, Liberia, Yugoslavia, and Haiti—Revisiting the Validity of Humanitarian Intervention Under International Law—Part I*, 20 DENV. J. INT'L L. & POL'Y 305 (1992)

Nawaz, M. *What Limits on the Use of Force? Can Force Be Used to Depose Oppressive Governments?* 24 INDIAN J. INT'L L. 406 (1984)

Reisman, W. *Coercion and Self-Determination: Construing Charter Article 2(4)*, 78 AM. J. INT'L L. 642 (1984)

Rodley, N. *Human Rights and Humanitarian Intervention: The Case Law of the World Court*, 38 INT'L & COMP. L.Q. 321 (1989)

Rougier, A. *La théorie de l'intervention d'humanité*, 17 REVUE GÉNÉRALE DE DROIT INT'L PUB. 468 (1910)

Ryan, K. *Rights, Intervention, and Self-Determination*, 20 DENV. J. INT'L L. & POL'Y 55 (1991)

Schachter, O. *The Legality of Pro-Democratic Invasion*, 78 AM. J. INT'L L. 645 (1984)

Scheffer, D. *Toward a Modern Doctrine of Humanitarian Intervention*, 23 U. TOL. L. REV. 253 (1992)

Schweigman, D. *Humanitarian Intervention under International Law: The Strife for Humanity*, 6 LEIDEN J. INT'L L. 91 (1993)

Schweisfurth, T. *Operations to Rescue Nationals in Third States Involving the Use of Force in Relation to the Protection of Human Rights*, 23 GERMAN Y.B. INT'L L. 159 (1980)

Simon, S. *The Contemporary Legality of Unilateral Humanitarian Intervention*, 24 CAL. W. INT'L L.J. 117 (1993)

Sornarajah, M. *Internal Colonialism and Humanitarian Intervention*, 11 GA. J. INT'L & COMP. L. 45 (1981)

Stowell, E. *Humanitarian Intervention*, 33 AM. J. INT'L L. 733 (1939)

Suzuki, E. *A State's Provisional Competence to Protect Human Rights in a Foreign State*, 15 TEX. INT'L L.J. 231 (1980)

Tesón, F. *Le Peuple, C'est Moi! The World Court and Human Rights*, 81 AM. J. INT'L L. 81 (1987)

Torrelli, M. *Les zones de securite*, 95 REVUE GÉNÉRALE DE DROIT INT'L PUB. 787 (1995)

Verwey, W. *Humanitarian Intervention Under International Law*, 32 NETH. INT'L L. REV. 357 (1985)

Wolf, D. *Humanitarian Intervention*, 9 MICH. Y.B. INT'L LEGAL STUD. 333 (1988)

Wright, G. *A Contemporary Theory of Humanitarian Intervention*, 4 FLA. INT'L L.J. 435 (1989)

2. Use of Force Generally

Akehurst, M. *Enforcement Action by Regional Agencies, with Special Reference to the Organisation of American States*, 42 BRIT. Y.B. INT'L L. 175 (1967)

Borchard, E. *Neutrality and Civil Wars*, 31 AM. J. INT'L L. 304 (1937)

Bowett, D. *Economic Coercion and Reprisals by States*, 13 VA. J. INT'L L. 1 (1972)

Chimni, B. *Towards a Third World Approach to Non-Intervention: Through a Labyrinth of Western Doctrine*, 20 INDIAN J. INT'L L. 243 (1980)

Cutler, L. *The Right to Intervene*, 64 FOREIGN AFF. 96 (1985–86)

Falk, R. *The Decline of Normative Restraint in International Relations*, 10 YALE J. INT'L L. 263 (1985)

Farer, T. *The Regulation of Foreign Intervention in Civil Armed Conflict*, 142 R.C.A.D.I. 289 (1974-II)

Farer, T. *Harnessing Rogue Elephants—A Short Discourse on Foreign Intervention in Civil Strife*, 82 HARV. L. REV. 511 (1969)

Fawcett, J. *Intervention in International Law*, 103 R.C.A.D.I. 343 (1961-II)

Feder, N. *Reading the U.N. Charter Connotatively: Toward a New Definition of Armed Attack*, 19 N.Y.U.J. INT'L L. & POL. 395 (1987)

Fenwick, C. *Intervention: Individual and Collective*, 39 AM. J. INT'L L. 645 (1945)

Friedmann, W. *Intervention in Developing Countries*, 10 VA. J. INT'L L. 205 (1970)

Gardam, J. *Proportionality and Force in International Law*, 87 AM. J. INT'L L. 391 (1993)

Gardner, R. *Sovereignty and Intervention: The Just Use of Force*, FREEDOM AT ISSUE (Mar.-Apr. 1985)

Gordon, E. *Article 2(4) in Historical Context*, 10 YALE J. INT'L L. 271 (1985)

Gunewardene, R. *Indo–Sri Lanka Accord: Intervention by Invitation or Forced Intervention?* 16 N.C.J. INT'L L. & COMM. REG. 211 (1991)

Henkin, L. *Force, Intervention and Neutrality in Contemporary Law*, 57 PROC. AM. SOC. INT'L. L. 147 (1963)

Higgins, R. *The Legal Limits to the Use of Force by Sovereign States: United Nations Practice*, 37 BRIT. Y.B. INT'L L. 269 (1961)

Kassar, N. *The Legal Limits to the Use of International Force Through the United Nations Practice*, 35 REVUE EGYPTIENNE DE DROIT INT'L 163 (1979)

Komarnicki, T. *L'intervention en droit international moderne*, 60 REVUE GÉNÉRALE DE DROIT INT'L PUB. 521 (1956)

Martson, J. *Coercion and Use of Force Short of War*, 55 BRIT. Y.B. INT'L L. 580 (1984)

McDougal, M. *Authority to Use Force on the High Seas*, 20 NAVAL WAR COLLEGE REV. 19 (1967)

Moore, J. *The Control of Foreign Intervention in Internal Conflict*, 9 VA. J. INT'L L. 205 (1969)

Potter, P. *L'Intervention en droit international moderne*, 32 R.C.A.D.I. 607 (1930-II)

Reisman, W. *Criteria for the Lawful Use of Force in International Law*, 10 YALE J. INT'L L. 279 (1985)

Rostow, E. *The Legality of the International Use of Force by and from States*, 10 YALE J. INT'L L. 286 (1985)

Schachter, O. *The Right of States to Use Armed Force*, 82 MICH. L. REV. 1620 (1984)

Schachter, O. *The Lawful Resort to Unilateral Use of Force*, 10 YALE J. INT'L L. 291 (1985)

Schachter, O. *In Defense of International Rules on the Use of Force*, 53 U. CHI. L. REV. 113 (1986)

Sohn, L. *How New is the New International Legal Order?* 20 DENV. J. INT'L L. & POL'Y 205 (1992)

Stowell, E. *La théorie et la pratique de l'intervention*, 40 R.C.A.D.I. 91 (1932-II)

Waldock, C. *The Regulation of the Use of Force by Individual States in International Law*, 81 R.C.A.D.I. 451 (1952-II)

Wright, Q. *The Legality of Intervention Under the United Nations Charter*, 51 PROC. AM. SOC'Y INT'L L. 79 (1957)

Wright, Q. *The Prevention of Aggression*, 50 AM. J. INT'L L. 514 (1956)

3. Human Rights

Alston, P. *The UN's Human Rights Record: From San Francisco to Vienna and Beyond*, 16 HUM. RTS. Q. 375 (1994)

D'Amato, A. *The Concept of Human Rights in International Law*, 82 COLUM. L. REV. 1110 (1982)

Delbrück, J. *International Protection of Human Rights and State Sovereignty*, 57 IND. L.J. 567 (1981–82)

Ermacora, F. *Human Rights and Domestic Jurisdiction (Article 2, §7 of the Charter)*, 124 R.C.A.D.I. 371 (1968-II)

Franck, T. *The Emerging Right to Democratic Governance*, 86 AM. J. INT'L L. 46 (1992)

Gottlieb, G. *International Assistance to Civilians in Armed Conflicts*, 4 N.Y.U.J. INT'L L. & POL. 403 (1971)

Meron, T. *Common Rights of Mankind in Gentili, Grotius and Suarez*, 85 AM. J. INT'L L. 112 (1991)

Reisman, W. *Sovereignty and Human Rights in Contemporary International Law*, 84 AM. J. INT'L L. 866 (1990)

Simma, B. & Alston, P. *The Sources of Human Rights Law: Custom, Jus Cogens, and General Principles*, 12 AUSTRALIAN Y.B. INT'L L. 82 (1992)

Trinidade, A. *The Current State of the International Implementation of Human Rights*, 1990 HAGUE Y.B. INT'L L. 3

4. Miscellaneous Legal Articles

Abbot, K. *Modern International Relations Theory: A Prospectus for International Lawyers*, 14 YALE J. INT'L L. 335 (1989)

Ago, R. *Positive Law and International Law*, 51 AM. J. INT'L L. 691 (1957)

Allott, P. *Language, Method and the Nature of International Law*, 45 BRIT. Y.B. INT'L L. 79 (1971)

Ames, J. *Law and Morals*, 22 HARV. L. REV. 97 (1908–09)

Bork, R. *The Limits of "International Law"*, 18 NAT'L INTEREST 3 (1989/90)

Bowett, D. *International Incidents: New Genre or New Delusion?* 12 YALE J. INT'L L. 386 (1987)

Burley, A. *International Law and International Relations Theory: A Dual Agenda*, 87 AM. J. INT'L L. 205 (1993)

Burley, A. *Toward an Age of Liberal Nations*, 33 HARV. INT'L L.J. 393 (1992)

Falk, R. *Casting the Spell: The New Haven School of International Law*, 104 YALE L.J. 1991 (1995) (book review)

Falk, R. *The Validity of the Incidents Genre*, 12 YALE J. INT'L L. 376 (1987)

Feldbrugge, F. *Good and Bad Samaritans: A Comparative Survey of Criminal Law Provisions Concerning Failure to Rescue*, 14 AM. J. COMP. L. 630 (1965–66)

Fuller, L. *Positivism and Fidelity to Law—A Reply to Professor Hart*, 71 HARV. L. REV. 630 (1958)

Green, L. *The Duty Problem in Negligence Cases*, 28 COLUM. L. REV. 1014 (1928)

Hart, H. *Positivism and the Separation of Law and Morals*, 71 HARV. L. REV. 593 (1958)

Henkin, L. *International Law: Politics, Values and Functions*, 216 R.C.A.D.I. 9 (1989-IV)

Lauterpacht, H. *The Grotian Tradition in International Law*, 23 BRIT. Y.B. INT'L L. 1 (1946)

Matheson, M. *The United States Position on the Relation of Customary International Law to the 1977 Protocols Additional to the 1949 Geneva Conventions*, 2 AM. U.J. INT'L L. & POL'Y 419 (1987)

McDougal, M. *International Law, Power, and Policy: A Contemporary Conception*, 82 R.C.A.D.I. 137 (1953-I)

Morgenthau, H. *Positivism, Functionalism, and International Law*, AM. J. INT'L L. 260 (1940)

Reisman, W. *International Incidents: Introduction to a New Genre in the Study of International Law*, 10 YALE J. INT'L L. 1 (1984)

Tieya, W. *International Law in China: Historical and Contemporary Perspectives*, 221 R.C.A.D.I. 195 (1990-II)

Weinrib, E. *The Case for a Duty to Rescue*, 90 YALE L.J. 247 (1980)

Zoller, E. *La definition des crimes contre l'humanite*, 120 JOURNAL DU DROIT INT'L 549 (1992)

B. International Relations

Chan, S. *Mirror, Mirror on the Wall . . . Are the Freer Countries More Pacific?* 28 J. Conflict Resol. 617 (1984)

Donnelly, J. *Human Rights, Humanitarian Intervention and American Foreign Policy: Law, Morality and Politics,* 37 J. Int'l Aff. 311 (1984)

Doyle, M. *Kant, Liberal Legacies, and Foreign Affairs,* 12 Phil. & Pub. Aff. 205 (pt. 1), 323 (pt. 2) (1982)

Gardner, R. *The Comeback of Liberal Internationalism,* Wash. Q. 23 (summer 1990)

Krauthammer, C. *The Curse of Legalism,* New Republic 44 (Nov. 6, 1989)

Mansfield, E. & Snyder, J. *Democratization and War,* Foreign Aff. 79 (May-June 1995)

Maoz, Z. & Abdolali, N. *Regime Types and International Conflict, 1816–1976,* 33 J. Conflict Resol. 3 (1989)

Will, G. *The Perils of "Legality",* Newsweek 66 (Sept. 10, 1990)

C. The United Nations and International Organization

Alvarez, J. *Judging the Security Council,* 90 Am. J. Int'l L. 1 (1996)

Boutros-Ghali, B. *Empowering the United Nations,* 71 Foreign Aff. 89 (Winter 1992–93)

Caron, D. *The Legitimacy of the Collective Authority of the Security Council,* 87 Am. J. Int'l L. 552 (1993)

Claude Jr., I. *The OAS, the UN, and the United States,* Int'l Conciliation No. 547 (Mar. 1964)

Farer, T. *The United Nations and Human Rights: More than a Whimper, Less than a Roar,* 9 Hum. Rts. Q. 550 (1987)

Franck, T. *Of Gnats and Camels: Is There a Double Standard at the United Nations?* 78 Am. J. Int'l L. 811 (1984)

Franck, T. *The "Powers of Appreciation": Who is the Ultimate Guardian of UN Legality?* 86 Am. J. Int'l L. 519 (1992)

Halderman, J. *Regional Enforcement Measures and the United Nations,* 52 Geo. L.J. 89 (1963)

Johansen, R. *Reforming the United Nations to Eliminate War,* 4 Transnat'l L. & Contemp. Probs. 455 (1994)

Khadduri, M. *The Arab League as a Regional Arrangement,* 40 Am. J. Int'l L. 756 (1946)

Lawrence, R. *United Nations Security Council Resolution 687 and its Aftermath: The Implications for Domestic Authority and the Need for Legitimacy,* 25 N.Y.U.J. Int'l L. & Pol. 593 (1993)

Meeker, L. *Defensive Quarantine and the Law,* 57 Am. J. Int'l L. 515 (1963)

Murphy, S. *The Security Council, Legitimacy, and the Concept of Collective Security After the Cold War,* 32 Colum. J. Transnat'l L. 201 (1994)

Picco, G. *The U.N. and the Use of Force,* Foreign Aff. 14 (Sept.-Oct. 1994)

Reisman, W. *Peacemaking,* 18 Yale J. Int'l L. 415 (1993)

Reisman, W. *The Constitutional Crisis at the United Nations,* 87 Am. J. Int'l L. 83 (1993)

Rosenstock, R. *The Declaration of Principles of International Law Concerning Friendly Relations: A Survey,* 65 Am. J. Int'l L. 714 (1971)

Schachter, O. *United Nations Law*, 88 Am. J. Int'l L. 1 (1994)

Stein, E. *The United Nations and Enforcement of Peace*, 10 Mich. J. Int'l L. 304 (1989)

Symposium, *Preferred Futures for the United Nations*, 4 Transnat'l L. & Contemp. Probs. 309 (1994)

Szasz, P. *The Role of the United Nations in Internal Conflicts*, 13 Ga. J. Int'l & Comp. L. 345 (1983)

Touval, S. *Why the U.N. Fails*, Foreign Aff. 44 (Sept.-Oct. 1994)

Urquhart, B. *For a UN Voluntary Military Force*, N.Y. Rev. Books 3 (June 10, 1993)

Watson, G. *Constitutionalism, Judical Review, and the World Court*, 34 Harv. Int'l L.J. 1 (1993)

Witten, R. *The Declaration on Friendly Relations*, 12 Harv. Int'l L.J. 518 (1971)

de Yturriaga, J. *L'organisation de l'unité africaine et les nations unies*, 36 Revue Générale de Droit Int'l Pub. 370 (1965)

D. Philosophy, Theology, and Just War Theory

Beitz, C. *Nonintervention and Communal Integrity*, 10 Phil. & Pub. Aff. 354 (1979–80)

Johnson, J. *Grotius' Use of History and Charity in the Transformation of the Just War Idea*, 4 Grotiana 21 (1983)

Mushkat, R. *When War May Justifiably be Waged: An Analysis of Historical and Contemporary Legal Perspectives*, 15 Brook. J. Int'l L. 223 (1989)

Rawls, J. *Justice as Fairness: Political not Metaphysical*, 14 Phil. & Pub. Aff. 223 (1985)

Slater, J. & Nardin, T. *Nonintervention and Human Rights*, 48 Politics 86 (1986)

Schachter, O. *Just War and Human Rights*, 1 Pace Y.B. Int'l L. 1 (1989)

Taylor, T. *The Concept of Justice and the Laws of War*, 13 Colum. J. Transnat'l L. 189 (1974)

Tesón, F. *The Kantian Theory of International Law*, 92 Colum. L. Rev. 53 (1992)

Von Elbe, J. *The Evolution of the Concept of the Just War in International Law*, 33 Am. J. Int'l L. 665 (1939)

Walzer, M. *The Moral Standing of States*, 9 Phil. & Pub. Aff. 209 (1978–79)

E. Studies of Specific Interventions

1. Pre–U.N. Charter Interventions

Kloepfer, S. *The Syrian Crisis, 1860–61: A Case Study in Classic Humanitarian Intervention*, 23 Canadian Y.B. Int'l L. 246 (1985)

Pogany, I. *Humanitarian Intervention in International Law: The French Intervention in Syria Re-Examined*, 35 Int'l & Comp. L.Q. 182 (1986)

2. Central Africa

Rousseau, C. *Chroniques de faits internationaux*, Revue Générale de Droit Int'l Pub. 1058 (1979)

3. Congo

Weisberg, H. *The Congo Crisis 1964: A Case Study in Humanitarian Intervention,* 12 VA. J. INT'L L. 261 (1972)

4. Cuba

Chayes, A. *Law and the Quarantine of Cuba,* 41 FOREIGN AFF. 550 (1963)
Meeker, L. *Defensive Quarantine and the Law,* 57 AM. J. INT'L L. 515 (1963)

5. Dominican Republic

Draper, T. *The Dominican Crisis: A Case Study in American Policy,* COMMENTARY 33 (Dec. 1965)
Fenwick, C. *The Dominican Republic: Intervention or Collective Self-Defense?* 60 AM. J. INT'L L. 64 (1966)
Nanda, V. *The United States' Action in the 1965 Dominican Crisis: Impact on World Order (pt. 1),* 43 DENV. L.J. 439 (1966), *(pt. 2),* 44 DENV. L.J. 225 (1967)

6. East Pakistan

Documents: Civil War in East Pakistan, 4 N.Y.U.J. INT'L L. & POL. 524 (1971)
Franck, T. & Rodley, N. *After Bangladesh: The Law of Humanitarian Intervention by Military Force,* 67 AM. J. INT'L L. 275 (1973)
Nanda, V. *Self-Determination in International Law: The Tragic Tale of Two Cities— Islamabad (West Pakistan) and Dacca (East Pakistan),* 66 AM. J. INT'L L. 321 (1972)
Nanda, V. *A Critique of the United Nations Inaction in the Bangladesh Crisis,* 49 DENV. L.J. 53 (1972)
Nawaz, M. *Bangla Desh and International Law,* 11 INDIAN J. INT'L L. 459 (1971)
Salzberg, J. *U.N. Prevention of Human Rights Violations: The Bangladesh Case,* 27 INT'L ORG. 115 (1973)
Schanberg, S. *Pakistan Divided,* 50 FOREIGN AFF. 125 (1971)
Talbot, S. *Ménage à Trois,* 50 FOREIGN AFF. 698 (1971–72)

7. Grenada

Audeoud, O. *L'intervention Americano-Caraibe á la Grenade,* 29 ANNUAIRE FRAN- ÇAISE DE DROIT INT'L 217 (1983)
Boyle, F. et al. *International Lawlessness in Grenada,* 78 AM. J. INT'L L. 172 (1984)
Dore, I. *The U.S. Invasion of Grenada: Resurrection of the "Johnson Doctrine?"* 20 STAN. J. INT'L L. 175 (1984)
Doswald-Beck, L. *The Legality of the U.S. Intervention in Grenada,* 31 NETH. INT'L L. REV. 355 (1984)
Fraser, H. *Grenada—The Sovereignty of a People,* 7 W. INDIAN L.J. 205 (1983)
Gordon, E. et al. *International Law and the United States Action in Grenada: A Report,* 18 INT'L LAW. 331 (1984)

Joyner, C. *The United States Action in Grenada: Reflections on the Lawfulness of Invasion*, 78 Am. J. Int'l L. 131 (1984)

Levitin, M. *The Law of Force and the Force of Law: Grenada, the Falklands, and Humanitarian Intervention*, 27 Harv. Int'l L.J. 621 (1986)

Moore, J. *Grenada and the International Double Standard*, 78 Am. J. Int'l L. 145 (1984)

Nanda, V. *The United States Armed Intervention in Grenada—Impact on World Order*, 14 Cal. W. Int'l L.J. 395 (1984)

Vagts, D. *International Law Under Time Pressure: Grading the Grenada Take-Home Examination*, 78 Am. J. Int'l L. 169 (1984)

Wheeler, L. *The Grenada Invasion: Expanding the Scope of Humanitarian Intervention*, 8 B.C. Int'l & Comp. L. Rev. 413 (1985)

8. Hungary and Czechoslovakia

Note, *Soviet and American Attitudes Toward Intervention: The Dominican Republic, Hungary and Czechoslovakia*, 11 Va. J. Int'l L. 97 (1970)

Wright, Q. *Intervention, 1956*, 51 Am. J. Int'l L. 257 (1957)

9. Iraq

Adelman, H. *Humanitarian Intervention: The Case of the Kurds*, 4 Int'l J. Refugee L. 4 (1992)

The Kurdish Crisis and Allied Intervention in the Aftermath of the Second Gulf War, 2 Eur. J. Int'l L. 114 (1992)

Harrington, M. *Operation Provide Comfort: A Perspective in International Law*, 8 Conn. J. Int'l L. 635 (1993)

Heidenrich, J. *The Gulf War: How Many Iraqis Died?* 90 Foreign Pol'y 108 (1993)

Schachter, O. *United Nations Law in the Gulf Conflict*, 95 Am. J. Int'l L. 452 (1991)

Stopford, M. *Humanitarian Assistance in the Wake of the Persian Gulf War*, 33 Va. J. Int'l L. 491 (1993)

Weston, B. *Security Council Resolution 678 and Persian Gulf Decision Making: Precarious Legitimacy*, 85 Am. J. Int'l L. 516 (1991)

10. Liberia

Ajomo, J. *Regional Economic Organisations: The African Experience*, 25 Int'l & Comp. L.Q. 58 (1979)

Kufuor, K. *The Legality of the Intervention in the Liberian Civil War by the Economic Community of West African States*, 5 African J. Int'l & Comp. L. 525 (1993)

Lillich, R. *Forcible Protection of Nationals Abroad: The Liberian "Incident" of 1990*, 35 German Y.B. Int'l L. (1992)

11. Panama

Alberts, D. *The United States Invasion of Panama: Unilateral Military Intervention to Effectuate a Change in Government—A Continuum of Lawfulness*, 1 Transnat'l L. & Contemp. Probs. 261 (1991)

D'Amato, A. *The Invasion of Panama Was a Lawful Response to Tyranny*, 84 Am. J. Int'l L. 516 (1990)

Farer, T. *Panama: Beyond the Charter Paradigm*, 84 Am. J. Int'l L. 503 (1990)

Hilaire, M. *The United States Intervention in Panama: Legal or Illegal under International Law?* 1990 Revue de Droit Int'l Sci. Dip. & Pol. 241

Maechaling Jr., C. *Washington's Illegal Invasion*, 79 Foreign Pol'y 113 (1990)

Miller, J. *International Intervention: The United States Invasion of Panama*, 31 Harv. Int'l L.J. 633 (1990)

Nanda, V. *The Validity of United States Intervention in Panama Under International Law*, 84 Am. J. Int'l L. 494 (1990)

Quigley, J. *The Legality of the United States Invasion of Panama*, 15 Yale J. Int'l L. 276 (1990)

Terry, J. *The Panama Intervention: Law in Support of Policy*, 39 Naval L. Rev. 5 (1990)

12. Somalia

Clark, J. *Debacle in Somalia*, 72 Foreign Aff. 109 (1992/93)

Crawford, S. *U.N. Humanitarian Intervention in Somalia*, 3 Transnat'l L. & Contemp. Probs. 2273 (1993)

Hutchinson, M. *Restoring Hope: U.N. Security Council Resolutions for Somalia and an Expanded Doctrine of Humanitarian Intervention*, 34 Harv. Int'l L.J. 624 (1993)

Murphy, S. *Nation-Building: A Look at Somalia*, 3 Tulane J. Int'l & Comp. L. 19 (1995)

13. Uganda

Chatterjee, S. *Some Legal Problems of Support Role in International Law: Tanzania and Uganda*, 30 Int'l & Comp. L.Q. 755 (1981)

Hassan, F. *Realpolitik in International Law: After Tanzanian-Ugandan Conflict "Humanitarian Intervention" Reexamined*, 17 Willamette L. Rev. 859 (1981)

Wani, I. *Humanitarian Intervention and the Tanzania-Uganda War*, 3/2 Horn of Africa 18 (1980)

Umozurike, U. *Tanzania's Intervention in Uganda*, 20 Archiv des Völkerrechts 301 (1982)

14. Yugoslavia

Banac, I. *The Fearful Asymmetry of War: The Causes and Consequences of Yugoslavia's Demise*, Daedalus 142 (Spring 1992)

Blum, Y. *UN Membership of the "New" Yugoslavia: Continuity or Break?* 86 Am. J. Int'l L. 830 (1992)

Weller, M. *The International Response to the Dissolution of the Socialist Federal Republic of Yugoslavia*, 86 Am. J. Int'l L. 569 (1992)

Index